8-22-73

Human Behavior in Ec

GEORGE KATONA

The Jossey-Bass/Elsevier
International Series

 Elsevier Scientific Publishing Company
Amsterdam

Human Behavior
in Economic Affairs

ESSAYS IN HONOR OF GEORGE KATONA

WITH CONCLUDING COMMENTS BY GEORGE KATONA

Edited by

BURKHARD STRUMPEL
JAMES N. MORGAN
ERNEST ZAHN

 Jossey-Bass Inc., Publishers

San Francisco · Washington · 1972

HUMAN BEHAVIOR IN ECONOMIC AFFAIRS

Burkhard Strumpel, James N. Morgan
and Ernest Zahn *(Editors)*

For the United States of America and Canada:
Jossey-Bass, Inc., Publishers
615 Montgomery Street
San Francisco, California 94111

For all other areas:
Elsevier Scientific Publishing Company
335 Jan van Galenstraat
Amsterdam, The Netherlands

Library of Congress Catalogue Card Number LC 72-87957

International Standard Book Number ISBN 0-87589-155-1

Manufactured in The Netherlands

FIRST EDITION

Code 7240

Preface

The twenty-five essays assembled in this volume are testimony to the impact of George Katona's work on social science and at the same time a state-of-the-art review of behavioral economics. Behavioral economics has a dual focus on content and methodology or, to put it differently, on specific problem areas and the approaches to study them. The major problem area is the role of the private household in economic affairs, neglected for so long both by scholars and practitioners in the field; the approach is the utilization and development of tools and concepts heretofore identified with other social sciences, most prominently psychology.

The development of the discipline, like any major innovation in science, was fraught with controversy, trial, error, and success. The controversy is still going on, and the editors have tried to recreate it in this volume, rather than to tone it down. Since George Katona remains one of the primary actors on this scene, it was only fair to grant him the opportunity to write a concluding chapter. The editors also felt it appropriate to include excerpts from a speech given by George Katona at a ceremony on the occasion of his retirement from teaching.

The volume opens with an introductory section in which the evolution of behavioral economics and the survey method is linked to the personality of George Katona, its main protagonist (Rensis Likert), and is seen in time perspective (James N. Morgan). The subsequent sections represent the major areas in which behavioral economics has been prominently applied.

The first section, entitled "Economic Psychology and Behavioral Science," deals with conceptual and methodological questions. It starts with a contribution by James Tobin in which the principles of Katona's work are reviewed in the light of the post-Keynesian theory of consumption. Daniel Katz subsequently draws attention to the broad range of psychological approaches to economic behavior. Burkhard Strumpel writes about a more general application of the models underlying psychological economics; he discusses how these models, developed and exemplified with an eye on consumer spending, can be applied to problems of long-term change in productive behavior. In this essay psychological variables additonal to Katona's package of attitudes and expectations come to the fore, such as goals and values, self-efficacy and fate control. Theodore Newcomb takes up the concept of expectations from the social psychological point of view, which is also treated by George Katona in the final essay of this volume. The Swedish psychologists Wärneryd and Olander continve this section by pointing to the potential of small-group and laboratory research in behavioral economics. Guy Orcutt discusses how micro-data collected in sample surveys may be organized and modeled more effectively for the decision-making of private households.

Robert Ferber and Francesco Nicosia open the section, "Understanding and Comparing Consumer Behavior," by developing a model of saving decisions of newly formed households, and test the model empirically. Robert W. Pratt, Jr., discusses the application of behavioral economics to market segmentation and forecasting in the marketing field. The three papers by Günter Schmölders and Bernd Biervert, Deborah S. Freedman, and Albert Lauterbach introduce a strong element of intercultural comparison to the volume — an area to which George Katona has recently devoted increasing attention.

The discussion of the role of consumer attitudes and expectations in economic forecasting began several decades ago. The contributions presented in the next section, "Predicting Consumer

Behavior," carry this discussion an important step forward. F. Gerard Adams and Lawrence R. Klein as well as F. Thomas Juster and Paul Wachtel deal with the central problems of model specification: to what extent and in combination with what other variables do attitudes and buying intentions anticipate aggregate demand? William C. Dunkelberg deals with a parallel question on the cross-section level. Harold T. Shapiro argues that a stock adjustment model in combination with income and unemployment data may be more successful in anticipating turning points in automobile demand than alternative formulations containing the *Index of Consumer Sentiment.*

In the following section, "The Consumer in a Changing Environment," the setting within which economic behavior takes place is reinterpreted by E. Scott Maynes and by Ernest Zahn. Whereas Katona views consumers as powerful on the economic scene and acting, if not rationally, by and large sensibly, Maynes points to the "micro-impotence" of the common man in the face of his macro-power and enters a plea for more research on consumer information. As if responding to that call, Gerhard Scherhorn and Klaus Wieken report on the impact of experimentally introduced nonadvertising information on consumer choice. Zahn takes up the question of consumer power or manipulation in the broader context of secular social change.

Some of the less optimistic perspectives of the latter section are followed by a discussion of "Poverty and Social Welfare", an area which recently has entered the orbit of behavioral economics. Starting out from the concepts of welfare theory, Kenneth Boulding maps some theoretical implications connected with analyzing nonmaterial aspects of well-being, nowadays frequently referred to as the quality of life. Poverty, for statistical and policy purposes, tends to be defined as a deficit in the minimum ratio of means to needs considered acceptable by society. Strategies for improvement can follow three avenues: increasing the earning power of the poor, reducing their needs, or transferring income. Each of the three following contributions takes up one of these areas. Harold W. Guthrie and Gordon F. Sutton argue that, given prevailing wage rates, a large number of average size families with full–time employed earners remain below the official poverty line. James D. Smith reports about research simulating a smaller family size by reducing the number of children born to poor families; the resulting decrease in needs would lift a considerable proportion of poor families above the poverty level. And Wilbur J. Cohen focuses on monetary transfers as an instrument of welfare policy.

Sylvia Kafka, Darryl W. Rhoades, and M. Susan Schwartz helped considerably in editing the volume. Virginia Eaton and Nancy McAllister contributed their remarkable secretarial and organizational skills. The editors are grateful to all of them.

BURKHARD STRUMPEL
JAMES N. MORGAN
ERNEST ZAHN

VIII

Contents

IX

X

Introduction

Courageous Pioneer:
Creating a New Field of Knowledge

RENSIS LIKERT

"Damn you, Likert," was the surprising comment made to me by a complete stranger in the lobby of a Cleveland hotel the first evening of the meetings of the American Economic and Statistical Associations in December, 1948.

I was more than a little startled. "What do you mean?" I said.

The stranger answered with a smile, "I have been hoping that the efforts of Katona and the Survey Research Center to demonstrate that consumer motivation can be measured and used to predict trends in the economy would fail. But they are not failing. These efforts are succeeding, and now I have to learn a whole new methodology. That means a lot of work ahead of me."

This comment by a competent economist reflects recognition of the initial phase of George Katona's pioneering work in the development of a new body of knowledge bridging a gap between economics and psychology. This field of work is now usually called psychological economics or behavioral economics.

When Katona started his work, the prevailing view among economists was that the general level of the total economy and major changes in this level were controlled by the actions of business and of government. Consumers were felt to have no influence, since their rate of expenditures was determined by their income, which in turn was controlled by the decisions of business and government.

Toward the end of World War II, some economists became concerned about the possible impact of consumer behavior in the immediate post-war period. One of these was Rolf Nugent, an economist at the Office of Price Administration. He was impressed by the findings in the studies by the Division of Program Surveys[1] of War Bond buying and redemption [1], [2] that most owners of Series E Bonds had no specific plans for the use of the funds invested. Moreover, plans for the redemption of the bonds changed very little from the first study of the Second War Bond Drive in 1943 through the summer of 1945.

Nugent pointed out that consumers, with their 32 billions of dollars in Series E Bonds, their cash, and their time and demand deposits, would have about 150 billions of dollars in liquid assets at the end of the war. If consumers decided suddenly at the end of the war to try to buy consumer durables and other products with their 150 billions, there would be a serious inflation, since the supply of consumer goods would be very limited. Nugent urged the Division of Program Surveys to expand the War Bond studies by interviewing samples of consumers to assess the probability that consumers would attempt to purchase large amounts of consumer durable goods immediately after the close of the war. If consumers were planning to do this, steps would have to be taken by the governement to prevent serious inflation, since the demand and purchasing power would far exceed the available supply of consumer durables.

The Division of Program Surveys sought the advice of Dr. Walter Stewart, Chairman of the group of economists at the Center for Advanced Studies at Princeton, New Jersey. He urged that Nugent's suggestion be implemented and suggested that the Federal Reserve Board would be the most likely source of support, since it would be the Federal agency most concerned with the control of inflation in the post-war period. He suggested that Governor Ransom, Vice-Chairman of the Board, would be much interested. In addition to Governor Ransom, Governor Evans was also ap-

---

[1] The senior personnel of the Division of Program Surveys of the Bureau of Agricultural Economics established the Survey Research Center at The University of Michigan on July 1,1946.

proached, since he previously, as head of the Agricultural Adjustment Administration, had found the sample surveys of the Division of Program Surveys of value.

With the support of Governors Ransom and Evans, the Board of Governors of the Federal Reserve System approved the financing of a pilot study in 1944. The proposed project was supported also by Chester Davis, President of the St. Louis Federal Reserve Bank, and by Woodlief Thomas, Assistant Director of Research of the Federal Reserve Board.

This pilot study was undertaken early in 1945, under the direction of George Katona and Eleanor Maccoby, by the Division of Program Surveys. It demonstrated that sufficiently accurate data concerning the distribution of ownership of liquid assets could be obtained through sample surveys to warrant undertaking a national study. The first nationwide survey of the ownership of liquid assets by consumers was conducted under Katona's direction in early 1946. It was called the National Survey of Liquid Assets. This title was used for the first annual survey and was changed in 1947 to the Survey of Consumer Finances, the title used for twenty-five years. The surveys represented a joint effort of several scholars in the Survey Research Center, who contributed to their management, planning, analysis, and the sampling and interviewing work. The contributions of Angus Campbell, James N. Morgan, John B. Lansing, Eva Mueller, Charles Cannell, and Leslie Kish may be singled out as particularly important.

The major objectives of the first nationwide survey, as defined by the Research Staff of the Federal Reserve Board, were to obtain the data needed to show (1) the distribution of the ownership of liquid assets among the population, and (2) the distribution of the expenditures for consumer durables during the previous year. The first objective was concerned with discovering how the ownership of liquid assets was distributed among the different segments of the population when grouped by income, occupation, age, and family size. The second objective dealt with expenditures for consumer durables when families were clustered in these same groupings.

At that time, the Research Staff of the Federal Reserve Board was not interested in the collection of data measuring consumer intentions to buy durable goods and plans for financing such purchases. The Research Staff felt that they could derive more accu-

5

rate estimates of the probable buying behavior by consumers of durable goods from data on the distribution of ownership of liquid .assets than from information on consumers' intentions to buy such commodities.

Katona explained to the Research Staff that it was necessary to ask consumers questions concerning their expectations, intentions, and plans, even though the Research Staff did not want the data. Methodological research had revealed that more complete and accurate answers on financial questions were obtained from respondents when these inquiries were embedded in questions concerning plans and aspirations.

The Research Staff's response to this methodological requirement was to say essentially, "If you need to ask such questions to obtain accurate financial data, go ahead and do so, but don't bother to tabulate the responses or report them to us." Katona, however, tabulated these consumer expectations and plans and reported them to the Research Staff.

An article by Ralph A. Young and Duncan Holthausen on the "Values and Limitations of Consumer Financial Surveys for Economic Research" (*Federal Reserve Bulletin*, March, 1947) discussed primarily contributions of liquid asset data to descriptive economics and devoted only a short section to the question "Do consumers plan? " by presenting the case both for and against the concept of consumer planning. Yet there was growing interest in psychological data. As early as June, 1947, an article in the *Federal Reserve Bulletin*, although entitled "Expenditures for Durable Goods", presented survey findings on consumer expectations and buying plans.

There was a major change in 1949. Toward the end of 1948 and the beginning of 1949, economic forecasts predicted that the United States economy was heading for a serious recession. This view was shared by the Research Staff of the Board. There was considerable skepticism, consequently, when, early in March, 1949, Katona gave the Research Staff a report showing that consumers were planning to spend about as much in 1949 for consumer durables as in 1948. Consumer intentions data showed that they planned to spend more for TVs and less for radios, but that, overall, they planned to spend as much in 1949 as in 1948. Consumer attitudes were slightly more favorable early in 1949 than a year earlier: prevailing expectations of declining prices made for favorable attitudes rather than indicating a recession.

If consumer expenditures for durables approached the magnitude called for by their intentions, the United States economy would have a fairly good year in 1949 and not a serious recession. The Research Staff was skeptical that consumers actually would implement their plans. One reason for this skepticism was the belief that incomes would decline. Furthermore, it was thought that the volume of goods produced would not permit purchases at the planned level. The Staff felt consumers just could not do what they said they planned to do and, consequently, would change their minds.

To test whether there was any evidence that consumers were changing their minds, Katona analyzed, by separate time periods, the interviews from the national sample. This analysis revealed no evidence of any changing of minds by consumers. Those interviewed toward the end of the interviewing period showed the same intentions as those interviewed one month earlier. Consumers appeared to be adhering to their plans.

In early 1949, good statistics on inventories were not available. But when the Research Staff sought to assess whether consumers were actually beginning to carry out their plans, they found evidence that this was the case. The evidence they obtained persuaded them that the consumers' intentions data should be taken seriously. They reported their conclusions to the Federal Reserve Board and a special report bound in green ribbons, not red tape, went to President Truman. By July, with inventories depleted, manufacturing schedules were rapidly accelerated. The evidence by then was clear that consumers were carrying out their plans and that 1949 would, indeed, be a good year.

This experience impressed the Research Staff sufficiently so that, when planning the 1950 study, they asked to have the consumer intentions data made available to them as soon as possible after the completion of the interviews. This required a preliminary tabulation of these data at extra cost, but they felt that having these results available promptly was worth the additional expenditure. The preliminary data were promptly published in the April, 1950, *Federal Reserve Bulletin*.

As Katona worked with the consumer motivation data, he became convinced that these variables should be measured more often than once or twice a year. Again he displayed faith, courage, and determination and obtained funds to support more frequent surveys. There have been three or four surveys a year of consumer intentions, expectations, and motivation since 1951 and quarterly surveys since 1960.

When Katona started his nationwide consumer surveys, the prevailing view was that the rate of consumer expenditures was not an independent factor affecting the level of economic activity. Increased or decreased rates of expenditures by business or government were viewed as the factors which determined whether we had good times or bad times. Consumers were felt to have little independent influence. They merely spent the flow of money that came to them. Amid considerable criticism and skepticism, Katona persevered in his view that consumers are important as an independent factor affecting the United States economy and its level of activity. The data he collected, and the analyses that he and his colleagues made, gradually demonstrated even to the most skeptical that consumer perceptions, expectations, and motivation can exercise a significant, independent impact upon our economy. The consumer sector of the economy has been shown to play an important role in determining whether we experience good times or bad.

One quarter of a century after Katona started his surveys for the Federal Reserve Board, the situation has changed greatly. Consumers are seen unquestionably as having discretionary purchasing power. They can and do make substantial changes in their rates of saving and of spending for consumer durables, travel, and leisure time activities. These changes exert a major influence upon the level of activity of the United States economy. The view is held rather widely now that changes in the perceptions, expectations, and motivations of consumers exert substantial, independent influence upon the United States economy and its general level of activity.

George Katona has had a major role in creating a new field of knowledge: psychological or behavioral economics. It has taken courage, faith, persistence, and creative thinking. He is still applying these attributes in his current activity of developing more sophisticated and adequate theories and concepts in the field of knowledge he has done so much to create.

REFERENCES

1 Cartwright, Dorwin P., "Surveys of War Finance Program", In *Conference of Consumers' Interest, Proceedings*, Philadelphia: University of Pennsylvania Press, 1947.
2 Cartwright, Dorwin P., "Some Principles of Mass Persuasion: Selected Findings of Research on the Sale of United States War Bonds", in *Human Relations* 2(1949), 253–67.
3 Katona, George, *Psychological Analysis of Economic Behavior*, New York: McGraw-Hill, 1951.
4 Katona, George, *The Powerful Consumer: Psychological Studies of the American Economy*, New York: McGraw-Hill, 1960.
5 Katona, George, *The Mass Consumption Society*, New York: McGraw-Hill, 1964.
6 *Survey of Consumer Finances* Conducted since 1946 by the Survey Research Center, Institute for Social Research, The University of Michigan. Findings published in the *Federal Reserve Bulletin* 1946–1959 and in monographs, issued by the Survey Research Center, each year from 1960 to 1971.

Reminiscences[*]

GEORGE KATONA

This is a time for reminiscing. Having been engaged in a variety of activities, it is not easy for me to discern a clear line of development. One thing I do know for sure, however. I have been lucky. I have had great and powerful benefactors who steered me toward what I now believe was the right path.

My first benefactor was Bela Kun. He staged a Communist revolution in 1919 and chased me out of Hungary. Without him I would have done what I had planned, namely, to study law in Budapest and enter the law office of my grandfather. Due to the Communist putsch, I went to the University of Goettingen in Germany and studied psychology.

A few years later there was little use I could make of my newly acquired Ph.D. in experimental psychology. But again something very favorable happened, the German hyper-inflation of 1922-23. Some of you may have read that the depreciation of money was so

* A session of the Nineteenth Annual Conference on the Economic Outlook, sponsored by the Department of Economics of The University of Michigan and held on November 19, 1971, was devoted to honoring George Katona on the occasion of his retirement from teaching duties. Part of the reply George Katona made to earlier speakers is reproduced here (with the permission of the Research Seminar in Quantitative Economics).

fast at that time that the governement printed money on one side only, leaving the other side blank. Therefore the money did not lose its value entirely: the blank side could be used for papering rooms, and this arduous, painstaking task was what the paper-hanger Adolf Hitler did for many months.

I got a job in a bank, where they paid us our wages at noon every day and gave us three hours free to spend the money before it lost its value. In 1923 I wrote a paper in which I persuasively argued that inflation was nothing but a manifestation of mass hysteria. The paper was widely quoted and got me good jobs as a journalist. But after having published the paper the thought occurred to me that it might be useful to study the matter. Prior to that time I had not studied economics, but this is what I began to do in 1923. Soon I discovered that my paper was all wrong, that inflation had both economic and psychological causes; but my later insights did not detract from the success of the paper.

In 1926 the great publicist, writer, and politician Gustav Stolper founded a new weekly, *The German Economist*. He offered me a job as Assistant Editor and I continued my economic education by writing articles on economics. The day after October 28, 1929 — the great crash on Wall Street — I wrote a lead editorial predicting that prosperity had ended and a depression was coming. I acted according to my prediction: In prosperous years a bachelor has a good life; not so in a depression. Therefore the day after publishing my editorial I did the best thing I have ever done in my life, I married.

My next great benefactor was Adolf Hitler. In 1933 he took over Germany and confiscated our paper. It was clear to me that I should go as far away as possible. I visited the American consulate in Berlin, sent my calling card to Mr. Messersmith, the Consul General (later Under Secretary of State), and told him that I did not come to interview him for *The German Economist*, but to ask him for an immigration visa to America. "Why do you want to go to America," he asked. "You know about free speech here under Hitler," I replied, "therefore let me say simply that you have a new President and I am very much interested in his economic policies and would like to observe the New Deal at close range." Mr. Messersmith looked at me for a few minutes, and then I got the visa.

When Marian and I approached New York harbor on the Cunard liner Berengaria in 1933, we remarked that we did not know a single American; we had not one American relative, friend, or acquaintance. But we had an advantage: we had some money. From 1930 to 1933 I was German correspondent of the *Wall Street Journal* and the Dow-Jones Ticker, hired my wife as secretary, incurred large expenses for cabling news — and let them pay all they owed me into an account with the Chase National Bank in New York. In spite of the bank failures, my assets were intact.

What does a stranger do in a new country? He tries to make money. I had an office with the prestigious address of 1 Wall Street in New York and gave advice to European investors. Fortunately something again intervened and pushed me onto the right path. In 1936 I was stricken by tuberculosis and it took three years until I recovered. During my illness it became clear to me that I should do something entirely different from what I had done before. My beloved teacher and friend Max Wertheimer, the founder of Gestalt psychology, obtained a grant for me from the Carnegie Corporation and I spent these years on a couch studying the psychology of learning. The result was a book entitled *Organizing and Memorizing*, published by the Columbia University Press in 1940. Its third edition was published in 1967.

But I was not fully satisfied with research in psychology. In 1939 World War II broke out in Europe. It provided the opportunity to integrate my interest in economics and in psychology. I gave a course at the New School for Social Research in New York City on the psychology of the war economy and wrote a book, finished and published after Pearl Harbor, with the title *War Without Inflation*. I tried to explain in that book that patriotism and cooperation would make price control, rationing, and high rates of taxation so effective that we might fight, for the first time in world history, a great war without inflation. The title of the book was also meant to imply that inflation without war was a distinct possibility.

In 1942 Jacob Marschak became the Director of the Cowles Commission for Research in Economics at the University of Chicago and inherited a project started by Theodore Yntema on business reactions to price control. I was appointed the Director of this project and organized sample surveys among businessmen. I wrote a paper on the methods I used and sent it to the leading survey expert, whom I had never met before. This was Rensis Likert, the Head of the Division of Program Surveys at the Department of Agriculture in Washington. For a few weeks I didn't hear anything; then the telephone rang and Dr. Likert said, without any reference to my paper, "Would you be interested in joining us here in Washington?" Thus began twenty-seven years ago, first in Washington and then in Ann Arbor, the last and happiest phase of my career — the period of belonging to and identifying with a growing organization, of planning and conducting the Surveys of Consumer Finances and the quarterly surveys of changes in consumer sentiment, and of developing psychological or behavioral economics.

A Quarter Century of Behavioral Research in Economics, Persistent Programs and Diversions

JAMES N. MORGAN

The retirement of a leader (or at least the retirement of his income) is inevitably the occasion for stock taking and a resetting of the sights. But it is dangerous and perhaps improper for those very close to the history to attempt to evaluate it. This contribution will therefore endeavor to summarize some history in such a way that others can evaluate it, but will also succumb to the temptation to opine about the best future directions for economics as a behavioral and social (as distinct from analytical) science.

The history of behavioral economics is largely the history of the Survey Research Center, and it is on that we focus, not trying to be encyclopedic or bibliographic. The federal Government, starting before World War II, has collected extensive data on consumer expenditures and incomes, and (in the Department of Agriculture) studied the utilization of food and clothing. A number of studies usually of subpopulations were conducted under various auspices. But the bulk of the national studies combining data on economic behavior or situations with a rich background of demographic, environmental, and attitudinal information, were done by the Survey Research Center.

When the mass exodus from the Division of Program Surveys, U.S.D.A., arrived in Ann Arbor to set up the Survey Research

Center in 1946, there was already a history of studies, and the first waves of the Survey of Consumer Finances, sponsored by the Board of Governors of the Federal Reserve System — support which persisted for nearly 15 years. It was an uneasy alliance, with the Board's concern for precise hard financial data and the Center's interest in attitudes and reasons why. There was never enough financial support for the methodological research on response error, nor enough flexibility to study why people made the economic choices they did.

It was the summer of 1949 when I first arrived in Ann Arbor. I had always thought that Elementary Education was as low as you could go in Education, but the Economic Behavior Program was lower — they were in the basement of University Elementary School. It was necessary even to duck when walking down the halls, because the pipes had been installed by short plumbers.

One of my first impressions of survey research was an episode where someone handed George Katona a sheaf of computer printout, which he riffled through. In less than a minute, he handed it back saying that it was incorrect. He was right, of course, the computer was wrong!

FOCUS AND COHERENCE

What gave coherence and stability to the research? In spite of many diversions and temptations, there was a focus on:
1. An interdisciplinary approach to the study of economic behavior or economic situations. It is the explanatory variables which are multi-disciplinary — from economics, sociology, psychology, and demography.
2. The use of personal interviews with a national sample as the basic data source. Once a national sample and a national field staff are available, the economic advantages are obvious. The overhead costs can be spread over many surveys, and one can make conclusions about the whole U.S. more cheaply than about one state or county.
3. A focus on salient, important, economic decisions where some genuine decision-making is likely to be taking place, and where mass shifts in the decisions can have major social impact. This

meant eschewing studies of brand choice, or of detailed expenditure allocations.

4. Repeated studies using sufficiently stable methodology so that changes and trends could be discovered. Probability samples and fixed question, open-answer interviewing and controlled coding allow us to see what has changed "out there".

5. Where possible, reinterviews and panels to study stability and change of individual families, in response both to individual and to national events.

6. Where possible, and particularly for George Katona's personal attention, a focus on mass changes, rather than on cross-section differences. And a focus on mass changes reflecting discretionary responses to national events.

The Surveys of Consumer Finances formed a useful base and nucleus for the research, but the interim smaller studies focused more directly on attitudes, expectations, optimism and confidence (and plans and major expenditures) and provided more frequent and richer assessment. One can argue that there was insufficient stability in the content and method for optimal testing of competing hypotheses. But one can also argue that there was too much attention to trends and not enough experimentation and innovation.

In fact, of course, the program of research that developed had to be forged out of the available research funds in a persistent application of the principle of second-best. Funds were never free, or unrestricted, or ample, and a good deal of negotiation, and mutual education, had to take place. What now may appear as a long series of surveys providing important trends was hammered together step by step through the persistence of George Katona, who kept his focus on the main targets.

CHANGE AND SPECIAL TOPICS

There was change, too, not just stability and persistence. The early focus in the Surveys of Consumer Finances on estimating saving gave way to a focus on discretionary saving and on consumer investment expenditures, the two most volatile and most easily measured components. And as consumer discretionary spending shifted somewhat from durables to travel and vacations, they were studied. When the income distribution appeared almost constant, studies were initiated to find out why some people stayed poor even in prosperity, and to examine the things they did that seemed likely either to improve or deteriorate their lot [13], [14].

And there were special studies and topics which were studied as the opportunity arose or it became obvious that they were important areas of change. Business decisions about industrial location and about financial institutions were studied on three occasions [4], [5], [6], [15], [16].

The third of these studies is a good example of the advantages of persistence in method and topic. Comparisons were possible with a simpler study ten years earlier. And since the early study had revealed a persistent tendency for Michigan businessmen to think of Ohio as a good location, the second study added an Ohio sample to discover whether Ohio was indeed better, or whether the grass merely looked greener on the other side of the fence.

Another major area of social change was in the provision for retirement and the decision when to retire. The advent of private pension plans to supplement Social Security, usually without much choice by the workers involved, allowed a study comparing those with and without such supplemental private pensions [3].

The regular surveys also provided information on people's notions of retirement as a purpose of saving, and their plans about when they would retire. In cooperation with the UAW a special study was done of two samples: a national sample and a sample of UAW workers 58–61 years old and mostly the potential beneficiaries of a supplemental early retirement benefit [2].

A follow-up of the UAW sample assured that the euphoria reported in the main study had not dissipated [1].

The evidence of a trend toward early retirement, and perhaps more importantly of a trend toward increasing bipolarization between those who can expect an adequate retirement, even early, and those who cannot, needs continuing surveillance. Major social policy issues are involved.

Diversity was encouraged also by bringing in other economists, and encouraging them to develop their own interests. Carnegie fellowships brought Lawrence Klein, Albert Lauterbach, Julius

Margolis, Guy Orcutt, and the author to the Center. John Lansing developed programs of research in travel and recreation, and in residental location and urban mobility [7], [8], [9], [11]. Eva Mueller worked with him on mobility of labor, and went on to study the impact of machine technology on the worker [10], [17].

The studies of asset preferences in the Surveys of Consumer Finances revealed what seemed to be substantial differences among those at the upper income levels. This led to a pilot study in Milwaukee and finally a national study of the affluent and their decisions about investment of savings.

There have been more panel studies, collecting more complex data across time; and some special studies of special subgroups, or even of chains of moves from one home to another [9].

Some areas of consumer behavior or situations required regular assessment, while others needed only an occasional measurement, and some things seem to have been done once, like auto accident compensation, lump sum settlements for injured workers, the impact of automation on the workers, early retirement.

If it looks like a program of research, it is not because we were able to finance everything we wanted to, or because we had great foresight (George Katona has more of it than most of us), but at least partly because it happened that way. And partly because so much needed to be done, most of which still needs to be done, that almost any start at moving away the veil of ignorance about household economic behavior would have seemed like a useful program of research.

The future may well see two trends, given some reasonable financial support:
1. More data designed to fit simulation models, not simple analysis nor time-series models.
2. More information on what matters to people — crude measurement, if you will, of social welfare and what affects it.

As more and more of the GNP goes through the public sector, it becomes more and more important to provide policy makers with good information on what people care about, like, or dislike, and how subgroups differ on these things. In this way, optimal packages of public policy can be designed so that it proves to be true that everyone pays taxes and everyone gets some benefits.

19

Even though funding was mostly for explicit studies, wherever it was possible methodological research was carried on. Split half samples proved not very useful. Often no differences appeared. If differences appeared, it was difficult to explain and understand them, or derive implications for future research designs. Reinterviews provide a number of validity and reliability checks, but again without much understanding. In one experiment people were asked about their asset and debt balances a year before, then handed a summary of what they had reported a year earlier on a previous interview. Very little was learned about *why* the discrepancies occurred, and it was not always even clear what the truth was.

What *has* been learned from all the various experiments and attempts at "trying something new", is that improvement will probably come only from a much more thorough knowledge of the dynamics of the interview and the process by which the respondent is motivated to perform his tasks [12]. As an oversimplification we can say that the main problem is the motivation of the respondent – sufficiently motivated, he can provide most of the information we need (or sign authorizations to those who can). In an age where "doing what is expected of one" is less and less likely behavior, the whole future of survey research will depend on learning how we can motivate people to work, and how we can minimize the burden we place on the respondent.

The problem of whom to interview has also been a continuing one. Some studies on decision making in the family and on who speaks accurately for whom in the interview have been done, but a great deal more needs doing. It is a difficult task because the whole of group–decision-making is involved, plus some special considerations having to do with who is most conscious of what really happens (has the most empathy with the other family members).

It is tempting to think of possibilities that do not require the respondent's cooperation, ranging from Don Campbell's unobtrusive measures (counting the liquor bottles in the garbage) to the use of records and files, or interviews with financial advisers and experts (lawyers). Our experience has been mostly negative. Records and files are not only narrow and incomplete, but are often inaccurate or difficult to work with. High income people claim that they delegate very little of their investment decisions to experts, using them mostly for information. Lawyers proved to know very little about the details of the cases of their own clients in auto accident cases, presumably because most were settled out of court and the detailed facts were not necessary, but also because once the case was over it was closed and forgotten by the lawyer, though not by the victim. There may well be a future in the use of records and files, but it is likely to be in conjunction with a personal interview that combines the various sources, and allows some understanding of *why*.

METHODOLOGY – ANALYSIS

Methodological development also proceeds in other aspects of the process of survey research. It has proceeded most in analysis methods and computer handling of data, and perhaps least in coding and content analysis – the translation from open answers to digital categories. There was a period in the development of computers when they restricted the freedom of the researchers rather than enlarging it. Numerical multiple regression was easy, but anything more flexible was difficult, including generating new variables (such as dichotomous or dummy variables). And the first few years of the substitution of the tape for cards were fraught with difficulties, particularly in file management, corrections of errors, and similar mechanics. When one generated a new variable and added it to a deck of IBM cards, either the same physical deck remained, or the new deck could be given the same name, but when any change is made to a tape, including correcting a single error, the data end up physically on a different tape which has a different identification number. The problems are obvious.

But progress was made, both in file management and in analysis programs. Tables showing association between classifications can be supplemented with various measures of association, including Cramer's V which has recently been shown to be identical with the mean square of the canonical correlations, treating each classification as a set of dummy variables [20].

Dummy variable regression programs have been supplemented

with more flexible searching procedures, searching for differences in subgroup means, or regression slopes, or regressions (means and slopes), or modal values [18], [19]. These procedures are more transparent, and impose far fewer assumptions (statistical or theoretical) on the data than such traditional approaches as factor analysis, clustering, and scaling procedures. The test of any data analysis procedure is not its mathematical elegance but whether it reveals in the data things about the real world that would not have been discovered otherwise. We are not in the business of testing explicit and detailed hypotheses but are selecting among any competing hypotheses about what affects what. We need efficient procedures for deciding what does *not* matter (either for the whole population or for any major subsegment of it), and then examining the patterns of what does matter, from which we may then work to develop better theory.

The need for such an approach is increased by the fact that the connection between what we measure and the constructs of our theories is at best tenuous, and at worst multiple. (Family size is a proxy for the need for housing, and at the same time for other demands on income that make less of a given income available to pay for housing.) The conventional solution of simultaneous equation models has so far not proven very useful. It seems to be difficult to develop a just-identified system of equations that is also realistic and meaningful. Before we focus too much attention on the best unbiased estimates of the parameters of a particular model, we need to provide some evidence that it is the proper model.

The variables that had to be used in such models were invariably proxies for too many different things. With panel data the possibilities expand and get more complex, but we are only rarely able to design a structural model that is both statistically appropriate and reasonably realistic. Too many absurd assumptions often seem required.

Similar considerations have restricted the use of such special procedures for dealing with limited dependent variables as probits, logits, etc. Similarly, instrumental variables or two-stage least squares have become accepted methods for dealing with errors-in-variables, but it proves to be difficult to find an instrumental variable correlated with an explanatory variable like income, but not correlated with the dependent variable. And in any case, the main problem often seems to be *not* getting the best unbiased estimate of a single coefficient, but finding out what combinations of things matter. In such complex analysis, other statistical problems are more important. In particular, the stability of findings that result from ransacking data is more crucial than possible bias in the estimates.

THE FUTURE

Where do we go from here? Do we need more detailed formal models, or more sociology, or more experiments, or more longitudinal studies, or more use of multiple data sources for the same unit, or more use of repeated measures to establish trends, or what?

It is tempting to say that we should use more structural models with the best modern econometric methods of estimation. Certainly the payoff in professional reputation is maximal in that direction. The experience of the past decades, however, is that the real world gets lost in a welter of assumptions and of purely statistical considerations, and that the resulting coefficients frequently have the wrong sign or size anyway. More elaborate methods for constraining the coefficients on the basis of a priori considerations would seem likely merely to hide the fact that the model did not fit the data, or vice versa.

This does not mean that the analytical framework in which the analysis of survey data is conducted can ignore complexities, feedbacks and interrelations. The relationships between the measured variables and theoretical constructs, and the general form in which the theoretical constructs are supposed to interrelate, must be spelled out.

Over the years, a substantial number of attempts have been made, with some success, to use attitudinal and expectational variables as part of the matrix of explanatory variables. Social psychology has thus been well represented. But have we neglected sociology? There are two possible ways in which sociological considerations would enter into the analysis of economic behavior. First, one might introduce explanatory variables representing group influences: reference groups, neighborhood environmental effects, etc. Second, one might look beyond the individual or family as the unit of analysis and analyze neighborhoods, cities, or other groups *taken as units*. The second of these is much less appealing, since it throws away much of the rich survey information, and leads to the use of ecological correlations (correlations among group means or other group measures). Such correlations have often been used when no other data were available, and much economic analysis is still being done with geographic units such as counties as the unit of analysis. The dangers are serious. Anything which varies a lot within the units but not between them cannot show its influence. And if the units are *defined* in terms of some variables, such as income, but not in terms of some others, such as family size, then the former will have its full influence revealed, and the latter will have most of its influence hidden. The analyst will conclude that family size does not matter and income does, merely because his data have only allowed the latter to vary.

But the use of explanatory variables suggested by sociology is another matter, and one worth more attention. It is true that we have tried in the past to use information about the block or the county to explain economic behavior, with indifferent success, and we are currently expanding the range of information about the local area so that we can look not just at the county, but at several different aspects of the county — unemployment level, increase in total employment, wage rates, the market for unskilled or female labor, etc.

The notion of "reference group" is more bothersome, since if the respondent defines his own reference group in response to questions using phrases like "people like you", "your best friend", "the people you grew up with", etc., we do not know whether to interpret the results as the influence of those people on the respondent, or as the respondent's selection of a reference group. In a current study we are asking about the respondent's siblings, on the argument that they may exert some influence on him or her, and were clearly not selected by the respondent. Even here we have to deal with the respondent's own perception of the status of the siblings, not with the actual "truth". His perceptions may well be more important in motivating his behavior, and hence be what we want most.

In general, expansion of the use of explanatory variables from psychology and sociology and political science deserves attention, and will require a lot of work since most of the tools developed in those fields have been developed for captive audiences, usually small nonrepresentative groups, and have generally not been validated in any real sense. We want things like attitudes, group influences, party loyalties, or values. To develop measures of social psychological or sociological variables that have some face validity to a respondent in voluntary personal interview, are meaningful to the widely heterogeneous types in our population, and have some credibility as measures of some theoretical constructs, is a large task. Hopefully they should also have a stable meaning over time, so one could rely on changes from one year to the next.

Another road to expansion or improvement of the variables used is the combining of survey data with other primary data sources relating to the same units. We might hope to improve the measurement of either the dependent variables (economic behavior, status, etc.) or of the explanatory variables in this fashion. To date, such outside sources have been used more for validity evaluations of data than as part of the basic data for analysis. Use has been made of insurance company reports on the coverage of medical insurance policies, hospital reports of expenses of individuals, police reports on auto accidents, auto registry reports of debts on cars, etc.

Over the years, the possibility of using other data sources has repeatedly arisen. Considerations of invasion of privacy, or the confidential nature of the outside sources, often inhibited attempts to secure and use such data, but the more important consideration was usually that the data were not sufficiently appropriate or useful. A classic example is Social Security records. If one secures a signed release from the respondent, it is possible to get a report on the status and history of his Social Security account. Even though the amount of earnings subject to the tax is limited, and has changed by looking at the tax paid the first quarter of each year, one can estimate the earnings subject to tax. But there may be several earners in the family, or an earner may have several jobs each paying Social Security taxes, or the individual may have more than one Social Security number — quite legally. And government employees and railroad workers are not covered by Social Security, nor are casual earnings, or some self-employment income. Hence, the added information would have to be combined with the survey data, and the total improvement in the quality of the data is uncertain, perhaps very small. If one believes that income reporting is affected by unwillingness to report income not reported for tax purposes, then the use of tax data or Social Security data is unlikely to help. If one thinks that it is the incidental earnings, mostly from self-employment, that are omitted, the same conclusions hold.

There is also the problem that in any real study, the cooperation of the respondents is crucial and not to be reduced by unnecessary demands, particularly that they sign something (quite threatening, or insulting when you have asked for similar information in the interview). And it is usually desirable to provide results reasonably promptly − difficult to do if the whole process of getting outside information and editing it must be done too.

It seems likely that the main future direction will be to use outside data largely in methodological studies and validity studies, attempting to develop better survey methods, rather than in data collection efforts. If and when we learn how to rouse the enthusiasm of the respondent to the point where he is so eager to give us the information that he finds it natural to send us to his bank or other record source, then we can consider extensive use of such sources. But for most data, if the respondent is that cooperative, the outside source will be unnecessary.

The use of data from similar respondents (same neighbourhood, or same demographic characteristics) as a kind of outside information about the individual respondent, is more promising. This is different from collecting data about the individual from outside sources, the data are about his *group* or his neighborhood. Particularly in the study of neigborhoods and satisfaction with housing and community, heavier-than-usual clustering of the sample, and the use of cluster averages as part of the explanatory factors for each individual, seem likely to be productive.

REINTERVIEWS AND PANELS

In recent years, there has been an increasing call for longitudinal studies − reinterviews and panels. The argument has been that

26

dynamic data on changes, particularly changes in attitudes, expectations, plans, but also in asset or debt balances, cannot be reconstructed from retrospective questions relying on people's memory. The Survey Research Center has conducted a number of such studies, and is currently engaged in a five year panel study which may extend to eight years for a crucial subgroup. As usual, our enthusiasm for the new and promising encourages us to underestimate the disadvantages and problems. It may be useful to mention a few of the latter:

First, the family, the usual unit of analysis, is not a stable unit. Over even a relatively brief period its composition changes. Where this is only the birth or departure of children, or even extra adults, it is not serious. But a substantial number of families experience change in head or wife. One can define a sample to include everyone in the initial families, and follow all the individuals who move out, but complex problems arise. If a daughter leaves home and gets married, we may have to interview the new husband.

If the individual is the unit of analysis, the girl will show up with a change in her individual income, and her "family income", the latter because it is a different family. If the family is the unit of analysis, there will be two different families in year two, each with a change in family income from year one that is affected by changes in the family structure. (The first year's family data appear twice in the record now.)

Second, there are problems of response rate, since each contact brings with it some losses, and the losses are cumulative if one requires the full set of records for the analysis. Response rates are generally higher on the later waves, as the recalcitrant are dropped, but the problem remains, particularly with the splitoffs.

Third, there are costs of following and interviewing people as the initial clustering which cut field costs is dissolved in a welter of moves. And as the past investment in each respondent gets greater, the amount it is worth spending to secure the next interview with him increases.

Fourth, there are possibilities of affecting the respondents by paying attention to them, or focusing their attention on the subject matter of the study. This does not seem to us a crucial matter, particularly with annual interviews. We know that most people can hardly remember the next day what a study was all about.

Fifth, there are costs of complexity all along the line. The number of possible variables measuring change that can be developed is astronomical, and problems arise whether one wants absolute change (which will be larger for those who have higher levels) or percentage changes (which will be larger for those who start lower). And with categorical measures such as occupation, how does one measure change? The problem of long record lengths — thousands of variables for each unit (family or individual) — can be handled, but only at the cost of computer time and expense.

ALTERNATIVE SOURCES OF DYNAMIC DATA

Given the expenses and other difficulties with reinterview studies, it is important that we explore alternative possibilities for securing dynamic data. For some studies, the use of retrospective questions relying on people's memories may be a real possibility. Studies have already collected occupational histories, and at least one has asked about the history of automobile purchases and disposals. And studies of family planning have asked for histories of births, contraception practices, etc. It would seem that one could rather easily study a family's history of changing family composition, location and housing.

Another possibility is the more intensive use of repeated cross-section samples. This has great flexibility since one can observe changes that need to be explained and identified, find earlier studies which contain the needed information, and repeat those studies. One can then search for subgroups of the population (identified in such a way that not too many people will have changed their subgroup membership) which have experienced the least and the greatest change. We now have flexible search techniques which can take a merged file from two studies at different time points, or in different places, and search for the subgroups with the largest and the smallest differences (absolutely or relatively) in some criterion variable like income or home ownership. The advantages of probability samples, reproducible methods, etc., can thus really be capitalized upon. The use of open-ended questions, and controlled content analysis in the central office, allows recoding of the earlier study to assure stability of methods.

28

Of course the obvious limitation of such a method is that the comparable groups can only be identified according to such demographic variables as race, sex, education, age (or date of birth), if one restricts analysis to groups with fixed membership. One can also look at groups according to residential location, occupation, or income decile, provided the interpretation of the analysis allows for the fact that the situation of the members of a group has changed, but part of the change may reflect the changing membership of the group, not changes in individuals' situations.

EXPERIMENTS

The implications of all this discussion are that the perseverance in studying important economic decisions and situations for representative national samples is worth continuing, and that various expansions and improvements are possible. The most focused-upon recent suggestion for change has been experimental manipulations of samples (usually of special subpopulations), as in the negative income tax experiments, or proposed experiments with housing allowances. Again, our enthusiasm for the possibilities should not blind us to the costs and problems. *First*, the desire to control the environment, and to measure the uncontrolled environmental forces, and perhaps to make the manipulation effective, encourages the restriction of experiments to a few geographic sites. But since one can never control the environment, the possibility of something unusual happening in each of the sites (or that they were unusual in the beginning in some way) is substantial, and "confounds" the experiments. Particularly since such experiments usually involve politically sensitive issues, the vocal concern of any local politician may be enough to "blow" the experiment.

Second, the manipulations never seem to be sufficiently close to the possibly permanent change, the effects of which are to be studied. A temporary guarantee, subsidy, etc., may well be treated differently from a permanent one; an experimental program limited to a few may produce a different response from a nationally accepted program. And the people's understanding of the program, not having it also clarified in the newspapers, by neighbors, etc., may well be less than the testing theory demands.

Third, since the experimental manipulations are often expensive, the number of families or individuals involved is usually restricted. Yet in any sample of families, a substantial number are subject to rather dramatic or compelling other pressures. Even in theory it is the marginal family that is supposedly affected by marginal changes. Hence, the experimental effects may be submerged in "noise" from other forces.

This problem occurs in any analysis of survey data, and requires some attention to locating subgroups which may be affected by a particular variable, not merely testing that variable's effect on the whole sample (however "multivariate" the regression analysis). But it is more serious with small samples restricted to a few areas and to special subpopulations. For instance, tight credit may have a substantial effect on young families without savings who have had several children recently (and need a lot of things) and who have a poor credit rating. Or differential trends in house prices versus rents may mostly affect older home-owners who can sell their homes and rent without paying capital gains taxes.

Fourth, there may actually be enough changes, and differently occurring in different states or counties, so that there are a number of natural experiments worthy of study, investing the funds in larger and broader samples. The issue is not so much sample size as representativeness.

Finally, there are some moral issues involved in experimenting with human populations. Are the behaviors we are trying to encourage really in their own interests? Are we producing temporary changes which would be good only if the program continued, getting them "hooked" on something they will not be able to continue with? Are we exposing them to the possibility of public criticism of their whole group? Any survey finding that generalizes is subject to the charge of stereotyping: the survey only says most X's believe Y but the common interpretation is to assume that any individual X believes Y. Many experimental manipulations expose individuals to temptations to cheat, and may put them under pressure in unfamiliar situations, and are likely to expose them to publicity. The survey organization collecting data to evaluate such a program can easily be thought to have been part of the program of enforcement against cheating, whatever the facts.

A THIRD BRANCH OF ECONOMICS

Whatever the future source of survey research on economic behavior, the increasing range of government policies affecting the consumer and worker raises a whole new area of investigation for survey research. We need better information on the diversity of desires, needs, tastes, values, and preferences of our citizens. Pareto optimality, in the theory of welfare economics, calls for assessing whether some solution is possible that leaves no one worse off, and at least someone better off. Real world policy issues often require assessing the gains and losses to various groups. It does not help to argue that utility cannot be measured, much less compared as between two individuals. Such measurements and comparisons are made by politicians all the time, and it would help if they had better information on which to base their decisions.

It is even possible that better information both about people's values and preferences, and about the information (or misinformation) and insights (or misunderstandings) on which they are based, would enable elected representatives to provide more leadership than otherwise. But at least we could avoid the sorry picture of warring proponents of alternative policies, each making his own assumptions about what will make the most people the happiest. The electoral process is far too slow and inefficient (and dominated by other forces like party loyalty) to do the job. Is it not appropriate to find out and make public any misunderstandings causing resistance to new public programs or policies of which elected representatives may be unaware?

So the future of survey research is entwined with the future of economics, for the behavioral findings of economic surveys provide the realism for the models of analytical economics, and perhaps some day the survey findings on the sources of satisfaction and dissatisfaction of different groups will provide the basis on which better public policies can be made and interpreted to the voters.

31

As economists, we should apply our own analytical tools to analysis of our own activities. Optimal resource allocation of the time and energy of economists among analysis, increasing our knowledge of economic behavior, attempting to measure what increases the welfare of which groups, and transmitting all three to the next generation (teaching and training), needs some attention. The poor fit between the sources and methods of funding, and the task to be done, should be the subject of some discussion. Survey research requires longer gestation periods and larger budgets than analytical economic research. Hence it is peculiarly hampered by insistence on annual funding, and by comparisons with projects which involve no new data collection. And coordination among the diverse activities of economists, so that the gains of specialization are not lost in the failure to coordinate or communicate, clearly needs attention and improvement. Analytical economists have tended to ignore cross-section data, even in the formulation of their models, while behavioral economists have tended to lose sight of the crucial concerns of analytical economists for data to fit their dynamic models, in the welter of other variables that must be allowed for in analyzing survey data, if only as "noise". And those concerned with policy have been impatient with both analytical economists and quantitative researchers, whose findings seemed too slow or not sufficiently focused on the problem. Better cooperation and mutual understanding are in order.

Those of us who have specialized in studying economic behavior, and in the use of personal interview surveys with representative samples of substantial and important groups, have to ask how we can improve the work, and whether expanding the scope-range of methods used will produce more gains than losses. There is so much research yet to be done, in so many areas of economics, that the opportunity cost of any decision is likely to be high.

What is the optimal mix of persistence and change, of continued work on one problem versus sensitivity to the crucial new problems of the day? It will be easier to answer this retrospectively after another twenty-five years have gone by, but the decisions must be made now.

REFERENCES

1 Barfield, Richard, *The Automobile Worker and Retirement, A Second Look*, Ann Arbor: Survey Research Center, Institute for Social Research, The University of Michigan, 1970.

2 Barfield, Richard, and James N. Morgan, *Early Retirement (The Decision and the Experience)*, Ann Arbor: Survey Research Center, Institute for Social Research, The University of Michigan, 1969.

3 Katona, George, *Private Pensions and Individual Saving*, Ann Arbor: Survey Research Center, Institute for Social Research, The University of Michigan, 1965.

4 Katona, George, *et al.*, *Business Looks at Banks*, Ann Arbor: University of Michigan Press, 1957.

5 Katona, George, and James N. Morgan, *Industrial Mobility in Michigan*, Ann Arbor: Survey Research Center, Institute for Social Research, The University of Michigan, 1950.

6 Katona, George, and James N. Morgan, "The Quantitative Study of Factors Determining Business Decisions", *Quarterly Journal of Economics*, 66 (February 1952), 67–90.

7 Lansing, John B., and Gary Hendricks, *Living Patterns and Attitudes in the Detroit Region*, Detroit Regional Transportation and Land Use Study, Detroit, 1967.

8 Lansing, John B., and Gary Hendricks, *Automobile Ownership and Residential Density*, Ann Arbor: Survey Research Center, Institute for Social Research, The University of Michigan, 1967.

9 Lansing, John B., Charles W. Clifton and James N. Morgan, *New Homes and Poor People: A Study of Chains of Moves*, Ann Arbor: Survey Research Center, Institute for Social Research, The University of Michigan, 1969.

10 Lansing, John B., and Eva L. Mueller, *The Geographic Mobility of Labor*, Ann Arbor: Survey Research Center, Institute for Social Research, The University of Michigan, 1967.

11 Lansing, John B., Robert Marans and Robert Zehner, *Planned Residential Environments*, Ann Arbor: Survey Research Center, Institute for Social Research, The University of Michigan, 1970.

12 Marquis, Kent, "Effects of Social Reinforcement on Health Reporting in the Household Interview", *Sociometry*, 33 (June 1970) 203–215.

13 Morgan, James N., Martin David, Wilbur Cohen and Harvey Brazer, *Income and Welfare in the United States*, New York: McGraw-Hill, 1962.

14 Morgan, James N., Ismail Sirageldin and Nancy Baerwaldt, *Productive Americans*, Ann Arbor: Survey Research Center, Institute for Social Research, The University of Michigan, 1966.

15 Mueller, Eva L. and James N. Morgan, "Location Decisions of Manufacturers", *American Economic Review*, 52 (May 1962), 204–217.

16 Mueller, Eva L. Arnold Wilken and Margaret Wood, *Location Decisions and Industrial Mobility in Michigan*, Ann Arbor: Survey Research Center,

Institute for Social Research, The University of Michigan, 1962.

17 Mueller, Eva L., *et al.*, *Technological Advance in an Expanding Economy: Its Impact on a Cross-Section of the Labor Force*, Ann Arbor: Survey Research Center, Institute for Social Research, The University of Michigan, 1969.

18 Sonquist, John and James N. Morgan, *The Detection of Interaction Effects*, Ann Arbor: Survey Research Center, Institute for Social Research, The University of Michigan, 1964.

19 Sonquist, John, Elizabeth Baker and James N. Morgan, *Searching for Structure*, Ann Arbor: Survey Research Center, Institute for Social Research, The University of Michigan, 1971.

20 Srikantan, K.S., "Canonical Association Between Nominal Measurements", *Journal of the American Statistical Association*, 65 (March 1970), 284–292.

Economic Psychology and Behavioral Science

Wealth, Liquidity, and the Propensity to Consume

JAMES TOBIN

The careers of the Consumption Function and George Katona have been intertwined since 1945. The consumption-saving decision has been a major subject of theoretical and empirical inquiry, to which no one has contributed more than Katona. A behavioral scientist by training and temperament, he brought to economic research quite a different bag of tools and insights from those of the technical economists. As a social psychologist, he was probably not surprised to find that he annoyed many of the brethern of his adopted scientific fraternity. What put them off was his disdain for utility-maximizing or profit-maximizing models of individual behavior, and his failure to base his statistical inferences and macro-economic conclusions on explicit formal system-wide models. But today we can appreciate, even from the perspective of economic theory and econometrics themselves, Katona's perception, prescience, and persistence.

Katona was the great entrepreneur of survey data collection, and for this alone the economics profession owes him an immense debt. In the early postwar years economists were still convinced that rigorous sophisticated methods could make time series of

* The research described in this paper was carried out under grants from the National Science Foundation.

economic aggregates disclose simple reliable macro-relations. This optimistic faith dominated in particular economists' research on saving behavior, thanks initially to the apparent statistical success of the Keynesian consumption function. But as primitive Keynesian functions failed and competing hypotheses of greater complexity were advanced to fill the vacuum, the importance of household survey data came to be appreciated. Meanwhile Katona and his colleagues in Ann Arbor and Washington were busy providing, in the annual Surveys of Consumer Finances, an invaluable data base. Moreover, Katona and the Survey Research Center pioneered in reinterview surveys: the profession's appetite for panel data of this type is now almost insatiable.

Katona's other major enterprise in survey data collection has been the continuous monitoring of consumer attitudes, expectations, and intentions. Indeed these are the data closest to his own theoretical and methodological interests. Economists have been slower to appreciate and to use these data than the more conventional demographic and financial information of household surveys. But this situation too is changing. One reason is that contemporary theories of saving behavior, portfolio choice, and inflation place great emphasis on economic agents' perceptions of their environment and expectations of its future. There is precious little information on these psychological variables — what they are, what their behavioral implications are, how they are altered by experience and learning — except what George Katona has collected. As economists move beyond the stage of regarding expectations as unobservable and representing them by untested functions of past observations, they will have to rely heavily on Katona's data, and on his interpretations as well.

Imitation and extension are flattery in science as elsewhere. The federal government and other agencies now collect, regularly or *ad hoc*, many of the kinds of survey and panel data in which Katona and his organization pioneered.

Economists concerned with consumption and saving behavior owe Katona a debt for insights and ideas as well as for data. He has always expressed skepticism of the tight mechanical relation of consumption spending to cash income, into which the Keynesian propensity to consume had evolved in lesser hands than those of its inventor. Katona saw two major developments in America and, with a lag, in other economies as well which make consumption a less and less predictable function of cash income. One is general affluence; as consumption spending becomes further and further removed from basic subsistence, both its direction and its timing become more discretionary. The other is the improvement of credit markets, the appearance and growth of institutions enabling consumers to borrow against houses, other durable goods, or simply their names and earning prospects.

To these reasons one might add a special consequence of the growth of affluence: increase in life expectancies and retirement spans. These have been accompanied by a shift in the socially accepted financial responsibilities of generations. Most Americans now expect, and are expected, to provide for their old age with their own resources and social insurance rather than to become charges on their children. Faced with this requirement, a household cannot, and as a result need not, follow the simple rule of spending as it earns.

These developments, in Katona's view, liberate consumer spending from dependence on contemporaneous cash income and make consumption-saving decisions, like any other area of discretionary behavior, a matter of psychology. The conventional economists' reaction to the news that contemporaneous cash income alone does not explain consumption is to add other "objective" explanatory variables: lagged incomes, wealth, liquid assets, etc. Katona's reaction has been to try to measure directly the attitudes and expectations that proximately govern households in exercising their discretion, and to seek in turn explanations of the formation of these proximate variables.

The two approaches are not as antagonistic as they have often seemed. Indeed, in the context of the current theory and econometrics of consumption and saving, they are convergent and complementary. That, at any rate, is the theme I propose to argue in this paper in honor of George Katona, as much to justify economic theory to him as him to the economic theorists.

INCOME AS LIQUIDITY AND AS WEALTH

Throughout its history the consumption function has been

characterized by intellectual tension between a liquidity and a wealth interpretation of income as the primary determinant of consumption. Both interpretations are present in the *General Theory* [8]. But the wealth interpretation is dominant; Keynes, after all, discusses the propensity to consume as a "psychological law". Nevertheless the liquidity interpretation came to dominate early statistical and econometric work, textbook expositions of multiplier arithmetic, and practical models of fiscal policy. Recent emphasis on permanent and lifetime income has brought the wealth interpretation to the fore.[1]

Which is the effective constraint on the current consumption of a household? Its liquidity, the resources it can mobilize to spend within a short period, a month, a quarter, a year or two? Or its wealth, human as well as nonhuman, the total of its present and future consumable resources, including prospective earnings from work? For a liquidity-constrained household, income is a source of cash and changes in income will be almost completely reflected in changes in consumption spending in a short time. For a wealth-constrained household, one year's income is by itself a small part of total wealth; like other variations in wealth, changes in current income will be shared among this year's consumption and all future years. Only if changes in current income inspire significant changes in estimates of future income and thus in total wealth will there be a large response in current consumption.

VOLATILITY AND STABILITY IN THE MARGINAL PROPENSITY TO CONSUME

Primitive evidence certainly supports Katona's observations that the *ex post* marginal propensity to consume is extremely volatile in the short run. In Figure 1, I have plotted, with apology for the use of so crude a device in this computer age, a scatter diagram of annual changes in per capita real personal consumption against contemporaneous changes in per capita real disposable income for the United States 1952–1970. The reference line has a slope of 0.91, which is the ratio of the full nineteen-year change in con-

---

[1] The standard references are [1], [4], and [10].

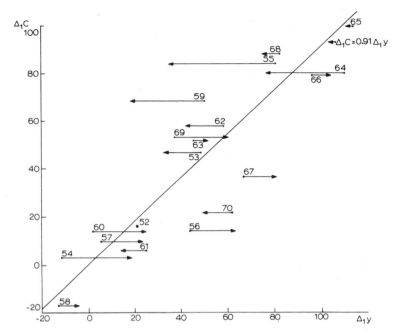

Fig. 1. Differences from previous year in per capita real disposable income ($\Delta_1 y$) and consumption ($\Delta_1 c$), 1952–1970 (1958 dollars).

sumption to the change in income over the period. The scatter speaks for itself. It would be even worse, of course, for quarterly data. Judicious expenditure of degrees of freedom on lag structure makes things better – see the consumption sector of any eco- nometric model. But the obstacles to substantial improvement by lagging income alone are indicated on the diagram by the horizon- tal arrows, which indicate how the designated point would shift if the horizontal variable included last year's income with weight up to one-half. About half the arrows point the wrong way.

Whether the volatility is greater postwar than prewar is not so clear. Figure 2 presents the same data for 1930–40, on a scale that compensates roughly for the difference in the magnitudes of in- come and consumption changes between the two periods. The reference line has the slope 0.78, based on comparison of 1933 and 1940, the biggest income difference during the period. Prewar deviations of consumption from the reference line were smaller than postwar in average absolute magnitude, both in dollars and in

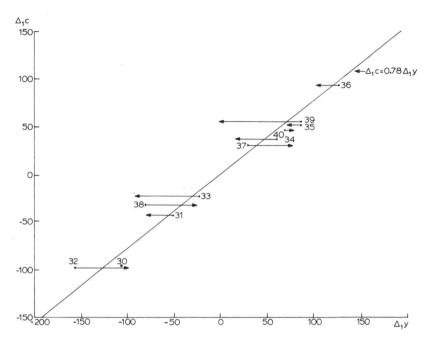

Fig. 2. Differences from previous year in per capita real disposable income ($\Delta_1 y$) and consumption ($\Delta_1 c$), 1930–1940 (1958 dollars).

relation to the average absolute size of income and consumption changes. But the prewar deviations were larger relative to average income and consumption levels.

Short-run volatility is consistent with a remarkable degree of long-run stability in the marginal propensity to consume. Figure 3 is derived from the same 1952–1970 data as Figure 1, but plots average differences from five and ten years earlier, instead of one year earlier. Since these deviations from the reference line in Figure 3 include averages of successive random elements in the one-year deviations of Figure 1, it is to be expected that they will have lower variance. But the improvement is greater than would be expected on this basis. For the ten-year differences, the standard deviation is .17 of that for the one-year differences, rather than $(1/10)^{1/2}$. For the five-year differences it is .27 rather than $(1/5)^{1/2}$. Evidently short-run fluctuations in the marginal propensity to consume are not independent. Although timing is erratic, a correction mechanism seems to operate to keep consumption,

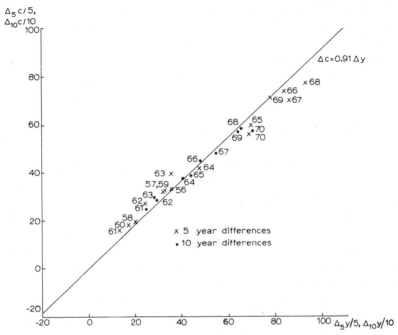

Fig. 3. Average annual differences from five or ten years previous in per capita real disposable income ($\Delta_5 y/5, \Delta_{10} y/10$) and consumption ($\Delta_5 c/5$, $\Delta_{10} c/10$) (1958 dollars).

saving, and income in fairly stable long-run relationship to each other. The task of theory is to explain both the short-run volatility and the long-run stability.

The role of disposable personal income in consumption functions illustrates the vacillation of the profession between the wealth and liquidity models. Although the choice of this income concept might be justified on both grounds, it is not really appropriate for either one. As a liquidity measure it would be a proxy for cash inflow. As a wealth measure it would be a surrogate for lifetime income or total wealth. Its most characteristic feature, the omission of direct taxes, makes sense in either case.

Department of Commerce DPI handles many items on a cash rather than accrual basis, and excludes both employer and personal contributions for social insurance. In these respects it is more liquidity than wealth oriented, but Paul Taubman has recently pointed out that it is far from a thoroughgoing cash income measure [13]. It is certainly a poor measure either of total wealth or of human wealth. It includes some but not all earnings of property; a major omission is corporate retained earnings. It omits earned supplements to wages and salaries. And of course it registers fluctuations of cash incomes of property and labor that households presumably smooth out in evaluating their wealth positions.

WEALTH AND LIQUIDITY: A TWO-PERIOD EXAMPLE

Consider, for example, the Fisherian consumer of Figure 4, with a life "cycle" of two periods. Suppose his wealth is entirely human wealth: his labor will yield cash incomes of y_1 and y_2 in the two periods. He can convert first-period income into second-period consumption at an interest rate of r. In a perfect capital market he can also borrow at this rate and convert future income into current consumption. His opportunity locus would be the line $C_2 C_1$, and let us suppose his chosen consumption sequence would be C^*. Should his initial income be y_1' instead, his opportunity locus will shift, parallel, to $C_2' C_1'$, and his chosen sequence will become $C^{*'}$. Normally, as in the illustration, both periods' consumption will share in the gain in total resources; the marginal

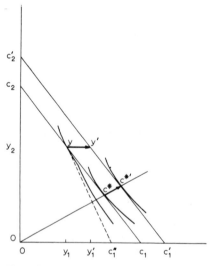

Fig. 4. Two-period consumption choice with and without liquidity constraints.

44

propensity to consume from current cash income is less than one. (If preferences are scale-free, indifference curves homothetic, C^* and $C^{*\prime}$ are on the same ray. The marginal propensity is simply the ratio of first period consumption to c_1 to C_1, the household's total resources evaluated in terms of first-period consumption, $y_1 + y_2/(1+r)$.) In this example the only constraint on the consumer is his wealth.

A pure and extreme case of liquidity constraint arises of the consumer of Figure 4 is not allowed to borrow future income, to convert second-period income y_2 into first-period consumption. This constraint forces the consumer to point Y, the consumption sequence $c_1 = y_1, c_2 = y_2$. His opportunity locus is $C_2 Y$, and in technical jargon he is at a 'corner' instead of 'interior' maximum of utility. The marginal propensity of current consumption with respect to current cash income is unity: $\partial c_1/\partial y_1 = 1$. This is indicated in Figure 4 by the horizontal path, YY', of response to an increase of initial income to y_1'.

The liquidity constraint need not be absolute. The consumer may be permitted to borrow against future income, but only at a penalty rate. The opportunity locus will be like $C_2 YC_1''$, and the consumer may still prefer the corner Y to any point interior to YC_1''. The current marginal propensity to consume is one, as before, at least for income decreases and small enough increases.

WEALTH AND LIQUIDITY IN THE LIFE CYCLE MODEL

The same points can be illustrated for a multi-period lifetime. I have set forth the life cycle model formally elsewhere, [15] and [2], and here I will only sketch it and illustrate it graphically. In Figure 5 the age of a consuming household from its formation to its death is measured horizontally, and against it is plotted the cumulative discounted labor income $Y(a)$ of the household up to each age a. This is the present value as of age 0 of the stream of income from 0 to a, with discount rates equal to the lending or saving rates available to the household. The flow of income $y(a)$, discounted to age zero, is the slope of the curve $Y(a)$. The value, as of age zero, of total life-time income is $Y(a)$. A similar path $C(a)$ may be drawn for discounted cumulative consumption. Assuming

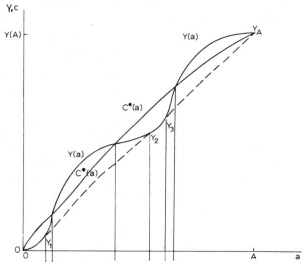

Fig. 5. Cumulative income Y and consumption C, constrained and unconstrained, in relation to household age a.

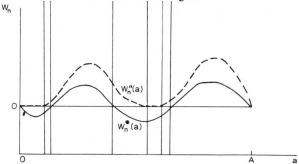

Fig. 6. Nonhuman wealth W, constrained and unconstrained, in relation to household age a.

that the household begins and ends with zero net nonhuman wealth — or with the same amount in value as of age zero — its lifetime budget constraint is that $C(A) = Y(A)$. (This implies $C(a) \leqslant Y(A)$ for all a — since consumption flow is nonnegative, $C(a)$ is nondecreasing in a.)

In a wealth model of consumption this is the only budget constraint. The shape of $Y(a)$ does not matter; any path $C(a)$ is available provided it ends up at the proper point. All wealth, human and nonhuman, future yields of labor as well as future yields of bonds and stocks, is available at its capitalized value for consumption now or at any future time. Wealth is completely fungible between periods.

With this freedom of choice, what consumption path will the household choose? This will depend on several factors: (1) the smaller its *subjective rate of time preference* and the greater the *interest rates offered in the market*, the more the household will tilt its consumption stream — the slope of $C(a)$ — in favor of later as against earlier consumption; (2) *household size and composition* vary over the life cycle, and there may be other age-related reasons for variation of consumption rates. With these factors taken into account, diminishing marginal utility of consumption in any one period is a strong force for equality of consumption between periods. The theory suggests a smooth consumption path $C(a)$. One with sharp changes of slope, that is of consumption rates, would probably be one with differences of marginal utility which the household could to its advantage erase by shifting consumption from a plush to a sparse year.

At this point a digression is in order to recall the role of Katona's Economic Behavior Program, especially of the late John Lansing, in developing the 'life cycle' concept and implementing it statistically. It was Jack Lansing who long ago saw the convenience and fruitfulness of regarding household age as a sovereign exogenous variable on which many other demographic and economic magnitudes were jointly dependent — family size and composition, labor force participation, income, consumption, wealth (see [9]). He saw before many of the rest of us that in handling household surveys this approach would often make more sense than regarding some of the jointly dependent variables as predetermined and regressing others upon them, as in the fitting and interpretation of Engel curves. It is also noteworthy that the long series of Surveys of Consumer Finances provides the best available data for estimating age—income profiles, on both a cross-section and sequential basis, for people of various occupations and educational attainments.[2]

---

[2] This has been painstakingly done by Robert Stearns [12]. Stearns has some success in showing that differences among households in current consumption are related to whole profiles, not just to current income. Some years earlier Harold Watts used SCF data for a similar purpose [16].

Returning to Figure 5, suppose that $C*(a)$ represents the utility-maximizing path. The difference $Y(a) - C*(a)$ is nonhuman wealth $W_n^*(a)$ at age a, discounted as usual to age zero. This may be negative at some ages, as in the illustration, because of borrowing against future labor incomes. The age-wealth profile $W_n^*(a)$ is also plotted in Figure 6. According to the life cycle theory, a household dissaves, saves, and dissaves, in order to smooth out in consumption the age-related fluctuations of its earnings.

With liquidity constraints, however, the household would not ever be able to have negative W_n. To the general wealth constraint $C(A) = Y(A)$ would be added $C(a) \leqslant Y(a)$ for all a. Alternatively, as in the two-period example above, a high penalty rate for borrowing could have the same effect as an absolute prohibition. The best liquidity-constrained path — with no negative net worth positions at any age — is $OY_1 Y_2 Y_3 Y_A$. Two segments of this path are liquidity-constrained, OY_1 and $Y_2 Y_3$. A best constrained C-path will have, as illustrated, tangencies to the Y path at the ages at which liquidity constraints become or cease to become effective, Y_1, Y_2, and Y_3 in the illustration. Otherwise there will be sharp discontinuities in consumption rates, inviting smoothing in order to bring marginal utilities closer together.

The liquidity-constrained age—wealth profile W_n'' is shown in Figure 6. It is of course always above the unconstrained age-wealth profile $W*_n$.[3]

Here, even more than in the two-period example, the effectiveness of liquidity constraints makes a difference in the current marginal propensity to consume (mpc). In the constrained case, this mpc is one during the stages of the life cycle at which the constraint is effective, and less than one at other ages. In the absence of constraint, all consumption within the horizon, future as well as current, will share in any revision of the household's estimate of the present value of its resources. The horizon may be

---

[3] In emphasizing the importance of household differences in liquidity in explaining their differences in saving, I return to my theme of twenty years ago [14]. Then I contended that simple lack of liquidity rather than lack of status aspiration explained the higher average propensity to save of Negroes. Their higher propensity as a group was largely due to the infrequency and limited amounts of dissaving among them, more likely the result of external constraints than of choice.

the remaining lifetime, as in the completely unconstrained case, or just the time until the liquidity constraint becomes binding, as in the interval $Y_1 Y_2$ in Figure 5. An increase in current disposable income alone will in these circumstances have only a fractional effect on current consumption; generally most of the increment in total resources will be saved for future consumption. Calculations for an unconstrained life cycle model for the United States population indicate an *mpc* from total wealth, human or non-human, of about .05-.07 [2, Part IV]. This would apply to a one-shot change in disposable income. It is a far cry from the estimate of one for liquidity-constrained consumers.

The wealth model and the liquidity model thus imply very different values of the short-run *mpc*, much smaller in the former case than in the latter. The mirror image is that they also imply very different responses to other parameters, larger for the wealth model than the liquidity model. Wealth-constrained households will, liquidity-constrained households will not, alter their current consumption in response to marginal changes in their illiquid resources — increases in expected future labor incomes, improvements in prospective retirement benefits, capital gains on houses and other imperfectly liquid assets. Wealth-constrained households will, liquidity-constrained households will not, respond to small changes in interest rates, either for lending or for borrowing. (In all these cases it is conceivable that large enough changes in the right direction will move a household from a corner to an interior point. For example, if future income declines enough the inability to borrow against it ceases to be a relevant concern.)

CURRENT INCOME AS AN INDEX OF WEALTH

Current income, in addition to being a constituent of total wealth, a small one for households of most ages, is a source of information about future incomes. This role may greatly magnify the short-run *mpc*. Whether it does or not depends upon how people read the changes in income which they experience. If their expectations are extrapolative, obviously, the effects will be stronger than if they are regressive. Here is one point on which the life cycle model must appeal to George Katona and other students of expectations.[4]

To formulate the point more precisely, the life cycle theory says that current year's consumption of a household of age a is a certain fraction γ_a of its total human and nonhuman wealth $W_h + W_n$. Human wealth W_h is $\Sigma_{i=0}^{A} (d_i)^i y_{a+i}$ where $y_a, y_{a+1}, y_{a+2}, \ldots$ is the stream of current and expected disposable labor income and the $(d_i)^i$ are the discount rates that convert these incomes to present values. Let the prior expectations of the income stream be $y_a^* + i$ and W_h^* the corresponding value of human wealth using the discount factors d_i. Suppose that the household obeys the following rule of revision of income expectations after learning the true value of y_a.

$$y_{a+i}/y_{a+i}^* = (y_a/y_a^*)^{\beta_i} \qquad (i = 1, 2, \ldots) \tag{1}$$

Thus $W_h = y_a + \Sigma_{i=1}^{A} (d_i)^i \, y_{a+i}^* (y_a/y_a^*)^{\beta_i}$, and

$$\partial c_a / \partial y_a = \gamma_a \left[1 + \Sigma_{i=1}^{A} \beta_i (d_i)^i (y_{a+i}^*/y_a^*) (y_a/y_a^*)^{\beta_i - 1} \right] \tag{2}$$

If all the β_i are zero, the *mpc* is simply γ_a, a parameter, as previously stated, of the order of .05–.07 on average. If all the β_i are one, $W_h = (y_a/y_a^*)W_h^*$ and the short-run *mpc* is

$$\gamma_a(W_h^*/y_a^*) = (c_a^*/y_a^*) (W_h^*/(W_h^* + W_n)) \tag{3}$$

Blowing disposable labor income y_a up by the ratio of total wealth to human wealth gives approximately total disposable income. So the short-run *mpc* in this case is equal to the average propensity to consume.

But of course there are many other possibilities, within and beyond these two special cases. We have no reason to believe the β_i to be constant over time or to be independent of the sources and circumstances of income change. We must expect revisions of income expectations resulting from information other than that conveyed by current income. Unlike the liquidity model, therefore,

---

[4] Besides the studies of Katona and his colleagues, reference can be made to [3], [6], and [11].

the wealth model gives us plenty of reason to understand the observed short-run volatility of the marginal propensity to consume.

The life cycle model has the substantial merit of providing an explanation of the long-run trend interrelations of consumption, saving, income and wealth. The theory predicts that in a demographic and economic growth equilibrium, in which households correctly foresee their lifetime incomes, their nonhuman wealth will follow a characteristic age profile (see Figure 6). The shape of the age–wealth profile will remain the same as incomes grow, assuming that technological progress raises proportionately the incomes of all age groups. Aggregate wealth is a weighted sum of the average wealth holdings of different ages, where the weights are the numbers of households of those ages. With a constant relative age distribution of the population, aggegrate wealth will, just like aggregate income, rise at the natural rate of growth of the economy, g, the sum of the rates of population growth and of technological progress. The aggregate wealth–income ratio will be a constant μ. The saving–income ratio will be $g\mu$. These ratios will be constant along any given demographic-economic growth path, but they will differ from path to path. The wealth–income ratio μ depends on, among other things, the interest rate, the rate of growth of population, and the rate of growth of per capita income.

The long-run aggregative implications of an unconstrained wealth model can be modified to allow for liquidity constraints of constant incidence, for example, always effective on typical consumers of certain ages. Such constraints will modify the characteristic age–wealth profile in the manner indicated in Figure 6 and raise μ above what it would be in the unconstrained case.

The merit of the life cycle model is to explain both (*a*) why the long-run saving–income ratio should be roughly constant, and (*b*) what determines the value at which it is constant. The model's essential properties hold even if a bequest motive for saving is introduced, provided that lifetime accumulation for transfer to the next generation is proportional to lifetime income. The model can probably also accommodate uncertainty and precautionary saving, a subject not discussed at all in this paper.

Critics complain that the model assumes a vastly unrealistic degree of foresight and rational calculus on the part of households. Similar criticisms are made of the maximize-present-value theory of the firm, which is in many respects analogous. In both cases theory assumes an objective and spells out its logical consequences. Real world households and firms doubtless employ many rules of thumb and shortcuts, and make many mistakes. That does not destroy the usefulness of the theory in pointing out the trends and relations implicit in the pursuit of these objectives. Perhaps the crucial assumption is that saving reflects purposeful behavior and is not just an unplanned random residuum. Purposeful saving is done for Christmas, taxes, vacations, college, retirement, and estates. Although households commonly speak of saving 'what is left over,' this is often a short-run technique of budget control rather than an indication that future and current needs are not balanced against each other.

There has been widespread agreement that purposeful foresight is involved in household consumption decisions, but disagreement about the length of the 'horizon'. Few consumers live literally hand-to-mouth in the sense that they are liquidity-constrained every hour or every day. People do smooth out their consumption and spending between paychecks and anticipate seasonal gaps between needs and receipts. Furthermore, there is plenty of evidence that horizons generally extend beyond one year. Friedman [4] suggests three years or so for his permanent income horizon; Modigliani and Brumberg [10] suggest a lifetime; others, emphasizing bequest motives, would span several generations. (Some dynasties, and some nonprofit institutions counted in the household sector in the national accounts, evidently have infinite horizons; consifer the Rockefeller family and Yale University.)

The model expounded above and illustrated in Figures 5 and 6 may help to clarify the concept of horizon. In its most inclusive and vaguest sense the word refers to the future period over which outcomes are of current concern and interest. In its technical meaning for consumption theory, it refers to the period over which resources are pooled and, speaking loosely, averaged to determine rates of consumption. This is the interval between effective liquidity constraints, as was illustrated in Figure 5. This interval may be a month for some consumers, and for others a year or two or three, or a lifetime. Knowing that whatever happens you will hit a liquidity constraint in a few years greatly simplifies the estimates and calculations relevant for current consumption. Incomes that will occur after date can be ignored; they will not arrive in time to relieve the constraints on current and near-term consumption anyway.

CONCLUDING REMARKS

The *mpc* for short-run variations of aggregate disposable income will evidently depend on how the change is split between liquidity-constrained and wealth-constrained housholds. The liquidity-constrained households will contribute an *mpc* of one to the average. The contribution of the remaining group will depend on their horizons and on how they re-estimate their human wealth as a result of changes in current income. Clearly it would be very desirable to identify the two groups and to collect relevant information from each. This would not be an easy task, but the model does provide a framework for the collection and organization of data.

Although the exposition and illustrations above stressed the possible illiquidity of future labor incomes, human wealth is not the only kind of wealth that may be illiquid. Future retirement benefits, under federal social security or private pension plans, cannot be turned into cash or pledged as security for loans. There are limits to the amounts that can be borrowed against houses, other consumer durable goods, and business proprietorships. These assets can be sold, it is true, but frequently only with sacrifices comparable to the penalty rate in the examples above: The reasons are familiar. Neither the markets for these assets nor those for rental of their services are perfect. Because of complementarities with the tastes or labor of their owners, durable goods and businesses often yield considerably more value in continued operation by their owners than they can realize in sale.

Liquidity constraint corners need not occur at zero current

saving. They may occur with positive 'contractual' saving, when a household is committed to accumulate illiquid wealth or to follow an agreed schedule of debt repayment. This will be true when these accumulations of equity fail to enlarge the household's credit lines, or do so only with interest penalties. Liquidity constraint corners may also occur with negative current saving, when a household is borrowing to the extent its credit line permits. Very likely there are a succession of credit lines with successively steeper penalties, and an effective liquidity constraint can occur at the threshold of any of them.

The unconstrained wealth model does not require, of course, that *all* human and nonhuman wealth be intertemporally fungible. It requires only that households always have sufficient liquid assets or credit lines so that they can offset as they wish the illiquidities of particular assets. Then they will never be forced into corners. Compelled to accumulate illiquid claims to retirement benefits, for example, they can if they please simply reduce other saving.

The desire to avoid liquidity binds in case of unfavorable surprises may induce more subtle and complex departures from hypothetical unconstrained consumption-saving paths. A well established finding from Michigan survey data is that among households suffering income reverses, those that have liquid assets reduce their consumption spending less than those that do not [9]. This observation conforms to the interpretation that the wealth model applies to the liquid asset holders while the others are liquidity-constrained. But it is conceivable that the fear of income decline previously led the first group to curtail consumption in favor of liquid saving. No doubt there are still plenty of liquidity-constrained households in the United States. We know, for example, that one-fifth of all households have no liquid assets and 45% have less than $ 500 [7]. Most of these households have low incomes and substantial installment debt. But households of this type certainly do not dominate in dollars the marginal consumption and saving dispositions in our economy. Those dispositions are dominated by households who have considerable short-run discretion, even if many of them have horizons shorter than their lifetimes. The strength of consumer spending in the face of the temporary tax surcharge of 1968 is a recent reminder that

American consumers are not slaves of their after-tax paychecks.

That is why we need George Katona. The wealth model offers him plenty of latitude. He is right that once consumption is not liquidity-constrained it is a highly psychological variable. Wealth itself is highly psychological. Recently something of an econometric identification problem has arisen as between wealth and consumer confidence as variables explaining items of consumer expenditure [3], [5], [6]. This is not really surprising. When Katona measures confidence, he is also measuring an important dimension of wealth.

But in the long run, attitudes and valuations are strongly governed by objective realities, and the purposes for which wealth is desired determine how much is accumulated. That is why the consumption—income relation is stable in trend while volatile quarter-to-quarter and year-to-year. That is why studies of consumer attitudes and behavior need to be embedded in a theoretical framework of rational accumulation.

REFERENCES

1 Ando, Albert and Franco Modigliani, "The Life Cycle Hypothesis of Saving", *American Economic Review*, 53 (March 1963), 55—84.
2 Dolde, Walter and James Tobin, "Wealth, Liquidity and Consumption", Cowles Foundation Discussion Paper No. 311, Yale University, 1971 (mimeographed), to be published in Federal Reserve Bank of Boston, Proceedings of Conference on Consumer Spending and Monetary Policy, 1971.
3 Fair, Ray C., "Consumer Sentiment, the Stock Market, and Consumption Functions", Econometric Research Program Research Memorandum No. 119, Princeton University, 1971 (mimeographed).
4 Friedman, Milton, *A Theory of the Consumption Function*, National Bureau of Economic Research General Series No. 63, Princeton University Press, 1957.
5 Friend, Irwin and F. Gerard Adams, "The Predictive Ability of Consumer Attitudes, Stock Prices, and Non-Attitudinal Variables", *Journal of the American Statistical Association*, 59 (December 1964), 987—1005.
6 Hymans, Saul H., "Consumer Durable Spending: Explanation and Prediction", *Brookings Papers on Economic Activity*, 1970, No. 2, 173—199.
7 Katona, George, *et. al., 1969 Survey of Consumer Finances*, Ann Arbor: Institute for Social Research, The University of Michigan, 1970.
8 Keynes, John Maynard, *The General Theory of Employment, Interest, and Money*, London: Macmillan, 1936.

9   Klein, Lawrence R., ed., *Contributions of Survey Methods to Economics*, New York: Columbia University Press, 1954, see paper by John B. Lansing, "Concepts Used in Surveys", pp. 9–48, as well as other contributions in this volume.

10 Modigliani, Franco and Richard Brumberg, "Utility Analysis and the Consumption Function: An Interpretation of Cross Section Data", in K. Kurihara, ed., *Post-Keynesian Economics*, New Brunswick: Rutgers University Press, 1954, 388–436.

11 Shuford, Harry L., "Subjective Variables in Economic Analysis: A study of Consumers' Expectations", unpublished Ph.D. dissertation, Graduate School, Yale University, June, 1970.

12 Stearns, Robert, "Life Cycle Earnings and Consumption: Evidence From Surveys", unpublished Ph.D. dissertation, Graduate School, Yale University, June, 1971.

13 Taubman, Paul, "Monetary Policy and Consumption (or a Chain is only as Strong as its Weakest Link)", 1971 (mimeographed), to be published in Federal Reserve Bank of Boston, Proceedings of Conference on Consumer Spending and Monetary Policy, 1971.

14 Tobin, James, "Relative Income, Absolute Income, and Saving", in *Money, Trade, and Economic Growth* (In Honor John Henry Williams), New York: MacMillan, 1951, 135–156.

15 Tobin, James, "Life Cycle Saving and Balanced Growth", in W. Fellner, ed., *Ten Economic Studies in the Tradition of Irving Fisher*, New York: Wiley, 1967, 231–256.

16 Watts, Harold W., "Long-run Income Expectations and Consumer Saving", in Thomas F. Dernburg, *et. al.*, *Studies in Household Economic Behavior*, New Haven: Yale University Press, 1958, 101–144.

Psychology and Economic Behavior

DANIEL KATZ

The development of the behavioral sciences has made explicit not only the interdependence of the various social disciplines in understanding human behavior, but also their overlapping in the phenomena they study. They all make psychological assumptions about the forces producing collective behavior even if the assumptions are not specifically formulated. In turn social psychology utilizes the knowledge of the other behavioral disciplines concerning institutional settings and the functioning of social systems. There is an interesting dialectical process involved in the growth of social science. On the one hand, our growing specialization narrows the scope of many investigations. On the other hand, as researchers dig more deeply into the problems of their special fields they encounter issues which need the help of other disciplines. Thus they sometimes find common cause with investigators in other sciences concerned with the same problem more than with members of their own profession.

We shall address ourselves to four major areas of such overlapping concern to psychology and economics that it is difficult at times to delineate the specialized interest of the economist and the psychologist: (1) The motivation and attitudes of the producer, (2) the motivation and attitudes of the consumer, (3) the decision-making processes of key groups of industrialists, bankers, and business leaders, and (4) the conflict and cooperative processes in society centering about the allocation of resources and rewards.

The psychologist's concern is with all aspects of motivation as they relate to performance. The economist traditionally has had a narrower interest in the relationship between productive accomplishment and monetary incentives to produce. To account for productivity more adequately, however, as in the phenomenal GNP increases in Japan in recent years, more aspects of motivation need to be explored than the monetary return to the producer.

Social psychology makes two distinctions which are directly related to the motivation to produce [16]. The first is between extrinsic and intrinsic rewards. The second is between individual and system rewards. Earlier treatments of motivation emphasized punishment and reward as external incentives, i.e., the carrot and the stick. With the increasing salience of ego needs the prevailing tendency is in accord with the field-theoretical distinction between *own* and *induced* forces in describing activities that are instrumental in securing need satisfaction compared to activities that are satisfying in themselves. The failure to recognize the differences in these two aspects of motivation is due in part to the fact that both forms of reward are correlated in our job structure. Positions that entail more interesting work are also those which receive higher compensation. The low skill, routine type jobs are more poorly paid than the jobs with variety and challenge. The correlation is not perfect, however, and people may take poorer paying jobs because they are more intrinsically satisfying. The distinction needs to be made, moreover, in that activities which are intrinsically rewarding are sustained and even lead to increased effort. There is a circular reinforcement with successful accomplishment, as Lewin and his students have demonstrated, with upward shifts in levels of aspiration following the attainment of lower levels [19]. Where work depends upon external incentives it will stop with removal of the extrinsic reward. Predictions about motivation to produce, then, are hazardous if based solely upon the manipulation of external incentives.

The second psychological distinction concerns the channeling of motivation. People move to get their share of extrinsic rewards but this does not necessarily mean that they work harder on their job assignments. If incentives are not tied to specific performance, there is little reason why they should. Many of the rewards in our industrial setup are geared to membership in the system and seniority in it rather than to the amount produced. This is true of fringe benefits such as unemployment compensation, pensions, and the health and recreational facilities of the organization. But even wage scales are often not related to the quality and quantity of the work of the individual producer. Wages frequently are set for workers based upon their classification in job categories and their seniority. Often wage raises are across-the-board cost-of-living increases. All the worker need do, then, in many organizations is to maintain some minimal level of performance to stay in the system. So long as he stays in the system he can enjoy its rewards.

The reason why external incentives are so infrequently applied in direct fashion to the productive efforts of the individual is the practical difficulty of separating out the individual's contribution to the joint product from that of his fellows in a complex production system. People are highly interdependent in their work and their cooperative interplay with respect to a group objective is critical. Not only is it difficult to identify each person's contribution and reward it equitably, but workers themselves resist such arbitrary distinctions. They often share responsibilities in getting a job done, whether or not this is formally recognized by the organization, but they also experience a common fate in terms of values and interests. Thus, when management introduces standards for individual compensation, the men develop their own informal standards and almost every member of the relevant group performs at that rate.

There are of course situations in which extrinsic rewards can be utilized to increase production and the conditions follow psychological principles which have been supported by research and experimentation. The reward has to be tied to the individual's own efforts so that he realizes more of it if he works harder and less of it if he falls behind. Reward increments from his point of view have to be sufficiently great to justify the increased effort. The reward system has to be reliable so that if he works harder and earns considerably more the job will not be retimed.

It is important, then, to realize that extrinsic rewards function differently depending upon whether they are individual or system rewards. System rewards do hold the individual in the system and so reduce turnover. It is true of course that very little turnover may be costly as well as high turnover. System rewards may also account for differences in the level of productivity between organizations rather than within organizations. If it takes a higher minimum level of performance to stay in one system than another, then we would expect the one system to be more productive if other things are held constant.

It can be maintained that economists have been justified in neglecting the distinctions psychologists would make about motivation and in being concerned only with broad considerations about the behavior of people in social systems. Why seek out refinements of motivation in the production process, since people are controlled and directed in industry by external constraints? For example, why bother about the internal aspects of motivation for workers on the assembly line? The amount they produce is determined by the speed at which the line moves and this is out of the control of the individual worker. There are three reasons for still being concerned with the problem of motivation. In the first place, it can affect the quality of performance, in this case the number of defective cars which may have to be recalled. In the second place, though the speed at which the line moves is not determined from hour to hour by the individual worker, he may play a role in determining the standard speed when his union negotiates the rate with management. Finally, there are many types of work which do not lend themselves to external controls in any complete sense, e.g., jobs in research and development, managerial or supervisory roles, etc.

Two opposed theories illustrate the differing emphasis upon motivation in the economic development of nations. One extreme would be the cultural emphasis upon technology. It would predict economic development as a function of the technological cultural base making progress an accelerating curve after some take-off point with deceleration after a long period of growth. The other extreme would be to predict the rate of economic development from studying the motivations of key individuals in the society. D. McClelland has taken this latter approach and has hypothesized that the need to achieve is basic to economic growth, that this motivation derives from the socialization practices of the society, and that as a result of such socialization there will be a sufficient number of achievement-striving entrepreneurs in the society to promote its growth [20]. In other words, McClelland would not predict the same outcome for all countries starting with the same technological base. The critical factor would be the degree of independence-training in the society resulting in different levels of the achievement syndrome for many of its people. McClelland, Atkinson, Veroff and their students have tested some of the specific hypotheses central to the theory. They do have strong findings that the need to achieve is a motive pattern of considerable stability in our society. The findings that such a motive pattern derives from independence-training in early childhood are suggestive rather than definitive. McClelland himself has highly interesting findings which show a significant relationship between need achievement as measured in children's readers and the relative economic progress of the country twenty-five years later. Economic development was measured by per capita income and by electric power production. The emphasis upon achievement themes in children's readers in 1925 correlated .25 with increases in per capita income and .53 for electric power in 1950 for some 22 nations [20, p.92].

The McClelland school dealt with one important form of internalized motivation, the need to strive to meet one's own standards of excellence. The achievement motive, so defined, is not elicited by all types of work assignment but by challenging and fairly difficult tasks. In economic development it is theoretically linked to the entrepreneur who is innovative and risk-taking. Some critical number of such high need achievers, McClelland argues, is important in the economic growth of a society. McClelland's thesis, as Katona points out, includes a sequence of three factors: (A) socialization leading to high need achievement, (B) a resulting number of entrepreneurs, and (C) a high rate of economic growth [13]. McClelland's research demonstrates a relationship between A and C but contains no direct measures of B, the number of entrepreneurs. This does not negate the contribution of McClelland but does qualify it.

61

Moreover, the McClelland approach does not attempt to take account of other forms of intrinsic motivation which could affect the level of economic productivity. During World War II the German industrial machine continued its effective functioning until the closing months of the war under great difficulties. A number of factors were involved, not the least important of which was the German training that work in itself was good and that being industrious was a virtue. Absenteeism and malingering were not only subject to penalties in the Nazi police state, but they were regarded as improper acts by the workers themselves. Now this emphasis upon work as a good is not the same as the need to achieve in that the former calls for sustained effort for routine, dull tasks as well as for interesting jobs. An achieving society may need both forms of internalized motivation, both the innovative efforts of the entrepreneurs and the dutiful performance of the majority in their daily, monotonous rounds. The need to achieve is an important dynamic of the developing capitalistic nation. All that may be needed, however, is a relatively small number of highly achieving entrepreneurs to furnish the spark. What may lead to significant economic advances may be this dynamic in combination with the older commitment to dutiful performance in the more traditional society. In other words, while the new spirit in the earlier period drove the minority of the Edisons, the Fords, the Carnegies, the Rockefellers and the Drews, the older psychological emphasis upon being a good worker still dominated the majority. One would predict on the basis of this hypothesis that a country will peak in its rate of economic growth while it still preserves the normative commitment of the older society for most of its people at the same time that a minority becomes infused with the achievement syndrome. It may be that the phenomenal development of the Japanese economy reflects just this combination of motivational forces. The rate of growth, then, would fall off rapidly as the Japanese become more modernized and lose the involvement in the norms of the older conventional society.

Attention needs to be given, moreover, to the way in which the emphasis upon types of motivation is utilized by organizations in a given society. Andrews compared two firms in Mexico [1]. The one followed traditional patterns with its emphasis upon authority and ascription. The second, as an American satellite, was heavily concerned with efficiency and productivity and with adapting bureaucratic structure to these objectives. This differential pattern was reflected in the kinds of people who moved up the ladder in the two companies. In the traditional firm there was no correlation between promotions and achievement motivation. In the more modern firm the correlation was clear and significant. Similarly, power motivation was not related to promotion in the modern company but was significantly so related in the traditional organization (see Table 1).

Table 1

CORRELATIONS, BISERIAL (r_{bis}) AND PEARSONIAN (r), IN FIRMS A AND P BETWEEN MOTIVE SCORE (n ACHIEVEMENT AND n POWER) AND THREE MEASURES OF ADVANCEMENT (JOB LEVEL, FREQUENCY OF PROMOTIONS, FREQUENCY OF RAISES)

Motive	Job level I or II		Promoted: Yes or No		No. raises	
	N	r_{bis}	N	r_{bis}	N	r
Firm A						
n Achievement	26	+.64	24	+.43	21	+.36
n Power	26	−.39	24	+.11	21	−.20
Firm P						
n Achievement	30	−.37	30	0.00		
n Power	30	+.38	30	+.34		

McClelland, like other psychologists, is too individually oriented in his theory of motivation to take full account of how people mobilize their energies to achieve their objectives. Though all motivation is individually generated, its direction can be either individual or social. The drive sources are within the person but his identification with his group can direct his energies toward group advancement rather than individual goals. Even Marx, who saw economic factors as central for understanding a society, was social-psychological in his theory of motivation and rejected an individualistic economic determinism. Workers, like members of other social classes, identified with one another and over time strove mightily for their group goal. Individuals would sacrifice their own selfish interests for the attainment of the objectives of the group. Though motives developed in the individual out of his own role in the social relations of production, they became crystallized and channeled as the worker realized that his comrades were similarly affected and could achieve changes through collective effort. Thus, Marx was not only ahead of the economists of his time in his conceptions of motivation but also ahead of much of present psychological theorizing.

The facts are that men will strive as energetically and as effectively to achieve group goals as they will for their own aggrandizement. The kibbutzim in Israel have dramatically demonstrated this point. They are as productive both in farming and in industry as the private sector of Israel if not more so. S. Melman's research, in fact, finds that kibbutzim factories in which community goals rather than personal profit are primary outproduce their counterparts in private industry [22].

One reason for the assumption of the primary importance of individual goals in assessing motivation to produce comes from our model for the allocation of rewards. In a private enterprise system the rationale is that rewards are distributed according to the individual's contribution to the outcome either through his investment of capital or of labor power. But this is an oversimplified picture of the functioning of the system. As we have already noted, many rewards are assigned on a system rather than an individual basis. In addition the tax structure seriously affects the logic of assigning rewards on a private enterprise basis. Finally, on the production side leaders utilize appeals directed at team spirit and collective effort. Cooperation is imperative among the members of any production subsystem but we have been slow in our research to study the conditions that would maximize motivation directed at collective objectives.

The values and motives which affect purchasing behavior and the consumption of commodities constitute a central area of psychological economics. The work of George Katona represents a major breakthrough in its treatment of the consumer as more than an economic model of man, in its reexamination of classical theories of consumption and its formulation of new conceptualizations about the mass consumer society [12], [14].

The traditional economic principle of purchasing as a function of amount of income is more applicable to a simpler subsistence economy than to the affluent society. What made the American nation remarkable was not the number of millionaires and not even the persistence of poverty among wealth. It was the widely-spread affluence with about half of the population receiving incomes in excess of the amount required for the basic necessities of life [14]. To summarize the Katona thesis, a large number of consumers thus enjoyed discretionary income. They could choose not only among types of goods and services but whether they wanted to save and invest some of their funds rather than to consume. As a result consumption could no longer be adequately predicted by knowing the level of income in the society. The willingness to purchase became a factor and to account for this willingness requires some knowledge of the attitudes, aspirations and expectations of people. It is important to establish the long-term factors such as personality predispositions and basic values which make for stable trends in consumer behavior in relation to short-term forces of new informational inputs about events.

The importance of recognizing long-term psychological determinants of the willingness to buy is a critical factor with respect to the business cycle. Katona holds that cyclical fluctuations have not been as great since World War II, partly because the typical consumer avoids excesses of behavior. In the last twenty-five years people have had more influence on the economy as consumers and this influence has been of a stabilizing character. Governmental controls are significant too, but public reaction has not been credited for the part it has played. In the first place, consumers are a large unorganized group in which the range of attitudes is greater than among homogeneous groups of business leaders. Hence, there is more operating in the way of checks and balance under the impact of news about events affecting the economy. In the second place, there is an habituation to either bad news or good news over a period of time. People do not go overboard in a boom period as they adapt to repeated optimistic stories. Nor do they necessarily panic with bad news as its impact becomes dulled with repetition. In the third place, the consumer tends to be conservative in his economic attitudes. He displays cautious attitudes even when times are good and maintains his confidence when times are bad [14].

The discretionary power of the consumer extends, moreover, beyond the purchase of material goods. It is in clear evidence in many forms of service and even has repercussions in the field of education. Young people feel that as the clientele for educational programs they should have a voice in the training they receive. They are attracted to institutions with varied and flexible programs, and they can exert pressures as consumers of educational services for different types of training. Moreover, people do seek the same sort of choice, in other matters of concern to them, which their discretionary purchasing power gives them in the marketplace. They seek responsive political institutions. In turn institutional leaders, while not accepting the notion that the customer is always right, give considerable attention to visible evidence of client demands. Mr. Dooley once observed that even the Supreme Court follows election returns.

The older economic model of purchasing and consumption geared to level of income represents a closed system. The approach of Katona is revolutionary in its conception of mass consumer society as a dynamic open system. The traditional model is static in its conceptualization of the factors of investment, production and consumption. It assumes a constant type of relationship — the higher the income, the greater the consumption, or the more consumed the less the investment in productive capital. The thesis of Katona not only shows the inadequacy of these distinctions but also points to a change process as the system develops. Consumers are not the passive recipients manipulated at will by the producer or his agents. They do not lie outside the system but are part of it. Their discretionary power and their investment activities influence the production as well as the consumption aspects of the economy. Over time the system is transformed from an operation directed by decisions of a few key leaders in business and banking concerned with the marketplace to a complex set of interacting decisions involving many people playing many roles. The consumer is not all-powerful but his behavior is not only an outcome of the system but an input into it as well.

The attribution of the consumer to a passive role in much that has been written about the American economy has some historical basis. Producers have been much better organized than consumers. Consumer groups and cooperatives have been few in number and their membership has been small. In the automobile industry, dominated by three major concerns, the millions of purchasers are an aggregate of individuals. The resources of the giant organization can be mobilized in its promotional and advertising efforts in an attempt to force its product upon the unorganized mass. One reason why market research has done so little to explore the needs, desires and values of people has been the confidence in the power of the corporation to impose its will upon the unorganized public. But even in an industry dominated by a few giant enterprises like the automobile industry, recent years have seen limitations to their power. A single voice can on occasion mobilize a large public. That a Ralph Nader could successfully challenge one of the most powerful corporations in the nation attests to the limits of the power of the producer. Nader was aided in his struggle by the fact that the corporation, in its attempts to silence him, had overstepped the bounds of the appropriate role. A more general instance illustrating the shift from the past in the recognition of public interest is the growing concern with ecology and the pollution of the environment. Industrial companies have responded with information campaigns to publicize their efforts in reducing their pollution. Words are easier than deeds, but there is a growing realization of the common interests of producer and consumer. The defeat of the efforts of the Nixon administration on its SST proposal may prove something of a turning point in that the Senate rejected a project proposed by the government to enhance national power and prestige relative to other nations. And the basic reason for the rejection was the interest of people in a better environment.

Production decisions thus no longer reside mainly in the hands of business leaders guided by narrow market considerations. The consumer has entered into the process not only through his discretionary purchasing power and through his activities as an investor, but also through his membership in the larger public. Even economic decisions, then, must recognize the public opinion process, for an aroused public can give greater priority to a cleaner environment than to increased productivity. In the past economists could neglect such social psychological considerations because they operated only at the boundaries of economic roles. So long as role players stayed within bounds, the simplified assumptions of our economic system worked. Increasingly, however, the once restricted roles of consumer, investor, and producer became intermingled. And what may be more significant, the interests of people as members of the community may transcend their narrower economic roles and heavily affect their decisions in these roles. It is no longer a matter of individuals exceeding the limits of the system and so being the exceptions to which psychological explanation is confined. The whole system is undergoing change in which role conceptions call for enlarged horizons. Both individual roles and the particular functions of subsystems may be moving toward a redefinition which sets broader limits for operations and which integrates general values with specific objectives. The Nuremberg Trials opened up the discussion of personal, role, and system responsibility for immoral behavior. The excesses of the Vietnam War have again made the issue salient. In less spectacular fashion the same questioning of role behavior divorced from social outcomes has been going on in many institutional settings. To the extent that we are moving toward such broadening of roles in practice, it becomes more important for economics and psychology to unite in their study and analysis.

DECISION-MAKING OF ECONOMIC LEADERS

Psychology and economics have a common interest in decision-making of leadership groups both from the point of view of how decisions are reached and of the influence of these decisions upon wider audiences. Economists emphasize the utility functions of such decision-making whereas psychologists follow less rational models about the total process.

It is sometimes assumed that, though the common man is subject to capricious impulse when he is not a slave of habit, the business leader follows more rational principles in reaching decisions. For one thing, the stakes may be higher for the industrialist than for the rank-and-file employee. For another, the executive is placed in a position where organizational facilities and expectations impose requirements for deliberation and problem solving. His ability to utilize organizational resources for rational analysis is supposedly one basis for his recruitment to the executive role in the first instance. There is some suggestive evidence indicating a greater attention to rational factors when more is at stake. G. Katona found that top asset holders conform more to the economic model of man than do average savers [14]. They are more concerned with hedging against inflation; they scrutinize their investments more carefully and shift their holdings to insure higher interest returns; and they study ways in which to minimize income and estate taxes. But by and large the differences are of degree between the small and large investor. Inertia and entrenched habits are common determinants of decisions, or lack of decisions, in both groups.

Officials and executives in economic organizations are in positions in which part of their role consists of activities related to problem analysis and solution. These constraints are often misperceived, however, in that they operate less as pressure toward a full rational attack upon the problem and more as forces pushing for a simplified model of the situation. March and Simon, in their clear and compelling analysis, agree that optimal standards are not employed for problem solving; rather, any satisfactory alternative will be utilized if it meets certain minimal criteria [21]. Instead of a thorough analysis of the difficulty the organization faces, the tendency is to take the symptoms as causes and even to ignore the problem in the hope that it will go away. In place of a consideration of a number of alternative solutions and an evaluation of their costs and gains, the first plausible solution is accepted. In place of innovation there is reliance upon old procedures and practices. Instead of research directed at ascertaining long-range outcomes, immediate feedback from limited operations is utilized. In place of a comprehensive long-range plan, related problems are approached in piecemeal fashion.

In describing decision-making within a business firm, R.M. Cyert and J.G. March further elaborated the conceptualization of organizational constraints upon problem solving [7]. The notion of an organizational goal directing the efforts of all members is a misleading simplification. There are many objectives of subgroups and individual members; the organization is a coalition of groups rather than an overperson. Policies and practices are the outcome of compromises and adjustments of parts of the coalition rather than the ideological program of moving effectively toward some single organizational objective. There is thus quasi resolution of conflict with some local autonomy in decision-making and some sequential organizational attention to the objectives of different subsystems. At one point in time the organization moves to satisfy its production people, another time its sales people, and so on. By taking one problem at a time the organization stumbles along without resolving the basic inconsistencies of such a vacillating course. Environmental factors produce uncertainties for the organization. Business firms try to reduce uncertainty by controlling the environment, or negotiating some arrangement, as in industry-wide practices about prices so as to avoid disastrous competition. This is not the rational problem solving of older economic models. Moreover, Cyert and March believe that the search procedures for generating alternatives for problem solution are biased. The bias is in the direction of the immediate problem, of a simple rather than a complex causal model, of the needs and experiences of the sub-units in the system.

A similar approach to the "satisficing" conception of March and Simon is the incrementalism stressed by Braybrooke and Lindbloom [5]. These authors point out that decisions tend to be incremental. Instead of a clearly formulated set of goals and a comprehensive program for their achievement, policy-makers make small, incremental changes in response to immediate pressures:

> Our program for the aged is not a program at all; it is not a comprehensively considered and coordinated policy. Rather, it consists of Old Age and Survivors' Insurance, special provisions for the aged under the income tax law, old age assistance provided through the cooperation of state and federal government, and county and municipal provision for the needy aged ... It has been developed – and goes on developing – as a sequence of decisions ... [5, p. 72].

Moreover, in attacking an important problem area the prevailing strategy is one of disjointed incrementation — the fragmentation of decision-making among many centers in imperfect communication with one another.

In budget-making a given bureau or department in times of prosperity will get a small percentage increase and in recession periods a small percentage decrease. In other words, instead of scrutinizing the budget as a whole in relation to priorities and accomplishments of the many subunits, the practice of administrators is to impose some increment or decrement across the board. Ease of administration governs decision-making rather than genuine problem solving. It would take long and arduous study to evaluate achievement and to determine priorities. Moreover, it is politically more feasible to impose a percentage increment or decrement on all units rather than to drop one completely or drastically penalize it. People may grumble but they accept the uniform treatment more readily than differential treatment. Studies by W.J. Gore [10] and A. Wildavsky [24] furnish empirical support for incrementalism in governmental budget decisions.

An organization by its very nature is a system of constraints in that it has limited functions and restrictions of communication to make operations possible. As J. Feldman and H.E. Kanter observe,

> Organizational decisions are constrained by the actions of the organization itself, by the physical and mental characteristics and previous experience of its members, and by the social, political and economic environment of the organization and its members [8, p. 619] ... The individual in the organization expects to have his decisions constrained, and within certain limits he accepts these constraints [8, p. 620].

For survival and effective functioning, organizations may build in mechanisms of an adaptive type which can create counter-forces to existing constraints. In fact, the fate of an organizational society may depend upon the speed with which we develop such adequate subsystems of this type. In the past most organizational decisions were limited in social space to the narrow interests of a single group and restricted in temporal consequences to the present or immediate future. The outcome has been the pollution of the environment and social conflicts and crises. Perhaps the most difficult psychological problem in this connection is the creation of a time perspective which will facilitate genuine planning. The resistances to extending our temporal frame of reference are many. There is a convincing reality to immediate payoffs as against more remote possibilities. The longer-range goals have been used in exploitive fashion as indicated in the old song about "pie in the sky". With an accelerated rate of change it is difficult to predict future developments. Generations are more separated on the basis of different experiences with no common temporal perspective. The cult of the now generation makes planning ideologically unattractive. Nonetheless, industry has found that it must replace its old five-year time perspective with longer-range thinking, and the hope is that this can be extended both temporally and socially both for industry and governmental structures.

Another critical problem in organizational decision-making is the availability of relevant information to the leadership. Organizations sometimes acquire significant information which somehow never reaches the top decision-makers at appropriate times. Often, too, organizations are biased in their information systems so that they can be captives to their own mistaken policies. The behavioral sciences need more research on the mechanisms by which data gathering and processing can maintain some degree of independence from operating functions and still furnish information appropriate for the problems confronting the organization. The issue is not one of perceptual distortions at the individual level but of reforming the structure of the organization.

THE ALLOCATION OF REWARDS AND RESOURCES

Social psychology has been slow to recognize the critical variables of the distribution of economic rewards in a society and the institutionalization of such distribution, i.e., not only the specific allocation but also the institutional mode for determining distribution. Thus it has been weak in dealing with conflicts of interest between groups which are the outcome of differential rewards. A common assumption among psychologists is that group conflict is largely a matter of inadequate communication and distorted perceptions and can be remedied by T-group methods. Though economists have done more with the problem than psychologists, they, too, have not made conflicts between interest groups their main concern. Labor relations and industrial conflict constitute a marginal area of study for economists. In fact, it was Harold Lasswell, a political scientist, who emphasized the centrality of the question "Who gets what, when, and how" [18].

Part of the reluctance to face the matter freely and openly is that the allocation of rewards readily triggers off questions of a normative character. For example, how equitable is the distribution system? How much socialism should be introduced into a free enterprise system or how much free enterprise into a socialist system? But there are many important questions calling for objective study which do not in themselves involve value positions. Social psychology, economics, and political science can join in furnishing more complete information on the following types of issues: Does the distribution system of the society create social classes and interest groups of a competitive or of a conflicting character? At the individual level what are the effects of such groupings on the values, aspirations, and behavior of people? How does the reward allocation within the nation affect its stance toward other nations? Is internal conflict externalized? Do dominant groups combine as in the industrial military complex to push the nation toward warlike policies?

There are few clear answers based upon systematic study to the many questions suggested by the concept of interest groupings and social class. The institutional distribution of rewards in capitalistic economies does provide a potential basis for social conflict. The important issue for the social psychologist is whether people in the same category of income and economic role identify with one another and see themselves as a group with common interests. Though there may be a latent structure with respect to social class, it is of minor significance if it remains latent. Social class can be used to predict differences in taste and attitude, but when it turns into class consciousness it can predict political behavior, orientations toward the basic values of the society, and social movements.

Various measures have been used to identify social classes. The simple approach of dividing people into income groups is often followed. For some purposes such divisions can be useful. Obviously, however, income differences are confounded with such factors as education and occupation. Rather than factor out single determinants it is often the practice to combine income, education and occupation into a single index of social status. The justification is that placing people in a single category such as income only gives us aggregates whereas taking account of characteristics they have in common such as education and occupation is closer to psychological groupings. It is widely acknowledged that in any survey of the population an objective index of social class is an essential background item. Though the investigator may not hypothesize relationships between his interests and social class, he has to be in a position to control on social class.

In place of, or in addition to, our objective measure of social class, many researchers utilize a measure of psychological identification (asking people what class they belong to). The logic of the procedure derives from H. Hyman's concept of reference groups [11]. The theory is that the individual utilizes some group as a frame of reference both for informational and sanctioning purposes. The difficulty is not with the concept of reference group but with the method of measurement. Subjective identification based upon one or two questions is not a very adequate measure of psychological groups. There is no systematic evidence to indicate that a question on subjective class identification is any better than the objective index of income, education and occupation. In fact the early study of R. Centers [6] found the latter question gave better correlations with liberal and conservative attitudes than did the former.

Another approach to the study of economic groupings comes from Marxian theory about social classes. His division of classes would be based upon sources of income rather than amount of income, i.e., whether income is from wages or from investment or business. There is, however, a high correlation between source of income and the common socio-economic index since the latter includes occupation as well as amount of income. The people who are not adequately taken into account are the mixed income types, such as the blue collar worker who rents rooms in his house, or the white collar worker who holds a few shares of stock. They are relatively few in number but are worthy of study as cases of likely misplaced upper class identification.

The Marxian notion of social class may be more useful, however, in suggesting questions concerning the individual's cognitive structure of social classes. Does he, for example, perceive members of his own class as having common interests which are directly opposed to the interests of another class? This would add specificity to the simple line of inquiry of perceived belonging to a social class. Trend questions along these lines should show whether class consciousness does increase over time or becomes attenuated as other groupings become more salient for people.

Even though there are economic interest subdivisions in society, their importance is mediated by the stability or instability of their personnel. If there is social mobility, if the sons of blue collar workers can go on to college, workers should show less strength of identification with social class. Nor does there have to be a great deal of upward movement for class consciousness to be affected. So long as there are some visible signs the resulting perception can be one of an open class structure. We do not know much about the amount of mobility necessary under various conditions for a diminution of class-consciousness. We do know, however, that with increasing opportunities and with increasing returns to lower class members, expectations rise rapidly as in the level of aspiration studies.

Empirical findings on social class and interest groupings in the United States, whether based upon objective or psychological measures, show fairly consistent patterns on two major dimensions [15, pp. 163-171]. Lower classes tend to be more liberal on social and economic proposals for reform and more Democratic in political allegiance than the upper classes. The strength of this relationship varies over time, but there is no doubt about its importance. On the other hand, the upper classes tend to be more liberal on civil liberties and the rights of the individual. Lower classes embrace an older ideology than those higher in social status, are less tolerant of deviants, and more authoritarian. Our interpretation of these findings is that interest grouping in American society is competitive and does not represent class conflict calculated to revolutionize society. These groups compete with one another for the rewards in the system, but they do not struggle to change the essential character of the system. The working class has not accepted or developed an ideology which is in opposition to the values of private enterprise. Their members

75

are more radical than employers, but just on those bread and butter issues that affect them directly. The unionism of the American labor movement has been a business unionism for the economic benefits of a given trade and was not directed at achieving a socialistic society. Union leaders have in fact been favorable toward war contracts which meant employment for their members. The identification is not with workers of the world but with members of one's own craft. In the same pattern of narrow self-interest some unions have restricted admission to their ranks and in some cases discriminated against blacks. There is some indication, however, that the labor unions of the future will pursue broader goals. Just as the narrow definition of the role of management is under pressure for revision in the direction of greater public responsibility, so, too, labor will move beyond specific demands for wage increases to programs for social betterment. It will not be a revolutionary class movement in the Marxian sense, but will seek broad reforms within the system.

The findings about the greater liberalism of the upper classes on noneconomic issues are consistent with our general hypothesis that social class differences are not essentially conflicting. According to the conflict theory one would expect the working classes to be in rebellion against the establishment, rejecting its values. The upper classes in resisting attempts to change would assert the validity of eternal verities. But it is the working classes who are more accepting of the traditional ideology and who lag behind the upper classes as changes in the values of the culture occur.

The supporters of the system are found as much among the workers as among their employers. It is the young from affluent homes who are more likely to seek subsystem changes than the old among the blue collar workers. In fact, the lines of cleavage in our society are more along age and ethnic lines than along economic lines. The militant students have been disappointed in finding that blue collar workers do not rally to their cause. The change forces are much more in age differences than in class differences. With accelerated rates of change in modern society, age differences widen into generational gaps. The values and motive patterns of a generation raised in relative economic abundance differ markedly from older values. There are those who see this as affecting social classes differentially. Hence, the children of the working class possessing more of the Protestant ethic than the middle class youngsters will replace them in positions of power very much as Pareto postulated in his theory of the circulation of the elite. The system will not change but the types of leaders recruited will. This thesis of "the blueing of America" has much to commend it, but it does not give proper weight to the generality of age differences across classes [2]. Though the ideological revolt has been centered in upper middle class youngsters, there is a pervasiveness of the new value systems among peer groups. It is probably true that there will be some circulation of the elite, but it is also likely that the young leaders who come to the fore, no matter what their background, will introduce social changes and will be amenable to certain types of social change. The society of the future will not be essentially the same as the society of the past.

Where changes have occurred in the past in the allocation mechanisms they have been more in the character of reforms rather than revolutionary modifications. Thus a graduated income tax does produce some shift in income distribution but does not destroy the private enterprise system. Social security benefits can be similarly characterized. Nonetheless these slow changes do have a cumulative effect over time and lead to the so-called middle way. The middle way is a private enterprise system with limitations on the return to capital based upon social rather than economic considerations and a free market limited by certain controls on wages and prices.

The middle way suggests that a society need not be of a piece in terms of its mode of distributing rewards. A pluralistic society may be pluralistic not only with respect to powerful unions counteracting big business, but also with respect to permitting different types of distributive arrangements, some capitalistic and others socialistic. The state of Israel from this point of view is more pluralistic than the United States because close to 42 percent of its economy is publicly owned and controlled by the government, the labor organization or the cooperative communities, and some 58 percent falls into the private sector. A pluralistic society may face more open struggles between its organized internal sectors than a homogenized social structure, but it has the advantage of providing more options for its citizens in ways of life.

Once interest groups are created within a society the question of their relationships becomes salient. Coalitions among them may result in the domination of some groups by others. Marx maintained that the coalition would follow the social relations of production, that employers in various industries would combine against workers. This has happened, but it is far from the whole story. In a given industry like the building trades there will be an effective coalition between builders and contractors and skilled workers. Both the contractor and skilled worker are in a privileged position as against the people in less skilled, more competitive fields. Alliances both implicit and explicit occur on the basis of a common stake in securing a higher proportion of the total fee.

One more coalition in the Marxian idiom is the industrial-military complex. Partly through the exchange of personnel in important posts there has been a linkage between the industrial and military elites. They exert their influence, the argument goes, for the expansion of American power abroad. The greater the expenditure for the military, the more industry profits. The more industry produces for the armed services, the greater the role of the military. Gabriel Kolko maintains that key business leaders pass in and out of bureaucratic posts in the Defense Department, staying long enough to influence policy and then returning to business [17]. Business careers become the aspiration of many military leaders. In 1959, he states, the 72 largest arms suppliers alone employed 1,426 retired officers, 251 of them being of flag or general rank. Kolko views this not as a coalition between the military and industry, but as the domination of the military and of government by big business. His interpretation, however, does not allow for the intervention of other forces which have led to the slowing down of the Vietnam War.

The countervailing forces of an aroused public and of political alliance have made the predictions from a simple industrial-military complex untenable. Instead of a monolithic political structure controlled by big business, the American political system is a loosely structured set of multiple groupings. Even within a major political party there are many parties for practical purposes — a presidential subsystem and a Congressional party, a national party and fifty state parties. Industrialists and bankers can exert great influence at strategic points in the total apparatus. But they cannot control the system even if they were themselves a unified, cohesive force — which they are not.

The notion of an industrial-military complex as the dominant determinant of foreign policy rests upon the assumption either (1) that there is a conscious coordination of these interests with power over related subsystems, or (2) that a cumulation of many piecemeal decisions is channeled in the same direction. The material on disjointed incrementalism in policy-making would argue against the first assumption. The second assumption would have to account for a single funneling of a multitude of smaller decisions, perhaps on the basis of common profit and power. But again there is evidence to indicate that many important sectors of the economy do not profit from the prosperity of the munitions industry. George Berkley goes so far as to assert that even "the military-industrial complex is seeking to extricate itself from the dubious, and often dismal, fortunes of war" [3, p. 18]. In addition, one must recognize a form of determinism which goes beyond the economic. As organizations or subsystems of the society develop around specialized functions, they take on values of their own justifying their functions. These different sets of values furnish a continuing dynamic for the various subsystems and make for a pluralistic society. Even the news media are affected in part by the value of furnishing information. Reporters do vie with one another in getting on the spot coverage. The TV networks gave unprecedented coverage to the war in Vietnam not because they were serving the Pentagon but because news was their business. In other words, though people are divided into interest groups on the basis of reward distribution, membership in other subsystems makes class consciousness not an overriding factor but just one important variable among many others.

We have discussed four substantive areas which have brought economists and social psychologists into close working relationships. Another type of influence worthy of note is the theoretical stimulation of one discipline from the models used by the other. Social psychologists have been affected by the economic model of exchange in a free market and have applied this concept to psychological transactions. Thibaut and Kelley have proposed a matrix for calculating successive gains and losses of two parties involved in interpersonal exchange [23]. The work of E. Jones and others is part of the same tradition [9]. Peter Blau has developed a theory of social exchange which develops the implications of a transactional approach for power and leadership in social systems [4]. Uneven exchanges can leave one party in a position of power because of obligations implicitly due him. A leader, however, can use up his power by expending it without securing rewards for his followers. The analogy of social power to money is imprecise, but the point is that specific models for interpersonal relationships can take their inspiration if not their elaboration from economic theory. In fact, the fit or misfit of theoretical models from one field to the data of another can help to advance both disciplines.

REFERENCES

1 Andrews, John D.W., "The Achievement Motive in Two Types of Organizations", *Journal of Personality and Social Psychology*, 6(1967), 163–168.
2 Berger, Peter L. and Berger, Brigitte, "The Blueing of America", *The New Republic*, 164 (April 3, 1971), 20–23.
3 Berkley, George, "The Myth of War Profiteering", *The New Republic*, 161 (December 20, 1969), 15–18.
4 Blau, Peter M., *Exchange and Power in Social Life*, New York: John Wiley & Sons, 1964.
5 Braybrooke, David, and Lindbloom, Charles E., *A Strategy of Decision*, New York: The Free Press, 1963.
6 Centers, Richard, *The Psychology of Social Class*, Princeton: Princeton University Press, 1949.
7 Cyert, Richard M., and March, James G., *A Behavioral Theory of the Firm*, Englewood Cliffs, N.J.: Prentice-Hall, 1963.
8 Feldman, Julian, and Kanter, Herschel E., "Organizational Decision Making", in J.G. March, ed., *Handbook of Organizations*, Chicago: Rand McNally, 1965, 614–649.
9 Gergen, Kenneth J., *The Psychology of Behavior Exchange*, Reading, Mass.: Addison-Wesley, 1969.
10 Gore, W.J., "Decision Making in a Federal Field Office", *Public Administration Review*, 16(1956), 281–291.
11 Hyman, Herbert H., "The Psychology of Status", *Archives of Psychology*, 269(1942).
12 Katona, George, *The Powerful Consumer*, New York: McGraw-Hill, 1960.
13 Katona, George, "Review of The Achieving Society", *American Economic Review*, 52 (June, 1962), 580–583.

14 Katona, George, *The Mass Consumption Society*, New York: McGraw-Hill, 1964.
15 Katz, Daniel, "Survey Methods in Psychological Research", In C.Y. Glock, ed., *Survey Research in the Social Sciences*, New York: Russell Sage Foundation, 1967, 145–215.
16 Katz, Daniel, and Kahn, Robert L., *The Social Psychology of Organizations*, New York: John Wiley & Sons, 1966.
17 Kolko, Gabriel, *The Roots of American Foreign Policy*, Boston: Beacon Press, 1969.
18 Lasswell, Harold D., *Politics: Who Gets What, When, How*, New York: McGraw-Hill, 1936.
19 Lewin, Kurt, *A Dynamic Theory of Personality*, New York: McGraw-Hill, 1935.
20 McClelland, David C., *The Achieving Society*, New York: Van Nostrand, 1961.
21 March, James G., and Simon, Herbert A., *Organizations*, New York: John Wiley & Sons, 1958.
22 Melman, Seymour, "Managerial Versus Cooperative Decision Making in Israel", *Studies in Comparative Development*, 6(1970–71), 47–58.
23 Thibaut, John W., and Kelley, Harold H., *The Social Psychology of Groups*, New York: John Wiley & Sons, 1959.
24 Wildavsky, A., *The Politics of the Budgetary Process*, Boston: Little, Brown, 1964.

Economic Behavior and Economic Welfare: Models and Interdisciplinary Approaches

BURKHARD STRUMPEL

INTRODUCTION

The development of economic thought has been guided by the necessity of dealing with pressing policy problems. Providing the framework for a scholarly analysis of one of these problems and helping society to tackle it, is the mark of a great economist.

Behavioral economics, a new brand of empirically-oriented social science first developed by George Katona, addresses itself to one of the principal problems of our day: the early recognition of changes in business activity — a problem of obvious importance to those who lived through the 1930's. A breakthrough in problem solving most frequently goes hand in hand with novel technology. The methodological innovation of behavioral economics was to explain changes in the economic system by analyzing actions and predispositions to action on the individual level. Katona established the connection link between individuals and the system, between the micro- and the macro-level of economic analysis. The economy, for him, is not the outgrowth of anonymously interacting statistical magnitudes such as commodities, prices, interest rates, and money, but rather the outcome of human behavior. Katona did not hesitate to step across the boundaries of recognized disciplines and to utilize any method or approach he found appropriate to understand human behavior as it related to economic problems.

Although his major contribution has been the explanation of short-term aggregate change, his real passion rests in understanding and explaining the economic behavior of private households. His background in psychology proved to be invaluable in the task he set for himself. Yet the application of psychological theories of behavior to economics raised novel and unusually difficult methodological questions. While psychology is primarily concerned with individual phenomena, he translated its theorems to the societal level and utilized its approaches and findings for social sciences primarily concerned with questions of change.

Katona calls behavioral change "the central problem pf psychology" [7, p. 30]. The basic feature of his model of behavioral change is the interaction between an exogenous stimulus (change in environment) and a behavioral response. He stresses the intervention of situational and contextual variables modifying this relationship. The former refer to the perception of the particular situation within which the stimulus occurs; the psychological theory of learning can be applied here, since this perception is dependent upon past experience. The latter refers to the unique attributes of the person confronted with the stimulus, his present attitude which is partly dependent upon his role and function; here the concepts of Gestalt theory are utilized.[1] Attitudes and expectations are measurable through eliciting verbal responses which reflect and summarize the modifications of the stimuli and the shaping of behavior.

The following stimulus → intervening variable → response

---

[1] Situational modifications of the stimulus are perceived by the individual through learning. Katona: "Human behavior is not repetitive. Doing the same thing the second time may differ from doing it the first time. There is maturation and there is learning. ...psychology is not concerned with reflexes that may be established by the neurophysiological structure one and for all. The structure itself is plastic. It is affected by previous actions". As to contextual effects Katona refers mainly to social roles: "The individual has a different role and function according to the group (whole) to which he belongs. It is not to be expected that the individual will behave the same way in different group situations" [7, p. 38].

paradigm, which is heavily indebted to, but not identical with, Katona's model [19], may help to clarify this approach:

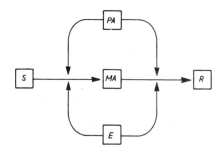

S = Stimulus (news event, information, personal experience).
PA = Prior attitudes (perceived "context", i.e., the existing set of attitudes, expectations, habits, motives, beliefs, and roles held by consumers).
E = Environment and its perception (the economic situation of the individual, his "terms of trade").[2]
MA = Modified attitudes (the set of attitudes, expectations, etc., as *changed* under the impact of the perceived stimulus).
R = Response (change in spending or saving behavior, incurrence of debt).

Different parts of the above model have been unequally covered by empirical research. Katona and his associates have systematically treated the relationship between MA and R, yet much remains to be done in incorporating PA and E as modification agents between MA and R. For the time being, we shall follow their example and elaborate on this centerpiece of the approach.

There is a whole range of psychological variables shaping economic behavior. We group these variables into two categories: preferences or values ("what people want"), and perceptions and expectations ("to what extent they think they will be able to achieve their goals"). Another group of psychological predispositions shaping economic action, namely *achievement orientation* (widely known through the work of David McClelland and John

---

[2] Under "terms of trade" should be understood the individual's terms of participation in market processes, such as the availability of work, wage rates, supply and prices of consumer goods and services.

W. Atkinson), contains elements of both. Closest to the economist's heart is the concept of expectations: if "tastes", or "preferences", are assumed to be the same over time, and if the "terms of trade" (i.e., the economic opportunities) do not change, then expectations (i.e., the subjective probability of success in reaching one's goals) should explain behavioral changes and ensuing aggregate trends. However, there are important analytical objectives in economics which require that we question the assumption that tastes, preferences, or values do remain the same over time[3]; this is the main contention of this paper. Long-term behavioral changes, intercultural comparisons of behavior — so crucial for the analysis of economic growth — and the micro-analysis of subgroups of a population, all require the consideration of what differences there may be and what changes may occur in people's tastes or values.

Different problems require different theoretical approaches. Katona's theoretical structure was developed and has been utilized primarily in connection with the problem of changes in economic activity. The question to be posed here is: in what form is his model, which has been uniquely successful in explaining short-term intertemporal changes, applicable to other behavioral economic problems. We shall consider various subject areas of behavioral economics within the context of appropriate psychological models. The next section will review the analysis of short-term intertemporal changes in purchasing behavior. In the following section, theoretical approaches to the role of private households as suppliers to the economic system of labor, skills, and savings will be discussed. In this context long-term (i.e., slow and mostly unidirectional) changes command the attention of social scientists. In addition to their role in the functioning of the economic system, the well-being of the private households themselves is an increasingly salient topic of analysis (the fourth section). It is particularly the welfare of poor or "marginal" groups which is in the public concern and requires thorough behavioral and psychological analysis. Recent preoccupation with the impact of socio-

[3] Economic analysis by and large has either neglected change in preferences or has banned it to the footnotes. There are rare exceptions, like Duesenberry's well-known book [2], which, however, treats level of aspiration as being determined solely by past income.

economic change on the "quality of life" raises new questions in the evaluation of welfare and the impact of changes in welfare [18]. Here the focus is on the interrelationship between economic action and the welfare of the individual rather than strictly related to the functioning of the system.

SHORT-TERM CHANGES IN PURCHASING BEHAVIOR

Katona's approach to explaining cyclical fluctuations in consumer durable spending is intriguing in its simplicity and realism. Spending for consumer durables is, to a large extent, postponable and thus "discretionary". Its timing is subject to "waves of sentiment" preceding changing levels in buying activity. Sentiment expresses people's "willingness to buy" as measured by their expectations and perceptions of their economic status and future, of the present state of and the outlook for the national economy, and of prices and buying conditions for consumer goods. Willingness to buy transforms a larger or smaller proprtion of disposable liquid or potentially liquid assets of the household ("ability to buy") into purchases.[4]

Short-term change in consumer sentiment depends on the information and experiences with which people are confronted. As mentioned earlier, people are conditioned by group processes as well as by the unique features of a given situation. "Good news" even in noneconomic areas makes for higher levels of spending. Generally it increases people's aspirations and their participation in economic processes. On the other hand, uncertainty and worry lead to a desire to remain liquid and keep commitments short. Unfavorable news concerning the environment, particularly about employment, inflation, wars, strikes, taxes and interest rates, tends to affect people's view of the future and create unfavorable attitudes. Occasionally, misgivings may change into fear with pressure to act, as in the case of a runaway inflation, but, barring extreme constellations, it is confidence rather than anxiety which leads to consumer action.

[4] For a detailed exposition of possible psychological and economic mechanisms explaining the impact of attitudes, see [8].

The major advantage of measures of attitudes is their ability to systematize and summarize the unsystematic impact of numerous variables that shape consumer spending. The impact of informational inputs on attitudes and behavior, although high on the agenda of behavioral economics, has not until recently been quantitatively analyzed.[5] Extensive data derived from questions addressed to respondents in quarterly surveys are available as base material. Respondents have been asked at regular intervals about the news items to which they attached significance, and about their reaction to certain salient political issues such as the war in Indochina, the new President, etc. Having expressed their opinions about the past and expectations for the future state of the economy, they were also asked "why" they thought as they did.

Katona's objective was not to explain and predict interindividual differences but rather aggregate fluctuations in behavior. Therefore, he quite rightly was never impressed with those of his critics who alluded to the so-called "time series—cross section paradox"; namely to the fact that, although attitudinal change corresponded very well with aggregate changes in demand in a time series, there was only a weak association between individual attitudes and purchases.[6] And insofar as he was interested in analyzing short-term phenomena, he could disregard tastes, preferences and achievement orientation, as well as all attributes of a person other than those which could be assumed to change in the short run in response to news, events of public concern, changes in the economic and political situation.

LONG-TERM CHANGES IN ECONOMIC BEHAVIOR

The impact of the economic decisions of private households on the economy goes beyond their short-term effect on changes in business activity. Private choices are also one of the determinants

---

[5] A first attempt by the author has just been made, see [19]. For a similar undertaking in the area of political behavior, see [3].

[6] These critics fell victim to the "ecological fallacy". Robinson proved as early as 20 years ago that one cannot generalize from individual to aggregate level and vice versa [16]. See also Katona's "On the Theory of Expectations" in this volume.

of long-term changes in the size, productivity and structure of an economy. In recent decades the economists' primary preoccupation with recession and unemployment has been supplemented by a concern with economic growth. Translated into our context, this implies that the focus on consumer demand as the most crucial behavior linking private households to the economic process has been replaced by a preoccupation with both demand and supply factors emanating from the consumer, the latter being represented primarily by the amount of labor and skills provided by households as well as by their saving activity. The pace of inflation as experienced during the late sixties reminds us continuously that, even though we have not solved the problem of unemployment, there are numerous periods, industries, and regions where the underemployment economy has become an overheated economy which frequently is prevented from further expansion by the limited availability of the right kind of labor, skills, and investment capital.

There is a ready, elastic response pattern of private households to the opportunities of a modern, growing economy which may be called *participatory*. The participative household is willing to exert much effort. Husbands often work long hours, or take on a second job, and wives seek gainful employment. Higher-level participation can also be achieved with unchanged work hours, by different, qualitatively higher inputs: skilled rather than unskilled labor, striving for occupational advancement, job mobility. This is the realm of educational and occupational choices. Finally, participation results from saving, creating conditions favorable for productive investment. Consequently, the linkage between the household and the economy is found in such behavioral areas as education, saving, labor force participation of women, job mobility, consumer demand, and willingness to work over time.

For these modes of behavior to become a legitimate subject of research, it is crucial not only that they exert potential influence on the system, but that they should actually be changing. And indeed there have been a number of significant changes in the productive behavior of Americans in the last years and decades. The following trends, for example, have made for new patterns in the quantity and quality of the labor supply and in saving:

The gradually growing labor force participation of married women.

The levelling-off in the reduction of working time that occurred in the first forty years of this century [6].

The unabated and still continuing increase in the proportion of young people attending college and graduate schools.

The rapid increase of people in their fifties and early sixties wanting to retire early and the growing number of those actually doing so [1].

An increasing number of young, college-educated people questioning traditional economic and material values and rejecting occupational careers (business) that express these values [15].

In the area of income allocation, the most notable change is the rise in the rate of saving by one whole percentage point in the United States in 1969–71. This phenomenon is most probably not exclusively of a cyclical nature.

It is hardly surprising that there are changes in economic behavior in periods such as ours with rapid social and cultural changes. Rising mass incomes and short work hours make it possible for many people to choose between saving and spending as well as between work and leisure. For some, a steady and continuous improvement in real income, common in modern society, is a reason to relax and to enjoy the fruits of prosperity. For others, it is a challenge to extend the range of goals even further and to increase their strivings. Thus the majority of private households in Western societies make their decisions in a setting characterized by discretion relating to income acquisition – job, work/leisure, educational choice – as well as to income allocation – choice not only between various consumer goods, but between saving and spending.

Large intercultural differences in economic behavior suggest that the amount of economic participation of private households is not solely a function of the economic status of the society. To cite just two examples treated in detail in a recently completed international comparison of economic behavior [10]: Labor force participation of German mothers is substantially lower than that of their American counterparts. This fact resulted in the high proportion of South European workers, mainly from Mediterranean countries, which now constitutes about 10 percent of the German labor force. The United States produces a much larger proportion of highly-educated scientists, engineers and other graduates with advanced degrees than European nations. There is little doubt that the edge the American economy maintains over Europe in areas like aerospace, electronics, and business management, can to a considerable extent be attributed to the large reservoir of highly-trained manpower, i.e., to the peculiar strength of educational aspirations and accomplishments in this culture.

Behavioral economics, in the tradition of George Katona, is called upon to measure and regularly monitor trends in economic behavior and the determinants of that behavior — both economic and non-economic — *before* they are manifested in the statistics. The individual choices on which these trends are based are not changed frequently and suddenly; they are shaped by changes in people's environment, situation, and opportunities as well as by trends in their psychological predispositions. Let us consider the latter in more detail.

If we observe people saving more or less, or working more or less than others or than they used to, our first superficial conclusion is simply that, in a cultural setting characterized by a certain freedom of choice, they want to do so. We are then looking at preferences, or tastes, or aspirations. This is an extension of Katona's original attitude-behavior paradigm which deals, strictly speaking, with the time distribution of purchases, i.e., with the question, "When will people do or buy whatever they anyway desire to do or buy? "

Aspirations have a qualitative and a quantitative aspect. Various nations, subgroups, and individuals differ both in what they want and in how much they want it; they differ both in the content and in the extent of aspirations. Some are saving-minded, others spending-minded, some are both. Some are concerned with occupational advancement, others have no interest in greater job responsibility, etc. Aspirations also have a dynamic aspect. There are differences in the structure or hierarchy of aspirations, i.e., in how their content and extent reacts to the fulfillment of past levels of aspirations.

Katona, in his critical study of the notion of saturation [7, p. 91], deals with the dynamics of the fulfillment of past levels of aspirations. In particular, he stresses the intimate relationship between optimism and levels of aspiration [9]. Aspirations, according to Lewin and his associates, tend to rise with accomplishment and to decline with failure [12]. Accomplishment encourages: formerly distant goals appear more realistic. Conversely, failure discourages aspiration. Yet, as Lewin has recognized, there certainly is not a one-to-one relationship between accomplishment (or failure) and the level of aspirations, much less such a relationship between accomplishment and aspirations of a specific kind, e.g., for home furnishings, recreational services, or even income generally.[7] A change in behavior, then, can come about through the implementation of one or more goals rather than through any basic change in the structure of the goals. Not only may concern with a particular goal often diminish with accomplishment while other, formerly less urgent goals come to the fore, but there are also indications that the process of goal adaption in the economic sphere unfolds with different intensity and speed for different people, nations, and subgroups. In other words, even though the level (not the margin) of aspirations might quite universally be moved upwards by accomplishment and reduced by failure, differences both in content and extent of this adjustment are doubtless substantial enough to necessitate measurement and explanation as well as to contribute to the explanation and prediction of behavior.

A monitoring and understanding of the levels and structures of aspirations — consumption, saving, income, career — may give an earlier, more complete, and more consistent picture of cross-section differences and time series trends than observations of *behavioral* differences and trends alone: earlier since aspirations are assumed to be formed in advance of action; more complete since they are observable among individuals who are not (yet) in a position to translate them into action, e.g., young people, people with rising incomes, or simply people who after having attained one type of goal will turn to a different one; more consistent since people's aspirations most probably are more stable phenomena than their behavior, the latter being more amenable to short-term situational and perceptional disturbance (see Katona's short-term

[7] We define "level of aspiration" as the sum of the level of attainment and the "margin of aspiration", i.e., as the sum of what one has and what one aspires to in addition. "Structure" or "hierarchy" of aspirations refers to the relative urgency of aspirations or the time sequence in which they are translated into action.

model as interpreted in the preceding section). Needless to say, these propositions require more thorough testing.

By no means is our intensive preoccupation with the psychological concept of aspiration tantamount to a depreciation of other approaches (e.g., environmental) to the explanation of economic behavior. The specific aspiration level of an individual may be related to social and family background, experiences, social norms of reference groups, past accomplishment, present economic situation, and other environmental variables. Rather, we view aspirations, in analogy to the role of attitudes in the Katona model represented in Section II, as measurable *intervening variables* which systematize and summarize the diffuse impact of various environmental forces on behavior.

In a recent study, the following question was asked for the purpose of evaluating the material aspirations of the respondents[8] :

> Now I have a question about your wishes: Are there any important things you and your family would like or do you have most of the important things you want? (If has wishes) What do you have in mind?

For each respondent, up to three responses were recorded. Table 1 reports data for those respondents who expressed a wish for: a new home, at least one item of durable goods, or any other material acquisition including "more money", vacations (if they required money), etc.

Responding to the above rather general open-ended question, 44 percent of the interviewed households heads mentioned material aspirations, some of them several. The largest number — 29 percent — expressed a desire for better housing; 20 percent, for durables (mostly cars). Since better housing is costly, it must be

[8] The subsequent data are taken from the project "Indicators of Changes in People's Goals, Opportunities and Economic Well-Being", conducted by the Survey Research Center of The University of Michigan with funds from the National Science Foundation. The primary concern of this project is the development of a set of social indicators of psychological predispositions of behavior. The survey was conducted in the spring of 1971. The sample consisted of 574 employed heads of complete families with small children (oldest child under 10 years) in the Detroit and Baltimore SMSAs and their wives. Official birth records and other sources were used for a random selection of households with children.

Table 1

CONSUMPTION ASPIRATIONS WITHIN DEMOGRAPHIC GROUPS

	Percent of Family Heads Who:			
	Want a new home	*Want to buy durables*	*Have material wishes**	*Number of cases*
All Family Heads	29%	20%	44%	574
Age of Family Head				
19-25 years	36	25	53	140
26-30 years	32	18	47	214
31 years or older	22	20	36	220
Education of Family Head				
0-11 grades	42	21	53	134
High school	31	23	49	177
College, no degree	26	20	44	140
College	16	17	30	121
Occupation of Family Head				
Professional, technical	18	16	32	139
Managers, officials	30	21	49	57
Clerical, sales	31	35	45	75
Craftsmen, foremen	28	19	47	127
Operatives, laborers, service workers	41	19	54	159
Race-Occupation of Family Head				
White white collar	22	21	39	238
White Blue collar	30	17	45	235
Black	48	28	56	88
Annual Income of Head				
Less than $ 12,500	35	24	50	399
$ 12,500 or more	17	13	32	158
Annual Family Income				
Less than $ 7,500	31	22	57	54
$ 7,500–9,999	43	25	50	125
$ 10,000–12,499	32	21	47	146
$ 12,500–14,999	28	22	42	96
$ 15,000 or more	15	15	34	132

Table 1 (continued)

Goal Ranked First by Family Head				
Prosperous life	36	28	50	170
Secure life	31	21	46	267
Important life	23	8	32	75
Exciting life	12	16	40	58
Importance of Prosperous Life to Family Head				
Ranked first	35	27	50	173
Ranked second	29	21	50	210
Ranked third	26	16	35	128
Ranked fourth	19	8	31	62

*In addition to the information used in categories (1) and (2), this category includes other material-oriented wishes.

borne in mind that discrepancies between wishes and reality are less easily overcome in this than in other areas of the consumer budget.

On the basis of Table 1, the following findings emerge: The number of spontaneously-mentioned material desires declines considerably with age, particularly after the age of 30 — and with college education. Furthermore, except for those in the lowest income bracket (under $7,500), the desire for new homes also declined as income rose — most markedly at the highest income level ($15,000 or more).

Two subgroups among white-collar occupations — professionals and managers — are far apart in their expressed level of aspirations. Managers score above average, professionals much further below average than any other subgroup.

The picture is markedly different between Blacks and Whites: Blacks are significantly more likely to express material desires, particularly for better housing. Here the frequent disequilibria prevailing among low-income families are further perpetuated through discrimination or fragmentation on the housing market [11].

A question about the relative importance placed by the head of the family upon either a prosperous, a secure, an important, or an exciting life indicated that such general values played a role in determining material desires. I shall discuss later the fact that those who chose prosperity and security as their prime goal in life expressed desires for material goods more frequently than those who preferred importance or excitement.

The findings suggest that material aspirations are shaped by many factors: socio-economic status, occupation, race, individual values. In the case of Blacks, the limitation of housing choices due to discrimination has to be added. The relationship between material desires and income seems to indicate that, in terms of housing, people do arrive at a high level of satisfaction of felt need as income rises; in terms of desires for other consumer durable goods the difference between people at different income levels was less pronounced.

The negative correlation between age and aspirations in only partly due to the common effect of income (older people in our sample received somewhat higher income). The relationship is the more remarkable since the sample comprised only a limited age range: all respondents had young children and were therefore at roughly the same stage of the life cycle. The weakening of aspirations in the thirties must thus reflect not only a different stage in the attainment of goals, but also a genuine realignment of values. That material desires decrease with age is confirmed by evidence from the *1968 Survey of Consumer Finances*. In that study, expressed wishes for "things to buy" decline from 75 percent for the 25–34 age group to 41 percent for those from 55 to 65, to 31 percent for those 65 and over. The German data presented in G. Schmölders' and B. Biervert's contribution to this volume reveal that older persons not only exhibit a lower level of aspirations but also actually have fewer possessions than younger people. For older people, goals tend to be reduced to accommodate reality. Realism is the order of the day, and the gap narrows between achievement and desire. In the U.S., too, those who are older worry less than those who are younger. They also care less and show symptoms of resignation to reality and its constraint [4].

The significant correlation between the priority accorded to one of several goals or values and aspirations for consumer goods opens the way to new concepts about economic behavior.

Values are affective states formed long before the resultant behavior; they are relatively stable personality attributes, they are generalized concepts, and effective in several spheres of action. As Milton Rokeach says [17. p. 4]:

Bypassing the problem of values and their relation to attitudes, we settled perhaps a bit too hastily for studies that deal with what I will call problems of persuasions to the neglect of what I will call problems of education and reeducation . . .We neglected the . . . effects of socialization, educational innovation, psychotherapy and cultural change on values. It was, therefore, our hope that in shifting from a concern with attitudes to a concern with values we would be dealing with a concept which is more central, more dynamic, more economical, a concept which would invite a more enthusiastic interdisciplinary collaboration.[9]

Applying some of Rokeach's basic value categories to economic behavior, two survey questions were developed for assessing people's goals and guiding principles in the economic sphere of their lives:

I would like you to tell me what you have found important in life. Would you please look at this card and tell me which of these is most important to *you* as a goal in *your* life, which comes next in importance, which is third, and so forth?

A Prosperous Life (having a good income and being able to afford the "good" things in life);

An Important Life (a life of achievement that brings me respect and recognition);

A Secure Life (making certain that all basic needs and expenses are provided for);

An Exiting Life (a stimulating, active life).

Would you please look at this card and tell me which things on this list about a job (occupation) you would most prefer, which comes next, which is third, etc.? (Income is steady; Income is high; There's no danger of being fired or unemployed; Working hours are short; Chances for advancement are good; The work is important, gives feeling of accomplishment.)

In a survey conducted in 1971 the conservative value, "security", was widely acclaimed as most important (46 percent). "A Prosperous Life", was ranked first by the second largest number (30 percent), while "self-actualizing" (Maslow) values — an "important" or "exciting life" — were of prime importance to

[9] "While attitude and value are both widely assumed to be determinants of social behavior, value is a determinant of attitude as well as of behavior . . If we further assume that a person possesses considerably fewer values than attitudes, then the value concept provides us with a more economical, analytical tool for describing and explaining similarities and differences between persons, groups, nations, and cultures" [17, p. 2].

Table 2

GOALS IN LIFE WITHIN DEMOGRAPHIC GROUPS

	Goal Ranked First by Family Head						
	Prosperous life	Secure life	Important life	Exciting life	D.K., N.A.[†]	Total	Number of cases
All Family Heads	30%	46%	11%	11%	*	100%	574
Age of Family Head							
19-25 years	30	52	6	11	1	100	140
26-30 years	35	45	10	9	1	100	214
31 years or older	25	45	20	10	*	100	220
Education of Family Head							
0-11 grades	40	46	8	6	*	100	134
High school	30	55	10	5	*	100	177
College, no degree	30	51	8	11	*	100	140
College	16	31	30	22	1	100	121
Occupation of Family Head							
Professional, technical	20	34	25	19	2	100	139
Managers, officials	39	35	14	12	*	100	57
Clerical, sales	31	49	9	11	*	100	75
Craftsmen, foremen	29	57	10	4	*	100	127
Operatives, laborers, service workers	35	52	6	7	*	100	159

Goal Ranked First by Family Head

	Prosperous life	Secure life	Important life	Exciting life	D.K., N.A.†	Total	Number of cases
Race-Occupation of Family Head							
White white collar	27	37	19	16	1	100	238
White blue collar	28	58	7	7	*	100	235
Black	47	41	10	2	*	100	88
Annual Income of Head							
Less than $ 12,500	31	50	10	9	*	100	399
$ 12,500 or more	28	37	20	13	2	100	158
Annual Family Income							
Less than $ 7,500	32	46	11	11	*	100	54
$ 7,500-9,999	31	54	6	8	1	100	125
$ 10,000-12,499	27	51	12	9	1	100	146
$ 12,500-14,999	33	48	8	9	2	100	96
$ 15,000 or more	30	32	24	13	1	100	132

*Less than .05 percent.

†Category includes: Don't know; not ascertained, and respondents who ranked two or more values first.

only 22 percent [see Table 2]. "A prosperous life" was most rarely selected by respondents with a college degree and by professionals (largely identical groups, of course). It was cited as the highest goal most frequently among such diverse groups as Blacks and managerial workers. Conversely, images like "important" or "exciting life" held the greatest attraction for those who held college degrees (52 percent as against an average of only 17 percent at lower educational levels) and thus are largely group-specific.

There are obvious and plausible parallels between higher levels of material desires and holding a "prosperous life" as one's highest goal. The question arises: What factors determine one's goals in life? Clearly, characteristics which change continuously throughout one's lifetime, such as income and age, play a less important role in the prediction of values than such persistent subcultural affiliations as race and occupation. Thus, goals or values may be expected to remain more stable than material aspirations, the latter, as we have seen, being related to income and age. However, stable as values may be for any one individual, they still bear a close relationship to such dynamic phenomena as education, race relations, and occupation so that, over a period of time, they may be expected to respond to changes in these areas. In other words, the frequency with which different values are expressed can be expected to change with societal trends like the educational revolution, changes in the role of Blacks in society, or the substantial increase in the proportion of professional workers in the labor force. This fact points to the potential of using the concept of values as a variable for the analysis of medium- and long-term changes in economic behavior.

Two issues should be mentioned in summary fashion since they are suggestive of the direction further research should take. Knowing about an individual's hierarchy of goals is not tantamount to knowing what behavior is deemed most suited to achieve the desired end. How does an individual perceive a particular action as affecting whatever goals he has? Furthermore, values or goals in life cannot be used to anticipate behavior without greater knowledge about people's perceptions of themselves: For instance, the goal or guiding principle, "a prosperous life", may have entirely different implications for a person who is or considers himself relatively well-off and for one who is not or does not so consider himself. For the former, it may help to explain a conservative, defensive posture, identification with the status quo; for the latter it may make for a restless, active type of decision-making in areas of work, career, and purchasing. Or a very strong preference for "work that is important, gives feeling of accomplishment" may activate one who is dissatisfied with his present job, as much as it may deactivate one who is satisfied. Finally and obviously, the same type of behavior may be the result of quite different values. For example, people may reduce their work load because of an increased dislike of work, an increased desire for leisure, or a decreased felt need for income. The list could be extended.

Values have long been accepted and used in the construction of basic theoretical concepts for the analysis of long-term trends. Much of the theory of social and economic changes (Max Weber, Talcott Parsons and David Riesman) is cast in terms of values and their changes. Values, like aspirations, tell us something in general terms about what people want. We are not yet in a position to supply strong empirical support for a theory linking values to behavior. Our attempt to provide some empirical flesh to the largely speculative theories of social change started by demonstrating that different values were held by different groups of the populations. It would be hard to believe that significant differences in values would not make for significant differences in economic behavior.

WELL-BEING OF PRIVATE HOUSEHOLDS

One of the great social problems with which behavioral economics is concerned, is the economic status and behavior of the poor and disadvantaged. The intensive study of poverty, its causes and consequences, and of strategies for intervention, is not prompted primarily by preoccupation with the economic system. The welfare of individual beings, not just of the nation, is at stake. This difference will require a reformulation of both the psychological and the behavioral variables to be employed in studying problems related to poverty. The researchers who deals with the effect of a household's decisions on the actor himself rather than on the system, will focus on behavior and mehcanisms capable of changing the household's economic status, such as personal efforts in areas of training, education and saving for future contingencies. He will, as James N. Morgan and James D.Smith have proposed [14], look at money-earning acts, connections to sources of information, acts of planning ahead, risk avoidance, real earning acts such as home maintenance and auto repairs, and economizing acts such as eating at home and avoiding nonessentials, regardless of their effect on commodity, labor or credit markets. Rather than directing our attention to differences in the spending, saving, and work choices of the mainstream of employed people in various degrees of affluence – as set forth earlier in this paper – attention must be focused on more specific areas of behavior: What makes or keeps part of the population out of the mainstream, of the labor market, of the pool for social mobility, or even of the "melting pot" altogether?

Our concern here is not with the question of *causation* of the present brand of poverty but rather with the *perpetuation* of poverty in which psychological variables certainly play a role. The vicious circle of poverty, discrimination, neglect, alienation, under-education, and unemployment has frequently been noted. One byproduct of the sequence is the failure of economic socialization in childhood and youth. One school of thought tends to see the perpetuation of poverty as a matter of values: It holds that people immersed in the poverty stratum *want* to live radically different life styles with less emphasis on work, occupational advancement, provision for the future, and material achievement generally. No doubt poverty, i.e., failure in a sphere which is highly stressed in Western cultures, does operate against identification with the values of the larger culture. We are not convinced, however, of the inevitability of the poor remaining within the circle of poverty. The economic socialization of all people in this nation, including its minorities, appears to result in such conformity of goals and values as to make virtually every adult want to live in economically secure circumstances, to have an occupation, to have his or her children attend school, and to acquire marketable skills, etc. This applies regardless of differences in values and goals touching on less basic issues of economic behavior, such as the *extent* of labor force participation, education, or saving. These less basic differences, which are expected to be useful for the explanation of behavioral differences as they exist in the mainstream, are discussed later in this paper.

Gurin and Gurin, in a set of studies on groups disadvantaged by economic and/or minority status — manpower trainees, "hard core" unemployed youths, black college students — have done extensive work designed to identify the psychological correlates of economic failure in the area of what they termed "expectancy/ fate control" rather than in the value areas [5]. Most early approaches to the problem of training or retraining the unemployed were based on the assumption that the problem lay in their goals and values or that they lacked the traditional achievement orientation. Consequently, action programs had a heavy "resocialization" emphasis, teaching trainees the "proper" attitudes and behaviors that would supposedly enable them to succeed in the job world. Recent research de-emphasizes the socialization deficit; it points to the lack of environmental rewards, of any possibility of controlling one's own fate, as causing frustration and discouragement. It tends to view the problem in "expectancy" terms, seeing the trainees' problems of motivation as tied to their assessment of the job market and the payoff they may expect. This has led to a much greater investment in on-the-job training programs, with the accent on clear job payoffs rather than individual value changes.

The implications of this interpretation are most intriguing for the interventionist. If people's perception of their environment and their opportunities makes for or prevents adaptation, the focus of the problem and its remedy lie in experiences of the present or of the recent past rather than in value "deficits". It suggests that maladaptation to the economic system as expressed most dramatically in hard-core unemployment is not mainly attributable to engrained and fixed personality traits but is rather a consequence of more recent experiences and thus can be influenced by changing the environment. Too little is yet known about the degree of stability or manipulability of these variables.

The chances of remedy through creating a more favorable environment in terms of improving individual expectations does not eliminate the need to consider the implications of the impact which a deterioration of the economic climate must also have on motivation. For the people losing their jobs, the cost of unemployment will have to be assessed in terms not only of immediate economic loss, but also of a more enduring negative restructuring of the unemployed's predisposition for economic action. And for the population as a whole, the very awareness of unemployment — and perhaps the threat of it — has a discouraging, deactivating effect even on those not immediately affected.

To cite another example: proposals for legislation requiring that incomes be maintained at fixed minimum levels may have to be viewed in terms not only of their effects on income distribution but also of their consequences for the motivation and expectations of the recipients. These schemes help to mitigate failure and prevent dislocation in one important domain of people's lives: material well-being. By so doing, they may prevent a restructuring of the expectancy/self-efficacy/ fate control syndrome from affecting working and other behavior. Conversely, a considerable income deficit may cause adverse repercussions in noneconomic areas of life — family cohesion, child care, health, and eventually work effort.

The differences and parallels between the attitudes/expectations syndrome as developed by Katona and the expectancy/fate control concept are evident. The one affects and predicts behavioral variation *within* the norms of the system; the other influences the degree of conformity with or alienation from the system. In both cases, it is a positive or a negative view of the environment which demonstrably has either activating or deactivating effects on economic behavior. If the environment is judged unfavorable or threatening, the subjective expectation of success in implementing one's goals and aspirations is diminished, both in the acquisition and the allocation of income.

CONCLUSION

This paper has advanced some thoughts about the role of noneconomic variables in the explanation of interindividual (cross-section) differences and long-term changes in economic behavior. Among psychological variables, we have explored the usefulness of aspirations, basic goals or values, and the expectancy/fate control syndrome. These concepts, like Katona's concept of attitudes, take the role of intervening variables summarizing a diverse assortment of present and past cultural/environmental influences. Katona's stimulus → intervening variable → response paradigm as he has used it in studies of short-term changes remains basically intact in the context of long-term and cross-section studies. However the catalogue of causative environmental variables or "stimuli" which sufficed for the former (mainly news about employment conditions, political events, etc.) must naturally be radically enlarged for the latter.

Family influence and economic socialization shaping basic values extend back ·to childhood and youth. Economic environment and experiences occurring as much as a few years ago are assumed to shape optimism and self-confidence and to be stable in the medium range; the occupational environment providing group norms and goal expectations is a matter of the present. There can be no doubt, that, apart from more engrained psychological dispositions, the social environment of a person, most prominently his peer groups, has a deep impact on his goals and behavior. Obviously, different areas of behavior are shaped by such factors to a different extent. Occupational identification, for example, may be expected to exert a strong influence on on-the-job behavior, career and educational decisions, a moderate influence on consumption decision, and practically none at all on saving decisions. Group norms and expectations can, but must not necessarily, result from or be in harmony with values. Often but not always, people will select the occupational and friendship groups where their values are matched by those of other group members.

The framework presented in this discussion cannot claim the virtues of simplicity and parsimony with which Katona's approach is so richly endowed. The reason was implied earlier. In a long-term approach, values or goals in life cannot legitimately be assumed to remain constant; thus they cannot be neglected — as they can in explaining cyclical changes. Complexity is not the only price exacted by research into the psychological predispositions of long-term behavioral change. Another is an imposed initial change from the macro- to the micro-level of analysis. For purely statistical reasons, the short-term model, after no more than a few years, yielded a sufficient number of observations of aggregate change in both attitudes and behavior to permit quantitative testing. By contrast, work on analyzing long-term macro-trends in the psychological predispositions of behavior must begin on the micro-level. In the absence of historical variables of a psychological nature, quantitative aggregate tests of our model are not feasible and will not be so for quite a while.[10] This leaves us with no option but to analyze differences on the cross section level, and to initially approach time series variance *per analogiam.*

REFERENCES

1 Barfield, Richard, and James N. Morgan, *Early Retirement: The Decision and the Experience*, Ann Arbor, Michigan: Survey Research Center, Institute for Social Research, The University of Michigan, 1969.

2 Duesenberry, James, *Income, Saving, and the Theory of Consumer Behavior*, Cambridge: Harvard University Press, 1949.

3 Erbring, Lutz, "Mass Publics and Political Events, On Modeling the Dynamics of Public Opinion: Theoretical Considerations, Research Design, and Progress Report", unpublished manuscript, Institute for Social Research, April, 1971.

4 Gurin, Gerald, Joseph Veroff, and Sheila Feld, *Americans View Their Mental Health*, New York: Basic Books, 1960.

5 Gurin, Gerald, and Patricia Gurin, "Expectancy Theory in the Study of Poverty", *Journal of Social Issues*, 1970.

6 Henke, Peter, "Leisure and the Long Workweek", *Monthly Labor Review*, 89(1966).

7 Katona, George, *Psychological Analysis of Economic Behavior*, New York: McGraw-Hill, 1951.

8 Katona, George, *The Powerful Consumer: Psychological Studies of the American Economy*, New York: McGraw-Hill, 1960.

9 Katona, George, "Consumer Behavior: Theory and Findings on Expectations and Aspirations", *American Economic Review*, May, 1968, pp. 19–30.

10 Katona, George, Burkhard Strümpel, and Ernest Zahn, *Aspirations and Affluence*, New York: McGraw-Hill, 1971.

11 Lansing, John B., Charles W. Clifton, and James N. Morgan, *New Homes and Poor People: A Study of Chains of Moves*, Ann Arbor: Survey Research Center, The University of Michigan, 1969.

[10] See however the attempt by McClelland [13] to measure the relationship between need achievement as contained in children's readers and the relative economic progress of the country twenty-five years later.

12 Lewin, Kurt, Tamara Dembo, Leon Festinger, and P.S. Sears, Chapter 10 in J.McV. Hunt, ed., *Personality and the Behavior Disorders*, Vol. 1, New York, 1944.

13 McClelland, David, *The Achieving Society*, Princeton: Van Nostrand, 1961.

14 Morgan, James N., et. al., *A Longitudinal Study of Family Economics*, Ann Arbor: Institute for Social Research, The University of Michigan, 1969.

15. Newcomb, Theodore M., and Kenneth A. Feldman, *The Impact of College on Students*, San Francisco: Jossey-Bass, Series in Higher Education, 1969.

16 Robinson, W.S., "Ecological Correlations and the Behavior of Individuals", *American Sociological Review*, 15 (June, 1950), pp. 351–57.

17 Rokeach, Milton, "A Theory of Organization and Change Within Value and Attitude Systems", manuscript of a talk, unpublished, 1970.

18 Strümpel, Burkhard, "Economic Life Styles, Values and Subjective Welfare — An Empirical Approach", Paper presented to the 86th Annual Meeting of The American Economic Association, New Orleans, December, 1971 (with the assistance of Richard T. Curtin and M. Susan Schwartz).

19 Strümpel, Burkhard, Jay Schmiedeskamp, and M. Susan Schwartz, "The Function of Consumer Attitude Data Beyond Econometric Forecasts", Paper presented to the 10th conference of CIRET (International Conference Business Tendency Surveys), Brussels, September, 1971.

Expectations as a Social-Psychological Concept

T. M. NEWCOMB

I suppose there is no notion that more characteristically permeates George Katona's work than that of *expectations*. He is quite explicit as to the formal status of the concept in his theoretical structure. It belongs to the family of intervening variables: "only in certain lower-order responses do we find a one-to-one correspondence between the stimulus and the response" [5, p. 34]. Among other intervening phenomena are attitudes — which (like habits and motives) are learned ways of "influencing how stimuli are perceived and how the organism reacts to them . . . The most important function of intervening variables is to organize. What fits in or what is consistent with our predispositions has the best chance of influencing us . . ." [3, pp. 54—55].

Expectations, in turn, are "a subclass of attitudes that point to the future, since our time perspective extends both backward and forward in a highly selective manner". As with other intervening variables, "two individuals' response to identical stimuli need not be the same. The same individual's response to identical stimuli at two points of time likewise need not be the same" [5, p. 34]. Expectations, like other attitudes, may be either enduring or variable, but "our concern is with attitudes that are variable because they are influenced by economic developments" [3, p. 57]. Thus the concept of expectations is placed in a psychological taxonomy and simultaneously in an economic context.

Thus Katona sees man as time-binding, and hence future behavior is likely to be influenced by how he relates what he has learned from past experience to future contingencies. But man is also so to speak people-binding; he is subject to social influences and often thinks, feels, acts — and expects — as a group member: "...the individual is a member of face-to-face groups and a part of society; therefore no real analysis of his motives, attitudes, and decisions is possible without taking into consideration the framework within which he functions" [3, p. 169]. Because it is this social-interpersonal area of his concerns that particularly overlaps with my own, I have chosen to examine the status of the concept of expectations in social psychology. How have other social psychologists made use of the concept, and in what ways have Katona's contributions been unique?

To answer the former question, I first consulted *A Comprehensive Dictionary of Psychological and Psychoanalytic Terms* [2]. I found that the term *expectancy* has a respectable status as "an intervening process variable (e.g., an attitude, or set) attributed to animals (or other men) as a parallel to what is subjectively experienced as an expectation; an acquired disposition whereby a response to a certain sign object or cue stimulus is expected to bring about a certain other situation. It is not to be read subjectively; it is inferred from an animal's behavior." *Expectancy theory* (attributed to E.C. Tolman) holds that "what is acquired in learning is a disposition to react to certain objects as signs for certain further objects." *Expectation* is "a tense and somewhat emotional attitude toward the prospect of a certain event." The statistical sense of the same term is also defined. Many associated terms — e.g., sign-gestalt-expectation, means-end expectancy — are also noted. No reference, however, is made to the use of any of these terms by social psychologists.

I then turned to the *Handbook of Social Psychology* [7], and combed the indexes of all five volumes for entries under "expectations" and "expectancy". I found 105 single-page references, together with three sections, totalling 53 pages, in which one of these words appeared in the section title. Thus, not less than 4% of the total 3,667 pages of printed text contained one of these words according to the index (done by computer, evidently). "Expectancy" occurred only about half as frequently as "expectation", and, interestingly, only in Volumes I, devoted mainly to "Systematic Positions"; II, entitled "Research Methods"; and III, entitled "The Individual in a Social Context". Volumes IV and V, entitled "Group Psychology and Phenomena of Interaction" and "Applied Social Psychology", respectively, had index referrals exclusively to "expectations". It is not always clear, from contexts, that the semantics of the two terms are distinct, but in general "expectancy" seems to stress psychological states, whereas "expectations" commonly refers to the content of what is expected – as in Katona's usage.

Very well then, a good many social psychologists use "expectational" terms fairly commonly. Or at least they do so of late; I found no such index entries at all in the first edition (1954) of the *Handbook* (perhaps the earlier one was not as thoroughly indexed).

The next question is *how* they use such terms. In terms of conceptual content, nearly all usages of the words fit fairly well into two broad classes. First (usually involving "expectancy"), the emphasis is on psychological states of "set", involving some sort of preparatory adjustment to anticipated events or situations. Non-occurrence of whatever is anticipated may be frustrating, and this suggests that motivational components are involved. Indeed, at least one writer [7, II, Berkowitz, "Social Motivation"], appears to use "incentive" and "expectation" in very similar ways. Indeed, Berkowitz notes that "much of the difference between S-R and expectancy analyses is largely semantic" [7, II, p. 78]. Rotter's theory of social learning is summarized [7, I, p. 109] as resting on three "basic concepts", related in the following way: "The *potential* that any behavior will occur is dependent on the individual's *expectation* concerning the occurrence of *reinforcement* . ." Other specific uses of the expectancy concept are suggested by the following phrases: (1) "Subjectively expected utility", as in the study of risk-taking; (2) "disconfirmed expectancy", with dissonance-like consequences.

Less clearly, the notion of "psychological set" is probably intended in discussions of humor and of art. Berlyne [7, III] notes that various "theories" of humor and laughter refer to unexpected denouements; he quotes Kant as referring to laughter as "an affection arising from the sudden transformation of a strained expectation into nothing". The "relief theories" stress decline or removal of threat or stress as a prime ingredient in humor. I find it interesting, incidentally, to contrast the phenomena of relief from unwelcome expectations with the dissonance of "disconfirmed expectancies" [7, I, pp. 378 ff.], since dissonance is not usually associated with "relief".

Child, in a fascinating chapter on "Esthetics" [7, III], refers to the "collation of expectation and outcome" in a discussion of complexity and cites attempts to trace "emotional meanings in music to the arousal of expectations and the consequences of that arousal" [7, III, p. 861]. He also discusses attempts to find "the meaning of music in the arousal and resolution of expectations" [7, III, p. 860]. The temporal nature of music presumably makes such an approach more applicable to music than to other forms of art.

My second category of usages refers not so much to intrapersonal as to outer, social influences. Thus the phenomena of socialization are associated with learning the expectations of a society, as part of its culture. Social structure includes patterns of action "Bound by ... rules of expectations" [7, IV, p. 285] and in some sense governed by norms and sanctioned expectations [7, IV, p. 295]. "Significant others" serve "to reinforce norms ... by exhibiting current expectations and sanctions" [7, IV, p. 307]. Roles are special cases of norms; "role expectations" provide a basis for the analysis of "the School as a Social System" [7, IV, pp. 462 ff.]. Analysis of the phenomena of leadership rests heavily on conflicts among roles — e.g., expected versus ideal behavior; expectations of superiors versus those of subordinates [7, IV, pp. 233 ff.]. Such usages appear often in other chapters, too [e.g., 7, V, "Social Psychology of Mental Health"].

But response to others' expectations is presumably not dissociated from one's own expectations. Thus A.F.C. Wallace is quoted to the effect that it is "the equivalence of expectations that permits a society to function adequately [7, IV, p. 336]. That is, an individual's *expectancy*, as a psychological state in such a society, is coordinated to the content of others' actual expectations. And so, in a sense, we come full circle. Expectation-like terms are widely used by social psychologists, sometimes in a narrow, technical sense, and often in rather common-sense ways. For some purposes, at least, different usages have meaningful relationships. Judging from one voluminous source, social psychologists would find it hard to get along without notions of expecting.

For Katona, as I have noted, such notions are indispensable. And — let there be no misunderstanding — this formulation of "expectations" is unmistakably a psychological one. They are, as I have noted, intervening variables — between the individual's residual of past experience and his behavior. He is primarily interested in them not as dependent (how they arise) but as independent (what they give rise to) variables. But this choice of interests imposes the necessity of describing *how* they give rise to some behaviors rather than to others. The following passage illustrates both Katona's, Gestalt-derived point of view and the nature of his reply to the foregoing question.

> Habitual behavior . . . may be inappropriate . . . Changes in the environment represent stimuli to which consumers as well as businessmen and economic policy makers respond. However, human response does not depend on stimuli alone. It is a function both of the environment and of the person involved. Stimuli elicit responses according to the psychological predispositions of the responding individual. Motives, attitudes, expectations, and aspirations are intervening variables that mediate between stimuli and responses. They influence both the perception of changes in the environment and the response to them [6, p. 10].

As his phrasing suggests, expectations can easily merge into aspirations which, according to a certain psychological terminology, are affective (dealing with desires and feelings) as distinguished from cognitive (dealing with "thought processes"). Several of the *Handbook* authors whom I have cited refer to the cognitive components of expectancy — e.g., Berkowitz [7, II, p. 78], who uses "the notion of expectancy . . . instead of stimulus-produced responses . . . there is a greater explicit emphasis on cognitive processes when expectancy constructs are employed." Katona, while recognizing this (and he would even, I suspect, insist upon it), is not thereby led to minimize the noncognitive aspects of expectations. The aspirational theme is of course most marked in his most recent book, *Aspirations and Affluence* [6]. Throughout this book aspirations — usually in the context of rising levels of it — recur as a kind of outcropping of bedrock. Indeed, in the opening chapter, a summary of "the major features of the modern form of adaptation" begins and ends with the theme, as these excerpts will show [6, p. 12].

> Progress or success makes for rising levels of aspiration.
> Rising income ... is seen as a personal accomplishment over which one has control ...Past changes are then projected into the future. Social learning ...comes easy ... New styles of living are readily adopted.
> Actions oriented to the future are undertaken ... By committing future income in advance, needs and wants exert great pressure toward obtaining a higher income.
> Productive effort is stepped up to meet rising levels of aspiration.

Aspirations presumably connote relatively much striving on one's own part, and expectations relatively much realism about influences other than one's own. But neither of them, for Katona, can be said to represent personal indifference in the sense of disembodied "pure thought".

I have so far dealt primarily with individual-psychological concepts, but Katona's work includes many references to social influences. I have noted that he sees man as people-binding and shall now examine the notion of expectations in this context.

In his discussion of "intervening variables" [3], he puts heavy emphasis on their social determinants. How the individual "feels, thinks, and acts is influenced by the group to which he belongs ... A person may identify himself with a social group, or with a political or national group" (reference groups). "One major principle applies to all these cases: swimming with the current is much easier than swimming against the current" [3, p. 55]. This proposition is linked, in somewhat oversimplified fashion in my judgment, to "the principle of social facilitation".[1] And, by no accident, one of the three chapters in the section titled "Psychological Findings" in this book, deals with "Group Belonging and Group Influence". It emerges clearly from these and other data that if

---

[1] More accurately, this term refers to "*enhancement* of a motivated behavior by social stimulation" [2], but I do not consider Katona's "free translation" far-fetched.

decision-making, purchasing, and saving are outcomes of expectations, the expectations are in important ways outcomes of group influences. Katona also takes note of the fact that "much of group influence is the result of uniform stimuli reaching people in similar situations" [3, p. 169], and does not necessarily imply direct interaction among them.

This latter point, reminiscent of F.H. Allport's distinction [1] between co-action and interaction within groups, is related to another of Katona's themes — "social learning." The term refers, literally, to similar kinds of learning on the part of aggregates of individuals, with or without direct interaction among them, and is generally operationalized in terms of changes in attitudes or expectations. The concept is uniquely Katona's and is of importance in his thinking.

Social learning derives from "the similarity of the information acquired by members of the same group, or by people with similar interests". But "only under certain conditions does uniform learning take place and influence people's opinions and attitudes in the same direction. Under other conditions the information acquired is not uniform, and cross-shifts of attitudes result" [3, pp. 76–77].

These conditions are ingeniously analyzed by comparing responses by the same populations at two times. When aggregate responses (categorized as optimistic or pessimistic) changed markedly during the interval, the respondents who had changed could be compared with those who had not. It turned out that the former had "learned something. [They had] acquired information about the economy which corresponded to the change in expectations." Nearly all respondents, in this case, either showed no change or became more optimistic. In other populations, at other times, total proportions of optimists and pessimists remained about the same, even though there were many individual changes in opposite directions. Katona's general principle here is that "substantial changes in mass attitudes reflect usually fairly uniform changes among very many people." [4, pp. 657–659], [3].

Being both a psychologist and an economist, Katona must come to grips with problems of "the macro and the micro", as most practitioners of either discipline alone do not. In an interesting chapter on "Social Cognition" he has this to say.

Learning and cognition [defined as "the process of acquiring information and knowledge"] are concepts of individual psychology. In a certain sense those terms are rightfully restricted to the individual. He alone is capable of learning. Saying that a group learns is a metaphor, implying there is some uniformity in the learning of all individuals belonging to the group. This statement indicates a special province of socio-psychological studies, namely, the examination of the similarities and the differences in the information acquired by group members. We shall be concerned mainly with the uniform features of the learning process among millions of unorganized consumers . . . The cognitive processes are [those] through which an individual or a people acquire their image of the environment [including] the meaning of, say, prosperity, depression, inflation, or deficits. These images result from a selective crystallization of past experiences as influenced by attitudes and expectations [5, p. 160].

In this chapter, perhaps unmatched for succinctness and clarity in applying a range of psychological (micro) concepts to economic (macro) problems, Katona brings to bear the principle of generalization of affect; the organization and polarization of information (specifically "news"); habituation; and the search for understanding (without, alas, a reference to Max Wertheimer, his beloved mentor). Also, in the same short chapter he deals with the macro-questions of the slowness and gradualness of social learning, and of the causes of similarity in attitudes and attitude changes (both uniformity of stimuli and the uniformity of people's cognitive processes).

No other social psychologist, to my knowledge, has organized a theoretical structure around the concept of expectations. No other has so artfully linked it, simultaneously, to other concepts with which both macro- and micro-social scientists are familiar. No other has so persistently and so usefully put it to work in the testing-ground of empirical studies. How shall we label such a man? Neither psychologist, nor economist, nor social psychologist will suffice. Let's just call him Mister Macro Micro.

REFERENCES

1 Allport, F.H., *Social Psychology*, Boston: Houghton Mifflin, 1924.
2 English, H.B., and Ava C. English, *A Comprehensive Dictionary of Psychological and Psychoanalytic Terms*, New York: Longmans, Green, 1958.
3 Katona, George, *The Powerful Consumer*, New York: McGraw-Hill, 1960.
4 Katona, George, "The Relationship between Psychology and Economics", In Koch, S., ed., *Psychology, A Study of a Science*, 6, New York: McGraw-Hill, 1963, 639—676.
5 Katona, George, *The Mass Consumption Society*, New York: McGraw-Hill, 1964.
6 Katona, George, Burkhard Strumpel, and Ernest Zahn, *Aspirations and Affluence*, New York: McGraw-Hill, 1971.
7 Lindzey, G., and E. Aronson, eds., *The Handbook of Social Psychology*, 2nd ed., vols. I—V. Reading, Massachusetts: Addison-Wesley, 1968—69.

117

The Place for Laboratory Experiments and Small-Sample Surveys in Economic Psychology

KARL-ERIK WÄRNERYD AND FOLKE ÖLANDER

INTRODUCTION

The purpose of this article is to discuss the fruitfulness of different research approaches in economic psychology. The main tradition in economic psychology is characterized by the use of large-sample surveys. Although the survey approach has met with little enthusiasm among psychologists, whose usual inclination is towards laboratory experiments, the opposite is true among economists. In this article the authors will argue that there is a place in economic psychology for laboratory experiments as well as for small-sample surveys, as distinguished from large-scale surveys.

We will first deal with the problem of defining economic psychology. Stipulative definitions of a research area are of little use in themselves. However, the way an area of study is conceived and the purposes for which the research is carried out do have import for the selection and formulation of research problems and the place allotted to various research approaches. A brief discussion of the content and objectives of economic psychology is therefore essential. We then present some illustrative examples of laboratory and small-sample survey research which has been carried out by ourselves and colleagues within the Economic Research Insitute at the Stockholm School of Economics. The discussion following thereafter points to some differences in frames of reference of economists and psychologists. Finally, we suggest some new tasks for research.

THE FIELD OF ECONOMIC PSYCHOLOGY

The concept, economic psychology, dates from the 1880s. Tarde [30] reports that he was first to use this concept in an article published about that time, although he concedes that the so-called Austrian School of Economics — Böhm-Bawerk and others — talked about economic psychology around the same time.

Tarde, a social psychologist, published a two-volume study *La Psychologie Economique* in 1902. As a psychologist, he criticized the psychological assumptions underlying economic theory. As Tarde defined economic psychology, it comprised the study of the psychological foundations of economic theory. He accused Adam Smith of failing to use psychological insights in propounding his economic theory, but rather keeping the two in separate compartments. Tarde's purpose in writing his voluminous study was to contribute to economics the insights he and his colleagues had gained in social psychology in order to replace the unrealistic psychology of economic theory. Tarde, best known for his work on the laws of imitation, stressed the social nature of the human being and the importance of social interaction which he thought should be the foundation of all psychology, including the psychology of economics. Some fifty years later, using the same title *La Psychologie Economique* [24] Reynaud discussed the development of economic psychology from around 1900 to mid-century. Reynaud presented no explicit definition of economic psychology but apparently, like Tarde, meant the psychological assumptions underlying economic theory. In later works, he developed the concept of economic psychology as an independent scientific area, a synthesis of economics and psychology. According to Reynaud it deals with "the subjective or mental aspects of economic problems" and thus utilizes concepts and methods from both economics and psychology, but also concepts and methods unique to economic psychology. Although Reynaud, like other French authors in economic psychology, is primarily interested in macro-economic problems, such as growth potential and thresholds in economic development, he includes micro-economic problems as well. It seems common in France to include industrial psychology, i.e., the study of psychological factors behind productive behavior, in the category of economic psychology. This is in good concordance with Tarde.

Whereas in the French tradition economic psychology is used in a broad sense comprehending all kinds of economic behavior, in the United States the tendency is to treat economic psychology primarily as consumer psychology. Among many psychologists the conception of the field is even further restricted, including only results originating from so-called consumer opinion surveys (*see*, for example, the well-known applied psychology textbook by Anastasi [1]). Sometimes the concept of economic psychology is used to cover only studies which relate to the macro-economic consumption function [23]. Undoubtedly, such delineations of the area are due to the influential research of George Katona and his co-workers, although Katona himself has provided no formal definition of economic psychology. Indeed he uses the term psychological economics or, more recently, behavioral economics almost interchangeably with the term economic psychology.

As the authors of this article conceive of economic psychology, it deals mainly with the psychological study of consumer choice behavior. By consumer behavior we, like many other behavioral scientists, refer not only to consumption but also to other aspects of the consumer and household roles in society, such as acquisition of income and household planning. Insofar as studies of entrepreneur behavior throw light upon the conditions of consumers and the relations between producer and consumer, we also include such studies within the subject area.

THE MANIFOLD PURPOSES OF RESEARCH IN
ECONOMIC PSYCHOLOGY

Psychological research in the area of consumer behavior has

until now been almost wholly inspired by demand from decision-makers in business and government. Psychologists have to an increasing extent been engaged by decisions-makers in marketing to do research on consumer behavior with a view to providing ideas and data as a basis for marketing, especially advertising activities. The bulk of research in the micro-economic area has had a clear orientation toward decision-making in business. Government economists have encouraged and sponsored psychological research in the macro-economic area, such as studies of saving behavior, of short-run forecasting, and of business and consumer reactions to economic-political measures. It should be noted, however, that much of Katona's work clearly is directed toward contributing to economics as a science and not simply toward offering data for immediate application.

In brief, at present three main purposes can be distinguished for research in economic psychology as the field is defined by us:

1. Providing data on — and to some extent also models of — individual and group consumer behavior, used primarily for marketing purposes.
2. Providing data on — and to some extent also models of — aggregate consumer behavior, used primarily by economists for economic policy advice and action, to a certain degree probably by business firms as well.
3. Contributing to economic theory, mainly on the macro-economic level, by providing realistic descriptions of consumer (and business) behavior.

Research for the first purpose is conducted at a fairly large number of institutions in several parts of the world: in commercial organizations, in departments of economics and marketing, and, to some extent also, in psychology departments. In the second and third areas, the Survey Research Center at The University of Michigan is well-known for its outstanding contributions, but there are few other institutions where studies with such aims are pursued.

Significant omission from the above list of purposes is something often designated as consumer interest. Consumer interest is now represented by more or less organized groups of consumers and in some countries through special government agencies. The common philosophy behind the actions of such groups and agencies is that the consumer should be provided with information, legal advice, and protection, and should also be aided in making his voice heard in the marketplace by means other than his buying power alone. The role that research has thus far played in this area has been, to say the least, inadequate. Thus, a fourth purpose should in our opinion be added to the three dominant ones already mentioned:

4. Providing data on and models for consumer (and business) behavior with the aim of serving consumer interests.

This purpose may, for example, involve research on effects of different designs in consumer education, on household information needs, and on household optimization problems. In the last part of this article the need for such research is further explored.

Economic psychology, as we conceive of it, by providing detailed and realistic descriptions of the behavior and decision-making of individual consumers and households is in a position to provide the foundation for the construction of consumer behavior models which could be employed by various agents: by consumers individually and in organized groups, by government for economic policy and for consumer education and protection, and by business firms. (The possibility of goal conflicts between these agents should of course not be forgotten.) A consequence of our view is that economic psychologists in their research should keep in mind the actual and potential use of their results in normative models and in some cases perhaps take the responsibility for developing such models.

We have emphasized the need for developing a descriptive theory of individual consumer behavior as a step towards the goal of helping government, business, and consumers to better decisions. There will, however, certainly be by-products of psychological studies of the consumer. One of these by-products could be the provision of data or small fragments of theory that could eventually lead to changes in micro-economic theory. It is to be hoped, of course, that in the long run general economic theory will be influenced by and benefit from any consolidated findings that may emerge from economic psychology. However, we are quite aware that isolated findings concerning individual consumer behavior (or even the rejection by means of experiments of some of the tenets of micro-economic theory) will not lead to a rapid reconstruction of economic theory. Thus, the goal of inserting wedges into the theoretical economist's picture of the world must be seen as secondary.

Another by-product of economic psychology could be to provide some building stones for general behavior theory. Economic behavior makes up a considerable part of everyday behavior. It is amenable to observation and experimentation; the events that can be studied are usually highly meaningful to the subjects (certainly in comparison with many other areas of behavior studied by psychologists, especially in their laboratories). Quite irrespective of any interest in economic or consumer problems, we think that psychologists and other behavioral scientists should take a closer look at the possibilities of using economic behavior as a testing ground for theories developed in other areas. If psychologists were to become more conversant with economic behavior, general behavioral laws could perhaps first be discovered and formulated in this area and then tested in other areas. A reallocation of some resources in psychology from the study of rats and college sophomores to the study of consumers could probably lead to a better understanding of human behavior.

THE CONTENTS OF ECONOMIC PSYCHOLOGICAL MODELS

Many normative models for the actions of consumers, as well as of government and business officials can be put forth with consideration of actual behavior. Descriptive theory does not seem to be a necessary prerequisite for constructing normative theories. Logical deductions from a few simple postulates are often considered sufficient. However, many business economists have come to the conclusion that useful normative models of management require reliable descriptions of how decisions are actually made, of the real goals pursued by entrepreneurs and managers, etc. Without such knowledge, both construction and implementation of normative models have little prospect of success.

In a similar vein, it appears desirable that normative models for individual consumer or household decision-making take into account more of the richness of actual consumer behavior. As psychologists, we are biased in favor of behavioral theory and are convinced that a rich description of household behavior needs to include not only economic, but also psychological and sociological variables.

There are several reasons underlying this belief. The first is based on an analogy. Researchers dealing with other spheres of individual economic behavior, such as managerial or employee behavior, have usually found it quite necessary to rely on social psychological variables and explanations in order to arrive at coherent descriptions of the behavior under observation. It seems highly probable, then, that there is the same need for comparable studies of individuals in their roles as consumers, where "non-economic" reasons can be suspected to be at least as important as in work behavior.

Another reason is that the use of psychological variables gives access to already existing theories and knowledge of individual behavior in similar but "nonconsumption" circumstances. Within psychology and other behavioral sciences, there exist theories of perception and cognition, of learning and motivation, of decision-making, of attitude change, of the importance of roles and social status, of communication and reactions to personal and imperso-nal influence, of diffusion processes. It seems hardly possible that these factors should be not at all involved in consumer behavior. Thus, to the extent that these research fields have provided valid observations concerning regularities in human behavior, the study of consumer behavior should benefit by taking such observations into consideration.

A third important reason is the following: The implementation of normative models requires some means by which the desired behavior can be brought about. In the case of consumers this is often attempted by means of legal or strictly economic measures such as making it financially easier or more difficult for house-holds to engage in certain behavior, or changing the consumer's environment through legal prescriptions for the sellers' activities. Such attempts to influence behavior by legal or economic-political measures are often unsuccessful unless supported by information or persuasion. Governments, federal banks, consumer agencies and organizations do in fact try to influence saving and spending patterns, the financing and planning of purchases, etc., by means of information, advertising, and propaganda campaigns and at least in some countries by means of regular education. Similarly, manufacturers try to influence consumer decisions not only by means of pricing and product and distribution policies, but also by carefully-planned advertising and other promotional activities.

Insofar as information and persuasion can be considered as a necessary and legitimate means by which to influence consumer decision-making, there is obviously a need for a psychological theory of consumer behavior. Human information processing cannot be studied as a purely economic event. There is a need for detailed knowledge of how individuals attend to, perceive and react to information, as well as for a mapping of the communication channels by which various categories of people keep in touch with their environment, in this case the economic environment. Without such knowledge attempts at changing consumer behavior by means of information are unlikely to succeed. Yet a large part of social psychological research deals with the human being only as an information processor, i.e. only with the effects of different types of informational or persuasive messages upon attitudes and behavior. Thus we have here a very important reason for trying to link consumer theory and psychological theory.

To take only one example of information problems, let us consider the role of information in the area of household saving. Our knowledge of the channels through which saving behavior and saving inclinations are influenced is very limited. There are many unanswered questions. Do attitudes and behavior in this area change at all, or are saving inclinations and attitudes to a large extent a function of habits founded in very early years? If and when changes in behavior and attitudes take place, are these changes then primarily a function of information obtained through mass media, through opinion leaders, through labor unions, through neighbors and workmates, or through other channels? And what information is disseminated through what channels?

Neither in Sweden nor in other countries has there been any great interest in studies of the channels by means of which it is possible to reach and influence the public in matters concerning saving and spending. This is a potentially fruitful field for economic psychological research.

In this particular respect, it is perhaps also justified to be somewhat critical of the work of the Katona group. In their work, few attempts have been made at investigating how the intervening variables that play such an important role in Katona's theories of economic behavior, above all attitudes and expectations, are related to environmental variables, particularly information diffused through mass media and personal contacts. It is often maintained that the possibilities of finding a pattern of environmental factors and antecedent events which determine the intervening variables are more or less nonexistent [8], [9], [11]. We have no doubt it would be a very difficult undertaking. However, if, as Katona maintains, attitudes and expectations are of great importance in determining economic action on the individual level then it is obviously also very important and worthy of much effort to find out about the factors that influence these variables. This is true, irrespective of whether the goal is to make a long-run forecast − it is not possible today to make any prediction of how attitudes and expectations will change in the long run − or if the goal is the one that we have primarily dealt with in this section, namely to hasten or counter, for example, by means of information and propaganda, a given development as it is in the process of evolving.

RESEARCH APPROACHES IN ECONOMIC PSYCHOLOGY

Economic psychology is often almost by definition associated with the use of large-scale surveys [1]. Morgan [16] seems to suggest that controlled experiments and small-sample surveys have not contributed to the economist's knowledge of consumer behavior. Katona often stresses the point that behavioral economics means a study of mass behavior. Piecemeal studies or the use of elaborate psychological methods are consequently not considered to be very useful.

It should be evident from our discussion that our conception of economic psychology and the purposes stated for research in this field involves research on a much broader set of problems than can be studied by large-scale surveys only. Consumer research for marketing purposes utilizes both large-scale surveys and intensive surveys of small samples and laboratory experiments. Certainly noncommercial research purposes could profit from the same wide range of research methods. Computers and computer simulation now permit larger and more complex sets of variables to be handled meaningfully, and the use of different methods could fill the need for more elaborate models of economic behavior.

By laboratory experiment is meant the conscious manipulation of one or more independent variables and registration of the effects in a setting that allows for the control of independent variables and potentially disturbing influences. A field experiment has the same characteristics, but the realistic setting usually permits less control of disturbing factors.

By small-sample survey we mean intensive interviewing with samples of say 30 to 200 respondents. The actual number is a less important difference from large surveys of the Survey Research Center type than the fact that the group is characteristically not a representative sample from a nationwide population or a considerable part thereof. Often the study is carried out on random samples from narrowly restricted groups or on mere convenience samples.

Psychologists generally view laboratory experiment as the main, if not the only way of building behavioral theory. Their training leads them to look for experimental designs and laboratory settings for the study of problems. Psychological research is characterized by the laborious accumulation of empirical data through small-scale studies and detailed data analysis guided by partial hypotheses. There are few global theories of behavior in psychology, and those psychologists who attempt to present such theories are viewed with suspicion in the research community.

TWO EXAMPLES OF CONTROLLED EXPERIMENTS

The following examples illustrate research problems with respect to which it was felt that experimental studies could give new insights. The first appears to have a certain relevance for micro-economic theory. The problem is whether price acts as an *indicator of the subjective quality or attractiveness* of a product. This question has to a surprising degree been neglected in economic literature. An exception is the discussion of the so-called

128

Veblen effect according to which consumers buy higher-priced goods in order to demonstrate pecuniary power. This might be one, but certainly not the only reason for finding a higher-priced product more attractive than a lower-priced one. Most economic scholars deny or disregard the function of price as an indicator of quality. Stigler, the well-known price theorist, goes so far as to assert [28, p. 44] that "No one has yet been able to find a demonstrable example of more of a commodity being purchased at a higher price (allowing for expectations of price changes . . .)."

Several reports published in the marketing literature (*see*, e.g., [5], [6], [13]) and comments heard in business quarters, give a quite different impression, namely, that there are cases when a high price gives rise to more demand than a low price. Certainly from a purely theoretical standpoint, there seems to be no a priori reason for belittling the role that price may play in indicating quality to a consumer, who is almost always subject to uncertainty with respect to many of the aspects of the purchasing situation, and who is on the lookout for any possible cue that may help him in his decision-making.

The principal procedure involved in the experiments carried out within our laboratory has simply been to divide subjects (e.g., housewives) into various experimental groups and to give the groups different information about the prices of a number of product variants within a certain product group. The price information has been given by means of normal price labels. In some cases other information has been systematically varied as well, e.g., information about the manufacturer. The dependent variable has mostly consisted of verbal or written judgments of the quality or attractiveness of the respective product variants; in some cases actual choices (with real outcomes) have been used instead. For a review of some of the studies carried out, *see* [20], [21].

The results obtained both in our laboratory and in other studies (*see*, e.g., [14], [27]) seem quite clearly to indicate that under certain circumstances (and in a laboratory situation), price does function as a cue for judging quality. The effects seem to be much more prominent in some cases and for some products than for others; however, so far little is known as to why this is so. In any case, it seems difficult to avoid the prediction (or speculation) that in some circumstances, the characteristics of which are largely unknown, higher price will lead to a higher demand for a product than a lower price (provided that customers are not given the impression that it is a matter of a *rise* in price). More detailed statements about the influence of price on the perception of quality would require first of all a systematic study of the influence of such factors as *product type, consumer characteristics* (income, education, product interest, etc.) and *size of price manipulation*. Many other factors probably affecting the size of the effect could undoubtedly be suggested.

It is rather difficult to see how a research question of the kind dealt with here could be studied with other than experimental techniques (e.g., with correlational methods). A natural next step in a research program concerning price as an indicator of quality would be to move the experiment out of the laboratory into the field, using actual buying behavior as the dependent variable.

The second example from our own research is a field experiment where an attempt was made by Seipel to study how consumers react to *premiums* [25], [26]. The operations and effects of this kind of sales promotion have seldom been subjected to empirical study. The main interest in Seipel's study was not focussed on implications for marketing, but rather on testing certain hypotheses about how people in general (and thus also consumers) react to *favors* and *gifts*.

One of Sweden's major food producers agreed to cooperate as the sponsor of an experimental premium offer. In Stockholm, 480 married housewives were randomly assigned to three experimental groups and one control group. In cooperation with the food producer a ceramic pot, with a retail value of about $2.50, was chosen as an attractive premium, and three levels of demanded reciprocation — low, medium, and high — were defined, In the condition of low reciprocation subjects were simply asked to mail a request for the pot; in the medium condition they were asked to include 50c value in stamps; and in the high condition, they were asked to include $ 1 in stamps and, in addition, to answer a short questionnaire about one of the company's products. The control group got no offer at all. The offer was mailed to the experimental subjects together with a letter from the company stating that they had been randomly selected for a special promotion. After the expiration of the offer, all subjects were interviewed by telephone.

Attractiveness of the premium offered was measured by the actual requisition rate in the various groups. Attitude toward the offer was established by direct questions. Questions were also asked concerning previous purchases of the company's products, buying plans, and the extent to which subjects has made comments to others about the offer.

The most striking result of the experiment was the following. *Fewer* subjects sent for the premium when it was offered free (but for a stamp on an envelope) than when 50c had to be paid. Clearly, making premiums free does not necessarily make them more attractive. There might, in effect, be a preference for fair reciprocation in relations between consumers and producers such as has been found in other experiments concerning favor-doing. Seipel suggests that receiving a free offer creates too strong an obligation to reciprocate, something that people generally resent, especially when they distrust the person or institution concerned. He finds support for these assumptions in data concerning the perception of the company's motives. When the gift was given free, suspicion with regard to the motives was definitely higher. As for purchases and buying plans, on the other hand, there was a tendency for the group where very low reciprocation was demanded to have bought more of the company's products in the weeks following the offer and to have more buying plans than the other experimental groups. In all experimental groups purchases and plans were much higher than in the control group.

All in all, the results form a rather intriguing pattern. Almost nonexistent demand for reciprocation definitely seems to have lowered the attractiveness of the premium. Nonetheless, and despite the fact that subjects in this group had no higher opinion than other subjects of the company's products, rather strong feelings of obligation seem to have been created (as judged from the purchasing behavior). If experiments like Seipel's, carried out in equally realistic circumstances, were to be replicated and to give similar results, even the theoretical economist might be puzzled: do people prefer goods that have to be bought at a certain cost to goods than can be had (almost) free of cost?

It is not possible here to review in any complete fashion the more or less continuous discussion of the psychological laboratory experiment as a research tool. (The reader is referred, for example, to [33], [34].) The main argument for the laboratory experiment as against correlational research is that the former permits a high degree of control and the complete disentanglement of extraneous factors from the independent variables under study. The controlled experiment serves the purpose of conceptual clarification by extricating and focusing on the variables that are interesting from the point of view of theory construction. The laboratory permits closer inspection of interesting phenomena, the testing of some variables for extreme values, the creation and study of rare events. The effects of events that have thus far not been encountered in reality can be studied in the laboratory. In particular, it is frequently possible to pretest in a laboratory situation the effects of messages of information and persuasion. There are, of course, limits to such studies, but as long as there is conceptual equivalence between reality and the laboratory a wide variety of phenomena can be subjected to laboratory study.

Critics of the laboratory experiment usually call attention to its artificiality. Even if a problem originates from realistic situations it has to undergo so many transformations to be dealt with in the laboratory that there may be little similarity between the problem actually studied and the initial problem. Admittedly, there is a question of how one can then be sure of conceptual equivalence. A second major argument against laboratory experiments is that there are doubts about the possibilities of generalizing the results to whole populations or important subgroups in the population. Replicated studies using groups from other populations would naturally serve to increase the credibility of experimental findings. Unfortunately, such replications are rare.

We certainly do not want to exaggerate the potential contributions to be made by the increased use of laboratory experimentation. The problem of the generality of results arrived at in the laboratory is serious. If such results are treated as preliminary and thought of mainly as sources of hypotheses to be further tested in representative survey research, there will probably be some agreement about the value of laboratory experimentation. This function has been called the heuristic analogue. We would go a little further than that. Laboratory experiments are not only important preambles to representative studies in economic psychology, but they may also allow for *follow-up studies* where certain relations found in surveys can be more closely examined. To us it seems that only a combination of approaches can provide a satisfactory description of consumer behavior. The exclusive use of large-scale surveys leaves large lacunae which can be filled only by research of a more intensive type.

TWO EXAMPLES OF SMALL-SAMPLE SURVEYS

We shall present two instances of research projects presently under way at our Institute, both employing the small-sample technique. The intention is to give examples of projects where the detailed study of a rather small (and homogeneous) group of subjects seems to constitute a useful research method, either as a preliminary to full-scale field investigations, or as a heuristic device in developing theories and hypotheses concerning consumer behavior.

Detailed studies of consumer decision processes have become rather frequent in recent years (*see*, e.g., [4], [19] for reviews). The studies attempt to determine, for example, the number of alternative products, brands, and shops considered in connection with a particular purchase; the role of various information sources in the process; the time sequence of the various steps in the decision process; and the planning horizon that consumers seem to employ. The work by Katona and Mueller [12] was, of course, one of the pioneer studies of this kind. In Sweden, both one of the authors, Wärneryd [32], and Wickström [35] have carried out such studies with respect to cars and household appliances, respectively.

Most studies of buying processes have been carried out as interviews "after the fact", i.e., a buyer of a particular item has somehow been identified and then interviewed about how he arrived at his decision. In a current research project (Lindfeldt and Ölander, in progress) an attempt is being made to enter consumer decision processes at a very early stage, to avoid exclusive reliance on retrospective reports. With the help of the Stockholm Board of Housing, the researchers are notified almost as soon as the young couples themselves when the latter are to receive their first offer of an apartment. As there is a constant shortage of housing in the Stockholm area, these young people have usually been waiting for an apartment for quite a long time, and the notice frequently arrives rather unexpectedly. Our assumption is that a number of decision processes are initiated at the moment the couple gets the notice.

By means of the panel study technique, these young couples are now being interviewed (each partner separately at the same time) three times within a six-month period concerning their purchasing plans and their actual purchases. Couples assigned to two control groups are interviewed only in the second or third panel wave so as to make possible an assessment of panel effects. The first interview is carried out within a few days after the couple has been notified and usually before they have moved into the new apartment. It is hoped that by thus studying plans in progress, it will be possible to get a fuller picture of the decision processes involved (in this case primarily decisions concerning furniture and household appliances). The different roles that husband and wife play in these processes can also be analyzed in some detail. The approach also permits detailed study of how priorities are set in the family, e.g., between a TV set and a washing machine, and of decisions concerning the financing of the purchases. The theoretical scheme underlying the design of the interviews is modelled after theories of decision-making found in other behavioral sciences and thus has a cognitive slant.

The sample studied in this investigation is not statistically representative of any larger segment of the population. The total number of households studied (in both the panel group and control groups) is about 150. Although some comparisons may be made as to demographic and social characteristics between the respondents and the general population, nothing can yet be said about the extent to which it may be proper to generalize the forthcoming findings. This particular study — being the first we have attempted of this kind — should perhaps be regarded as a methodological exercise to test the applicability and reliability of the measuring instruments, to assess the size of panel effects, and to study other procedural problems. In considering the merits and demerits of such a small-scale study it should be borne in mind that researchers are unlikely to find necessary funds to collect detailed data about individual decision-making processes, involving several interviews with each person in a household spread out over a certain time, for a large sample statistically representative of the whole population (or some large segment of it). Also the sheer problem of strictly defining a population for a large-scale study of "decision processes just begun" would in our case have been overwhelming.

We believe, however, that the intensive study of small samples can provide interesting data both for consumer behavior theory and for use as background information in attempts to educate or influence consumers. Particularly in applied work of the latter kind, knowledge of the ways that *some* consumers go about planning their purchases, collecting their information about products, prices and stores, dividing decisions among household members, etc., is usually preferable to not possessing this knowledge about *any* consumer. We tend to believe that the same argument may also be valid when the purpose is to develop theory.

Now to our second example of a small-sample study. Within micro-economic theory, the income of an individual is treated as an exogenous restriction placed upon his economic behavior. Income (and wealth) according to this viewpoint, provide the boundaries within which the individual can make decisions about consumption and saving. However, several researchers have recently begun to question the relevance of this point of view. Morgan [15] has suggested that "the whole concept of income as a simple exogenous variable in the household sector begins to seem invalid." For similar comments, *see*, e.g., [17], [29]. There are, of course, a number of actions that it is at least theoretically possible for the individual person or household to take in order to influence his (its) income. Moonlighting, overtime work, the housewife's gainful employment, and change of jobs are some of the possibilities that can alter income rather quickly. Income can, of course, also be influenced by long-term decisions regarding retraining, change of place of living, etc.

In a pilot study recently carried out at our unit [7] an attempt was made to map out in some detail the process, including motivational and cognitive factors, that governs the individual's choice of income. Since the study was of a very exploratory character, we chose for investigation a situation where the possibility of earning more money was readily available to all but where the decision to do so or not was quite voluntary. The subjects chosen were employees of a government office in Stockholm where there were ample opportunities for overtime work, and where it was possible for the investigators to obtain reliable data about the individuals in question, including data about their overtime work. All respondents were female and unmarried. A rather comprehensive interview was carried out with the subjects, asking questions about their incomes and expenditures, their attitudes towards saving, consumption and work, their dispositions towards economic planning, their felt need for achievement, etc.

Among the various findings were the following. The tendency to acquire extra income was totally unrelated to discretionary spending power (ordinary income minus taxes and certain outlays such as rent). The need for extra income was obviously determined by other factors. Certain differences in consumption patterns were found among those who did much and those who did little or no overtime work. For example, the former spent more money than the latter on vacations, cigarettes, liquor, and restaurants. In this particular instance, it was also found that overtime work was associated with difficulties or lack of planning. Observations concerning differences in saving propensity, in attitudes to saving, and in planning ability between overtime workers and others, led the investigators to put forward for further research the idea that thrifty people with good planning ability are (a) able to avoid certain kinds of expenses and thus able to save more and (b) more able to plan their economy as a whole and thus to avoid the need for replenishment of income. The findings concerning planning also provided the stimulus for a field experiment (with a representative sample from one segment of the Stockholm population), which is presently being carried out, and in which certain of the experimental subjects are paid for keeping a record of their incomes and outlays in the course of a month's time. The goal is to investigate whether the insights into one's own economy that a person may get during that period, can change planning and economic behavior (including income acquisition) in the following period of time.

The study just referred to was not only being conducted on a small scale (102 interviews) but, for reasons mentioned above, has been confined to one locality. To put it bluntly, the sample is far too specific and the reliability and validity of the observations (both of economic and psychological magnitudes) too little known to allow broad generalizations at this stage. Still, we shall attempt to further support our contention that there is some value in this type of study.

SOME REFLECTIONS ON THE USE OF THE SMALL-SAMPLE SURVEY IN ECONOMIC PSYCHOLOGY

The comments made about laboratory experiments hold true in many respects for small-sample surveys as well. Intensive interviewing can provide a lot of interesting data about the persons interviewed and give a descriptive richness that cannot be achieved in large-scale surveys. With small samples it is possible, with specially-skilled interviewers, to use a blend of lengthy attitude scales and informal questions. On the other hand, sampling errors are considerable, and even if random samples are used, they are usually representative of very narrowly-defined groups, not of nationwide populations. Actually, convenience samples are usually used because of the reluctance of many randomly-selected respondents to participate in time consuming and sometimes boring interviews. Small-sample studies may be seen as pilot studies [16], or as a heuristic device which helps the researchers involved to clarify their own ideas and hypotheses concerning a particular sphere of consumer behavior. Small-sample studies doubtless have a place in economic psychology for generating hypotheses to be further studied by means of large-scale surveys, controlled experiments, and simulations. Like laboratory experiments they can also serve the function of follow-ups of larger-scale studies in which the ecological distribution of the phenomena under study has been ascertained and where interesting relationships in need of further clarification have been found. Whether such studies will provide

In another context, one of us [22, pp. 23–26] has recently discussed the problem of studying change from the psychologist's point of view. He challenges the notion that only those psychological variables which show appreciable changes over time can profitably be used in the analysis of changes in consumption and saving. The major argument against that notion is that *interactions* between stimuli (environmental changes) and, say, personality characteristics may be of great interest. Economic-political measures as well as other changes in general economic variables may have different effects on groups of people having varying personality characteristics, and these differential effects can hardly be explained or predicted without knowledge of the distribution of personality characteristics in the population [31] and without experimental and other studies concerning the nature of such interactions.

The representativeness of results from psychological research is a complicated issue. It has two main facets: the need (1) to study representative samples of subjects – a factor largely related to the problem of finding the necessary funds – and (2) to study representative situations. Psychologists have often sinned in both respects, studying conveniently-selected subjects in nontypical situations. There is, however, among psychologists an expanding interest in the ecological validity of situations studied both in the laboratory and in the field. More careful considerations of situational representativeness may perhaps increase the credibility of their studies in the eyes of the economist.

Although economists sometimes seek psychological data to aid in their work, all too often they seem to be unaware of the potential contributions of psychology to the study of certain types of problems. Indeed we venture to remark that economists are often prone to act as "macro-psychologists" as, for example, when they give advice – or criticize – government with respect to economic policy. They talk freely about attitudes, habits, and motivation relying on assumptions that do not strictly belong to economic theory. In such cases the use of behavioral science methods, such as small-sample surveys and experiments, especially if replicated under varying circumstances, could perhaps give a firmer foundation for recommendations.

usable insights into economic behavior at the micro level and thus provide some of the impetus for the formulation of richer and more detailed economic hypotheses and theories, largely remains to be seen.

There are apparently many differences between the psychologist's and the economist's views concerning the pursuit of scientific knowledge. One difference we have already touched upon. Many psychologists are apt to generalize quite freely from very restricted studies. While conceding that the results arise from artificial situations, they nevertheless put trust in theories developed through such studies and then frequently argue — mainly on the basis of laboratory studies of economic behavior — that the economist's assumptions about human behavior are fundamentally wrong. The economist finds the laboratory evidence too scanty and contends that he is correct about economic behavior in the long run and on an aggregate level. There is certainly a need for discussions between psychologists and economists to attempt to resolve their differences and to consider such things as the psychological underpinnings of economic theory and the possibilities of related research. These discussions would also have to attack the problems of aggregating data from psychological studies, where the unit of study is usually the individual and where social interdependencies are stressed, thus making aggregation rather difficult.

There are other differences between economists and psychologists. The former are less interested in how things *are* [16], than in *changes* and in what happens as a consequence of changes. The latter are frequently content with the description of relationships between variables of interest at one particular point of time, and any changes in behavior that are studied usually deal with momentary reactions to specific (molecular) stimuli in the individual's immediate environment. Both economists and economic psychologists have strongly maintained that in studies of economic behavior the changes in gross behavior over time are of primary interest [10].

In most industrialized societes, including some socialist countries, there is an increasing interest in consumer affairs, sometimes characterized as consumerism. Consumer affairs have begun to occupy important positions on political party programs in at least some countries in Western Europe. In the U.S. there is lively debate on consumer interests which is likely to have consequences in the form of legislation and cooperative efforts among consumer groups. It is conceivable that the debate will also affect the choice of problems in academic research on consumer behavior. In our opinion there should be such an impact. There is at present very scanty knowledge about consumer behavior, relevant to consumer education and consumer participation.

It is easy to give examples of research within economic psychology that should be useful to consumer educators in their attempts to provide consumers with better information and better decision models. From the few examples of our own research mentioned earlier in this paper, it seems obvious that consumer agencies and organizations could use the results of experiments concerning the relationships between price and subjective quality for the purpose of mapping out areas in which people seem particularly apt to be misled by price in their choices, and directing consumer education accordingly. That there are product fields in which the correlation between quality in a functional sense and price is low − or even absent − thus making it generally bad strategy to judge quality by price, has been demonstrated by Morris and Bronson [18].

Data concerning household planning and how planning and other economic behavior are connected also appear to be essential in a variety of cases where attempts are made to influence consumer behavior or to ameliorate the situation. Thus studies of decision-making and general planning within households can provide consumer educators with the data necessary for an informed choice of target groups, message content, and media vehicles in their educational activities. Consumer participation is often viewed by businessmen as a potential threat to business, the degree of the threat being a function of the degree of consumer participation. We would merely note here that there is no doubt that the modern consumer, judging by results from surveys and mass media debates, often experiences a sense of powerlessness when faced with developments in the marketing area. Neighborhood stores suddenly disappear, shopping centers crop up far from urban centers, the assortment of commodities in well-known stores change, certain brands and products that were thought to be satisfactory are replaced by varieties that seem inferior. Studies of how widespread the feelings of helplessness and frustration are, as well as a mapping of their correlates, should be a task for economic psychology.

We believe that the whole area of consumer participation is one in which research can be put to profitable use. Some examples can be given. In Great Britain and in Sweden there are special local consumer committees in some urban areas. Such groups could be studied from many points of view. What do they accomplish in terms of environmental changes and in terms of their own satisfaction? What channels do they have for communication and how do these channels function?

In general, studies of the way in which consumers are able to *communicate* with producers and impress their wishes and ideas upon them are sorely needed. Whether or not one is of the opinion that the traditional market place provides an adequate system of communication between consumer and producer, it seems important to study empirically the extent to which individual consumers or consumer groups today act or find it possible to act as senders of information to business and industry. The most interesting area to choose for a closer look at the communication channels between consumers and producers might be the area of new product development, where there are several indications that two-way communication is very rare [2], [3].

It is to be hoped that future developments of empirical research in economic psychology will include systematic and large-scale attacks on issues such as those outlined in this section. Consumer behavior can be studied from several points of view. It is imperative that one of them be the point of view of the consumer himself. However, an important prerequisite for obtaining the substantial increase in economic resources which would be necessary for an expansion of research on consumer behavior with a view to serving the consumer interest, would be that the parties concerned − government and consumer groups − be convinced that such research can produce useful results. On the other hand, until interested researchers are provided with adequate funds it would be difficult to prove the value of this kind of research. It remains to be seen how the vicious circle may be broken.

CONCLUDING REMARK

In this article we have attempted to set forth certain thoughts concerning economic psychology as an area of research. It would be our hope that our conception of economic-psychological research may contribute to arousing greater interest among psychologists in economic behavior. Partly on the basis of our own experiences, we tend to feel that for many psychologists consumer behavior is seen *either* as an area for marketing research — regarded as unattractive because of perceived demands for the direct applicability of results or for ideological reasons — *or* as economic psychology in its most restricted sense (related solely to the consumption function) and then viewed as too narrow and theoretically uninteresting.

Considering the range and importance of consumer problems in today's societies, whether affluent or developing, one is, however, forced to the conclusion that interdisciplinary research attacks are necessary. Economists need more understanding of the research approaches favored by behavioral scientists and the latter would profit from learning more about economic behavior. A precondition for more extensive collaboration is that other aspects of consumer behavior than have hitherto been stressed in research be made subject for study, and that new purposes for consumer research be added, as suggested in this article.

REFERENCES

1 Anastasi, Anne, *Fields of Applied Psychology*, New York: McGraw-Hill, 1964.
2 Buzzell, Robert D., and Nourse, Robert E., *Product Innovation in Food Processing: 1954–1964*, Boston: Harvard University, Graduate School of Business Administration, 1967.

3 Cohen, Dorothy, ed., "Communication Systems between Management and the Consumer in Selected Industries", Hampstead, N.Y.: Hofstra University, 1969 (mimeographed).

4 Engel, James F., David T. Kollat, and Roger D. Blackwell, *Consumer Behavior*, New York: Holt, Rinehart and Winston, 1968.

5 Fog, Bjarke, *Industrial Pricing Policies*, Amsterdam: North-Holland, 1960.

6 Gabor, André, and C.W.J. Granger, "The Pricing of New Products", *Scientific Business*, 3 (August, 1965), 141–50.

7 Julander, Claes-Robert, and Folke Ölander, "Inverkan av konsumtions-motiv och sparandemotiv pa hushallens inkomst" [The Influence of Consumption and Saving Motives on Household Income], Stockholm: The Economic Research Institute at the Stockholm School of Economics, 1970 (mimeographed).

8 Katona, George, "Attitude Change: Instability of Response and Acquisition of Experience", *Psychological Monographs*, 72, no. 10, 1968.

9 Katona George, *The Powerful Consumer*, New York: McGraw-Hill, 1960.

10 Katona, George, "The Relationship between Psychology and Economics", in S. Koch, ed., *Psychology: A study of a Science*, Vol. 6, New York: McGraw-Hill, 1963, 639–76.

11 Katona, George, "Consumer Behavior Theory and Findings on Expectations and Aspirations", *American Economic Review*, 58 (May, 1968), 19–30.

12 Katona, George, and Eva Mueller, "A Study of Purchase Decisions", in L.H. Clark, ed., *Consumer Behavior: The Dynamics of Consumer Reactions*, New York: Harper, 1954, 30–87.

13 Knauth, Oswald, "Considerations in the Setting of Retail Prices", *Journal of Marketing*, 14 (July, 1949), 1–12.

14 McConnell, Douglas J., "Effect of Pricing on Perception of Product Quality", *Journal of Applied Psychology*, 52 (August, 1968), 331–34.

15 Morgan, James N., "The Anatomy of Income Change", in R.F. Kosobud and J.N. Morgan, eds., *Consumer Behavior of Individual Families over Two and Three Years*, Ann Arbor, Mich.: University of Michigan, Institute for Social Research, 1964, 18–41.

16 Morgan, James N., "Contributions of Survey Research to Economics", in C.Y. Glock, ed., *Survey Research in the Social Sciences*, New York: Russell Sage Foundation, 1967, 217–68.

17 Morgan, James N., Martin H. David, Wilbur J. Cohen, and Harvey E. Brazer, *Income and Welfare in the United States*, New York: McGraw-Hill, 1962.

18 Morris, Ruby T., and Claire S. Bronson, "The Chaos of Competition Indicated by Consumer Reports", *Journal of Marketing*, 33 (July, 1969), 26–34.

19 Nicosia, Francesco M., *Consumer Decision Processes*, Englewood Cliffs, N.J.: Prentice-Hall, 1966.

20 Ölander, Folke, "The Influence of Price on the Consumer's Evaluation of

Products and Purchases", in B. Taylor and G. Wills, eds., *Pricing Strategy*, London: Staples, 1969, 50−69.

21 Ölander, Folke, and Jan Forslin, "The Influence of Price on the Attractiveness of Consumer Products", unpublished manuscript.

22 Ölander, Folke, and Carl-Magnus Seipel, *Psychological Approaches to the Study of Saving*, Urbana, Ill.: Bureau of Economic and Business Research, 1970.

23 Perloff, Robert, "Consumer Psychology in Academia", paper read at the XVIIth International Congress of Applied Psychology, Liège, July 25−30, 1971.

24 Reynaud, Pierre-Louis, *La Psychologie Economique*, Paris: Rivière, 1954.

25 Seipel, Carl-Magnus, "Konkurrens med presenter och tjänster" [Marketing with Presents and Services], Stockholm: The Economic Research Institue at the Stockholm School of Economics, 1970 (mimeographed).

26 Seipel, Carl-Magnus, "Premiums − Forgotten by Theory", *Journal of Marketing*, 35(April, 1971), 26−34.

27 Stafford, James E., and Ben M. Enis, "The Price-Quality Relationship: An Extension", *Journal of Marketing Research*, 6 (Nov., 1969), 456−58.

28 Stigler, George J., *The Theory of Price*, revised ed., New York: Macmillan, 1953.

29 Suits, Daniel B., "The Determinants of Consumer Expenditures: A Review of Present Knowledge", in D.B. Suits and others, *Impact of Monetary Policy*, Englewood Cliffs, N.J.: Prentice-Hall, 1963, 1−60.

30 Tarde, Gabriel, *La Psychologie Economique*, 2 vols., Paris: Alcan 1902.

31 Tobin, James, and F. Trenery Dolbear, Jr., "Comments on the Relevance of Psychology to Economic Theory and Research", in S. Koch, ed., *Psychology: A Study of a Science*, Vol. 6, New York: McGraw-Hill, 1963, 677−84.

32 Wärneryd, Karl-Erik, "Bilägaren och bilköpet" [The Car Owner and the Car Purchase], Stockholm: The Economic Research Institute at the Stockholm School of Economics, 1961 (mimeographed).

33 Wärneryd, Karl-Erik, "Can Results from Laboratory Experiments be Generalized to Situations outside the Laboratory? " in P. Lindblom, ed., *Theory and Methods in the Behavioral Sciences*, Stockholm: Svenska Bokförlaget/Norstedts, 1970, 73−89

34 Weick, Karl E., "The Laboratory Experiment", in J.G. March, ed., *Handbook of Organizations* Chicago: Rand McNally, 1965, 194−260.

35 Wickström, Bo, *Konsumentens märkesval* [Consumer Brand Choice], Göteborg, Akademiförlaget/Gumperts, 1965.

144

Micro-Analytic Simulation
for Personal Decision-Making*

GUY H. ORCUTT

How does the future depend upon choices to be made between alternative courses of action? This is what every policy-maker needs to know. Knowing the answer does not resolve all of a decision-maker's problems, of course, since there is the question of values and objectives. However, it helps, and if decision-makers cannot be expected to have appropriate values or to ascertain appropriate values from their constituencies, what can we expect of them? Some individuals might even be so rude as to suggest that if decision-makers cannot bring to bear appropriate values then even a suitably programmed computer might do a better job of using information and spewing out commands.

Since action without some knowledge of consequences hardly befits a man, a lot of effort has gone into finding out consequences of actions. In a rather basic sense this is what all experimental and much of nonexperimental observational science is all about. But isolated bits of knowledge about consequences of actions seldom satisfy the decision-maker who cares. Such a person wants to know more than just the direct and immediate

* Thanks are due to philosopher Jack Barense of the Yale Institution for Social and Policy Studies. He was especially helpful in getting me to see the need for the concluding cautionary remarks.

consequences of actions that might be called into being. He or she wants to know the totality of effects. While it may not be obvious to such a person, a model obviously is needed.

Tracing out the implications of any action requires a model because each step in the tracing out requires application of some piece of understanding often expressible in the form of an equation with an output variable which is taken to be dependent in a specified way on one or more variables used as inputs into the equation. A system of such equations is by common usage called a model and so is what the person who cares needs to have. Not any old model, of course, but one which will enable the decision-maker to successfully trace out the consequences of contemplated actions through many steps.

Model builders seeing the need seek to fill it, even if the intended beneficiaries of such help may upon occasion fail through lack of insight, or perhaps of confidence in the state of the arts, to recognize the need themselves. But model building and even more the achievement of understanding essential to useful model building are difficult, time consuming, and expensive. Thus it is understandable that model builders have perforce tended to focus on the needs of business decision-makers or of public decision-makers at the federal level. After all, billions of dollars and the welfare of millions may hang in the balance.

All this is true, but smaller units, including individuals and families, also have their decision-making problems. Don't they have a need to know, if that is possible, about secondary and tertiary consequences of their contemplated actions? Of course they do, since it is their welfare, presumably, that the rest of the social structure is supposed to serve.

In this connection, one other matter at least deserves mention. One consequence of the development of useful decision-making tools for decision-makers in large bureaucracies is to facilitate the growth of these bureaucracies and to favor the concentration of power in the hands of those who run them, since they may be the only ones in a position to effectively use this knowledge. Perhaps the balance towards more and more centralization of power needs to be reversed, or at least checked. That, in any case, is the author's point of view.

The point then of this paper is to present some basic ideas on how knowledge can be organized and used more effectively in the service of decision-making by individuals, families, and other relatively small behavioral units. The next section points out four developments which make the proposed new development at least feasible, if not easy and inexpensive. The following section briefly describes micro-analytic models and their solution and use. The final section presents the key ideas underlying the proposed development of micro-analytic simulation for personal decision-making.

FACILITATING DEVELOPMENTS

Although the proposed new decision-making tool would not have been feasible in the past, it soon will be because of developments which have taken place in the areas of data accumulation, data storage and retrieval, data analysis, modeling of social systems, and the use of Monte-Carlo simulation techniques. One of the key developments making this new tool possible was the recognition of the importance of having a rich variety of cross-sectional and time-series measurements relating to individuals and family units and the creation and employment of highly competent and successful sample survey organizations. The importance of the role played during the last three decades by George Katona along with Rensis Likert, Angus Campbell, Leslie Kish, Jim Morgan, the late John Lansing, and others of the University of Michigan Survey Research Center, cannot be overstressed in this connection.

A second key development of the last half century which now makes it possible to develop a significant micro-analytic tool for personal planning, is that of statistical methods for designing experiments, and for carrying out multivariate analysis of bodies of data derived from the natural experiments which are continually being performed by the million on the micro-behavioral units of our society. It is these statistical methods which now enable man to learn from planned experimentation and from studying the outcomes of choices made by individuals in natural situations some things of value about the consequences of alternative personal choices.

A third key development, of the last two decades, which is

certainly essential to the application, if not the development, of the proposed new tool, is the computer revolution which is taking place with such rapidity and such far-reaching and poorly-understood consequences. It is this development which by reducing costs per unit of computing by several orders of magnitude, has made it feasible to solve and use micro-analytic models by means of comprehensible and rugged Monte-Carlo simulation methods. This is clearly essential since, so far at least, alternative ways of solving and using micro-analytic models of appropriate realism have not been developed.

The fourth development facilitating the future creation of a new tool of micro-analysis for personal planning, is that of micro-analysis of social systems. The concept for this type of modeling of a social system is barely a decade-and-a-half old, and significant realizations are much younger. The significance of this development for the present proposal is partly conceptual, since clearly it is a type of micro-analytic simulation which is being proposed. It is more than this, however, in that a micro-analytic model of the population of individuals and families, is needed as an environment for operation of the proposed new tool for aiding individual and family decision-making. It also is the case that existing micro-analytic models of the population of individuals and families already contain a model of the individual person and of the individual family. These models will need to be extended in various ways for the proposed new tool, but they do provide an excellent start on a key ingredient which will be needed.

MICRO-ANALYTIC MODELS

A distinctive feature of micro-analytic models is that at least some of their components correspond to micro-components of the social system modeled. In the real system we can identify several different types of decision-making units — individuals, families, firms, labor unions, local governments. Micro-analytic models, like the real system, contain a population or populations of decision-making units composed of a relatively small number of different types of such units and a relatively large number or population of one or more of the types [12].

While being of the same general statistical type as other models of economic systems, micro-analytic models are, nevertheless, the most general in terms of their statistical structure. Each major type of model of a national economy may include stochastic elements, each may use lagged dependent variables as part of what is treated as given, and each may be expressed as a system of finite difference equations. However, micro-analytic models are more general in that they may contain a population of any kind of component, instead of a single case of each kind, as is true with both Leontief-type and aggregate-type national income models. Figure 1 presents a flow diagram of the type of micro-analytic model sketched out in Orcutt *et al.* [13].

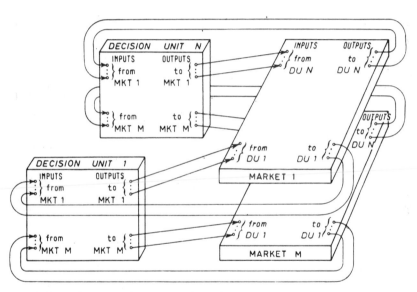

Fig. 1. Flow diagram of an economic system.

An example of an early useful development and application of a static micro-analytic model without a significant behavioral content is provided by Joseph A. Pechman [15]. A model used by Nelson McClung and Gail Wilinsky in analyzing negative income tax and family maintenance programs, represents an evolution of this type of micro-analytic modeling with limited provisions for advancing the initial sample representation of the population forward in time. It was developed for President Johnson's Income

Maintenance Commission and is currently being applied and further developed at the Urban Institute for estimating the cost and distribution of impacts of a variety of welfare and health programs.

In addition to the dynamic demographic micro-simulation model reported on in the book by Orcutt *et al.*, several other related models have been developed. Ridley and Sheps [17] developed *REPSIM* to study the relative importance of various demographic and biological factors on natality. Barrett [1] reported on a human reproduction model similar to *REPSIM*. Hyrenius and Adolfsson [9] developed a fertility simulation model for use with age cohorts. A demographic microsimulation model has been reported by Hyrenius *et al.*, [10] and results obtained with this model have been reported by Holmberg [7]. Schulz [18] reports on a microanalytic model developed earlier as a Yale thesis. With this model he traces out twenty year implications of the existing and alternative social security laws for individuals 45 or over in 1960. Horvitz *et al.* [8] describe *POPSIM*, a dynamic demographic model designed for computer simulation of the principal demographic processes occurring in human populations. This is a micro-simulation model which can be used for simulating either cohort or period data. Sprehe and Michielutte [21] report on the development of a micro-analytic simulation model as a step in the development of a system of social accounts and Pryor [16] reports on the development and use of a micro-analytic model for investigating the impact of social and economic institutions on the size distribution of income and wealth. Bryan and Carleton are developing and promoting micro-analytic simulation as a tool for policy analysis in the monetary and fiscal area [2], [3]. Orcutt *et al.* [14] report on an extensive micro-analytic simulation effort that has been under way at the Urban Institute during the past two years. This effort is focussed on questions associated with poverty, inequality, and growth.

MICRO-ANALYTIC SIMULATION FOR PERSONAL DECISION-MAKING

The applications of the micro-analytic models now under development at the Urban Institute all involve deriving unconditional or conditional predictions about the U.S. population or about major subpopulations of the U.S. population. Expected output includes tabulations resulting from classification of the U.S. population according to selected variables. This type of output will be like the innumerable tables derived from U.S. census data. A wider range of variables will be available for use in classifying individuals and families into cells. Annual instead of decennial output will be possible. In addition, output for hypothetical development and use of policy will be feasible. Averages, variances, and covariances of all micro-variables will be available and development of aggregative time series will be possible.

While the richness of potential output about the U.S. population and about major subpopulations is great, compared with available macro-analytic models, our present approach does not permit generation of predictions relating to relatively small subpopulations, such as represented by the population of a city, county, state, or single year age cohort. Neither does our present approach permit generation of useful predictions about specific families or specific individuals.

The fundamental reason for these limitations is that we represent any population and its associated distribution by a sample of individuals from the population. With a sample of ten to one hundred thousand individuals it is possible to achieve an exellent representation of the U.S. population in its full multivariate richness. Unfortunately, the laws of sampling are such that, for a given adequacy of representation, nearly as large a sample is needed to represent a population of a few hundred thousand as is needed to represent a population of two hundred million. This might be a large enough sample to permit calculation of some mean values, but even these would have large sampling variances. Estimation of even single variate distributions would be out of the question.

The situation is even worse when it comes to generating predictions relating to specific families or individuals. Here the problem is of a slightly different nature. Our operating characteristics are designed to predict aspects of individual and family behavior and experience. Nevertheless, they are probabilistic relationships. That is, they predict such things for individual units in any given year such as probabilities of death, marriage, divorce, etc. The use of probabilistic operating characteristics reflects the limited nature of our knowledge about behavior of individual units. The probabilistic component of prediction at the micro-level may be narrowed down as our understanding grows. Nevertheless, it is bound to be a dominant feature of our understanding, and hence of our models, for the foreseeable future.

The difficulty in using out models in generating predictions for individuals or for individual families, is that such predictions should be in the form of probability distributions. Unfortunately, while our models implicitly contain a basis for such predictions, our present provisions will not enable us to obtain explicit estimates of probability distribution for specific individuals or families. The problem is that only one concrete life is traced out for any one individual in any one simulation of the entire U.S. population. It is obtained by translating each probability distribution as it is computed for the individual into a concrete action by means of a random drawing from the distribution. This provides a fine Monte-Carlo method of obtaining information about derived distributions relating to the U.S. population, since tens of thousands of life paths are traced out in any simulation run. It does not do for any one individual because only a single life path, out of the innumerable number of possible life paths for the individual, is traced out. In general, this may result in but a single drawing from each derived distribution of interest.

The range of application of our micro-analytic models could be extended to predictions about specific individuals and families as follows: The data set for a specific family, or for a specific individual and associated family, could be repeated one or more thousand times and used as a second sample along with the main sample representing the U.S. population. Members of this second sample would be tagged so as not to be included in tabulations for the U.S. population. Nevertheless, members of this second sample would be subjected to the repeated application of the same operating characteristics as are applied to members of the U.S. sample. Since concrete behavior for each member of this second sample would also be obtained by the use of random drawing from computed probability distributions, it is evident that the thousand or more replications of any individual would each go its own way. A given simulation run would thus generate a thousand or more life paths for the individual or family. Each such life path would represent a random drawing from the population of life histories implicitly determined by the operating characteristics of the model used. Since a thousand or more such life paths would be traced out, it would be feasible to summarize and tabulate results so as to estimate derived probability distributions of interest for the replicated individual and his family.

By making successive runs with everything held constant except the behavior or treatment of a replicated individual, it would be possible to determine the implied consequences for the individual of given behavioral or treatment changes. For example, such changes might consist of introduction of family limitation, extension of schooling, postponement of marriage, alteration of eating habits, etc.

In presenting the basic idea for extending the range of application of our models, one important consideration has been glossed over. Why not run simulations with just the replicated individual or family of interest? Just as we must provide a family to serve as part of an environment for an individual to grow within and to interact with, we also need the U.S. population to complete the environment needed for an individual or family over time. The need could occur in a number of different ways, but the most pressing reason for needing the U.S. population is so that each of the replicated individuals can find a suitable mate as determined by application of the marriage operating characteristics.

Interaction of the sample composed of a replicated family with the main sample could influence the behavior of the main sample in undesirable ways, if steps were not taken to avoid this. Tabulations for this secondary sample can and would be kept quite separate from tabulation for the U.S. sample. Output generated with the main sample would be available for use in applying operating characteristics to members of the replicated sample; the reverse would not be permitted. Marriage between members of the replicated sample would not be permitted, since this would be equivalent to marrying brother and sister. Members of the replicated sample would marry in the regular way with members of the main U.S. sample with one difference. Any member of the main sample marrying a member of the replicated sample would be replicated at the time of marrying. The replication would be transferred into the sample of replicated individuals and families. The individual replicated would be left in the main sample, and his or her marriage, if and when it occurs, would be completed in the usual way with someone from the main sample.

Extending the range of application of our models to yield results about subpopulations which while numbering in the tens of thousands or more are still small relative to the total U.S. population also seems possible. The appropriate approach seems to involve use of a second sample to represent the subpopulation along with a primary sample to represent the U.S. population. Operation and interaction of the two samples would be carried out much as in the above case of a second sample made up of replicated individuals. Again, output from the main sample would be available in applying operating characteristics to members of the second sample, but the reverse would not be permitted. Tabulation for the two samples would be kept separate, and of course different blow-up factors would be needed, since individuals and families would have a higher probability of being in the sample for the subpopulation than in being in the sample for the U.S. population. Some additional complications might result in handling marriage and migration. These have not been fully worked through but are thought to be manageable.

The importance of extending the range of application of microanalytic models to facilitate prediction for subpopulations, such as cities and states, seems obvious. The desirability of extending the range of application to facilitate probabilistic predictions for specific individuals and families seems less obvious, but may be of greater fundamental importance.

Well before the year 2000 computing costs may have dropped, and the availability of useful operating characteristics may have increased to the point where nearly every individual might frequently find it worthwhile to see probabilistic predictions tailored to his specific history, current status, and alternative courses open to him. But long before such a speculative development takes place, it will be economically feasible to develop and use limited versions of such a capability to assist individuals and families in making certain decisions. Key decision areas that might well be candidates for early consideration include life style; occupational and career choices; marriage and family planning choices; location, spending, and saving choices; as well as health and longevity related choices.

Before ending this essay, certain cautionary remarks are in order. What has been presented is a basic idea for extending the potential range of application of micro-analytic modeling and simulation. However, the major problem in achieving useful micro-analytic simulation for personal decision-making is and will remain that of acquiring useful knowledge about how outcomes depend upon choices made.

It appears that divorced men have substantially higher death probabilities than married men of apparently similar characteristics. However, this hardly can be taken to mean that, if by an act of choice, such men had not become divorced, they thereby would have avoided higher risk of untimely death. The legal fact of divorce may be merely a common correlate in our society for all sorts of more basic factors. Avoidance of divorce may be quite feasible without significant alteration of the really critical factors.

We know that the average income is much higher in some counties of the United States than in other counties. Does it follow that, if a resident in a poor county hears about this and therefore moves by choice to a much richer county, that he will thereby have greatly improved his chances for a high income? Individuals make choices and we believe that their choices do greatly affect their futures. But learning how futures of individuals do in fact depend upon choices made by them is not easy, and many mistaken judgments seem inevitable. Micro-analytic simulation for personal decision-making is technically feasible, but its utility will be dependent on the adequacy of the understanding built into micro-analytic models actually used. While the ideas presented in this paper could facilitate the use of knowledge about causal relations, they clearly could not be a useful substitute for needed knowledge, nor for application of personally acquired knowledge not incorporated in any model. To acquire essential new knowledge probably requires sophisticated analysis of both planned and naturally occurring experiments.

One other cautionary remark seems obvious but should constantly be kept in mind. Any model and any simulation system available for assisting in personal decision-making also will be available to corporations, government, and other organizations. New possibilities for abusive as well as constructive uses will be opened up. Nothing proposed in this paper will contribute very directly to improving mans's ability and resolve to see that both his machines and his organizations are and remain his servants, rather than his blind masters. At best, development of micro-analytic simulation for personal decision-making will serve only to extend to the individual for his own uses some of the decision-assisting facilities available to government and large corporations.

REFERENCES

1 Barrett, J.C., "A Monte Carlo Study of Reproduction", presented at the Society for Human Biology Symposium, London, 1967.
2 Bryan, W.R., and W.T. Carleton, "Short-Run Adjustments of an Individual Bank", *Econometrica*, 35 (April, 1967), 321–47.
3 Carleton, W.T., and W.R. Bryan, "Deposit Expansion and Federal Reserve-Banking System Interaction: A Micro Unit Simulation", 1971 (mimeographed).
4 Giesbrecht, F.G., and G. Ranney, Demographic Microsimulation Model POPSIM I: Manual for Program to Generate the Initial Population, Closed Core Model, Technical Report No. 2, Project SU-285, Research Triangle Institute, 1968.
5 Giesbrecht, F.G., G. Ranney, and J.R. Chromy, Demographic Microsimulation Model POPSIM II: Manual for Programs to Generate the Initial Population, Open Core Model, Technical Report No. 4, Project SU-285, Research Triangle Institute, 1968.
6 Giesbrecht F.G., and L. Field, Demographic Microsimulation Model POPSIM II: Manual for Programs to Generate Vital Events, Open Core Model, Technical Report No. 5, Project SU-285, Research Triangle Institute, 1969.
7 Holmberg, I., *Demographic Models: DM4*, Report #8 Demographic Institute, University of Goteborg, Sweden, 1968.
8 Horvitz, D.G.; F.G. Giesbrecht, B.V. Shah, and P.A. Lachenbruch, "Popsim, A Demographic Microsimulation Model", *International Union for the Scientific Study of Population*, General Conference, London, September, 1969.
9 Hyrenius, H., and I. Adolfson, *A Fertility Simulation Model*, Report #2, Demographic Institute, University of Goteborg, Sweden, 1964.
10 Hyrenius, H., I. Holmberg, and M. Carlsson, *Demographic Models: DM3*, Report #5, Demographic Institute, University of Goteborg, Sweden, 1967.
11 Lachenbruch, P.A., J. Klepfer, and S. Rohde, Demographic Microsimulation Model POPSIM I: Manual for Programs to General Vital Events, Closed Core Model, Technical Report No. 3, Project SU-285, Research Triangle Institute, 1968.

12 Orcutt, G.H., "A New Type of Socio-Economic System", *Review of Economic Statistics*, 58 (Sept., 1957), 773–97.

13 Orcutt, G.H., M. Greenberger, J. Korbel, and A.M. Rivlin, *Microanalysis of Socio-Economic Systems: A Simulation Study*, New York: Harper, 1961.

14 Orcutt, G.H., G. Peabody, and S. Caldwell, "Microanalytic Simulation: A Demographic Model", Social Statistics Section, Proceedings of the American Statistical Association Meetings in Detroit, December, 1970.

15 Pechman, J.A., "A New Tax Model for Revenue Estimating", reprinted in *Studies in Government Finance*, Brookings Institution, Washington, D.C., 1965.

16 Pryor, F.L., "The Impact of Social and Economic Institutions on the Size Distribution of Income and Wealth: A Simulation Study", 1971 (mimeographed).

17 Ridley, J.C., and M.C. Sheps, "An Analytic Simulation Model for Human Reproduction with Demographic and Biological Components", *Population Studies* (March, 1966), 297–310.

18 Schulz, J.H., *The Economic Status of the Retired Aged in 1980: Simulation Projections*, U.S. Dept. of Health, Education, and Welfare, Social Security Administration, Office of Research and Statistics, Research Report No. 24, 1968.

19 Sprehe, J.T., and R.L. Michielutte, "Simulation of Social Mobility: Toward the Development of a System of Social Accounts", a paper prepared for the "Theoretical and Methodological Issues" section of the annual meeting of the Eastern Sociological Society, April 19, 1969.

20 Sprehe, J.T., and R.L. Michielutte, "Problems and Prospects in Simulating Large-Scale Social Change", December, 1969 (mimeographed).

21 Sprehe, J.T. and R.L. Michielutte, "Simulation of Large-Scale Social Mobility: Toward the Development of a System of Social Accounts", Final Report on NSF Grant No. GS-2311, 1971.

22 *The President's Commission on Income Maintenance Programs – Technical Studies*, U.S. Govt. Printing Office: 1970, 0-379-518.

Understanding and Comparing Consumer Behavior

Newly Married Couples and Their Asset Accumulation Decisions*

ROBERT FERBER AND FRANCESCO NICOSIA

This paper has two main purposes. First, following a brief discussion of the reasons for the construction of the Illinois–Berkeley panel of newly married couples, a conceptual and general framework for the study of asset accumulation decisions is presented. Second, results of an empirical test of some parts of the framework using data of the Illinois–Berkeley panel are given and a number of hypotheses are developed for future study of consumer asset decisions.

* Professor of Economics, also Director of Survey Research Laboratory, University of Illinois; and Professor of Business Administration, and in the Survey Research Center, University of California at Berkeley. We acknowledge with many thanks financial support received from the Ford Foundation and Educational Foundation of the American Association of Advertising Agencies (AAAA) in setting up and continuing this panel. We would also like to express our appreciation to Lucy Chao Lee for assisting with the empirical analysis. A very preliminary version of this paper was presented at the annual meetings of the American Psychological Association, Miami Beach, Florida, September 5, 1970.

As a "natural" unit in our culture, the family has been studied in a variety of ways by several branches of the social sciences. For many centuries, various characteristics of the family have been observed for census and taxation purposes. This interest in the family has been naturally present in the economics literature.

Several premises and operational definitions of past studies of the family, or household, need to be reassessed as society enters the beginning stages of affluence [10], [11]. It has become clear that one of these definitions — that of household — has to be examined more closely. Usually, past and present marketing studies of household behavior in the marketplace record families' spending and saving by interviewing one member of a household.

The conceptual, methodological, and empirical shortcomings of this practice are well known. The economic and para-economic behavior of a family is a multi-person decision process.

Evidence suggests that this is true even for relatively minor choices. One brand of breakfast cereal may be bought by a housewife acting as the purchasing agent for her husband. In the case of another brand (or family type), the purchase may result from the mother's preference for the package design (convenience in storing and handling) *and* from her child's desire for special gifts or coupons. In the first case, the appropriate unit of observation is obviously the husband. The second situation, which is probably more common, is more complex. Not only are there two units of observation (mother and child), but the choice results from the interaction among, at least, two persons' preferences. The release of this interaction into a purchase may be subjected to influences and constraints of economic, psychological, and social nature.

There are basic and applied questions where this multiplicity of relevant units of observation and their interactions cannot be ignored. In these cases, micro-economic theory does not suggest guidelines for deeper inquiries into the structure of family behavior. Studies based on behavioral theories have unfortunately concentrated on facets other than economic, e.g., the noneconomic dimensions of marriage. Furthermore, the conceptual and empirical strength of many of these studies usually does not meet the requirements of applied disciplines such as marketing. After the pioneering studies in the fifties [9], the marketing community has given progressively more attention to economic family behavior. From the well-known symposium on household decision-making in 1961 [4] to the work by Davis [2] and the explorations into what is a husband—wife interaction [12], the results of this marketing literature are promising.

Habitual Behavior, Marriage, and Panel Designs

Basic and applied studies of family economic behavior, however, face a difficult methodological problem. As is well known, most so-called consumer behavior is habitual. Thus, as in many other disciplines, researchers find it extremely difficult to identify the structures that underlie and comprise such behavior. In the physical and related disciplines, this situation is referred as the problem of inferring the content of a box which is closed to direct observation; here, methodological inventiveness, mathematical rigor, and the art of statistical inference have been the major ingredients for handling this problem satisfactorily.

Applied disciplines have been developing not only an awareness of this problem but also their own methodological devices. In principle, we should be able to vary family behavior experimentally so that, given some initial notion of what underlies this behavior, and given a set of disturbances and our recording of the reactions to them, we should be able to identify gradually the structures making for the observed behavior. This principle has been implemented in many studies concerning a variety of problems. The experimental study of a family, in laboratory or real life conditions, however, is not easy to implement.

Substantive insights into family behavior and methodological developments have suggested alternatives to traditional experimental designs. The substantive insights were first discussed informally by a group of researchers at the Bureau of Applied Social Research [5], [13]. Briefly, the notion was that life itself provides disturbances to man's habitual behavior. In the case of family behavior, examples of these natural disturbances are the birth of a child, a family death, change in residence, and of course marriage. These events tend to create readjustments that directly or indirectly involve buying and saving behavior and other para-economic

163

styles of life. So far, the change in residence disturbance has attracted the most attention.[1]

In our case, we have focused on marriage. It is clear that marriage is a natural disturbance which probably contains the largest potential for the study of substantive and methodological problems. Each spouse-to-be will differ in a variety of ways – in cultural heritage, social and economic background, psychological make-up, and so forth, including habitual behavior in a variety of areas (from personal hygiene to reading, radio listening, and TV viewing habits). Dating and engagement may have provided not only some sorting device to identify the appropriate partner but also varying degrees of, shall we say, rodage. Yet, short of compulsory premarital cohabitation, most couples find themselves in a relatively new and constrained situation after marriage. Consciously or not, they must resolve their differences, disengage from many of their past routines, and build a new *menage a deux*.

The methodological developments that underlie our study of newly married couples concern panel designs and analyses. Although proposed in the forties by Lazarsfeld, panels have gained recognition rather slowly. In some sense this has avoided the usual overenthusiasm and overbuying of a new idea and the unfortunate but usual and premature dismissal of the entire idea. Over the years, the research community has had time to assess the many pros and cons of this survey design.[2] In particular, it has become clear that panels provide the means of recording complex chains of changes that may follow disturbances introduced in a system at rest either experimentally or "naturally" (i.e., by life occurrences) [14], [6, pp. 97–101].

The Illinois–Berkeley Panel of Newly Married Couples

This panel reflects the increasing interest by social scientists and marketing researchers in the family. We decided that our understanding of family economic behavior can be improved if we can

[1] *See* [16]. For studies more sharply focused on marketing implications, *see* [1], [12].
[2] Among the most comprehensive reviews, *see* [3], [17]. For a discussion of the applicability of panel designs and analyses to different marketing management questions, *see* [14], [15].

observe how it is formed from its very beginning. We also decided that a panel design would be an appropriate method to record the formation of habitual styles, and thus that a panel is a vehicle for data analyses to reconstruct the structures comprising family decision-making.

These are in brief the major features of the panel. Given the exploratory nature of the study, we did not want a national sample nor did we want to observe our couples in the often bewildering complex environment of a large city. To the contrary, we wanted one or two small cities, as reasonably closed or self-contained (economically and socially) as possible. We settled for Peoria and Decatur, Illinois, both between 100,000 and 250,000, industrial, and relatively isolated from other major urban centers.

Ideally, it would have been desirable to begin at least with subjects at the engagement stage; this was beyond our financial resources. Our population was all couples in those two cities married during the summer months of 1968. They were interviewed for the first time in late September and early October. This first wave produced 313 interviews of about an hour length. The same couples were reinterviewed four times (Spring and Fall 1969, and Spring and Fall 1970), and the data from these five waves are used in this analysis.

Marriage will cause many changes in life styles of both spouses. But, given our limited resources, we had to select a few behavior areas and a few possible processes that may underlie such changes. Within these constraints, the choice was especially guided by the desire to observe areas of basic importance to the family institution, to the economy, and possibly to a society that is beginning to experience the cultural costs and paradoxes of affluence.

First of all, therefore, we decided to interview only young couples. Our criterion was the age of the head of the household — 30 years or younger. We began by thinking about financial matters, that is, how do our couples receive income, manage it, spend it? Over the various waves we have concentrated in various degrees on recording their saving decisions (amount and type), use of credit, purchase of different types of insurance, and purchases of household durables. Many of these data enter into the model of asset accumulation presented in this paper.

How do young couples decide how much to spend and how much to save of their income, and in what form to put their savings?[3] Such decisions are among the most important made by newlyweds, for the consequences may relate not only to their future economic welfare but the probable success of the marriage itself. Yet virtually no work seems to have been done on this subject. The only studies even remotely related are the few economic analyses of the factors related to family asset holdings and the sociological studies of the causes of marital break-ups.

The focus of our inquiry is on asset accumulation decisions by newlyweds. First, we present a conceptual framework for such decisions for both financial and nonfinancial assets, and incorporate within this framework many different types of factors that enter into these decisions. Moreover, an attempt is made to present such a framework in dynamic terms, to allow for changes in the couple's saving and savings objectives with the passage of time. After having indicated exactly what sort of decisions we are trying to explain, we present the econometric specification of the part of the model we are testing.

Asset Accumulation: A Decision Sequence

Three types of asset accumulation decisions are considered within the present framework. They are:
1.   How much should be saved out of current income?
2.   Into what assets should the saving out of current income be put? Or, if there are dissavings, what should be the source of these dissavings?
3.   Given total wealth as the sum of prior wealth and current saving, how should this wealth be allocated among alternative assets (and debts)?

To some extent, these decisions are interdependent. As a first approximation, however, we shall assume that for analytical purposes these decisions can be treated as sequential through time, in the sequence that they are presented. In econometric terms, this

[3] Throughout this paper "saving" refers to current accumulation, i.e., saving out of current receipts, and "savings" to stock of wealth at a particular time.

permits us to formulate a recursive model, which offers certain advantages for the estimation of parameters. Moreover, from the point of view of decisions analysis, this assumption is not implausible. Certainly, decisions on total saving in the current period are likely to precede decisions on how to allocate these funds; and it also seems plausible that the allocation of one's total wealth (including current saving) is likely to be reconsidered after it is known what current saving is likely to be.

To be sure, in practice these decisions are likely to be more of an iterative nature, but if the iterations follow the same recursive pattern as here postulated, the analytical results are likely to be essentially unchanged.

In effect, from the point of view of model specification, we have two sets of decisions to explain — one set regarding current saving and one set regarding total wealth. Within our recursive framework, it is desirable to consider each set separately.

Current Saving

Consciously or not, any consumer unit has to make two decisions regarding current saving — how much and in what form. The "how much" most likely comes first, partly because it is interrelated with expenditure decisions which generally take priority and partly because such evidence as is available (as well as the advice of home economists) suggests that the form of saving be determined by the amount of saving among other things. Even in the case of contractual saving, such as payroll deduction for a pension or home mortgage payments, the initial decision has to depend on the amount of saving that will be available. Admittedly attitudes, motivations, expectation level, and types of aspirations may partly determine this amount; allowance for some of these factors is made in the model.

Accordingly, the amount saved S_t, in a particular period t, by a couple is hypothesized to depend on the following factors:

Current income (Y_t), the usual budget constraint, that may be relatively strong for a young couple.[4]

---

[4] In future analyses we shall explore whether the strength of this constraint varies according to the couples' aspirations and other characteristics.

Attitudes toward saving versus spending (A_t), as indexes of the desire to save.

Financial and other resources made available by parents and relatives (F_t), a factor of particular importance for newlyweds.

Felt need for acquisition of household and related goods (N_t), especially relevant once more for newlyweds.

Our first equation in general form is, therefore:

$$S_t = f(Y_t, A_t, F_t, N_t). \tag{1.1}$$

Next, we consider the determinants of the amount saved, S_t^i, in period t, in form of saving i, by the couple. Since by our recursive system S_t is already determined, we may consider the proportion saved in form i, as the variable to be explained, that is, $P_t^i = S_t^i/S_t$. However, many if not most couples may save nothing in a particular form; this aspect of the problem is best divided in two — who saves in that form (D_t^i), and how much (P_t^i). The former variable (D_t^i) would seem to depend on the following:

Attitudes toward saving in that particular form (A_t^i), as an absolute index of desire to save in that form.

Attitudes toward saving in that form relative to saving in general (A_t^i/A_t), as a relative index of desire to save in that form.

Educational background of the financial decision-maker (E_t), for evidence suggests that the more educated are more amenable to investing in variable-dollar rather than fixed-dollar forms.

Total saving (S_t), for as total saving rises, allocation into different forms becomes more likely.

Communication and promotional impact (C_t^i) on our subjects of messages promoting that form of saving.

This equation, really a set of equations, is:

$$D_t^i = g_i(A_t^i, A_t^i/A_t, E_t, S_t, C_t^i), \text{ for } i = 1, \ldots, m. \tag{1.2a}$$

The second variable, P_t^i, may be considered to depend on essentially the same set of variables as in (1.2a) with the addition of P_{t-1}^i, since saving in a particular form, once begun, is likely to become a habit. Also, this equation applies only to the subsample that does save in that form. The equation can be represented as:

$$P_t^i = g_i \left(A_t^i, A_t^i / A_t, E_t, S_t, C_t^i, P_{t-1}^i \right), \text{ for } i = 1, \ldots, m \text{ for}$$
only those couples for whom $D_t^i \neq 0$. 　　　　(1.2b)

In other words, there are conceptually $2m$ equations, one for each form of saving. In practice, however, only $2m-1$ equations are needed, since one equation of the allocation is determined by the fact that $\Sigma P_t^i = 1$.

Although S_t and P_t are the principal economic variables entering into current saving, from a decision point of view it is desirable to move one step further and consider the determinants of the attitudinal and advertising variables $- A_t$, A_t^i and $C_t^i -$ because these are not only current but are potentially manipulable. Our hypotheses on their determinants are as follows: General attitudes toward saving (A_t) depend upon:

Educational background of the financial decision-maker (E_t).

Total savings, or wealth, expected at end of period (W_t^e), on the premise that the more savings one expects to have, the more favorably disposed one is toward saving.

Long-run goals of couple (G_t), for some goals will require more saving than others, and more incentive to do so.

This equation is, then:

$$A_t = h \left(E_t, W_t^e, G_t \right). \qquad\qquad (1.3)$$

Attitudes toward saving in a particular form (A_t^i) are assumed to be determined by:

E_t, as above.

W_t^e, because as assets are expected to be accumulated it is well known that certain forms take precedence over others.

D_t^i, for familiarity reasons, and because ownership, even by inheritance, may itself influence attitude.

C_t^i, assuming that more ad impact is related to more desire to save.

Z_t^i, a set of personality characteristics of the husband and wife possibly relevant to saving behavior, as specified in the next section.

The resulting general form is:

$$A_t^i = h_i\,(E_t, W_t^e, D_t^i, C_t^i, Z_t^i),\ \text{for } i = 1, \ldots, m. \qquad (1.4)$$

This is a set of m equations, each with different parameters. Communication and promotional awareness (C_t^i) may be said to be determined by:

E^t, as before.

D_t^i, for reinforcement reasons, namely that ownership may make a person more alert to promotional messages for that asset.

A_t^i, for those more motivated are more likely to be receptive to promotional messages.

Readership of magazines, newspapers and use of other media (M_t) which makes possible exposure to such messages.

Z_t^i, for the same reasons as before.

Hence, this equation is:

$$C_t^i = k\,(E_t, D_t^i, A_t^i, M_t, Z_t^i). \qquad (1.5)$$

It should be noted that the m assets can be as specific or as general as desired, and that "assets" may also include debt categories as well as nonfinancial assets such as durable goods.

Wealth

The wealth of a couple, or a consumer unit, represents the summation of all past saving, i.e.:

$$W_t = T_{t-n} + \sum_{t-n}^{t} S_t,$$

where

n is the age of the family unit; and

T_{t-n} is the initial wealth at the time of formation of the unit.

Alternatively, for our purposes we can consider W_t as determined by the wealth at the start of the previous period plus current saving, i.e.:

$$W_t = W_{t-1} + S_t. \tag{1.6}$$

This is an especially useful approach if no data are available on inheritances and gifts of assets from parents as it is true so far in the present case.

By this definition, given the prior determination of S_t through Equation (1.1), W_t is fully determined. It remains, then, to consider the allocation of W_t among the various asset categories. As with saving, however, it is best to divide this problem in two — who owns a particular asset, and how much. The former variable, H_t^i, is postulated to depend on:

Attitudes toward saving in that form (A_t^i), for the same reason given for P_t^i, in Equation (1.2).

Attitudes toward saving in that form relative to saving in general (A_t^i/A_t), for the same reasons as before.

Long-run goals (G_t), as before.

Educational background of financial decision-maker (E_t), as before.

Total wealth (W_t), for some assets become more important than others as W_t increases.

Impact on decision process of messages about that asset (C_t^i), as before.

Personality characteristics (Z_t^i), as before.

The equation, in general form, is:

$$H_t^i = k_i \ (A_t^i, A_t^i/A_t, G_t, E_t, W_t, C_t^i, Z_t^i), \text{ for } i = \ldots, m. \tag{1.7a}$$

The allocation of wealth $(V_t^i = W_t^i/W)$ is assumed to depend on the same set of variables plus the allocation in the preceding period, V_{t-1}^i, because of the very strong likelihood of habit formation, especially as applied to those having this form of wealth. The equation is:

$$V_t^i = k_i\,(A_t^i,\,A_t^i/A_t,\,G_t,\,E_t,\,W_t,\,C_t^i,\,Z_t^i,\,V_{t-1}^i),\text{ for }i-1,\ldots,$$

m for couples for which $H_t^i \neq 0$. (1.7b)

As with Equations (1.2), this is a set of $2m$ equations, though for empirical analysis only $2m-1$ equations are required.

The decision components of this equation are A_t^i and A_t, and these are already explained by Equations (1.3) and (1.4). Hence, for the present purposes, the model is complete.

Recapitulation

We have a model of $6m + 1$ equations to explain the following dependent variables:

(d1) amount of saving (S_t); and allocation of saving among different forms (S_t^i);

(d2) saving in a particular form (S_t^i), and allocation of saving among these forms;

(d3) attitudes toward saving in general (A_t), and toward specific assets (A_t^i);

(d4) advertising impact on saving form i (C_t^i); and

(d5) total wealth (W_t), and allocation of wealth among different assets (V_t^i).

(d6) ownership of particular assets (H_t^i),

in terms of the following purely exogenous variables:

(e1) income (Y_t);

(e2) other resources available (F_t);

(e3) felt need for goods (N_t);

(e4) education (E_t);

(e5) expected wealth (W_t^e),

(e6) exposure to advertising (M_t),

(e7) personality characteristics (Z_t), and

(e8) long-run goals (G_t) of the couple.

The general estimation procedure can be outlined as follows:

1. Estimate A_t^i and C_t^i simultaneously from the sets of two simultaneous equations from (1.4) and (1.5).

2. Estimate A_t from (1.3).

3. Estimate S_t from (1.1) and Step 2.

4. Estimate D_t^i and P_t^i from (1.2) and Steps 1 and 3.

5. Estimate W_t from (1.6) and Step 3.

6. Estimate H_t^i and V_t^i from (1.7) and Steps 1 and 5.

The role of intervening variables was introduced by George Katona some time ago, with his emphasis on the importance of attitudes and other variables of a psychological nature in influencing economic behavior [8]. The present model builds on his earlier work in introducing a few such variables at various stages of the decision process, and indeed by including the concept of attitudes as a determining factor on behavior. It should be stressed, however, that this general framework is subject to modification based on empirical results.

A PARTIAL TEST

A full test of the model presented in the preceding section is not yet possible, partly because not all the data have as yet been collected and partly because time restrictions have not permitted carrying out all the tests that could be made with the available data. More specifically, the data presently available (from Waves 1–5) include, among the dependent variables, various components of attitude toward saving in the form of specific assets (d3), communication awareness (d4), total wealth (d5), and ownership of particular assets and their allocation (d6). The exogenous variables available include income (el), other resources (e2), felt need for goods (e3), ownership of the particular form of savings (e4), education (e5) of both husband and wife, exposure to advertising (e6), some personality measures (e7), and data on savings plans and savings priorities, a distant proxy for long-run goals (e8).

Variables currently not available that would be expected to play important roles in our model are the amount of saving and its allocation in a particular period (d1), expected wealth (e6), and specific long-run goals (e7).[5]

Inasmuch as the available data pertain only to the wealth and its components of the couples, only Equations (1.4), (1.5) and (1.7) of the model can be tested at this time. These equations do, however, constitute a self-contained submodel of their own, serving to determine the holding of particular assets and the amounts held. Such a test therefore is of interest as applying not only to the validity of a part of a larger model, but also the validity of a model of wealth allocation.

For statistical testing, four variants of this submodel are considered, all variants utilizing (1.4) and (1.5) to determine attitudes toward the asset and awareness of advertising for it. The variants differ in the determination of the allocation of wealth, as follows:

1. This variant utilizes (1.7a) and (1.7b) to determine, first, which couples own a particular asset, and second, for the owners only how much is owned in terms of the share of the total portfolio (V_i).

2. This variant utilizes (1.7a) to determine, as before, which couples own a particular asset. In place of (1.7b), however, a second equation (1.7c) is used to estimate how *much* is owned (W_i), in logarithms (to reduce effects of a few very large amounts).

3. Instead of the two-stage process, (1.7a) and (1.7b), a single equation (1.8) is used to estimate (V_i), including couples not owning that asset. In effect, this variant is a test of the superiority of the two-stage approach relative to Variant 1.

4. As another test of the effectiveness of the two-stage approach, Equations (1.7a) and (1.7b) are replaced by a single equation

[5] Actually, some data are available on this subject, dealing with type of job hoped for ten years ahead, urge for advancement, and felt pressure to move ahead. However, it was not felt that these variables would be particularly significant in the present case.

(1.9) estimating the *amount* owned (W_i) in a particular asset. The result is then compared with that from Variant 2.

Five asset forms were tested — savings accounts, U.S. government bonds, marketable securities, real estate (including own home), and life insurance and pension plans. All equations were tested in linear arithmetic form. As noted earlier, however, logarithms were used for financial magnitudes, including income, debt, and total net wealth. Although the preceding formulation served as the basis for selecting variables, the actual variables used in the equations were many more than those listed, primarily for two reasons. One was that, where data permitted, separate variables were used for husband and wife. This was done partly to investigate whether separate husband—wife effects on portfolios seemed to exist, a major topic of interest underlying this panel operation. Second, in view of the exploratory nature of this study, a number of personality and attitudinal variables were included for testing, especially since it was not clear a priori which were likely to be most influential.

The variables used in each case are listed in abbreviated form in the tables that follow and a complete list is given in the appendix as well as the form of the variable used.

The results from fitting Equations (1.4) and (1.5) to the data are shown in Table 1. The dependent variables are, respectively, the rank of that asset form as desirable for saving (6 as the highest, 1 as the lowest), and awareness of advertisements for that form of saving mentioned by the couple, the latter as a dichotomous variable. In fact, Equation (1.5) could be fitted to only three of the asset forms, because awareness of advertisements for savings accounts and for life insurance were virtually universal among this group. Rank of the asset form may not be the best form of attudinal variable to use, but it would certainly seem to be one possibility, and data for it were available.

The independent variables include two personality measures, namely, tendency toward extravagance on the part of the husband or the wife and the extent to which each member of the couple feels that life holds opportunities. With the former variable, one would expect negative relationships with attitudes toward different assets, with the exception of perhaps pensions and in-

Table 1. BETA COEFFICIENTS AND GOODNESS OF FIT OF EQUATIONS (1.4) AND (1.5)

Variable[a]	(1.4) Asset Ranking[b]					(1.5) Ad Awareness[b]		
	A1	A2	A3	A4	A5	C2	C3	C4
Rank of given asset[c]	–	–	–	–	–	.02	.15#	-.07
Education, h	-.06	-.10	.40**	-.03	-.14	.10	-.18#	.07
Education, w	.07	-.04	-.08	-.06	.10	-.25**	-.04	-.03
Priority of saving, h	.12	-.14	.06	-.03	.02	-.02	-.24*	-.28**
Priority of saving, w	-.04	-.20	-.03	-.05	.07	-.07	.11	.21*
Extravagance, h	.01	.01	.02	-.00	-.10	-.06	.01	-.09
Extravagance, w	-.11	.10	-.04	.03	.07	.05	-.05	.08
Life holds opportunities, h	.01	-.04	-.05	-.04	.08	.00	-.09	-.08
Life holds opportunities, w	.13	.05	.04	-.03	-.08	.16*	.09	-.06
Holding Debts	-.15#	-.05	.07	-.03	-.04	–	–	-.05
Has a goal for total savings	–	–	–	–	–	.04	.08	.01
Plans to save in that asset	-.07	-.00	.09	-.14#	.17*	.02	.00	.01
Ads noted for that asset	-.00	.02	.13#	-.08	-.12	–	–	–
Owns given asset	.02	.15#	.18*	.13	.19*	.02	.12	.11
R^2	.06	.07	.31	.05	.11	.09	.17	.08
Adj. R^2[d]	.00	.00	.25	.00	.04	.02	.10	.01

Sample size

#Significant at .10 level   a   h–husband, w–wife.
*Significant at .05 level   b   The column headings denote the following assets:
**Significant at .01 level   1   –savings accounts
                                2   –U.S. Government bonds

3   –marketable securities
4   –real estate (including own home)
5   –life insurance and pensions
c   Highest rank 6; lowest, 1
d   Sample size was 174 throughout

surance toward which a person with extravagant tastes may feel favorably disposed in order to be covered for personal catastrophe. With the other personality variable, one would expect positive relationships, especially in the case of such variable dollar holdings as securities and real estate.

In fact, as is evident from Table 1, few significant relationships at all are apparent. In the case of Equation (1.4), only the regression for securities appears to provide a meaningful fit. The relationships illustrated by this equation serve to bring out an anomaly which is reinforced by the later results, namely, a tendency for the husband and wife to disagree with each other not only on their attitudes toward particular assets, but also in the distribution of their portfolio. Thus, in the present case a couple is likely to take a more favorable attitude toward investing in securities as the education of the wife *increases* and as the education of the husband *decreases*. The other significant coefficients in this equation also present somewhat of a paradox, suggest that with increased awareness of advertising for securities or with ownership of any of that asset, the couple has a more favorable opinion of securities. In the case of Equation (1.5), the results in Table 1 indicate little evidence for the usual views that interest in a particular commodity, or service relates to advertising awareness. Indeed, higher priority of saving in a particular form seems to reduce awareness of ads, except for the wife's saving priorities for real estate. Education also seems to mitigate against ad awareness, four of these six coefficients being negative, including the only two significant at the .10 level or beyond.

Admittedly, however, the goodness of fit is not appreciable for any of these assets. These results can only be treated as suggestive of what the true relationships may be after a more thorough analysis and with more observations.

The beta coefficients and the goodness of fit obtained from fitting the three equations corresponding to Variants 1 and 2 to estimate holdings of each of the five assets are presented in Table 2. It should be noted that the sample size varies substantially between the equations attempting to explain whether the particular couples hold a given asset form and those attempting to explain how much or what percent of the portfolio is in that form; in the latter case only those couples are included that own the particular asset.

177

Table 2. BETA COEFFICIENTS AND GOODNESS OF FIT OF EQUATIONS (1.7a), (1.7b) AND (1.7c)

Variable[a]	(1.7a) Ownership of Asset					(1.7b) Share of Portfolio, owners only					(1.7c) Amount Owned, owners only[b]				
	H1	H2	H3	H4	H5	V1	V2	V3	V4	V5	W1	W2	W3	W4	W5
Rank of given asset	.02	.14#	.18*	.07	.18*	-.01	.08	.27#	.07	.08	.01	.36#	.31#	-.00	.06
Education, h	-.03	.04	.20*	-.07	.21*	.05	.08	-.08	.03	-.05	.20#	.16	-.03	.01	-.04
Education, w	.05	.02	-.22	-.00	-.09	-.08	-.20	-.30	-.05	.05	-.05	-.29	-.12	.06	.14#
Priority of saving, h	-.23*	.03	.09	.24*	.07	-.04	-.76#	-.40	-.32*	.07	-.00	-.23	-.49#	-.19**	.06
Priority of saving, w	.08	-.06	-.01	-.10	-.10	-.06	.69#	.06	.36*	-.09	.05	.14	.19	.20**	-.05
Extravagance, h	-.12	-.00	-.06	.01	.19*	-.10	.27	.13	.19#	.19*	-.15#	.18	.01	.04	.02
Extravagance, w	-.00	-.05	-.05	-.20*	-.05	.08	.05	.02	.10	.12	.03	-.12	.05	.12*	.15*
Life holds opportunities, h	-.03	-.02	.02	-.05	.05	-.12	-.08	.00	.17	.13	.02	-.18	.06	.07	.03
Life holds opportunities, w	-.02	.02	-.06	.09	-.05	.02	-.02	.29#	-.15	-.24**	-.10	-.46**	.07	-.05	-.20**
Percent of 1969 income saved	.01	.07	-.12	.15*	.03	-.17*	-.09	.06	.03	-.02	.02	-.09	-.11	.02	.14#
Relative level of 1969 saving	-.23	.07	.17**	-.06	.02	.02	-.13	.01	.07	.03	.02	-.00	-.05	.08	-.04
Log of income	.02	.01	.08	.24**	.10	-.19*	-.15	-.48***	-.05	-.13	-.03	.45*	-.04	-.13*	.10
Log of wealth	-.01	.17*	.27**	.11	-.04	-.08	-.59**	.34	-.19	-.09	.42**	.09	.60**	.82**	.53**
Log of debts	.11	.11	.03	.25**	.12	-.40**	-.03	-.23	.12	-.20*	-.35**	.07	-.27	.13*	-.19*
Goal for total saving	-.09	.04	-.01	-.13	.03	.03	.32#	.14	-.04	.10	.10	.06	.17	-.02	.09

Plans to save in that asset	.23**	.30**	.28**	.15**	.01	.08	.10	-.08	-.07	.11	.13	.41*	.01	-.02	-.06
Ad exposure to that asset	-.01	.02	.12	.08	-.03	-.16*	-.31	-.03	.06	-.04	-.09	-.27	.04	-.01	-.09
R^2	.13	.19	.41	.36	.15	.37	.61	.70	.21	.19	.30	.69	.63	.82	.44
Adj. R^2	.04	.11	.35	.29	.06	.28	.25	.47	.05	.09	.20	.40	.34	.79	.37
Sample Size	174	174	174	174	174	133	36	40	100	151	133	36	40	100	151

Sample size

#Significant at .10 level
*Significant at .05 level
**Significant at .01 level

a h –husband, w –wife.
b   Subscripts denote the following assets:
   1 –savings accounts
   2 –U.S. Government bonds
   3 –marketable securities
   4 –real estate (including own home)
   5 –life insurance and pensions

179

The goodness of fit seems to be appreciably better than for the first two equations of the model, and many more coefficients are statistically significant at the .01 level or beyond. However, the adequacy of a particular function form clearly varies substantially with the type of asset. The most respectable showing overall would seem to be that of the functions for securities, which explain 35 percent of the variation in ownership of the asset, 47 percent of the variation of the share of portfolio for the owners, and 34 percent of the amount owned, all adjusted for degrees of freedom. The functions also make a very respectable showing for real estate ownership, explaining 29 percent of the variation in ownership, only 5 percent of the share of the portfolio, but a very substantial 79 percent of the variation in the amount owned (much of the latter because home ownership is included in both sides of the equation).

The explanation of the variation in ownership of the other three assets (Equation 1.7a) is rather low, the adjusted R^2 varying between 4 percent and 11 percent. Much better explanations are provided in those cases of the amounts owned. The proportion of the total variance in the share of the portfolio or in the amount owned generally varies between 20 percent and 40 percent, with the exception of the share of the portfolio in life insurance where the value of the adjusted R^2 is only .09.

Before considering which variables are primarily reponsible for these relationships, it is preferable to examine the results obtained from fitting the two equations corresponding to Variants 3 and 4 since, as will be noted shortly, many of the same patterns appear in all four variants. The latter set of results, fitting the data to Equations (1.8) and (1.9), are shown in Table 3. It will be recalled that these equations correspond to Equations (1.7b) and (1.7c), with the exception that the entire sample is included in each case to see whether the two-stage process of first explaining ownership and then amount or percent owned is superior to doing both at the same time.

The answer to this question would seem to be mixed. On the one hand, the goodness of fit of one-stage Equations (1.8) and (1.9) is generally appreciably less than that of corresponding Equations (1.7b) and (1.7c). However, these levels of goodness of fit are generally well above that of the function that pinpoints owner-

Table 3. BETA COEFFICIENTS AND GOODNESS OF FIT EQUATIONS (1.8) AND (1.9)

Variable[a]	(1.8) Share of portfolio, total sample					(1.9) Amount Owned, total sample				
	V1	V2	V3	V4	V5	W1	W2	W3	W4	W5
Rank of given asset	.04	.09	.29**	.10	.12	-.00	.17*	.20**	.01	.18**
Education, h	.03	.02	.05	-.05	.03	.02	-.01	.18*	-.11#	.14
Education, w	-.02	-.04	-.19*	-.02	-.00	.04	.03	-.22**	.00	.00
Priority of saving, h	-.18#	-.01	-.07	.10	.04	.21*	.00	.05	.15*	.17#
Priority of saving, w	.03	.10	-.04	.03	-.09	.07	-.05	.05	-.06	-.18#
Extravagance, h	-.14#	.09	-.05	.08	.22**	-.12	.02	-.08	.06	.20**
Extravagance, w	.06	-.01	.01	-.16*	.09	.01	-.00	.00	-.10*	.06
Life holds opportunities, h	-.11	.01	-.03	.02	.12	.01	-.02	.02	-.03	.06
Life holds opportunities, w	-.01	.02	.09	.03	-.22**	-.07	-.00	-.05	.05	-.12#
Percent of 1969 income saved	-.15#	-.06	-.09	.14#	-.03	-.06	.04	-.11	.02	.03
Relative level of 1969 saving	-.07	.06	.12#	-.03	.04	-.17*	.07	.12#	.02	.03
Log of income	-.15#	-.01	-.13#	.20*	-.12	-.10	.07	.06	.05	.00
Log of wealth	-.11	-.07	.51**	.01	-.03	.36**	.17	.23*	.65**	.46**
Log of debts	-.27**	.03	-.07	.27**	-.11	-.04	-.05	-.05	.20**	-.11
Goal for total saving	-.03	.16*	.06	-.13#	.10	-.04	.08	.06	-.06	.10
Plans to save in that asset	.16*	.17*	.04	.09	.11	.27**	.35**	.31**	.08#	.04
Ad exposure to that asset	-.11	-.17*	-.05	.11	-.05	-.07	-.02	.07	.04	-.05
R^2	.28	.11	.37	.24	.17	.22	.21	.39	.70	.33
Adj. R^2	.20	.02	.30	.16	.08	.13	.13	.32	.67	.26

Sample size

a   h—husband, w—wife.
b   Subscripts denote the following assets:
    1 —savings accounts
    2 —U.S. Government bonds
    3 —marketable securities
    4 —real estate (including own home)
    5 —life insurance and pensions

\# Significant at .10 level
* Significant at .05 level
** Significant at .01 level

ship, Equation (1.7a). Given the low goodness of fit of that equation for assets such as savings accounts, U.S. government bonds, and life insurance, the two-stage procedure could not be expected to yield any better results than the one-stage procedure in terms of explaining the percent or the amount held of a particular asset. However, Equations (1.7b) and (1.7c) would seem to be generally superior to Equations (1.8) and (1.9), respectively, in estimating portfolio shares or absolute amounts owned, *given* that the couple owns the particular asset.

With regard to the significance of particular types of variables on these relationships, a number of tentative inferences can be made, some of which seem rather surprising. In particular:

1. The ranking accorded a particular asset is not always highly correlated with ownership of that asset or amounts owned. The primary instances where such positive relationships exist are for U.S. government bonds and for marketable securities.
2. The two personality variables affect ownership of the assets in diverse ways. As hypothesized, couples where one member (especially the husband) tends to be extravagant are more likely to own life insurance and pensions, and to have more of their assets in that form. Extravagant tendencies otherwise usually appear to be negatively correlated with ownership of marketable securities and of real estate, with some exceptions. The other personality variable, if life holds opportunities, seems to manifest its main effect through the wife. The more likely she is to hold this opinion the less likely is the couple to hold government bonds or life insurance and the more likely is the couple to hold marketable securities.
3. As one might expect, the indicators of general well-being and of wealth affect appreciably the ownership of particular assets. The wealth variable would seem to be most important, exerting a strong positive influence on all assets held except for government bonds. At the same time, wealth is also positively correlated with whether any government bonds or marketable securities are owned and tends to be negatively correlated with the share in the portfolio of all the five assets covered except for marketable securities. The income variable is also significant, primarily in influencing ownership of real estate, acting to reduce the portfolio share in savings accounts and marketable

securities but to increase the amount owned in government bonds. Debts are positively correlated with ownership and amounts owned in the form of real estate (mainly because mortgages are included in debts) and are inversely correlated with ownership of savings accounts.

4. An "intentions" variable in the form of stated plans to save in a particular asset is highly positively correlated with ownership of four of the five assets, and is also seen to affect amounts owned in government bonds. Thus, an intentions variable in the case of saving may be of real value for future prediction although in this case the comparison is between current ownership and future plans rather than the more usual comparison between current plans and future ownership.

5. As in the case of Table 1, reported exposure to advertisements for a particular type of asset appears to have no discernible effect on ownership of that asset or amounts owned. Indeed, the only coefficient statistically significant at the levels used in this study is negative.

6. These results tend to bring out, possibly for the first time, that both the husband and the wife may exert strong influence on the saving behavior of the family and, moreover, that this influence may be in opposite directions. Thus, education of the husband is seen to influence asset ownership significantly (at the .01 level or beyond) five times. Education of the wife affects ownership in these five sets of equations three times. Yet, in every case where the coefficient of education of one member of the couple is statistically significant, the education coefficient of the other member has the opposite sign! The most striking instance occurs on the amount owned of marketable securities of the total sample, Equation (1.9), where the husband's education is strongly positively correlated with amount owned while the wife's education exhibits an even stronger negative correlation.

This suggestion of possible internal conflict receives further support from comparison of the husband—wife coefficients on priority of saving. The husband's coefficient is significant nine times, the wife's coefficient four times, and in every instance the husband's coefficient and the wife's coefficient have opposite signs, including four pairs where both coefficients are significant!

183

The evidence from the two personality variables is also in the same direction though not nearly as strong. Of eighteen times in which one or the other coefficients of the pair is statistically significant, the husband—wife coefficients have opposite signs nine times. There is no instance here of both coefficients being significant at the same time.

At the least, it would seem that there is little agreement between husbands and wives on saving practices or priorities. Clearly, the question of husband—wife interrelations in saving behavior (as well as on spending behavior) is a subject that merits much further study.

CONCLUSIONS

This study of the asset accumulation decisions of young married couples has attempted to provide a general framework for explaining such decisions and has provided some empirical tests of a part of this framework. The results are mixed, as one might expect in an exploratory study of this type.

The weakest part of the model would seem to be the explanation of saving attitudes and of exposure to advertising. In the former respect, much more work remains to be done, partly in investigating what is the most appropriate dependent variable and partly in considering what other factors may enter into the explanation of attitudes. Alternatively, one might not seek any explanation of this type of variable on the ground that it is essentially exogenous to the explanation of economic decisions. However, this is not an idea we are prepared to accept as yet without much further testing.[6]

The puzzling results are with regard to the exposure of the young couples to advertising, both in low goodness of fit for explaining this variable and in its lack of significance in explaining asset decisions. A number of other tests might be run before these findings can be accepted at face value, since it is indeed hard to believe that advertising of the magnitude practised by some

[6] As Katona has argued, the distinction between economic and noneconomic forces is often very tenuous. *See*, for example, [8], [7, pp. 219–32].

184

financial institutions is without effect. Possibly this is due to the use of this variable in dichotomous form, which for some assets means its exclusion altogether because of advertising awareness by the total sample. Here the panel feature of the study could prove very useful, since questions can be asked of the panel members in future waves on such matters as the reasons for particular attitudes toward advertising and of the relative influence they feel advertising has in guiding their investments among many other variables.

Although the financial behavior variables are reasonably well explained by the model, room for improvement here also exists, particularly in pinpointing which couples do and which couples do not own particular types of assets. In any event, however, the results would seem to suggest three major future lines of study in the explanation of asset accumulation decisions. First, it would be more meaningful to treat ownership of all types of assets as interdependent, so that ownership of any one asset is a function of ownership of other assets. Such interdependence is logical not only from a financial but also from a psychological point of view, e.g., home ownership may be regarded as a form of insurance. Building on the results of the present study, such an approach should be more easily manageable.

Second, the practice in the past of treating a couple (or a family) as a unit may well have been a mistake, for this study provides evidence that when it comes to asset decisions husbands and wives may not agree with each other. Hence, an explanation of these decisions may lie not in treating the family as a unit but in considering each of its major component parts and of how they interact with each other.

Third, attitude and personality variables are also found to influence asset behavior and need to be included along with the usual economic variables in models of this type. How best to do so remains a mystery.[7] This is yet one more case where economic behavior and noneconomic factors have to be brought into juxtaposition, something that George Katona has been advocating for more years than we would like to recall.

[7] One other approach tried here that met with no success was to treat the Equations (1.4) and (1.7) as a true recursive system with the estimated attitude from (1.4) used as an independent variable in (1.7). The results were no different than before.

Asset ranking — 1 (lowest) to 6 (highest).

Ad awareness, dichotomy — 1 (1 or more ads), 0 (none).

Ownership of asset, dummy variable — 1 (yes), 0 (no).

1. Savings accounts and shares, including certificates of deposits, all types of savings institutions.
2. U.S. Government bonds, bills and notes.
3. Marketable securities, including common and preferred stock and all bonds except U.S. Government.
4. Real estate investments, including own home.
5. Life insurance and pension plans, all types including Social Security.

Amount owned of asset, current dollar values, securities and real estate at market values, life insurance and pensions at amounts paid in.

Education, highest grade completed — none (0) to graduate school (17).

Priority of saving — 0 (lowest) to 5 (highest).

Handling of income — 0 (use as available) to 7 (advance plans for spending and saving).

Extravagance, tendency toward, sum of four scale questions — 0 (none) to 4 (high).

Life holds opportunities, dichotomy — 0 (no), 1 (yes).

Specificity of expense budget — 0 (none) to 3 (high).

Has goal for total savings, dichotomy — 0 (no), 1 (yes).

Plans to save in that asset, dichotomy — 0 (no), 1 (yes).

Percent of 1969 income saved, actual percent, positive or negative.

Relative level of 1969 saving compared to last year, trichotomy — 0 (low), 1 (same), 2 (high).

REFERENCES

1 Andreasen, Alan, "Geographic Mobility and Market Segmentation", *Journal of Marketing Research*, 3 (November, 1966), 341–348.
2 Davis, H.L., "Dimensions of Marital Roles in Consumer Decision Making", *Journal of Marketing Research*, 7 (May, 1970), 168–177.
3 Ferber, Robert, *The Reliability of Consumer Reports of Financial Assets and Debts*, University of Illinois Bureau of Economic and Business

Research, Studies in Consumer Savings No. 6, 1966.

4 Foote, N.N., ed., *Household Decision-making*, New York: New York University Press, 1961.

5 Glock, C.Y., and F.M. Nicosia, "Sociology and the Study of Consumers", *Journal of Advertising Research*, (September, 1963).

6 Green, P.E., and D.S. Tull, *Research for Marketing Decisions*, Englewood Cliffs, New Jersey: Prentice Hall, 1970.

7 Katona, George, "Expectations and Decisions in Economic Behavior", In Daniel Lerner and Harold D. Lasswell, eds., *The Policy Sciences: Recent Developments in Scope and Method*, Stanford: Stanford University Press, 1951.

8 Katona, George, *Psychological Analysis of Economic Behavior*, New York: McGraw-Hill, 1951.

9 Katona, George, and Eva Mueller, "A Study of Purchase Decisions", in Lincoln H. Clark, ed., *Consumer Behavior, The Dynamics of Consumer Reaction*, New York: New York University Press, 1954.

10 Katona, George, *The Powerful Consumer*, Psychological Studies of the American Economy, New York: McGraw-Hill, 1960.

11 Katona George, *The Mass Consumption Society*, New York: McGraw-Hill, 1964.

12 Kelly, R.F., and M.B. Egan, "Husband and Wife Interaction in a Consumer Decision Process", In P.R. McDonald, ed., *Marketing Involvement in Society and the Economy*, Chicago, Illinois: American Marketing Association, (August) 1969.

13 Lazarsfeld, P.F., W.H. Sewell, and H.L. Wilensky, eds., *The Uses of Sociology*, New York: Basic Books, 1967.

14 Nicosia, F.M., "Panel Designs and Analysis", P.D. Bennett, ed., *Economic Growth, Competition, and World Markets*, Chicago, Illinois: American Marketing Association, (September) 1965.

15 Nicosia, F.M., R. Pratt, Jr., A. Andreasen, D. Granbois, and J. Engle, *Longitudinal Analysis*, New York: Free Press (Macmillan) forthcoming.

16 Rossi, Peter, *Why Families Move*, Chicago, Illinois: National Opinion Research Center, 1955.

17 Sudman, Seymour, "On the Accuracy of Recording of Consumer Panels", *Journal of marketing Research*, 1 (May, 1964), 14–20; 2 (August, 1964), 69–83.

Marketing Applications of Behavioral Economics

ROBERT W. PRATT, JR. *

INTRODUCTION

Management philosophy guiding American industry during the twentieth century has taken three broad directions. During the period 1900 to 1930, concern was focused primarily on problems of production; between 1930 and the late 1940's, orientation switched to problems associated with distribution systems; since the late 1940's, increased attention has been directed toward the end consumer [15]. The philosophy manifested in this latter orientation is widely referenced in business literature as the "marketing concept".

The essence of the marketing concept is simply that the mix of goods and services offered by a seller in the marketplace must be responsive to predetermined needs and wants of potential buyers. Evolution of this concept represents explicit recognition on the part of marketing management that American consumers are confronted with a growing array of choice, and the options to choose are being exercised. Under these conditions, it is essential to market goods and services that are matched to consumer wants. In attempting to bring about this match, businessmen have turned for

* Manager, Business Research & Forecasting Operation, Major Appliance Business Group, General Electric Company.

189

assistance in ever-increasing numbers to social scientists. Concurrently, a number of economists have been working to temper selected elements of traditional economic theory with psychological theory in order to better explain certain aspects of economic behavior. This general area of study is now identified as "behavioral economics".

It is not a coincidence that growing application of the marketing concept has been paralleled by growing application of behavioral economics to marketing problems. Application of either to marketing requires acceptance of the premise that an understanding of the "why" of human behavior is essential to both formulation and evaluation of effective marketing programs. Regardless of the route by which one arrives at this premise, techniques for implementation are found within the same body of social science theory. Application of the marketing concept, particularly as it relates to consumer durable goods, depends heavily on application of principles from behavioral economics.

The objectives of this chapter are threefold. First, to summarize major changes in American society that underlie both development of the marketing concept and evolution of behavioral economics. Second, to describe concepts and theories that provide the basic foundation for behavioral economics. Finally, to explore potential and actual applications of behavioral economics to the development of marketing policies and practices. The chapter is written primarily for marketing practitioners.

CHANGING CONSUMER ENVIRONMENT

During the period since World War II, the American culture has been experiencing rapid and continuous change. Perhaps the two words that best describe the general consumer environment that exists today are "change" and "choice". The rate of change and the fact of choice have combined to greatly complicate the related tasks of understanding and predicting consumer behavior. At the risk of oversimplification, the first section of this chapter will discuss a limited sampling of factors that are related directly to the increasing ability of American consumers to exercise choice. Not only has each of these factors undergone dramatic change in recent years, but also information about each is essential to the formulation of effective marketing programs.

Consider first the dimensions of economic choice presently available to American consumers. Although poverty has not been eliminated in the United States, one of the major features that makes present-day American society unique in world history is the fact that "the majority of families now have discretionary purchasing power and constantly replace and enlarge their stock of consumer goods [13, p.3]". The single most significant "revolutionary change" in the United States is inherent in "the common man's ability to use some of his money for what he would like to have rather than for what he must have...[13, p.6]." This last point cannot be emphasized too strongly. In less than three decades, America has witnessed the growth of a large middle class endowed with sufficient income to permit individuals and families relatively wide latitude in deciding how available monies are spent. The single most important condition that enables a family to purchase goods and services — and, if sufficiently large, to exercise meaningful choice among alternatives — is after-tax income.

In terms of current income, how well off is the "common man"? The majority of American consumers currently enjoy a level of real income unmatched in world history. In 1970, per capita disposable income in current dollars reached $3,357, up from $1,937 in 1960 — an increase of 73.3 percent. Over the same decade, median family income increased 75.6 percent, from $5,620 to $9,870. Moreover, approximately 50 percent of all disposable personal income is now "discretionary". Thus, on average, 50 cents of each after-tax dollar is spent for "necessities"; that is, expenditures over which the buyer exercises little choice. But buyers do exercise a great deal of choice in allocating the "discretionary" 50 cents. A question of great concern to market analysts, then, deals with understanding the *process* by which these choices are made.

In addition to current income, there are other factors which contribute significantly to the ability of an American family to spend in excess of short-term earnings, thus facilitating a range of choice. These include the availability of increasing levels of liquid assets, ready access to installment credit, and protection against uncertainty provided, for example, by availability of a wide assortment of insurance programs, such as medical insurance, workmen's compensation, unemployment compensation, and social security. The widespread presence of income security provided by these programs is a relatively new phenomenon on the American scene.

Education is still another important area of change that has had a profound impact on the processes by which consumers reach decisions, and hence on the formulation of marketing programs. Levels of formal education have increased and are expected to continue to increase with each new generation. By 1980, over 80 percent of the young will be completing high school, and 16 percent will be going on for at least 4 years of college. In contrast, in 1940, only 38 percent of the young were completing high school, and only 6 percent were completing four years of college. Perhaps more important, continued learning, as provided, for example, by night school attendance, company retraining programs, and travel, has had an important influence on the increasing diversity and rate of change in life styles. A propensity to learn, and hence to change, has become a fundamental characteristic of the American consumer.

Finally, the ability to exercise choice is greatly enhanced by long-term trends toward increased availability of leisure or "discretionary" time — holidays, vacations, sabbaticals, and now the four-day work week. One alternative use of discretionary time is, of course, assuming a second or even a third job. Thus, among other things, the freedom to allocate time will make it possible for a large number of families to make considered decisions regarding the amount of income they need or want.

The foregoing paragraphs highlight broad areas of change with which the market analyst must be concerned on a continuous and intensive basis. The impact of these changes is widespread. As stated in the introduction to this chapter, they have caused a redirection of management attention away from problems of production and distribution toward a focus on needs and wants of end consumers. In accomplishing this redirection, concepts and theories from behavioral economics have found increasing application. Before turning to these applications, the reader should be introduced to basic principles of behavioral economics as they pertain to marketing; these principles are discussed in other contexts elsewhere in this book.

384

During the second decade of this century, marketing began to receive attention as an independent area of study within the broader discipline of economics. Most early marketing scholars were trained economists. Not surprisingly, therefore, early marketing theories were generally extensions of traditional economic thought, and traditional economics was first and foremost a deductive science. Faced with a given situation, "rational" consumers would behave in a predictable fashion. What represented "rational" behavior, however, was defined in the minds of economists, not in the minds of consumers. Sales would respond to changes in price. Borrowing would respond to changes in interest rates. Thoughts or feelings of individual buyers or borrowers played no part in these formulations. The human element was absent. Consumers were considered to be passive; it was assumed that, as a group, they would react in a known way to a given stimulus. As long as the postulated relationships held, there was no need for economists to become concerned with individual or group behavior.

With the advent of a large and relatively affluent middle class in the United States, deductive theory became less useful as a basis for understanding and predicting behavior. The consumer moved to center stage. In seeking to understand his needs and wants, marketing management turned for assistance to social scientists from a number of disciplines. The present section of this chapter provides an overview of the way in which selected theories and concepts from economics and psychology were brought together following World War II to develop a set of basic principles which, collectively, provide the foundation for behavioral economics. The following section of the chapter will discuss actual and potential applications of these principles to marketing.

Virtually all research in the field of behavioral economics is an outgrowth of pioneering work done by George Katona and his colleagues at the University of Michigan's Survey Research Center. In his basic treatise, the essence of Katona's work is captured in these words:

> ... the basic need for psychology in economic research consists in the need to discover and analyze the forces behind economic pro-

cesses, the forces responsible for economic actions, decisions and choices. . . "Economics without psychology" has not succeeded in explaining important economic processes and "psychology without economics" has no chance of explaining some of the most common aspects of human behavior [7, pp.9-10].

The starting point for Katona's work is found in Keynesian economics; specifically, in the Keynesian consumption function. Keynes wrote that aggregate consumption is a stable function of aggregate disposable personal income [14]. Katona states, first, that aggregate consumption is a function of disposable personal income *plus a willingness to spend that income*, and, second, that "willingness to spend" is measurable. At a given time, "willingness to spend" is considered to be a function of the relative degree of optimism or pessimism felt by consumers.

It is in the measurement of "willingness to spend" that Katona turns to psychology. Principles from psychology that have contributed importantly to the development of behavioral economics are identified in the paragraphs that follow.

Marketing management is well aware that consumer response to a given stimulus (e.g., TV or radio advertisements, point-of-purchase displays, packaging, price changes, extended warranties) is likely to differ among individuals at a single point in time and differ for the same individual at two or more points in time. Why? The answer lies in an understanding of the manner in which individuals perceive and interpret stimuli. George Smith offers a succinct statement of the problem in marketing terms.

> We have to know what is going on inside the person. For example, we want to know what images, memories, and emotions are elicited by an illustration for life-insurance copy. Is the reader put into a mood which causes him to start reviewing his insurance holdings and plan for the future, or does the picture strike him as trivial, silly, or overdone so that he passes it by? We want to know, if possible, the basic gratifications involved in the consumption of toilet soap and wine, and in the use of automatic dishwashers and convertibles. Satisfactory answers to these and hundreds of similar questions represent cash value for advertisers, publishers, and manufacturers because then they can bring both their products and their appeals more nearly into line with consumers [26, p.4].

Smith goes on to suggest that research must "focus attention on *the whole battery of inner conditions that play a dynamic part in a person's buying or not buying, responding favorably or unfavorably to some communication* [26, p.5]".

Smith's "inner conditions" are referred to by Gestalt psychologists as "intervening variables". A list of such variables would include motives, beliefs, assumptions, prejudices, attitudes, aspirations, feelings, emotions, expectations, social values, and more. These variables are postulated to function within an individual; they provide the psychological framework within which perceived environmental stimuli are organized and interpreted. The end result of this internal process leads to overt behavior.[1] Further, the structure of intervening variables is constantly changing through time as a result of new learning and experience. One consequence of constant change is that the same stimulus will bring about different patterns of overt behavior at different points in time. Thus, learning theory must play an important role in behavioral economics, as must the theory of motivation.

Virtually all buying behavior is both "rational", in the sense that the term is defined by psychologists, and motivated.[2] Motivated behavior can be thought of as "behavior that is instigated by needs within the individual and is directed toward goals that can satisfy these needs [18 p.56]". Within this definition, a fundamental objective of all marketing programs must be to offer products or services that will serve as goals toward which need-oriented behavior will be directed. Although simple in theory, application is complicated seriously by the fact that overt behavior is almost always motivated by a combination of needs, some reinforcing and others offsetting or in conflict.[3] The presence of a multiplicity of both motives and goals accounts for the fact that a well-conceived sales campaign must be designed to appeal to a variety of needs, not just one. Thus, advertising campaigns frequently specify both "primary" and "secondary" appeals.

Another aspect of motivation that has gained wide attention

[1] For a discussion of the basic theory, *see* [16]. For examples that illustrate the Gestalt theory of perception and learning, *see* [27].

[2] For a discussion of the difference between rational and irrational behavior, *see* [4]; *see also* [8]. Katona's article outlines a theoretical framework for the study of rational buying behavior.

[3] For a discussion of "Multiplicity of Motives", *see* [12, pp.663-66].

among market analysts is aspiration theory. A great deal of the basic research in this area has been completed by Kurt Lewin and his associates [17]. Lewin found that most individuals aspire to goals that are just beyond their immediate grasp. If the goals are achieved, they are reformulated upward; if they are not achieved, a downward adjustment is in order. Katona's use of measures of optimism and pessimism to predict aggregate buying behavior is, essentially, an application of Lewin's aspiration theory. As summarized by Katona:

> Gratification of needs does not mean saturation; instead it results in the raising of sights, provided people are optimistic and confident about the future. New wants arise when more pressing wants have been satisfied. Frustration, disappointment, or a pessimistic outlook make for feelings of saturation.[4]

In the area of upward adjustment of aspirations, it is well documented that a large proportion of those purchasing consumer durables are replacing products with which they have little or no mechanical difficulty. Their dissatisfaction with the product is psychological; one important reason for their decision to replace is that they perceive and are attracted by innovations in product design [19]. In marketing surveys, respondents' reasons for dissatisfaction with present products can be frequently categorized as "psychological obsolescence". For example, one study completed by General Electric Company concluded that a significant number of expressed dissatisfactions with major appliances had nothing to do with the particular appliance asked about; rather, they referred to features or performance characteristics that the respondent would like to have [5].

If there is any doubt about the importance of motivation theory to marketing, that doubt can be quickly dispelled by a review of marketing literature. Marketing textbooks and articles that draw on motivation theory number well up in the hundreds. Essentially, research in this area is a manifestation of the desire to implement the "marketing concept". "The goal is to understand the 'why' of behavior, to become 'customer oriented', to view the

[4] See [11, p.100]. For additional information regarding the relationship between levels of aspiration and buying behavior, see [12, pp.666-670]; see also [10, especially Chapter 8]; and [7, pp.91-98].

world as the customer views it [22, p.115]." As one economist aptly writes:

> ... consumers are *players* on the economic stage, not merely puppets. They do not automatically spend a certain proportion of an income increase when they receive it. Instead, their changing expectations and aspirations are an important determinant of *changes* in the shape of the consumption function [24].

To the extent that material presented in this section can be summarized, the foregoing paragraphs add up to this: High levels of discretionary purchasing power in the American economy tend to negate traditional deductive theories of buying behavior. In order to understand the decision process by which consumers allocate discretionary income (and discretionary time), one must first understand certain concepts and theories applicable to the broad area of human behavior — concepts and theories that are equally relevant to the narrower problems of buying behavior. The most important of these are the concept of intervening variables and the theories of motivation and learning. The introduction of these theories and concepts into the search for a better understanding of consumer buying behavior has resulted in rapid growth and development of the discipline of behavioral economics.

APPLICATIONS OF BEHAVIORAL ECONOMICS TO MARKETING PROBLEMS

How have the theories and concepts discussed in the preceding section of this chapter been brought to bear on marketing problems? In an important sense, the application of behavioral economics to marketing is just beginning. Yet a start has been made, and the rate of progress is increasing. The present section of this chapter will discuss potential and actual applications of behavioral economics to three general types of marketing problems — understanding decision processes, market segmentation, and forecasting. Reference will be made to both published and unpublished empirical research.

The most fundamental application of behavioral economics to marketing is in gaining an understanding of the problem-solving process that precedes a purchase decision, whether the process is terminated by a decision to buy or a decision not to buy. The reason for this is that every element in a marketing program is designed to meet the same criterion. Each must exert maximum influence on short- and/or long-term purchase decisions of potential customers.

Principles from behavioral economics are most directly applicable to buying situations in which a consumer is likely to consider alternatives and make a genuine decision, as contrasted to purchases resulting from habit. Katona has listed six "expenditures and conditions which cause consumers to reflect and make. . . genuine decisions before making a purchase"[13, pp.289–290].

1. Expenditures which are subjectively thought to be major and which are fairly rare. Many of these expenditures are large (e.g., a house or, in many but not all cases, a car, etc.), but some may be small and yet of great importance to the buyer (as, for instance, a dress or a present for a specified occasion).
2. Unsatisfactory past experience, especially disappointment of expectations.
3. Some (by no means all) purchases of new products or the first purchase of a product.
4. Awareness of a difference between one's customary behavior and that of the group to which one belongs or an important reference group.
5. Impact of strong new stimuli or precipitating circumstances; these stimuli may consist of general news (threat of war, inflation, etc.) or of news regarding specific products, which may be transmitted by advertisers.
6. Certain personality characteristics, often associated with education.

Note that the above list does not restrict consideration of alternatives to large-ticket durables. In fact, from the standpoint of research strategy, techniques for studying decision processes find wide application in the study of habitual buying behavior. To understand why this is true, consider the nature of habits.

> ... goal-oriented behavior must gratify a need if it is to be repeated. The behavior must be reinforced; gratification of a need provides the incentive for repeat behavior when the same need reoccurs in the future. Continuous reinforcement of a particular mode of behavior underlies the formulation of habits. Habits, then, are response patterns that have become automatic to given stimuli [22, p.120].

In marketing, habitual behavior is evidenced most often in purchase patterns for frequently-purchased convenience goods, such as grocery products. Getting consumers to accept new products or to switch brands is essentially a problem of introducing an alternative response (goal) that will be perceived by the individual and cause him to reconsider a previous decision; once an habitual behavior pattern has been arrested, a new decision must be reached. The new decision may, of course, be to continue the previous pattern.

There are two general research strategies used by market analysts to study habitual behavior. One requires the researcher to locate a group of respondents who are actually in the decision process; the second requires creation of an artificial situation in which respondents are forced to repeat the decision-making process. One approach to implementing this latter strategy is this:

> ... the researcher must first measure the consumer's attitude toward the brands in a particular product group; second, disturb the consumer's environment and brand choices; and third, study the process through which the consumer develops new brand attitudes. Thus, the researcher uses some disturbance in the consumer's life to trigger the entire decison-making process and, thereby, tries to identify and measure all the interacting cause and effect relationships involved in the decision process. . .[3, p.4].

The sum of the above is that the "why" of buying behavior, regardless of the type of product or service involved, cannot be researched directly. An understanding of habitual buying behavior is gained by studying the decision processes by which habits are established or broken. Thus, all "why" research concentrates on decision processes.

A search of the literature indicates that most published research on decision processes, as that work relates to specific areas of marketing, has been undertaken by individuals trained in one or more of the social sciences. One example can be found in Katona's early efforts to understand and predict spending and saving patterns. That work, however, was restricted to a relatively high level of aggregation; questions asked were framed in economic, not marketing, language.

In a landmark study published in 1954, Katona and Mueller did extend their research to questions of general interest to marketing management [9]. Katona defined the area of study by asking these questions: "Spending on what? Should an automobile or refrigerator be bought, and if so, which brand, which model, at which price, through which dealer [9, p.31]?" These are marketing questions!

The Katona-Mueller study examines major dimensions of the purchase decision for four relatively expensive household appliances. For purposes of comparison, recent buyers of sport shirts were also interviewed. Following are general conclusions reached by the authors.

> We did *not* find that all or most purchases of large household goods are made after careful consideration or deliberation; that all or most such purchases require a long planning period; nor that all or most such purchases are preceded by extensive information seeking or shopping around. . . In general, we may conclude that consideration of alternatives and of consequences, discussion with family members, and extensive information seeking tend to occur when buyers feel that they have discretion to act and when, subjectively, it matters greatly to them how they act [9, pp.34–35].

For reasons discussed above, a large part of the estimated $600,000,000 spent annually on marketing research in the United States is applied to gaining insights into various aspects of the dynamics of decision-making. Very little of this research is published, however, and what is published is frequently outdated. To provide the reader with some idea of the extent to which principles from behavioral economics are applied by those engaged in commercial marketing research, the paragraphs that follow set forth selected observations and empirical findings based on this writer's experience with General Electric Company.

First, some observations regarding both analytical techniques and explanatory variables. Regardless of the particular dependent variable being studied, market analysts spend a major part of their time endeavoring to better explain variance. As a result of the environmental changes discussed earlier in this chapter, the task is becoming more difficult each year. This is particularly true when one is attempting to understand relatively complex processes, such as those associated with decisions. Regardless of the number of explanatory variables available, or the accuracy of measurement, bivariate analysis often fails to disclose interactions among a multiplicity of variables that may contribute importantly to an understanding of the phenomenon represented by the dependent variable. Rarely, if ever, will a single independent variable serve to "explain" a complex dependent variable.

Among market analysts, one response to this problem has been rapid innovation in analytical techniques. The accelerating rate at which new techniques are being developed is dramatically illustrated in Figure 1.

But techniques alone have not solved the problem. Regardless of analytical techniques used, demographic and other descriptive variables have become less and less efficient in explaining variance.

THE GROWTH RATE OF INNOVATION IN
ADVERTISING-MARKETING RESEARCH

1930-1969

NUMERICAL TAXONOMY
INTERACTIVE PROCESSING
COMPUTER CONTROLLED EXPERIMENTATION
ATTITUDE SEGMENTATION
CONTINUOUS GAMES
ADAPTIVE CONTROL THEORY
GRAPH THEORY
STABILITY THEORY
RENEWAL THEORY
MONTE CARLO TECHINQUE
DYNAMIC PROGRAMMING
GEOMETRIC MODELING
SEMANTICS
NON-STATIONARY MARKOV CHAINS
INFORMATION STORAGE AND RETRIEVAL
LEARNING THEORY
DECISION THEORY
SIMULATION
LINEAR PROGRAMMING
MARKOV CHAINS
SCALING THEORY
TIME SAMPLING
EXPERIMENTAL DESIGN
OPERATIONS RESEARCH
FACTOR ANALYSIS
MOTIVATIONAL RESEARCH
REGRESSION METHODS
PROBABILITY SAMPLING
OPINION POLLS
A. C. NIELSEN STORE AUDIT

1930 1935 1940 1945 1950 1955 1960 1965 1970

Source: This chart was presented by Benjamin Lipstein during a panel discussion titled "The Mathematical Revolution and the Management of Marketing Communications". *See* [6, p.43].

While application of multivariate techniques has helped, the key to completing operationally-useful explanatory research lies in greatly expanding the character of variables being measured and made available for analysis. There is a trend in marketing research toward regular measurement of psychological and sociological variables, such as attitudes, expectations, buying plans, life styles, and social values. In many instances, these variables and the techniques used to measure them can be traced to published work in behavioral economics. In situations where the marketing problem deals directly with questions of spending and savings, frequently the case in research done by banks and other financial institutions, principles and techniques from behavioral economics can be applied directly.

Turning to a specific General Electric example, recorded here to demonstrate the potential value of psychological and behavioral data, one objective of a national reinterview study involving 6,355 families was to determine the factor, or combination of factors, that best describes households that are active in the appliance market during a twelve-month period. The basic purpose was to provide a description of the U.S. appliance market that would offer a useful framework within which to formulate marketing programs for individual products or group of products. The research strategy was to move, first, from a profile of the aggregate market to a profile for the product(s) in question and, finally, to a definition of target segments within the total potential market.

Multivariate analysis designed to identify active households leads to two major conclusions.

1. At a point in time, the number of households actively shopping for any one appliance (indeed, for any combination of appliances) is relatively small; hence, the target audience for a product promotion is correspondingly small. Further, as attention is moved from a line of appliances to a specific appliance or brand, the number of potential buyers for whom marketing effort is relevant becomes increasingly smaller.

2. A dominant number of the variables that describe active segments tend to occur infrequently (for a single household) or are subject to rapid change. That is, they reflect either (1) recent changes (e.g., moved, married), or (2) expectations and/or attitudes that "tend to change infrequently, radically, and simultaneously".[5]

Expectations and attitudes that were used in this analysis included the following:

Attitudes toward different brands.

Satisfaction with home furnishings.

Whether this is a "good time to buy".

Expected income change during next twelve months.

Expected changes in employment (respondent or spouse) during next twelve months.

Intentions to purchase one or more household appliances (from among a list of twenty-nine).

Intentions to purchase an automobile.

Intentions to make other home improvements.

Intentions to change place of residence.

For a wide range of analytical work involving multivariate techniques, these variables, or variables like these, play an important role in explaining variance. As a group, they are similar to many of the variables that appear in Katona's published works.

A second part of the study described above was directed toward identifying major factors associated with different levels of buying activity in the appliance market. By concentrating only on active households, the analysis provided an in-depth look at factors that describe the fifty percent of all U. S. households that purchase one or more appliances during a year. One important conclusion was that, "as analysis of active households becomes more comprehensive, an increasing number of 'change' and/or subjective variables (i.e., expectations and/or attitudes) enter the picture." In one A.I.D. analysis,[6] eight of twelve splits were accounted for by this type of variable. In short, as the analysis became more detailed, variables that are subject to rapid change, such as expectations and attitudes, made an increasingly important contribution to the explanation of variance.

---

[5] *See* [7, p.55]. The word "simultaneously" is used here to refer to similar changes among a large number of people.

[6] The Automatic Interaction Detector (AID) program is a multivariate technique for identifying combinations of variables that maximize differences among subgroup means, thus accounting for a larger proportion of the total sums of squares of the dependent variable than would be accounted for by any other combination of variables. For a complete description of this program, *see* [25].

A major conclusion from this study was this: "If a large number of key variables that define an appliance market are subject to rapid change, then one major input to the formulation, evaluation and adjustment of marketing strategies and programs through time (including, of course, sales forecasts) should be the measurement of these key variables on a frequent or continuous basis." Conclusions of this type are responsible for the rapid proliferation of continuous marketing information systems within American industry.

Market Segmentation

American consumers are becoming different, one from the other, on a growing number of dimensions. As indicated earlier, the pace of long-term change in our general environment — for example, as reflected in increasing affluence, rising levels of education, and more "discretionary" time — is accelerating. But these changes frequently hide the dynamics that lie beneath the surface. Consider these contrasts (all of which are directly relevant to the planning of marketing programs):

1. More families are changing their place of residence each year than at any time in the past, yet a lack of willingness to move among some population segments is considered by many planners to be cause for major concern. For example, as a result of ethnic or other ties, many blue-collar workers resist moving from areas of high unemployment to areas where their skills could be employed.

2. While affluence is recognized as a fact of life in the United States, poverty remains a major national concern.

3. Despite rising incomes and the availability of an ever-increasing array of material goods, there is some evidence that American families are becoming less enchanted by "things". Perhaps Veblen's conspicuous consumption has become a cultural anachronism. But while some people are turning away from "things", others are looting stores to get what they believe they deserve.

On almost any dimension, consumers are becoming increasingly heterogeneous. The concept of "market segmentation", which was nurtured in the 1950's and grew to maturity in the 1960's, has taken its place among the basic instruments of the market planner who must develop a blueprint for selling at a profit in an environment of explosive and accelerating change. The basic approach to segmentation is simply to define a group of potential customers who are alike on one or a number of relevant dimensions; to design a product or a product line specifically for this group; and to use the total marketing program (e.g., distribution, advertising, after-sale service) to gain maximum market share within the target segment. Once the total market has been divided into segments, a decision can be made to ignore some segments or to allocate a disproportionately large quantity of marketing effort to other segments, with the goal of gaining and holding high levels of market penetration. Particularly in fast changing markets, like those for consumer electronics, one can point to examples of companies operating profitably with a one or two percent share of the total national market, but with a relatively large share of a carefully defined market segment.

Segments can be structured using any characteristic, or combination of characteristics, of the population to be segmented. Although socioeconomic variables provide a widely used starting point, market analysts are constantly seeking additional variables that can be used to better define segments (i.e., in variance-analysis terms, to minimize variance within segments and maximize variance between segments). For example, Yankelovich has proposed a method for segmenting markets based on the scaling of psychological and sociological characteristics of consumers (e.g., values, needs, attitudes).[7] Benson has developed a technique for determining the market franchise for individual products and brands by combining concepts and techniques from psychology and mathematics [2, p.63–83], [1, p.320–335]. The same techniques can also be used to determine a potential franchise by

[7] See [28]. Yankelovich's early research in this area led to introduction of a syndicated service in 1970, The Yankelovich Monitor, "designed to give marketers of consumer goods and services information on social trends comparable to the information they now receive on economic, population, sales and media trends". This service holds promise of providing marketing analysts with a substantial quantity of information about behavioral variables on a continuing basis.

defining a segment of consumers whose needs are not being met by products presently on the market.

Turning again to General Electric data, variables of the type listed above (i.e., attitudes, expectations, and intentions) are frequently combined with standard socioeconomic information to define market segments. The general procedure involves three steps:

1. First, multivariate techniques are used to identify combinations of variables that minimize within-group variance and maximize between-group variance. In actual application, it is sometimes necessary to accept a relatively low R^2 because the total number of segments in which different marketing strategies can be employed has a practical limitation — generally in the neighborhood of five or six.

2. Second, segments are compared using characteristics pertinent to the marketing problem under study. These might include, for example, socioeconomic characteristics, attitudinal data, characteristics of the buying or shopping process, characteristics of the product or service being marketed, brand share, and so on.

3. Third, a marketing strategy is formulated for each segment. This task includes allocation of total marketing resources across segments, as well as determination of specific elements of the marketing program within each segment — these elements would include, for example, advertising message content and media selection.

Information necesssary to complete this type of analysis is available to General Electric through its Consumer Market Information System, a continuous reinterview panel initiated in January, 1967 [23].

To illustrate the first step outlined above, in the multivariate analysis designed to determine factors associated with different levels of activity in the appliance market (referenced earlier), one segment of relatively heavy buyers was found to have the following characteristics:

Head of household is a professional or manager.

Head under forty-five years old.

Recently moved to a new residence.

Income increased in past twelve months.

Respondent thinks now is a good time to buy.

Respondent is dissatisfied with way home is furnished.
In a second segment, households with a relatively low level of activity in the appliance market had the following characteristics:

Operatives, laborers, etc.,

Head forty-five years old or older.

Annual income less than $6,000.

The attitude and "change" variables associated with heavy buyers are most likely to occur when a relatively high proportion of purchases by households in a segment are "discretionary". When purchases are mandatory, such as many of those made by members of the low-activity segment defined above, attitudes and expectations play a lesser role.

Once segments have been defined, further analysis can be completed both within and across groups. The type of output frequently generated is illustrated by reference to a project undertaken to analyze the monochrome TV market. One of a number of dependent variables used was screen size. As in the previous example, the first step involved use of multivariate analysis to "determine what variable, or combination of variables, best predicts the screen size purchased." Five segments were defined; attitudes, expectations and/or intentions played a part in the definition of four of these. Once this step had been completed, selected characteristics were compared across segments. Examples for three of the five segments are summarized in Table 1.

For management of any one brand, analysis across and within segments provides substantial information about structure of the total monochrome television market. Information of this type is extremely useful for both tactical and strategic planning. For example, Brand C is in command of a small-screen segment that represents sixteen percent of total industry unit sales. Consumers buying these sets are relatively affluent; further, their new sets, on average, are being added to an already large inventory of TV receivers. As an aside, given the data shown in Table 1, Brand C management would immediately wish to know brand composition of these inventories. To what extent are Brand C small-screen portables being purchased by brand-loyal customers?

Turning to strategy, each brand has a wide range of alternatives. Brand C, for example, could attempt to hold market share in the small-screen segment and increase share in the large- and medium—

Table 1

COMPARISON OF SELECTED CHARACTERISTICS FOR THREE
SEGMENTS OF TELEVISION BUYERS (MONOCHROME SETS
ONLY)

	Segment Identification (based on screen size)		
	Large Screen	Medium Screen	Small Screen
Segment's share of all 12-month purchases	11%	26%	16%
Average screen size purchased	21.2"	18.5"	13.3"
Brand share (selected brands):			
Brand A	21%	24%	13%
Brand B	19	12	9
Brand C	8	13	20
Model purchased:			
Portable	51%	76%	95%
Table or console	49	24	5
Mean number of sets in household prior to purchase	1.4	1.8	2.7
Mean family income	$ 8,500	$ 9,700	$ 12,600

SOURCE: General Electric Consumer Market Information System
(1969 data).

screen segments. Another alternative would be to exit the large-screen segment altogether and attempt to gain a much larger share of small-screen business. Particularly if the small-screen segment were forecast to grow over time, one appeal of this latter strategy would be the potential for more efficient use of marketing resources (e.g., advertising dollars, square footage of warehouse space, number of retail outlets, and so on).

Clearly, there are numerous strategic alternatives available to each brand, but the purpose of this chapter is not to discuss strategic planning. The critical point in the above example is that the segments, themselves, are virtually always defined by a combination of variables. If they are available for analysis, the combination, with rare exception, will include one or more psychological or sociological variables; that is, the types of variables that have been developed within the framework of behavioral economics. Without these variables, it would be impossible to achieve the levels of between-segment variance that are being achieved today. There is every reason to expect that improved measurement, coupled with the introduction of new variables, will allow even better segmentation in the future.

Forecasting

Regardless of institutional affiliation, policy makers now recognize that consumers play an active and important role in the well-being of the economy. It would be difficult to find a serious analysis of the contemporary economic scene that does not reference consumer sentiment and its potential or expected impact on the general economic health of the nation. Public mood has assumed a prominent position among variables used to forecast consumer buying behavior.

How is consumer sentiment measured? A growing number of household surveys, both here and abroad, are asking about attitudes, expectations, and anticipated future behavior, including buying behavior. The vast majority of this research has been initiated by economists and is addressed to economic questions, most frequently to questions designed for use in forecasting.[8]

In addition to the Michigan studies directed by Katona, which have continued without interruption over the past twenty-five years, major empirical studies have been conducted, or are presently being conducted, by the U. S. Bureau of the Census, the Federal Reserve Board, The Conference Board, Consumers' Union, the National Bureau of Economic Research, and numerous marketing research companies, including Sindlinger & Company and R.H. Bruskin Associates. Private companies have also been active in the area; notable examples include panel research completed by General Motors and General Electric. To the knowledge of this

[8] For a summary of much of this work, *see* [21].

writer, measurements of consumer sentiment or confidence obtained from one or more of these sources are incorporated in all quantitative techniques used to forecast short- and intermediate-range sales of consumer durables.

How useful have these measures been in forecasting product demand? A review of published results leads to the general conclusion that accuracy of predictions *based on buying intentions alone* has been less than impressive. When attitudinal and other information are combined with results of buying-intentions questions, however, such as is done to construct the Michigan *Index of Consumer Sentiment*, accuracy of prediction for major categories of consumer expenditures has been improved greatly. In fact, the Michigan Index has proven to be a useful leading indicator of aggregate expenditures for consumer durable goods.[9]

CONCLUDING COMMENTS

In summary, behavioral economics is contributing in a number of important ways to the solution of marketing problems. One major contribution is represented by the growing body of empirical techniques and findings that add to our understanding of the processes by which consumers allocate available economic resources among alternatives.

A second major contribution is found in published theoretical and empirical work designed, first, to measure various psychological and sociological variables (e.g., attitudes, expectations, intentions, social values, and so on) and, second, to test the ability of these variables to assist in both understanding and predicting buying behavior. These variables find direct application in every area of marketing, including the three discussed in this chapter — understanding decision processes, market segmentation, and forecasting. As the range of consumer choice increases, as it inevitably will, and as market analysts become more attuned to techniques from behavioral economics, application of these variables to marketing problems will become commonplace.

By summarizing the nature of behavioral economics and its

[9] For an evaluation of the effectiveness of the Michigan Index for forecasting discretionary spending by consumers, *see* [20].

application to marketing, this chapter implicitly recognizes the enormous contribution of one individual, George Katona. In concluding these remarks, that recognition should be made explicit. By means of extraordinary scholarship, manifested in his teaching, research, and writing, Katona has established behavioral economics as an accepted interdisciplinary approach to understanding a vital aspect of human behavior. This is, indeed, a unique achievement.

REFERENCES

1 Benson, Purnell H., "Consumer Preference Distributions in the Analysis of Market Segmentation", *Emerging Concepts in Marketing*, Chicago: American Marketing Association, 1962.
2 Benson, Purnell H., "Psychometric Procedures in the Analysis of Market Segmentation", *Innovation: Key to Marketing Progress*, Chicago: American Marketing Association, 1963.
3 Bucklin, Louis P., and James M. Carman, *The Design of Consumer Research Panels: Conception and Administration of the Berkeley Food Panel*, Berkeley: Institute of Business and Economic Research, 1967.
4 Bursk, Edward G., "Opportunities for Persuasion", *Harvard Business Review*, 36, 5 (Sept.-Oct., 1958), 114-15.
5 General Electric Company, *Consumer Satisfaction With Household Appliances*, Unpublished report dated March, 1970.
6 Hale, William S., ed., *16th Annual Conference Proceedings*, Advertising Research Foundation, Inc., 1971, 43.
7 Katona, George, *Psychological Analysis of Economic Behavior*, New York: McGraw-Hill Book Company, Inc., 1951.
8 Katona, George, "Rational Behavior and Economic Behavior", *Psychological Review*, 60, 5 (Sept., 1953), 307-18.
9 Katona, George, and Eva Mueller, "A Study of Purchase Decisions", in Lincoln H. Clark, ed., *Consumer Behavior: The Dynamics of Consumer Reaction*, New York: New York University Press, 1954, 30-87.
10 Katona, George, *The Powerful Consumer*, New York: McGraw-Hill Book Company, Inc., 1960.
11 Katona, George, "Long-Range Changes in Consumer Attitudes", in C. Lininger, ed., *Dynamic Aspects of Consumer Behavior*, Ann Arbor: Foundation for Research on Human Behavior, 1963.
12 Katona, George, "The Relationship Between Psychology and Economics", in Sigmund Koch, ed., *Psychology: A Study of Science*, New York: McGraw-Hill Book Company, Inc., 1963.
13 Katona, George, *The Mass Consumption Society*, New York: McGraw-Hill Book Company, Inc., 1964.

14 Keynes, John Maynard, *The General Theory of Employment Interest and Money*, New York: Harcourt, Brace & Company, 1935.

15 King, Robert L., "The Marketing Concept", in G. Schwartz, ed., *Science in Marketing*, New York: John Wiley & Sons, Inc., 1965.

16 Kohler, Wolfgang, *Gestalt Psychology*, 2nd Ed., New York: Liveright Publishing Corporation, 1947.

17 Lewin, Kurt, *et al.*, "Level of Aspiration", in Joseph M. Hunt, ed., *Personality and the Behavior Disorders*, New York: Ronald Press Company, 1944.

18 Morgan, Clifford T., *Introduction to Psychology*, New York: McGraw-Hill Book Company, Inc., 1956.

19 Mueller, Eva, "The Desire for Innovation in Household Goods", in Lincoln H. Clark, ed., *Consumer Behavior*, New York: New York University Press, 1958.

20 Mueller, Eva, "Ten Years of Consumer Attitude Surveys: Their Forecasting Record", *Journal of the American Statistical Association*, 58 (Dec., 1963), 899-917.

21 Pearl, Robert B., *Methodology of Consumer Expenditures Surveys*, U. S. Bureau of the Census, Working Paper No. 27, Washington: U. S. Bureau of the Census, 1968.

22 Pratt, Jr., Robert W., "Consumer Behavior: Some Psychological Aspects", in George Schwartz, ed., *Science in Marketing*, New York: John Wiley & Sons, Inc., 1965.

23 Pratt, Jr., Robert W., "Using Research to Reduce Risk Associated With Marketing New Products", *Changing Marketing Systems*, Chicago: American Marketing Association, 1967, 98-104.

24 Schmiedeskamp, Jay, "People Are What Economics is All About", Unpublished paper presented in honor of Professor Colston E. Warne, Amherst College, May 10, 1969.

25 Sonquist, John A., and James N. Morgan, *The Detection of Interaction Effects: A Report of a Computer Program for the Selection of Optimal Combinations of Explanatory Variables*, Monograph 35, Ann Arbor: Survey Research Center, Institute for Social Research, The University of Michigan, 1964.

26 Smith, George H., *Motivation Research in Advertising and Marketing*, New York: McGraw-Hill Book Company, Inc., 1954.

27 Wertheimer, Max, *Productive Thinking*, New York: Harper & Bros., 1959.

28 Yankelovich, Daniel, "New Criteria for Market Segmentation", *Harvard Business Review*, (March-April, 1964) 83-90.

Level of Aspiration and Consumption Standard: Some General Findings

GUENTER SCHMÖELDERS AND BERND BIERVERT*

This contribution analyzes German data with respect to a problem which has occupied George Katona intensively: aspirations versus saturation in the affluent society. In particular, we shall investigate the relations between equipment level, the level of aspirations, consumption standards (these terms to be explained below), and such explanatory variables as income, age, and stage in the life-cycle. Since we were not interested in the analysis of consumer interest in any single product, the 29 durable items included in our surveys were divided into classes and assigned weights corresponding approximately to the average price of each item and reflecting the ratio of estimated value among the different groups of goods. We limited ourselves to a weight which expressed the ratio of values among goods. As the objective of our surveys was not the explanation of demand for single durables or groups of durables, the use of such indices appeared all the more justified.

The *equipment level* was defined as the sum of durables available in the household, weighted according to their estimated

* The authors are indebted to Miss Gisela Neuerburg for computer analysis of the data presented in this chapter. G. Neuerburg, *Determinanten des Konsumstandards, Kölner Diplomarbeit*, WS 1971/72.

value.[1] The *level of aspiration* was defined as the sum of weighted durables, the acquisition of which would realize the household's conception of an appropriate standard of living.[2] As the level of aspiration designates the gap between the actual level of consumption and the desired level of consumption, a household's *standard of consumption* was defined as the sum of its level of consumption plus its level of aspiration.

If the two components of the standard of consumption — the level of aspiration and the equipment level — are considered separately, the finding emerges that the latter is correlated to income while the former is not. Ownership of durable goods increases progressively up to 900 DM monthly income and then continues to increase, although at a decreasing rate (Table 1). By contrast, the level of aspiration responds little to variations in income. The aspirations of households with an income under 600 DM are below average; and although the level of aspiration does increase slightly within the next income group (700 DM), further increases in income do not result in further increases in aspirations. Indeed, in the highest income bracket, a remarkable drop in the level of aspiration may be noted.

The factor of saturation represents a major problem in determining the relationship between income and demand. This saturation is expressed by a relatively flat curve of needed goods which in the highest income bracket may even turn in a negative direction. The point of saturation is reached much sooner with respect to the requirements of subsistence than to luxuries. The flat curve of the level of aspiration, expressed by our data, and the negative ratio of increase of the level of aspiration over 1,500 DM income, point to tendencies which Morgan noted for the U. S. as early as 1958: Expenditure for "consumer investment goods" at that time — contrary to previous times and to conditions in other countries at the same time — could be represented by an Engel curve; this suggests that in the U.S. many durable goods had at that time already begun to be considered as necessities. Today, this explana-

---

[1] The question was: "Can you tell me from this list, which durables your household owns? " (For list of durables *see* Appendix.)

[2] For this purpose the question was: "In your opinion, which durables do you still need to be able to say: 'Now I have an appropriate standard of living'? "

Table 1

CONSUMPTION STANDARD AND INCOME (IN DM)[a]

Total net income of household (monthly)	N	Equipment Level[b]	Level of Aspiration[b]	Consumption Standard[b]
		a	b	a + b
0– 599	305	488	299	718
600– 699	201	594	301	896
700– 899	488	768	305	1073
900– 999	200	878	287	1166
1000–1499	267	1006	303	1309
1500 and more	133	1190	207	1397
All households	1594	785	279	1065

a   The data are taken from a survey directed by the *Forschungsstelle für empirische Sozialoekonomik*, Köln, 1969; they are based on a random sample representative of all households in the Federal Republic of Germany and West Berlin ($N = 1682$).

b   "Equipment level", "level of aspiration", and "consumption standard" show the averages of an index calculated from 29 durables presented to the interviewed households (*see* Appendix).

tion seems to be applicable to the Federal Republic of Germany: As incomes increase more and more, former luxuries are included into the purchase horizon of average households. At the same time the significance of these goods changes. They lose their character as "luxuries" accessible only to persons with higher incomes. These assumptions are supported by a general trend toward saturation observed by other authors [8].

In considering the relation between income and level of aspiration, we must not forget, however, that the level of aspiration was measured on the basis of a broad though limited choice of consumer goods. Inclusion of items representing a higher order of wants would probably weaken the negative tendency of the level of aspiration in the upper-income class. If new or additional goods or goals are offered to a household, it is possible to arouse new desires [6, p. 151].

215

Regarding the list of goods included in our study, our findings indicated that "rising" occupational status was linked to a rising equipment level (Table 2). An interesting comparison of workers on one hand, with employees, civil servants and professionals on the other hand, revealed that a larger percentage of the former than of the latter owned refrigerators, washing machines, television sets, radio-phonographs and freezers, and an equally large percentage of both the former and of the latter owned a car, although the workers' average income was lower. Nonmanual workers were found to prefer higher expenditures for furniture, typewriters, and similar objects.

Hamilton, using data from another study of the *Forschungsstelle für empirische Sozialoekonomik* (Research Center in Empirical Economics) [13] has pointed out that there are still significant differences between the consumption levels of manual and nonmanual occupational groups, and of the working class and middle class [5]. He found that the consumption patterns of the

Table 2.1

CONSUMPTION STANDARD (IN DM) AND OCCUPATIONAL GROUPS

Occupation of Head of Household[a]	Monthly Income (Average)	Equipment Level	Level of Aspiration	Consumption Standard	N
		a	b	a + b	
Group A	1399	1045	345	1400	240
Group B	1251	962	261	1224	194
Group C	976	861	335	1197	324
Group D_1	826	806	336	1142	382
Group D_2	732	677	346	1023	298

a   Group A : Professionals, upper management and civil servants.
     Group B : Self-employed, craftsmen.
     Group C : Medium and lower employees and civil servants.
     Group D_1: Skilled workers.
     Group D_2: Unskilled workers.

best-paid workers corresponded to those of lower-paid workers rather than to those of middle-class groups with the same income. To Hamilton, it is a "lack of incentives" on the part of the working class which determines the leveling of consumption patterns.

A comparison of the consumption standard of occupational groups indicated that workers did not differ significantly from persons belonging to other occupational groups with similar income (Table 2.2). The differences were far greater among income groups than among occupational groups. Hamilton's findings have obviously changed in the course of the last decade insofar as differences in consumption between manual and nonmanual occupations have become more equalized. As to the level of aspirations,

Table 2.2

CONSUMPTION STANDARD, OCCUPATIONAL GROUPS AND INCOME

Income up to 699 DM	N	Consumption Standard
Group A	23	937
Group B	25	1093
Group C	65	1090
Group D_1	96	948
Group D_2	39	953
Income 700–999 DM		
Group A	58	1202
Group B	94	1189
Group C	184	1192
Group D_1	254	1145
Group D_2	171	1147
Income 1000 DM and more		
Group A	148	1466
Group B	70	1339
Group C	63	1289
Group D_1	27	1345
Group D_2	65	1347

the two occupational groups do not differ significantly from each other. More and more households are looking for a "standard package" of goods; since wants can be "learned", they arise or are created among the working class in an affluent society by the influence of mass communication media and contacts with the middle class.

The differences in the ownership of consumer goods which, according to our study, may be traced to differences in education appear to be small and could also be due to influences of income (Table 3). An exception are the households with "Abitur" (high school graduates) and higher education with an income of less than 700 DM who are less well provided with consumer goods than those with less formal education; they have, however, very high levels of aspiration. Presumably this group is primarily made up of student families whose long-term income expectations are high and thus lead to a high level of aspiration. If one extends the level of aspiration from consumption aspirations for durable goods to the entire range of spending, it appears that individuals with a high school education report desires much more frequently (57 percent) than those with secondary school (41 percent) or elementary school education (with apprenticeship 35 percent, without apprenticeship 30 percent).

For all three status criteria (income, occupation, education) a

Table 3

CONSUMPTION STANDARD (IN DM) AND EDUCATION

Education	Monthly Income (net average)	Equipment Level	Level of Aspiration	Consumption Standard	N
		a	b	a + b	
Elementary school	651	606	261	868	450
Apprenticeship	886	813	288	1101	886
College	1149	914	266	1180	251
University	1618	1045	323	1368	94

similar tendency concerning the standard of consumption showed up at first glance: the higher the status of the group in each category, the higher the standard of consumption. However, since income obviously has a strong influence on the level of consumption, that one factor had to be eliminated before the effect of the other two factors could be seen. When that was done, it became clear that the level of consumption standard was primarily determined by income. This finding emphasizes the importance of the absolute level of income, if conceptions of an appropriate standard of living are to be transformed into actual consumption. The achieved equipment level showed substantial differences for each income class. Other studies in earlier years also failed to find any significant correlation of occupation and income to the frequency and size of demand for durable goods [9].

The equipment level of households was found to be influenced by the stage of the life-cycle. The introduction of the life-cycle concept into our studies of consumption and aspirations represents a transition from a static to a more dynamic approach. Though the data concerning the structure of a family are usually collected in cross-section studies, they may also be used in a longitudinal analysis so as to represent the behavior of the same group of households during the complete family life-cycle [14, p.2].

Influences of the life-cycle can be observed both in the areas of earning and of spending. For our purposes, we broke down the individual stages of life as follows:

1st phase: Young people, no children (average income of husband 837 DM; total family income 1137 DM).

2nd phase: Young family, children under 6 years (1034 DM/1111 DM).

3rd phase: Normal family, children over 6 years, living with their parents (1005 DM/1085 DM).

4th phase: Adult family, three adults and more (931 DM/1391 DM).

5th phase: Older people, one or two adults, no children at home, (699 DM/835 DM).

Changes in the life-cycle are reflected in the standard of consumption (Table 4).[3] A parallel development between equipment level and income within the different phases of the life-cycle can be stated very simply: The average income of the head of the household and the average level of ownership of durables are lower in the first and last phase than in the other phases; both reach their peak in the second phase. In most studies, differences in consumer behavior are traced to income rather than to life-cycle. Yet, if one breaks each stage of the life-cycle into three income classes, the relationship between equipment level and stage of life still holds: Young people and young families — regardless of income bracket — stand out as having a significantly higher level of

Table 4

CONSUMPTION STANDARD (IN DM) AND LIFE-CYCLE

Life-Cycle	Monthly Income (net average)	Equipment Level	Level of Aspiration	Consumption Standard	N
		a	b	a + b	
Young people	826	875	461	1336	93
Young family	1034	980	415	1395	288
Normal family	1005	865	322	1188	440
Adult family	931	835	241	1076	383
Older people	699	536	134	671	364

ownership. The same result is reached if we break down the households according to age groups (Table 5). Families whose head is under 34 years of age are, in all income brackets, significantly better equipped than older households. If one takes into account the size of the household, the households composed of three or four persons generally reach the highest level of ownership; in households of five persons and more the possession of durable goods decreases (Table 6) [3, p.80].

[3] Describing the changes in the standard of consumption during the life-cycle, the variables concerning age and size of the households are dealt with separately in order to be able to prove a possible specific influence of one of these factors on the levels of consumption and aspiration.

220

Table 5

CONSUMPTION STANDARD (IN DM) AND AGE

Age Head of Household	Monthly Income (net average)	Equipment Level	Level of Aspiration	Consumption Standard	N
		a	b	a + b	
34	951	918	440	1359	372
35—44	1004	873	336	1209	398
45—54	975	824	271	1096	355
55 years and more	743	610	137	747	555

Table 6

CONSUMPTION STANDARD (IN DM) AND SIZE OF HOUSE-HOLD

Size of Household	Monthly Income (net average)	Equipment Level	Level of Aspiration	Consumption Standard	N
		a	b	a + b	
1—2 persons	722	583	213	796	595
3—4 persons	998	909	323	1233	750
5 and more persons	1004	875	301	1177	326

Despite the above-average equipment of their households, young families are not at all satisfied with their situation. Their aspirations concerning standards of consumption far surpass those of older families; the levels of aspiration decline over the life-cycle. This result is again independent of income. Breaking down the households into groups according to the age of the husband emphasizes even more strongly the variations in the levels of aspiration. Within each income class there are significant differences between the several age groups: Households with heads under 34 years of age have the highest level of aspiration. Considering the size of the households those best equipped are those with the highest aspirations, thus, with the highest *standard* of consumption.

A decline in the household's equipment, which starts in the third phase of the life-cycle, is not completely overcome by the children's financial contribution in the fourth phase. Although the average income of the head of the household decreases, total income of the household reaches its highest level in this phase. Yet the contribution of working children to the household income seems not to be used for renewal or additions to the stock of consumer goods. People think rather of accumulating funds for the future households of their children, who will leave the parental household at the end of this phase. The desire to add to existing durable goods seems to be weak. The level of aspiration of the adult household falls under the overall average. A second indicator provided further evidence that these households were relatively more content: Only 32 percent of the households still had "unfulfilled wishes" in the fourth phase of life-cycle as compared to 45 percent in the third, 47 percent in the second, and 55 percent in the first phase.

Older households no longer think of an expansion of their stock of consumer goods but rather strive to maintain its level. Their equipment and their aspirations are rather low as compared to younger households. Schelsky has said that in the "area of consumption" the ideal of old age is an expansion of needs, although he goes on to admit that the old-age pension is a restrictive factor [12]. Our findings contradict the former notion: purchases of new products and additions to equipment require a dynamic attitude which weakens with growing age, especially since old-age pensions are indeed very restrictive.

The standard of consumption and its determining factors were ascertained through a cross-section analysis. Basically, we can therefore only indicate trends with regard to the behavior of younger, middle-aged, and older families. There is no proof that the pattern of behavior of the older group will repeat itself with those who are now young. One may rather assume that the level of aspiration of young households will never decrease to the level of today's pensioners. But neither can it be denied that there exists a group whose expansion of needs comes to a stop as a result of their age. In a certain measure, this conclusion retains its validity for every generation to come.

Our findings concerning the effects of age on consumption and aspirations run parallel to reports of the *Gesellschaft für Konsumforschung*, analyzing the demand structure for the years 1953 and 1962 [4]. In 1953, 81 percent, and in 1962, 69 percent of the households interviewed expressed intentions to buy; in the group of persons under 30 years of age, in 1953, 87 percent, and, in 1962, 77 percent had such intentions. The percentage decreased with increasing age. Among persons between 50 and 64 years of age in 1953, 81 percent and, in 1962, 64 percent still had intentions to buy; those over age 64, only 65 percent in 1953, and in 1962 49 percent had such intentions. These figures reveal not only distinct differences among the several groups at a certain period, but above all the extent of the changes that occurred between the two dates considered. Between 1953 and 1962, the average percentage of households with intentions to buy dropped by 12 percentage points. The reduction was most significant in groups which earlier contained a relatively small proportion of households willing to buy, and was smallest in those groups with the highest proportion of households willing to buy.

The rate of increase and decrease in equipment during different phases of the life-cycle, which was observed by us for all households, varies but little among the different status groups, although it does appear that the higher the occupational status the later in life does the household equipment level reach its peak. This is probably related to the growth of income; top income and highest equipment level are reached in the same phase.

The size of the household plays an important role in the determination of the equipment level in households. Households consisting of 3—4 persons have considerably larger equipment levels than 1 or 2 person households (Table 6). But it is not sufficient to know the size of a household to determine a household's equipment level: Younger households without children are better equipped with durables than older families whose children have already left. In this case, it is not the size of the household but rather the position in the life-cycle which results in a certain level

223

of consumption, in one case directed toward expansion, in the other case toward conservation.

Contrary to the conclusions which were reached by David [2], who found the household's size to play a greater role than the phase of the life-cycle in determining the level of equipment, in our analysis, the life-cycle was found to be the better explaining variable [10]. The size of the household is important only insofar as it determines the increasing and decreasing level within the cycle, but not the absolute equipment level. The factor of age also has less influence than the life-cycle on the level of consumption [10]. The size of the household contributes only little to the explanation of the level of aspiration, but the two factors, age and life-cycle, show a closer connection with the level of aspiration. Life-cycle is of eminent importance for the determination and

Table 7

CONSUMPTION STANDARD AND EXPECTATIONS REGARDING THE GENERAL ECONOMIC TREND[a]

Expectations	N	Equipment Level	Level of Aspiration	Consumption Standard
		a	b	a + b
Income up to 699 DM				
Better	73	605	341	947
Same	292	530	265	796
Worse	53	580	230	810
Income 700–999 DM				
Better	154	838	341	1179
Same	408	810	312	1122
Worse	55	746	204	951
Income 1000 DM and more				
Better	105	1137	281	1418
Same	235	1057	277	1334
Worse	32	988	269	1257

a   The question was: "Looking at the economic situation in the Federal Republic, will it be better, the same, or worse a year from now?"

explanation of the consumption standard, as it correlates positively — more than any other factor — with the equipment level as well as with the levels of aspiration. Among various attempts to prove that life-cycle determines economic behavior, only those were successful that did not eliminate income [15, p. 55], [6, p.125], [11, p.149]. Our results, however, show that, even after the elimination of income effects, the strong influence of the life-cycle still prevails. The different phases of the cycle should to an ever larger extent gain significance for the differentiation of the standard of consumption.

The influence of *attitudes* and *expectations* on short-run consumer behavior in West Germany can no longer be denied [1]. The influence on behavior is apparent whether the expectations relate to the households' own financial situation or to the general economic trend. Optimists have not only a higher equipment level but also show higher aspirations and thus a higher consumption standard then pessimistic or indifferent households, though the differences are not very great (Table 7). Our findings in this respect clearly confirm those of Katona and his colleagues [8].

A rather high percentage of households can usually be observed in surveys whose level of consumption seems to correspond to their idea of an appropriate standard of living. Asked about additional purchases of consumer goods, they do not report further wants, i.e., their level of aspiration drops to the value of zero. The following considerations come to mind:

- The theory of saturation, according to which the intensity of a want decreases with increasing satisfaction, maintains that the desire for further durable goods will continue to decrease as the equipment level continues to increase, until at the moment of absolute saturation, the consumer's felt needs have completely ceased to exist.[4]
- The theory of the level of aspirations, according to which aspirations depend on experiences of success or failure. In the area of consumption, success reveals itself in a high level, and failure in a low level of consumption — the level being judged according to earlier consumption levels, or according to levels achieved by other groups.

[4] This sentiment of saturation usually exists only temporarily: "But the feeling of saturation may be temporary, at least in the absence of repeated severe shock"[7, p.21].

In our studies, households which had levels of **aspiration** for equipment below the average, also had low levels of **achievement**. Thus, the hypothesis concerning levels of aspiration was confirmed:

Persons with low achievement and little success reduce their aspirations or suppress them completely; "saturation" in this case is the result of a high degree of resignation.

Levels of consumption are greatly influenced by success or failure in various spheres of life (income, education, occupation), as well as by personal characteristics regarding a person's dynamism required for implementing a high level of consumption.

APPENDIX

DURABLES SELECTED FOR THIS RESEARCH

Cars	Kitchen furniture
Furniture	Sun chairs
Color TV	Tape recorder
Washing-machine	Bookcase
Dishwasher	Electric stove or gas stove
Complete furniture for camping	Refrigerator
Carpet, carpet floor	Radio
Music cupboard	Radio for Car
TV — black-white	Grill
Stereo, HiFi	Silver cutlery
Deepfreezer	Typewriter
Camera (more than 150 DM)	Vacuum cleaner
Mangle	Bicycle
Couch	Tea-cart
Electric sewing machine	

REFERENCES

1 Biervert, B. and H.J. Niessen, "Consumer Attitudes and Purchase Plans — Consumer Surveys in The Federal Republic of Germany and Their Informational Value", Paper for the 10th CIRET conference, Brussels, 1971.
2 David, Martin H., *Family Composition and Consumption*, Amsterdam: North Holland Publishing Company, 1961, 52.

3 Ferber, Robert, "Factors Influencing Durable Goods Purchases", In L.H. Clark, ed., *Consumer Behavior*, 2, New York: New York University Press, 1955.

4 *Gesellschaft für Konsumforschung, Nürnberg: Die Bedarfsstruktur im Käufermarkt*, Nürnberg, 1953; *Die Bedarfsstruktur*, 1962, Nürnberg, 1962.

5 Hamilton, R.F., "Affluence and the Worker – The West German Case", *American Journal of Sociology*, 71 (1965/66), 144–52.

6 Hörning, K.H., *Ansätze zu einer Konsumsoziologie*, Freiburg, 1970.

7 Katona, George, "Consumer Behavior: Theory and Findings on Expectations and Aspirations", *American Economic Review*, 58, No. 2 (May, 1968), pp.19–30.

8 Katona, George, B. Strümpel, and E. Zahn, *Aspirations and Affluence: Comparative Studies in Western Europe and the United States*, New York: McGraw-Hill, 1971.

9 Klein, L.R., and J.B. Lansing, "Decisions to Purchase Consumer Durable Goods", *Journal of Marketing*, 206 (1955/56) 109–32.

10 Lansing, J.B., and L. Kish, "The Family Life Cycle as an Independent Variable", *American Sociological Review*, 22 (1957), 512–19.

11 Lydall, H., "Life Cycle in Income, Saving and Ownership", *Econometrica*, 23 (1955).

12 Schelsky, H., "Die Bedeutung des Berufes in der modernen Gesellschaft", *Unser Verhältnis zur Arbeit*, Stuttgart, 1960, B. 52.

13 Schmölders, Günter, *Der Umgang mit Geld im privaten Haushalt*, Berlin: Duncker und Humblot, 1969.

14 Schmucker, H., *Der Lebenszyklus in Erwerbstätigkeit, Einkommensbildung und Einkommensverwendung, Allgemeines Statistisches Archiv*, Nr. 40, 1956.

15 Schrader, A., *Die soziale Bedeutung des Besitzes in der modernen Konsumgesellschaft*, Köln/Opladen, 1966.

Consumption Aspiration as Economic Incentives in a Developing Country - Taiwan*

DEBORAH S. FREEDMAN

Most work on the psychological determinants of consumption has been limited to Western countries, with only a few such studies in developing countries [11], [12]. Even for developed countries, economic theory has only recently given recognition to the role that psychological factors play in economic decisions. A basic element in Keynesian economic theory is that consumption is a function of income. However, Professor Katona's work has shown that the relationship between income and consumption is affected by psychological factors. It is not sufficient for consumers to have the ability to buy; they also must be willing to make the purchases. His studies have shown that there is a large discretionary element in consumption purchases in Western countries, due to such factors as the large proportion of consumers with incomes above subsistence levels, the availability of credit and savings account balances, and the large part of consumption purchases devoted to durables [5]. In such situations, the decisions made by individuals about whether or not to buy will be influenced to a

* This project was financed by a grant from the Population Council. It also received some assistance from the Population Studies Center at the University of Michigan. Field work and coding were done by the Taiwan Provincial Institute of Family Planning, under the direction of Dr. Tom Sun, Director.

considerable extent by their attitudes and expectations. Studies of the psychological determinants of consumption behavior, under conditions where consumers have some latitude, have made important contributions to economic policy by providing more informed and accurate forecasts of the consumption component of aggregate demand.

Similar studies for developing countries become meaningful when enough economic development has been achieved so that a sizeable proportion of the population has incomes which allow some margin for discretionary spending. How high income levels must be to allow for more than bare subsistence is, of course, a relative matter. Even in India, for example, where incomes are very low, most of the poor exercise some discretion in consumption in that they manage to finance out of their meagre incomes relatively sizeable expenditures for ceremonials.

This study investigates the role which psychological factors play in determining consumption in one developing economy. It presents some findings on consumer aspirations for modern goods in Taiwan, which has experienced an unusually rapid rate of economic growth in the last decade. Income levels are still low in Taiwan; G.N.P. per capita in 1968 was only $265. But there has been a substantial improvement in living standards since 1951; real per capita income has doubled and there is no evidence of increased inequality in the distribution of incomes. The rapid growth in incomes has opened new options in consumption to most families in Taiwan.

We are interested in the attitudinal factors influencing the consumption of modern goods and services. Obviously, income is always a constraint to consumption, but, in itself, it is not sufficient to explain consumption decisions. Two other factors are involved − the potential consumer must want the new items enough to be interested in purchasing them, he must aspire to buy; and he must feel it is a good time to buy. This paper is concerned only with the former − the growth of aspirations.

The analysis is concerned only with aspirations for modern goods and services − modern consumer durables, more modern housing, and modern recreational services. Studies of aspirations in Western countries have concentrated on these same goods and services, identifying them as highly valued goals for improved living standards [7]. Such items are new and usually highly desired in developing countries. Purchases of such modern goods and services should be particularly influenced by economic attitudes and expectations. In the first place, since these items are fairly new, their purchase should not be governed by habit. Instead, a much more considered decision, weighing alternatives, must be made to purchase them, with the potential consumer's attitudes one important factor in the decision process. Secondly, the marginal utility of such goods and services should be considerably greater than that of more conventional goods and services. They are not basic necessities and are things which many persons do not yet own but which almost everyone would like to have. Psychological factors should be particularly important in determining aspirations for these modern goods and services.

We distinguish here between wants and aspirations. Wants are universal, and few persons have everything they desire. Our definition of aspirations is less inclusive. In the first place, aspirations must seem possible of attainment. Aspirations are reality-oriented; the horizons of most individuals have some relation to their levels of accomplishment. In addition, an aspiring individual must feel that the goods in question are worth the cost to him. In this study aspirations were ascertained by asking individuals which specific goods and services they hoped or planned to buy. Of course, such expressions may contain some element of self-delusion. Yet, the fact that such aspirations are not universally expressed and are at widely disparate levels for different goods and services makes them seem quite credible. Such survey data on expressed aspirations have proved extremely useful in understanding changes in consumer demand in the United States.

The first part of this analysis will investigate what kinds of socio-economic characteristics and attitudes are related to expressed aspirations for more modern goods and services. A second line of analysis will investigate the economic behavior, other than consumption, of families who express different aspirations. Is the desire to enjoy modern consumption associated with other forms of modern behavior? Do families with high aspirations plan rationally? Do they save more or less? Do other aspects of their economic behavior seem beneficial or detrimental to development efforts? Development economists frequently view consumption solely as a cost, to be kept to an irreducible minimum so as to maximize production of investment goods. They attach little weight to consumption goals as incentives for evoking from individuals a more sizeable and more rational economic effort. This is surprising, since one of the basic tenets of economic theory is the importance of incentives in motivating economic behavior. The author's previous study of consumers of modern durables in Taiwan found that individuals who had above-average holdings of modern durables also had above-average savings and used innovative business practices — behavior presumably favorable to development [3].

A priori, it seems likely that families with high consumption goals would exhibit modes of behavior which seem favorable to development. The desire for new goods should lead families to reassess their present consumption patterns more critically and to plan their budgets to facilitate the new purchases. It might encourage individuals to augment their incomes by doing additional work or by investing in their business or farm. It could even encourage long-range family planning to insure that family size does not conflict with desired living standards. Since any change from traditional ways involves difficult adjustments, families must be motivated to adopt new ways, and the desire for modern consumption could provide the motivation. No attempt will be made to establish a causal relationship between consumption goals and economic behavior. Instead, the investigation will center on whether aspiring families in Taiwan do in fact display distinctive economic behavior.

The first part describes the data and method of analysis. It describes in some detail the consumption variables used, including the index measures constructed to measure present consumption levels and consumer aspirations. Since many of the socio-economic characteristics which are related to consumption aspirations are inter-correlated, multiple classification analysis (MCA) is used to determine the relationship of each variable to aspirations after adjusting for the effects of the other variables. The second part will present the antecedents of high consumption aspirations. The third part will deal with economic behavior patterns associated with high aspirations.

This study is based on interviews in the summer of 1969 with a cross-section of 2300 Taiwanese husbands whose wives were in the child-bearing ages.[1] The survey had as its central purpose an analysis of the economic correlates of fertility behavior. Unlike most fertility surveys, it designated the husband as the respondent in an effort to increase the reliability of reporting on economic matters. In addition to collecting demographic data, questions were asked about economic attitudes, family income, savings behavior, present consumption, and aspirations for future consumption.

The survey collected information on three forms of modern consumption — ownership of modern consumer durables, use of modern recreational services, and the quality of housing. Questions also were asked about the respondent's plans or desires to increase his consumption of such goods and services.

The respondent was asked whether his family owned each of 15 modern consumer durables which are listed below, together with the frequency with which they were owned.

Modern Objects	Percentage of Families Owning
Clock or Watch	88
Bicycle	76
Electric Fan	74
Sewing Machine	67
Electric Rice Cooker	48
Radio	43
Radio-Record Player Combination	32
Gas Burner	24
Television	23
Motorcycle	21
Refrigerator	14
Camera	10
Record Player	6
Washing Machine	4
Air Conditioner	1

[1] It included only families where the wife was less than 42 years of age.

It is indicative of the popularity of modern durables that so many of these items are owned by a fairly large proportion of the families. Many of these items were not even on the market ten years ago and some, such as television, became available only within the past few years. These goods have become popular at a fairly early stage of economic development in Taiwan since the growth in income is very recent and income levels are still quite low. Of course, some of these durables are fairly inexpensive; an electric rice cooker costs about ten dollars. But even this is a sizeable expenditure relative to income levels, and many of the items which are owned by a sizeable minority — such as a motorcycle, refrigerator, or television set — cost at least $100–200. The survey families owned, on the average, 5.3 modern objects; 26 percent of the families owned 3 or less while 20 percent had 8 or more. The mean number of different items owned by a family is used as a measure of the consumption of modern durables.[2]

Consumption of modern recreational services was obtained by asking the respondents how often they attended movies in the last couple of years, how often they ate in restaurants during the past year, and whether, within the past five years, they had taken any pleasure trips which involved staying away from home overnight. Movies are the most popular recreation form, with much fewer reporting that they ate out or took a trip. Nine percent of the respondents went to the movies frequently, an additional 24 percent went with some regularity, and another 30 percent reported sporadic attendance. Eleven percent of the respondents had eaten out in a restaurant at least once during the preceding year, while 20 percent had taken at least one vacation trip during the preceding five years. An index measure was constructed for consumption of all recreational services, with different weights reflecting the frequency of participation.[3]

The information on housing quality consisted of the enumerator's reports about the type of neighborhood and the kind of construction materials utilized for both walls and floors and the

[2] Alternative weightings were considered, such as including duplicate items in the total count or using approximate values as weights. Each presented more difficulties than it solved, and the number of different items owned seemed the best measure of participation in modern durable consumption.

[3] For a more detailed description of the construction of these consumption measures, see [4].

respondent's reports on floor space, type of cooking fuel, and availability of modern plumbing facilities. Flooring materials ranged from fairly primitive mud floors (in 34 percent of the dwellings) to modern terrazzo floors (in 10 percent). Fifty-five percent of the respondents reported having a private toilet, 51 percent said they had running water inside their dwelling, and 26 percent said they used modern fuels — gas and electricity — for cooking. A scale of housing quality was constructed which allotted roughly equal weight to each housing characteristic on a low to high modernity continuum.

The survey asked several questions about the respondent's plans or desires to increase his consumption, both of modern durables and recreational services, and to improve his housing. Out of this information, a composite score was constructed to measure total consumption aspirations.

After the interviewer had listed the modern durables owned by the respondent, he questioned the respondent about his desire for additional objects as follows: "Are you hoping to buy some (more) of these objects in the future or would you say that they are not worth the cost to you?" If they hoped to buy some, they were asked which they thought they might buy some day. Forty-five percent of the families said they might buy at least one more object. Though all these families indicated they might buy more durables, some were more interested than others, and an attempt was made to measure the intensity of their interest by asking, "Are there any of these that you *plan* to buy in the next year or two?" Only two-fifths of those who thought they might buy some durables had plans to purchase any during the next year or two. Any respondent who said he might buy a modern durable was assigned some weight in the consumption aspirations index; those who reported plans to buy were considered more aspiring.

Each respondent was asked if he wanted increased use of modern recreational services and, if so, which ones he favored. More than half said that they did want more. More respondents mentioned pleasure trips than any other form of recreation. Eighty-four percent of those who wanted more recreation mentioned trips as a desired expenditure, and half mentioned trips exclusively. This gives some indication of the interest of families in Taiwan in expanding their horizons. This new consumption activity is very apparent in Taiwan; sight-seeing buses are a common sight.

235

very apparent in Taiwan; sight-seeing buses are a common sight.

Aspirations for improved housing were obtained by first asking if the respondent felt his housing was satisfactory; twenty-nine percent felt their housing was very satisfactory, while the remainder was either less satisfied or was dissatisfied with their current housing. Those who were not very satisfied were asked, "Do you plan to do something in the future to try to improve you housing?" Seventy percent said they had such plans, which, as they described them, varied from plans for explicit improvements to vague expressed hopes. Any respondent who mentioned a plan to improve his housing was considered to be aspiring, but those who mentioned plans for specific large-scale improvements were considered more aspiring than those who mentioned plans for minor repairs or had no specific plans.

The consumption aspiration index was constructed as follows:

Reply	*Points Assigned*
Respondent indicated he planned to improve his housing and mentioned specific plans for major changes	2
Respondent indicated he planned to improve his housing but is uncertain as to plans or mentions only minor changes	1
Respondent said he might buy a consumer durable, but had no specific plans to buy one in the next year of two	1
Respondent said he might buy a consumer durable and mentioned specific plans to buy one in the next year or two	2
Respondent said he wanted to use more of the modern recreational services	1

The possible scale scores ranged from 0, for those with no aspirations, to 5 for those with the highest aspirations. The mean score was 2.0 and the scores were distributed as follows:

Score	Percent of Families
0	19%
1	20
2	22
3	20
4–5	19
	100%

This composite aspiration index is used as a measure of aspirations throughout the analysis. A detailed analysis showed that the relationship of the independent variables to aspirations was similar whether the dependent variable was the total aspiration index or each of the separate components.[4] The use of the index measure gives a summary view of total consumption aspirations and simplifies the presentation of the findings. Only when we related present consumption levels of modern goods and services to aspirations did it seem important to relate present consumption of housing, durables, or services to aspirations for that particular item.

Other economic variables used in the analysis include the amount of savings the family had accumulated since marriage[5], whether consumption purposes were stressed as important reasons for saving[6], yearly income per adult household member[7], and the respondent's comparison of his present income with both past and expected future income. Income per adult appears to be a more meaningful measure than family income in a society where 43 percent of the surveyed couples live in some form of extended family.

[4] Although the direction of the relationship was the same, the relationship was stronger when the total aspiration index was the dependent variable.

[5] Respondents were asked first if they had accumulated savings in any form since marriage (a check list of seven possible savings media was used here), and if they responded positively, they were asked to compare the amount saved to two months, six months, or a year's income. This furnished a rough measure of the amount of savings; 38 percent of the sample had accumulated some savings.

[6] The respondent was asked whether he thought it was important to save. Seventy-eight percent of the sample agreed that it was important. Almost no one disputed the importance of saving, but a sizeable group, 19 percent, said they were unable to save. The group who felt saving was important was then questioned about their main purposes for saving and were grouped into those

The multivariate analysis of the data relies on multiple classification analysis (MCA) [1]. For each subclass of the independent predictor variables MCA provides (a) the mean of the dependent variable expressed as a deviation from the grand mean for the whole sample (the unadjusted deviations), and (b) the deviation of each subclass mean of the dependent variable, after the effect of other independent variables has been removed (the adjusted deviations). MCA also provides two other statistical measures: (a) a multiple correlation coefficient $-R^2$, and (b) a beta coefficient for each predictor variable, which gives some indication of the ranking of the independent variables in the order of the strength of their relationship.[8]

THE ANTECEDENTS OF CONSUMPTION ASPIRATIONS

What kinds of families want more modern goods and services? There should be considerable differences in how families perceive their needs for such items, since they are not basic necessities nor is their purchase dictated by tradition. How families perceive their needs is likely to depend both on their present socio-economic status and on their attitudes and expectations.

We start with a basic core of four demographic and socio-economic variables — income per adult, husband's education, wife's education, and wife's age — which seem relevant to con-

who stressed consumption purposes, those saying consumption purposes were less important, and those who mentioned only nonconsumption purposes for saving.

[7] A list was made of all the household members, separated into adults (15 and over) and children. If adults shared more than half their income with the group, they were considered to be members of one economic household.

[8] MCA is a special form of regression analysis — in which the explanatory variables represent membership in subclasses rather than numerical values. Its particular advantages are: (1) it can be used with independent variables which are unordered (use of family planning) or lack an interval scale (education, plans for children's education), and (2) it requires no assumption about the functional relationship of the dependent and independent variables. For example, using MCA we could see that aspirations are affected by whether a family has zero as against some positive savings but not by the amount of savings.

sumption aspirations. Then we add other economic variables in turn to see what additional effect they have in explaining aspirations. We would expect income levels to be positively related to consumption aspirations, since aspirations are usually influenced by one's ability to buy. Wife's age was included to explore possible generational effects. Education of husband and wife has proved to be a good measure of modernization; previous studies in Taiwan have shown education to be positively related to such variables as income, occupational status, family planning behavior, modern attitudes, and the consumption of modern durables [2].

Table 1

RELATIVE IMPORTANCE OF SOME MAJOR DETERMINANTS OF CONSUMPTION ASPIRATIONS (AS MEASURED BY BETA COEFFICIENTS OBTAINED IN *MCA* ANALYSIS)

	Beta coefficients derived from regressions						
	(1)	*(2)*	*(3)*	*(4)*	*(5)*	*(6)*	*(7)*
Husband's Education	.14	.13	.12	.12	.07	.11	.09
Wife's Education	.14	.13	.13	.13	.09	.10	.11
Age of Wife	.04	.04	.04	.04	.04	.03	.04
Income per Adult	.10	.08	.09	.07	.04	.07	.07
Past Income Change	†	.10	†	†	†	†	†
Expectation for Future Income Change	†	†	.17	†	†	†	†
Combined Past and Future Income Change	†	†	†	.16	†	†	†
Mass Media Exposure	†	†	†	†	.27	†	†
Ownership of Modern Durables	†	†	†	†	†	.09	†
Housing Quality	†	†	†	†	†	.14	†
Consumption of Services	†	†	†	†	†	.32	†
Educational Plans for Children and Knowledge of Costs	†	†	†	†	†	†	.20
R^2 (Adjusted)	.08	.09	.11	.12	.12	.16	.11

† Omitted from the regression

Table 1 shows the beta coefficients obtained when different groups of variables are used, in turn, to explain consumption aspirations. The four core variables (*see* Regression 1) explain only a small part − 8 percent − of the variance. Income is less important than either husband's or wife's education in explaining aspirations. Wife's age has a negligible effect.

Income per adult has a positive relationship to aspirations, but the relationship is not strong (*see* beta measure in Table 1). The adjusted deviations (*see* Table 2) show that income differentiates only the extreme categories.

Since aspirations are concerned with future purchases, the more relevant income variable may not be current income, but instead

Table 2

RELATION BETWEEN SOCIO-ECONOMIC CHARACTERISTICS AND ASPIRATIONS TO CONSUME (MEAN INDEX VALUE FOR CONSUMPTION ASPIRATIONS = 2.1)

	No. of Cases	Mean Index Score	Deviations from Sample Mean Score	
			Unadjusted	Adjusted
Income Per Adult[a]				
NT $ 6,000 or less per year	786	0.7	−.4	−.2[b]
NT $ 6,000−9,000 per year	422	2.0	0	0
NT $ 9,001−12,000 per year	312	2.2	.1	.1
NT $ 12,001−16,000 per year	281	2.4	.3	.1
NT $ 16,001−20,000 per year	166	2.4	.3	.1
NT $ 20,000 and over per year	209	2.6	.6	.3
Husband's Education				
Less primary graduate	475	1.5	−.6	−.4[b]
Primary graduate	1083	2.1	0	0
Attended Jr. or Sr. High	258	2.4	.3	.2
Senior High Grad. or more	327	2.6	.6	.2
Wife's Education				
No formal education	779	1.6	−.5	−.3[b]
Primary attended	208	2.1	0	.1
Primary graduate	896	2.3	.2	.1
More than primary grad.	260	2.6	.6	.2

	No. of Cases	Mean Index Score	Deviations from Sample Mean Score	
			Unadjusted	Adjusted
Expectation for Future Income Change				
Expect some Increase	421	2.7	.7	.5[b]
Expect no Change	503	1.9	−.2	−.2
Expect some Decrease	387	2.1	.1	.1
Uncertain	865	1.8	−.2	−.2
Comparison of Present Income with Income 5 years ago				
Better Now	446	2.5	.4	.3[b]
Same	940	1.9	−.1	−.1
Worse Now	781	2.0	−.1	0
Combined Past and Future Income Change Variable				
Cumulative Gains (++)	181	2.9	.8	.6[b]
Intermittent Gains (One Plus)	364	2.5	.4	.3
No Gains (No Plus)	764	1.9	−.1	−.1
Mass Media Exposure				
Least Exposure	714	1.4	−.6	−.5[b]
↑	591	2.0	0	0
↓	496	2.5	.4	.3
Most Exposure	371	2.8	.7	.6
Consumption of Services				
None	720	1.5	−.6	−.5[c]
↑	520	1.9	−.2	−.2
↓	560	2.4	.4	.3
Most	327	3.0	.9	.9
Housing Quality				
Lowest	509	1.8	−.3	.2[c]
↑	528	2.0	0	.2
↓	651	2.1	.1	−.1
Highest	439	2.2	.2	−.4
Ownership of Modern Objects				
1−3 Objects	569	1.8	−.2	.1[c]
4−5 Objects	626	1.8	−.3	−.1
6−7 Objects	501	2.4	.3	.1
8+ Objects	431	2.4	.3	−.1

Continued Table 2

	No. of Cases	Mean Index Score	Deviations from Sample Mean Score	
			Unadjusted	Adjusted
Education Aspirations and Knowledge of Costs				
No aspirations beyond junior high	416	1.4	−.7	−.5[b]
Expects high school: no knowledge of costs	209	1.7	−.4	−.3
Expects college: no knowledge of costs	902	2.1	.1	0
Expects high school: knows costs	79	2.3	.2	.3
Expects college: knows costs	569	2.6	.6	.4

a   One NT $ = 2.5 cents U.S.
b   Adjusted for wife's age, income per adult, wife's education, and husband's education.
c   Adjusted for wife's age, wife's education, husband's education, income per adult, consumption of services, ownership of modern objects, and housing quality.

some measure of permanent income which reflects long-term purchasing power. We do not have a direct measure of permanent income, but education may give some indication of its magnitude, since it is one of the most important avenues for increased incomes. Educated individuals may well expect that their life-time income will reflect their additional training and adjust their aspirations accordingly. The fact that education has a stronger relationship to aspirations than does current income (*see* beta measures in Table 1) suggests that permanent income might be more related to aspirations.

Though permanent or long-term income probably affects consumption aspirations more than current income, the actual long-term trend in an individual's income may have less influence on aspirations than does his perception of his financial position. Does he feel better off now than previously, and does he expect to do better in the future? There is always uncertainty about the future course of events, and individuals will differ in their outlook, partly because their prospects do differ, but also because some are more optimistic than others. Similarly, the appraisals that individuals make of their current financial situation relative to the past contain a large subjective element. An individual who is worried about his financial situation will be reluctant to buy, even though he may have the money, while one who sees his situation as increasingly prosperous is likely to plan for the new purchases he feels will then be possible.

The data show that in Taiwan the respondent's assessment of his financial situation does affect his aspirations; families who are optimistic have high consumption aspirations. The respondents were asked: (1) whether they felt they were better off now compared to five years ago, and (2) whether they expected to be better off five years hence. Despite the fact that average per capita incomes in Taiwan increased 25 percent during the five years prior to the survey, only 20 percent of the respondents reported being better off now; two-thirds blamed higher living costs for the lack of improvement. Families who felt their situation had improved were more aspiring (*see* adjusted deviations) though the differences are not large. There is a more pronounced positive effect on aspirations if a family is optimistic about its future income. (*See* beta measure and adjusted deviations in Tables 1 and 2.) When expectation for future income is added to the four core variables in Regression 3, it increases explained variance from .08 to .11. Families who feel they will be more successful in the future are interested in improving their standard of living.

The respondents who are most optimistic are those who report an improvement in their present situation and, in addition, expect further improvement in the future — a group Katona describes as having "cumulative gains". His work shows that in the United States this group is more likely to express buying intentions [6]. Instead of being satured by the higher consumption levels which their success had made possible, their acquisitions have served to arouse new wants. A similar analysis was done for Taiwan. In comparing his present financial situation with his past or expected future situation, a respondent could report a gain (+), a deterioration (−), or stability (=).[9] Thus a respondent who reported that he was better off now than in the past but expected to be worse off in the future, would be rated (+−). Those who reported (++) trends have "cumulative gains"; those who combine a (+), either past or future, with a (−) or (=) in the other direction, are considered to show "intermittent gains", while the remainder − some combination of (−) and (=) − showed "no gains". The multivariate analysis showed the group with "cumulative gains" to be most interested in additional modern comsumption, the group with "no gains" to be least interested, and those with "intermittent gains" to be intermediate in their aspirations. This is consistent with Katona's findings for the United States. In both Taiwan and the United States, couples who feel optimistic about their financial situation want to consume more modern goods and services.

Age has no effect on consumption aspirations in Taiwan. This contrasts with the situation in the United States and in Western Europe, where younger families are more likely to express buying intentions. One explanation for this difference may be that the recency of economic development in Taiwan has not afforded the older generation an appreciably longer period in which to acquire modern goods.

Education of both husband and wife shows a strong relationship to consumer aspirations. As mentioned previously, education usually increases an individual's expected long-term earning potential, and this is likely to increase his aspirations. But education also has a more direct effect on aspirations, since it is the most important force for bringing people into contact with new ideas and new ways of behavior. Education alters traditional patterns of behavior and opens up many new possibilities, including the availability of new types of goods and services. The adjusted deviations in Table 2 show that respondents who are less than primary school graduates are least aspiring; those with more than a primary certificate are most aspiring.

Mass media exposure is another measure of modernity which shows a strong relationship to aspirations. This variable measures the degree to which people are exposed to newspapers, magazines,

[9] Some respondents said they were uncertain about what their income would be five years later; they are not included in this analysis.

244

television, and radio. The mass media serve as an important avenue through which contact is made with a larger world, and thus act as a modernizing force. More specifically, exposure to mass media can affect aspiration levels in various ways; it can inform the individual about specific economic events which may affect him, it can make him aware of what is available on the market with respect to new goods and recreation services, and it exposes him to advertising.

After adjusting for the effects of income, education and age, mass media exposure has a regular sizeable relationship to aspirations. The addition of mass media exposure reduces the beta measure for education; evidently education influences aspirations partly via the mass media. When mass media is used together with education, income and age to explain aspirations, it adds 4 percent to the explained variance (*see* Regression 5). Modern families, whether the measure of modernity is education or exposure to mass media, do expect higher living standards, and specifically want more modern goods and services.

A family's aspirations for more modern goods and services should be influenced by the amount they are already consuming, but the relationship is somewhat equivocal. Aspirations are not static and the gratification of one's desires can lead, not to satisfaction, but to the development of new and different wants. In the United States, buyers of new appliances were found to be particularly frequent among owners of "traditional" appliances (cooking ranges, washing machines, etc.) [9]. An earlier study in Taiwan found that families who already had a relatively high number of modern objects were most likely to have purchased the newly available television sets and refrigerators [3]. Of course, this does not necessarily happen; the gratification of desires can lead instead to a feeling of saturation. Whether acquisitions result in saturation or instead beget more needs, depends, in great measure, on the consumer's attitudes and expectations. Insecurity and anxiety about the future may contribute to a feeling of saturation, while optimism will tend to raise the consumer's sights to new possibilities. For example, in Germany, where, despite continued prosperity, economic attitudes are less optimistic than in the United States, many families who have acquired a certain level of consumption say that "they have enough". Families in the United

States are more likely to adjust their goals upward with rising levels of living [7].

The level of aspirations for modern goods and services in Taiwan is affected by the quantity a family already enjoys. When the three consumption variables are used in addition to age, income and education, the explained variance increases from 0.08 to 0.16 (*see* Table 1, Regression 6). The total explained variance is not large but compares favorably with results in other socio-economic cross-section studies. When we look at the gross relationships, we find that aspiration levels are positively related to all kinds of modern consumption. The more a family enjoys of modern durables, good housing, or recreational services, the higher its aspiration levels.

Once an adjustment is made for the effect of income, age and education[10], however, the nature of the net relationship is quite different as among the three consumption variables. The present level of ownership of modern objects shows no net relationship to the aspiration index. Families who already own a large number of durables are just as aspiring as families with very few. A family's appetite for modern consumption apparently is neither satiated nor stimulated by past acquisition of modern durables. Families who own better housing, on the other hand, are considerably less likely to want additional modern consumption; the initial positive relationship becomes negative when an adjustment is made for age, income and education. The differences are not large, but families with the best housing are below average with regard to aspirations.

Consumption of recreational services has the strongest relationship to aspirations. The aspiration level of the families who consume the most recreational services is almost twice that of those with none, and this difference remains after adjusting for age, income and education.

Since a composite index was used for consumption aspirations, it was uncertain if the relationship found between achieved consumption and total aspirations would hold for each of the three components of the aspiration index, or whether they have differing relationships which partly offset each other when combined into a total index. Therefore, an *MCA* analysis was run in which

[10] The results are similar when the three consumption variables are also held constant.

246

each component of the aspiration index — aspirations to acquire durables, to improve housing, and to enjoy recreational services — was used in turn as the dependent variable together with income, age, education, and the three consumption measures as independent variables.

Ownership of modern objects which had no relation to the total aspiration index also had no relation to any of the individual aspiration variables. Housing quality, which was negatively related to total aspirations, is negatively related only to aspirations for more housing, but shows no relationship to aspirations for services or modern objects. Thus, the negative relationship between housing and total aspirations is due entirely to the negative relationship with aspirations for improved housing. Apparently, families in Taiwan who already have relatively good housing feel no need to upgrade their housing standard. An informal examination of the shops in Taiwan appears to support this; in contrast to the great variety of clothing and durables for sale, not many items are available for home beautification or improvement.

Consumption of services is positively related to aspirations for all three kinds of consumption, affirming the relationship found with total aspirations. It is easy to understand why such families would want more recreational services. A taste for modern recreation can be quickly acquired and, unlike durables, its enjoyment depends on continuous expenditures. But it is less easy to understand why these families are more likely to want all kinds of modern consumption. In a previous study, we found that exposure to mass media and education both were more strongly related to consumption of services than to other consumption measures [2]. It may be that high consumers of modern services are more assimilated into the modern sector and so more interested in modern consumption.

In sum, attitudinal factors are significantly related to aspirations for modern goods. Optimism is an important factor in explaining aspirations; actual income matters less than expectations for future income. The more a couple has been exposed to modern influences, as indicated by their education and exposure to mass media, the more likely they are to want more modern goods and services. Continuous changes in tastes affect the relationship between present consumption levels and aspirations, by deter-

247

mining the extent to which different items are perceived as needs. In Taiwan, achieved consumption levels have differential effects on aspirations. Once a family has an adequate house, it no longer yearns to improve it, so quality of housing is negatively related to housing aspirations. Present ownership levels of modern objects have no effect, either positive or negative, on the desire to acquire more. Where recreational services are concerned, however, there is a strong positive relationship between present use and aspirations; the more people have already obtained, the more they want.

ECONOMIC BEHAVIOR PATTERNS ASSOCIATED WITH HIGH
ASPIRATIONS

We now ask whether high levels of consumption aspirations are associated with particular kinds of economic behavior which could be beneficial or detrimental to Taiwan's development effort. Aspirations for modern goods and services can have an impact on many aspects of family behavior. They could have a negative influence on saving patterns by increasing consumption propensities. It is also possible that couples with a strong desire for a better standard of living would be less willing to expend funds for their children's education. To the extent these patterns prevail, consumption aspirations could have a negative effect on economic development. Conversely, there are ways in which consumption aspirations might be likely to have a favorable impact on development. Consumption aspirations could motivate couples to plan and budget more carefully so as to allow more leeway for modern consumption. This would necessitate a realistic analysis of present spending patterns. The desire for more consumption could also lead to more work effort. Ruth Mack presents convincing arguments that in the United States consumption aspirations have influenced income by motivating individuals to work harder [8]. Consumption aspirations could also affect long-range family plans by motivating families to raise their living standards by having fewer children. A finding that high consumption aspirations are associated with patterns of economic behavior which seem favorable to development would not prove that aspirations promote development, but it would at least show that such aspirations certainly are not incompatible with economic development, and, instead, are likely to be a positive influence.

The data show that consumption aspirations do not have a negative impact on saving behavior in Taiwan. Thirty-nine percent of the interviewed couples said that they had accumulated some savings since they were married, and couples who want more modern goods and services are more likely to have savings than non-aspiring couples (*see* unadjusted deviations in Table 3). When a multivariate analysis was used to explain savings behavior, adjusting for the effects of income, education and age, 30 percent of the non-aspiring couples had savings as against 49 percent of the most aspiring couples. This is a substantial difference, and the adjusted deviations show the relationship to be monotonic — the higher the aspiration score, the higher is the percentage who save.

Undoubtedly, some of these savings are earmarked for later consumption; couples who want more modern goods and services are likely to save so that they can buy. But, the savings of high aspirers are not oriented mainly towards consumption. The respondents were asked what they regarded as the main purposes for saving.[11] The largest proportion — 40 percent — singled out the education of their children as the most important purpose for saving, but many other purposes also were mentioned. Thirteen percent mentioned emergencies or old age, and 11 percent mentioned investing in a business; only 7 percent mentioned the purchase of large consumer items, while 10 percent mentioned housing improvements. When the respondent was asked to check which of a list of possible reasons for saving he considered very important, an additional 40 percent checked housing, and 10 percent checked consumer purchases, while an additional 63 percent checked emergencies or old age, and 35 percent checked the children's education. Obviously, the accumulation of reserve funds is highly regarded, but mostly for long-range goals rather

[11] Each respondent was asked if he felt it was desirable to save. Almost no one said it was not desirable, but twenty percent said they were unable to save. All those who felt saving was desirable were asked, "what are your main purposes for saving"? and up to two purposes were recorded. They were then shown a list of ten possible reasons for saving and asked to check whether they regarded each reason as very important, less important, or not important at all.

Table 3

RELATION BETWEEN CONSUMPTION ASPIRATIONS AND THE PERCENTAGE OF FAMILIES WHO HAVE ACCUMULATED SAVINGS (MEAN PERCENTAGE WHO SAVE = 38%)

Consumption Aspirations	Number of Cases	Mean Percentage Who Save	Deviations from Mean	
			Unadjusted	Adjusted*
Lowest	402	21	− 17%	−9%
↑	423	27	− 11	−6
	465	37	− 1	−1
↓	438	48	10	5
Highest	410	56	18	10

*   Adjusted for income per adult, husband's education, wife's education, and wife's age.

than immediate consumption. Many of the respondents may at various periods save so that they can buy some desired item, but once this goal is achieved, they continue to save for other purposes.

Additional evidence for this is provided by the saving behavior of families who have already achieved a high level of modern consumption. After controlling for income, education and age, couples who have better housing, or more modern objects, or make more use of modern recreational services, are all more likely to have accumulated savings than are couples who consume less. It is quite possible that some of these purchases were made with savings accumulated for that purpose, but the saving habit seems to have persisted after the purchases were made. Certainly at the time of the survey these couples had managed simultaneously to achieve high levels of modern consumption and to accumulate reserve funds.

The data show a behavioral pattern which seems favorable to development; families are more likely to save if they want modern goods and services, and their savings are accumulated mainly for purposes other than consumption.

Aspirations for modern consumption also could have an impact on economic development by motivating families to plan and budget more carefully. Though no direct evaluation can be made of budget practices, we do have a measure of how aware the respondent is of the costs of one large item in the family budget, namely the expense involved in raising children. An index measure was constructed to measure how aware the respondent was of the financial burden of children.[12] The extent to which a family is aware of the opportunity cost of additional children should depend in part on the importance placed on alternative uses of income. This appears to be the case in Taiwan. When the financial burden of children index is used as the dependent variable in a multivariate analysis, consumption aspirations proved to be one of its most important determinants.[13] The higher a couple's aspirations for modern consumption, the more aware it is of the cost of raising children. The adjusted deviations in Table 4 show that consumption aspirations have a consistent relationship of some magnitude to awareness of the financial burden of children, even after adjusting for education and income.[14]

Although aspiring families are quite aware of the costs of children, this does not indicate any intention to enjoy consumption by denying educational opportunities to their children. Taiwan fathers express very ambitious education plans for their sons; 67 percent expect to send their sons to college[15], and the higher a respondent's consumption aspirations, the more likely he is to express college expectations. Of course, some of these education plans may be unrealistic, since 64 percent of the respondents indicated they had no idea what it would cost to send their sons to college. But parents with high education aspirations, who are knowledgeable about the costs involved, express higher consumption aspirations than do parents who have the same educational

[12] The respondents were asked a number of questions about the advantages and disadvantages of small versus large families, about what accounted for their present economic position (relative to 5 years previous), and whether they had plans for their children's education, etc. For a more detailed description of the index, see [10].

[13] Only husband's education showed a stronger relationship.

[14] Specifically, this regression held constant husband's education, wife's education, income per adult, number of living children, and husband's employment status. See [10].

[15] An additional 13 percent expect to send their sons to high school. Taiwan fathers also have high educational aspirations for their daughters: 48 percent expect to send them to college.

Table 4

RELATIONSHIP BETWEEN CONSUMPTION ASPIRATIONS AND
INDEX SCORE FOR THE FINANCIAL BURDEN OF CHILDREN
(MEAN INDEX SCORE FOR FINANCIAL BURDEN OF CHIL-
DREN = 2.4)

Consumption Aspirations Index	Number of Cases	Mean Index Score	Deviations from Mean	
			Unadjusted	Adjusted*
Lowest	390	2.0	−.4%	−.3%
↑	420	2.2	−.2	−.1
	455	2.5	.1	.1
↓	438	2.5	.1	.1
Highest	405	2.8	.4	.3

*   Adjusted for husband's education, wife's education, income per adult, number of living children, and husband's employment status.

goals but are ignorant of the costs. A variable was constructed which combined the husband's educational expectations for his sons and his knowledge of the costs involved (*see* Table 2). After adjusting for the effects of income, education and age, families who combine high education aspirations and an awareness of the costs involved have high consumption aspirations. Those unaware of the costs of education express low consumption aspirations, and, within this group, consumption aspirations are positively related to the level of educational aspirations. High consumption aspirations are not held at the expense of educational aspirations; they are characteristic of couples who want to give their children a good education, even though they have some knowledge of the costs involved.

The desire for modern goods and services, insofar as they make couples more aware of the cost of children, may contribute to more rational budget decisions. The desire for a better standard of living also can affect longer range plans. Most developing countries, including Taiwan, regard their current rates of population growth as harmful to economic growth. Consumption aspiration can be a positive factor in the development effort, if they motivate couples to adopt family planning to limit family size.

Table 5

RELATIONSHIP BETWEEN CONSUMPTION ASPIRATIONS AND
THE PERCENTAGE OF COUPLES CURRENTLY USING CONTRA-
CEPTION, FOR WIVES 30 YEARS OR OLDER (MEAN PERCEN-
TAGE CURRENTLY USING CONTRACEPTION = 55%)

Consumption Aspirations Index	Number of Cases	Mean Percentage Using Contraception	Deviation from Mean Unadjusted	Adjusted*
Lowest	115	40	−14%	−10%
↑	127	53	− 1	1
	172	55	1	1
↓	149	61	6	4
Highest	138	64	9	6

* Adjusted for age of wife, wife's education, husband's education, and income per adult.

An analysis of the determinants of fertility behavior shows that consumption aspirations have a strong relationship to contraceptive use. Since contraception is used in Taiwan mainly to limit family size (and relatively little for spacing), its use is most prevalent among older wives who have already achieved their desired number of children. When a multivariate analysis is made of the use of contraception, consumption aspirations prove to be an important determinant for wives 30 years and older (*see* Table 5).

In that age group, after adjusting for the effects of income, education and age, couples who have high aspirations for modern consumption are 36 percent more likely to use contraception than the lowest aspiring group; this is a considerable difference. These older families apparently are aware of the trade-off between additional children and a higher standard of living, and plan rationally to reconcile their life plans.

Consumption aspirations also were one of the few economic variables which showed any relationship to contraceptive use or ideal family size for younger women.[16] Two of the most difficult problems faced by Taiwan's family planning program are how to

[16] Statements about ideal family size are less meaningful for older women since many are reluctant to express an ideal below their actual parity.

interest younger women in using contraception, and how to motivate families to want fewer children. Most couples want three or four children (Mean Ideal size = 3.8 children); this is not consistent with Taiwan's population goals. Consumption aspirations affect both contraceptive use and ideal family size for the younger couples. Younger couples with high aspirations are more likely to practice contraception and to want fewer children than are less aspiring couples, after adjusting for the effects of income, education and age. The differences are modest — a range of 10 percentage points for contraceptive use and .5 of a child for ideal family size between the highest and lowest aspiring group — but they suggest that younger families also are not unaware of the opportunity costs of children.

The desire to consume more modern goods and services should encourage families to add to their incomes by doing additional work. It was impossible, within the time constraint of the questionnaire, to include enough questions on the amount of work effort expended to explore this problem fully. However, the survey did collect data on the working status of wives and on whether the respondent or his wife held an extra job.

Wives are more likely to work if they help in a family enterprise; 78 percent of the wives of farmers were employed as against 41 percent for wives of businessmen, and only 30 percent for wives of wage and salaried workers. A separate analysis was made of the determinants of wife's employment status for each of these employment groups, using as independent variables wife's education, wife's age, income[17], area of residence, age of youngest child, and type of family.

Consumption aspirations have no relationship to the working status of wives for either businessmen or farmers, perhaps because their decision to work depends on the needs of the family enterprise. But if the husband is a wage and salaried worker (a modern employment relationship which is increasingly prevalent), consumption aspirations are positively related to wife's employment status. For these couples, the adjusted deviations (*see* Table 6) show a net difference of some magnitude in the percentage of

[17] The analysis of farmers and business owners is handicapped by the fact that husband's income (as distinct from family income) was only available for wage and salaried workers.

Table 6

THE RELATION OF CONSUMPTION ASPIRATIONS TO THE
PERCENTAGE OF WIVES EMPLOYED, FOR WAGE AND SALA-
RIED WORKERS (MEAN PERCENTAGE OF WIVES EMPLOYED,
FOR WAGE AND SALARIED WORKERS = 30%)

Consumption Aspiration Index	Number of Cases	Mean Percentage of Wives Employed	Deviation from Mean Unadjusted	Adjusted*
Lowest	204	25	− 5%	−5%
↑	173	27	− 2	−1
	230	28	− 1	0
↓	218	33	4	3
Highest	230	33	4	3

* Adjusted for wife's education, wife's age, husband's income, area of
residence, age of youngest child, and type of family.

working wives as between the groups with the highest and lowest
consumption aspirations; the percentage of wives working in the
highest aspiring group is about one-third larger than for the group
with the lowest aspirations.

An analysis was also made of what determined whether either
the husband or wife[18] held an extra job. Twenty-four percent of
the couples had an extra job, with the respondent's employment
status being by far the most important determining factor. Fifty-
one percent of the farm couples reported an extra job, as against
15 percent for wage and salaried workers, and only 8 percent for
businessmen. The gross relationship between consumption aspirations and the percentage having an extra job is not meaningful.
But after controlling for employment status, education, income
and age, the adjusted deviations show a regular and positive,
though modest, relationship between aspirations for modern consumption and having an extra job (see Table 7).

Though the data are somewhat meagre, they indicate that

[18] In almost all cases, it was the husband who held the extra job, but occasionally he reported that his wife had an extra job. All couples in which either
the husband or wife had an extra job are included in the analysis.

Table 7

THE RELATION OF CONSUMPTION ASPIRATIONS TO THE
PERCENTAGE OF COUPLES WHO HAVE AN EXTRA JOB
(MEAN PERCENTAGE OF COUPLES WHO HAVE AN EXTRA
JOB = 24%)

Consumption Aspiration Index	Number of Cases	Mean Percentage having an Extra Job	Deviations from Mean	
			Unadjusted	Adjusted*
Lowest	408	24	−1%	−3%
↑	426	27	2	−2
	463	25	0	0
↓	437	25	1	2
Highest	410	21	3	3

*   Adjusted for income per adult, husband's education, wife's education, wife's age, and husband's employment status.

couples with high consumption aspirations do expend some additional work effort via an extra job or employment of the wife.

CONCLUSIONS

This study has shown that economic attitudes play an important role in determining aspirations for modern goods and services in Taiwan. The data also show that couples with high consumption aspirations display other modern economic behavior. It is a reasonable inference from these data that aspirations appear to be a positive force in Taiwan's development effort.

Even though income levels are much lower in Taiwan than in the United States or Western Europe, Taiwan couples do manage to buy modern goods and services and are interested in increasing such consumption. Just as in Western countries, economic attitudes and expectations play an important role in determining consumption aspirations in Taiwan. The data show that an individual's perception of his long-range financial situation has more impact on aspirations than does his current income. Couples who are more in touch with modern influences, via education or the mass media, are more interested in modern consumption. Tastes for modern goods and services are not easily satiated in Taiwan; the more modern recreation a family enjoys, the more it wants, and only in the case of housing does acquisition lead to a feeling of saturation.

It is likely that discretionary consumption — for such items as modern goods and services — will become increasingly important in Taiwan. For example, both education levels and exposure to mass media are rising as well as income, and it is precisely the families who are educated and use mass media who were shown to want more modern consumption. As economic growth continues, consumption demand should be increasingly affected by economic attitudes. The survey findings on the nature of these relationships should contribute to economic analysis and decison-making. They also suggest the desirability of additional studies, since these relationships may change over time.

The findings support the view that consumption aspirations are likely to have a positive impact on economic development. High consumption aspirations do not have an adverse effect on either the accumulation of savings or educational aspirations. Couples who want modern goods and services are more likely to have savings than are less-aspiring couples, and these savings, for the most part, are accumulated for purposes other than consumption. The growth in private savings in Taiwan substantiates this relationship. The volume of private savings has increased tenfold between 1959 and 1967; this has occurred at the same time as the boom in consumption of modern durables. Couples who want modern consumption have no intention of improving their living standard by sacrificing their children's future; instead, they express high ambitions for their children's education.

The desire for modern goods and services does seem to motivate couples towards behavioral patterns which could facilitate such consumption. Their ability to plan is undoubtedly enhanced by the fact that they are more realistic than less aspiring couples about the cost of raising a family, and more aware of the costs of education. The desire for a higher standard of living seems to increase their awareness of the opportunity cost of children. Not only are they cognizant of the trade-off, but they take positive action to keep their family size to the desired level. Families who want modern consumption use family planning to avoid unwanted

257

children and, to a lesser degree, indicate they want smaller families. Couples who want modern goods and services are industrious. The data suggest that the wives of wage and salary earners (the modern and rapidly growing segment of the labor force) are more likely to be in the labor force if the couple has a high level of wants. The data also show a high incidence of extra jobs among aspiring couples.

All these relationships suggest that families with high consumption aspirations will take some positive action to satisfy them. In each case, these new modes of behavior are favorable to the development effort. The kind of individuals who are most able to contribute to development — those who are better educated and more modern — are more aspiring. At the same time, aspiration levels seem to evoke patterns of behavior which contribute to development. Aspirations can exist only if there is some possibility of attainment. This suggests that a development plan which promotes investment by restricting the availability of consumption goods to the bare minimum may entail some negative implications for development.

REFERENCES

1 Andrews, Frank, James N. Morgan and John Sonquist, *Multiple Classification Analysis*, Ann Arbor: Survey Research Center, University of Michigan, 1967.
2 Freedman, Deborah S., "The Role of Consumption of Modern Durables in a Developing Economy: The Case of Taiwan", Ph.D Dissertation, University of Michigan, 1967.
3 Freedman, Deborah S., "The Role of the Consumption of Modern Durables in Economic Development", *Economic Development and Cultural Change*, 19, No. 1 (Oct., 1970).
4 Freedman, Deborah S., "The Relationship of Fertility Behavior to the Consumption of Modern Goods and Services in Taiwan". Unpublished paper.
5 Katona, George, *The Powerful Consumer*, New York: McGraw-Hill Book Co., 1960.
6 Katona, George, "Consumer Behavior: Theory and Findings on Expectations and Aspirations", *American Economic Review*, Papers and Proceedings of the 80th Annual Meeting of the American Economic Association, Washington, D.C., Dec. 28–30, 1967.

7 Katona, George, B. Strumpel and E. Zahn, *Aspirations and Affluence, Comparative Studies in the United States and Western Europe*, McGraw-Hill Book Co., 1971, 62.

8 Mack, Ruth, "Trends in American Consumption and the Aspiration to Consume", *American Economic Review*, Papers and Proceedings, 46 (1956), 55–69.

9 Mueller, Eva, "The Desire for Innovations in Household Goods", In L.H. Clark, ed., *Consumer Behavior*, III, New York: Harper & Brothers, 1958, 13–37.

10 Mueller, Eva, "Economic Motives for Family Limitation". Unpublished paper, University of Michigan, 1971.

11 Strumpel, Burkhard, "Consumption Aspirations: Incentives for Economic Change", *Social and Economic Studies*, Institute of Social and Economic Research, University of the West Indies, 14, No. 2 (1965), 183–93.

12 Strumpel, Burkhard, "Preparedness for Change in a Peasant Society". *Economic Development and Cultural Change*, University of Chicago, 13, No. 1 (1965), 203–16.

The Social Setting of Consumer Behavior in Latin America

ALBERT LAUTERBACH

INTRODUCTION

This paper is concerned with the social environment in which consumer actions in Latin American societies are typically embedded. Of necessity the investigation will be essentially of a non-quantitative nature. Systematic data from survey research and similar sources are mostly nonexistent or, at best, confined to one big city area such as Santiago. Those household surveys that have been undertaken in Latin American countries have concentrated almost entirely on factual data of income and consumption; questions and analysis of an attitudinal or motivational character have been quite rare.

Most writers in this field, it is true, have pointed out the low consumption level of the masses. But this situation has invariably been seen in historical or institutional terms such as the low income of most people and the profit orientation of consumer-goods production. This is the approach, for example, of one of the earliest elaborate works on the subject, by Poblete-Troncoso [11]. In his 428-page investigation of the underconsumption of food, clothing, and housing in South America hardly any thought is given to consumer preferences and behavior patterns; stimulation of consumption can be achieved only through an appropriate income policy. Only once [11, p.413] does he mention, among the *social* measures that could be taken, "raising the workers' way of life (*cultura*), on the economic level, with a view to better utilization of the wages and elimination of useless and damaging expenditures."

One needs to realize, of course, that this was written at a time when discretionary income was all but nonexistent for the overwhelming majority of Latin Americans. To some extent, but a diminishing one, this is still true for sizeable groups of the Latin American population. This, however, is a logical place to present, with more then the standard emphasis, the usual warning against excessive generalizations with regard to Latin America. Not only are there enormous differences in incomes and consumption habits among countries, but even more striking differences exist between the residential sections and the shanty towns of Lima or Caracas, between the middle class of São Paulo and the peasants in the periodically drought-ridden Northeast of Brazil, and quite frequently between the luxury of a palatial home and the subhuman living conditions of its next-door neighbors in many a city.

This paper is essentially distilled from scattered empirical evidence available, especially in Chile, and from personal observations over some fifteen years. It will begin with a brief account of structural aspects of Latin American societies, then continue with a discussion of "dualistic" society and its consumption patterns under Latin American conditions. This will be followed by an examination of the urbanization process in its effect on consumption habits, of the demonstration effect of industrialized societies on changing consumption patterns in Latin America, and of some specific influences on these patterns such as prolonged inflation. The concluding section will evaluate the impact on consumption patterns of the recent striving in Latin America for greater social consumption, of a new nationalism, and of revolutionary changes in society.

SOME STRUCTURAL ASPECTS OF LATIN AMERICAN SOCIETIES

Historically, all the Latin American societies have been based on *agriculture*. To some extent this is still true today but in an ever diminishing degree. The reduction of the agricultural basis applies not only to the shrinking relative (and in some cases, absolute) importance of agricultural production compared with the growing share in GNP of manufacturing and the services, but also to the proportion of the total population which lives on agriculture or inhabits rural areas. Industrialization was originally based in many areas on agricultural products but it is gradually becoming more diversified. Even more important, the semi-feudal legacy of Latin American agriculture, which has greatly influenced the relations and mutual attitudes of owners, managers, and workers in incipient industries, is now on its way out in substantial parts of South America and the Caribbean, although it remains strong in Central America.

The Indian, African and Ibero-European heritages, in a great variety of mixtures, have been basic factors in shaping the Latin American way of life and consumption patterns. The Indian element is especially influential in Peru, Ecuador, Bolivia, and Guatemala; the African element in the Atlantic and Caribbean areas; the Ibero-European element largely in the upper and middle classes of many countries. It should not be thought, however, that the way of life and consumption pattern necessarily follow skin color. The term "Indian", in particular, has largely a socio-economic and cultural, not merely an ethnic connotation in Latin America. The Indians in this sense, like some other socio-economic groups, live outside the national markets and, as a rule, do not speak the "national" language.

A related long-range and, in a sense, structural feature of Latin American societies which has greatly influenced their consumption patterns has been rooted in the far-reaching *foreign impact* on their economic life. Although this impact has been emphasized (and often exaggerated) in recent years in various theories of the economic dependence of Latin America, there is an important nucleus of truth. It ranges from colonial exploitation to later patterns of foreign investment largely in primary products. It is seen in the semi-feudal legacy of colonialism with corresponding limitations of the home market, concentration of exports on one raw material, in the demonstration effects of foreign consumption patterns and in the more recent attempts to counteract this legacy from the past, partly by import substitution and partly by inter-American or subregional (e.g., Andean and Central American) integration of markets and eventually of investment and manufacturing. It is especially the export dependence of Cuba on sugar, Ecuador on bananas, Chile on copper, Brazil and Colombia on coffee, and so forth, which has encouraged in recent years a strong reaction, sometimes of a revolutionary character, against the perceived dependence of Latin American production, consumption, and way of life rooted in emulation of the industrialized countries. In fact an attitude, especially among students and professionals, favoring social radicalism and rapid change in society — including basic changes in public administration making it better equipped for socio-economic development — has come to be a quasi-structural characteristic of Latin America in our period. It has begun to modify profoundly the social setting of consumer behavior there.

The family, however, remains for the time being the decisive unit in Latin America's social, economic, and political life. In the upper and middle strata, business activity or land ownership is typically considered one important expression of a family's striving for social status. But this meaning of the family usually does not apply to the low-income, low-status groups, especially those of a "marginal" character. In these latter groups the family without a male household head (or with one which it shares with one or two other families) is a frequent occurrence. The role of women as heads of many families and as their principal or only provider, shapes the consumption pattern of these often large families.

The short-range view which has traditionally dominated business actions as well as consumer decisions, has partly reflected low economic levels with the corresponding lack of financial reserves; and partly it has resulted from the prevailing cultural patterns. The hand-to-mouth way of life is still perceived by many as the only possible one, at least under the unstable conditions in which they and their groups or country have always lived.

Casual work habits are widespread among workers and management alike, although they coexist with backbreaking, long working days of peasants and housewives whenever there is no alternative. Consumer aspirations are on the rise, but their fulfillment is not necessarily associated with systematic work performance or with a hurried way of life. At the same time, Latin Americans are capable of peak performance when sufficiently stimulated by social or group aspirations, especially when these are combined with pecuniary incentives.

However, the striking inequality of income distribution imposes a severe limit on both work performance and consumer desires. The differences among countries in per capita GNP levels are very large, with Argentina and Venezuela having the highest levels (close to or above $900 in 1968) and Bolivia and Paraguay the lowest levels (less than $300 per capita) among the South American countries. Within each country there also exists a glaring inequality in income distribution, as shown in Tables 1 and 2.

Table 1

INCOME DISTRIBUTION IN LATIN AMERICA

Income Groups	% of total income	Average income (regional average = 100)	Average income per capita[a] (dollars)
20% poorest	3.1	15.5	60
30% below median	10.3	34.0	130
30% above median	24.1	80.0	310
15% below highest 5%	29.2	194.0	750
5% highest	33.4	680.0	2,600

a   These figures refer to 1965, but are expressed in terms of 1960 dollars.
     SOURCE: ECLA, "Estudio Económico de América Latina, 1969", part III.

The population of Latin America is much farther from representing a fairly homogeneous body of consumers than is the population of the United States or the Scandinavian countries, for example. It has, of course, been argued by many that low income levels of the majority of the population and also an inequality of income distribution often accompany low productivity. The latter is indeed a characteristic of all the Latin American economies in varying degrees, although there is a fairly widespread trend toward higher productivity levels. However, gains in productivity, in-

Table 2

PERCENT COMPOSITION OF THE PRINCIPAL INCOME GROUPS,
BY COUNTRY

Country	20% poorest	30% below median	30% above median	15% below 5% highest	5% highest
Argentina and Uruguay	–	3.9	12.9	36.6	23.6
Brasil	49.6	40.8	35.5	11.8	20.0
Colombia	3.9	13.0	7.8	2.6	7.8
Chile	–	2.6	5.2	7.9	7.8
Mexico	9.1	18.1	20.1	26.1	18.0
Peru	2.5	5.8	5.2	4.6	5.0
Venezuela	1.8	2.5	4.9	4.9	7.6
Other countries[a]	33.2	13.3	8.4	5.5	10.2
Total	100.0	100.0	100.0	100.0	100.0

a   Central American and Caribbean Countries (except Cuba), Bolivia, Ecuador, and Paraguay
SOURCE: ECLA, 1969. op. cit.

creases in income, and rising consumer aspirations do not necessarily occur at the same pace.

A corresponding unevenness also characterizes the *cultura* (way of life) of the low-income groups that represent the great majority of Latin American populations. Overwhelmingly, housing conditions are quite bad by the standards of richer countries; not only slums of a "permanent" nature, but various types of shanty towns – the *ranchos* in Caracas, *barriadas* in Lima, *callampas* in Santiago, *favelas* in Rio de Janeiro, *villas miseria* in Buenos Aires, and so forth – keep forming overnight even where older ones have been cleared out. Rural housing conditions tend to be even worse than urban slums; in particular, cleanliness and orderliness are more easily found in poor city areas than in the countryside. Rational household management according to "Western" standards is rare in either case and so is systematic consumer decision-making.

The social limitations come to a peak in the case of the "marginal" groups of Latin American populations. This is not the place to enter into all the current definitions of social marginality; a United Nations publication states,

> Marginality is a structural situation, not merely a psychological condition manifested in specific individuals, although it may be the cause of such a condition. It is characterized by non-participation in the prevailing social structures, combined with the impossibility of acting without reference to all or some of them: a non-participation accompanied by the aspiration to secure at least a minimal share in the assets of a given society [14, p.88, 116].

The same study points out that monetary income in these groups is always very low, in fact, below what can be considered a minimum subsistence level, but with considerable disparity: it is not unusual for the ratio between minimum and maximum income levels within this group to be 1:4. The corresponding culture or subculture of poverty develops its own mechanisms, through mutual helping out within the extended family or otherwise, for making up for some of the glaring shortcomings of consumption facilities.

Father R. Vekemans [5], on the basis of an extensive study of the phenomenon of marginality, describes it in the following terms: "superposition" of European and African cultures upon the indigenous population, with far reaching socio-economic effects; lack of "pertinence" associated with marginal populations (their feeling that they "do not matter" to the more fortunate groups, a feeling which is shared by the latter); values, attitudes, and aspirations of the rural populations concerned and the characteristics of the extended family in rural areas, which are then transferred to marginal groups of new city dwellers; and nonparticipation mentioned above. The same study arrived at certain data on consumption and living conditions in Latin America which are listed in Table 3.

A more specific investigation by *DESAL* of urban marginality as evidenced by conditions in Greater Santiago [6] between May and July 1966, based on 1,037 interviews covering a universe of

Table 3

COMPOSITION OF CONSUMPTION IN LATIN AMERICA

	Total			High and Middle Income			Low Income Groups		
	Total (millions of dollars)	%	Per capita (dollars)	Total (millions of dollars)	%	Per capita (dollars)	Total (millions of dollars)	%	Per capita (dollars)
Food	7,560	52	76	3,000	36	150	4,560	75	57
Non-food products	3,290	23	33	2,500	30	125	790	13	10
Textiles, footwear, and clothing	1,150	8	11	840	10	42	310	5	4
Other products of current use[a]	1,570	11	16	1,090	13	55	480	8	6
Durable consumer goods	570	4	6	570	7	28	–	–	–
Services[b]	3,630	25	36	2,900	34	145	730	12	9

a Includes beverages and tobacco, chemical and pharmaceutical products, paper and printing, and other manufactured goods.

b Includes housing, domestic service, transportation and other services.

   SOURCE: DESAL [5].

268

113,479 dwellings, arrived at an estimate of 27.8 percent of the total population of Greater Santiago as being marginal. Inhabitants 15 years old or less accounted for one-half of the total; 54 percent of the dwellings were in planned areas; 30 percent in areas of spontaneous settlement, and 16 percent in deteriorating central zones. *Callampas* (mushroom or shanty towns) represented only 12 percent of the total dwellings. A large part of the marginal group lived a great distance from the main commercial and working centers. One-half of the dwellings were lightly built, a dangerous condition in a zone of frequent earthquakes. The interior equipment of many marginal dwellings was found to be relatively acceptable: one-half of them had toilet, kitchen, drinking water and light; 57.8 percent of the sites were owner-occupied, 31.5 percent rented, 10,7 percent were illegally occupied; among the dwellings, 65.8 percent were owner-occupied, 4.6 percent illegally occupied. Illiteracy was relatively low, especially among men, but the schooling experienced was very limited.

The principal motive for migration to Santiago was found to be hope to get work, or better-paid work than before. Most people felt that their situation was better than before migration, and their social mobility had increased. Two-thirds did not indicate occupational aspirations or only low ones; but their occupational and educational aspirations for their children were markedly higher than for themselves.

Another empirical survey of occupation and marginality, defined differently, was carried out recently by ECLA in two large cities, Santiago (Chile) and Guayaquil (Ecuador). "Marginality" was defined here in terms of the lowest occupational levels according to the kind of work and position. The questionnaire included questions on frequency and preferred location of market shopping; distribution of family expenditures including food, transport, entertainment, and education; buying on credit; aid received in terms of money, food, or clothing, and any compensatory performance for the benefit of the aid-givers; friendship and *fiesta* habits, and so forth.

The condition of marginality heavily overlaps with unemployment. The *DESAL* investigation found 7.7 percent of the marginal population to be unemployed, compared with 6.0 percent of the total population; the rate among women was 8.6 percent, among men 7.3 percent. Moreover, among the employed marginal population the earnings of most were quite low, and only 62.6 percent had social security compared with 74.7 percent in the general employed population.

The phenomenon of marginality constitutes one of the most important differences between the structure of the consumer population in Latin America and its structure in North America and Europe, where some similar phenomena exist but not on any comparable scale. As mentioned already, marginality overlaps with another widespread problem in large parts of Latin America, unemployment and underemployment. This phenomenon has been so persistent that it must be considered a structural characteristic of most Latin American economies. Hopes during the fifties that an accelerated rate of economic growth, especially of industrialization, would take care of unemployment and its elusive but no less extensive twin scourge, underemployment, have clearly not been fulfilled, as the latest work by Prebisch cautiously admits [12].

THE "DUALISTIC" SOCIETY AND ITS CONSUMPTION PATTERNS

More than any other factor, the traditional inequality of the distribution of income and wealth, along with widespread unemployment, in most of Latin America has aroused strong movements in recent years for fundamental change in the socioeconomic arrangements that have long put severe limitations on domestic consumers' markets and, even more crucially, have prevented in many countries the establishment of an integrated society. This phenomenon has often been characterized as a "dualistic" society, though the concept has been exposed to some criticisms: the separation between the large tradition-bound Indian population of, say, Guatemala and Ecuador, and the relatively modernized Ladino or Mestizo groups, not to mention the small Europeanized or Americanized upper-class minority, is by no means absolute and has been slowly but constantly shrinking. This trend applies in various ways to education, social mobility, and consumer markets. Yet, at this point there is still a striking gap between the ways of life of the indigenous or otherwise "marginal" groups on the one hand, the rest of the population on the other hand.

The remaining self-sufficient consumption in the traditional rural sectors, most of all in the countries with a large indigenous population, is still extensive, but the factors of change are growing and resistance to it is decreasing. Even in somewhat isolated Indian communities such innovations as European-type clothing, especially among men, radios, and beds are gradually spreading. Mass communication media, especially the transistor radio, influence even the illiterate rural dweller. So does two-way migration both of seasonal and other types. The growth of community development and agrarian reform agencies, and the expansion of public transport services that pass through rural areas, round out the picture.

This process, however, should not be interpreted as meaning that the social integration of consumption patterns is anywhere near completion. For some time to come, discretionary spending in Latin America will remain confined to a rather small, but growing, minority of the population. Besides this there are substantial, often restrictive influences on the consumption of many persons and groups from governmental actions such as price and import policies, subsidies, tax policies, and wage legislation. Moreover, the long-range trend of the proportion of government consumption in relation to private consumption has been upward in most countries.

To sum up this section, consumption patterns in large areas of Latin America are still characterized by the existence of large groups of people, in some cases the majority, who live outside the national and international markets; who follow in their patterns of consumption, their own cultural and historical traditions; who are too poor and ignorant (or else not motivated) to adopt the consumption habits and preferences of the more "modern" sector of society; and who have no financial or cultural opportunity to engage in discretionary spending. Industrialization, government intervention, and other influences, however, have been steadily undermining this historical pattern of "dualistic" division of Latin American societies. One of the most important influences in this direction has been the urbanization process.

The process mentioned has been unmistakable and, in all probability, irreversible. In 1940, Latin America had only four cities with more than one million inhabitants; by 1960 the number had risen to ten, and by 1980 it is expected to reach twenty-eight [14, p.95]. Countries with an especially high level of urbanization are Argentina, Uruguay, and Chile. The phenomenon of urbanization has by no means been identical with that of industrialization, although there has been some overlapping.

The urbanization process is changing the urban settlement preferences. Garden suburbs with supermarkets and shopping centers, all heavily dependent on the automobile, are spreading in many cities along with the survival and expansion of shanty towns where people still depend for supplies on the itinerant vendor and the small nonspecialized shop. Many one-time-upper-class sections near the center of cities deteriorate and come to house low-income groups. At the same time, new settlements of lower-income groups also spring up in what only yesterday was farm land or desert. Public programs and regulations have had some effect in Bogotá and Santiago, for example, but the entire pattern is more often chaotic than not. It includes a considerable concentration of the younger age groups in the peripheral settlements, including many new families of teen-agers. There is some evidence that small urban centers, such as provincial capitals and centres of diversified manufacturing or industries dependent on local raw-materials (steel, petroleum, fishmeal), are growing even faster than the big cities.

At any rate, an important effect of urban growth on consumption patterns results from the fact that the per capita income of the urban population, despite its sizeable share of "marginal" groups, considerably and increasingly exceeds the per capita income of the remaining rural population.

Some observers have argued that the increasing urban concentration of the population will supply stimuli to "modern" consumption and corresponding investment. A recent study, however, comes to a different conclusion:

> Rapid urbanization, under some circumstances, may supply a stimulus to higher capital investment in consumer goods for an ex-

panding market as urban living increases needs and furnishes cash income. It has not worked out this way in Latin America. . . because the low and uncertain urban incomes are scarcely sufficient to cover costs of the basic necessities of food, clothing, and shelter. Relatively few urban workers attain occupational stability and most of them are unable to progress to higher stages in what is considered the normal pattern of demand: housing stability, purchase of some durable goods, improvement of housing and "extension of comforts" through purchase of a wide range of durable consumer goods, education for children, followed by accumulation of savings in order to protect the standard of living attained [pp. 103f.].

Actually the consumption effect of the recent urban growth has been rather contradictory. The potential for growing consumption with more leeway for discretionary spending is there, but the implementation of this potential is hampered by the shortcomings just mentioned. Even so the difference between urban and rural living is marked. A recent study in Peru [7, p.53] of long-range supply and demand trends for agricultural products found that the per capita indices of consumption were much higher in urban areas for meat, eggs, vegetables, milk and derivatives, and fats and oils; in rural areas the indices were higher for starchy roots, dried vegetables, and sugar. The quality of nutrition thus was substantially higher in urban areas.

A related, much-discussed question is whether or not life and consumption in the urban slums generally represent an improvement over the rural alternative under prevailing Latin American conditions. Scattered evidence indicates that as a rule the shantytown dwellers consider their urban existence superior to their rural past. To appreciate this apparent attitude, one must remember that the typical slum has deplorable sanitary conditions and often no sewers, that many shacks have no windows, that they often can be reached only over narrow, steep paths, that some of them are easily washed off a cliff by heavy rains, that garbage collection is at best confined to places where vehicles can get to, and that electricity for lighting and appliances is often unavailable or frequently interrupted. It is true that some of these same sections show a fair number of TV antennas (usually, but not always, with a TV set under them!), refrigerators, and cars. Whether or not this is to be considered "rational" depends on the definition of the term and on the motivation in each case; it may variously represent a status device, a demonstration effect, or simply the fact that in many settlements shacks are interspersed with relatively durable houses.

To complicate further the situation, shack-dwellers as a rule gladly accept rehousing to newly built developments but do not always feel happy there for long, either because the resettlement has interfered with their old community relations, or because of the general change involved in their accustomed way of life.

For further appreciation of the social situation, it is necessary to keep realizing the fact that the rise of shanty towns and urbanization in general has been accompanied by a severe spread of unemployment and underemployment, which has greatly affected income and consumption. In particular, there has been a heavy concentration in slum areas of young people, many of whom are employed or underemployed.

However, the pattern of urban growth is itself undergoing rapid changes, largely connected with the simultaneous growth of middle sectors and of mass communication media. The traditional dichotomy of the very rich and the very poor with nothing much in between still applies to some countries in Central America, for example, but is less true of various areas with a large middle sector such as São Paulo, Buenos Aires, Santiago, and Mexico City. These areas, accordingly, now enjoy a growing basis for "modern" types of consumption. Their consumers' preferences are increasingly exposed, at the same time, to spreading mass communication media along with demonstration effects from other parts of the world. They are gradually being conditioned to diversification of manufactured consumer goods, sometimes with planned obsolescence or skillful packaging. The importance of domestic service in the expenditure pattern of the middle sectors has been decreasing, while spending for some other services, such as foreign travel and air transportation, has been rising. Savings habits vary from one country and income group to the other, but in many cases saving is interpreted as a step to eventual consumer spending, especially on durable goods such as refrigerators, vacuum cleaners, and washing machines.

The number of automobiles has increased conspicuously as shown in Table 4. Automobile ownership has been concentrated in the large cities, especially their upper- and middle-class areas, but

Table 4

OWNERSHIP LEVELS FOR TV RECEIVERS, RADIOS, AND
AUTOMOBILES (IN THOUSANDS)

	TV Receivers	Radios (per 1,000 inhabitants)	Automobiles (per 1,000 inhabitants)		
			1950	1960	1967
Argentina	1,900 (1967)	348 (1967)	18.5	22.6	50.8
Brasil	2,500 (1966)	95 (1964)	3.8	7.6	17.9
Chile	55 (1966)	187 (1962)	6.6	7.6	12.4
Colombia	400 (1966)	115 (1967)	2.8	5.6	7.3
Mexico	1,792 (1967)	239 (1967)	6.7	13.4	20.1
Peru	275 (1966)	186 (1966)	4.0	7.9	15.7
Venezuela	650 (1965)	179 (1967)	14.0	36.4	48.1

SOURCES: TV Receivers — United Nations, *Statistical Yearbook,*
1968, Table 217.
Radios — United Nations, *Statistical Yearbook 1967*, Table 211, and
Statistical Yearbook 1968, Table 216.
Automobiles — For 1950 and 1960, *El Transporte en América Latina*,
United Nations publication, Sales No 65.II. G.7, Table 71; for 1967,
United Nations, *Statistical Yearbook, 1968*, Table 155.

is spreading rapidly both in its social and geographic distribution.
Car prices are extremely high under the impact of import duties
and taxes, but driving habits typically disregard the serious financial loss (let alone the personal injuries) resulting from each of the
numerous accidents. Perception of the mere possibility of careful
driving is simply nonexistent in many areas and groups of people.
Traffic congestion in the business sections, parking, and air pollution have become serious problems in many Latin American cities
(as in other parts of the world); a few cities try to counter these
evils by building up an efficient, cheap, and expanding system of
public transportation. At the same time the spread of personal car
ownership has been changing the traditional uses of leisure time in
some big-city areas at an amazing pace.

Television is growing rapidly (Table 4). Thus far the proportion
of foreign-produced programs has been high. The advertising effects of TV on consumption, frequently with the help of viewing

in clubs or neighbors' houses (against a small fee) in the lower-income areas, may turn out to be substantial, but this remains to be seen over a longer period.

The emergence of the transistor radio has made this communications medium available to people in areas without electricity. There is some evidence of high priority being given to radios by low-income families with little financial leeway. (There is also widespread demand among them for bicycles, sewing machines, and flashlights.) Radio programs, of course, are accessible even to illiterates and can follow consumer preferences for popular music and, in some areas, for programs in indigenous idioms.

THE DEMONSTRATION EFFECT OF INDUSTRIALIZED SOCIETIES

The communication media just mentioned, along with the impact of foreign movies, tourism in both directions, and sophisticated methods of advertising have combined to lead to an ever-growing pressure on the Latin American consumer, even the one with little discretionary purchasing power, in the direction of emulating the consumption preferences and habits of consumers in industrialized countries; a pressure which, to be sure, not always succeeds in uprooting ingrained cultural traditions but which has substantially affected the middle sectors, in particular.

At this stage of the development process in Latin America, the most important demonstration effect of consumption patterns from industrialized countries appears to consist in their potential anti-saving implications. The effectiveness of this influence depends on many local factors including the presence or absence of inflation and its length, the phase of the development process reached, the persistence of traditional factors either of the indigenous or the colonial type, and many others. Having said this, one cannot but point out the effect of "premature" consumer aspirations (i.e., those preceding the achievement of fairly high or markedly rising levels of output and productivity) upon the formation of capital and the development process as a whole. It has, of course, been claimed that higher consumer aspirations will help create a hitherto nonexistent mass market and thus induce a backward-linkage effect toward stimulating industrial production and, with it, higher incomes. This is not the place to discuss all the implications of the dichotomy involved; but it has, at least, not yet been proven that blind emulation in Latin America of North American and European consumption patterns without, or far ahead of, a concomitant adjustment of savings and work habits, will actually lead to faster development.

As in some other parts of the world, anti-saving attitudes may be of special importance in the formative stages of the younger age groups which account for a high proportion of the Latin American population. In most Latin American countries the proportion of the young has grown during the 1960's; only in Argentina and Uruguay, and to some extent also in Chile and Cuba, has the age structure been showing a rise in the proportion of older people. For Latin America as a whole the large proportion of young among consumers and savers, or more accurately potential savers, is likely to continue.

Can Latin America then be expected to yield to the demonstration effect of industrialized societies with respect to consumption patterns, including mass markets, standardization of products and preferences, tolerance of urban blight, and everything else? To some extent this has taken place, but certain limits to such emulation have also become clearer. In the first place, Cuba has already (and Chile will perhaps) changed many of its previous consumption trends as a result of political changes of a revolutionary nature. Such changes in consumption, to be sure, are in a large degree of a compulsory character; but some part of the change is likely to be of a voluntary and permanent nature. The new consumption policy favors public consumption over private and tends to restrict the range of choices available to the individual.

As mentioned earlier, an even greater limitation to full acceptance by Latin America of consumer habits and preferences from the North is rooted in the strength of cultural differences that — under the surface of momentary emulation of other people's ways — are actually surviving in a large degree. They could sooner or later lead to a counter-trend with nationalist or other reassertion of cultural identity, as they have in some places already. It is unlikely that *all* of the supposedly rational consumer preferences from industrialized countries will conquer Latin America in a permanent sense. Moreover, we can expect continuing great differences among Latin American nations, for cultural and historical reasons. Actually, the scanty comparative data available on specific consumer goods used in various Latin American countries during the 1960's [15] show considerable variations (sometimes, it is true, due to governmental restrictions or promotion campaigns) in the consumption of such goods as beef and grains, although there has invariably been a substantial and sustained increase in the use of gasoline.

By way of sidelight, an investigation in Taiwan of the role of durables consumption in economic development yielded the finding that

> The characteristics and economic behavior of the families who buy modern durables in Taiwan is inconsistent with the idea that such consumption necessarily decreases savings and capital formation, and, thus, impedes development efforts. Instead, the families who are modern in consumption are characterized by a complex of characteristics, attitudes, and behavior which, on the whole, are likely to be beneficial to the development process. There is also a suggestion of the possibility that rising aspirations may increase productivity enough to support increasing levels of both consumption and saving [8, pp.47f.].

This conclusion appears to be based on the widespread assumption that development must essentially represent an imitation of the consumption, production, and values of the "developed" West; an assumption which, incidentally, has been disproved by "development" in the East along its own lines. Different interpretations of the development process are certainly possible. The direction of the causation involved appears to be left open in the investigation cited; does saving depend primarily on the availability of savings institutions and stable money? Does saving increase the appetite for consumption, consumption the appetite for saving, either one the motivation for higher productivity, or do they all have a common basic cause? In any case, whatever may be the merits of the Taiwan study, it leaves the question open whether its results are applicable to Latin America as a whole or any large part of it. The study does not seem to preclude the possibility that elsewhere there may be growing consumption without much higher productivity and savings, as a result of dissaving or income redistribution. In other words, motivation for higher consumption may exist for long periods *without* the other motives mentioned; or there can be a substantial gap in time between aspirations and actual ownership. This appears to be the case in most of Latin America.

SOME SPECIFIC INFLUENCES ON LATIN AMERICAN CONSUMPTION
PATTERNS

Government intervention in social living conditions has been closely connected with, and sometimes counteracted by, that tenacious phenomenon of some (but not all) Latin American economies: *inflation*. The variation of the index of consumer prices (growth rate of annual averages) in the period 1965-69 [9] has been as follows: Uruguay 72.3, Brazil 30.0, Chile 24.2, Argentina 20.4, Peru 11.0; on the other hand, Venezuela 1.4, Mexico 3.1, and Guatemala 2.2. Some of these figures are illustrative rather than exact, and they do not allow for earlier peaks of consumer price inflation which in individual years exceeded 70 percent in Chile (1954) and 100 percent in Brazil (1963).

The case of Chile is of special interest in this respect since the inflation in that country, with some breathing spells, is the oldest in all of Latin America [10]. It dates back, in its acute phase, to the 1930's. There is no consumer in the country who has lived in a noninflationary economy for longer than two to three years, or whose parents have. One can expect, therefore, a prevalence of deeply rooted attitudes based on inflationary experiences and expectations when faced with consumer decisions. Two survey studies of recent years throw some light on this matter.

The first [3] was focused on consumer credit for the purchase of durable goods, especially with regard to the high interest rates charged, in some cases at an annual rate of more than 100 percent. The survey was based on 151 interviews with producers and distributors of such goods in the Santiago area. An estimated 55 percent of sales transactions were carried out on credit over an average period of 7.2 months and at a compound interest rate of 4.7 percent *per month*. Down payment averaged 14 percent of the price. The interest rate charged was presented to the consumer in the form of the difference between cash payment and installment prices, the average difference being 9.9 percent. Credit sales amounted to 28 percent of total sales for textiles, 30 percent for footwear, 64 percent for clothing, 70 percent for furniture, and 90 percent for automobiles (100 percent for the cheapest category!). A tendency toward both a longer credit period and a larger down payment was observed. So was a high interest-rate elasticity of the demand for credit over the years, with some additional influence of the total debt previously contracted by the consumer concerned.

It was further found, however, that as a rule the interest rate charged is not explicitly mentioned during the transaction and is usually unknown to the buyer; for certain goods it goes as high as 12 to 14 percent per month. Different buyers often obtain different terms according to their bargaining ability in comparison with that of the seller. In the stores of greater importance the cash price is increasingly assuming the role of mere window-dressing. The variety of interest rates charged also reflects the organization of the respective market, the market information available, the cost of administering the credit, taxes, and insurance, the risk of payment in depreciated money, and the additional risk of changes in the interest-rate structure. The rate of inflation expected by the sellers was found to correspond closely to projections from government sources. The rate of non-payment was quite low but delays in payment were very frequent. The producers of durable consumer goods acted to some extent as financing agency for the distributors of these goods who, in turn, financed the consumers' purchases.

The other study referred to [2] [4], focused on demand projections to 1980. That part of it which refers to family income first lists a number of government measures which may have affected the results obtained: changes in the length of the work day, promotion of the production of poultry, meat, and eggs, restrictions on the sales of beef, and income redistribution through salary adjustments and tax policy. Allowing for these influences as well as the effects of continuing inflation, this survey of 2,428 families interviewed in the four largest cities (Santiago, Valparaíso-Viña del Mar, Concepción and Antofagasta) over a 12-month period from October, 1963, to September, 1964, with changing composition of the family sample from week to week, yielded the result described in Table 5. The patterns of food consumption were found to differ

Table 5

CONSUMPTION STRUCTURE BY INCOME LEVELS, EXPRESSED AS PERCENT OF TOTAL CONSUMPTION EXPENDITURE, 1963-64

	1st quartile income, 0-209[a]	2nd quartile income, 210-319[a]	3rd quartile income, 320-519[a]	4th quartile income, 520 and over[a]
Vegetables and vegetable products	26.4	25.1	25.3	20.4
Wheat and flour products	21.8	18.7	16.1	12.7
Milk and milk products	7.7	9.0	9.9	10.6
Poultry and eggs	2.7	3.8	4.7	6.9
Beef and beef products	15.0	17.3	17.1	19.4
Pork and pork products	1.2	1.4	1.6	3.5
Other meats (rabbit, duck, etc.)	0.1	0.2	0.2	0.4
Seafood and products	3.9	3.7	3.9	3.7
Fruits	4.7	6.1	7.3	9.7
Pastries and sweets	7.4	6.3	6.5	6.9
Beverages	5.2	5.1	4.5	2.6
Miscellaneous, incl. fats and oils, fuel, etc.	3.0	2.5	1.7	1.8
Total consumption expenditure[b]	100.0	100.0	100.0	100.0

a   1964 Escudos.
b   Allowing for rounding.

SOURCE: *Chile: Demand and Supply Projections for Agricultural Products, 1965-80*, Catholic University of Chile, under contract with the U.S. Department of Agriculture, Santiago, 1969, pp. 44 ff.

substantially according to income groups, though there were some additional differences in consumption habits between white-collar and blue-collar workers of the same income group. Specifically, the lower income groups spent a higher proportion of their total consumption expenditure on bread, flour, and potatoes than did the higher income groups; the opposite was true of beef, poultry, eggs, and fresh milk. The qualitative composition of food consumption thus was less satisfactory in the lower income groups than in the upper, a phenomenon not unknown in other parts of the world even where there are no major deficiencies in the food quantities consumed.

Another specific influence of considerable importance has resulted from the widespread preference of consumers for imported goods, especially those from economically advanced countries. This preference has been due to a variety of factors: the colonial past and continuing national inferiority feelings; the use of imported goods as a status device in the case of cars and electric appliances, in particular; and perceived superiority of imported goods with respect to quality, often but not always, borne out by the facts. This time-honored preference has been counteracted in recent decades by a public industrialization policy based on import substitution; but the whole phenomenon of import preference and the counteraction to it have affected relatively little the low-income, and especially the "marginal", groups which consume only a few manufactured products.

Thus far the tastes described reflect chiefly the value system of the middle and upper classes. Studies of consumption in Trinidad have shown that the richer a person is the higher a proportion of his income he spends on luxury items with a high import content [13, pp.227f.].

With certain changes under way in the value systems, and in the socio-economic and political influence of the low-income groups, the time-honored phenomenon of smuggling and black markets for imported goods may also undergo considerable changes, especially in the longer run. This, indeed, is likely to be part of a far more fundamental transformation of Latin American values and consumption patterns in the direction of greater emphasis on social consumption and on educational aspirations of the individual.

NATIONALISM, REVOLUTIONS AND CHANGING CONSUMPTION
PATTERNS

Large parts of Latin America have been shaken out, since 1959, from the traditional structure of society and consumption that was described in the first Section of this chapter. Castro's revolution in Cuba could still be interpreted as a unique occurrence, but events in Chile since late 1970, the persistence of violence in various parts of Latin America, and other indications point to the seriousness of forces for fundamental changes in society, and to the gradual loss of ground on the part of forces — still quite strong in various areas of Latin America at this point — of a rigid conservatism mostly based on large land-ownership and *caudillo* militarism. The movements for change typically combine two elements: a nationalism directed especially against foreign ownership of basic resources but also against the emulation of North American or Western European ways of life; and a drive for political and economic rules by peasants and workers led on by university students and radical politicians. The major decision which Cuba took after 1959, and which Chile has been facing more recently, concerns the method through which such changes are to be achieved: is the social revolution and the resulting new society going to be democratic or totalitarian?

Whatever may be the answer to this question, the new society might produce some kind of social asceticism designed to make it recoil from the perceived excesses of foreign-type individual consumerism of the upper and middle classes. It is also possible, of course, that such ascetic attitudes will merely rationalize objective supply shortages during a transition period, if not a longer period, resulting from abrupt changes in ownership, capital shortages, exchange difficulties, or chaotic procedures in carrying through needed changes in land tenure and credit allocation. It is also possible that the social asceticism mentioned will take the form of forced savings in one way or another.

The nationalist element in the social movements concerned may take the form, among other features, of favoring "criollo" or native products over a "yanqui-type" consumerism which is regarded by critics not only as undignified but as inappropriate for the (historically seen) poorly integrated or structurally weak societies of Latin American countries. The nationalist element may be combined with a drive for greater social consumption, particularly in education but also in public housing, health, and perhaps transportation. As a result "the powerful consumer" may not be so powerful, as an individual, in the Latin America of the near and middle future. Conceivably he might become more effective in the longer run, though the basic question raised earlier about the prospects for eventual "modernization" or else for persistence of cultural differences in consumption, respectively, must remain open for the moment.

REFERENCES

1 Beyer, Glen H., ed., *The Urban Explosion in Latin America*, Ithaca, 1967.
2 Catholic University of Chile, Economic Research Center, *Chile: Demand and Supply Projection for Agricultural Products 1965–1980*, Santiago, 1969.
3 Córdova, F., L. Múxica and G. Wagner, "Algunos Aspectos del Crédito al Consumo", *Cuadernos de Economia*, Universidad Católica de Chile, Santiago, 1968, Vol. 16.
4 CORFO (Corporación de Fomento de la Producción), "Efectos de la Estructura des Consumo sobre el Crecimiento del Sector Industrial", Publicacion No. 52a/70, Santiago, 1970 (mimeographed).
5 DESAL, (Centro para el Desarrollo Económico y Social de América Latina), "Marginalidad en América Latina", 2 vols., Santiago, 1967 (mimeographed).
6 DESAL, "La Marginalidad Urbana: Origen, Proceso y Modo", 2 vols., Santiago, 1968 (mimeographed).
7 Dirección de Estadística, Convenio de Cooperación Tecnica, *Perú: Proyecciones a Largo Plazo de la Oferta y Demanda de Productos Agropecuarios Seleccionados 1970–1975–1980*, Lima, 1969.
8 Freedman, Deborah S., "The Role of the Consumption of Modern Durables in Economic Development", *Economic Development and Cultural Change*, 19 (No. 1, October, 1970).
9 *Notas sobre la Economía y el Desaviollo de América Latina*, No. 62, January 16, 1971, based on data from the International Monetary Fund and the United Nations Monthly Statistical Bulletin.
10 Pinto S.C., Aníbal, *Chile, un Caso de Desarrollo Frustrado*, Santiago, 1962.
11 Poblete-Troncoso, Moises, *El Subconsumo en América del Sur; Alimentos, Vestuario y Vivienda*, Santiago, Chile, 1946.
12 Prebisch, Raúl, *Change and Development: Latin America's Great Task*, Report submitted to the Inter-American Development Bank, Washington, 1970.

13 Seers, Dudley, "A Step towards a Political Economy of Development", *Social and Economic Studies*, University of the West Indies, 18 (No. 3, September, 1969).

14 United Nations, Economic Commission for Latin America, *Social Change and Social Development in Latin America*, New York, 1970.

15 Unión Panamericana, Departamento de Estadística, *América en Cifras 1967*, Part 5, Section 353, Washington, 1969.

Predicting
Consumer Behavior

Anticipations Variables in Macro-Econometric Models

F. GERARD ADAMS AND LAWRENCE. R. KLEIN*

THE ROLE OF ANTICIPATIONS

For many generations economists have made use of such subjective concepts as "expected", "anticipated", "desired", or "planned" and have usually represented these magnitudes by distributed lags or other surrogates on the grounds that direct objective measurements were not available. Not so with the research programs of George Katona, who takes the approach that since consumer expectations, attitudes, and other subjective feelings are important for economic behavior, we, as economists, should go directly to the agents of action and ask them what these subjective variables are at regular intervals of time.

Measurement of subjective variables associated with economic units (firms, households, bureaus) received large impetus from George Katona's work, and grew to a status that would not otherwise have been achieved. It is the purpose of this essay to look into the independent contribution of anticipatory variables in forecasting with econometric models. We are not arguing for either

* The authors wish to thank Vijaya Duggal for help beyond the call of duty. Nariman Behravesh provided valuable research assistance.

the survey approach or the formal model-building approach, but for their joint use to improve the contributions of both to the overall objective of getting more forecast accuracy for the economy.

Although George Katona's principal work has been with attitudinal variables obtained from consumer surveys, we are going to look further afield into investment surveys and statistics of advance commitments — consumer attitudes, investment intentions, and housing starts. We are aware of inventory expectations, sales expectations, employment expectations, and price expectations; but these variables are not going to be used in our present investigation, partly because they are not very reliable and partly because they do not appear to be productive in getting us to our main objective. Orders variables are already in our models and appropriations variables could be similarly introduced but have not been used in the Wharton Model, which forms our basic econometric point of reference[1].

The most important aspect of the anticipatory variables that we are going to deal with is their *lead time*. They involve answers to questions about the future or about things that indicate future developments. To some extent, we shall use variables that include some future commitments. In a dynamic economy like ours where big changes can occur on short notice, certainly within one year, it cannot be assumed that anticipatory variables remain firm as indicators for more than three to six months. They are mainly of use as predictors for short-run business cycle analysis. At most they are indicative of some aspects of the economy for one year, but are more likely to be valid for a shorter period. Consumer attitudes probably erode faster than business investment intentions and housing starts. Investment planning deals with major time-consuming projects that need much advance planning. They also have some degree of commitment, possibly contractual. This gives them firmness and less flexibility than comsumer attitudes. Housing starts are physically evident commitments but are usually phased into completion in less than one year.

[1] Wharton Models have been formally used in regular forecasting exercises since 1963, but in this paper we are going to use the new, 1971, version of the Model, called Wharton Mark III. It is our third generation of Wharton Models.

Anticipatory variables provide a short look ahead and can be compiled without much delay. George Katona and his colleagues at the Survey Research Center can ascertain consumer attitudes on a nationwide basis in less than one month with good information on a horizon of up to six months. Housing starts are regularly reported every month on the basis of data collections with no more than a month's delay. Investment surveys, like consumer surveys, are usually quarterly and take no longer to execute. We therefore have a quick resource for short-run analysis.

Another dimension of anticipatory variables, related to their lead time, is their degree of firmness. The anticipatory variables in the consumer sector are the least firm of those used in economic forecasting. Opinions or attitudes could, under pressure, change almost overnight, and buying plans frequently appear to be statements of purchase probability rather than firm intentions. There is enough stability in many of these data so that they are good predictors, but they are not as firmly based as are other anticipatory variables. Orders can be cancelled; construction plans can be either curtailed or expanded. Therefore investment intentions, even if measured by contracts or appropriations, are not fixed until completion. They are subject to revision, but probably less frequently than consumer attitudes. A housing start is probably more fixed than investment intentions, but even in this case revision is possible through partial cancellation or modification of building plans.

Anticipations are going to be used in the present study in as a structural a way as possible. They are not going to be used simply as broad indicators of behavior in the economy as a whole; they are going to be related to specific types of behavior. At impact they will be highly localized, but their complete system effects will be traced through the whole economy by solving simultaneous dynamic equations.

In the case of consumer attitudes, the measured subjective variables will be related to consumer expenditures and residential constructions. We shall not draw any direct inferences about the effect of consumer attitudes on total production, employment, or income — only on specific types of consumer expenditures, which, in turn, will have some effects on aggregate activity.

Similarly, investment intentions will be studied in direct relation to capital formation. It will be through econometric analysis of an entire equation system that the effect of intentions in the economy as a whole will be inferred. Housing starts will be studied in relation to residential construction outlays, and their broader influence on the whole economy will have to be transmitted through residential construction expenditures.

ALTERNATIVE SCHEMES FOR USING ANTICIPATIONS

One of the main features of the present study is that anticipations will be used, if possible, in a closed system. Most frequently, these variables have been used as *predetermined* indicators because of their well-known lead time. This has been a passive use of such variables. Given their quantitative standing on some date and their approximate lead time, they have been used as indicators of specific types of behavior up to the end of their valid horizons.

In contrast with the use of anticipatory variables as predetermined variables over the duration of their (brief) lead time, we shall try to "explain" anticipations as well as actual behavior. One such scheme to be considered is a prediction-realization sequence.

In the initial phase, equations are developed to explain anticipations. In the received theory of investment, actual capital outlays are made a function of current and past values of production, relative price of output and capital rental, stock of capital. The equation may be written as

$$I_t = \sum_{i-0}^{P} w_i\, X_{t-i} + \sum_{i=0}^{q} x_i\, (\tfrac{P}{c})_{t-i} + \sum_{i=0}^{r} y_i\, K_{t-i} + e_t$$

If anticipations have a lead time of six months (two quarterly time units in the scale of t), they might be explained by

$$I_t^a = \sum_{i=0}^{P} w_i\, X_{t-i-2} + \sum_{i=0}^{q} x_i\, (\tfrac{P}{c})_{t-i-2} + \sum_{i=0}^{r} y_i\, K_{t-i-2} + e_t$$

This is the same equation that is used to explain I_t, except that everything occurs two quarters earlier. If this equation can be established as an estimate using data on I_t^a, X_{t-i-2}, $(\tfrac{P}{c})_{t-i-2}$, K_{t-i-2}, we can compute the system by adding a realization equation that explains $I_t - I_t^a$ as a function of X, p/c, K, their historical

292

changes, and other variables. The two equations — one explaining I_t^a and the other explaining $I_t - I_t^a$ — provide enough equations to keep the system in which they are included closed. This scheme has been seriously considered previously but not fully implemented.[2] This general scheme is somewhat modified in our specification estimated below for investment. Investment intentions are estimated as in the equation just given for I_t^a but as there are two anticipations for each quarter's investment in the SEC—OBE surveys — one with two quarters' lead time and one with one quarter's lead time — we have made the second anticipations variable for a given quarter a function of the first anticipations variable, as well as distributed lags in the usual objective explanatory variables.[3]

Instead of specifying a *realization* equation directly, we make actual investment outlays a function of distributed lags in first and second anticipations and of current values in the usual objective variables.

A related scheme, but one that is less formal in the association between equations that explain the standard objective variable and the corresponding anticipatory variables, is one that simply tries to explain anticipations by other endogenous variables — not necessarily lagged and not necessarily the same ones that explain corresponding expenditure behavior. The endogenous explanation of consumer attitudes may appear to be a considerably different equation from that explaining consumer durable expenditures, but that is no problem from the viewpoint of generating all endogenous variables in a closed system.

In a previous attempt to introduce anticipatory variables in the Wharton Model, we developed equations in which anticipatory variables played an *auxiliary* role; i.e., they were simply included as additional variables together with standard objective variables to determine if the subjective factors have an independent (supplementary) explanatory contribution to make [5]. A consumer attitudes index, investment intentions, and housing starts were intro-

[2] See the chapters by Dale Jorgenson and Robert Eisner in [4].
[3] Throughout this paper we will refer to the anticipations variable with two-quarters lead time as "first anticipations", and the variable with one-quarter lead time as "second anticipations". These traditional names will be used despite the fact that anticipations expressed still earlier are now available at times.

duced as separate variables in consumption, investment, and housing equations respectively.

The auxiliary type relationships were used only for short solutions over the two-quarter lead time of the anticipations. In the present study such equations will be one of the alternatives considered. They will be used in longer extrapolations together with equations for the anticipatory variables.

The appropriate scheme for integrating anticipatory variables into the demand equations of a macro-model depends on the nature of the anticipations and on the demand category to be considered.

Consumption does not depend firmly on buying plans, and nonspecific consumer sentiment data can be seen as supplementing the objective determinants of consumer spending. Adams and Green [2] have explained attitudes in terms of changes in labor market conditions. Hymans [8] has linked such functions to endogenous explanation of consumer purchases. For the explanation of consumer attitudes, Hymans has used such variables as changes in disposable income, stock prices, and consumer prices. His results are moderately good, but leave much error in the endogenous generation of consumer attitudes. This will show up in solutions beyond the lead time of one or two quarters. Our procedure will be along the same lines for the consumer sector, but the equation for endogenous treatment of consumer attitudes is a transformation of a distributed lag in changes in unemployment and consumer prices. To some extent, these equations for consumer attitudes are purely empirical, for a widely accepted theory to explain them is not available.

With regard to business fixed investment, the OBE Model has relied on investment intentions for predictions of capital formation [9]. Subsequently, the OBE econometricians developed an independent investment function that depended only on standard objective variables. They used this equation for longer simulations. They also tried the following procedure: For the first two quarters of a forecast, use the anticipations variables

$$I_t = I_t^q$$

where I_t^q is taken with lead time from an earlier survey of intentions. They used the first anticipations from the previous quarter's survey to predict investment two quarters ahead and the second anticipations to predict investment one quarter ahead.[4] For the third and future quarters ahead, they used the standard function with only objective variables. The difficulty with this approach is that it may provide a discrete jump at the switching point between the second and third quarters ahead. This difficulty is avoided in our approach by using the same investment functions for all prediction periods, feeding into them actual values of the anticipations when they are available or endogenously estimated values when actuals are not available.

In some of our equations, we have also adopted Jorgenson's suggestion [4] of investment as a distributed lag on anticipations and as noted above, we made use of a modified realization approach.

The well-known housing model of Sherman Maisel established particular relationships between starts and capital expenditures on residential construction.[5] There are many detailed aspects to Maisel's model, but the principal idea is that starts depend on income, credit market conditions, relative prices, and possibly other standard objective variables of a macro-model. Similarly average value per start depends on objective economic variables. Expenditures are estimated from

$$(I_h)_t = \sum_{i=0}^{P} w_i \, V_{t-i} \, (H_s)_{t-i}; \qquad \sum_{i=0}^{P} w_i = 1$$

where I_h = capital outlays for residential construction
V = average value per start
H_s = housing starts
w_i = weight factor

In this equation, expenditures are expressed as a moving average of the value of starts. Presumably this is approximately the same formula that national income statisticians use for phasing-in starts to get expenditures. An alternative approach is to estimate the

---

[4] Friend and Thomas [7] have argued that such direct use of the investment anticipations compares favorably with other formulations in prediction. It is not clear, however, why this should be so.
[5] *See* the chapter by Sherman Maisel in [4].

distributed lag coefficients of residential construction on starts [6]. Brady's work [3] has suggested that it may be important to distinguish between various classes of housing starts.

Our variation of the Maisel model is both more and less detailed. Single family starts are separated from multi-family starts. In this respect our model is more disaggregated than Maisel's, but not as much as Brady's, and introduces what seem to be important behavioral differences between owner-occupiers and landlords. Otherwise, our model is more aggregative and somewhat cruder than Maisel's. Expenditures on residential construction, in constant prices, are made a function of income, credit terms, and relative prices as standard objective variables.

Credit availabilities have been measured by a proxy based on the differential between long and short interest rates. These variables are available from the financial sector of the Wharton Model; whereas more specific flows of funds to lending institutions, such as those used by Fair and Brady, are not. We take a further step into the realm of anticipatory variables by including the index of consumer attitudes, for these are relevant to house buying as well as to purchases of cars or other consumer durables. Single family starts are specified to depend on income, credit conditions, relative prices, consumer attitudes, and trend. Multiple family starts depend on the same class of variables but are not directly related to the index of consumer attitudes.

Two variants of equations have been run. One explains total non-farm residential construction directly; introduces starts as "auxiliary" variables in the sense explained above; and uses Maisel's fixed time phasing for the independent variables. The other distinguishes between construction of new homes and additions and alterations and estimates the time lag between starts and residential construction put-in-place.

In all three sectors — consumption, business fixed capital formation, and residential construction — we have joint explanation of anticipatory variables and the corresponding GNP component. We are thus able to make use of anticipatory lead time for very short run predictions and then to generate future estimates of the anticipatory variables for prediction beyond the lead-time horizon. The various alternative approaches outlined here will all be tested in complete system solutions.

The basic alternatives compared below are:

Version I. — Objective variables version: Consumption, investment, and residential construction are explained entirely in terms of objective variables using the standard equations of the Mark III Wharton Model.

Version II. — Anticipations as auxiliary variables: Anticipations have been introduced into the equations simply as supplements to the other variables in the equations as in earlier versions of the Wharton model.

Version III. — Anticipations in a realizations framework: Anticipations have been used in this version as direct forecasters of the fixed investment in a realizations type format. This has not been possible for consumer purchases of automobiles, where the Version III equation simply drops the unemployment variable. Version III may also be characterized as the approach which puts greatest weight on the anticipations variables.

SINGLE EQUATION RESULTS

The equations incorporating anticipations variables are evaluated from a single equation point of view in this section. In view of space limitations, only the standard errors, $\bar{R}^2$, and Durbin-Watson statistics of the Version I equations, those in the standard version of the Mark III model, are shown. An alphabetic index of variables is presented in the Appendix.

Consumption

The numerous empirical studies of consumer attitudes and buying plans have produced consensus, if not agreement, with regard to the usefulness of this material in consumption functions. On the basis of earlier work and some additional empirical experimentation, it appears that attitudinal variables contribute particularly to the explanation of consumer purchases of cars, but have little or no effect on other consumer purchases. Broad consumer anticipations like the SRC Index of Consumer Sentiment, and

297

surrogates for them, have been useful in time series but buying plans variables have shown considerably less promise [1].[6]

The direct use of buying plans as predictors and their integration into realization functions do not appear warranted. Empirical analysis was focused on the use of the SRC *Index of Consumer Sentiment* (CSI) and other anticipatory variables as auxiliary variables in the automobile purchases equation.

Numerous equations were tested incorporating the CSI variable, and/or other objective variables which could influence consumer anticipations. Stock prices were not used, however, since they pose forecasting difficulties in their own right. Strangely, the filtered version of the CSI variable used by Hymans [8] works less well over the time period considered here than does the CSI index in its original form. Other proxies for attitudes, for example weekly hours in manufacturing industry, make a contribution to explaining auto purchases but generally are not as statistically significant as the CSI variable.

The best equations obtained were:[7]

Table 1
Automobile Purchasing Functions
Version II   (1)

$$CA\text{-}MHTR = \underset{(5.98)}{0.06612} * (Y\text{-}TR/PC) + \underset{(2.32)}{29.9426} * LIQUID$$

$$-\; \underset{(4.39)}{4.3000} * DS + \underset{(1.27)}{1.023} * CR$$

$$-\; \underset{(1.23)}{10.380} * (PA/PC) - \underset{(1.27)}{0.2552} * UN$$

$$+\; \underset{(2.71)}{0.2814} * (CA\text{-}MHTR)_{-1} + \underset{(1.43)}{0.8877} * (IL/IS)_{-4}$$

$$+\; \underset{(1.54)}{0.0525} * CSI_{-1} + \underset{(1.44)}{0.0831} * \Delta CSI_{-2}$$

$$-\; \underset{(1.24)}{21.094}$$

$$\overline{R}^2 = .9714 \; SE = 1.091 \; DW = 1.760$$

[6] Juster's recent work with purchase probabilities is conceptually between explicit "plans to buy" and broad attitudinal measures. Unfortunately there is not yet a sufficiently long time series of the purchase probabilities index to allow serious simulation tests.

[7] Definitions of variables are given in the Appendix. The estimation period for all equations is 1953.3 to 1970.1.

Table 1 continued

Version III

$$CA\text{-}MHTR = 0.0653 * (Y\text{-}TR/PC) + 34.8092 * LIQUID \qquad (2)$$
$$\phantom{CA\text{-}MHTR = } (5.89) \qquad\qquad\qquad (2.81)$$
$$\phantom{CA\text{-}MHTR =} - 4.3779 * DS + 0.9136 * CR$$
$$\phantom{CA\text{-}MHTR = } (4.45) \qquad\quad (1.14)$$
$$\phantom{CA\text{-}MHTR =} - 10.5138 * (PA/PC) + 0.3214 * (CA\text{-}MHTR)_{-1}$$
$$\phantom{CA\text{-}MHTR = } (1.24) \qquad\qquad (3.24)$$
$$\phantom{CA\text{-}MHTR =} + 0.8019 * (IL/IS)_{-4} + 0.0697 * CSI_{-1}$$
$$\phantom{CA\text{-}MHTR = } (1.29)$$

$$\phantom{CA\text{-}MHTR =} + 0.08122 * \Delta CSI_{-2} - 27.239$$
$$\phantom{CA\text{-}MHTR = } (1.40) \qquad\qquad (1.65)$$
$$\phantom{CA\text{-}MHTR = xxxxxxxxxxxxxxxxx} (2.22)$$

$$\bar{R}^2 = .9711 \; SE = 1.096 \; DW = 1.851$$

Version I Statistics $\qquad\qquad \bar{R}^2 = .9688 \; SE = 1.316 \; DW = 1.593$

Except for the consumer sentiment variables, Equation (1) is exactly as in Version I, the standard Wharton Model. When the CSI variables are included, the contribution of unemployment becomes nonsignificant and this variable has been omitted in Equation (2). The other coefficients are not much affected by the presence of the anticipations variable. The CSI variable results in only very modest improvement in the explanatory power of the auto equation.

In the explanation of CSI, as well, numerous alternative formulations and variables were explored. As above, we did not use stock prices despite the evidence that they could be useful on a single equations basis. Surprisingly a simple formulation:

$$CSI = .7565 \, CSI_{-1} - 3.4625 \Delta UN - 93.1000 \, (PC\text{-}PC_{-3})$$
$$ (13.44) \qquad\quad (4.09) \qquad\quad (4.02) \qquad\qquad\qquad (3)$$
$$ + 24.5840$$
$$ (4.58)$$

$$\bar{R}^2 = .8351 \; SE = 2.3529 \; DW = 1.6737$$

where CSI is simply a distributed lag function of change in unemployment and consumer prices, works best. This version of the equation is used to explain forward values of CSI endogenously.

As in the original version of the Wharton Model, separate investment equations have been estimated for three industrial categories,
mining and manufacturing, regulated industries, and commercial
and other.

In the Version II formulation, the anticipations variables have
simply been added to existing equations, testing whether they
contribute information not already incorporated in the objective
determinants of investment. For this purpose it has been assumed
that the prediction period of the OBE-SEC investment anticipations corresponds to their time lead, two quarters for the so-called
"first anticipations" and one quarter for the "second anticipations" and that businessmen make an accurate allowance for
change in prices of capital goods. This means that the anticipations
can be introduced as single values (not distributed lags) with the
indicated time lag and deflated by the capital goods deflator of the
time the investment is effected.

The general form of the equation is:

$$I_t = f(\lambda_i (\theta) Z_i, EP1_{t-2}, EP2_{t-1})$$

where

I_t – investment at time t,

$\lambda_i (\theta) Z_i$ – distributed lags of i objective variables, and
$EP1_{t-2}$ and $EP2_{t-1}$ – *OBE-SEC* first and second investment anticipations, deflated by business fixed investment
deflator for time t.

Empirically such an equation could turn out to be equivalent to a
realizations function. Suppose the effect of the lag terms of the
objective variables is absorbed by the anticipations, the equation
would indicate that investment depends on anticipations as modified by those terms of the objective variables which intervene
between the time anticipations are formulated and investment is
put in place. In other words, realized investment would be a function of plans and of realizations of the anticipated objective variables. However, the empirical results, Table 2, do not support
such a notion.

Table 2

VERSION II BUSINESS FIXED INVESTMENT FUNCTIONS[8]

$$IPMM = -3.765 + 7.238 * CPMM_{-1} \qquad\qquad (4)$$
$$(1.73)\quad(3.24)$$

$$+ .5770 * EPMM2_{-1} + .2048 * EPMM1_{-2}$$
$$(4.83)\qquad\qquad(1.78)$$

$$+ \sum_{i=0}^{5} a_{4i} XMM_{-i} + \sum_{i=0}^{15} b_{4i} (UCCMM/PMM)_{-i}$$

$$[.0238] \qquad\qquad [-14.7732]$$
$$P = .0058 \qquad\quad P = -3.1864$$
$$i = -4 \qquad\qquad i = -3$$
$$\bar{R}^2 = .9919\ SE = .4473\ DW = 1.413$$

Version I Statistics $\qquad\qquad \bar{R}^2 = .9811\ SE = .6830\ DW = .6079$

$$IPR = -2.356 - .0244 * KR_{-1} \qquad\qquad (5)$$
$$(1.48)\quad(1.96)$$

$$+ .7764 * EPR2_{-1} + .0630 * EPR1_{-2}$$
$$(3.63)\qquad\qquad(.337)$$

$$+ \sum_{i=0}^{35} a_{5i} XR_{-i} + \sum_{i=0}^{4} b_{5i} XMF_{-i}$$

$$[.2923] \qquad\qquad [.0427]$$
$$P = .0148 \qquad\quad P = .0131$$
$$i = -11 \qquad\quad i = -1$$
$$\bar{R}^2 = .9915\ SE = .3423\ DW = 1.399$$

Version I Statistics $\qquad\qquad \bar{R}^2 = .9845\ SE = .4625\ DW = 1.1040$

$$IPC = 2.553 + .02792 * KC_{-1} + .1923 * EPC2_{-1} \qquad (6)$$
$$(3.30)\quad(8.56)\qquad\qquad(1.33)$$

$$+ \sum_{i=0}^{7} a_{6i} XC_{-i} + \sum_{i=0}^{15} b_{6i} (UCCC/P)_{-i}$$

$$[.7246] \qquad\qquad [-341.9020]$$
$$P = .1258 \qquad\quad P = -49.6543$$
$$i = -3 \qquad\qquad i = -4$$

[8] The sum of the distributed lag coefficients is shown in square brackets. Underneath the sum is shown P, the peak absolute value of the lag coefficients, and i, the timing of the peak value. Due to space limitations, the lag coefficients and their t-values are not included in the text. They are available from the authors on request.

$$\bar{R}^2 = .9671 \ SE = .9593 \ DW = .6510$$

Version I Statistics $\qquad \bar{R}^2 = .9679 \ SE = .9475 \ DW = .6910$

Inclusion of anticipations reduces the standard error of estimate in these equations for IPMM and IPR. In the IPC equation, the effect of anticipations is not significant, and the Version II equation is marginally worse than the Version I formulation. The coefficient of the anticipations is statistically significant in the other equations, but it is smaller than unity[9] even in the cases (IPR and IPMM) where the categories of investment covered and the anticipations variables correspond. In contrast to the realizations interpretations, the lagged objective variables continue to have a significant effect. The anticipations must consequently be seen as auxiliary variables in this scheme.

Version III forces the investment equations into a realizations function mold. Following Jorgenson it is assumed that investment is a distributed lag function of the anticipations in contrast to the typical realization function formulation which takes the anticipations as direct predictors (with an implied coefficient of 1.0) of investment. However, investment plans may be modified after they have been made so that it is appropriate to introduce intervening variables, objective variables which provide information on the period between the formulation of investment plans and their realization. The general functional form used here is

$$I_t = f(\lambda_{1,2}(\Theta) \ EP_{1,2}, Z_i)$$

where $\lambda_{1,2}(\Theta)EP_{1,2}$ are distributed lags of the first and second investment anticipations and Z_i are objective variables occurring after the anticipations are formed. In contrast to Version II, the distributed lag here applies to the anticipations which are forced to account for lagged values of the objective variables, since only

---

[9] In view of multicollinearity, statistical considerations determined whether first or second anticipations or both were included.

current (or briefly lagged) values of the latter are used. These functions put much heavier weight on the anticipations than the

Table 3

VERSION III REALIZATION INVESTMENT FUNCTION

$$IPMM = -3.268 - 7.701 * UCCMM/P \qquad (7)$$
$$(3.07) \quad (2.43)$$

$$+ 6.113 * CPMM_{-1} + .01627 * XMM$$
$$(4.67) \qquad\qquad (4.26)$$

$$+ \sum_{i=0}^{4} a_{7i}\, EPMM1_{-2-i} + \sum_{i=0}^{4} b_{7i}\, EPMM2_{-1-i}$$

$$[-.2972] \qquad\qquad [1.1029]$$
$$P = -.0831 \qquad\qquad P = .5134$$
$$i = -1 \qquad\qquad\quad i = -1$$
$$\overline{R}^2 = .9951 \; SE = .3479 \; DW = 1.586$$

$$IPR = -.3786 + .2066 * XR \qquad (8)$$
$$(.763) \quad (4.74)$$

$$-.0111 * KR_{-1} + \sum_{i=0}^{4} a_{8i}\, EPR1_{-2-i}$$
$$(2.43)$$

$$\phantom{+ \sum_{i=0}^{4}} [.8307]$$
$$+ \sum_{i=0}^{4} b_{8i}\, EPR2_{-1-i}\; P = .2800$$
$$\phantom{+ \sum_{i=0}^{4} b_{8i}\, } i = -3$$
$$[.0595]$$
$$P = .4581$$
$$i = 0$$
$$\overline{R}^2 = .9878 \; SE = .4096 \; DW = 1.296$$

$$IPC = -3.920 + .0823 * XC \qquad (9)$$
$$(.624) \quad (2.31)$$

$$-14.297 * UCCC/PCOM + .0065 * KC_{-1}$$
$$(.512) \qquad\qquad\qquad (.472)$$

$$+ \sum_{i=0}^{4} a_{9i}\, EPC2_{-1-i} + \sum_{i=0}^{4} b_{9i}\, EPC1_{-2-i}$$

$$[-.5517] \qquad\qquad [.70108]$$
$$P = -.4201 \qquad\qquad P = .2461$$
$$i = -4 \qquad\qquad\quad i = -1$$
$$\overline{R}^2 = .9620 \; SE = 1.0302 \; DW = .686$$

Version II formulation. The Version III investment functions, shown in Table 3, also improve on functions without anticipatory variables. But in comparison to the Version II equations, the equation for IPMM is an improvement; whereas for IPR and IPC the realization formulation is not quite as good. The distributed lag coefficients of the anticipations carry negative signs in some instances. It should be remembered that the first and second anticipations are in effect two readings, one quarter apart (at time $t-2$ and $t-1$), on the same investment to be carried out at time t. The inclusion of both anticipations means that the interpretation of the coefficients is somewhat precarious. In the case of the equation for IPMM (Eq.7) the sum of the coefficients over the entire lag period for EPMM1 is $-.297$ and for EPMM2 it is 1.103. Writing in terms of the first anticipation, the effect is $(-.297 + 1.103)$ EPMM1 $+ 1.103$ (EPMM2$-$ EPMM1).

The first anticipation has an impact of .806 and a revision of the anticipations has a somewhat greater effect of 1.103. In the case of IPR the effect of the first anticipation can be calculated as .890 but revisions of anticipations only have a small effect of .060.

The objective variables in these equations, intended to catch the impact of changes in the investment after investment plans are made, have been included only when the results had directions of effect in agreement with prior notions.

Equations to explain the anticipations variables themselves have been formulated in the same way as in the model equations for investment. It is assumed that investment plans are a function of objective variables for activity, user cost, and capital stock or capacity utilization. The function for the second anticipations includes the first anticipations as a variable. They may be considered a form of "revisions of anticipations" equations. The functions selected are shown in Table 4.

The equations explaining the first anticipations are quite similar with regard to coefficients and lag structure to the original equations explaining investment in terms of objective variables only. In the equations for the second anticipations the objective variables remain statistically significant, but, as we would expect, these coefficients are much smaller since the first anticipations are included in the equation. Here again the empirical evidence suggests that the first anticipations play an "auxiliary" role and that the

Table 4

FUNCTIONS FOR INVESTMENT ANTICIPATIONS

$$EPMM2 = -\,2.648 + .7624 * EPMM1_{-1} \tag{10}$$
$$(1.03)\quad(8.81)$$

$$+\,4.0512 * CPMM_{-2} + \sum_{i=0}^{5} a_{10i}\,(XMM_{-1})_{-i}$$
$$(1.74)$$
$$[.0343]$$
$$P = .0106$$
$$i = -1$$

$$+\sum_{i=0}^{15} b_{10i}\,(UCMM/PMM)_{-1_{-i}}$$
$$[-12.8062]$$
$$P = -2.8030$$
$$i = -3$$

$$\overline{R}^2 = .9901\; SE = .5070\; DW = 2.241$$

$$EPMM1 = -\,10.169 + 16.236 * CPMM_{-3} \tag{11}$$
$$(2.35)\quad(5.64)$$

$$+\sum_{i=0}^{5} a_{11i}\,(XMM_{-2})_{-i} + \sum_{i=0}^{15} b_{11i}\,(UCMM/PMM)_{-2_{-i}}$$
$$[.1401]\qquad\qquad\quad[-49.3650]$$
$$P = .0313\qquad\qquad\quad P = -8.0960$$
$$i = -2\qquad\qquad\qquad i = -3$$
$$\overline{R}^2 = .9715\; SE = .8523\; DW = .647$$

$$EPR2\;\; =\;\; 1.7259 - .00996 * KR_{-2} \tag{12}$$
$$(1.44)\qquad(.984)$$

$$+\,.6666 * EPR_{-1} + \sum_{i=0}^{36} a_{12i}\,(XR_{-1})_{-i}$$
$$(7.17)$$
$$[.3233]$$
$$P = .0128$$
$$i = -18$$

$$+\sum_{i=0}^{33} b_{12i}\,(UCCR/PXR)_{-1_{-i}} + \sum_{i=0}^{4} c_{12i}\,(XMF_{-1})_{-i}$$
$$[-39.7899]\qquad\qquad\qquad[-.0075]$$
$$P = -2.1591\qquad\qquad\qquad P = -.0053$$
$$i = -10\qquad\qquad\qquad\quad i = -4$$
$$R^2 = .9912\; SE = .2296\; DW = 2.591$$

Continued Table 4

$$EPR1 = 2.196 - .05765 * KR_{-3} \qquad (13)$$
$$(1.12) \quad (3.76)$$

$$+ \sum_{i=0}^{36} a_{13i}(XR_{-2})_{-i} + \sum_{i=0}^{33} b_{13i}(UCCR/PXR)_{-i}$$

$$\begin{array}{cc} [1.0100] & [-94.2582] \\ P = .0401 & P = -4.2204 \\ i = -17 & i = -13 \end{array}$$

$$+ \sum_{i=0}^{4} c_{13i}(XMF_{-2})_{-i}$$

$$[.0490]$$
$$P = .0224$$
$$i = -1$$
$$\overline{R}^2 = .9775 \; SE = .3894 \; DW = 1.907$$

$$EPC2 = 1.086 + .00858 * KC_{-2} \qquad (14)$$
$$(1.99) \quad (4.40)$$

$$+ .6179 * EPC1_{-1} + \sum_{i=0}^{10} a_{14i} \Delta (XC_{-1})_{-i}$$
$$(6.49)$$

$$[.3393]$$
$$P = .0434$$
$$i = -6$$

$$+ \sum_{i=0}^{15} b_{14i} \Delta (UCC/PCOM)_{-1-i}$$

$$[-166.5655]$$
$$P = -18.1043$$
$$i = -4$$
$$\overline{R}^2 = .9679 \; SE = .6402 \; DW = 2.365$$

$$EPC1 \cdot = 4.813 + .01866 * KC_{-3} \qquad (15)$$
$$(12.6) \quad (14.4)$$

$$+ \sum_{i=0}^{10} a_{15i} \Delta (XC_{-2})_{-i} + \sum_{i=0}^{15} b_{15i} \Delta (UCC/PCOM)_{-2-i}$$

$$\begin{array}{cc} [.7936] & [-507.3583] \\ P = .0999 & P = -58.3565 \\ i = -5 & i = -4 \end{array}$$
$$\overline{R}^2 = .9355 \; SE = .8498 \; DW = .914$$

coefficients do not fully describe a "revision" of anticipations process.

Residential Construction

Two alternative approaches to explaining residential construction have been tested. As before, Version II seeks simply to add supplementary anticipations variables − single and multiple housing starts and CSI − to the present Wharton Model residential construction equation. The alternative Version III approach establishes a more direct estimated distributed lag relationship between construction of new housing and includes separate treatment of additons and alterations.

The original Wharton Model residential construction equation uses Maisel's average time phasing relationship between housing starts and construction-put-in-place as weights for Fisher type distributed lags on the monetary tightness and the relative price terms. The same weighting scheme has been applied to the anticipations variables added to this equation. The Version II equation

$$(16)$$

$$IH = 14.656 + .0088 * Y \; .6047 * \sum_{i=0}^{2} w_i \, (IL - IS)_{-i}$$
$$\quad (2.84) \quad (2.66) \quad (2.83)$$

$$+ \; 9.692 * \sum_{i=0}^{2} w_i \, HSM_{-i} + 7.954 \; \sum_{i=0}^{2} w_i \, HS1_{-i}$$
$$\quad (9.90) \qquad\qquad\qquad (11.35)$$

$$+ \; .06230 * \sum_{i=0}^{2} w_i \, CSI_{-i} - 13.7470 * \sum_{i=0}^{2} w_i \, (PH/PR)_{-i}$$
$$\quad (3.52) \qquad\qquad\qquad (2.998)$$

$$\bar{R}^2 = .9129 \; SE = .5853$$

$$w_0 = .41 \qquad\qquad DW = .786$$
$$w_1 = .49$$
$$w_2 = .10$$

Version I Statistics $\qquad \bar{R}^2 = .5777 \; SE = 1.289 \; DW = .3968$

shows significant coefficients for multiple starts and single starts and for CSI. The objective variables continue to be statistically significant but with substantially smaller coefficients. The degree of explanation achieved is spectacularly higher than in equations without anticipations variables.

The Version III approach equations use a different disaggregation, one more appropriate for relating residential construction and housing starts. Total residential construction is broken down:

$$IHT = INHU + AA$$

where INHU = construction of new houses

and AA = additions and alterations and non housekeeping residential construction are explained separately. Note that INHU includes farms since the current housing starts statistics usually include farm housing.[10] The value of new residential construction (in 1958$) is explained in terms of single and multiple starts and the lagged average real value per start.

$$(17)$$

$$INHU = -12.447 + 1.0224 * (INHU_{-1}/(\sum_{i=1}^{3} w_i \, HST_{-i})$$
$$ (7.12) \quad (8.88)$$

$$+ \sum_{i=0}^{3} a_{17i} \, HS1_{-1} + \sum_{i=0}^{3} b_{17i} \, HSM_{-i}$$

[12.4672]	[11.7426]
$P = 5.4413$	$P = 4.7054$
$i = 0$	$i = 0$

$$\bar{R}^2 = .9534 \; SE = .3990 \; DW = 2.314$$

$$w_0 = .41$$
$$w_1 = .49$$
$$w_2 = .10$$

This is a statistical approximation of the OBE procedure of translating starts into construction put in place.

It is interesting to note that the distributed lag for single and multiple starts is practically the same and conforms closely to the phasing used in the Version II equation.[11] The lagged average value per start (in 1958$) carries a coefficient slightly greater than unity, indicating an upward trend in real value per start. As a result of the inclusion of this variable the coefficients of single and multiple starts are of about equal value.

Additions and alterations, a residual item which poses some

---

[10] Since nonfarm residential construction is contained in the model, it is obtained by subtracting farm residential construction, as exogenous variable, from IHT.

[11] The phasing is as follows: DISTRIBUTED LAG WEIGHTS

	HSI	HSM	Version II Phasing
Quarter t	.44	.40	.41
$t-1$	.42	.40	.49
$t-2$	.18	.20	.10

seasonal adjustment problems, is explained very simply in terms of a time trend, a seasonal correction dummy, the consumer sentiment index, and the distributed lag on housing construction prices.

$$AA = 23.493 + .0269 * TIME + 1.0 \ PAA \qquad (18)$$
$$(11.1) \quad (13.8)$$

$$+ \sum_{i=0}^{5} a_{18i} \ (PH/P)_{-i} + \sum_{i=0}^{5} b_{18i} \ CSI_{-i}$$

$$[22.2411] \qquad\qquad [.0303]$$
$$P = 6.1478 \qquad\qquad P = .0098$$
$$i = -1 \qquad\qquad\quad i = -1$$
$$\overline{R}^2 = .8705 \ SE = .2143 \ DW = .7307$$

Interestingly, the short term fluctuation of residential additions and alterations are picked up by a distributed lag on consumer sentiment, which has a highly significant effect in this equation.

The explanation of housing starts is visualized in terms similar to those used to explain residential construction in the Version I equation. Since the factors affecting single starts are likely to differ from those affecting multiple starts, the two classes of starts have been considered separately.

The equations used are:

$$HS1 = -1.427 + .0056 * (Y-TR/PC) \qquad (19)$$
$$(1.48) \quad (5.08)$$
$$- .02277 * TIME - .09703 * TIGHT$$
$$(7.028) \qquad\qquad (2.32)$$

$$+ \sum_{i=0}^{8} a_{19i} \ (IL-IS)_{-i} + \sum_{i=0}^{8} b_{19i} \ (PH/P)_{-i}$$

$$[.2348] \qquad\qquad [1.3255]$$
$$P = .0368 \qquad\qquad P = -.9554$$
$$i = -5 \qquad\qquad\quad i = -1$$

$$+ \sum_{i=0}^{4} c_{19i} \ \Delta \ CSI_{-i}$$

$$[.0144]$$
$$P = .0064$$
$$i = -1$$

$$\overline{R}^2 = .9057 \ SE = .0644 \ DW = 1.326$$

$$HSM = 1.9196 - .1249 * TIGHT \qquad\qquad (20)$$
$$(2.50) \quad (3.90)$$
$$+ .00233 * (Y - TR/PC) + \sum_{i=0}^{8} a_{20i}\,(IL - IS)_{-i}$$
$$(7.26)$$
$$[.1745]$$
$$P = .0267$$
$$i = -5$$

$$+ \sum_{i=0}^{8} b_{20i}\,(PR/P)_{-i}$$
$$[-2.5017]$$
$$P = -.4677$$
$$i = -2$$
$$\bar{R}^2 = .8761 \ \ SE = .0643 \ \ DW = .510$$

Both kinds of starts are sensitive to monetary tightness. This has been indicated here by a nonlinear effect of the interest rate differential as a proxy variable. The difference between the long and the short interest rate is introduced with a distributed lag, and it enters once again in the form of the "TIGHT" dummy which catches those unusual periods of monetary crisis when the short rate exceeds the long rate. Both equations have an income effect. The price effect is on the price of houses for single starts and on the price of rentals in the case of multiples. Single housing starts have a negative time trend in accord with recent developments. Remarkably, the single starts are significantly affected by changes in consumer sentiment, multiple starts are not. The degree of explanation achieved is quite good.

SYSTEM SIMULATION RESULTS

Full system dynamic simulations of the anticipations equations as part of the Wharton Model were carried out for the period 1960.1 to 1970.1. The simulations make use of the entire model except for the tax functions; taxes are treated as exogenous.[12]

[12] Exogenizing taxes tends to increase the errors of the model as compared to a simulation of the complete system since errors in the endogenous tax estimates would tend to offset errors elsewhere in the system. However, the comparisons made here are not likely to be affected. No constant adjustments, which would also tend to reduce forecast error, were made.

Table 5

SIMULATION RESULTS

		Version I				Version II				Version III			
		Forecast Period (Quarters)											
		1	2	3	4	1	2	3	4	1	2	3	4
CA	RMSE	1.137	1.275	1.359	1.393	1.061	1.172	1.315	1.381	1.063	1.140	1.267	1.331
	|%E|	3.122	3.652	3.948	4.019	3.019	3.499	3.864	4.039	3.086	3.498	3.846	3.900
	$\bar{E}$	.183	.252	.282	.315	.105	.147	.205	.245	.061	.094	.153	.198
IP	RMSE	1.679	1.871	2.071	2.223	1.243	1.479	2.041	2.138	1.092	1.297	1.800	2.167
	|%E|	2.305	2.668	2.908	3.058	1.579	1.938	2.830	2.921	1.481	1.766	2.407	3.005
	$\bar{E}$	.070	.249	.303	.360	-.002	.052	.065	.156	-.028	-.018	-.078	-.084
IPMM	RMSE	.706	.840	.942	1.015	.469	.767	.944	.956	.358	.438	.739	.972
	|%E|	2.940	3.481	3.838	4.173	1.770	2.105	3.755	3.944	1.517	1.711	2.924	3.914
	|$\bar{E}$|	.084	.219	.228	.240	.035	.057	.030	.077	.007	.021	-.006	-.004
IPR	RMSE	.429	.422	.438	.475	.323	.352	.416	.445	.356	.400	.450	.461
	|%E|	2.190	2.186	2.317	2.459	1.596	1.822	2.198	2.240	1.828	2.017	2.241	2.313
	$\bar{E}$	.025	.038	.054	.068	.011	.024	.046	.052	.022	-.017	-.006	.010
IPC	RMSE	1.025	1.087	1.126	1.158	.953	1.046	1.134	1.191	.949	1.013	1.092	1.208
	|%E|	4.045	4.338	4.578	4.702	3.810	4.203	4.650	4.825	3.610	3.870	4.370	4.850
	$\bar{E}$	-.039	-.008	.021	.051	-.048	-.028	-.010	.028	-.012	-.022	.065	-.090
IH	RMSE	1.431	1.443	1.496	1.682	.730	1.089	1.248	1.292	.636	1.240	1.744	2.087
	|%E|	5.521	5.572	5.622	6.552	2.680	3.661	4.283	4.586	2.374	4.634	6.756	8.237
	$\bar{E}$	-.084	-.078	-.088	-.027	-.028	-.034	.013	.101	.026	.048	.023	-.144

Continued Table 5

		Version I				Version II				Version III			
		Forecast Period (Quarters)											
		1	2	3	4	1	2	3	4	1	2	3	4
GNP $	RMSE	4.141	6.117	7.756	8.474	3.785	5.716	7.597	8.365	3.739	5.383	7.131	7.984
	|%E|	.485	.730	.939	1.020	.445	.687	.938	1.014	.441	.656	.888	.972
	$\bar{E}$	.350	.541	.776	1.191	.167	.189	.413	.876	.074	.039	.186	.537
1958 $													
GNP	RMSE	4.068	5.506	6.434	6.707	3.741	5.009	6.125	6.425	3.653	4.720	5.680	6.006
	|%E|	.532	.699	.839	.878	.487	.634	.808	.864	.474	.605	.767	.804
	$\bar{E}$	.916	1.180	1.473	1.888	.736	.817	1.069	1.516	.640	.659	.845	1.195
P	RMSE	.0027	.0036	.0043	.0055	.0027	.0035	.0042	.0054	.0027	.0042	.0042	.005
	|%E|	.204	.265	.332	.413	.199	.266	.325	.404	.201	.261	.321	.392
	$\bar{E}$	-.001	-.001	-.002	-.002	-.001	-.001	-.002	-.002	.0009	-.0013	-.0016	-.001
C	RMSE	2.349	3.009	3.857	3.987	2.240	2.803	3.396	3.830	2.229	2.728	3.248	3.645
	|%E|	.474	.609	.765	.831	.461	.573	.720	.807	.461	.571	.697	.765
	$\bar{E}$	.416	.631	.783	.958	.314	.463	.617	.793	.256	.383	.523	.687
W $	RMSE	1.946	3.178	4.200	4.830	1.906	3.113	4.151	4.840	1.905	3.093	4.101	4.783
	|%E|	.386	.710	.919	1.017	.382	.691	.912	1.014	.384	.686	.900	1.006
	$\bar{E}$	.170	.378	.544	.807	.135	.294	.437	.704	.116	.256	.383	.640
UN	RMSE	.261	.450	.584	.659	.254	.435	.573	.656	.254	.431	.564	.643
	|%E|	4.102	7.542	10.233	12.290	3.977	7.166	9.895	11.999	3.961	7.001	9.568	11.619
	$\bar{E}$	-.203	-.027	-.029	-.034	-.016	-.010	-.003	-.005	-.012	-.001	.009	.012

RMSE = Root Mean Square Error |%E| = Percent Absolute Error $\bar{E}$ = Mean Error

Runs embodying Version II equations (1), (3), (4), (5), (6), (10), (11), (12), (13), (14), (15), (16), (19), (20) and Version III equations (2), (3), (7), (8), (9), (10), (11), (12), (13), (14), (15), (17), (18), (19), (20) are compared with Version I, the standard version of the Model. Results for forecast simulations for one-quarter, two-quarter, three-quarter, and four-quarter forecasts are summarized in Table 5.

Looking first at the GNP components which are directly affected by the equation changes (shown in the first page of the Table) substantial improvements are apparent in the predictions for investment and housing. For consumer purchases of automobiles there is also an improvement but it is relatively smaller.

The additional information provided by anticipations data is most important for the early quarters when the actual data on anticipations are used in the equations. As the forecast is extended beyond this point, the estimates of anticipations used are themselves endogenous and the gain in accuracy diminishes.

The modest gain obtained in the simulation of CA is not surprising in view of the analogous single equation result. Consumer sentiment has a net effect in reducing RMSE in Version III, particularly, where the unemployment variable has been omitted entirely. But, of course, consumer sentiment is closely related to the employment situation so that much of the impact of consumer attitudes has already been incorporated in the unemployment variable used in the Version I equation. It is interesting however to note that the formulation using the attitude variable shows less positive bias (a lower mean error, $\bar{E}$) than the Version I equation.

In the case of business fixed investment, the greatest improvement occurs with IPMM. RMSE is reduced almost by one-half in the one- and two-quarter forecasts and remains a little lower even in the third and fourth quarter. The realizations function formulation (Version III) gives consistently better results in this case. Again the anticipations appear to reduce bias. The results are less clear for IPR and IPC. Beyond the first quarter forecasts the gains are quite small, and while Version III is best for IPC, the "auxiliary" Version II works best for IPR. As was apparent in the single equation results as well, the anticipations data seem to be less firmly linked to investment in these categories than they are for manufacturing and mining.

313

With regard to residential construction, the anticipations equations reduce RMSE almost by one-half for the one-quarter predictions and by lesser amounts in subsequent quarters. Some improvement remains even in the four-quarter predictions. Surprisingly, however, the more disaggregated Version III equations do less well after the one-quarter forecasts than the Version II equations, and after two quarters even less well than the Version I formulation. Why this should be so is not clear. There is reason to question the validity of the underlying data breakdown, and that may explain the failure of the more disaggregated equations in Version III to give as good results as the simpler versions.

Results of the forecast simulations for aggregative statistics are shown on the second page of Table 5. In view of the considerable improvement for the GNP components, we might have hoped for a larger decrease in the error statistics for the GNP aggregate. Despite the effects of offsetting errors[13], we do find a systematic reduction in Version II and III below the error statistics of the Version I simulation that makes no use of anticipations variables. This improvement ranges from $.4 to $.8 billion in the RMSE for GNP in current and constant dollars (Version II compared to Version I). It is noteworthy that the reductions in error, though modest, are sustained for as long as four quarters. We fully expected to find most of the impact of anticipations in the first two quarters. At the same time the bias of the forecasts is reduced particularly in Version III.

---

[13] One offset is related to the inventory determination equations of the Wharton Mark III model. The latter explain the movement of inventories in terms of an approximation of the identity

Inventory Change = Production − Sales.

If current production exceeds sales, inventories are being accumulated; if sales exceed production inventories are being reduced. The approximation to this identity substitutes GNP final demand components to take the role of sales. On the production side of the identity, proxies for investment demand enter with lags. This means that in the very short run a change in the prediction for IP, or IH, is partially translated into an offsetting change in inventories.

There is almost no impact on the price forecasts, and the improvement in the estimates for unemployment is very small.

The separate effect of the anticipatory variables for consumption, investment, and residential construction is shown in Table 6. For these simulations, only the equations introducing anticipations relevant to one GNP component at a time have been changed (using Version III equations for consumption and investment and Version II equations for residential construction). Other equations remain as in Version I. The results show that in each case the use of anticipations variables results in a small improvement in the forecast of aggregate GNP.

CONCLUSIONS

The survey data on consumer sentiment pioneered by George Katona are only one type of anticipatory material on economic developments. We have suggested in this study that these data must be fitted into the structure of econometric models in a logical and specific way, not as broad cyclical indicators. Consumer attitudes help to explain consumption; investment anticipations relate to various types of investment; and housing starts signal the movement of residential construction. While the forecasting horizon of the anticipations themselves may be limited, we have fitted them into the model endogenously, using the actual data when available and the endogenous estimates of the anticipations for later periods. The anticipations have been cast in the role of auxiliary variables in one formulation and into a realizations equation framework in another.

We conclude from these calculations that the anticipatory variables are indeed useful in prediction. On a single equation basis and in full system simulations, the inclusion of the anticipations improves prediction for the relevant components of GNP, particularly for one- and two-quarter predictions. The net contribution of the consumer attitudes is relatively modest. This does not mean that consumers fail to react to their feelings about economic prospects. Rather it reflects the presence of a proxy for attitudes, the unemployment rate, in the original consumer purchases of autos equation. The impact of anticipatory variables is greater in

315

Table 6

SEPARATE EFFECTS OF ANTICIPATORY VARIABLES

Anticipations Variables in:

		CA (Version III equations)				IP (Version III equations)				IH (Version II equations)			
		Forecast Period (Quarters)											
		1	2	3	4	1	2	3	4	1	2	3	4
GNP $	RMSE	3.963	5.836	7.507	8.337	4.029	5.928	7.700	8.494	4.018	5.888	7.431	8.08
	|%E|	.474	.718	.945	1.030	.471	.695	.932	1.021	.474	.710	.903	.98
	Ē	.124	.149	.319	.749	.301	.424	.629	1.038	.338	.497	.708	1.09
GNP 1958$	RMSE	3.880	5.157	6.070	6.366	3.948	5.281	6.341	6.692	3.983	5.348	6.193	6.42
	|%E|	.513	.669	.819	.868	.511	.666	.816	.879	.522	.683	.808	.83
	Ē	.663	.744	.973	1.399	.874	1.059	1.294	1.673	.925	1.175	1.458	1.85

RMSE = Root Mean Square Error; 1% E = Percent Absolute Error; Ē = Mean Error.

the business fixed investment and housing equations where anticipatory information is likely to be more firm. For aggregate GNP, the improvement in RMSE amounts to $.4 to $.8 billion and persists even in four-quarter forecasts.

The last word has not been said on the usefulness of anticipations data in macro-economic models. This study suggests that, properly integrated into the framework of structural equations, anticipations variables can make an important contribution to improved prediction of the components of GNP and to a lesser extent to the prediction of aggregate economic activity.

APPENDIX
LIST OF VARIABLES

C	** PERSONAL CONSUMPTION EXPENDITURES
CA	** PERSONAL CONSUMPTION EXPENDITURES ON AUTOS & PARTS
CDA$	NONPASSBK. SAVINGS OF PUBLIC AT MEMBER BANKS
CPMM	WHARTON CAPACITY INDEX, MFG & MINING
CR	DUMMY: CONSUMER CREDIT–REG W
CSI	MICH CONSUMER SENTIMENT INDEX
CUR$	CURRENCY COMPONENT OF MONEY SUPPLY, SA
DAA	DUMMY FOR BAD SEASONAL; NONZERO IN 68.2,69.2,69.3,70.1
DD$	DEMAND DEPOSIT COMPONENT OF MONEY SUPPLY, SA
DS	DUMMY: AUTO SUPPLY SHORTAGE 48.1–2,48.3–4,49.1,53.3
EPC1	* 1ST INVEST ANTICIPATION, COMMERCIAL – ADVANCED 2 QTR
EPC2	* 2ND INVEST ANTICIPATION, COMMERCIAL – ADVANCED 1 QTR
EPMM1	* 1ST INVEST ANTICIPATION, MFG+MINING – ADVANCED 2 QTR
EPMM2	* 2ND INVEST ANTICIPATION, MFG+MINING – ADVANCED 1 QTR
EPR1	* 1ST INVEST ANTICIPATION, REGULATED – ADVANCED 2 QTR
EPR2	* 2ND INVEST ANTICIPATION, REGULATED – ADVANCED 1 QTR
HS1	SINGLE UNIT NEW PRIVATE HOUSING STARTS INCL FARM, SA
HSM	TOTAL NEW MULTIPLE UNIT HOUSING STARTS, SA
IH	** FIXED INVESTMENT IN NONFARM RESIDENTIAL STRUCTURES
IHAA	** INVESTMENT IN RESIDENTIAL ADDITIONS & ALTERATIONS, SA
IHT	** FIXED INVESTMENT IN TOTAL RESIDENTIAL STRUCTURES, SA
IL	MOODY'S TOTAL CORPORATE BOND YIELD
INHU	** INVESTMENT IN NEW RESIDENTIAL STRUCTURES
IP	** IPC+IPMM+IPR
IPC	** COMML & OTHER P+E INVEST.
IPMM	** MINING+MFG. P & E INVESTMENT
IPR	** INVEST IN REG P & EQUIP.
IS	RATE ON 4–6 MO. PRIME COMM'L PAPER
KC	** CAPITAL STK IN COMMERCIAL & OTHER
KR	** CAPITAL STK IN REGULATED IND
LIQUID	(CUR$+DD$+TD$–CDA$)/(Y∗PC)
MHTR	** MOBILE HOMES & TRAVEL TRAILERS PURCHASES

317

P		IMPLICIT PRICE DEFLATOR FOR GNP
PA		AUTOS & PARTS DEFLATOR
PC		IMPLICIT DEFLATOR FOR PCE
PCOM	**	COMM. AND OTHER GPO DEFLATOR
PH		IMPLICIT DEFLATOR FOR NONFARM RES. STRUCT.
PMM	**	MANUF. AND MINING GPO DEFLATOR
PR		RENTAL COMPONENT OF CPI
PXR		REGULATED GPO DEFLATOR
TD$		TIME DEPOSITS SA
TIGHT		INTEREST RATE DUMMY = 1.0 WHEN IS > IL; 0 OTHERWISE
TIME		TIME TREND, 1948. 1 = 1
TR		TRANSFER PAYMENTS RECEIVED BY PERSONS
UCCC		USER COST OF CAPITAL, COMMERCIAL INDUSTRIES, EQUIP'T
UCCMM		USER COST OF CAPITAL, MFG. & MINING, EQUIPMENT
UCCR		USER COST OF CAPITAL, REGULATED INDUSTRIES, EQUIP'T
UN		UNEMPLOYMENT RATE, ALL CIVILIAN WORKERS
W$		COMPENSATION OF EMPLOYEES
XC	**	GPO, COMMERCIAL AND OTHER
XMM	**	GPO IN MINING, MFG.
XR	**	GPO IN REGULATED IND.
Y		DISPOSABLE PERSONAL INCOME DEFLATED BY PC

*   Investment anticipations are deflated by deflator for business fixed investment at time investment is to be put in place.

**   1958$

REFERENCES

1 Adams, F.G., "Consumer Attitudes, Buying Plans and Purchases of Durable Goods", *Review of Economics and Statistics*, November, 1964.

2 Adams, F.G., and E.W. Green, "Explaining and Predicting Consumer Attitudes", *International Economic Review*, 1965.

3 Brady, E.A., "An Econometric Analysis of the U.S. Residential Housing Market", Working Paper #11, Federal Home Loan Bank Board, Washington, D.C., November 30, 1970.

4 Duesenberry, J. (ed.), *et al., The Brookings Quarterly Econometric Model of the United States*, Chicago: Rand McNally, 1965.

5 Evans, M.K., and Lawrence R. Klein, *The Wharton Econometric Forecasting Model*, Philadelphia: Economics Research Unit, University of Pennsylvania, 1968, 2nd rev. ed.

6 Fair, R.C., *A Short-Run Forecasting Model of the U.S. Economy*, Lexington, Massachusetts: D.C. Heath and Company, 1971, Chap. 5.

7 Friend, I., and W.C. Thomas, "A Reevaluation of the Predictive Ability of Plant and Equipment Anticipations", *Journal of the American Statistical Association*, June, 1970.

8 Hymans, S.H., "Consumer Durable Spending: Explanation and Prediction", *Brookings Papers on Economic Activity*, 2, Washington, D.C.: The Brookings Institution, 1970.

9 Liebenberg, M., .A. Hirsch, and J. Popkin, "A Quarterly Econometric Model of the U.S.: A Progress Report", *Survey of Current Business*, May, 1966.

Uncertainty, Expectations, and Durable Goods Demand Models*

F. THOMAS JUSTER AND PAUL WACHTEL

INTRODUCTION

A number of studies have explored the use of survey data on consumer expectations models of durable goods demand (*see* Mueller [8], Brookings-SSRC [2], Maynes [7], Juster [5], Juster-Wachtel [6]). For the most part these are single equation models, with the dependent variable generally automobile rather than total durable goods purchases. Expectational variables typically used in such models are the Survey Research Center Index of Consumer Sentiment, A, and an expected or planned purchase variable, p, derived either from Survey Research Center (SRC) data or from the methodologically similar survey conducted by the U.S. Bureau of the Census.

In previous papers, the authors (Juster [5] and Juster-Wachtel

* This paper is part of a larger program of research being conducted by the National Bureau of Economic Research in cooperation with the U.S. Bureau of the Census. The program is supported by a grant from the National Science Foundation, as well as by other funds of the National Bureau. We are indebted to Teresita Rodriguez and Jayati Mitra for research assistance on the project. The paper has not been reviewed or approved by either the staff or directors of the National Bureau.

[6]) have explored the question of equation specification for expectational variables in durable goods demand models, and the optimal mix of objective variables like income or price and expectational variables like consumer sentiment or buying plans. The findings are representative of those reported in other studies: the Index of Consumer Sentiment ordinarily makes a significant contribution to the explanation of the cyclical variability in automobile purchase rates, but its presence tends to result in unstable regression coefficients; the expected purchase variable contributes to the explanation of both trend and cyclical movements in purchase rates but tends to be sluggish in reflecting the full extent of the cyclical movements; permanent income makes no net contribution to an explanation of the variance in purchases of durables if an expected purchase variable is included, and more generally, the only "objective" economic variables that play an important role in a fully specified expectational model are transitory income and, possibly, relative prices.

This last finding — that permanent (expected) income plays no role in durable goods demand models when expected purchases are included — may appear to some readers as a striking and unusual result. It is neither: after all, expected purchases represent plans reported by households with full knowledge of their past and present financial situation, and it ought to be mainly unforeseen changes in financial status that would explain actual purchase behavior relative to purchase expectations.

THE UNCERTAINTY HYPOTHESIS

The purpose of this paper is to suggest a specification which is consistent with the conceptual content of the consumer expectation measures, and in addition seems to capture the best features of both the consumer sentiment and expected purchase variables in a formal statistical sense. We also explore the question of deriving optimal quarterly forecasts for models that use expectational (or other) variables where the analytically relevant time span is not necessarily a single quarter but may be a six-, nine-, or twelve-month span.

We hypothesize that expected purchases or plans represent the household's best (single-valued) estimate of future purchase rates. However, this estimate may be a biased measure of future purchase behavior because it takes no account of the dispersion of purchase expectations due to uncertainty. For example, the point estimate of expected purchases reported by each household does not have to represent the mean value of some distribution: it could easily be the mode. If so, the point estimate would be a biased estimate of the mean whenever the distribution was skewed. Alternatively, the point estimate could represent a mean value but the influence of intervening events in a realization function might be asymmetrical. That is, favorable intervening events might have little influence on purchases in a realization function when the general economic climate is pessimistic, but a strong influence when the climate is optimistic, and vice versa for unfavorable intervening events.

Next, we hypothesize that the Index of Consumer Sentiment is a variable that reflects not only the general state of consumer optimism or pessimism, but also the impact of consumer uncertainty in the sense of either an asymmetrical disperion about the mean or an asymmetrical influence of intervening variables. While the Index of Consumer Sentiment summarizes movements in a number of variables, a major part of its time series variance is due to movements in two components: responses to questions about short-term business prospects in the economy as a whole, and responses to questions about whether the present is a "good or bad time to buy major durables and appliances". Both of these components can reasonably be viewed as either an optimism-pessimism yardstick or as a reflection of the state of consumer uncertainty about economic events relevant to purchase decisions. Thus, when the consumer sentiment index is improving, optimism is growing and uncertainty is being dispelled, and vice versa when the index is deteriorating.[1]

---

[1] In the context of this paper the question whether the Consumer Sentiment Index measures optimism-pessimism or some phenomena best described by a term like uncertainty is a purely semantic one with no operational content. For future research, however, the distinction is substantive; there may be better ways to measure uncertainty if that is what the consumer sentiment index actually reflects.

Empirical Specification

This hypothesis can readily be made operational. The role of expected purchases, p, is straightforward: it serves as an estimate of the expected purchase rate, given the "typical" amount of uncertainty. But during periods when uncertainty (or optimism) is changing, estimates based on expected purchases need to be corrected by a measure of the extent of deterioration or improvement. The fact that correction is needed suggests, as noted above, either that expected purchases are a biased measure during periods when uncertainty is changing (e.g., consumer purchase expectations do not fully register the probable influence of changing uncertainty on subsequent behavior), or that events which impinge randomly on purchase expectations when uncertainties are stable do not impinge randomly when uncertainties are shifting (e.g., favorable unforeseen events may have a stronger influence on behavior when uncertainty is being dispelled and optimism is growing, while unfavorable unforeseen events may have a stronger influence when uncertainty is increasing and pessimism is growing). Either interpretation specifies the same empirical model.

The empirical tests relate purchase rates for automobiles to three independent variables. The first is expected purchases, measured by either buying intentions or purchase probability. Intentions can be obtained either from SRC sources or from Census Bureau (QSI) sources, while purchase probabilities are obtained from the recently initiated Census Bureau Survey of Consumer Buying Expectations (CBE). QSI intentions are used in preference to SRC data whenever possible because QSI has smaller sampling error. Thus purchase expectations are a linked series consisting of SRC buying intentions when no other information is available, QSI intentions when these become available, and CBE mean probabilities when this series supplants QSI intentions. The second variable is designed to measure changes in uncertainty, and we test several variants based on the SRC Index of Consumer Sentiment. The third variable reflects the influence of events that were presumably unforeseen and hence not reflected in either survey measure. For this purpose we use U, the unemployment compensation.[2] Both expected purchases and change in uncertainty are measured at the beginning of the forecast period, while U is measured concurrently with purchases. Hence the model produces contingent rather than pure *ex ante* forecasts; operational use requires that future values of U be obtained from outside the system. Alternatively, the user can produce a set of forecasts contingent on unobserved values of U.[3]

Since all three of the independent variables are measured per household, and since expected purchases are measured as unit sales rather than expenditures, the dependent variable is the proportion of households purchasing a new automobile. Other possible determinants of durables demand such as income and prices do not enter the model directly, as noted above, but only through their influence on the expected purchase variable.[4]

We test a number of alternative ways to use the Index of Consumer Sentiment, A, as a measure of change in uncertainty. For comparison with other studies, A and ΔA are tested. To capture changes in the state of uncertainty however, neither of these variables seems appropriate: purely random movements in A or ΔA would have just as much influence on the empirical results as the systematic movements that ought to be more closely related to changes in uncertainty. Our suggested empirical proxy for the desired measure is the change in A during periods when changes are either large or persistent, hence when uncertainty can be thought of as unmistakably increasing or decreasing.

For determining whether or not a change in A is systematic, we suggest an arbitrary but reasonable criteria: If A changes in the same direction for three or more consecutive quarters, the change is defined as systematic. For the empirical specification of the model, only the third and all subsequent change in the same direction can be used. Alternative criteria are: Sentiment must change by a "large" amount over two consecutive quarters, in which case the second and all subsequent changes in the same direction are defined as systematic;[5] or if A has been increasing (decreasing) for

[2] The insured unemployment rate is preferred because it is a cyclically sensitive measure of unemployment in the permanently attached work force.

[3] The use of U introduces a possible simultaneity bias. The forecast equation may best be considered as part of a larger econometric model, but this question will not be examined here.

[4] As we show in [6], none of the conclusions in the paper would be affected by including either income or price variables in the model.

enough quarters or by a large enough amount for its change to be counted as systematic, a one-quarter change in the opposite direction will not break the string, if in the next quarter A resumes its movement in the original direction and reaches a new local high (low) level.[6]

More formally, the dummy variable Z defines systematic changes in the Index of Consumer Sentiment. The primary criteria and two alternatives define Z as:

$$Z = 1 \text{ if } \Delta A_{t-i} \text{ for } i = 0, 1, 2 \text{ are of the same sign}$$
$$\text{or if } |\Delta A_t + \Delta A_{t-1}| \geqslant$$
$$\text{or if } Z_{t-2} = 1 \text{ and } Z_{t-1} = 0 \text{ and } |\Delta A_t| > |\Delta A_{t-1}|$$
$$Z = 0 \text{ otherwise}$$

The logic underlying the selection of these criteria is simple enough. The attitude index will always show some kind of change between any two periods, and the observed change may be either real or a random abberation. Two consecutive movements in the same direction will occur about once in four trials if the true movement is random, and this frequency is higher than one would like. But three consecutive changes in the same direction, given no real change in the true index, will occur only about once in eight trials, which seems a reasonable empirical limit to the acceptance of a movement as systematic when it is in fact random. Thus, our criteria are much less likely to accept a random change as a real one than to reject a real change as random; this is the way we prefer to weight the choices.

For the empirical analysis, we define the variable $Z\Delta A$, where ΔA is the change in A and $Z = 1$ when the change in A is systematic as defined above. The $Z\Delta A$ variable is thus a nonlinear and interactive transformation of ΔA, and meets the analytical requirement for a variable that captures only genuine changes in the underlying state of consumer uncertainty. The model is thus one

[5] A "large" change is taken to be one of 7 percentage points or more in the A index, which has a base of $1963 = 100$. That also corresponds to approximately two standard sampling errors in A.

[6] The most recent change will be counted as a systematic change in consumer uncertainty because the previous quarter proved (in retrospect) to be an abberation.

326

in which expected purchases are taken as an unbiased estimate of future behavior unless uncertainty has been systematically shifting. In this case expected purchases will not fully reflect the shift, except with a lag, and will tend to underestimate (over-estimate) purchases whenever uncertainty has been decreasing (increasing).

Empirical Findings

The basic empirical results are shown in Table 1. Regressions are estimated for three dependent variables — automobile purchase rates during the three-month, six-month, and nine-month periods, respectively, following the expected purchase survey (x_3, x_6, and x_9, shown in Panels A, B, and C). Independent variables are a weighted measure of expected purchases (p^*, defined as $.6p_t + .3p_{t-1} + .1p_{t-2}$), the unemployment rate (U_3, U_6, or U_9, depending on the time span of the dependent variables), and at least two variables reflecting changes in uncertainty. The latter include the lagged Index of Consumer Sentiment, (A_{t-1}), the lagged change in A (ΔA_{t-1}), weighted lagged A and change in weighted lagged A (wA_{t-1} and $w\Delta A_{t-1}$, with the first and second lags weighted equally), and the interaction variables $Z\Delta A_{t-1}$, $wZ\Delta A_{t-1}$, and $wZ'\Delta A_{t-1}$.[7] For this set of variables, Z is defined to be 1 when A is changing systematically, Z' is defined to

---

[7] The Index of Consumer Sentiment in the current quarter is based on a survey taken during the quarter, therefore the index is always used in lagged form. The variables are defined by:

$$\Delta A_{t-1} = A_{t-1} - A_{t-2}$$
$$wA_{t-1} = .5\,(A_{t-1} + A_{t-2})$$
$$w\Delta A_{t-1} = .5\,(\Delta A_{t-1} + \Delta A_{t-2})$$
$$Z\Delta A_{t-1} = Z_{t-1}\,\Delta A_{t-1}$$
$$wZ\Delta A_{t-1} = .5\,(Z_{t-1}\,\Delta A_{-1} + Z_{t-2}\,\Delta A_{t-2})$$
$$wZ\Delta A_{t-1} = .5\,(Z'_{t-1}\,\Delta A_{t-1} + Z'_{t-2}\,\Delta A_{t-2})$$

Throughout the paper t subscripts refer to quarters and numerical subscripts refer to months.

The weighting scheme is essentially a smoothing device that average the variable prefixed by w and its lag. The question of optimum weighting is discussed below.

Table 1

ALTERNATIVE SPECIFICATIONS OF CONSUMER UNCERTAINTY VARIABLES, ANTICIPATORY MODELS OF AUTOMOBILE DEMAND, 1956 I – 1968 IV

PANEL A: x_3, three-month purchase rate dependent

Const.	p^*	ΔA_{t-1}	$Z\Delta A_{t-1}$	$wZ\Delta A_{t-1}$	A_{t-1}	wA_{t-1}	$wZ'\Delta A_{t-1}$	U_3	SDD_3	DW	SEE	$\bar{R}^2$
.2301 (1.6)	.1309 (9.7)	-.0036 (.9)	.0095 (1.7)					-.0313 (3.1)	-.1196 (3.4)	1.41	.0585	.8800
-.1184 (.5)	.1272 (9.8)			.0070 (1.4)				-.0238 (2.3)	-.1252 (3.8)	1.41	.0546	.8956
-.1774 (.8)	.1267 (.9)			.0083 (1.9)	.0037 (1.6)			-.0223 (2.2)	-.1252 (3.9)	1.42	.0538	.8936
.2091 (1.5)	.1322 (10.3)			.0183 (2.4)		.0043 (2.0)	-.0068 (1.1)	-.0285 (2.9)	-.1210 (3.6)	1.49	.0555	.8922

PANEL B: x_6, six-month purchase rate dependent

Const.	p^*	ΔA_{t-1}	$Z\Delta A_{t-1}$	$wZ\Delta A_{t-1}$	A_{t-1}	wA_{t-1}	$wZ'\Delta A_{t-1}$	U_6	SDD_6	DW	SEE	$\bar{R}^2$
.2696 (1.2)	.2767 (13.1)	-.0043 (.7)	.0281 (3.3)					-.0228 (2.8)	-.1210 (2.3)	1.02	.0869	.9298
-.0218 (.1)	.2766 (14.1)			.0308 (4.4)	.0027 (.9)			-.0177 (2.3)	-.1424 (3.1)	.89	.0772	.9446
-.0320 (.2)	.2758 (14.1)			.0317 (5.0)		.0031 (1.0)		-.0174 (2.3)	-.1414 (3.1)	.88	.0769	.9450
.2136 (1.0)	.2803 (14.8)			.0410 (3.8)			-.0072 (.8)	-.0192 (2.6)	-.1353 (2.9)	.93	.0773	.9444

Continued Table 1

PANEL C: x_9, nine-month purchase rate dependent

Const.	p^*	ΔA_{t-1}	$Z\Delta A_{t-1}$	$wZ\Delta A_{t-1}$	A_{t-1}	wA_{t-1}	$wZ'\Delta A_{t-1}$	U_3 U_9	SDD_3 SDD_9	DW	SEE	$\bar{R}^2$
.2272	.4283	−.0024	.0518					−.0163	−.1797	1.13	.1069	.9512
(.8)	(15.6)	(.3)	(4.9)					(2.3)	(2.8)			
.5929	.4338			.0638	−.0043			−.0165	−.1874	.83	.0980	.9590
(1.4)	(16.4)			(6.9)	(1.1)			(2.5)	(3.2)			
.6109	.4356			.0624		−.0047		−.0163	−.1932	.84	.0976	.9593
(1.6)	(16.4)			(7.5)		(1.3)		(2.5)	(3.2)			
.2559	.4241			.0586			−.0003	−.0157	−.1779	.80	.0993	.9579
(.9)	(16.7)			(4.2)			(.03)	(2.3)	(2.9)			

Note: Independent variables defined in the text. The dependent variable, x_t, is S/H, where S is unit sales of new automobiles to households and H is the number of household units. The units for the purchase rates are actually x_t, $x_t + x_{t+1}$, and $x_t + x_{t+1} + x_{t+2}$, respectively, where x is seasonally adjusted at annual rates. All equations are estimated with an appropriate strike dummy variable, SDD.

329

be 1 when A is *declining* systematically, and the weighted constructs give equal weights to the first and second lags. Estimates are fitted to quarterly data over the period 1956 I to 1968 IV, and missing values, of which there are several all prior to 1962 in both the p and A series, are interpolated linearly.[8]

The first equation in each panel has lagged change in attitudes (ΔA_{t-1}) and the comparable interaction variable $Z\Delta A_{t-1}$: the coefficients will indicate whether the interaction measure of uncertainty is better than a straightforward attitude change variable. The evidence is conclusive: all of the variance explained by attitude change is due to the effect of permanent changes in attitudes, i.e., changes which proved to be systematic. During other periods, attitude change has no influence on purchases.

The second and third equations have the weighted interaction variable $(wZ\Delta A_{t-1})$ and either attitudes (A_{t-1}) or weighted attitudes (wA_{t-1}): the test here is to determine whether the interaction variable substitutes wholly or partly for A, which is the variable most often used in other studies. The results are reasonably clear-cut. For the three-month purchase period, both the interactive variable and the weighted sentiment variable are on the borderline of statistical significance, but for the six- and nine-month purchase periods the interaction dominates the level of consumer sentiment. In general, weighting improves the performance of the sentiment level variable, but not by very much. On the other hand, weighting greatly improves the performance of the interaction variable, as discussed more fully below.

The fourth equation tests for an asymmetrical influence of the interaction variable. If this variable is significantly more effective when uncertainty is increasing (e.g., when sentiment is deteriorating), the $wZ'\Delta A_{t-1}$ would be significantly positive, and if the entire effect of the interaction variable were due to its influence when uncertainty was increasing, the $wZ\Delta A_{t-1}$ variable would become nonsignificant when the Z' interaction is included. The results give no indication of asymmetry: $wZ'\Delta A_{t-1}$ never comes close to statistical significance in any of the equations.

[8] A recent paper by Hymans [4] indicates that interpolation by regression methods gives about the same results as a simple linear interpolation. Our own results suggest that omission of the missing quarters gives virtually the same results as simple interpolation.

The other variables in each equation behave as expected. Expected purchases are always highly significant, and the unemployment rate is always significant at the 5 percent level though not usually at the 1 percent level. The very high significance level of the p^* variable in due in good measure to the fact that it is the only independent variable with a time-trend, and there is a pronounced upward trend in the dependent variable.

Table 1 shows that the suggested specification is generally superior in explanatory power to the usual one of treating the sentiment variable as linear. Thus, not only is the suggested nonlinear interactive variable consistent with the view that systematic changes in the state of uncertainty (or in optimism) are the relevant dimension for proper specification of the model, but the suggested variable is also superior by the usual measures of statistical fit.

Parameter Stability

A second and more critical test concerns the stability of the regression coefficients in the model. Table 2 is designed to examine this question. We show regression coefficients for two models — one including p^*, U and A_{t-1}, the other p^*, U and $wZ\Delta A_{t-1}$ — for a number of different time spans covering the period for which the models can be estimated (1953–68). The first three equations show results for the full 1953–68 period, and for two subperiods characterized by a differential amount of sampling error in the measurement of p^*. Because estimates of p must be based on the relatively small sample SRC data prior to 1960, sampling errors are larger before 1960 than for the 1960–68 period, when either QSI or CBE can be used. The next four equations start with 1956 and examine periods of different lengths.

The evidence suggests that the interactive specification has considerably greater stability when estimated for different time spans, and that coefficients estimated from the 1953–59 period, when the SRC version of the expected purchase variable must be used, are markedly different from coefficients estimated for the 1960-68 period when the Census Bureau's buying expectations

Table 2

TWO EQUATION SPECIFICATIONS ESTIMATED FOR DIFFERENT TIME SPANS, 1953–1968

Sample Period	Const.	p_t^*	A_{t-1}	U_3	SDD_3	$\bar{R}^2$	DW
PANEL A: x_3 dependent, sentiment level independent							
53 III to 68 IV	.1856	.0722	.0068	-.0561	-.1371	.7764	.83
	(.8)	(5.0)	(2.8)	(4.7)	(2.7)		
53 III to 59 IV	.7425	.0599	.0028	-.0807	-.0879	.5049	.65
	(1.2)	(1.2)	(.4)	(2.3)	(.7)		
60 I to 68 IV	-.4842	.1135	.0091	-.0310	-.1502	.8493	1.58
	(1.5)	(3.7)	(3.2)	(1.9)	(3.7)		
56 I to 62 IV	.2522	.0976	.0027	-.0377	-.0825	.7326	1.17
	(.6)	(3.2)	(.6)	(1.8)	(1.4)		
56 I to 64 IV	.2196	.1196	.0014	-.0388	-.1105	.8458	1.08
	(.6)	(8.2)	(.4)	(2.3)	(3.0)		
56 I to 66 IV	-.2781	.1259	.0054	-.0207	-.1268	.9040	1.29
	(1.0)	(10.1)	(2.1)	(1.6)	(3.3)		
56 I to 68 IV	-.2577	.1236	.0055	-.0232	-.1212	.8933	1.34
	(1.1)	(9.6)	(2.8)	(2.3)	(3.7)		

PANEL B: x_6 dependent, sentiment level independent

	Const.	p_t^*	A_{t-1}	U_6	SDD_6	$\bar{R}^2$	DW
53 III to 68 IV	.7000 (1.5)	.1580 (5.7)	.0090 (2.0)	−.0565 (4.8)	−.1566 (1.8)	.8017	.50
53 III to 59 IV	2.795 (2.4)	.1910 (2.3)	−.0111 (1.0)	−.1164 (3.6)	−.0120 (.1)	.5804	.59
60 I to 68 IV	−.9952 (1.8)	.2425 (4.4)	.0165 (3.6)	−.0245 (1.6)	−.1550 (2.4)	.8915	.86
56 I to 62 IV	.5617 (.8)	.2339 (4.7)	.0019 (.3)	−.0393 (2.4)	−.0338 (.4)	.7896	.77
56 I to 64 IV	.5217 (.9)	.2581 (10.9)	.0005 (.1)	−.0401 (3.0)	−.0599 (1.0)	.8984	.74
56 I to 66 IV	−.7317 (1.5)	.2538 (11.5)	.0118 (2.8)	−.0141 (1.3)	−.0719 (1.1)	.9250	.77
56 I to 68 IV	−.4833 (1.3)	.2532 (11.4)	.0099 (3.1)	−.0209 (2.4)	−.1112 (2.1)	.9234	.67

333

Continued Table 2

	Const.	p_t^*	$wZ A_{t-1}$	U_3	SDD_3	$\bar{R}^2$	DW
PANEL C: x_3 dependent, interactive variable independent							
53 III to 68 IV	.6337 (4.8)	.0947 (7.6)	.0223 (4.5)	-.0556 (5.2)	-.1403 (3.1)	.8117	1.02
53 III to 59 IV	.9730 (3.2)	.0534 (1.4)	.0220 (2.5)	-.0670 (3.1)	-.1033 (1.0)	.6131	.78
60 I to 68 IV	.1026 (.4)	.1441 (5.3)	.0247 (3.4)	-.0275 (1.7)	-.1571 (3.9)	.8545	1.59
56 I to 62 IV	.4715 (2.3)	.1065 (4.4)	.0033 (.6)	-.0445 (3.7)	-.0764 (1.4)	.7333	1.21
56 I to 64 IV	.3471 (2.6)	.1217 (9.1)	.0032 (.6)	-.0413 (3.8)	-.1103 (3.0)	.8471	1.12
56 I to 66 IV	.2193 (1.6)	.1336 (10.9)	.0078 (1.8)	-.0329 (3.2)	-.1215 (3.1)	.9014	1.33
56 I to 68 IV	.2100 (1.5)	.1323 (10.3)	.0114 (2.7)	-.0288 (2.9)	-.1223 (3.7)	.8919	1.38

Continued Table 2

	Const.	p_t^*	$wZ\Delta A_{t-1}$	U_6	SDD_6	$\bar{R}^2$	DW
PANEL D: x_6 dependent, interactive variable independent							
53 III to 68 IV	1.038	.2066	.0503	-.0440	-.1933	.8718	.78
	(4.4)	(9.6)	(6.1)	(4.6)	(2.7)		
53 III to 59 IV	1.495	.1461	.0519	-.0467	-.2065	.6949	.72
	(2.7)	(2.3)	(3.0)	(2.0)	(1.2)		
60 I to 68 IV	.0085	.3043	.0545	-.0199	-.1840	.9212	1.03
	(.02)	(7.2)	(5.4)	(1.6)	(3.3)		
56 I to 62 IV	.6630	.2323	.0222	-.0297	-.0820	.8354	.89
	(2.2)	(6.7)	(2.5)	(3.0)	(1.0)		
56 I to 64 IV	.4257	.2631	.0205	-.0284	-.0837	.9168	.85
	(2.0)	(13.2)	(2.6)	(3.1)	(1.6)		
56 I to 66 IV	.2132	.2807	.0311	-.0196	-.1057	.9425	.93
	(1.0)	(14.6)	(4.7)	(2.4)	(1.9)		
56 I to 68 IV	.2065	.2812	.0340	-.0191	-.1434	.9449	.88
	(1.0)	(14.9)	(5.7)	(2.6)	(3.1)		

Note: variables are defined in text and note to table I

335

survey, with its smaller sampling error, is the basis for measuring expected purchases.[9]

The difference in stability shows up most strongly in the six-month span data. Comparing the four time spans that begin with 1956 I and extend to 1962 IV, 1964 IV, 1966 IV and 1968 IV, respectively, the specification with the sentiment level variable has the following characteristics: the intercept declines systematically from +.56 to −.48, a difference of −1.04; the p^* variable ranges narrowly from .234 to .258; the sentiment variable ranges from .0005 to .0118, and two of the four coefficients are nonsignificant; and the U_6 variable ranges from −.040 to −.014 and is not significant in one of the spans. In contrast, the interactive or uncertainty specification shows, for the same time spans, an intercept that also declines monotonically but only from .66 to .21 for a difference of .45; a p^* variable with the same relatively narrow range from .232 to .281, an interactive variable that ranges only from .021 to .034 and is always significant at conventional levels, and a U variable that ranges from −.030 to −.019 and is always significant at conventional levels.

[9] A more precise look at the results in Table 2 can be made in terms of various statistical tests applied to the regressions for two independent sample periods, 1953 III to 1959 IV, and 1960 I to 1968 IV. First of all, the Chow test [1] can be applied to examine the hypothesis that the structure of the equation is the same for the period using SRC data and the period using QSI-CBE data. The test will reject the null hypothesis (that the coefficients in the two relations are equal) if the F value is above the actual value. The actual value at the 5 percent level of significance $F(5.52)$ is 2.40 which is not exceeded by any of the sets of results from Panels A to D. Thus, the hypothesis that the differences in the vector of coefficients is due only to sampling variation is not rejected.

A priori, we expect the importance of the survey variables (particularly p^*) to be different for the two periods. A simple test for the difference of the means of two normally distributed variables can be applied. The small sample result found in Hoel [3, pp. 276−79] can be used to test the hypothesis that the coefficients of p^*, $wZ\Delta A_{t-1}$ and A_{t-1} are equal in the two sample periods. The null hypothesis is rejected for the p^* coefficients in the Panel C and Panel D data. For the alternative sentiment variables the null hypothesis is rejected only for the A_{t-1} variable in Panel B. The coefficient of the $wZ\Delta A_{t-1}$ variable is not significantly different in any of the tests.

The quantitatively large differences in the coefficients for overlapping time periods (rows 4-7) cannot be readily tested because the samples are not independent.

The weakness of the A_{t-1} specification for forecasting is discussed below. The forecast errors are much larger than the fit period errors while the interactive specification does not deteriorate in the forecast period.

LENGTH OF LAG

Although the above results indicate that a two-quarter weighted construct is superior to a single-quarter value for the uncertainty variable, it is possible that other weighting schemes would be better yet. The two quarter weights of .5 were chosen arbitrarily because it is often difficult to distinguish among alternative lag structures.

A priori, we expect the most recent change-in-uncertainty value to have a stronger influence on behavior than more remote values, hence we require the weights to decline monotonically. Since we prefer to avoid transformations that use lagged dependent variables, our procedure consists of assigning linearly declining weights to different numbers of past values of the $Z\Delta A_{t-1}$ variable, and noting the pattern of improvement in statistical fit. We calculated the proportion of variance explained by a series of equations all of which contain a common dependent variable and three independent variables: weighted purchase expectations, p^*, the insured unemployment rate, U, and $\Sigma w_i Z\Delta A_{t-1}$, where i varies from one to seven time periods.

Figure 1 shows the pattern in explained variation as the length of the lag varies. The optimizing value of i is at least 4 and sometimes higher, depending on the time span of the dependent variable. The improvement in fit is monotonic until the peak value is reached. When x_3 is the dependent variable, $\bar{R}^2$ is maximized with a lag of six quarters; for x_6, the optimum lag is four quarters. The evidence is, therefore, that changes in the state of consumer uncertainty have an impact on purchase behavior for an extended period of time into the future, and purchase expectations will be a biased estimate of future purchase rates during most time periods because of the extent of these lagged influences of uncertainty change.

337

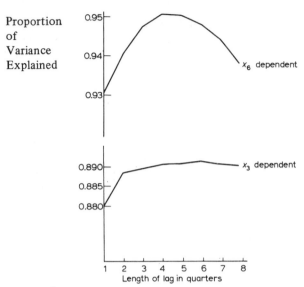

Fig. 1. $\bar{R}^2$ FOR ALTERNATIVE LAGS ON $\Sigma w_i Z A_{t-1}$, 1956–68.

OPTIMAL QUARTERLY FORECASTS

In the previous three sections, constructed survey measures were used to forecast the purchase rate for alternative and continuous time spans. Neither the expected purchase rate nor the interaction version of the Index of Consumer Sentiment contain any a priori time dimension. The same forecast specification performs reasonably well when the dependent variable is defined for a number of different time spans, with the result that a number of different quarterly purchase rate forecasts can be obtained from the same general specification. The problem is thus to derive an optimal forecast for purchase rates in specific quarters, e.g., t, $t+$ 1, and $t+2$. Optimality is defined as the best *ex post* explanation of the purchase rate, given unforeseen strike effects and taking account of current transitory phenomena. It is also of interest to see if the *ex post* performances of the alternative specifications in Table 2 differ.

The forecast specification, termed F, is the same for each forecast span;[10] the strike and transitory specification is given by $\sum_{q}^{n} T_i$

[10] The most recent survey is used as it measures the latest revisions in expectations. However, the horizon over which those expectations hold is not known a priori.

where i is the time span in months of the period being forecast. A forecast equation for the current quarter is given by (1). For the next quarter

$$\sum_1^3 x_i = \alpha F + \beta \sum_1^3 T_i + u_1 \tag{1}$$

a direct forecast is available from (2) and an indirect one by combining (3) and (1): equation (3) provides a forecast of the purchase rate for

$$\sum_4^6 x_i = \alpha F + \beta \sum_4^6 T_i + u_2 \tag{2}$$

$$\sum_1^6 x_i = \alpha F + \beta \sum_1^6 T_i + u_3 \tag{3}$$

a six-month span, hence a forecast for the last three months of that span can be obtained by subtracting an estimate of equation (1) from an estimate of equation (3).

Denoting these direct and indirect estimates as x_i^D and x_i^I, respectively, we can derive a decision rule for the optimal estimate, x_i^o. The linear combination of x_i^D and x_i^I that minimizes the mean square error over the period of fit is used. That is, we minimize $E[a + b_1 x_i^D + b_2 x_i^I - x_i]^2$, which is the same as regressing x_i on the direct and indirect estimates.

The same procedure can also be used to estimate an optimal forecast for the span $\sum_7^9 x_i$. A direct estimate is obtained from equation (4); the indirect estimate subtracts the optimal estimate for $\sum_4^6 x_i$ and the estimate of $\sum_1^3 x_i$ from equation (1), from an estimate of the nine-month span in equation (5). The weights are then derived in the same manner as above.

$$\sum_7^9 x_i = \alpha F + \beta \sum_7^9 T_i + u_4 \tag{4}$$

$$\sum_1^9 x_i = \alpha F + \beta \sum_1^9 T_i + u_5 \tag{5}$$

For the empirical analysis we test two specifications of the forecast function, F. In the first, buying intentions and the lagged consumer sentiment index, p_t^* and A_{t-1}, are used. In the second, intentions and the weighted interaction (uncertainty) variable, p_t^* and $wZ\Delta A_{t-1}$ are used. E-quations (1)–(5) are estimated for the period 1956 through 1964, and the optimal weights are based on experience during that period. The specification of T_i for each equation is the appropriate strike dummy and the insured unemployment rate for the time period of the dependent variable.

As least-squares estimates, the optimal estimates must have *fit period* errors that are smaller than the errors of the direct and indirect estimates. In the *forecast period* the optimal estimates are not necessarily better; they are optimal in the sense that there is no a priori way to choose between the direct and indirect estimates. The procedure reduces the potential for error when there is no a priori criterion for choosing the appropriate use of the survey variables.

A summary of results is contained in Table 3 for the $p_t^*, wZ\Delta A_{t-1}$ and p_t^*, A_{t-1} specifications, respectively. The indirect estimates tend to have larger weights than the direct estimates. For the less distant forecast quarter, the weights are more evenly divided. For the interactive specification the RMSE of forecast are only slightly larger than the RMSE of fit. For the fit period, the indirect estimates are preferred but in the forecast period, this holds for seven- to nine-month spans but not for four- to six-month ones. Thus the weighting scheme substitutes for the absence of a priori information about the relative accuracy of direct and indirect estimates.

Table 3 also provides a comparison of the forecast performance of the two specifications. The p_t^*, A_{t-1} specification does uniformly less well in both forecast and fit periods, especially the former, presumably reflecting the greater instability in that specification noted in the first part of the paper. Also, the root mean square errors are relatively larger in the forecast period than in the fit period with this specification. The instability of this specification is illustrated by the optimal forecast for the seven- to nine-month span. The linear combination that reduces the fit period RMSE yields a forecast period RMSE that is larger than the errors of either the direct or indirect estimates. For all other results the RMSE of forecast of the optimal estimate lies between the two.

340

Table 3

ROOT MEAN SQUARE ERRORS OF OPTIMAL FORECASTING

Equation Specification	Error for:	
	Fit Period 56 I - 64 IV	Forecast Period 65 I - 69 II
$p_t^*, wZ\Delta A_{t-1}$ Form of Equation		
Time span $\sum_{1}^{3} x_i$	.0461	.0651
Time span $\sum_{4}^{6} x_i$		
Direct	.0421	.0507
Indirect	.0371	.0529
Optimal[a]	.0369	.0514
Time span $\sum_{7}^{9} x_i$		
Direct	.0525	.0871
Indirect	.0516	.0548
Optimal[b]	.0496	.0663
p_t^*, A_{t-1} Form of Equation		
Time span $\sum_{1}^{3} x_i$	.0463	.0642
Time span $\sum_{4}^{6} x_i$		
Direct	.0497	.1046
Indirect	.0447	.0885
Optimal[c]	.0445	.0944
Time span $\sum_{7}^{9} x_i$		
Direct	.0551	.1537
Indirect	.0537	.1473
Optimal[d]	.0524	.1691

Note: Mean purchase rate (x_t) is 1.12 in fit period, 1.36 in forecast period. All purchase rates are seasonally adjusted at annual rates.

a   Equation is: $x^0 = -.0171 + .8561 \, x^I + .1592 \, x^D$
b   Equation is: $x^0 = -.0476 + .6271 \, x^I + .4152 \, x^D$
c   Equation is: $x^0 = -.0285 + .9220 \, x^I + .1033 \, x^D$
d   Equation is: $x^0 = -.0761 + .8547 \, x^I + .2129 \, x^D$

The current quarter purchase rate fit and forecast errors are virtually identical for the two specifications.

The dependent variable used in the forecast analysis is the proportion of households purchasing a new automobile. The purchase rate is in percent per year and is derived from automobile expenditures in billions of dollars, M, average price of new cars, V, and the number of households in thousands, H. The purchase rate, X is defined as $(M/H)/V$. The expenditure series M is the personal consumption expenditure component of gross auto product from the National Income Accounts.

The estimate of number of households, H, is obtained by interpolation of the annual data published by the Census Bureau in the *Statistical Abstract of the United States.* For the last two years, the estimates of H are obtained directly from the Census Bureau's Survey of Consumer Buying Expectations.

The average car price is a weighted average of the seasonally adjusted average prices of new foreign and new domestic cars obtained from the Commerce Department.

Explanatory variables include a set of survey variables described below, an unemployment variable, and a strike dummy. The unemployment rate is the insured unemployed rate from the Business Conditions Digest (BCD series number B1, 45).

The strike dummy is used for automobile strikes in 1964 IV and 1967 IV and a steel strike in 1959 IV. The strike dummy is designed to account for unforeseen effects on the purchase rate and is therefore altered for different purchase rate time spans. When current quarter purchase rates are being predicted, it has a value of one in the strike period and zero otherwise. For predicting a six-month span the unforeseen effects call for a +1 dummy in the quarter prior to the strike and +.25 in the quarter of the strike. For predicting a nine-month span, the +1 appears two quarters prior to the strike and +.25 just before the strike and zero otherwise. These are based on the cumulative effect of a strike dummy which takes on a value of +1 during the strike quarter, $-.75$ one quarter after, $-.25$ in the second quarter and zero otherwise. An appropriate strike dummy is included in all regressions.

The survey variables are of two basic sorts. First of all, A is the familiar SRC Index of Consumer Sentiment. The data are reproduced in *Business Conditions Digest* (Series Number C1, 435). The survey was not taken in every quarter prior to 1962 and missing quarters are interpolated linearly. Since the survey is taken at various times during the quarter the index is always used in lagged form. The other survey variable, p^*, is constructed from SRC, QSI, and CBE survey sources as described below.

From 1953 through 1959 the only source of buying intentions data is Survey Research Center data. The data are taken from several publications and are not available in a consistent form nor, as noted, for every quarter. Therefore, some processing is necessary to put the raw data in useful form. The basic data are taken from Okun [9, p.446] and from various issues of the *Survey of Consumer Finances*.

From 1953 I to 1956 I, Okun provides data for eight of thirteen quarters in the form of intentions (measured by the sum of *will buy, will probably buy*, and one-half the *maybe* responses) for new and used cars. The new and used car intentions are assigned weights of .6 and .3 respectively. From 1956 on, second- and fourth-quarter surveys are available with the data classified by *will buy, will probably buy*, and *may buy* new autos. Weights of .7, .5, and .3, respectively, were assigned as well as a .3 weight for used car purchase plans and a .4 weight for *don't know* responses. The first quarter data are available in a new-used classification with *don't know* responses allocated. Consistent weights for these classifications based on the mean size of each category were calculated (.32 for used cars, .54 for new cars). The two sections of the SRC data were then linked on the basis of an overlap period.

Missing quarters were interpolated and the series seasonally adjusted with the X-11 moving seasonal program. After adjustment, the missing quarters were corrected to be interpolations of the seasonally adjusted data. The SRC portion (1953–60) of the basic intentions series was then linked to the level of the QSI-CBE portion based on an overlap period. The derivation of the QSI-CBE portion follows.

For 1960–66, the Census Bureau's *Quarterly Survey of Intentions* is used; for 1967 on, CBE purchase probability data are used.

First we construct a weighted measure of the basic QSI intentions data: six-month definite, probable, or possible new car plans are assigned weights of .7, .5, and .3, respectively, twelve-month plans are assigned a weight of .3, used car plans a weight of .2, and *don't know* responses a weight of .3. For CBE data, six- and twelve-month car purchase probabilities were given equal weights. The resulting variable was then regressed on the purchase rate, seasonal dummy variables, and dummies for the effect of interviewer training session and survey type (QSI vs. CBE). The coefficients on the last two dummies were used to adjust the weighted plan variable for those net effects. The entire series was then seasonally adjusted with the Census X-11 (moving seasonal) program.

The resultant intentions variable, p, is always used in weighted form, p^*, which draws upon three surveys of expected purchases. The current quarter survey value and two lagged surveys are weighted .6, .3, and .1, respectively. The current survey is included because the Census Bureau surveys are taken at the beginning of the quarter although they do not become available until the middle.

The Z variable is a dummy assigned a value of 1 when there is a systematic change in A as defined in the text, and a value of 0 otherwise.

More complete documentation of the data, is available from the authors upon request.

REFERENCES

1 Chow, Gregory, "Tests of Equality Between Sets of Coefficients in Two Linear Regressions", *Econometrica*, 28 (1960).
2 Duesenberry, James, et al., eds., *The Brookings Quarterly Econometric Model of the United States*, Rand McNally, 1965.
3 Hoel, Paul G., *Introduction to Mathematical Statistics*, 3rd ed., John Wiley and Sons, Inc., 1962.
4 Hymans, Saul H., "Consumer Durables Spending", Paper prepared for the Second Meeting of the Brookings Panel on Economic Activity.
5 Juster, F. Thomas, "Consumer Anticipations and Models of Durable Goods Demand: The Time-Series Cross-Section Paradox Re-examined", In Jacob Mincer, ed., *Economic Forecasts and Expectations*, New York: Columbia University Press, 1969.

6 Juster, F. Thomas, and Paul Wachtel, "Anticipatory and Objective Models of Durable Goods Demand", *American Economic Review,* 1972, forthcoming.

7 Maynes, E. Scott, "Consumer Attitudes and Buying Intentions: Retrospect and Prospect", September, 1966 (mimeographed).

8 Mueller, Eva, "Ten Years of Consumer Attitude Surveys: The Forecasting Record", *Journal of the American Statistical Association*, 1963.

9 Okun, Arthur, "The Value of Anticipations Data in Forecasting National Product", in *The Quality and Economic Significance of Anticipations Data*, Princeton for NBER, 1960.

The Impact of Consumer Attitudes on Behavior: a Cross-Section Study

WILLIAM C. DUNKELBERG

Since the development of anticipatory statistics in the early 1950's, there has been a continual controversy over the usefulness of these data in predicting and understanding consumer behavior. Early efforts to isolate the contribution of measures of consumer attitudes and expectations met with rather limited success [30], [32]. As the methodology for collecting and interpreting these statistics was developed, and as the number of observation points increased, it became clearer that aggregate models of discretionary spending and saving that included measures of consumer sentiment were clearly superior to those which included only the so-called "objective" economic variables [4], [18], [27], [31], [35], [37], [38].

Cross-section tests of the importance of the attitude measures, however, offered little support to the contention that sentiment, as measured, was a significant determinant of spending and saving by individuals or selected groups of individuals [2], [39]. In retrospect, the cards seemed to be stacked against the discovery of such an effect. First, the data used were collected on an annual basis. The theory of attitude formation advanced by George Katona, the developer of the anticipations measures, asserted that among individuals, attitudes may be short lived, subject to revision in response to a changing environment. Data periods as long as a year could submerge major shifts in sentiment that might occur. The second major difficulty was one of specification. The sentiment measures in operational form consist of the responses to a large number of questions. No single question can be relied on to be an equally effective indicator of general attitudes and expectations for all consumers. Thus, the sentiment measure in the cross-section test should be reasonably broad based, encompassing the responses to questions of different dimensions. Similarly, the dependent variable in the analysis should be a broad measure of expenditures, not consumer outlays for a particular good such as automobiles. In general, cross-sections tests have not adequately dealt with this problem, using far too specific measures for expenditures and for attitudes.[1]

This paper presents evidence from cross-section tests that substantiates the time-series findings concerning the importance of consumer sentiment. The first section of the paper demonstrates the value of sentiment measures, broadly defined, in explaining variations in consumer discretionary spending. The spending measure is also defined to include nearly all major types of expenditures that might be considered discretionary. The next two sections re-examine the relationship between buying plans and attitudes and compare their relative predictive performances, noting that buying intentions tend to be oriented toward a particular type of expenditure, while attitudes are more diffuse in their orientation.

[1] Tobin's 1959 study [39] dealt most effectively with this problem, using net outlay on cars and durables as the dependent variable and a 4 question index. Tobin eliminated all but 652 of 1032 cases of a 1952/53 panel for various statistical reasons and normalized all financial variables to the income of the family unit. The index employed a +1, 0, −1 scale and was based on questions 1, 3, a combination of 12 and 14, and a version of 2 which asked about the expectation of making more money (the 1 year expectation version of 2). It should be noted, however, that even if the problems of comprehensiveness and time span were solved, individual measurement error inherent in cross-section data (and averaged out in the aggregate) would still impair attempts to estimate the effects of attitudes and expectations on individuals' behavior.

Since the consumer has limited financial resources, various types of expenditures must be substitutes for each other within this constraint. Because discretionary spending can take many forms, the expenditure variable must be as broadly defined as possible lest we conclude that the optimist fails to make such expenditures only because we have omitted some types of spending from the measure.

Similarly, the measure of sentiment must encompass a large number of dimensions to raise the probability of including factors of concern to the consumer. All consumers express opinions about expected inflation or about expected business conditions. There is no assurance that these opinions will be of importance to an individual's behavior, however. There will be different concerns across individuals, and the importance of particular factors or events will vary over time. Much of this problem as it relates to interpersonal differences on specific events is eliminated by the general nature of the questions asked (Appendix A). But even the more general questions may singly fail to represent the multifaceted attitude complex of consumer sentiment.

For the cross-section tests, a comprehensive expenditure variable including expenditures on cars, durables, additions and repairs to the home, vacations, and sports and hobby equipment (less the value of any items traded in) was constructed using reinterview data from the *1967* and *1968 Surveys of Consumer Finances.* For a description of the studies, *see* Katona *et al.* [22], [23].

An index of sentiment was also constructed for each individual, based on the responses to the five questions used to construct the *Index of Consumer Sentiment* developed by Katona [21]. Two points were given for a favorable response to the question and no points were awarded for an unfavorable response. Inbetween answers (such as "the same" or "no change") received one point. Thus a respondent could score as high as ten points or as low as zero. The questions used to construct the index are noted by an * in Appendix A.

There were 1921 respondents in the study, interviewed in January, 1967, and January, 1968. No families whose household head exceeded sixty years in age were included in the study.

Change variables were constructed by differencing reported levels in the two surveys. Variables used in the analysis are defined as follows:

$E67$	Total net outlay on cars, durables, additions and repairs to the house, vacations, and sports and hobby equipment during 1967.
$Y66$	The level of 1966 family income reported in January, 1967.
$Y67$	The level of 1967 family income reported in January, 1968.
$A66$	The value of the sentiment index constructed as of January, 1967.
$A67$	The value of the sentiment index constructed as of January, 1968.
AGE	The age of the family head in years.
$MOVE$	Assigned a value of one if the family moved in 1967, zero otherwise.
INT	Assigned a value of one if in January, 1967, respondent indicated he definitely or probably would buy a car (new or used) in 1967, zero otherwise.

Table 1 presents a multivariate analysis of individual discretionary expenditures during 1967, denoted $E67$. Equation (1) indicates that both income during 1966, $Y66$, and the level of optimism (as measured by the index constructed) at the beginning of 1967, $A66$, are significant in the equation. Income change over the year 1967 is added in equation (2). The performance of the equation is noticeably improved, but even with the level of 1966 income and income change during 1967 in the equation, sentiment at the beginning of the year remains significant.

In equation (3), sentiment change during 1967 is added to the formulation presented in equation (2). The income coefficients and their significance remain unaltered. The sentiment change variable makes a significant contribution to the formulation, even in the presence of the level of sentiment at the beginning of the year and the income and income change variables.

Age of the family head is added in equation (4) as a proxy for life-cycle variations in expenditures. Its contribution is negligible, perhaps because a nonlinear representation of its effect is more appropriate. A one-zero dummy variable is also added, *one* for all families that moved during 1967, *zero* for all others. Moving is frequently associated with new outlays on durables, repairs to the

Table 1

DISCRETIONARY EXPENDITURES, OPTIMISM, AND EXPECTATIONS

Dependent Variable: Discretionary Expenditures in 1967 ($E67$)

Predictors	Equation Number:				
	(1)	(2)	(3)	(4)	(5)
$Y66$	.07928 (.00466)	.08170 (.00464)	.08082 (.00464)	.08145 (.00468)	.07677 (.00462)
$Y67-Y66$[a]		.04890 (.00840)	.04650 (.00844)	.04563 (.00842)	.04597 (.00834)
$A66$	48.988 (16.860)	43.025 (16.750)	73.49 (18.453)	74.886 (18.530)	62.9050 (20.2730)
$A67-A66$[b]			47.677 (20.463)	48.740 (20.656)	42.2830 (18.2470)
AGE				3.3358 (3.3042)	
$MOVED$				344.78 (101.25)	
INT					632.22 (91.11)
$CONSTANT$	215.90	185.73	−12.01	−216.01	−14.05
R^{-2}	.146	.160	.163	.168	.184
SE	1532	1519	1517	1513	1498

Number of cases: 1921
a $Y67-Y66$ Income change during 1967.
b $A67-A66$ The change in the sentiment index value during 1967.

home, vacations en route, and other discretionary expenditures not normally made by the family. Its contribution is significant, but does not alter the coefficients or significance of the income and attitude variables.

Since automobile purchases make up a significant component of discretionary expenditures, buying plans for cars at the beginning of 1967 (measured at the same time as $A66$) were introduced to compare relative performances. The intentions variable, *INT*, was given a value of *one* if the respondent reported that he definitely or probably would buy a car (new or used) in 1967, the period of measurement for the expenditure variable. A value of *zero* was assigned for all other cases. Buying plans clearly made a significant contribution to the formulation, adding two percentage points to the R^2 obtained in equation (3). The impact of the attitude variables (in terms of the size of the coefficients) is slightly diminished as is the effect of the level of 1966 income. Both the attitude and the income variables remain significant in the formulation, however.

Since the average net outlay on all cars in the sample was about $1400, the coefficient on the intentions variable understates the expenditures on cars. This may be due to one or more of the following considerations: (1) optimism will directly explain some of the variation in automobile expenditures; (2) not all intenders actually buy a car (about sixty percent do); (3) no differentiation was made between new and used car buying intentions; and (4) if consumers do not buy a car in any particular year, they may spend their incomes on other items, reducing the differences in average discretionary expenditures between car buyers and other consumers.

On balance, the evidence presented in Table 1 clearly indicates that a significant relationship between consumer spending behavior and measures of consumer attitudes and expectations can be found when the model is reasonably specified. The problem created by the use of one year observation intervals was not eliminated in this analysis since the reinterviews were taken one year apart. This fact would seem to add significance to the performance of the attitude measures, for if shorter time periods were used and consequently expenditures were less tied to current income flows, the performance of the sentiment measures could be expected to improve while the effects of income measures would become less significant as would the performance of the intentions variable.

CONSUMER SENTIMENT AND PERSONAL CHARACTERISTICS

The sentiment measures, however, could always appear to be

statistically related to expenditures if differential concentrations of attitudes were systematically related to other characteristics which determined spending behavior; for example, newly formed families are typically frequent purchasers of durable goods and may generally be more optimistic than other groups in the population. A large number of individual characteristics are highly correlated with expenditures. Appendix B presents a partial list of those found to be particularly useful in explaining differences in spending behavior in work done at the Survey Research Center [5], [22], [23]. For aggregate analyses most of these variables are of little consequence, since their distributions change very slowly over time.

If measures of attitudes and expectations are systematically related to these variables, then the attitude measures will explain differences in spending behavior, but not necessarily for causative reasons. Using a statistical technique developed at the Survey Research Center, the AID program [36], a population can be partitioned into subgroups based on a set of characteristics (in this case, those presented in Appendix B) in such a way as to maximize the variance of the dependent variable between groups. The resulting model is neither linear nor additive and the algorithm is similar to a stepwise regression technique.

Using the sentiment measure $A67$ as a dependent variable and the set of variables presented in Appendix B as predictors, the characteristics which best explain differences in attitudes can be isolated. The results of this analysis are presented in Figure 1. Ten percent of the variance in attitudes ($A67$) was explained.

The analysis indicates that low values of the sentiment measure are typical of individuals who have low pay and little education (group 6), particularly if they have no special occupation or are retired (group 10). Sentiment is highest for families with high incomes, especially when the family head is young with a prestigious job (group 9) or is over 45 years of age (group 5). Given the correlation between occupation, education and income, the differences might well be described as dependent on income (or expected income as the age differences in groups 4 and 5 suggest). Since income is also highly related to spending, it is possible that the explanatory power of the attitude index is derived to a significant degree from its correlation with income.

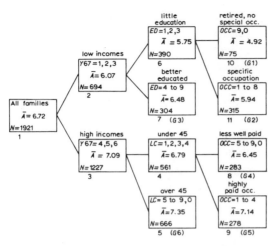

Fig. 1. GROUP DIFFERENCES IN ATTITUDES

A	measurement of sentiment as of January, 1968	*ED*	education of head
*Y*67	1967 family income	*OCC*	occupation of head
		LC	family live cycle
See	Appendix B for an explanation of code values.		

To control for this effect, the results of the AID analysis can be converted to a new variable which explains differences in attitudes dependent on income, occupation, age, and education. Six dummy variables (*G*1 to *G*6) were constructed based on class membership in the AID groups as follows:

	New Variable Name	*Mean Sentiment Index*	*Number of cases*
Family income under $7500			
Education 0 to 11 grades			
Occupation code 0,9	*G*1	4.92	75
Occupation code 1 to 8	*G*2	5.94	315
Education: high school or more	*G*3	6.48	304
Family income above $7500			
Under age 45			
Occupation code 0, 5 to 9	*G*4	6.45	283
Occupation code 1 to 4	*G*5	7.14	278
Age 45 or over	*G*6	7.35	666
All families		6.72	1921

If the correlation of the sentiment index with these characteristics contributes, at least in part, to its explanatory capabilities, then including these groups ($G1$ to $G6$) in the explanatory equation should, to a large degree, control for this:[2]

$$
\begin{aligned}
E67 = 376.63 \; + \; & .0689 & Y66 \; + \; & .0451 & (Y67\text{-}Y66) \\
& (.0055) & & (.0085) & \\
+ \; & 61.970 & A66 \; + \; & 40.410 & (A67\text{-}A66) \\
& (20.871) & & (18.635) & \\
- \; & 164.76 & G1 \; - \; & 387.57 & G2 \\
& (196.57) & & (118.18) & \\
- \; & 330.95 & G3 \; - \; & 255.92 & G4 \\
& (113.35) & & (111.39) & \\
+ \; & 5.45 & G5 & & \\
& (110.38) & & R^2 & = .172 \\
& & & SE & = 1511
\end{aligned}
$$

Equation (1) shows that even with a set of variables representing systematic interpersonal differences in sentiment (as represented by the index constructed), there still remains a statistically significant relationship between the level of optimism and its change during the year and the level of discretionary expenditures made in 1967.

As a further test of the contribution of the sentiment measure, the expenditure variable, $E67$, was regressed on the set of predictors shown in Appendix B to remove all the effects of important personal characteristics on discretionary spending. Nineteen percent of the variation in $E67$ was explained. The residuals from this regression represent variations in expenditures that cannot be explained by the characteristics listed in Appendix B. Regressing the expenditure *residuals* on the level of sentiment at the beginning of the period, $A66$, indicated that the R^2 in the equation would have been improved by a minimum of five percent (one percentage point in R^2) by including the sentiment variable in the regression. Using a sentiment variable adjusted for interpersonal differences related to the characteristics listed in Appendix B (i.e., the residuals from the analysis presented in Figure 1, each individual's sentiment index deviation from his appropriate

[2] Of the six AID groups, the dummy variable $G6$ was excluded from the analysis because it contained the largest number of cases.

AID group mean), the results were also significant, suggesting a minimum improvement in R^2 of at least 2.5 percent. Thus, even when interpersonal differences in attitudes that might be related to spending behavior are removed from the sentiment measure, and the expenditure measure is purged of all variation related to objective personal characteristics, measures of consumer sentiment still make significant contributions to the explanation of consumer behavior in a cross-section study.

CONSUMER SENTIMENT AND THE FORMATION AND FULFILLMENT OF BUYING PLANS: THE CASE OF AUTOMOBILES

The relative performance of specific measures of buying plans and more general measures of consumer sentiment has also been the subject of much debate. Early cross-section studies showed that actual purchases were generally much more frequent, as a proportion, for intender groups than for nonintenders. However, intenders generally made up but a small proportion of the population, and most of the actual expenditures were made by nonintenders, reducing the usefulness of the cross-section estimate as an indicator of aggregate expenditures in the time period of the sample.

As a time series on buying intentions was developed, analysts began incorporating it into aggregate expenditure models, again with little success. It was asserted that the major difficulty was in the lack of precision in the measurement of the intention variable, and that the variable was not properly specified in a dichotomous buy/not-buy form.[3] More sophisticated methodology was developed but there has been little progress (although it is still too early to judge the success of the newer procedures). The most recent aggregate analyses incorporating measures of attitudes and of buying plans have shown them both to make significant contribu-

---

[3] Even though individual observations may be measured with considerable error, aggregating over a large number of cases eliminates unsystematic bias in responses. It is not clear that increasing the accuracy of the measurement of individual buying plans will improve much on the aggregate estimates, although Juster's work makes it clear that sampling error is an important consideration.

tions to the explanation of consumer spending, a reasonable result, substantiated by earlier evidence cited in this paper and the cross-section findings presented in this section [4], [17].

Measures of attitudes, expectations, and buying plans are all anticipatory data in the sense that they are oriented toward behavior in some future period. It is frequently argued that the formation of an optimistic (or more optimistic) outlook precedes the formation of more specific spending plans which in turn precede expenditures. This does not imply that measures of sentiment should necessarily temporally precede measures of buying plans in an empirical model of expenditures. The relevant lag for sentiment measures must be determined by its relationship to expenditures other than through the attitude-buying plans mechanism. The inclusion of buying plans directly in the empirical relationship already incorporates the explanatory variance of the process of intention formation and the extent to which it depends on consumer attitudes.

The formation of buying plans is also clearly not solely dependent on the formation of optimistic expectations and attitudes. To a significant degree, intentions data reflect replacement demand, at least in terms of disequilibria between the actual and desired stock of durables. To the extent that such expenditures are discretionary (operationally, associated with relatively small disequilibria in the related stocks in the consumer portfolio), it seems likely that the making of the actual expenditure would require the coexistence of the intention and the favorable attitudes and expectations which contributed to the formation of the buying plans. Should the factors which seem to be motivating an intended expenditure cease to exist, it seems unlikely that the intention will continue to exist or that the expenditure will be made. Other events, such as income change, may also influence the fulfillment of buying intentions, although this type of effect may also show up in changes in optimism.

The timing of the formation and the various states of certainty or specificity of the anticipatory variables have other implications. If it is true that the formation of attitudes precedes the formation of more specific behavior indicators, such as buying intentions, then a measure of the number (or percentage) of "optimists" might include almost all of the "discretionary intenders" as well as a number of individuals who have the potential of becoming intenders and finally purchasers. Measures of intentions will include the set of individuals who will be buying out of necessity and those who are already committed discretionary purchasers, but will not include *potential* discretionary buyers whose plans will crystallize at a later date. Buying out of necessity may or may not be associated with the attitudinal measures, but this is not the likely source of volatility in expenditures anyway.

For individuals, buying intentions are likely to be good predictors of spending, but only for the *specific* types of expenditures to which they relate. Because of their specific orientation and their frequent dependence on the need for replacement of specific

Table 2

CAR BUYING INTENTIONS BY OPTIMISM INDEX

January, 1968 Car Buying Intentions, Next 12 Months	All Families	Optimism Index, January 1968 (A67)				
		0-2	3-4	5-6	7-8	9-10
Will buy	15.4%	6.6%	10.5%	11.9%	14.2%	26.4%
Probably will buy	1.2	1.6	1.3	.7	1.3	1.5
Might buy	7.3	8.2	6.6	6.7	7.8	7.4
Will not buy	75.5	83.6	81.2	79.9	76.0	64.2
NA, DK	.6	*	.4	.8	.7	.5
Total	100.0%	100.0%	100.0%	100.0%	100.0%	100.0%
Expect to Buy						
New car	11.6%	6.6%	9.6%	8.0%	11.7%	18.4%
Used car	10.5	9.8	8.3	9.3	10.1	14.1
NA which	1.9	*	.4	2.2	1.8	2.8
No car	76.0	83.6	81.7	80.5	76.4	64.7
Total	100.0%	100.0%	100.0%	100.0%	100.0%	100.0%
Number of cases	1921	61	229	538	703	390

*Less than 0.05%

Table 3

NET OUTLAY ON DISCRETIONARY ITEMS BY OPTIMISM IN-
DEX

Net Outlay on Cars, Durables, Additions and Repairs, Hobby Items and Vacations, 1967 (E67)	All Families	Optimism Index, January 1967				
		0-2	3-4	5-6	7-8	9-10
No such expenditure	13%	17%	23%	14%	12%	6%
Less than $ 500	28	35	34	28	28	22
$ 500-999	19	21	15	20	17	22
$ 1000-1999	17	15	12	16	19	21
$ 2000-2999	10	4	8	10	10	12
$ 3000 or more	13	8	8	12	14	17
Total	100%	100%	100%	100%	100%	100%
Number of cases	1921	75	274	530	686	356

items, they are not likely to be good predictors of total discretionary spending. An individual who does not intend to buy a car may still make large expenditures in the period under consideration; or, an intender who does not buy a car as planned may spend on other items.

Measures of sentiment do not have these restrictions and are likely to be better indicators of total spending, since more of the probable spenders are likely to be identified by these measures, as they are not specifically oriented to particular expenditures. For these reasons, attitudes may be better predictors of specific and total expenditures at the aggregate level, and possibly better predictors of total spending by individuals, than buying plans. Both types of variables are related to spending behavior, but through mechanisms which need not and frequently will not be the same. A behavioral model using both types of variables, perhaps interactively, might well prove to be the superior formulation.

Table 2 indicates that in January, 1968, the proportion of very optimistic families (index scores at 9 and 10) that expected to buy

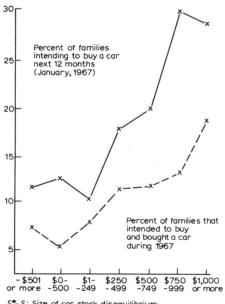

Percent of families intending to buy a car next 12 months (January, 1967)

Percent of families that intended to buy and bought a car during 1967

$S^{*}-S$: Size of car stock disequilibrium

Fig. 2. BUYING PLANS AND THEIR FULFILLMENT BY
CAR STOCK DISEQUILLIBRIUM

a car in the next twelve months (new or used) was nearly four times higher than that for pessimistic families (index scores of two or less). In general, the frequency of buying intentions rises with the level of optimism as measured by the index used. The level and frequency of large discretionary outlays is also related to the senti-ment measure (Table 3).

Figure 2 shows the relationship between the percentage of families intending to buy a car in 1967 and the calculated disequi-librium in the stock of cars owned by the 1921 families in the study.[4] The expected (or desired) stock of cars (denoted S^{*}) was calculated for each family based on its characteristics and the observed relationship between these characteristics and the actual value of all cars owned by families (including nonowners). S^{*} is then compared to the actual value of cars owned, S, and the difference between the two represents the disequilibrium.

The difference should provide an index of the adequacy of the car stock. A recent purchase would likely leave S high relative to S^{*}, making a purchase less probable in the current period. A large deviation between S^* and S indicates the need for additions to the car stock (although the gap may also reflect the preferences of the family and not represent a disequilibrium at all; the composition of the car stock is also ignored by the measure S). Thus, other things being equal, the larger the disequilibrium, the more likely the individual is to have firm buying plans (reported that he would or probably would buy a car in 1967 when interviewed in January, 1967), and the more likely he was to fulfill those plans.

Equations (1) and (2) in Table 4 combine the impact of the two determinants of buying intentions discussed in this section: the measured disequilibrium in the car stock (the calculated difference between the expected and actual value of all cars owned) and the level of consumer sentiment. Equation (1) incorporates $S^* - S$ (the expected stock less the actual value of cars owned at the beginning of 1967) as a measure of the disequilibrium, equation (2) uses $(S^* - S)/S^*$, the relative size of the disequilibrium.

Buying plans early in 1967 are clearly related to the level of sentiment, $A66$. However, the statistical relationship between the car stock disequilibrium and buying plans is much stronger in both formulations, reflecting the importance of the dependence of intentions on this disequilibrium.[5] Both optimism and the disequi-

---

[4] The expected stock of cars, S^*, was calculated for each individual from a regression of the computed value of all cars owned, S, as of January, 1967, on the age, education, occupation and race of the family head, the value of liquid asset holdings, the level of disposable income in 1966, region and place (urban-rural) of residence, the family size, and the number of family members earning \$600 or more per year. All predictors were measured as of January, 1967. The sample mean for 1921 families (no families with head aged over 60) was \$1100. The maximum value that could be predicted for S^* was about \$5000, the minimum about $-\$1000$. Negative values were not truncated to 0. S^* is more appropriately thought of as the *typical* or *expected* value of the car stock owned by families with a given set of socio-economic and demographic characteristics. Whether or not this is an individual's *desired* stock of cars cannot be ascertained from the data. There is also no reason to assume that consumers were collectively "in equilibrium" in the survey year so that the equilibrium estimates may be systematically biased even if the model is properly specified. Families were classified as intending to buy a car if they reported that they definitely or probably would buy a car in the next twelve months.

[5] In Kosobud and Morgan [24, p.48], the most significant variable in the predictive equations for car buying intentions is the age of the newest car owned.

Table 4

MULTIVARIATE ANALYSIS OF CAR BUYING INTENTIONS

	Dependent Variable: Intended to Buy a Car, January, 1967 (INT)	
Predictors	Equation	
	(1)	(2)
$\dfrac{Y66}{1000}$	.00668 (.00113)	.00726 (.00114)
$A66$	.01160 (.00411)	.01247 (.00410)
$\dfrac{S^*-S}{1000}$	.05043 (.00901	
$\dfrac{(S^*-S)/S^*}{1000}$		.87471 (.14484)
Constant	.029	.011
R^2	.04	.04
SE	.373	.373

INT 1 if intended to buy a car in the next twelve months, 0 otherwise.
$Y66$ The level of family income in 1966.
$A66$ The value of the sentiment index in January, 1967.
S^* The expected value of the car stock, January, 1967.
S The measured value of the car stock, January, 1967.

librium are significantly related to buying plans.

The *fulfillment* of buying plans is also dependent on the level of sentiment and the car stock disequilibrium [equations (1) and (2), Table 5]. Income is still an important determinant of automobile buying, independent of its effect on the desired stock of cars, S^*. Sentiment change carried the expected sign but did not make a significant contribution to the equation (although its performance appeared better than of the income change variable).

Unfortunately, little of the total variation in buying intentions

Table 5

MULTIVARIATE ANALYSIS OF FULFILLMENT OF BUYING PLANS FOR CARS

| Predictors | Dependent Variable: Intended to Buy AND Bought a Car in 1967 | |
| | Equation | |
	(1)	(2)
$\dfrac{Y66}{1000}$	.00474 (.00091)	.00503 (.00092)
$\dfrac{Y67\text{-}Y66}{1000}$	.00126 (.00166)	.00129 (.00136)
$A66$	.01145 (.00403)	.01212 (.00404)
$A67\text{-}A66$	.00547 (.00363)	.00584 (.00364)
$\dfrac{S^*\text{-}S}{1000}$	.02912 (.00722)	
$\dfrac{(S^*\text{-}S)/S^*}{1000}$		.44812 (.11639)
Constant	−.0243	−.0345
R^2	.029	.028
SE	.299	.299

or their fulfillment could be explained. A dummy variable dependent measure probably makes the estimation of the effects more difficult, and perhaps intended expenditures or actual expenditures by intenders would be superior measures for estimation purposes, especially where the car stock disequilibrium is part of the model. It may also have been more reasonable to restrict estimation to only those consumers who originally expressed an intention to buy, rather than using all consumers. But, to the extent that buying plans and their fulfillment can be explained, consumer sentiment does appear to be important.

If earlier data on the failure of attitude measures to perform at the micro-level have contributed to an unwillingness of the profession to accept such measures as useful in aggregate analyses, then perhaps this study has, to a major degree, eliminated that reticence. It would appear that attitudes play a major role in determining expenditure variations, even when annual observations are used. It appears that data collected over shorter periods would provide even stronger evidence (possibly as much through a relative decline in the importance of objective variables in determining expenditures as by an increase in the significance of sentiment measures).

Buying intentions were shown to depend on consumer attitudes as well as on more objective variables like income and the adequacy of the car stock. The fulfillment of these plans also depended on consumer sentiment. Used jointly, both attitudes and intentions make significant contributions to the explanation of spending variations, both at the micro-level and in time-series equations.

From the forecaster's point of view, these measures are indeed difficult to incorporate directly into objective models. Sometimes, they are strong enough to confound the estimation of the effects of objective variables in short-term models. And, with good reason, forecasters are more reluctant to forecast sentiment than they are to predict income or government spending. Yet, many of the major forecast errors in econometric models are traceable directly to the consumer sector and the difficulty of predicting expenditures. This seems to suggest the need for increased effort aimed at integrating sentiment measures into the models rather than at explaining why they might be omitted.

APPENDIX A

MAJOR QUESTIONS USED BY SRC TO MEASURE ATTITUDES AND EXPECTATIONS

*1. We are interested in how people are getting along financially these days. Would you say that you and your family are *better off* or *worse off* financially than you were a *year ago?*

*2. Now, looking ahead, do you think that *a year from now* you people will be *better off* financially, or *worse off*, or just about the same as now?

3. Are you people making as much as you were a year ago, or more or less?

4. How do you think your total family income for this year, 19 , will compare with the past year, 19 , will it be much higher, a little higher, about the same, or lower?

*5. Now turning to business conditions in the country as a whole, do you think that during the next twelve months we'll have *good* times financially, or *bad* times, or what?

6. Would you say that *at present*, business conditions are better or worse than they were *a year ago*?

7. And, how about *a year from now*, do you expect that in the country as a whole business conditions will be better or worse than they are *at present*, or just about the same?

*8. Looking ahead, which do you say is more likely, that in the country as a whole we will have continuous good times *during the next five years* or so, or that we will have periods of widespread unemployment or depression, or what?

9. Speaking of prices in general, I mean the prices of things you buy, do you think they will go up in the next year or so, or go down, or stay where they are now?

10. Would you say that these (rising, falling, unchanged) prices would be to the good or bad or what?

11. During the *last few months* have you heard of any favorable or unfavorable changes in business conditions?

*12. About the things that people buy for their homes — such as furniture, house furnishings, refrigerator, stove, TV and things like that. *Generally speaking* do you think now is a good or a bad time to buy major household items?

13. Generally speaking, do you think now is a good time or a bad time to buy a house?

365

14. Speaking now of the automobile market, do you think the next twelve months or so will be a good time or a bad time to buy a car?

15. Do you *expect* to buy or build a house for your own use during the next twelve months?

16. Do you expect to buy a car during the next twelve months or so? Does anyone else in the family here expect to buy a car during the next twelve months?

16a. Will it be a brand new car or a used car?

*Questions used to construct the index.

APPENDIX B

PREDICTORS USED IN AID ANALYSIS OF ATTITUDES AND DISCRETIONARY EXPENDITURES

Age of Head of Family
1. Under 25
2. 25-34
3. 35-44
4. 45-54
5. 55-64
6. 65 and over

Race of Head of Family
1. White
2. Non-white

ED *Education of Head of Family Unit*
1. 0-5 grades
2. 6-8 grades
3. 9-11 grades; some high school plus non-college schooling
4. 12 grades; completed high school (12 years)
5. Completed high school plus other non-college training
6. College, no degree (included junior colleges)
7. College, Bachelor's degree
8. College, advanced or professional degree
9. *NA, DK*

LC *Life Cycle*

Under Age 45
1. Unmarried, no children
2. Married, no children
3. Married, youngest child under 6
4. Married, youngest child 6 or over

Age 45 or over
5. Married, has children
6. Married, no children, head in labor force
7. Married, no children, head retired
8. Unmarried, no children, head in labor force
9. Unmarried, no children, head retired

Any Age
0. Unmarried, with children

Marital Status of Head
1. Married
2. Single
3. Widowed (widower)
4. Divorced
5. Separated
6. Separated - husband away in service
9. *NA*

OCC *Occupation of Family Head*
1. Professional, technical
2. Managers, officials
3. Self-employed business-men, artisans
4. Clerical, sales
5. Craftsmen, foremen
6. Operatives
7. Laborers, service workers
8. Farmers, farm managers
9. Miscellaneous
0. Retired

Y67 *Total Family Unit Income, 1967*
1. Under $2,999
2. $ 3,000- 4,999
3. $ 5,000- 7,499
4. $ 7,500- 9,999
5. $10,000-14,999
6. $15,000 or more

Y66 *Total Family Income, 1966*
0. Under $1,000
1. $ 1,000- 1,999
2. $ 2,000- 2,999
3. $ 3,000- 3,999
4. $ 4,000- 4,999
5. $ 5,000- 5,999
6. $ 6,000- 7,499

                                              7. $ 7,500- 9,999
                                              8. $10,000- 14,999
                                              9. $15,000 or more

ΔY   *Total Family Income Change During 1967*
     0. $5,000
     1. $2,000-4,999
     2. $1,000-1,999
     3. $500-999
     4. $200-499
     5. $199 to −199
     6. −$200 to −499
     7. −$500 to −999
     8. −$1,000 to −1,999
     9. −$2,000 or more

Percent of Income Change During 1967

1.	20% or more
2.	15% to 19%
3.	10% to 14%
4.	5% to 9%
5.	4% to −4%
6.	−5% to −9%
7.	−10% to −14%
8.	−15% to −19%
9.	−20% or more

Optimism Index, January, 1968
1. 0-2 points
2. 3-4
3. 5-6
4. 7-8
5. 9-10

Optimism Index, January, 1968

xx   Actual Index Value
     Maximum value = 10
     Minimum value = 0

REFERENCES

1 Adams, F.G., "Consumer Attitudes, Buying Plans and Purchases of Durable Goods", *Review of Economics and Statistics*, XLVI (November, 1964).
2 Adams, F.G., "Prediction with Consumer Attitudes: The Time Series-Cross-Section Paradox", *Review of Economics and Statistics*, XLVII (November, 1965).
3 Adams, F.G., and E.W. Green, "Explaining and Predicting Aggregative Consumer Attitudes", *International Economic Review*, 6 (September, 1965).

4 Dunkelberg, William, "Forecasting Consumer Expenditures with Measures of Attitudes & Expectations", Unpublished doctoral thesis, University of Michigan, Ann Arbor, 1969.

5 Dunkelberg, William, and F. Stafford, "Debt in the Consumer Portfolio: Evidence from a Panel Study", *American Economic Review*, (September, 1971).

6 Evans, Michael K., *Macroeconomic Activity, Theory, Forecasting & Control*, New York: Harper & Row, 1969.

7 Ferber, Robert, "On the Stability of Consumer Expectations", *Review of Economics and Statistics*, XXXVII (August, 1955).

8 Ferber, Robert, "Anticipation Statistics and Consumer Behavior", *The American Statistician*, (October, 1966).

9 Ferber, Robert, and P.A. Piskie, "Subjective Probabilities and Buying Intentions", *Review of Economics and Statistics*, XLVII (August, 1965).

10 Fisher, J.A., "Consumer Durable Goods Expenditure, with Major Emphasis on the Role of Assets, Credit, and Intentions", *Journal of the American Statistical Association*, 58 (September, 1963).

11 Flechsig, T., "Evaluation of Survey Techniques for Measuring Consumer Anticipations", *American Statistical Association: Proceedings of the Business and Economic Statistics Section*, September, 1962.

12 Friend, Irwin, and F.G. Adams, "The Predictive Ability of Consumer Attitudes, Stock Prices, and Nonattitudinal Variables", *Journal of the American Statistical Association*, 59 (December, 1964).

13 Hymans, Saul H., "Consumer Durable Spending: Explanation and Prediction", In Okun and Perry, eds., *Brookings Papers on Economic Activity*, 2, Washington, 1970.

14 Juster, F.T., "Some Experimental Results in Measuring Purchase Probability for Durables and Some Tentative Exploration of Time Series Demand Models", *American Statistical Association: Proceedings of the Business and Economic Statistics Section*, September, 1967.

15 Juster, F.T., "Prediction and Consumer Buying Intentions", *American Economic Review, Papers and Proceedings*, May, 1960.

16 Juster, F.T., "Consumer Buying Intentions and Purchase Probabilities: An Experiment in Survey Design", *Journal of the American Statistical Association*, 61 (September, 1966).

17 Juster, F.T., "Consumer Anticipations and Models of Durable Goods Demand", in J. Mincer, ed., *Economic Forecasts and Expectations*, NBER, New York: Columbia University Press, 1961.

18 Juster, F.T., and P. Wachtel, "A Note on Uncertainty Expectations and Durable Goods Demand Models", Unpublished manuscript.

19 Katona, George, *The Mass Consumption Society*, New York: McGraw-Hill Book Co., 1964.

20 Katona, George, "Anticipations Statistics and Consumer Behavior", *The American Statistician*, 21 (April, 1967).

21 Katona, George, and Eva Mueller, *Consumer Attitudes and Demand, 1950-1952*, Ann Arbor, Mich.: Survey Research Center, University of Michigan, 1952.

22 Katona, George, William Dunkelberg, Jay Schmiedeskamp, and Frank Stafford, *1968 Survey of Consumer Finances*, Ann Arbor, Mich.: Survey Research Center, University of Michigan, 1969.

23 Katona, George, William Dunkelberg, Gary Hendricks and Jay Schmiedeskamp, *1969 Survey of Consumer Finances*, Ann Arbor, Mich.: Survey Research Center, University of Michigan, 1970.

24 Kosobud, R.F, and J.N. Morgan, *Consumer Behavior of Individual Families Over Two and Three Years*, Ann Arbor, Mich.: Survey Research Center, University of Michigan, 1964.

25 Kuh, Edwin, "The Validity of Cross-Sectionally Estimated Behavior Equations in Time Series Applications", *Econometrica*, 27 (April, 1959).

26 Lansing, J.B., and L.R. Klein, "Decisions to Purchase Consumer Durable Goods", *Journal of Marketing*, 20 (October, 1955).

27 Maynes, E. Scott, "An Appraisal of Consumer Anticipations Approaches to Forecasting", *American Statistical Association: Proceedings of the Business and Economic Statistics Section*, 1967.

28 McNeil, John M., and Thomas L. Stoterau, "The Census Bureau's New Survey of Consumer Buying Expectations", *American Statistical Association: Proceedings of the Business and Economics Statistics Section*, 1962.

29 Mueller, Eva, "Consumer Attitudes: Their Influence and Forecasting Value", *The Quality and Significance of Anticipations Data*, A Report of the National Bureau of Economic Research, Princeton, N.J.: Princeton University Press, 1960.

30 Mueller, Eva, "Effects of Consumer Attitudes on Purchases", *American Economic Review*, 48 (December, 1957).

31 Mueller, Eva, "Ten Years of Consumer Attitude Surveys: Their Forecasting Record", *Journal of the American Statistical Association*, 58 (December, 1963).

32 Okun, Arthur M., "The Value of Anticipations Data in Forecasting National Product", *The Quality and Significance of Anticipations Data*, A Report of the National Bureau of Economic Research, Princeton N.J.: Princeton University Press, 1960.

33 Peterson, Richard L., and W.D. Dunkelberg, "Short Run Variations in Aggregate Spending Behavior", Research Paper #54, Graduate School of Business, Stanford University, 1971.

34 Peterson, Richard L., and W.D. Dunkelberg, "Short Run Fluctuations in Aggregate Savings Rates", Research Paper #61, Graduate School of Business, Stanford University, 1971, Presented at the Western Economics Association Meetings, Vancouver, 1971.

35 Shapiro, Harold T., and Gerald E. Angevine, "Consumer Attitudes, Buying Intentions, and Expenditures — An Analysis of Canadian Data", Paper presented at the Canadian Economics Association in Calgary, Alberta, June 5, 1968.

36 Sonquist, John, and James Morgan, *The Detection of Interaction Effects*, Ann Arbor, Michigan: Survey Research Center, University of Michigan, 1964.

37 Survey Research Center, "Fifteen Years of Experience with Measurement of Consumer Expectations", *American Statistical Association: Proceedings of the Business and Economics Statistics Section* 1962.

38 Suits, D.B., and G.R. Sparks, "Consumption Regressions with Quarterly Data", *Brookings Quarterly Econometric Model of the United States*, Ed. by J.S. Duesenberry, G. Fromm, L.R. Klein, and E. Kuh, Chicago: Rand-McNally, 1965.

39 Tobin, James, "On the Predictive Value of Consumer Intentions and Attitudes", *Review of Economics and Statistics*, XLI (February, 1959).

40 Tobin, James, "On the Predictive Value of Consumer Intentions and Attitudes: A Final Remark", *Review of Economics and Statistics*, XLI (August, 1959).

The Index of Consumer Sentiment and Economic Forecasting: a Reappraisal*

HAROLD T. SHAPIRO

INTRODUCTION

The possible usefulness of attitudinal data in forecasting the level of "discretionary" consumer expenditures (consumer durables, particularly automobiles) has been a matter of some controversy ever since George Katona and his colleagues at the Survey Research Center (SRC) at the University of Michigan first began (some two decades ago) their pioneering efforts to measure consumer attitudes and study their influence on household behavior. There was broad agreement that consumer attitudes and psychology have an important role in determining discretionary spending, but whether these factors played an independent role whose effects could be clearly isolated, or whether the use of variables directly measuring changes in consumer sentiment was clearly more efficient in forecasting consumer expenditures than the alternative of combining other types of variables in more complex patterns, remained an open issue. In recent years, the debate has once again intensified as economists have tried to understand their failure to predict recent patterns in consumer durable spending in

* I am indebted to R. Hokenson for valuable assistance in all aspects of the preparation of this study.

the United States. Interestingly enough the re-examination of this issue has been especially prevalent among econometricians despite (because of?) the fact that the great majority of the econometric consumption equations currently in use as forecasting tools allow no role for variables directly measuring consumer attitudes.[1]

The current debate has two distinct streams of investigation. The first stream represents a continuation of the traditional issue of whether or not the inclusion of a consumer attitude index (usually derived from the SRC's Index of Consumer Sentiment, ICS) in an equation explaining consumer durable expenditures improves the model's ability to explain or forecast this category of consumer expenditure. In this area the current research seems to support the view of previous studies that the attitude index helps, but not much unless one begins with a hopelessly naive model of consumer behavior. The second, and more novel aspect of the current investigations centers around attempts to explain the ICS itself. In particular, this effort involves attempts to isolate a stable relationship between the ICS and other easily measurable variables of economic activity such as changes in income, unemployment rates, rates of inflation, and changes in equity prices. Hymans [5], for example, has recently claimed some success in this area.[2]

One of the significant results of the current debate is that George Katona has once again served notice to the profession that he is not entirely satisfied with our understanding of the issues involved and, therefore, with the tests performed and the results achieved. In his most recent published comments [7], he once again sets forth the model of human behavior underlying the construction of the ICS and, at least by implication, challenges us to review more carefully our efforts in this area. The purpose of this paper is to respond by confronting, in a way quite different from previous studies, two of the main issues raised by Katona in his recent comments, namely:

1. The hypothesis advanced by Katona that the mechanism generating changes in consumer attitudes (as measured by the ICS) is not a stable function over time of a finite set of determining variables.

---

[1] A notable exception is a recent model by R. Fair [4].
[2] For an earlier attempt in this area see Adams and Green [1].

2. The predictive value of the index should be evaluated primarily in terms of its contribution during periods of substantial change, especially in those periods where the direction of consumer activity has shifted.

The second section of this paper reviews the importance of the stability of the mechanism generating consumer attitudes in the context of the behavioral theory underlying the construction of the ICS and presents some empirical evidence on this issue. The third section evaluates in a new and hopefully more meaningful fashion the usefulness of the ICS in forecasting consumer expenditures on automobiles — with special emphasis on those periods dominated by shifts in activity.

STABILITY

The basic model of human behavior that underlies the construction of the ICS postulates that changes in discretionary expenditures are not solely a function of such economic determinants as income, prices, etc., but that "intervening" variables such as attitudes, expectations, etc., influence both the consumer's perception of his economic environment and his response to it. Further, the model postulates that while we can measure changes in the "intervening" variables, the mechanism governing these changes will change over time. That is, since the mechanism itself is unstable, its parameters cannot be isolated by standard statistical analysis and can be revealed only by a continuous series of household surveys. Thus, the collection of attitudinal data will remain an important continuing obligation if we wish to understand the fluctuations in consumer sentiment, and to predict their effects on consumer behavior. In this situation there is no replacement for the surveys themselves.

The hypothesis regarding the stability of the mechanism generating consumer attitudes has, to date, remained an untested conjecture. Hymans [5] and Fair [3], however, have certainly raised some doubt about its validity by isolating, from the data of the last ten to fifteen years statistical relationships capable of explaining fifty percent of the *variance of the change* in the ICS, using unemployment rates, equity prices, and inflation rates as determining variables. Further, Hymans [5] has shown that that component of the ICS which his equation does explain is the component most responsible for the contribution of the attitude index in improving forecasts of consumer expenditure. Neither of the above researchers, however, investigated directly the stability of the relationship explaining the attitude index over the sample period.

In order to test this proposition of stability, we present two rather similar models relating the ICS to measures of aggregate economic activity, stock prices, and the rate of inflation. The specification of the equations derives directly from the work of Hymans [5], and the two models differ only in the measure employed to reflect the level of aggregate economic activity. Model (A) uses constant-dollar disposable income net of transfers as the appropriate measure, while Model (B) uses an unemployment rate for the purpose. Estimates of the parameters (by ordinary least-squares) of both these models based on quarterly data covering the whole sample period (1956.1-1970.2) are as follows[3] (figures in parentheses are t-values):

Model (A)

$$ICS = 138.64 + 29.13 \left(\frac{SP_{t-1}}{SP_{t-2}}\right) - 181.44 \frac{PCED_{t-1}}{\frac{1}{8}\sum_{i=1}^{8} PCED_{t-i}}$$
$$\quad\quad (2.15) \quad (3.89) \quad\quad\quad\quad (3.61)$$

$$+ 52.77 \frac{DYK^*_{t-1}}{\frac{1}{8}\sum_{i=1}^{8} DYK^*_{t-i}}$$
$$\;\;(1.71)$$

$$+ .59\, ICS_{t-1}$$
$$\quad (5.83)$$

$$R^2 = .83 \quad\quad\quad\quad\quad D.W. = 2.1 \quad SEE = 2.71$$

---

[3] The ICS variable itself is available only sporadically before 1961.4. The missing data were estimated either by interpolation, or by using Model (A) fitted to the initially available data points. Our results were insensitive to these alternate procedures.

Model (B)

$$ICS = 319.36 + 29.48 \left(\frac{SP_{t-1}}{SP_{t-2}}\right) - 300.14 \quad \frac{PCED_{t-i}}{\frac{1}{8} \sum\limits_{i=1}^{8} PCED_{t-i}}$$

$$(3.18) \quad (3.89) \qquad\qquad (3.40)$$

$$- .83\ UM_{t-1} + .56\ ICS_{t-1}$$
$$(1.79) \qquad\quad (4.79)$$

$$R^2 = .83 \qquad\qquad D.W. = 2.1 \quad SEE = 2.73$$

where   *ICS*   SRC's index of consumer sentiment.

   SP   Standard and Poors Index of Industrial Common Stocks (1941-43 = 10).

   PCED   Implicit Deflator for Consumer Expenditures (National Income Accounts) (1958 = 100.0).

   DYK*   Seasonally Adjusted Disposable Income Net of Transfers. Billions of 1958 Dollars.

   UM   Unemployment Rate (Men 20 Years and Over), (Percent).

The parameters of both model (A) and model (B) were also estimated from data generated over two nonoverlapping sub-periods of the sample (1956.1-1960.3, and 1960.4-1970.2) in order to test the hypothesis that the observations in these two periods were generated by the same mechanism. For this purpose we employed the F-test suggested by Chow [2]. The results are presented in Table 1, and do not reject the hypothesis that the data in both periods were generated by the same mechanism. Additional experiments with other possible subdivisions of the sample period were carried out, but the results were uniformly the same. The data did not reject the hypothesis of stability. The primary driving variables in both models, namely stock prices and price expectations, retain their strong influence in all subperiods of the sample tested. These influences at least, therefore, have a continuous and steady influence on the formation of consumer attitudes. Further, the estimated values of the ICS, derived from these equations fitted over various portions of the sample period, play a significant role in models explaining consumer expenditure on automobiles. That part of the ICS that was left unexplained by these models, however, played no such role. Thus, the unexplained component of the index seemed to play no role in predicting behavior.

Table 1

SUMMARY STATISTICS NECESSARY TO TEST STABILITY OF REGRESSION COEFFICENTS

	Model (A)	Model (B)
Sum of Squared Residuals from Pooled Regression (Q_1)	391.604	394.172
Sum of Squared Residuals from Separate Regressions (Q_2)	360.666	366.042
$Q_3 = Q_1 - Q_2$	30.938	28.130
Computed $F = \dfrac{Q_3/k}{Q_2/(m+h-2k)}$	.823	.738
Critical $F_{.05}$*	2.40	2.40

*If $F > F_{.05}$ we reject hypothesis of stability.

It is important to note that these results by themselves do not necessarily imply that consumer attitudes and expectations are a function of economic determinants alone, since much of the variance in stock price, for example, may come from some other source. Further, the lagged value of the sentiment index also plays an important role in the equation. The results do imply, however, that a stable model of consumer attitude formation can be isolated from readily available data on income, inflation rates and equity prices, and that for some purposes (e.g. short-term forecasting), this information may be used in models of consumer behavior in place of the survey results.

There have been a number of investigations of the extent to which movements in the *Index of Consumer Sentiment* can improve a model's ability either to explain or forecast consumer durable expenditures. Virtually all these studies have proceeded by formulating various models of consumer expenditure and then investigating the effects of specifying an additional variable directly measuring consumer attitudes. If this additional variable made a "significant" contribution to the explanation of expenditures over the sample period, and then perhaps also made an additional contribution to forecasts one or two periods beyond the sample, it was concluded that "attitudes" did have a important independent role to play. It seems to me, however, that if we wish to isolate the role of "attitudinal variables" in improving our ability to *forecast* consumer behavior that this is an inadequate set of procedures. The appropriate way to evaluate a model's ability to predict (for example, a particular turning point in automobile expenditures) is to restrict the model's access to information to a data period ending prior to that event. A model's ability to predict a particular turning point — *ex post* — after one has been allowed to make use of this particular information in estimating the model's parameters is of limited relevance to the forecaster. What a forecaster must predict is unknown future events which lie outside the sample period of the data which he has available. The following procedure, therefore, suggests itself.

1. Estimate a model from the data generated over an initial sample period (say 1954.1-1958.1).
2. Use the model to forecast changes in the variables of interest over the next few quarters.
3. Update the model by re-estimating its parameters using data from the initial sample and from the quarters just forecast.
4. Use the "new" model to forecast for the next few quarters.
5. Repeat steps (3)-(4) as you move through time.

The important property of this procedure is that forecasts are never being made of events within the sample period. You are always forecasting events outside the sample period. To investigate, within this framework, the usefulness of an index of consumer sentiment, for example, in decreasing forecasting errors, you simply formulate alternate sets of models explaining consumer behavior (both with and without variables directly measuring attitudes) and evaluate their relative forecasting performance when generating forecasts along the lines suggested in steps (1) to (5) above.

For purposes of this study we formulated four different models designed to explain consumer expenditure on automobiles. One of the models (I) is composed of a number of simple rules and cannot be used without information on consumer attitudes. The remaining models are formulated in two different versions (A) and (B), one without variables directly representing consumer sentiment (A) and one with such variables (B). Each of these models is used, under the procedures set up above, to generate forecasts over the period 1958.1-1969.2. These forecasts are then compiled in summary form and compared in order to draw certain conclusions regarding the contribution of the variables representing changes in consumer sentiment. We begin, therefore, with a brief description of the models used.

Model (I)

Our first model is a rather naive model designed solely to predict the direction of change in automobile expenditures. It is composed of two rules.
1. If there is no change in the index of consumer attitudes being used, then the direction of change in expenditures this period will be the same as last period.
2. If there is a change in the index of consumer attitudes, the direction of change in expenditures will follow the direction of change in the attitude index.
Although this is a very simple model it has a number of advantages, principally, it is cheap and easy to use. It will predict changes in the direction of change only when the attitude index is changing its direction.

Model (II-A)

This is a simple autoregressive model of auto expenditures, which can be written as follows,

$$CAUTOK = a_0 + a_1 CAUTOK_{t-1}$$

where $CAUTOK$ =   consumer expenditures on autos and parts in the national income accounts, adjusted to remove mobile homes, in billions of 1958 dollars, seasonally adjusted at annual rates.

The parameters of this model were initially estimated by ordinary least-squares over the sample period 1954.1-1957.4. The model was then updated every two quarters and then used to forecast two quarters ahead. If the estimated residuals showed signs of first order autocorrelation the parameters were re-estimated using a first order Markov transformation of the data. Further, in the period subsequent to the 1964 auto-strike, a dummy variable reflecting the effects of auto strikes (in 1964 and 1967) was added to the equation.

Model (III-A)

Our third model is also a simple characterization of consumer behavior which specifies auto expenditure as a simple function of lagged disposable income net of transfers.

$$CAUTOK = b_0 + b_1 DYK^*_{t-1}$$

As with Model (II), we began by estimating the parameters of this model by ordinary least-squares from data generated in the initial sample period 1954.1-1958.4. The estimates were then updated every two quarters for use in forecasting over the following six-month period. Unfortunately, until the early 1960's we could not isolate stable coefficients for either b_0 or b_1. For purposes of forecasting, therefore, Model (III) is considered a type of hybrid, using the equations of Model (II) for the period prior to 1962.1. As with Model (II), all estimates were corrected for first-order serial correlation in the estimated residuals where necessary and provision was made for the effects of auto strikes subsequent to 1964.

Model (IV-A)

This is a standard stock adjustment model with disposable income net of transfers, unemployment rates, and relative prices as determinants of desired stock [5]. As with the above model, auto strike effects were allowed to enter subsequent to the 1964 auto strike. The equation actually estimated can be expressed as follows.

$$CAUTOK = c_0 + c_1 DYK^*_{t-1} + c_2 UM_{t-1} + c_3 \frac{AUTOD}{PCED} + c_4 KA_{t-1}$$

where $AUTOD$ = Gross auto product deflator, 1958=100.
KA = actual auto stock, end of quarter multiplied by four to accord with the annual rate of income and auto expenditure.

This model was updated every *four* quarters beginning in 1958. For the first six years (through 1962.4) unemployment rates and prices played no role in the equation and were dropped from the relationship. As with the above model, the parameters were estimated by ordinary least-squares with first order Markov transformations of the data where necessary.

Models (II-B), (III-B), (IV-B)

These models are analogous to models (II-A), (III-A), and (IV-A), with the exception that they all introduce a variable (denoted as J) directly measuring changes in consumer attitudes as an additional factor in explaining and forecasting expenditures on automobiles. The variable used is a "filtered" version of changes in the *Index of Consumer Sentiment* — first suggested by Juster and Wachtel [6] and further investigated by Hymans [5]. The purpose of this "filtering" mechanism is to isolate the meaningful changes in the *Index of Consumer Sentiment*. It is defined as follows.

$J =$ 0.5 ΔICS_{-1} + 0.5 ΔICS_{-2} if (*a*) ΔICS_{-i} for $i=1,2,3$, are all of the same sign; or if (*b*) ΔICS_{-i} for $i=1,2$ are of the same sign and $|\Delta ICS_{-1}| + |\Delta ICS_{-2}| \geq 7$; if neither (*a*) nor (*b*) is fulfilled, the variable takes on the value of 0.

The procedure followed generated 25 separate sets of parameter estimates for each of Models (II) and (III), in both versions, and 13 different sets of estimates for Model (IV), the latter being updated only every four quarters. Although no formal tests were performed to investigate the hypothesis of stability in the generating mechanism each time the sample was enlarged, the estimated parameters in fact change very little over much of the period. Little is to be gained by presenting all 126 sets of parameters estimates here, and thus, I confine myself to presenting, for purposes of illustration, the parameter estimates for each of these models based on two different sample periods. The first set of estimates are based on data generated through 1965.4, the second set on data through 1969.4. The estimates are tabulated in Table 2.

In generating forecasts from those models we allowed our "forecaster" one additional bit of insight. We assumed that the forecaster took advantage of the errors made in recent quarters by the model currently in use and adjusted the model's forecast accordingly. We allowed the model's "raw" forecast to be altered by the average of the last two estimated residuals from the regression equation used to estimate the model's current parameters. Thus, if the model had been consistently overestimating (underestimating) expenditures in the most recent past, the "raw" forecast was adjusted to get the model "back on track". Summary measures of forecasts and forecast errors for these various models are presented in Tables 3 through 6.

Table 3 contains certain summary measures of the overall forecasting performance of those models over the entire sample period. A number of general observations can be made from the evidence presented here, namely:

1. The addition of the filtered version of the ICS, substantially reduces the mean absolute error and the root mean square error of the forecasts made by the simpler models, Models (II) and (III).

2. It has virtually no effect on the ability to forecast automobile

Table 2

PARAMETER ESTIMATES FOR MODELS (II), (III) AND (IV) COMPARISON OF ALTERNATE SETS FROM TWO DIFFERENT SAMPLE PERIODS

Model	Sample Period	$\hat{a}_0$	a_1	$\hat{b}_0$	$\hat{b}_1$	$\hat{c}_0$	$\hat{c}_1$	$\hat{c}_2$	$\hat{c}_3$	$\hat{c}_4$	$\hat{\gamma}_0$*	$\hat{\gamma}_1$†	$\hat{e}$‡
(II-A)	1954.1-1965.4	1.115φ	.961								1.614		0.0
(II-A)	1954.1-1969.4	.658φ	.986								1.692		0.0
(II-B)	1954.1-1965.4	1.437φ	.944								1.618	0.231	0.0
(II-B)	1954.1-1969.4	.546φ	.992								1.743	0.186	0.0
(III-A)	1954.1-1965.4			-7.758	0.089						1.447		0.832
(III-A)	1954.1-1969.4			-10.425	0.098						1.518		0.780
(III-B)	1954.1-1965.4			-7.875	0.090						1.456	0.388	0.791
(III-B)	1954.1-1969.4			-11.239	0.100						1.648	0.341	0.754
(IV-A)	1954.1-1965.4					12.961	0.202	-.711	-19.528	-.152	1.606		0.614
(IV-A)	1954.1-1969.4					17.713	0.156	-.618	-23.051	-.096	1.592		0.643
(IV-B)	1954.1-1965.4					14.128	0.183	-.813	-19.334	-.130	1.588	0.148	0.627
(IV-B)	1954.1-1969.4					18.760	0.137	-.766	-22.104	-.075	1.725	0.305	0.492

*   Coefficient on auto strike dummy variable

†   Coefficient on filtered ICS variable (J)

‡   Estimated first order autocorrelation coefficient. Where this takes a non-zero value the parameters were estimated using a first order Markov transformation of the data

φ   Estimates "insignificant" at the 5% level

Table 3

SUMMARY MEASURES OF FORECASTS AND FORECAST ERRORS IN MODELS OF CONSUMER AUTO EXPENDITURE

Model	Period	Mean Absolute Change	Mean Absolute Error	Mean Error	Root Mean Square Error
(I)	1958.1-1970.2	n.a.	n.a.	n.a.	n.a.
(II-A)	1958.1-1970.2	.866	1.477	.115	2.100
(II-B)	1958.1-1970.2	.784	1.365	.223	1.754
(III-A)	1958.1-1970.2	1.231	1.740	.299	2.356
(III-B)	1958.1-1970.2	1.143	1.586	.558	2.051
(IV-A)	1958.1-1970.2	1.070	1.080	.031	1.378
(IV-B)	1958.1-1970.2	1.186	1.096	.013	1.466
Actual	1958.1-1970.2	1.255	n.a.	n.a.	n.a.

expenditures through the more complicated mechanism of a stock adjustment model. In fact, in the example taken here, the results are somewhat worse when using the attitude variable.

3. Simple models do poorly.

Table 4 is divided into two sections. Both give some additional summary data comparing the forecasting performance of our models which concentrate on the model's ability to forecast the direction of change in automobile expenditures. The top part of the table, however, contains statistics covering the whole sample period, while the bottom section summarizes the model's forecasting performance only for those periods of the sample which were not dominated by a smooth trend in expenditures. This latter section is provided so that we may deal more effectively with Katona's request that we evaluate the contribution of the index in those periods not characterized by smooth movements in expenditures. The following observations are suggested by the statistics gathered in this table – confining our attention for the moment to the second section of the table.

1. Model (II), the autoregressive model, is not better than the simple set of rules summarized in Model (I). This is so regardless of whether or not we use attitude indices. Information on changing consumer attitudes does nothing to salvage the ability of this model to correctly forecast the direction of change in

385

Table 4

FORECASTS OF QUARTERLY CHANGES IN CONSUMER AUTOMOBILE EXPENDITURE DISTRIBUTED BY TYPE OF CHANGE AND TYPE OF ERROR FOR VARIOUS FORECASTING MODELS

Model	Time Period	Total	Number of Forecasts of Quarterly Changes				
			Direction of Forecast Change Correct		Directional Errors[c]		
			Under-Estimates[a]	Over-Estimates[b]	Type 1	Type 2	Total
(I)	1958.1-1970.2	50	n.a.	n.a.	9	9	18
(II-A)	1958.1-1970.2	50	20	7	13	10	23
(II-B)	1958.1-1970.2	50	22	4	16	8	24
(III-A)	1958.1-1970.2	50	16	8	19	7	26
(III-B)	1958.1-1970.2	50	19	8	18	5	23
(IV-A)	1958.1-1970.2	50	21	13	13	3	16
(IV-B)	1958.1-1970.2	50	24	12	11	3	14
(I)	1958.1-1961.2/1966.2-1970.2	31	n.a.	n.a.	8	9	17
(II)	1958.1-1961.2/1966.2-1970.2	31	8	6	7	10	17
(II)	1958.1-1961.2/1966.2-1970.2	31	9	4	10	8	18
(III)	1958.1-1961.2/1966.2-1970.2	31	9	5	10	7	17
(III)	1958.1-1961.2/1966.2-1970.2	31	10	8	8	5	13
(IV)	1958.1-1961.2/1966.2-1970.2	31	9	16	3	3	6
(IV)	1958.1-1961.2/1966.2-1970.2	31	8	17	3	3	6

a   Predicted change is less than actual change

b   Predicted change exceeds actual change

c   Sign of predicted change $\neq$ sign of actual change

Type 1 – Predicted change negative, actual change positive

Type 2 – Predicted change positive, actual change negative

expenditures. Both models (I) and (II) incorrectly forecast the direction of change well over half the time.

2. Model (III) represents little improvement over Models (I) and (II), unless it is allowed to make use of information on changes in the ICS. The introduction of attitudes into this model substantially improves its ability to forecast the direction of change correctly. Of these first five models, only Model (III-B) correctly predicts the direction of change over half the time. (Batting average is 0.581.) This model is, therefore, able to make effective use of changes in consumer sentiment in forecasting expenditures.

3. Models (IV-A) and (IV-B) are far superior to the others, being able to predict the direction of change correctly about 80 percent of the time — confining ourselves to that part of the sample dominated by more volatile shifts in expenditures. Within the framework represented by these models, however, information on changing consumer attitudes does not improve the forecaster's ability to predict the direction of change in expenditures.

If we consider statistics covering the entire sample period (top half of Table 4), roughly the same conclusions obtain. In this context, however, Model (I) performs relatively well. The reason is that it does best in the period dominated by a smooth upward swing in expenditures (1961.3-1966.1). The other models continue to make numerous small errors during this time. When things are simple, therefore, it is efficient to use simple models.

Table 5 presents statistics summarizing the model's ability to predict turning points in consumer expenditure on automobiles. Information is presented regarding the number of turning points correctly predicted, as well as the number of false signals generated by each of the models. For our purposes, a turning point was defined as a change in the direction of change in expenditures of at least 5 percent of its previous level. Thus only "major" turning points are considered. There were twelve of these during the entire forecast period. Of all the statistics presented, these in Table 5 and in Table 6 (to be discussed below) are the most relevant to establishing the role of changing consumer attitudes in forecasting major shifts in consumer expenditure behavior. A number of interesting observations are suggested by the statistics presented.

Table 5

FREQUENCY OF TURNING POINTS[a] AND ERRORS IN QUARTERLY FORECASTS OF CHANGES IN CONSUMER AUTOMOBILE EXPENDITURE

Model	Period	Number of Turning Points					Percentage of	
		Observed	Predicted	Correctly Predicted	Missed	Falsely Predicted	Observed Turns Missed	Predicted Turns False
(I)	1958.1-1970.2	n.a.	n.a.	n.a.	n.a.	n.a.	n.a.	n.a.
(II-A)	1958.1-1970.2	12	7	0	12	7	100.0	100.0
(II-B)	1958.1-1970.2	12	8	0	12	8	100.0	100.0
(III-A)	1958.1-1970.2	12	4	0	12	4	100.0	100.0
(III-B)	1958.1-1970.2	12	8	1	11	7	92.0	88.0
(IV-A)	1958.1-1970.2	12	8	3	9	5	75.0	63.0
(IV-B)	1958.1-1970.2	12	10	4	8	6	67.0	60.0

a   A Turning Point here was defined as a change in the direction of change of at least 5% from the previous value. In the actual series these changes occurred at the following dates: 1958.1, 1958.4, 1959.4, 1960.1, 1961.2, 1966.2, 1966.3, 1967.1, 1967.2, 1968.3, 1970.1. "Strike" related effects were ignored.

Table 6

FORECASTS OF MAJOR "EXPENDITURE SHIFTS"[a] IN CONSUMER AUTOMOBILE EXPENDITURE

Model	Period	Actual Number of "Expenditure Shifts"	"Expenditure Shifts" Predicted	"Expenditure Shifts" Predicted Correctly	"Expenditure Shifts" Incorrectly Predicted
(I)	1958.1-1970.2	22	n.a.	n.a.	n.a.
(II-A)	1958.1-1970.2	22	15	5	10
(II-B)	1958.1-1970.2	22	11	6	5
(III-A)	1958.1-1970.2	22	20	6	14
(III-B)	1958.1-1970.2	22	20	7	13
(IV-A)	1958.1-1970.2	22	21	14	7
(IV-B)	1958.1-1970.2	22	23	14	9

a   An expenditure shift is defined as a change in expenditures amounting to more than 5% of its previous value.

1. Model (II), as one might expect of an autoregressive scheme, predicts none of the actual turning points correctly, although it does manage to provide us with seven or eight false signals!
2. Model (III) does little better, but as before, the introduction of information on consumer attitudes into this mechanism substantially alters the nature of the forecasts generated. In general, forecasted expenditures become a much more volatile series. One turning point is now correctly predicted, but the number of false signals generated by (III-B) is almost double that generated by its more naive counterpart (III-A). On the whole, it seems to me that the "B" version of this model can only be judged very marginally superior (if at all) to the "A" version.
3. Once again the stock adjustment mechanism provides the best forecasts, correctly predicting the largest number of turning points, and generating the fewest false signals. Once again, however, this mechanism is unable to make use of information on changes in consumer attitudes to improve its forecasts.

Table 6 catalogues the models' success in forecasting major changes in automobile purchases ("expenditure shifts"), whether or not these changes represent turning points. For our purposes, an expenditure shift is defined as a change in expenditure amounting to more than 5 percent of its immediately preceding level. During the entire forecast period (1958.1-1970.2) there are twenty-two such shifts in expenditure. The forecasts generated by Model (IV) again dominate all the others. The two models in this category correctly predict two-thirds of the expenditure shift, compared to one-third or less for Models (II) and (III). Further, they provide relatively few false signals. Once again, however, the introduction of filtered information on the change in consumer sentiment adds nothing to the forecasting performance of these stock adjustment models. Models (II) and (III) lag far behind in overall performance, but we should note that information on attitudes does seem to dramatically reduce the number of false signals generated by Model (II).

This study has attempted to address two problems: First, the stability of the mechanism or pseudo-mechanism generating consumer attitudes; here we studied the stability of the mechanism isolated by Hymans[5] designed to "explain" variations in the ICS. We found the ICS to be a stable function of a limited number of explanatory variables and that the predicted values of the ICS generated by this mechanism played their expected role in models explaining consumer expenditure. Thus, at least over the period and models investigated in this study, other readily available data on income, inflation rates, and stock prices could be substituted for the survey result in preparing short-term forecasts of consumer discretionary spending. Second, we studied the contribution of variables directly measuring changes in consumer attitudes to the forecasting performance of models designed to explain discretionary consumer spending. Here we generated the actual forecasts in what seems to us to be a more relevant framework than previous studies. Our analysis concentrated heavily on times of rapid change in the direction of consumer spending. On the whole, we found that, at least within the framework of the models discussed above, information on consumer attitudes made a negligible contribution to the quality of the forecast. Thus, although variables directly representing changes in consumer sentiment continuously played a "significant" role in explaining variations in consumer expenditure during all the sample periods tested, they provided no additional ability to forecast events in the immediate post-sample periods.

In many respects, however, this analysis must simply be considered yet another beginning. The series of tests performed was hardly exhaustive, and it is very difficult to judge whether they are in any sense optimal. Other tests, with somewhat differently specified models may yield different conclusions.[4] I think, however, that the forecasting procedure presented here (producing post-sample forecasts only) is a more appropriate way to approach

---

[4] Our experiments were limited to the models discussed above, although we did experiment with varying forms of the ICS in place of the filtered variable (J) presented here. None of the forms we tried yielded different conclusions.

this problem, and I hope future studies will retain this aspect of the current investigation.

APPENDIX: A BROADER PERSPECTIVE

The continuous series of household surveys carried out by Katona and his colleagues at the Survey Research Center (SRC) over the last two decades provide a potentially rich body of data concerning many aspects of consumer behavior. Although public attention has often focused on the *Index of Consumer Sentiment* (ICS), Katona and his colleagues have shown an equal interest in the analysis of the large body of additional and supplementary information provided by these surveys. Presumedly, this additional analysis enabled them to better understand the implications of particular movements in the ICS, as well as to gain further insights concerning consumer behavior.

> ... surveys on changes in consumer attitudes yield much more information than what is summarized in the *Index of Consumer Sentiment*.[5]

Thus one would expect that the forecasts of consumer durable spending by the staff of the Survey Research Center might be superior to that produced by "outside" researchers relying on the "raw" published index (ICS) alone. Further it would be interesting to investigate whether the collection and analysis of this household survey data over the last two decades have helped those most closely associated with this activity develop important insights into the dynamics of consumer behavior. Fortunately, there is a record of published material that bears on both of these issues.

Since 1954, Katona and other senior members of the SRC's staff (principally Eva Mueller) have annually presented (at the University of Michigan's Annual Conference on the Economic Outlook) an analysis of the consumer sector and of the outlook

[5] *The Economic Outlook for 1967*, Proceedings of the Fourteenth Annual Conference on the Economic Outlook, University of Michigan, Ann Arbor, 1967, p. 116.

392

for consumer durable spending. The published *Proceedings* of these conferences provide a record both of the forecasts made and of the principal issues raised by the SRC staff in their analysis of the consumer sector. I have used the information in these records to investigate the following two issues: (1) the quality of the forecasts made by Katona and his colleagues at these annual conferences; (2) whether in retrospect this published record indicates any issues concerning consumer behavior on which Katona and the SRC staff developed valuable new insights as a result of their work with the survey data. I will deal with each of these issues separately below, but my analysis of the record indicates that the quality of the forecasts were as good as could reasonably be expected of any forecast of this volatile component of consumer spending (consumer durables), and that Katona and the SRC staff did in fact develop very early (well in advance of the economics profession in general) a number of valuable insights on consumer behavior.

The SRC Forecasts of Consumer Durable Spending

The evaluation of the annual SRC forecasts required a more subtle approach than I had originally anticipated. The principal reason for the difficulty was that the forecasts (even the conditional forecasts) are not often expressed in clearly unambiguous terms, and it is not always clear which of the conditional forecasts presented was the main or preferred forecast. I, therefore, adopted the following three-step procedure.

1. From the published *Conference Proceedings* of each year I extracted a number of *verbatim* quotes which seemed to me to best characterize their position. Although I took some care in the selection, obviously some arbitrariness was involved in this procedure. As a minimal check, each of the final selections was evaluated by a number of my colleagues and students. The quote or series of quotes from a given year were then "packaged" as a single forecast. In all, sixteen such forecasts were prepared, covering the years 1956 through 1971.
2. A questionnaire was then prepared which asked the respondents to classify each of the "packaged" forecasts presented as to whether it represented a forecasted increase or a forecasted

decrease in consumer durable spending for the following year. The forecasts were presented in an arbitrary chronological order on the questionnaire and in such a way that the respondent had no way of knowing which year each referred to. The purpose of the questionnaire was to determine the nature and consistency of the information being transmitted by these forecasts and to classify more precisely, where possible, the SRC forecast for that year. If response opinion varied substantially regarding a particular forecast, it was classified as a "no change" situation. A two-thirds plurality of respondents was required to un-ambiguously characterize a forecast.

3. The SRC forecasts, as classified by the respondents[6], were then compared to the historical record.

The results of this procedure were as follows. First, fourteen of the sixteen forecasts were unambiguously classified by the respondents. The respondents were divided in their interpretations of the forecasts for 1962 and 1971.[7] Second, the historical record shows that on an annual basis there were four downturns in constant dollar expenditure on consumer durables in the period 1956 through 1971 (1965, 1958, 1961, and 1970). The SRC forecast predicted three of these (1958, 1961, 1970) and generated only one false signal when a downturn in expenditures was forecasted for 1967. This latter year was characterized by a very small increase in constant dollar expenditure on total durables, although there was a small decrease in the automobile component. On this basis, Katona and the SRC staff have a very creditable forecasting record indeed.

Before leaving the area of forecasting, it is interesting to note a number of issues on which the SRC provided extremely useful and accurate forecasts of certain secular changes in the American economy. They were among the first to recognize the following phenomena.

[6] Fifty questionnaires were tabulated. All respondents were professional economists.

[7] The forecast for 1971 is interesting in that although it correctly and unambiguously called for a continued high savings rate, it (apparently) wavered on the issue of whether expenditures on durables would be up or down.

1. Changing housing patterns and their effects on the demand for housing and other durables.
2. Rapidly rising demand for services such as medical care, government services, education, etc.
3. Recognition of the growing incongruity of private opulence and public poverty.
4. Predicted that the 1960's would be a decade characterized by more inflation, but that people would cease to worry quite as much about it (would continue to purchase despite high prices).

Issues In Consumer Economics

As one rereads the continuing contributions of Katona, Mueller, Lansing, and Morgan to the annual Conferences on the Economic Outlook, there are a number of themes which appear over and over again in their analysis of consumer behavior. I would like to take this opportunity to note five of those which underlay their approach from the early 1950's on and which in my opinion represented important insights concerning consumer behavior.
1. *Portfolio Analysis.* An early focus on the need for a portfolio analysis of consumer behavior. Given the data limitations, most of their early studies concentrated on the accumulation of financial assets and installment debt.
2. *Permanent Income, Expected Income, and Wealth.* Developed the notion that the consumption of nondurables and services would respond, with a lag, to permanent or expected income, with transitory income going either to savings or expenditures on consumer durables. Consistent with their development of portfolio analysis, they recognized the role of Net Worth on consumption expenditures.
3. *Life Cycle Models.* Their analysis clearly indicates an appreciation of the existence of "life cycle consumption habits" and the effects of this on the aggregate data.
4. *Stagnation Thesis vs. Aspirations Economy.* Have continuously fought against the notion that the current stock of durables (including housing) represented a point of saturation or near saturation. (In the 1950's the idea of saturation was still a serious issue!) Rather, they advanced the hypothesis that in the affluent American society, a "needs" economy is replaced by an

"aspirations" economy. The basic idea here is that continued decades of accomplishment have reinforced consumer optimism so that consumers both desire and strive for change — continually upgrading their aspirations and their demand for consumer durables.

5. *Price Expectations and Asset Preferences.* Clearly recognized the potentially important effects changes in price expectations have on asset preferences.

The only puzzlement in all this is that the economics profession as a whole did not seem to recognize either the nature or importance of these early contributions — but that is a subject for another paper.

REFERENCES

1 Adams, F. Gerard, and Edward W. Green, "Explaining and Predicting Aggregate Consumer Attitudes", *International Economic Review*, VI (September, 1965), 275–93.
2 Chow, G.C., "Test of Equality Between Sets of Coefficients in Two Linear Regressions", *Econometrica*, 28 (July, 1960), 591–605.
3 Fair, R.C., "Consumer Sentiment, The Stock Market, and Consumption Functions", *Econometric Research Program Research Memorandum No. 119*, Princeton University, September, 1971.
4 Fair, R.C., *A Short-Run Forecasting Model of the U.S. Economy*, Lexington, Mass., 1971.
5 Hymans, Saul H., "Consumer Durable Spending", *Brookings Papers on Economic Activity*, (1970).
6 Juster, F.T., and Wachtel, P. "Uncertainty Expectations and Durable Goods Demand Models" (in this volume).
7 Katona, George, "Consumer Durable Spending", *Brookings Papers on Economic Activity*, (1971).

The Consumer in a
Changing Environment

The Power of the Consumer

E. SCOTT MAYNES

INTRODUCTION

This paper focuses on the macro-power and the micro-impotence of consumers, and the challenges they pose in 1971 for economists and for the Economic Behavior Program (EBP) of the Survey Research Center (SRC), the institution which George Katona did so much to create.

The first part identifies the macro-power of consumers as the power to bedevil standard econometric models, their makers, and their users. It goes on to show how George Katona's great invention – the consumer anticipations approaches – is, by its logic, well-suited to the forecasting of turning points in discretionary spending. Finally, it suggests two areas where research relating to the consumer anticipations approaches is likely to have large payoffs.

The second part deals with the micro-impotence of consumers. Our present economy should, according to received economic doctrine, serve up the best quality products at their single, lowest prices. Instead, consumer markets are characterized by the coexistence of high and low prices, high and low quality, high and low price-per-unit-of-quality, as well as dishonored promises. And consumers are unable to do anything about it. Why is it that consumers are so ill-served? The culprit is consumer information. Often consumers cannot obtain and/or will not act upon the information they possess. With its information component in poor repair, the reward-punishment mechanism at the heart of our market economy works badly.

This diagnosis challenges economists to integrate the cost of information into the theory of markets and to recognize and champion the notion of a public interest in the provision of consumer information. It challenges EBP, which for a generation has undertaken research designed to explain and predict the behavior of consumers, to shift ground in part and undertake research on behalf of consumers.[1]

THE MACRO-POWER OF CONSUMERS

In their aggregative behavior, consumers do possess power — the power (among other things) to bedevil economic forecasters and policy-makers. This power was exercised most recently in the Summer of 1969 when consumers, in the face of still-rising real disposable income, perversely slowed their rate of automobile purchases and thus contributed to the 1969-70 recession. The volatility of aggregate expenditures on consumer durables has yet to be accepted and digested by the economics profession. The point requires expansion.

It was Keynes who got our profession off on the wrong foot in this matter. In the *General Theory* Keynes argued that aggregate consumption is a "fairly stable function" of aggregate income, thus assigning a passive role to consumers in aggregate income determination. Had Keynes defined consumption as "services enjoyed" as Friedman [7] and Modigliani-Brumberg [19] later did, he would probably have been right. But he did not. Instead, Keynes stated explicitly that the drawing of the line of demarca-

---

[1] Any research, regardless of the purpose for which it was conceived, will help consumers if it favorably affects economic policy and understanding. By the same token, research designed to help consumers may in fact not help them. The point I make here is that this is a viewpoint which has not been emphasized in the SRC research program. For an exception, see [20].

tion between consumer-purchasers and investor-purchasers is un-important [15, p.61]. That Keynes did not bother about con-sumer investment is understandable in view of its probably small magnitude in the Britain of the 1930's and in view of the lack of statistical data at the time.

Nonetheless, Keynes was wrong. Juster's careful, statistical com-parison of cyclical variations of various components of aggregate investment in the private sector shows that for 1947-62 household expenditure on automibiles and other durables represents, in either absolute or relative terms, a highly volatile component of GNP [10, p.84]:

	Cyclical Variation Measured:	
	Absolutely	*Relatively*
Component of GNP	*Standard Deviation*[a]	*Coefficient of Variation*[a]
Household durables	$1.05 billion	.066
Enterprise durables	0.85	.075
Household structures	0.50	.081
Enterprise structures	0.25	.043
Nondurables and services	Not estimated	.010

a   After removal of time trend.

What's more, if "household expenditures on durables" was nar-rowed to include only expenditures on new automobiles, it would probably become the single most volatile component [17, p.114].

The volatility of consumer expenditures on durables, so well documented in Juster's data, has been only partially digested by economists. On the positive side, both the Wharton [6] and the Brookings—SSRC [24] econometric models acknowledge the variability of aggregate automobile expenditures by specifying separate equations for the forecasting of this component. On the negative side the "news" of the volatility of consumer durables expenditures has yet to reach writers of macro-economic texts and their audiences. For example, such representative macro-texts as Bailey [2], Dernburg and McDougall [5], and Smith [22] contain no intimation whatsoever of the nonpassivity of the durables com-ponent of aggregate consumption expenditures.

We turn now to the crucial question of the forecasting of the nonhousing portion of consumer investment. It is our thesis that George Katona's great invention, the consumer anticipations approaches, is well-adapted by its logic to the forecasting of this component; but, first a matter of history and description.

Katona was among the first to argue the error of Keynes' views on the consumption function and to assert the instability of aggregate consumption expenditures in the short-run. Working from a background of Gestalt psychology, Katona argued — as early as 1946 [14], but more completely in 1951 [13] — that large expenditures are discretionary, subject to "genuine decisions", as contrasted with habitual behavior. Hence, large expenditures could not be viewed as automatic responses to changes in the values of such standard economic variables as disposable income.

This discretionary view of large expenditures led almost directly to the invention by Katona of the consumer anticipations approaches to the short-run forecasting of discretionary expenditures, especially automobiles. Two variants of the consumer anticipations approaches have developed: the *attitudes* variant and the *buying intentions* variant. Both utilize periodic consumer surveys to collect subjective data on consumer attitudes and buying intentions, respectively. Suitably processed into indices, these become inputs for forecasts, either by themselves or, preferably, in conjunction with standard economic variables. The attitudes variant collects information regarding the consumer's evaluation of his own current and prospective financial position, his appraisals of current and expected business conditions, and of the market for consumer durables. The buying intentions variant collects information regarding what is, in essence, the unconditional, subjective probability of purchase for some specified reference period (3, 6, 12, 24 months ahead).

Other papers in this volume have undertaken careful reviews of the predictive performance of the consumer anticipations approaches under various formulations. It is sufficient to note here that the consumer anticipations approaches have successfully forecast the following turning points in automobile expenditures which were ill-forecast by conventional models: the 1949 downturn, the 1955 peak, the 1957-58 recess, the 1962 aborted recession, the 1969-70 downturn. Lest the reader be unduly carried away, he should be warned that the SRC *Index*, when placed in a sophisticated econometric model, is statistically significant at the 2-sigma level, but no more [6, p.8].

An aspect of the consumer anticipations approaches which has been underappreciated is their different logic. Almost all pre-existing "scientific" systems of forecasting — even the most so-phisticated econometric models — represent some form of extra-polation. This implies, first, that parameter values remain constant or change in prespecified ways. Not so the consumer anticipations approaches. In the latter, for example, a given increase in dis-posable income can have a different influence at different times on the subjective probability of purchase as measured. This could arise because the *perception* of a given change in income was favorable under certain circumstances and unfavorable under others. In conventional models these variable responses would have to be specified in advance. In the consumer anticipations approaches the consumer decision-makers themselves record their differential responses to the identical stimuli.

A second assumption of conventional forecasting system is that the weights assigned to different variables remain constant or change in prespecified ways. Again, not so in the consumer antici-pations approaches. Since both buying intentions and consumer attitudes are subjective, they permit the decision-maker to take account of *any* variable (or any interactions) and also to change the weight assigned to any variable at any time. Thus, the decision-maker who gave little emphasis to "price expectations" in the Heller era of price stability in the early Sixties may now assign great importance to that variable.

Summing up, the logic of the consumer anticipations approach-es imparts advantages of flexibility and economy to the two variants. They are flexible in that they can reflect changes in para-meter values and weights that were not specified in advance. They are economical in that the effects of many variables and many interactions are summarized in a single portmanteau variable.

If changes in parameter values and the weights of variables tend to occur at cyclical turning points, this characteristic of the con-sumer anticipations approaches would account for their outstan-ding performance at cyclical turning points.[2]

[2] For an analysis of the record of the consumer attitudes approaches as *turning point indicators*, cf. [17, pp. 119–21].

Consumer anticipations have been successful in forecasting aggregate expenditures for automobiles and relatively unsuccessful with respect to houses and nonautomotive durables. In the case of houses, the lesser success is probably due to the fact that supply conditions are more variable than for automobiles. If consumers are able to anticipate changes in supply conditions accurately, such changes would not constitute a barrier to a good predictive performance. But it seems unlikely that they can. (This is, of course, a testable hypothesis.)

Purchases of nonautomotive durable goods, requiring smaller outlays typically, are probably less subject to "genuine decisions" and hence less suited to the consumer anticipations approaches.

With respect to automobiles the past success of the consumer anticipations is well established [8]. Future developments are not so well focused. I would pose two major challenges of a methodological nature to those who would wear the mantle of George Katona. Both have their roots in past failures.

The first relates to buying intentions. Though the detection of the 1969-70 downturn in automobile expenditures was scored as a success for the consumer attitudes variant, it must be counted a failure for buying intentions. While the SRC *Index of Consumer Sentiment* (attitudes) clearly signaled a major downturn in automobile purchases [25], the Census Bureau's *Current Buying Expectations Survey* foretold continued high spending for automobiles [4]. Why? Though no one can be certain, I would attribute the failure of the buying intentions at this turning point to their unconditional nature. Respondents are asked: "What are the chances that you will purchase a new automobile in the next 6 (12, 24) months?" Replies which are in essence subjective probability judgements obviously make certain assumptions regarding expected income, employment, prices, etc. For a large cross-section sample in ordinary times favorable unexpected (unassumed) changes in these variables probably tend to be offset by unfavorable, unexpected developments. It is my conjecture that in late 1969 and early 1970 unexpected developments of an unfavorable nature outweighed favorable developments, thus accounting for a shortfall from the predicted purchase level for automobiles.[3]

Whether this conjecture is correct or not, this line of reasoning suggests the desirability of exploring the difficult area of measuring and using *conditional* subjective probabilities of purchase. For example, one might ascertain how subjective probabilities of purchasing a new car are affected by income increases of different sizes. One might go further and ascertain the subjective probabilities of receiving different-sized income increases.

The second challenge arises from what has come to be known as the consumer attitudes—buying intentions paradox [1]. The paradox is this: buying intentions are successful cross-section as well as time-series predictors of automobile purchasers. On the other hand, the cross-section relationship between consumer attitudes and subsequent purchase behavior has, if anything, marginal statistical support [1] while the time-series relationship is firmly established [8].

Why? My hypothesis is that random errors of measurement, greater in degree for attitudes (where, unlike the case of subjective purchase probabilities, there are no "natural" referents), obscure the underlying cross-section relationships.[4] In the time series, on the other hand, these random errors tend to cancel one another, leaving the basic underlying relationships revealed.

Whether this hypothesis is correct or incorrect, it is clear that research designed to improve the measurement of both attitudes and buying intentions is in order. It poses, in its most generalized form, a research objective of overwhelming importance to all the social sciences — the devising of measures of subjective variables (such as attitudes and buying intentions) which are inter-personally and inter-temporarily valid. Success in this enterprise would have immense payoffs wherever questions are used to elicit subjective data. For the same outlay it would enable researchers to uncover relationships now obscured by random errors. Alternatively, the current level of precision could be obtained from smaller samples and smaller expenditures, an important objective when personal interviews cost as much as $50 each.

---

[3] At a meeting at the Bureau of the Census in May, 1970, Dr. F. Thomas Juster indicated that he had (independently) arrived at approximately the same interpretation.

[4] As George Katona has pointed out, there exist two situations in cross-section analysis where measured attitudes are irrelevant to subsequent automobile purchase behavior: (1) where the sample family has just purchased a new car; (2) where families purchase new cars at regular intervals, e.g., every two years.

A comparison of techniques presently used with proposed ideal techniques may lay bare the nature of the problem and even suggest possible solutions.

The Survey Research Center forms its *Index of Consumer Sentiment* by assigning and summing values as follows to a set of five questions of the following type:

"Would you say that you and your family are better off or worse off financially now than you were a year ago?"

Response Categories:	Better Now	Same	Worse Now	Uncertain
Assigned Scale Values:	2	1	0	Omitted

The Current Buying Indicators Survey of the Bureau of the Census obtains its buying intentions data from questions of the following form:

"What are the chances that you or any member of your family living here will buy either a new or used car during the next 6 (12, 24) months?"

Response Categories: 0 10 20 30 40 50 60 70 80 90 100

Once respondents have selected a response category, CBI forms an index by assigning to each category an estimated probability of automobile purchases, based on *ex post* purchase rates observed in earlier surveys.

As to the questions themselves, although CBI appears to permit respondents to choose among the integers from 0 through 100, in practice the respondent must select one from among eleven categories just listed.

The proposed ideal scale would have the following properties:
1. *The number of categories should be large.* A possible ideal scale might consist of the integers from 0 through 100. This characteristic stems from the assumption that attitudes represent a continuum, that survey respondents can make reliable discriminations along this continuum, and finally that these discriminations are related to subsequent behavior.

If in fact respondents can discriminate to the extent suggested by a 101-category scale and if there exists a high correlation between such categories and durable goods spending, then it seems plausible that the three categories currently used by SRC seriously reduce the probability of detecting any underlying cross-section correlation. (Assuming a $0-1$ dependent variable and zero response errors, [11] shows that a 3-category scale has

89 percent of the power of a multi-category scale. Neither condition holds here.)

The need for accurate measurement of subjective probabilities of purchase also suggests the use of a many-category scale. With the 11-category CBI scale mentioned above, about 70 percent of respondents report their subjective probability of purchasing a new car in 12 months as 0. Given the condition of one's car, possible favorable developments (promotion, pay increases, the elimination of a family's contingent liabilities) and other factors likely to affect subjective probabilities favorably, it seems plausible that a substantial proportion of the households now recorded as having "zero" subjective probability of purchase do in fact have a positive, though "small", subjective probability of purchases. A detailed scale would permit such near-zero subjective probabilities to be recorded and their usefulness for prediction to be tested.

2. *The categories of the scale should have numeric designations.*
This characteristic is proposed because numbers are assumed to have similar (not identical!) meanings for different people. Not so, words. Common experience can supply innumerable examples where different individuals apply different verbal (scale) labels to identical phenomenon.

The use of numerical designations should reduce, though not eliminate, this source of error. It will probably still be true that some individuals will be "conservative" and others "liberal" in attaching numerical scale values to identical stimuli. The devising of means of calibrating the differential responses of different individuals poses a major challenge in the development of better scales.

3. *Its boundaries should be clearly defined.* As noted before, the scale we propose would consist of the integers from 0 to 100. Respondents would be told that 0 means "couldn't be worse" while 100 means "couldn't be better".[5]

Under this convention the numerical boundaries, 0 and 100, would be precisely defined. However, "couldn't be worse" and "couldn't be better" may convey somewhat different notions to different individuals, and hence introduce some error. Thus far, this a problem from which no escape is in sight.

[5] I am indebted to John Neter not only for this suggestion, but also for discussions which helped clarify and refine many of the ideas in this section.

4. *Its intervals should be equal for everyone.* Though one can assert that a movement from 93 to 94 on a 101-point interval scale *should* represent the same degree of change as a movement from (say) 53 to 54, the work of S.S. Stevens [23] suggests that, in practice, the movement from 93 to 94 represents a larger change than the movement from 53 to 54.

   If careful investigation should further confirm Stevens' expectation, then it would be appropriate to investigate the use of transformations to convert the *de facto* scale of unequal intervals to a scale of uniform intervals.

5. *It should be simple, understandable.*

6. *There should be no pressure on boundaries.* This characteristic stems from a desire that the scale almost always be capable of registering deterioration or improvement, as compared with values previously reported.

   Existing SRC scales violate this requirement badly. In the illustrative question, once a respondent has answered "better off" there is no way of signaling further improvement.

One final comment regards the *use* of such an ideal scale. Though it is plausible that survey respondents can be taught to use a scale such as that proposed, it is clear that individuals do not customarily register their sentiments in this manner. This observation suggests two practices in the use of such scales. The first would be that the respondent be given enough "training" so that he thoroughly understands the scale. The second is that reinterviews be used and that respondents be told their previous responses. (See [21] where such a technique was used to obtain more accurate reports of expenditures.) This practice, it is hoped, would reduce errors arising in the process of locating oneself on a strange scale.

Regardless of the merit of these particular suggestions, the challenge of developing inter-personally and inter-temporally valid measures of subjective variables should be high on the research agenda, not only of George Katona's successors, but of many other social scientists as well.

Try yourself on the following "test" of the functioning of markets. Consider the price paid per $1,000 of protection (*not* face value) by a standard insured person for a straight life insurance policy, sometimes called "ordinary life" or "whole life". If among 88 reliable companies the *lowest priced* company charges $4 per $1,000 of protection, what does the *highest priced* company charge? Is it $4, $4.10, $4.25, $4.50, $5, $7.50, $10, $13, $20? Obviously, your answer will reveal your belief as to how well life insurance markets work.

If markets for life insurance were informationally perfect — meaning that consumers could, with little effort, come to know the correct price — then the highest price charged should be in the close vicinity of $4. Unhappily, to calculate the true "price of protection" with any accuracy, one must be a hardworking student of insurance, endowed with considerable mathematical ability, possessed of considerable data-collecting and computer time, and ready to make fairly strong assumptions.[6] With this explanation it should come as no surprise that consumers are not able to ascertain the lowest price and hence that this market does not work well. The result is that the highest price is $13, a whopping three times greater than the lowest price [3].

In this example consumers were unable to ascertain price. Since all the insurance companies were "reliable" (rated B+ or better by *Best's Insurance Manual*), quality differences were of no importance except to the extent that consumers might be willing to pay more to deal with a "friendly" agent or one they knew. In our second example the inability of consumers to assess quality lies at the heart of the market failure. This example concerns coffee urns and stereo receivers. According to *Consumer Reports* (May, 1969) list prices for a representative set of 19 coffee urns ranged from $13.95 to $45.95. Of the 19 tested, 5 were "check-rated", meaning that these models were "significantly superior" to other models tested. For the check-rated urns, list prices were as follows: $14, $26, $35, $40, $42. Similarly, in August, 1970, *Consumer Reports* check-rated stereo receivers with prices listing from

[6] For example, in the case of participating policies it is usually assumed that the path of future dividend payments will conform closely to that of the past.

$270 through $450. Why is it that higher prices for equivalent quality can persist? My tentative answer is that consumers are unable and/or unwilling to obtain and act upon the relevant quality and price information.

We are now ready to undertake a systematic analysis of the informational imperfections of consumer markets and of the consequent micro-impotence of consumers.

Conditions for Effective Functioning of Markets

The consumer's role in a well functioning market is to identify and reward good performance on the part of sellers. To perform his role effectively, the consumer in turn needs to know the following:

1. What products, brands, sellers exist and where to buy;
2. What characteristics of a product are desirable ("general product information");
3. The extent to which particular product-brand-seller combinations possess the desired characteristics;
4. Prices of product-brand-seller combinations.

It goes without saying that consumers must not only possess the required information, they must be willing and able to act on it, all at low cost.

Additional conditions are that there exist numerous alternative brand-seller combinations, and that resources be mobile.

Markets and Consumers in 1776

Consider the functioning of retail markets in 1776, notable as the year in which Adam Smith published his *Wealth of Nations*, the first satisfactory analysis of the working of a market economy.

In general, the amount of information required then was much less than now. In the rural, small town markets of that time, the identity and location of sellers were common knowledge, available at almost zero cost. What is more, the number of choices to be made was much less than now: due to smaller incomes, access to fewer products, and fewer sellers.

At the same time information was easier to obtain. Products were simple. From common experience people knew what characteristics of products were desirable and the extent to which particular items possessed them. Consider the horse as transportation. No one had any difficulty in understanding how a horse "worked". And, despite a classic literature on "horse trading" and the people taken in thereby, most people could identify good-performing and poor-performing horses.

The main defect of these local markets was structural: the small size of the market led to local monopolies. Little wonder that this is the defect which economic theory has stressed from that time to this.

Monopoly aside — and this is an important exception — consumers could usually identify good and poor performance on the part of sellers. Under these conditions the reward-punishment system at the heart of a market economy worked well. The presumably selfish motivations of sellers were channeled to a constructive end through an effective market. Markets tended to be cleared by a single low price.

Consumers and Markets Now

Two hundred years later the picture has changed drastically. The volume of information which consumers require is now massive. Why? In the first place, consumers have more income to spend. Secondly, there are more products, brands, and sellers. Thirdly, not only are there more products and brands, but variants of brands have proliferated.[7] As every car buyer knows, you must decide on body type, "line", transmission, motor size, type of brakes, trim, numerous accessories. The same phenomenon applies, though on a reduced scale, to other products which until recently were single-variant products. Fourthly, model changes are becoming more frequent, except (thankfully!) for automobiles.[7] Finally, given urbanization and the automobile, each consumer now has access to more product-brand-seller combinations.

At the same time the cost of obtaining price and quality information is now vastly higher. Here we properly count as costs not only money outlays devoted to the search for information, but also such subjective but real factors as the utility of activities given

[7] These points were suggested to me by John Hancs, Director of Marketing Information for Consumers Union.

411

up in order to undertake shopping (e.g., the tennis game sacrificed) and the disutility shopping itself may have for an individual. As Staffan Linder has so cogently pointed out [16], affluence has brought us more goods, but we are still stuck with the 168-hour week. Interpreted: time is worth more now; hence, the cost of shopping has increased drastically. The task per se of obtaining price-quality information has become more difficult. The accumulated experience of the consumer and his acquaintances, acquired at near-zero cost, no longer enables the consumer to know prices and qualities. The culprit, of course, is the technical complexity of products. To solve the life insurance problem cited at the beginning of this section, one must be an insurance scholar, or be able to hire such a person, or to locate and digest his results. None of these is easy. And an analogous problem exists for most modern products. This difficulty applies to the ascertaining of prices and the extent to which a brand posesses the desired characteristics as well as knowing what characteristics are desirable. Regarding the latter, we may ask rhetorically: Who — before Ralph Nader — had any idea whatsoever of the characteristics of a "safe" automobile?

The widespread dissemination of price and quality information is not sufficient to assure the effective functioning of markets. Consumers must be willing to *act* on the information. Everyone "knows" that new automobile prices are bargainable, but many consumers find bargaining distasteful or lack the essential skills or the supporting information. Similarly, even if most consumers were aware of the extremely wide range of prices for a standard package of automobile insurance ($129 to $227 for a "standard" package for an identical driver in Minneapolis),[8] many would not make the effort to search out the lowest priced company.

While the local markets in which consumers deal have deteriorated informationally between 1776 and 1971, they have improved structurally. Due primarily to the automobile, urbanization, and the development of mail-order organizations (especially from 1900 to 1940), the typical consumer today has access to a larger

---

[8] Data were obtained by a graduate student in Home Economics at the University of Minnesota from a set of seven insurance companies thought to include both low- and high-priced companies. When the data were deflated roughly to take account of quality, the range narrowed somewhat from $98 to $78.

412

number of product-seller-brand combinations and hence less often faces a local monopoly. But not all structural developments are favorable. While the consumer typically has access to more local sellers, the number of brands may be smaller, due to economies of scale in both production and selling.

The net effect — a judgement, of course — is the coexistence for the same product of high and low prices, good and poor quality, high and low prices-per-unit-of-quality.

To be more specific, I would argue that, because consumers do not and/or cannot obtain and act on relevant price-quality information, the reward-punishment mechanisms on which we have been relying to discipline the strong, but selfish motivations of sellers do not work. The consequences are everywhere observable: poor quality, unsafe products, dishonored warranties, consumer grievances, and consumerism.

The Challenge to Economists and SRC

The foregoing analysis poses numerous challenges to economists and to the Survey Research Center. Three are singled out here for further discussion.

Many may not be convinced by the illustrative evidence or the argumentation of the previous section. What is greatly needed is careful documentation of the imperfections of consumer markets. Specifically, we need to ascertain for a representative set of consumer goods just how much variation exists in local markets with respect to price, quality, and price-per-unit-of-quality. If convincing evidence is obtained of substantial variations on these variables, then we may properly conclude that markets are operating badly and turn our attention to further diagnosis and to consideration of corrective actions.

A study of the imperfections of markets poses some intriguing conceptual problems. What, for example, are the boundaries of the consumer market in which price variation is to be measured? Rational shopping procedures imply that a consumer continue searches for information ("shopping") as long as the expected gain from the search exceeds the expected cost of the search. But costs will properly include such subjective matters as the individual consumer's distaste for shopping. And the expected gain will be dependent upon his perception of variations in price and quality.

Another challenging conceptual problem is the specification of "quality". Since higher quality is an offset to higher prices, deflation of money prices by a measure of quality is a prerequisite to any conclusion that markets are working badly. In real life, choices involving quality differences are made every day by everyone. And at least two million of the best educated families purchase and use the quality measurements provided in *Consumer Reports* by Consumers Union. Nonetheless, quality is a problem which economics has swept under the rug. The analysis of the previous section suggests that the inability of consumers to discern accurately differences in quality is a key element in the failure of markets. To test this hypothesis, it is necessary to conceptualize and measure quality. It is difficult to imagine an organization better equipped to document the imperfection of consumer markets than EBP-SRC.

Intellectual curiosity aside, there are two compelling reasons for undertaking such a study. In the first place, before remedial steps can be taken, numerous groups in the economy — professional economists, politicians, civil servants — need to be convinced that markets do perform badly. Secondly, such a study would reveal to intelligent consumers the substantial payoffs which are to be had in response to effective searches.

A second major challenge is the development of a theory of markets incorporating both the cost of information and quality differences. A "good" theory incorporates the chief elements of reality, and no more. If the analysis of the previous section is approximately correct, then theories which fail to incorporate the cost of information and differences in quality will mislead rather than illuminate. The challenge here to economists is to improve the body of economic theory and thus our understanding of the economic system.

An additional reason for suggesting the development of an information-explicit and quality-explicit theory of markets is that theory tends to organize the professional efforts of the economics profession. The existence of a theory of markets focusing on structural defects as the source of market failures has given rise to the field of industrial organization. It has also channeled the efforts of a large body of economists towards the elaboration of theory in

414

this area as well as the development and evaluation of appropriate policies. In contrast to industrial organization, the activities of Consumers Union in the production and distribution of quality information and the "consumerism" movement have been almost bereft of direct support from the economics profession. In my judgement, the incorporation of the cost of information and quality differences into the theory of markets would do much to change this.

A third major challenge, suggested but not implied by the analysis of this section, is that economics should undertake research not just *about* consumers, but *on behalf of* consumers. Given that the need to make consumer choices is universal, it may be argued that economists have a responsibility to assist consumers in making better choices — at a level of abstraction and reality which is useful. It is my further suggestion that the viewpoint of the consumer provides a fresh and fruitful way of approaching a subject.

As an example of the latter, consider the consumption function. Vast efforts have been expended by our profession seeking to develop and test theories explaining how consumers do in fact divide their income between consumption and saving. But turn the question around and you have a subject which is almost untouched: what fraction of its income *should* a family save, year in and year out? Specify that the household wishes to save for (1) the children's college education, and (2) retirement income, and (when detailed) you have a researchable problem.

A second example concerns life insurance. It is an interesting socio-economic question to ask whether families purchase enough life insurance to provide the level of after-death income for survivors which the husband-wife really want. If they fail to do so, they suffer from a life insurance "deficit". An interesting research problem, on which the author has already conducted a pilot study [17], is to ascertain the size, distribution, and determinants of the life insurance deficits of American households.

But research on behalf of consumers could also involve the devising and testing of policies designed to improve the informational functioning of markets. We can estimate, for example, that businesses spent about $67 billion in 1970 on the production and

415

distribution of price and quality "information". This was composed as follows.[9]

Advertising	$21 billion
Sales promotion	
(direct sales)	7
Personal selling	36
Public relations	. 3
Total	$67 billion

These business expenditures on consumer information were financed by what comes to a 10.9 percent "sales tax" on consumer spending: that is, prices on the $616 billion of consumer spending were set high enough to permit businesses to recover the $67 billion they expended on consumer information.

[9] I am indebted to Professor Ivan Ross for this estimate of business expenditures for consumer information purposes. Sources were as follows:

(a) Advertising − $21 billion. From S. Banks, R. Reisman, and C.Y. Yang, *Advertising Age*, June 7, 1971, p.27.

(b) Sales promotion − $7 billion. From A.W. Frey and J.C. Halterman, *Advertising*, 4th Ed., New York: Ronald Press, 1970, p. 40.

(c) Personal selling − $36 billion. There exists no satisfactory estimate of expenditures on personal selling. However, Brink and Kelley are quoted in Boyd and Levy as asserting the existing of a 3-to-1 or 4-to-1 relationship between expenditures for personal selling vs. advertising. Splitting the difference and applying the 3 1/2-to-1 ratio to 1970, we estimate total personal selling expenditures at $72.8 billion. We assume arbitrarily that one-half of the efforts of sales personnel are devoted to informing and persuading and hence arrive at the $36 billion estimate (= 1/2 x $72.8 billion). Cf. Harper W. Boyd, Jr., and Sidney J. Levy, *Promotion: A Behavioral View*, Englewood Cliffs, N.J.: Prentice-Hall, 1970, p. 10.

(d) Public relations − $3 billion. Our estimate for public relations expenditures is even cruder than those for other components. We accept a forecast by Kalman Druck (*Business Week*, July 2, 1960, p. 42) that public relations expenditures, estimated at $2 billion in 1960, would be $6 billion in 1969. We assume, again arbitrarily, that one-half of public relations expenditures activities are directed toward consumers.

(e) Aggregate personal consumption expenditures − $616 billion. From *Survey of Current Business*, July, 1971.

Is this arrangement, sanctioned by long usage, in the best interest of consumers? That price-quality information provided by businesses is biased by exaggeration or omission we know from both common experience and from a priori argument based on the self-interest of sellers. Nonetheless, business-provided price-quality information might be acceptable if we could be reasonably sure that consumers could "see through" the distortions and omissions. Unfortunately, due to the complexity of products and other factors influencing the cost of obtaining information, they cannot.

It follows, then, that some of the information-providing resources now controlled by businesses should be shifted to consumer control. How? By levying a tax (a "Truth Tax"?) on business promotion expenses (the four categories listed above); the proceeds would be transferred to a consumer-controlled "Consumer Information Corporation". Such a corporation might produce, assemble, and disseminate both positive and negative accurate consumer information. With an independent source of financing – the Truth Tax – and with independent control (provided by a board elected by consumers), such an institution might go a long way in improving the informational functioning of markets.

This is but an example of innovations which should be developed and tested to improve the functioning of markets.

Summing up, it is my suggestion that society would be well served if economists in general, and SRC in particular, were to shift a considerable portion of their efforts from research *about* consumers to research *on behalf of* consumers.

REFERENCES

1 Adams, F. Gerard, "Predicting with Consumer Attitudes: The Time Series–Cross Section Paradox", *Review of Economics and Statistics*, Nov., 1964.
2 Bailey, Martin, J., *National Income and the Price Level*, New York: McGraw-Hill, 1971.
3 Belth, Joseph M., *The Retail Price Structure in American Life Insurance*, Bloomington, Ind.: Bureau of Business Research, Indiana University, 1966.
4 Bureau of the Census, Current Population Reports, *Consumer Buying Indicators*, Series P-65, No. 27 (Aug. 22, 1969).

5 Dernburg, Thomas F., and Duncan M. McDougall, *Macro-Economics, The Measurement, Analysis, and Control of Aggregate Economic Activity*, New York: McGraw-Hill, 1968.

6 Evans, Michael K., and Lawrence R. Klein, *The Wharton Econometric Forecasting Model*, Philadelphia: Economic Research Unit, University of Pennsylvania, 1967.

7 Friedman, Milton, *A Theory of the Consumption Function*, Princeton: Princeton University Press for NBER, 1957.

8 Hymans, Saul H., "Consumer Durables Spending: Explanation and Prediction", *Brookings Papers on Economic Activity*, 2 (1970).

9 Juster, F. Thomas, "Comsumer Anticipations and Models of Durable Goods Demand", in Jacob Mincer, ed., *Economic Forecasts and Expectations*, New York: Columbia University Press for NBER, 1970.

10 Juster, F. Thomas, *Household Capital Formation and Financing, 1897–1962*, New York: Columbia University Press for NBER, 1966.

11 Kalton, Graham, "A Technique for Choosing the Number of Alternative Response Categories to Provide in Order to Locate an Individual's Position on a Continuum", Survey Research Center, unpublished memoranda, 1966.

12 Katona, George, *The Powerful Consumer*, New York: McGraw-Hill, 1960.

13 Katona, George, *Psychological Analysis of Economic Behavior*, New York: McGraw-Hill, 1951.

14 Katona, George, and Rensis Likert, "Relationship between Consumer Incomes and Saving: The Contribution of Survey Research", *Review of Economic Statistics*, Nov., 1946.

15 Keynes, J.M., *The General Theory of Employment, Interest, and Money*, New York: Harcourt, Brace, 1936.

16 Linder, Staffan B., *The Harried Leisure Class*, New York: Columbia University Press, 1970.

17 Maynes, E. Scott, "An Appraisal of Consumer Anticipations Approaches to Forecasting", in American Statistical Association, *1967 Proceedings of the Business and Economics Section*, Washington: Americal Statistical Association, 1967.

18 Maynes, E. Scott, and Loren V. Geistfeld, "The Life Insurance Deficit of American Families: A Pilot Study", draft manuscripts to be submitted, 1971.

19 Modigliani, F., and R. Brumberg, "Utility Analysis and the Consumption Function: An Interpretation of Cross-Section Data", in Irwin Friend and Robert Jones, eds., *Proceedings of the Conference on Consumption and Saving*, Vol. II, Philadelphia: Wharton School, 1960.

20 Mueller, Eva, and George Katona, "A Study of Consumer Purchases", in Lincoln Clark, ed., *Consumer Behavior*, Vol. I, New York: New York University Press, 1954.

21 Neter, John, and Joseph Waksberg, *Response Errors in Collection of Expenditure Data by Household Interviews: An Experimental Study*,

U.S. Department of Commerce, Bureau of the Census, Technical Paper #11, Washington: Government Printing Office, 1965.

22 Smith, Warren L., *Macro-Economics*, Homewood, Ill.: Irwin, 1970.

23 Stevens, S.S., "A Metric for the Social Consensus", *Science*, Febr., 1966.

24 Suits, Daniel B., and Gordon R. Sparks, "Consumption Regressions with Quarterly Data", In James S. Duesenberry, Gary Fromm, Lawrence R. Klein and Edwin Kuh, eds., *The Brookings Quarterly Econometric Model of the United States*, Chicago: Rand McNally and Co., 1965.

25 Survey Research Center, *The Outlook for Consumer Demand*, quarterly reports, Ann Arbor, Michigan: Survey Research Center.

26 Torgerson, Warren S., *Theory and Methods of Scaling*, New York: Wiley, 1958.

On the Effect of Counter-Information on Consumers*

GERHARD SCHERHORN AND KLAUS WIEKEN

The balance of power[1] between producers and consumers in consumer goods markets is regularly unbalanced in favor of the producers for the following reasons: (1) The producers are in a stronger *market position* because of their relatively small number, their size, and the heterogenity of the goods being offered; (2) The consumer supplies himself with neither sufficient nor accurate *market information* before he buys. George Katona and Eva Mueller were the first to provide empirical evidence on how little information consumers do have before they buy [5].

To understand why so many consumers make their buying decisions on the basis of wrong or incomplete market information, it seems useful to differentiate between "capability" and "readiness"

* This article is a first brief report on the results of a larger empirical study which was undertaken in 1969 and 1970 by the *Institut fuer angewandte Verbraucherforschung*, Cologne, and which is just being completed. The study was designed and supervised by Gerhard Scherhorn; co-workers are Hildegard Jahn-Schnelle, Hannelore Kluten, and the co-author Klaus Wieken. Translated into English by E. Hartjens. The study was supported by the *Landesamt fuer Forschung* of the State of Nordrhein-Westfalen.
[1] The market power of a participant in a market is the measure of his ability in an exchange situation to increase his own real income at the expense of the real income of the other participant, in other words, the ability to enforce his own conditions against the will of the other [3].

in the search for information. The fact that many consumers are not *capable* of providing themselves with market information is a consequence of insufficient education. They possess neither the capacity for a rational means-end calculation nor the techniques for gathering and analyzing the required information. Very few people have, for example, the requisite knowledge to judge the quality of raw meat, or a refrigerator, or to see through deceptive selling techniques, or to understand the "fine print" on a bill of sale.

Furthermore, consumers very often are neither ready nor willing to inform themselves sufficiently before they buy. On the one hand, this is due to their inability to seek out accurate information, which in turn leads to discouragement about the possibility of ever getting a precise picture of the supply situation. On the other hand, this unwillingness is due to the complexity of markets. In most markets the spatial dispersion of supply and the high degree of product differentiation make acquiring information a most difficult and discouraging task. This is so because the consumer lacks the substantial resources needed to inform himself from neutral sources about the competitive suppliers of a product, about their addresses and prices, and about the condition and quality of their products.

A corollary of the above is that consumer education alone is not sufficient to improve the readiness of consumers to inform themselves before buying. One must also make the market situation itself more transparent in order to reduce the high cost of gathering the necessary information. This opaqueness of the market is partly produced by the suppliers themselves. The strategies they use may be called "camouflage" and "deception". The suppliers *camouflage* a product when they neglect to take steps which would clarify its position in the market, for example, by indicating the price per unit (i.e., per ounce, per sheet, etc.), data of production, or date beyond which it should not be used. By *deception*, we mean that by means of product design, packaging, or advertisement the consumer is wrongly led to believe:

1. that one brand is better or equal in regard to certain characteristics than another, or
2. that the brand is substantially improved in regard to certain characteristics, or

3. that one brand is equipped with more of certain useful characteristics, or free of certain harmful characteristics than competitive products.

To improve their market situation suppliers of consumer goods have two classes of strategies at their disposal. By eliminating competition they strengthen their *position* in the market. By "camouflage" and "deception" they decrease the market information available to consumers and thus force them to make choices based on false or insufficient information.

Whether a consumer's preference for a special brand is based on real or imagined advantages can be determined empirically by informing him about actual differences among products and then checking the extent to which he examines his options when making a subsequent buying decision. If the consumer's preference withstands the information provided, it may be assumed that the supplier's advantageous market position was based on an actual heterogeneity of the supply. If his preference does not withstand the test of conflicting information, then it must be assumed that the supplier's position was based on false or insufficient consumer information.

What we call *counter-information* is information prepared or distributed in the consumer's interest in order to prevent the camouflaged and misleading information of the producer from determining the consumer's choice. Therefore, it is the purpose of counter-information either to influence consumer preferences when they are first formed or to alter them afterwards.

There has been little research done on the effects of counter-information, but a number of research findings about attitude change are applicable to this area.

First, we must determine the conditions under which attitudes can be influenced while they are in the process of being formed. In the case of consumer attitudes about products, one can assume that the consumer is ready to accept information about the products concerned. But the problem with counter-information is that it runs counter to other information emanating either from the product itself, from advertisements, or from other consumers of the products. The confrontation with contradictory information can easily cause feelings of incompetence, anxiety, and resignation on the part of the consumer, and lead to apathetic behavior. Thus, the more comfortable or easily available information tends to be accepted. Counter-information is able to avoid this disadvantageous effect only if it is measured out in small doses and presented credibly. How credible consumer information becomes is mainly dependent on the credibility of its source, the objectivity of its content, and the uniformity of its formal presentation.

The task of counter-information changing *existing* attitudes is more difficult. In this case two barriers have to be overcome: the selective perception which hinders the consumer from accepting information which is in opposition to an existing inclination, and the psychological resistance of that person who has accepted contradictory information as being true, but who exhibits mechanisms of resistance which save him the trouble of changing his attitude. Both of these barriers are founded in man's tendency to avoid cognitive dissonance − in this case between knowledge and attitudes.[2]

In this situation there seem to be two ways of bringing about changes in existing attitudes. *First*, one can try to establish cognitive dissonance *ad hoc*, hoping that it will be displaced, not by the rejection of the information, but rather by a change of attitude. Naturally, to be successful the stimulus must be strong enough so that the information is neither filtered out nor rejected.[3]

Second, one can try to compose and present information in such a way that it *may* create dissonance but does not have to. A learning opportunity is created which may or may not be perceived as such by the individual. In this case one gives up the idea of using a powerful stimulus to draw information together and rather relies on rewards which develop out of the individual's own disposition. For instance, one might connect information about the quality of one brand of a product with the argument that, because the competing brands are more expensive though not

[2] The most important theoretical statements dealing with the problem of attitude change [2], [4], [6] all start from the hypothesis that the individual aims to achieve congruence [8].

[3] The conscious establishment of dissonant situations requires a much greater effort than the transmittal of neutral information. Available survey results indicate that the consicious establishment of dissonance improves the effect of counter-information only a little. Only among groups with extreme opinions does it seem to be worthwhile to use techniques which establish dissonance in order to achieve the desired attitude changes [7].

better, money could be saved by buying this particular brand.

Commercial advertising long ago discovered the possibilities of counter-information which are embedded in the second method, and has tried to counter with the same type of technique. For instance in the German advertising for the detergent DASH (USA: TIDE) it is openly admitted that the product is more expensive than other competing detergents. But this admission is counteracted by showing satisfied customers who, because they are obviously convinced that the quality justifies the higher price, won't change their minds even after seeing an opportunity to save money.[4]

Such attempts at immunization confirm the potential effectiveness of counter-information.[5] Suppliers try to reinforce the consumer who buys a more expensive product than is obviously necessary because this particular type of consumer holds internalized, culturally-derived principles of action which demand that he choose the cheapest among qualitatively equal brands, and the best from equally expensive ones.

It is in the producer's interest to overcome these principles of action through effective advertising. It is in the consumer's interest to have these principles activated through counter-information, for instance, by information proving to the consumer that the cheaper brands of a product, which he considers worse than the more expensive ones, are in fact just as good.

In order to check if counter-information of this type is able to change consumer preferences, the *Institut fuer angewandte Verbraucherforschung* carried out the following study:

Two West German consumer markets were studied: the market for gasoline, and the market for detergents. They both have the following in common:

a) certain brands having a large proportion of the market and a well-known image,

---

[4] Methods of reducing dissonance after a purchase have been used relatively often [1].

[5] The relatively unsuccessful information campaign against smoking cigarettes does not contradict this. Unlike other areas, smoking is a need which can be addictive. The appeals of counter-information – low probability of becoming seriously ill at some point – are often too weak to counter the addictive needs of people who are already heavy smokers.

b) the existence of brands and brand-free varieties of the product with a small proportion of the market, and regional or local rather than national distribution,

c) sharp differences in prices between the better and the less well-known brands,

d) qualitative similarity of all brands offered on the market.

Qualitative similarity, of course, does not imply that in those markets all varieties of the products were absolutely equal with regard to all relevant characteristics of quality. By this we mean rather that they all equally fulfilled the basic conditions required by the car or the wash. At the beginning of the survey there were enough independent comparable tests available to determine that gasoline and detergents were qualitatively similar by our definition.

In the first stage of the survey (in the beginning of July, 1969), we studied the two markets according to their structure and performance and, among other things, identified the range of price differences. In twelve locales in the Federal Republic of Germany regular gasoline, with nationwide distribution, for instance, was sold at prices which in a given area differed by as much as 13.5 percent from the maximum price of the local product. The average deviation of the lowest price from the highest price for regular gasoline was over 8 percent, for super (high test) gasoline more than 7 percent. In the case of national brands of detergents the highest prices were on the average 57.4 percent over the local minimum prices.

In the second stage of the survey we interviewed two random samples of about 900 drivers and about 1690 detergent users. The items studied were: number of brands of the product bought, frequency and quantity of consumption, preference for a brand and dealer, degree of information about qualitative and price differences, etc.

In the third stage we concentrated on two local partial markets and interviewed an area sample of 180 drivers and 165 housewives. It was the purpose of this survey to study more thoroughly than is possible in a nation-wide sample, the attitudes, preferences, and information of the local consumers, and to prepare another survey which followed.

Those respondents who in this survey expressed the belief

426

that there were considerable differences in quality among expensive and cheaper gasoline or detergent brands then received two letters of information from the *Institut fuer angewandte Verbraucherforschung.* The first letter was sent a couple of weeks after the survey, and the second followed the first by a month. In these letters, the respondents were informed as objectively and convincingly as possible about the qualitative similarity of brands of gasoline or detergents, and the degree of local price differences and the savings possibilities resulting therefrom.

Four weeks after the second letter, this particular group of people was questioned a second time. This was now three months after the original survey. The results of this survey showed not only that counter-information could be effective but also that it is necessary. In the original interviews only 1/4 of the West German drivers expressed no preference for a particular gasoline brand or brand names in general. The other 3/4 bought expensive gasoline because of preferences which resulted from misinformation about quality. Only 1/8 of German housewives had no preferences for certain brands of detergents or brand name detergents in general. The other 7/8 bought expensive detergents because of preferences resulting from misinformation about quality.

The attitude of drivers who bought expensive (brand name) gasoline was partly conditioned by the fact that they preferred the service of a particular gas station. More than 1/4 of the drivers who preferred certain gasoline brands gave as a reason the good service at the gas station of that particular brand, but most of them preferred their regular brand because they thought that it was qualitatively better or because they were used to it.

In buying detergents, the preference for certain dealers played a smaller role because most stores carry both expensive as well as cheaper detergents. Here the belief in the superior quality of the more expensive brand and long personal habit were definitely the dominant factors in the decision-making.

From these examples we can see what extraordinary effects the producers' strategies of camouflage and deception can have. Less than 30 percent of the gasoline and detergent buyers were sufficiently informed of the fact that there were no considerable differences in quality between the different brands. Because *clarity about quality* (measured as ability to recognize the qualitative similarity of products) was relatively low, it is understandable that knowledge about price differences did not lead to price-conscious behavior. *Clarity about price* was very high, especially among gasoline buyers. In the first survey of a local market for gasoline, almost 9/10 of the drivers were able to give the name and address of the gas station with the lowest price, almost 1/3 knew two or three such gas stations. Clarity about prices of detergents, though lower, was by no means low. About 60 percent of the detergent buyers in the representative sample said that in their areas there were cheaper detergents available than the one they had last bought.

The picture changes, of course, if one measures clarity about price, not by knowledge of the mere *existence* of price differences, but rather by how well consumers were informed about the *actual range* of prices and real price differences. Most people were able to make only relatively imprecise estimates about the latter. Nevertheless it can be said of both product studies that, of the two most important conditions for a rational buying decision (degree of information about quality, and prices of the varieties of a product which are available to the consumer), the level of clarity about prices was higher than the level of clarity about quality.

Therefore, the main interest of our study became how the belief in the superior quality of better-known and more expensive brands could be corrected through counter-information. The first reaction of the consumer to the informative letters was generally positive. Although many of them said in the second survey that they had been very surprised when they had received the letter, most had found the material to be quite interesting. Only a small portion of the respondents felt angry or bothered. Some of these suspected the whole thing to be an advertising campaign. Almost all the respondents read both letters and could remember essential points of their contents during the second interview. For many, not all of the information was new, and about 1/3 stated that they had already heard or read *everything* before. Only a few had doubts about the credibility of what they had read; most believed the information to be true.

Four effects of counter-information were evident:
1. It improved the clarity about quality differences.
2. It increased the clarity about price differences.

3. It reduced preferences for the products usually bought.
4. It changed purchasing behavior to a certain extent.

Clarity About Quality

Of the gasoline buyers who before the survey had been convinced that more expensive brands were of better quality, only 27 percent did not change their minds after reading the letters; 48 percent became convinced of the similarity in quality, although up to that point they had either believed the opposite or were not sure. Another 19 percent had become uncertain. Before, they had been convinced of the existence of differences in quality, and now they gave inconsistent answers.

However, among the detergent buyers, 45 percent were not influenced by the informative letters to revise their belief in the qualitative superiority of the better-known and more expensive brands. The other 55 percent were generally convinced by the counter-information that all detergents tend to meet the same standards of quality.

Clarity About Price

Among the gasoline buyers in the survey, considerably more respondents were able to cite the price of the cheapest gasoline more precisely after receiving the counter-information. Before, only about 30 percent were capable of giving true or almost true statements, while afterwards almost half were able to do so. Thus, even though the letters did not contain this information, the market became much clearer to a small, but not insignificant, portion of the respondents through individual observation instigated by the letters. Some of the respondents went so far as to patronize the less expensive independent stations.

In the case of detergents, 40 percent of the respondents could not say before receiving the counter-information, whether there were cheaper brands than the one they preferred. After receiving the information, however, only 20 percent were unable to state at least approximately the price differences between brand name detergents and cheaper detergents.

429

Brand Preferences

After receiving the counter-information almost 1/2 of the drivers (45 percent) were willing to buy cheaper gasoline more often in the future. While, at the time of the second interview, the larger portion of this group had already changed their behavior, a smaller portion said they would change in the future. Fifty-five percent of the drivers did not want to change their buying behavior in the future despite the information. Two-fifths of these still based their argument on the "poorer quality" of cheaper gasolines. They could not be convinced by counter-information. Others had different arguments, mainly the service and convenient location of their "regular" gas station.

Buyers of detergents less frequently revised their preferences because of improved clarity about quality. After receiving counter-information only 1/3 of the buyers interviewed were ready to buy the detergent which was actually the cheapest. Another 25 percent while expressing a desire to be "price conscious", still did not want to give up buying well-known brands. The rest wanted to stay with "their" brand.

Buying Behavior

Asked if they had bought cheap gasoline more often or less often since the first interview, 38 percent of the drivers who had been supplied with counter-information stated that they had gone to "independent" gas stations more often; the other 72 percent had not changed. Thus, under the influence of two informative letters, more than 1/4 were ready to buy cheap gasoline more often or at least to try it. In the case of detergent buyers, at the time of the second interview, after receiving the information, 64 percent had again bought a detergent. Of this group 1/2 had again decided on their usual brand. The others had changed their brand; 2/3 of these had bought cheaper detergents.

These results of our counter-information experiment reveal tendencies which we are convinced would be verified through replication. The results have special importance if one takes into consideration the fact that the counter-information used was of remarkably low intensity. No television films or magazine articles, illustrated booklets, or verbal influence were employed — just two moderate letters of information. The introduction of more effective means over a longer period of time would certainly have produced much stronger effects.

REFERENCES

1 Donelly, Jr., J.H., and J.M. Ivancevich, "Post-Purchase Reinforcement and Back Out Behavior", *Journal of Marketing Research*, 7 (1970), 399.
2 Festinger, L., *A Theory of Cognitive Dissonance*, Palo Alto, California: Stanford University Press, 1957.
3 Gaefgen, G., "Die Marktmacht sozialer Gruppen", *Hamburger Jahrbuch fuer Wirtschafts- und Gesellschaftspolitik*, 12 (1967), 46.
4 Heider, F., "Attitudes and Cognitive Organization", *Journal of Psychology*, 21 (1946), 107–12.
5 Katona, George, and Eva Mueller, "A Study of Purchase Decisions", In Lincoln H. Clark, ed., *Consumer Behavior, The Dynamics of Consumer Reaction*, I, New York: New York University Press, 1954, 30–87.
6 Tannenbaum, P.H., "The Principle of Congruity in the Prediction of Attitude Change", *Psychological Review*, 62, 1955, 42–55.
7 Smith, E.E., "The Power of Dissonance Techniques to Change Attitudes", *Public Opinion Quarterly*, 25, 1961, 626–639.
8 Zajonc, Robert, B., "The Concepts of Balance, Congruity and Dissonance", *Public Opinion Quarterly*, 24 (1960), 280–96.

The Consumer Society:
Unstinted Praise
and Growing Criticism

ERNEST ZAHN

When Katona's book *The Powerful Consumer* was published in 1960, the title of Galbraith's book *The Affluent Society* (1958) was already on everyone's lips. This title had quickly come to be a popular catchword. The growing literature about disclosed or alleged effects of the rising standard of living upon society and culture had culminated in Galbraith's work, which was said to teach economics in the Age of Opulence. Katona's work was more limited in its range — primarily to the role of the consumer in the economy. Yet it had a great deal to say about the whole economy. It treated problems in great detail and developed ideas which had been tested. It was less provocative, gave significant information, and contributed substantially to a modern theory of economic behavior.

When four years later Katona's book *The Mass Consumption Society* (1964) appeared, it became evident that social science research on economic behavior, as developed by Katona, had not only led to a better understanding of the modern economy, but had indeed become a major contribution to the knowledge of modern society. Under Katona's aegis the study of consumer behavior, once mainly a statistical analysis of the composition of expenditure and saving, developed into the empirical analysis of an

433

important set of human activities and human expectations, of social interaction, social cognition, and social change. It had, of course, long been recognized that "the consumer" should not be viewed as an isolated individual whose behavior could be explained as a function of economic variables. Shortly after World War I, Hazel Kyrk wrote in a highly regarded but now forgotten book that the study of consumption was "the study of almost all the motives and desires which move men to action" [8, p.94]. It was in Katona's work that this study evolved into what is now called modern psychological economics. Sociology has not been excluded from its scope. Katona brought into focus the fact that the family household – the consumer unit – functioned as the center of a social group faced with the need to make wise decisions and to respond to the challenging demands of a changing world. When purchasing behavior was studied as decision-making in such areas as household innovation and investment with due attention paid to such factors as the changing role of the woman, the patterns of authority in the family, and standards of education in the making of such decisions, consumer research became social research in the fullest sense of the word. In his role as consumer, the individual was seen as an increasingly active participant in both economic processes and social developments. It became evident that the consumer was capable of generating income and of shaping new habits of living, interacting with his environment and responding to the opportunities offered by a higher standard of living.

In this article I would like to comment briefly on the effects of affluence as viewed and interpreted in some contemporary writings, in public discussion and popular books reflecting widespread sentiment and people's search for understanding. I would like to approach these manifestations as a part of the developments following the end of the Second World War, as an aspect of social change during these twenty-five years.

By the beginning of the 1960's "Man in the affluent society" had become a fashionable subject for conferences. Economists, sociologists, psychologists, businessmen, and representatives of the churches wished to be heard. A mass audience demanded opinions. The affluent society, it appeared, had discovered itself. This did not occur in the United States alone. At that time there was much talk in Germany about that country's "economic miracle". Its architect was said to be Professor Erhard, that well-nourished cabinet member who later became chancellor. His ample face and figure breathed an air of solidity and conservatism and appeared in cartoons as the embodiment of prosperity. Dietary habits had not yet become part of the progressive conscience of sophisticated consumers. As in feudal and peasant communities where the consumption of wealth was directed to the comfort of the ruling class, the rounded stomach and pink cheeks appeared endowed with status and claim to respectability. The complexion of abundance remained associated with the air of distinction. A higher level of living was remembered as a privilege of the old elite, as a mark of the master, as Veblen would have said. Indeed, the European consumer bore a likeness to Veblen's concept rather than to that of David Riesman or William H. Whyte as they viewed the contemporary American scene. European consumer behavior revealed conservative attitudes. Having recovered its legs and its consciousness, bourgeois society gave expression to its achievement in the old symbols of the traditional social order and its value system. Economic progress was expected to restore the traditional way of life.

The term "era of restoration" has long been used by historians to denote the period following the defeat of Napoleon and the Congress of Vienna (1815). In the literature of history and political science the word "restoration" is associated with a "reactionary spirit," the failure to achieve any fundamental reorientation and a lack of genuine innovation. But in the years following the end of World War II there was in Europe a deeply-felt need for restoration. The generation that had suffered from the greatest war in history lived to see the rebuilding of cities, the reconstruction of factories, and the regaining of a private livelihood as a dazzling process. This was particularly the case in Germany where clearing away ruins helped restore self-assurance as it figuratively represented clearing away the recent history. Young people in their twenties, who had been trained for war and had worn uniforms, now became trainees in industrial corporations and turned to grey flannel suits. The attributes of the business elite were readily adopted by the cadets of the meritocracy. The "fabulous fifties" went down as years of conspicuous production and conspicuous consumption, as the decade of triumphant business. The conspicuous behavior of consumers in Europe has often been explained by the suddenness with which the improvement in material well-being came about and by a lack of any habitual standards for appropriate responses to affluence. Material gain and economic progress were applauded and admired. Economic growth was visible to the man in the street. Productivity spoke for itself. There was no need to justify the pursuit of economic activity and the making of profits, because all this was associated with the improvement of everyone's living conditions. Last but not least, the rising standard of living was perceived as a proof testifying to the superiority of the capitalist system in the competition with the socialist states, a confrontation which presented itself as the "cold war" and was a matter of concern to many people who remained anxious about the future.

It was not long, however, before affluence became a subject of censure. Criticism of modern society soon turned to criticism of what had been achieved. As in many other fields the United States had already led the way. The first translations of daring and provocative interpretations of the contemporary American culture were greedily devoured by many members of the European middle classes. Thoughtful and somewhat melancholic comments about the ups and downs of civilizations and a conventional indignation about mass society had in earlier years paraded as a sign of education and as evidence of good taste. The same sort of people who in 1930 were fascinated by Ortega y Gasset and Oswald Spengler in 1950 turned to David Riesman and C. Wright Mills. American scholars had impressively depicted modern man in his new role of consumer and employee. In journalistic writings Riesman's concepts became widely used as stereotypes. The consumer was said to be lonely and lost in a crowd of "other-directed" people, finding it "hard to be someone," needing guidance and love and looking for approval by his neighbors or peer groups. Guidance, indeed, became less and less accepted from the traditional institutions of society. Instead, it was more and more received from a new "voice of authority": "the opinions of others", "the generalized other" as reflected in the mass media. Values and behavioral norms of the parental generation were questioned by the younger generation. One of the many characteristics of the consumer society has been not the vertical but the horizontal spread of new ideas and new ways of living.

The eloquent presentation of psychological insight and knowledge about the contemporary culture, combined with an emotional attack on the undesirable aspects of mass culture, appealed to the aesthetic bias of those people who cultivated a nostalgia for the "good old times". The gap between the technical sciences and the humanities, between the practical world and the world of the arts, so vividly described by C.P. Snow, began to grow. The greater the alienation between the two disciplines, the more prejudiced became the attitudes on both sides toward their respective mentality and métier. When the consumer society was portrayed as a hunting ground for hidden persuaders, status seekers and waste makers, the latent suspicion of business in many minds guaranteed applause and approval. In the days of Chaplin's movie "Modern Times" professional moralists had aimed the weight of their censure at mass production; now they turned to mass consumption. The consumer himself seemed pleased. He appeared eager to be taught that economic progress and material wealth did not automatically lead to freedom and hapiness, to social justice and democracy. Did he have a feeling of guilt? There is sufficient evidence that the majority of Germans today find that their compatriots "live beyond their means" and that the standard of living is "too high" [7]. Affluent society has begun to doubt itself. Affluent society has begun analyzing itself. Affluent society has become an increasingly critical society, concerned about well-being.

It is noteworthy that this should have happened in a process where the same mechanisms of want satisfaction, which were questioned by social critics, responded to the new demand for popular culture and knowledge emerging among critical consumers. Madison Avenue successfully responded to the "higher" wants and aspirations. Advertising stories switched from "mother-in-the-kitchen" to a sophisticated family engaged in cultural pursuits. In business conferences the catchword of the sophisticated consumer became the signal for a reconsideration of marketing policies. The new type of consumer was recognized as the consumer in the new suburbia: college educated, achievement oriented, innovation minded. But there was not yet the provocative

consumer, the dissenting young and their adult mentors, representing radical discontent and striving for a "counter culture," which
diverges from the values and ideas that have been the mainspring
of our society since the beginning of the Age of Discoveries [14].

It has sometimes been argued that this evolution of "higher"
cultural wants and aspirations was mainly or merely the consequence of more free time and leisure, stimulating curiosity and the need
for amusement. This is not true. Masses of people, for example,
study magazines with the express intention and expectation of
attaining a new "social orientation". As one authority in this
field has put it: "Leisure time seems to be the new social riddle on
which extensive reading and studying has to be done"[9, p.295].
The appearance of more sophistication among consumers is essentially related to the emergence of a genuine new need: the need to
understand what is happening and changing in the environment.
Where old standards governing behavior are abandoned or rejected,
the finding of new ways of behaving and living becomes a problem, be it in the field of household management and home life,
marriage and family, child-rearing and education, leisure and fashion, occupational choice, work organization or politics. David
McClelland is right when he says: "Norms governing behavior must
exist, must come from somewhere, if the society is not to become
disorganized" [11, p.193]. Aspirations for knowledge and information are essentially aspirations to achieve competence by
acquiring means and standards for the mastery of the environment. Adaptive behavior has become increasingly dependent on
the development of intellectual and human capacities. Cultural
interests, therefore, are more than merely a hobby.

People also want to understand the greater and more complicated problems of society and culture. This is often difficult without adequate intellectual training. In 1961, T.H. Marshall wrote:
"There is an area of modern literature about social questions
through which the reader travels with the help of neatly simplified
maps, guided by signposts which tell him in clear and incisive
terms exactly where he is and where he will get to by whichever
road he chooses to take" [10, p.280]. Today, literature about our
society is a subtle matter of supply and demand. Much of this
literature is highly critical. Capitalistic market systems have proven
to be adaptable even to the commercial exploitation of social

protest and to political ideas attacking capitalism. The culture of social protest flourishes by the grace of the profit motive. There is ample supply of reflections on the technocratic society and its opposition. Where people are inclined to project their personal problems and dissatisfactions onto the environment with the expectation of viewing them as an aspect of the malaise of the society, they can readily find theories to fit their needs. Many critics of modern society quickly discovered the meaning of the concept that the media had developed into a "new voice of authority" substituting for the old traditions. Communications outlets soon found themselves not only in the role of suppliers of information and guidance in all sorts of matters; they discovered at the same time that they could gain power. Capitalistic society does not persecute its opponents. It may rather highly reward them when their criticism responds to the structure of widespread sentiment and to what has been called the revolution of rising expectations. Even this situation is not without its detractors, however, and has recently been denoted by Herbert Marcuse as "repressive tolerance".

Where do new standards of consumption and of social behavior come from today? Who sets them and who controls them? Who are the power holders in the economy and what are their bases of legitimacy? Questions like these are being asked by an increasing number of young college-educated people questioning traditional economic and material values and rejecting occupational careers in business that express these values. A new generation, representing, perhaps, a new phase of the affluent consumer society, appears eager to change the behavior of producers and consumers. Conventional advertising, directed to the comfort and convenience of a pampered consumer, encounters indignation among many groups aware of the disastrous poverty in the underdeveloped world, the malaise in the West, and the great technological, educational, and political challenges of the second half of the century. Rising levels of aspirations motivate underprivileged groups to attain desired ends by action. The need to justify action has led to a new interest in ideologies. The concept of alienation, initially referring mainly to the life of the exploited worker, is increasingly used with reference to the other-directed consumer. The old argument that the unequal distribution of wealth and economic power makes for

439

a disproportionate application of productive resources to serve the interest of the few has been modified; it has been extended to the marketing process so that it includes the setting of standards for consumption and the control of behavior. Galbraith's assertion that wants are increasingly being created by the process by which they are satisfied has been readily adopted by the New Left. The fact that the statement as such does not explain the social and psychological nature of such a process – which remains essential for the assessment of what Galbraith has in mind – makes it useful for demagogues. Ideas of the most brilliant scholars may respond to widespread sentiment and serve the interests of groups. Ideas – whether or not preconceived and prejudiced – play a part in that process which Katona has described as the generalization and spread of affect. We shall have to make more and more studies on the spread of affect, on people's response to social conflict, and on their attitudes toward social change.

At the same time we should not overlook the fact that effective criticism, challenging polemics, and public controversies remain a necessary and fermental element in a sound democracy. Even over-simplification, exaggeration, and provoking statements may some-times lead to the path to the truth. Once the things that "must be said" have been expressed and articulated with necessary pungen-cy and piquancy, it is possible in a second round to moderate and reduce the assertions to the "normal" measure. Modern demo-cracy is expected to function as a mass democracy in the sense that more and more people are expected to accept responsibility and to participate in critical discussions about important issues. In daily television, public issues are discussed before the eyes of a mass audience, and the most subtle theoretical questions, which formerly belonged to and still require the professional competence of a minority, have now become the concern of masses of people. It must be recognized that, despite the spread of higher education, many people still lack the intellectual training for the adequate understanding of complicated issues. It must, at the same time, be recognized that not the level of school education, but the nature of people's attitudes, their perceptions, and, especially, the degree of their involvement in the issue, will determine their readiness to accept or to reject a particular idea, theory or policy. The "right" choice among ideas and policies offered in the political market place is much less a matter of intellectual training than it is a matter of civic attitudes, civic education, and diligent citizenship.

Many sociological studies that appeared during the fifties and early sixties were concerned with what was called the political apathy of the people, an oft-heard complaint in those days. Lack of genuine political interest seemed to have become part of the profile of the consumer society. Are the communications media escaping from politics? David Riesman asked this in *The Lonely Crowd* (1950). Daniel Bell argued in *The End of Ideology* (1960) that the decade of the fifties was marked by the decline of radicalism, by the exhaustion of the political ideas — particularly marxism — that had dominated the intellectual scene. He felt it necessary to plead for a new critical view of society, stressing the point that an anti-ideological perspective did not have to be identified with conservatism. "One can be a critic of one's country without being an enemy of its promise" [3, p.17]. In Germany, Helmuth Schelsky characterized the young of the postwar years as the sceptical generation [14]. One could often hear it said in those days that the German people were "fed up with politics" and that the youth had practical and prosaic views, ambition only to possess material goods and to enjoy a bourgeois way of life. Today, by contrast, politics dominate the Western universities. It is being argued that the choice and determination of desirable ends to be attained by society should precede the process of science and give direction to both teaching and research. Whatever may be said about this comprehensive and controversial issue, the emerging new sentiments, aspirations, and actions of young people have greatly stimulated innovation and the necessary reform of institutions. The new sentiments must be well understood irrespective of whether or not the underlying theories are correct. We must become aware of what Alvin Gouldner has called "an unfilled theoretical need" deriving from a gap between the new structure of people's sentiments and the older theories which do not function to organize or to serve these sentiments. The predicted "end of ideology" has not come. Instead, Gouldner predicts the end of traditional academic sociology in his work *The Coming Crisis of Western Sociology* (1971), where Marxist sociological tradition, neglected by American sociologists, is reconsidered in order to open a way to new conceptions. Theodore Roszak believes that the alienated young are giving shape to something that looks like the saving vision that our endangered civilisation requires, and that there is no avoiding the need to understand and to educate them in what they are about [14, p.1]

Affluent society, lonely crowd, organization man, meritocracy, counter culture: all such book titles are characteristics and names of modern society and not without meaning. T.H. Marshall has argued that one should pay attention to such phrases, as those who introduce or quickly adopt them often express a genuine experience at a specific time. The nature of social systems can sometimes be revealed by the subtle analysis of the names given to them. Such names often reveal perceptions and expectations. According to Marshall the term "affluent society" denotes a standard of values, rather than a level of living. It denotes a dominant spirit, a consensus with regard to certain key points and key issues of the social system. This common attitude is reflected in the concept which, therefore, helps to sustain the system. Marshall has compared the connotation of the term "affluent society" with the concept of "welfare state" — a label "tied by somebody or other round the neck of the British society in the 1940's" [10, p.281]. The transformations of Britain's old industrial society during the first half of the 20th century came to conceptual and emotional expression in the "spirit" of the Welfare State. It marked the attack on the standard of the prosperous mid-Victorian decades when people spoke of a prosperous country in spite of the fact that very large groups were still poor. "The poor were the common soldiers in the economic army, and were adequately equipped, so they thought, for their task; the indigent were the casualties who must be carried off the field and treated by separate service" [10, p.283].

The term "welfare state" denotes the deliberate use of mechanisms superseding and modifying the market forces in order to achieve for all people subsistence and security. The mechanisms include such things as rent and price control, rationing and various kinds of social insurance, administered in different ways in different countries. In Britain, Holland, Germany and — especially — Scandinavia, the concept of national social policy has long been accepted by public opinion as a meaningful notion. As Marshall shows, the spirit of the British Welfare State reached maturity during the war when people became aware of the necessity of collective efforts in the face of a common danger. The "mutual service society of the war" was expected to become "the mutual benefit society of the peace". This, as we know, did not work out quite as the protagonists had hoped. The institutions and procedures were questioned in a subsequent phase in which they failed to achieve what had been acclaimed. The social policy of the Welfare State remained associated with austerity; it did not stop inflation, it often subsidized the middle class rather than the poor, it was not successful in the field of education, and – most important – many social problems had disappeared or changed in character with the rising standard of living and the coming of the "affluent society" [10, p.299].

The term "affluent society" first became a label of the modern American society. The American society has again and again been characterized by sociologists as "a society which places a high premium on economic affluence and social ascent for all its members" [12, p.146]. In his famous classic, Robert Merton demonstrates the importance of incentives for success provided by the established values of the culture. If these values extol certain common success goals above all else for all people, whereas at the same time the access to the approved modes and means of reaching these goals is restricted by the actual social organization (for instance, class differentials), a deviation from these modes and innovation are likely to occur. As Merton shows, poverty is not an isolated variable operating in precisely the same fashion wherever found; when poverty and associated disadvantages are linked with a cultural emphasis on material success as a dominant goal, rates of criminal behavior rise. Poverty is thus less highly correlated with crime in southeastern Europe than in the United States. "In this setting, a cardinal American virtue, 'ambition' promotes a cardinal American vice, 'deviant behavior' " [12, pp.146–47].

Americans are said to be characterized by a willingness to respond to any unusually competitive social environment and to make use of the opportunities offered by society. The word "opportunity" here refers to economic and social achievement – a connotation which the equivalent word in many foreign languages does not have. Thus, the affluent American society is not to be understood merely as a society with a high standard of living where large-scale production is sustained by mass demand at an ever-rising level. The American society is essentially characterized by that cultural system of norms and values, e.g., self-reliance, ideas and beliefs which favour a responsive common attitude toward affluence. If there exists such a thing as a "spirit" of the affluent society, it would have to be understood as a basic set of dynamic attitudes which makes people see themselves as the active producers of that affluence rather than as the passive recipients of its benefits.

This is the underlying optimism which George Katona discovered among large groups of American consumers and denoted with the word "consumer confidence". A similar dynamic element, termed "civic competence", was discovered and investigated by Gabriel Almond and Sidney Verba in the behavior of the American people as citizens in their community and as members of the larger society [2]. In order to make sense, the ideal concept of an affluent society must include that type of "political culture" which Almond and Verba describe as "civic culture". The value system of the culture and the social norms of behavior are related to the perception of social processes and to the individual willingness to participate; they are related to the perception of opportunities and the degree of willingness to act. The motivation to respond to material improvement and to social opportunities cannot wholly be explained by psychology; motivation is a sociological problem as well. We might now ask in what way specific cultural values and institutional factors may determine whether or not specific developments, for instance an improvement in living standards or a more democratic political organization, are perceived as progress in the minds of the people, leading to responsive and adaptive behavior. The crucial question is not how prosperous or how democratic a society is according to economic or institutional criteria, but to what extent this society is able to respond to both prosperity and democracy in such a way that desired ends are attained.

In *Aspirations and Affluence*, a study of international differences in economic behavior, it has been shown that differences in social values between North America and Western Europe have an impact on people's responses to affluence [7]. Indeed the very differences in the nature and extent of the economic progress of

444

industrialized nations with different social and cultural settings were found to have been determined to some extent by the latter factors. Content analysis of the connotations attached in different languages to such words as "affluence", "welfare", "well-being", etc., can reveal different sets of values. Although the phenomena signified by the term "affluent society" are to be found more or less in all highly-industrialized societies, the concept retains an American characteristic. By contrast, the European concept of "welfare state" cannot conceal its origin and its connection with European social and political thought. From a cultural and institutional point of view, Western and Northern European countries — with the possible exception of Switzerland — represent welfare state societies rather than genuine affluent societies. In much of Europe the state is expected to play a relatively more responsive and responsible role in shaping conditions of life. Research for the above-mentioned study of international difference gave reason to believe that in good times, Europeans are more inclined than Americans to say that the government did a good job and that the institutions and organizations of the country functioned satisfactorily. Conversely, in bad times, they are more likely to blame government and business for failure. On the whole, it was found that Europeans are less inclined than Americans to attribute either success or failure to their own behavior.[18]

If we accept Marshall's point that the concepts of the affluent society and the welfare state stand for opposed ideologies, we ought to add that the basic principles are not irreconcilable. These principles might be defined in terms of two opposed issues: (1) opportunity for individual accomplishment, and (2) intervention for social justice. The first stands for liberty, the second for equality. Both are complementary aspects of the same indivisible effort of making our social world livable and acceptable for all people. Either of the two may deserve priority in a specific historical situation. Either of the two can be overemphasized and become a dominating philosophy at the cost of the other. In the fifties, the principles of the welfare state came under attack in many countries and the affluent society was applauded; at the beginning of the seventies, the attack on the spirit of the affluent society began to take shape, and voices are being heard again demanding better institutions and policies for social planning and control. In the minds of many people, the word welfare is associated with social services and social policy, with pensions, insurance, family allowances, and fringe benefits of various kinds.

Economists have stressed the point that we must not assume that total well-being is greater when the overall level of production is higher than when it is lower. Nor must we assume that overall well-being is necessarily greater when the network of welfare institutions and services is more comprehensive. Both a higher level of production and a more comprehensive network of welfare institutions must be viewed in connection with a higher level of wants and aspirations, necessitating a higher level of want satisfaction. Just as more and more people are demanding an increasing variety of new consumer products, also they are demanding an increasing variety of social services provided by the state, including such varied things as meals in school, methods of birth control, marriage counselling, and adult education.

Well-being depends on wants, expectations and aspirations. A plea for more well-being need not be a plea for less affluence. Nor must a plea for more well-being necessarily result in a demand for an extension of social action by the State. Promoting well-being is to be recognized as a common task, assigned to all organized groups of society and, not to the least degree, to the individual people themselves. It would be wrong to assume – as it is in fact tacitly assumed by many – that business exists mainly for the satisfaction of "private wants", that "public needs" are to be met by the government, and that any shift of emphasis from "private wants" to "public needs" would require a greater part to be played by the state. Private wants and public needs are not necessarily opposed. The content of both concepts is determined by cultural values and norms of conduct. Indeed, many public needs have in recent years become private wants. Business will have to do much in the future to meet them. Marshall, referring to those critics of the welfare state who point to the benefits of a higher standard of living, says: "If it is necessary to remodel the machinery of the Welfare State to fit the conditions of the Affluent Society, it is equally essential to change the spirit of the Affluent Society to fit the principles of the Welfare State" [10, p.301]. The fundamental ideas of the welfare state and the fundamental principles of a business enterprise ought to be the same and to meet in the concept of well-being. If one agrees that well-being does not automatically flow from affluence and social welfare services but remains a task to be achieved by deliberate human effort, the discussion, then, can only hinge on the question of who should do what and by what means, and how should both goals and means be determined.

The question of what government and business should do for the welfare and the well-being of the people requires a realization of what it means that the people themselves have come to play an increasingly active part, both in economic processes and in shaping new ways of living. Katona's studies have clearly demonstrated the vital role of this greater latitude of action on the part of individuals. In the context of his work, the concept of aspirations is crucial. Affluence — defined as "more for the many rather than much for the few" — cannot be properly understood without an understanding of the dynamic role of aspirations. If affluence stands for income and the ability to buy, aspirations refer to attitudes and the willingness to buy. There is the level of living and the level of aspirations. Both can be quantitatively determined. To summarize Katona's findings: The increased power of consumers has been shown to exist in their greater latitude of action and discretion. The decisions of people in their private households were recognized as being just as important as the economic decisions of business and government. It was pointed out that consumers' decisions depend on levels of aspirations, which rise with achievement: the perception of improvement and of progress generates higher aspirations rather than saturation. It was demonstrated that both income and confidence determine effective demand, and that people's perceptions, motives, and expectations may differ from economic "facts". It was proved that trends and fluctuations in attitudes can be measured and predicted and that reasons for such fluctuations can be discovered and analyzed. But can we assess the meaning of such findings from a sociological point of view?

The analysis of the development of consumer aspirations reveals the specific needs of a typical family household in the different phases of the life cycle. Critics who equate the abundance of consumer goods with gadgetry and waste, and the striving for a higher standard of living with "materialistic" attitudes, usually forget the challenging problems which present themselves to people in the changing environment of an "open society" which is becoming more and more dynamic. A higher income poses the question of how to spend or invest it in home and family. The shorter workweek raises the question of what uses should be made of increased leisure. Educational and occupational opportunities must be met with the willingness and wisdom to develop one's capacities and to respond to the demands of a competitive work environment. The education of children, in earlier times no major problem, has become a large factor in determining social status, quite the reverse of the situation in the old class society where social and economic status determined the achievable level of education. Keeping up with the changing work organization, efforts to survive within the contradictions and crises of bureaucratized systems, and the risk of failing to adapt oneself to new roles and circumstances are concomitants of social mobility. The longer life span makes it necessary to prepare for old age and to adapt oneself to it. Geographical mobility requires the successful tackling of transportation and communication problems. The urban way of life confronts the citizen with the deterioration of the cities, growing delinquency, and increasing air pollution. It is in these latter areas that public needs are beginning to be felt as private wants by more and more people, so that more and more people respond to proposals for action. The more our material situation improves, the more we are struck by those things which remain unsolved or even grow worse.

Indeed, man in the affluent society is a subject which involves the whole complex of conditions under which all members of that society and of other societies live today. Poverty, therefore, must be included. There are new forms and new perceptions of poverty [13]. Poverty shows up all the more blatantly wherever affluence exists next to it, rendering inequality insufferable and intolerable. Poverty is also an aspect of the spread of great expectations. Amid Victorian prosperity the poor did not protest the way they do today. Today poverty raises its voice in the unlivable slums and ghettos of American cities and has become one of the greatest challenges to the nation. In the developing countries poverty increases, paradoxically, as a consequence of progress as improved means of fighting illness and infant mortality increase survival without a parallel growth in income and food production. It is now impossible to speak about the effects of affluence without thinking of those people throughout the world who have no share in it.

Taking issue with Galbraith's much-discussed ideas on private opulence and public poverty, Katona summarized his views as follows:

> It is precisely the wanting and striving for improvement in private living standards that form the solid basis of American prosperity. Only if the so-called private opulence increases still further can we hope to overcome public poverty. The question is not one or the other; it is both or none. . . people are willing to exert great effort if the effort helps them to achieve their own concrete goals, namely, a better life for themselves and their children [5, p. 65].

At the same time, Katona has also shown that private wealth may result in an extension of personal concerns. In a process of "extension of the ego" individuals may become more prepared to identify themselves with public issues and problems arising from the dangers that threaten our society. We may well ask under what circumstances and conditions such a process is likely to occur.

It is possible that in the future more and more public needs will become felt as private needs and that more and more people will respond to meaningful proposals for tackling such problems as air pollution, traffic congestion, urban renewal, housing, and education. The participation of the people will be needed. As solutions will imply behavioral change and behavioral adaptation, social science research will be needed to discover "social indicators", attitudinal predispositions and possible directions of change. Social research will have to precede and to become an integral part of the development of plans and proposals, in the same way as it has become a part of the process of marketing consumer products. Essentially there should be no difference between the marketing of new products and the development and introduction of necessary community services desired by the people as a part of their well-being. Public policy has a lot to learn from business policy, and business policy, on the other hand, will have to meet a new challenge. In the same way as business in the 1950's came to discover the "sophisticated consumer" it should now come to discover and to understand the "critical consumer" concerned about well-being. Once it was said that emphasis should shift from the marketing of specific products to the cultivation of style. Now, we need a further shift to the humanization of our social environment, to efforts in the search for more desirable ways of living. Will we be able and are we willing to realize this?

Perhaps Katona has expressed too great an optimism. He has said that social learning may bring forth more desirable changes among consumer needs. "Instead of arguing that there is too much manipulation of consumers a good case might be made for the thesis that they are not manipulated enough in the sense of not being helped to acquire sufficient information and knowledge" [6, p.245]. We should not forget that well-being does not depend only on the availability of sufficient information and knowledge. Using Katona's own concepts, we may say: There is the ability to know and there is the willingness to know. Behavior is not only a function of the ability to know. The way people think and their reactions to information and knowledge depend on their interests and positions in the society. Social prejudice, unlike simple misconceptions, is actively resistant to evidence that would unseat it [1]. There are conflicting interests and systems of power. This points to a need to go beyond the psychological approach to economic behavior and to include sociology in the studies. This can be done following the way Katona has led. Katona has demonstrated that people, in their role of consumers, act as a stabilizing force in the economy. If this is possible, there is no reason why they as citizens should not also be able to act as a stabilizing force in the society. And why should one not express optimism? Another famous psychologist from Europe who also came to the United States as a refugee, Erich Fromm, has recently published a book on *The Revolution of Hope*. Fromm believes that we worship production and consumption as the idols of our time. But in his call for action toward a humanized technology he, too, presents a theory of optimism which after all is not so very different from essential ideas expressed by Katona in his theory of expectations. Hope is the mood that accompanies faith, Fromm says. "Faith, like hope, is not prediction of the *future*; it is the vision of the *present* in a state of pregnancy". [4, p.14] It is, indeed, our basic orientation to life and the quality of our expectations which will determine the further processes of social change in the time of growing social conflict.

REFERENCES

1 Allport, Gordon W., *The Nature of Prejudice*, New York: Addison-Wesley Publishing Company, 1958.
2 Almond, Gabriel A., and Sidney Verba, *The Civic Culture: Political Attitudes and Democracy in Five Nations*, Boston: Little Brown & Company, 1965.
3 Bell, Daniel, *The End of Ideology*, New York: Collier Books Edition, 1961.
4 Fromm, Erich, *The Revolution of Hope*, New York: Harper & Row, 1968.
5 Katona, George, *The Mass Consumption Society*, New York: McGraw-Hill, 1964.
6 Katona, George, *The Powerful Consumer: Psychological Studies of the American Economy*, New York: McGraw-Hill, 1960.
7 Katona, George, Burkhard Strümpel, and Ernest Zahn, *Aspirations and Affluence*, New York: McGraw-Hill, 1971.
8 Kyrk, Hazel, *A Theory of Consumption*, Boston: Houghton Mifflin Company, 1923.
9 Lowenthal, Leo, "Biographies in Popular Magazines", in B. Berelson and M. Janowitz, *Reader in Public Opinion and Communication*, enlarged ed., Glencoe, Illinois: The Free Press, 1953.
10 Marshall, T.H., *Class, Citizenship and Social Development*, New York: Doubleday & Company, 1964.
11 McClelland, David C., *The Achieving Society*, paperback ed., Glencoe, Illinois: The Free Press, 1967.
12 Merton, Robert K., *Social Theory and Social Structure*, rev. and enlarged ed., Glencoe, Illinois: The Free Press, 1957.
13 Morgan, James N., *et al.*, *Income and Welfare in the United States*, New York: McGraw-Hill, 1962.
14 Roszak, Theodore, *The Making of a Counter Culture*, London: Faber & Faber, 1970.
15 Schelsky, Helmut, *Die skeptische Generation*, Düsseldorf: E. Diederich, 1962.
16 Snow, C.P., *Two Cultures and Scientific Revolution*, Cambridge University Press, 1959.
17 Wilensky, H.L., and C.N. Lebeaux, *Industrial Society and Social Welfare*, Free Press–Macmillan, enlarged paperback ed., 1965.
18 Zahn, Ernest, *Meningsvorming en Maatschappelijke Orde*, Amsterdam: de Bussy, 1971.

451

Poverty and Social Welfare

Human Betterment and the Quality of Life

KENNETH E. BOULDING

Judgements of better or worse, that is, value judgements, are an essential element in human activity, and indeed I would argue, in the activity of all living creatures. Certainly any kind of behavior which involves choice implies some kind of welfare function, preference function, value function, or betterment function, whatever we like to call it, which at least orders the alternative states of the future about which choice is being made. Decision-theory is a set of mathematical variations on the theme that "everybody does what he thinks is best at the time." By definition, that which is chosen is presumably regarded as better on the betterment scale than those things which are not chosen, the betterment scale simply being the ordering of states of the universe on a scale of better or worse. All behavior involving choice, therefore, and all valuation imply a betterment function which we can write

$$B = f(\text{the universe})$$

which simply means that of any two perceived states of the universe, we can tell which one is better and which one is worse, unless they are both equally good, in which we have what the mathematicians unkindly call a "weak ordering". In practice, of course, we may replace the "universe" in the argument of this function by "the relevant environment", though it is often quite hard to draw a line between what is relevant and what is not. I prefer the solar system when it has a visible comet and I prefer a universe when it has a super novae visible on earth, so that human valuation extends out a very long way.

When faced with a function as large and complex as the betterment function, there is a strong tendency to try to reduce it and to simplify it, though I shall argue that it is probably wise to try to resist these tendencies, as they nearly always result in replacing the "true" betterment function with a false one. Thus, there is a strong tendency to identify one element of the universe as a measure of betterment. We see this even in language, where "up" is regarded as good and "down" is regarded as bad. In speaking about the betterment function, indeed, I have frequently used the expression, "How do we know which way is up?" and everybody understands, at least in English, that "up" means better. The more one thinks about it, however, the odder this relationship seems. If I am upstairs in the morning, it is certainly better to go down to breakfast. If I have been on the top of a mountain for an hour, it will almost certainly be better to go down. If I am a skin diver, it is certainly better to go down. Why "up" gets such a good press, therefore, is really quite puzzling. Why, for instance, is it regarded as good when stock prices go up and bad when they go down? It is perhaps because we associate "down" with uncontrollable crashes, such as falling off a cliff, whereas climbing "up" is a rather steady exercise of our own virtue. When the stock market goes up, it redistributes assets in a different way than when it goes down, but why on earth should one be better than the other? It is really a little puzzling. It is true, of course, that a capitalist society operates more successfully under inflation than under deflation, because it is easier to raise prices and money-wages then it is to lower them, but then this in turn may be related to this absurd prejudice we have that up is good.

A similar fallacy is involved in "the bigger the better". Bigness, of course, is related to upness, simply because when a thing gets bigger, whatever number measures this increases; we think of an increase as up. We can think of many cases indeed in which "the bigger the worse".

456

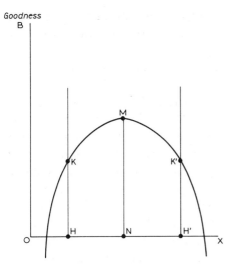

Fig. 1. Betterment function

This leads to a fundamental proposition regarding the betterment function, that most relationships between B and any particular element in the universe are not only nonlinear but exhibit some kind of a maximum, that is, if we plot a section of the betterment function, as in Figure 1, with any particular variable of the universe, say X, on a horizontal axis and "goodness" on the vertical axis, the curve will tend to exhibit a maximum at M. For any element in small quantities, below the optimum that is, the more of it there is the better. Beyond the optimum, the more of it there is, the worse. This indeed is the famous principle of the Aristotelian mean. When a poor man gets richer, it is clearly better; when a rich man gets richer, this may easily be worse, even for him, that is, increased riches may be a burden. In small quantities, pride is self-respect and the more the better; in large quantities, it is arrogance and the more the worse. Every virtue becomes a vice if there is too much of it; every vice becomes a virtue if there is little enough of it. The Aristotelian mean indeed is a direct consequence of the principle of diminishing marginal utility, utility being simply the economists's name for value or betterment. That is, the more of any particular element in the universe, the less valuable is an increment of it. It is possible, of course, though unlikely, that the maximum value could be at an infinite quantity of a particular variable, even with diminishing marginal utility, though ordinarily we would expect the maximum value to be at some finite amount.

Economists have pointed out, quite rightly, that usually we cannot reach the maximum of the betterment function, which would be bliss, because we are constrained by various scarcities, that is, out of all conceivable states of the relevant environment of any particular decision-maker at any particular moment only a subset of these states are open to him, that is, the "feasible set", and the problem of decision, therefore, is to find that element within the feasible set which is best on the B scale. Thus, in Figure 1, if OH is the feasible set, that is, the only amounts of X which are obtainable lie to the left of H, then H will be chosen in preference to any other quantity of X because it is clearly better than any other. We should notice, incidentally, an obvious point but one which is often overlooked, that if the feasible set is OH', beyond the optimum amount OM, we will choose less than the maximum feasible amount of X, ON rather than OH'. Economists are so accustomed to scarcity that they often implicitly assume that all positions are in the range OM, so that the chooser will always be pressing to the feasibility boundary, but this is not necessarily the case. It is by no means impossible for the best choice to lie within the feasibility boundary, in which case it is no longer true that "the more the better". All "bads", or negative goods, fall in this category.

Economists tend to have a very limited notion of what are the elements that lie within the argument of the betterment function. In neoclassical economics, for instance, it is usually assumed that for the firm the only significant variable is Profit, and that often measured as an income rather than as a rate of return. Thus, B is supposed to move towards the better when profits go up, and is not supposed to move when any other element changes, provided that profits remain the same. This is clearly unrealistic. Even the most profit-oriented organization will usually increase profit by sacrificing something else – such as reputation or leisure, so that the betterment function clearly always includes variables besides profit. In the neoclassical economics, also, the consumer or the household is supposed to maximize utility, which could be just another name for betterment, but the argument of this utility function consists only of quantities of commodities purchased, subject to the constraint of the fixed amount of money spent. The formal solution to this problem is, of course, the principle of equimarginal utility, that is, that the optimum distribution of the fixed quantity of money expended among the various lines of expenditure is such that an additional dollar added to each line of expenditure would increase total utility by the same amount.[1]

The restriction of the variables in the argument of the neoclassical utility function to quantities of commodities consumed, is of course highly arbitrary, but it is very easy to expand the number of variables. I have argued, for instance, that stocks of commodities or states of being are probably more significant in the utility function than quantities produced or consumed. For many things we get satisfaction out of use, not consumption. It is by wearing a suit of clothes that we gain utility, not by wearing it out. This is not to say, however, that certain rates of consumption and changes, varieties, and so on, may not also be variables of the utility function. We get utility out of being well fed, but we also get it out of eating, which is not quite the same thing.

Neoclassical welfare economics, both of Pigou and of Pareto, assumes usually that the only variables in the utility function are quantities of commodities purchased or possessed by a single individual or at best, perhaps, a family. This is the principle of independence of utility on which the famous Paretian optimum rests. This, again, seems quite unnecessarily restrictive. Selfishness, that is, independence of utilities, is a highly special case; it is, in fact, merely the zero on the scale of benevolence and malevolence. My perception of the welfare of others, or even the wealth or income of others, is clearly a significant variable in the argument of my utility function. I feel benevolent towards a person if my perception of an increase in his income, wealth, or welfare, increases my

---

[1] This particular formulation assumes a cardinally measurable utility, but the principle can easily be reformulated in a form that assumes that utility is only ordinally measurable. The reason why the assumption of cardinal measurement is usually unnecessary is that maxima survive any transformations which do not involve reversals of order. Thus, the significance of Figure 1 would remain unchanged no matter how much we stretched or retracted the figure in the vertical direction, provided that the order of all horizontal straight lines remained the same.

own utility. I similarly feel malevolent if my perception of an increase in his income, wealth, or welfare, diminishes my utility. We can argue, indeed, that selfishness, that is, zero malevolence or benevolence, is not only a very rare case, but is likely to be dynamically unstable. Both benevolence and malevolence are learned by processes of interaction, similar to what have been called "Richardson processes".[2]

Thus, when two people A and B come in contact with each other, if A reacts favorably in a way that pleases B, B will react in a way that pleases A, A will react still more in a way that pleases B, B still more in a way that pleases A, and so the process will go on, with increasing benevolence until some kind of equilibrium is reached, at some level of mutual benevolence. On the other hand, if A reacts unfavorably, B may also react unfavorably, A still more unfavorably, B still more unfavorably and so on, until an equilibrium is reached at a level of negative benevolence, or malevolence, with both parties disliking each other and hence each increasing his utility if he perceives that the other's position is worsened. Even a quite casual relationship, such as with a store clerk, is likely to exhibit a mild degree of benevolence, engendered by the conventions of courtesy. Other relationships, such as that with the traffic cop, may develop equally mild relationships of malevolence. With people in close and intimate contact, such as a husband and wife, selfishness is very rare indeed. The relationship almost always develops either quite high benevolence or quite high malevolence because of the sheer dynamics of intense interaction. Selfishness is only likely to be stable, therefore, where interaction is very low or nonexistent. This is a phenomenon of which economists almost universally have failed to take account. Yet there is no reason why rates of benevolence cannot be added to the variables of the utility or betterment function.

The obvious fact that benevolence and malevolence are learned in processes of interaction raises a still more difficult problem, that the whole utility function is learned in the process of growing up and socialization. The utility function, presumably, does have some genetic base or predisposition. The taste of some substances,

---

[2] These are processes similar to arms races, first studied by Lewis F. Richardson, *see* [1].

for instance, seems to be physiologically disagreeable. We are only physiologically comfortable within a certain range of temperatures. Hunger, thirst, and sexual desire certainly have physiological machinery underlying them. Nevertheless, the particular form which utility functions assume is determined mainly by the learning process of the child as he grows up in a particular culture. A child who grows up in Japan develops a taste for raw fish, dried octopus, and is horrified by cheese. A European tends to reverse these preferences. Similarly some cultures develop preferences for monogamy, some for polygamy, some for piety, some for worldliness, some for peacefulness and some for militancy, and so on, almost indefinitely. Human instincts are now generally discredited. Certainly nobody believes any more that there is an instinct of workmanship, and what we seem to have are rather diffuse physiological drives, the specific expression of which, even in the case of sex, has to be culturally learned, largely through the reward structure.

Once we admit that utility or betterment functions are learned, however, neoclassical economics, especially welfare economics, falls apart at an alarming rate. There is general assumption underlying neoclassical economics that preference or utility functions are given and are not to be questioned. This is the famous principle of consumer sovereignty and of what Galbraith has called the "accepted sequence", from the consumer or the voter directing, or at least influencing, the producer or the government. If preference functions can be taken as given, some interesting propositions, such as the famous marginal conditions of welfare economics, can be derived by a process of impeccable logic, for instance, the proposition that the optimum price structure is that which corresponds to the structure of alternative costs.[3]

These propositions unfortunately completely fall apart when we are faced with the fact that preferences are learned from parents, relations, friends, teachers, preachers, peers, newspapers, advertisements, radio, TV, political speeches, and especially from conversations. Classical welfare economics, believing in what I have called

[3] This, incidentally, is the real meaning of the economists' otherwise absurd preoccupation with perfect competition, which would, it if were possible (which it is not) give us a relative price structure corresponding exactly to the structures of alternative costs.

the "immaculate conception of the indifference", tends towards the view that there is something illegitimate or evil about persuasion. Preferences are supposed to spring, pure and undefiled, from the deep wells of our unchangeable personalities. This, unfortunately, is a romantic illusion, proving incidentally, what I have always suspected, that economists are romantics at heart, believing in the real Me inside this corruptable veil of persuadable flesh, and believing also that this real Me is pure in heart, inspired neither by envy or by pity, selfishness being the purest of all human virtues, totally unspotted from contact with a corrupting world.

To say that values or preferences are learned, then, is simply to say that man is teachable, but this means also that he is persuadable. Teachability is legitimated by the assumption that there is truth which can be learned, and that there are processes by which the learning of error can be corrected. In the case of values and preferences, we have much less confidence in the existence of some objective truth, although hardly anybody believes really that values are either purely arbitrary or purely subjective. The evolutionary process at least imposes certain standards of survival value on those preferences which do in fact survive. A society with a strong preference for suicide and infanticide will probably not be around very long, and so we are quite unlikely to observe it. Everything that exists, including preference functions, presumably exists because it has some sort of survival value, even if that is only temporary.

Survival value, however, is not enough to give us anything which corresponds in the value field to "truth", for a great many different preference functions may have equal survival value. There can be coexistence of cultural species and species of preference functions just as there can be coexistence among the living species of a stable ecosystem. We have to recognize, however, that coexistence may be a function of the discontinuities and "nichiness" of the environment. This is certainly true in the biosphere. The more harsh and the more homogeneous the environment, the fewer species are likely to coexist in it. A heterogeneous environment with many niches is likely to have many different species, because, one ought to add, there is not perfect competition, but protected "markets" for many species up to a certain quantity.

It is impossible to prove, therefore, that Galbraith's "revised sequence", according to which producers and governments persuade consumers and citizens to take what is offered, is necessarily "bad", even though we may legitimately have a certain prejudice against it. The fact that all values are learned and learned ultimately by persuasion or by a system of rewards and punishments means that we cannot rule out the persuasion as inherently illegitimate. Otherwise, we would rule out learning of values altogether. On the other hand, we do have a strong feeling that not all persuasion is legitimate, as some of it involves "conning" or cheating. At one end of the scale we have the obvious cheats — the confidence men, the shills, the hucksters, demagogues — and at the other end, of course, we have the teachers, true prophets, the professors, wise parents, the statesmen, and so on, who also are frequently engaged in persuading people, presumably for their own good. Unfortunately, however, there is no easy way of telling what constitutes a person's own good, particularly once we leave the realm of the more the merrier, or the bigger the better. Is a person who is happily deceived by spiritualist or astrologer, even a patent medicine, necessarily worse off than he would have been if he had not been so deceived? This is a very uncomfortable question. We know enough about Hawthorne effects, placebo effects, and so on, to suggest that not even objective truth is always a positive variable in the betterment function. In front of this quaking morass, traditional welfare economics looks as clear, cheerful, and enlightened as the gentle, optimistic, eighteenth century deism out of which it grew. Once we abandon it, we face a slippery mass, a hell of uncertainty and doubt, from which perhaps only a good Calvinist doctrine of election can save us.

If subjective betterment is a morass in which delusion and deception may be preferable to truth and enlightenment, we may save the day by moderating our demands. Instead of insisting on a betterment function whose argument is the universe, can we break the problem down into subsystems about whose properties and dynamics we can hope to have some more secure and subjective knowledge? This at least is a strategy which seems worth a try. We might begin by looking for variables which can serve as indicators within the betterment function, where there is wide agreement as to the general nature of the relationships involved.

We might begin with health. There is wide agreement that it is better to be healthy than sick, and we have a pretty accurate subjective information apparatus, as well as a great deal of objective measurement, which can tell us how sick we are, although there have been cases, of course, in which the patient improved right up to the point of death. Even in this very obvious relationship, however, there are real doubts and difficulties. Should we prolong the lives of people who are too miserable to enjoy life and who have no chance of recovery? An enormous crisis would be created by any real medical breakthrough in aging, which might lead to the prolongation of human life beyond the "allotted span". We must certainly face the fact that there is an optimum age of death, though it is hard to say exactly where it is. The ideal would presumably be a healthy life for everybody until the moment of death at the optimum age. The most uncomfortable truth of economics, however, is that none of the best things of life is free, and that everything has its price, and even perfect health would exact social costs, which we are already beginning to feel in the shape of the shift in the age distribution away from the triangular form which was universal in pre-technical societies (with large numbers of young people and decreasing numbers of people of successively older ages), into the rectangular age distribution, which we are rapidly approaching today, with approximately equal numbers of people at each age up to the age of death.

We have still not faced up to the social consequences of this change in terms of increasing conservatism, decreased opportunities for advancement, and an unsatisfactory life pattern which may easily involve a maximum welfare in youth and declining welfare through middle and old age.

The problem arises because hierarchies tend to be triangular, with a few people at the top and a lot of people at the bottom. If the age distribution is triangular, then those who survive have a good chance of rising. If the age distribution is rectangular, everybody survives, say, to age seventy, but the older a person gets, the less chance he has of finding a suitable and rewarding role. It may be indeed that the "youth problem" of the last ten years has been the result of a quite temporary shift in the age distribution towards youth as a result of the "bulge" in births from 1947 to 1961, and that the "age problem" which we may face in the future is going to be much more severe and intractable. One ends up with the thought of a nightmarish society in which everyone is perfectly healthy, but in which in the interest of social stability and desirable life patterns, the lowest income percentile of each age group is painlessly put to death every year, thus restoring the triangular age distribution. This solution, like a lot of other rational solutions of problems, begins to look alarmingly like Dean Swift's "modest proposal" for solving the population problem by eating the babies.

If not even health can be relied on as an objective standard for human betterment, it is clear that wealth is even more shaky. It is only the most unreconstructed economist who believes that a rise in per capita GNP is always good. It is not merely that the GNP itself is a grossly inaccurate measure, even of economic welfare [2], as it includes within it the production of a considerable quantity of "bads" as well as goods. But even if we could get an accurate measure of average economic welfare, in terms, say, of the true per capita Net National Product, this could still not be used as a monotonic betterment indicator. We might, for instance, have an increase in the per capita Net National Product which is accompanied by more unequal distribution. An increase, for instance, might all go to the top five percent of the population with the rest becoming even worse off. This is not to deny of course that an increase in the Net National Product is frequently very good, for real wealth and income are likely to follow the law of the Aristotelian mean, so that an increase in the wealth of the poor people is likely to be better than an increase in the wealth of the rich. This, of course, is the famous economic principle of the diminishing marginal utility of money with increasing wealth, which cannot be proved and indeed to which there may be exceptions, but which commands a good deal of informed approval.

If neither health nor wealth are adequate indices or betterment, what about pleasure? Here, of course, we run into severe problems of measurement and very severe problems of interpersonal comparisons. Physiological pleasure is also a very deceptive indicator of betterment, and again clearly follows the Aristotelian law; when we have little, more is clearly good, but the frenetical pursuit of more is probably not worth it. In any case, the *reductio ad absurdum* of the pleasure principle would be the pleasure wire, an electrode into the pleasure center of the brain (this apparently can already be done with a rat), which would keep the human being indefinitely in a condition of absolutely meaningless physiological ecstacy. Drugs would be a very mild problem compared to this, and they are bad enough.

If pleasure is a fluctuating physiological state, only valuable as a goodness indicator in small quantities, we may be able to do better with happiness, the pursuit of which is a classical American occupation. It may be thought of as a general condition or predisposition of a person involving, as it were, his personal net worth, or what I have sometimes called the "net moral worth", that is, a person's evaluation of his own person and the environment in terms of property, status, roles, relationships with other people, and so on, which surround him. Happiness, however, is also very hard to measure, except again perhaps at the lower end of the scale.

Things are no easier when we try to go on to "joy", an illusive but nevertheless real concept relating to the fulfillment of the whole life identity and potential, which is even more difficult to identify and measure than happiness. Still, one would like to encourage psychologists to work on these problems, which are surely not inherently insoluble. Even if we cannot get very reliable measures for the individual, by the famous principle which I have sometimes called "Katona's Law", that the summation of ignorance produces knowledge, we may find an operation or instrument with self-cancelling random factors which will give us a much better measure for a hundred or a thousand individuals than we can get for one.[4]

We can argue further that the search for individual measures of betterment is likely to be frustrated because individuals derive their significance and identity and even their net moral worth from the society of which they are a part, and we cannot really, therefore, separate individual measures of betterment from social measures, such as justice, freedom, equality, participation, democracy, or on the other side, alienation, tyranny, and so on. There is something in this argument. On the other hand, if individual

[4] As George Katona has shown, asking one person whether he will buy an automobile next year provides totally unreliable information. Asking a thousand people and summing the answers produced is quite astonishingly reliable.

measures of betterment are difficult, social measures are even harder. Justice, for instance, has been an ideal of society, certainly since Plato, but its measurement even in the roughest possible terms is extremely elusive. Thus, we have to postulate a "Justice function",

$$J = f(\text{things relevant to Justice}).$$

The significant argument here is always some kind of distribution of power or status, income or whatever else may be distributed in the society. This in itself is difficult to describe, simply because it can only be treated as a scalar, for instance, in the Gini index, by doing gross violence to the multidimensionality of the distribution concept itself. Even if we get over that one, we are then faced with at least two different concepts of justice. One is the distribution according to desert, the other is distribution according to need. These two may have very different betterment functions. Thus, an equal distribution makes for a very high "Justice value" on distribution according to need, very low on distribution according to desert. This is a dilemma which has plagued the human race for a long time and will almost certainly continue to plague it into the future.

The justice functions are closely related to the betterment functions for such social characteristics as equality or freedom. On either standard of justice, our evaluation of equality depends on our estimation of the actual distribution of either need in the one case r desert in the other. It is much easier to assess equality of ne' in some particular variables, such as health, education, legal rights, civil rights, and so on, than it is in such cases as esthetic and recreational tastes. This problem arises very clearly under conditions of wartime rationing, where even in the case of food, it is a fundamental principle that some basic foodstuffs should be left unrationed, simply because calorie requirements for different individuals vary so enormously that equal distribution of food would not be according to need. The idea of equal distribution of tickets to football games or to the opera is clearly absurd. This is where freedom comes in. We need freedom because of diversity and non-measurability of needs. If all human beings were exactly alike, we could put a low value on freedom, for the political

467

authorities could easily find out what is best for everybody and simply do it. It is the diversity, unpredictability, and essential randomness of the human being which force us to put a high value on freedom.

We must now face a problem, however, which we have hitherto neglected, which is that of the interrelationships among the variables in the argument of the betterment function. These are profoundly related because of the principle of scarcity. We have seen earlier how we can divide the conceivable states of the universe into a feasible set and an infeasible set by a feasibility boundary. If the ideal state of the universe is in the infeasible set, then the best we can do is reach the feasibility boundary and then at this point we are almost certain to find that many different variables of the argument are competitive, in the sense that the more we have of one the less we can have of the other. That is to say, the feasibility set is extremely likely to be convex. This means in evaluating the betterment derived from an increase in one variable of the argument, we always have to take into account the effects of possible decreases, or perhaps increases, of other variables, some of which may be "goods", that is, things an increase of which makes things better, and some of which may be "bads", that is, things an increase of which makes things worse. We are then virtually forced into a kind of "marginal betterment" analysis which soon involves us in something like a set of shadow prices, which however in this case is just another name for the unspeakable embarrassment of absolute measures of the good. Thus, if we increase power production, which is good, we will also increase air pollution, which is bad. How much of one is worth how much of the other? In the case of things which have a market price, this gives us some kind of relative value structure or structure of rates of substitution, which is at least a base from which we can start. Difficulties arise, however, in the case of public goods and public bads, or even private bads, where these do not have a market, and hence nothing emerges out of the system which gives even a shadow price from which to begin our calculations.

The problem becomes even more difficult when we go to the larger social variables, such as justice, equality, and freedom. Here again, there may be a kind of "production function" of these things. We can often only get more equality by the sacrifice of individual freedom, and also perhaps by the sacrifice of productivity, as the Cuban and Chinese experiences suggest. Whether more equality is better than less depends on our valuation of these other things which have to be sacrificed in order to get it, as well as on our valuation of equality itself. And in the absence of any adequate political market, these evaluations are extraordinarily hard to do and open up opportunities for extraordinarily diverse judgements. It is hardly too much to say that ideological conflicts are a result of the diversity of judgement regarding both the production functions and of great social variables, and also in regard to the preference functions. Sometimes, indeed, quite small divergences of preference can lead to very large diversities of judgement as to what is preferred, especially where the variables concerned are either easily substitutable or even negatively substitutable, that is, cooperative rather than competitive.

It is clear that no easy answers emerge from this analysis. Nevertheless, these problems are not hopeless. We may not be able to solve the large problem of the total betterment function, and even the use of the smaller variables, such as health and wealth, as we have seen, run into grave difficulties. Nevertheless, we may be able to identify certain processes within the social system in which there is wide agreement on the question of whether the dynamics of the process goes from bad to better or from bad to worse. I have argued, indeed, that we may be wasting our time to try to find a social optimum, because over large areas of the field the betterment function is a plateau of weak orderings, in which one position of the universe is neither very much better nor very much worse than another. On the other hand, the plateau may have cliffs, that is, in some cases, quite a small move of the social system may lead to sharp worsenings or even to irrecoverable disaster. We need to be aware of these discontinuities. There may also be slippery slopes that lead toward cliffs. The "no no's", that is, the moral and legal prohibitions of society, are the fences that we try to build at the top of the cliffs or on the slippery slopes that lead to them. Sometimes, of course, we build fences where there are no cliffs, which may teach people the disastrous lesson that there are no cliffs. Finding out where the cliffs are, however, is remarkably difficult and takes a great deal of social learning.

Some of these "slippery slopes" can be identified fairly easily, such as drug addiction. Others are more difficult, such as commodity addiction, which is what the radical economists accuse the American economy of promoting. We can also identify perverse reactive processes, such as arms races, or the mutual learning of malevolence, as we have noted earlier. The identification and understanding of these perverse dynamic processes is perhaps the major key to social betterment. Our present therapeutic industries, such as medicine, education, and perhaps law, are all too much concerned with individual therapy and not enough concerned with what might be called the therapy of subcultures, or the therapy of social structure. This, however, is a field far beyond the scope of the present paper and merely underlines the essential argument in all these matters — that we still have a very long way to go.

REFERENCES

1 Richardson, Lewis F., *Arms and Insecurity*, Chicago: Quadrangle Books, 1960.
2 Sametz, A.W., "Production of Goods and Services: The Measurement of Economic Growth", in Sheldon and Moore, eds., *Indicators of Social Change*, New York: Russell Sage Foundation, 1968.

The Role of Earning Rates in Determining Poverty*

HAROLD W. GUTHRIE AND GORDON F. SUTTON

The premise for the research reported here is that any population of the United States at any point of time will contain a subgroup that is in poverty[1] and that this subgroup is determined and created by the normal functioning of the socio-economic system. Poverty is, therefore, not an aberration but a normal consequence of our cultural arrangements and any serious attempt to remove poverty as a social problem must resort to drastic action that will change the structure of the system. The point of departure for this paper is taken by moving from the assertions above to an examination of the conditions of poverty as these appear to be associated with a hierarchy of occupations an the earnings yielded by those occupations. Our social welfare policy for alleviating or removing poverty will then be reviewed in the light of the implications of occupational differences in earnings.

* The research on which this paper is based has been supported in various ways by the U.S. Office of Economic Opportunity, the University of Massachusetts, the University of Illinois, and the Urban Institute. The views expressed here are those of the authors and should not be imputed to the supporting institutions.
[1] By the current official definitions developed by the Social Security Administration.

Several years ago Harold Wilensky and Charles Lebaux contrasted "residual" and "institutional" conceptions of social welfare. The residual view, which they held characterizes the approach to welfare in the United States, presumes that, ". . .social welfare institutions should come into play only when the normal structures of supply, the family and the market, break down" [1, p. 138]. By contrast, the "institutional" conception defines social welfare as a central function in the society.

The Wilensky and Lebeaux "residual" conception is of special interest here for it presumes a society in which social policy is market-oriented, wherein the concern for social policy planning regarding the economy exceeds that for individuals or, indeed, groups of individuals. In such a society, concerns regarding macro-economic policy affecting the price level or the rate of growth of gross national product override concern for the welfare of persons who become unemployed or who have inadequate earnings. The welfare of individuals or disadvantaged subgroups is always assumed to be a matter to be disposed of by the individuals and their relationship to the market system. Only in the most extreme adverse circumstances will they be offered institutionalized support.

Working from the perspective of the "residual" conception, we are able now to look more closely at the role of the "normal" structures – family and market – of support in the society. For our purposes, it is important to view family and market as interrelated. That is, building upon Wilensky and Lebeaux, we propose that the "normal" support of individuals in the society grows out of (1) direct participation in the labor market, or (2) through the labor force participation of others joined in a family relationship. Thus, the occupation of the breadwinner becomes important in a sustenance connection for both breadwinner and his dependents. The part of the social system that determines family or individual support is, then, the complex set of economic market relationships and mores that affect the way persons earn income by working. When we consider this set of relationships in the context of the economic system, we typically conclude that a supply of labor is formed by a large population with variable qualifications for different types of work. We also conclude that a demand for labor is formed by a large population of employers with variable needs and preferences for the number and type of workers that they can employ profitably. The theoretical view of the interaction of the supply of and demand for labor is that each prospective worker will be employed at a wage rate equal to the value of his marginal contribution to the product of his labor as it is valued in a competitive market for goods and services. This market is dominated by the incomes of consumers and their tastes.

Our social view of the market for labor and of the mores that impinge upon it is that a member or members of each family, with exceptions, must work at a job to earn the income he wants to spend on goods and services. There is, in general, a social obligation on the breadwinner of each family to support his family. There is also an implicit assumption that any person who wants to work will have the opportunity to work and will be able to support his family above the level of poverty. Exceptions are made in that the aged, the disabled, and children without a breadwinner are given meager public support.

In providing this support the prevalent public attitude among those who do not need public support is that the recipients could, if they only wanted to, find work that would provide enough income to keep them out of poverty. This attitude has been expressed in strong terms in the legislative activity concerning the Family Assistance Plan. Not only is there a work requirement for beneficiaries; there remains strong support for denying benefits to families in which there is an able adult male.

One approach to further understanding why and how poverty is inherent in our present culture is to examine systematically four factors that determine poverty status:

1. *Wage adequacy*. It is a fact that many persons in our society fulfill the cultural norm of working 50–52 weeks but do not earn enough to maintain a family of four persons above the poverty line.
2. *Job security*. A person may be adequately waged, on a full year work basis, but his income may fall below the poverty line if he does not work a full year.
3. *Additional earners*. A husband, as the principal breadwinner, may lack income to bring his family above the poverty line because of either or both wage inadequacy and lack of job security. Yet the family can have enough income to keep it out

of poverty if the wife or another family member also works.

4. *Size of family*. A husband and wife, through some combination of the husband's full-year earning rate and his job security and the wife's earnings, may have enough income for four persons, but they may be in poverty nevertheless if they have more than four persons in the family.

These four factors, singly and in interaction, provide a framework for a static analysis of poverty. Although it is expected that research efforts under way will lead to an integrated analysis of the role of these four factors in determining the poverty population, the research reported here is concerned only with the first factor, wage adequacy. This analysis is expected to provide a model that can be tested in a subsequent, more extensive, analysis.

AN EARNINGS MODEL

The earnings model to be used for assessing wage adequacy attempts to disaggregate a highly complex labor market by considering highly specific occupation groups. This by no means assures that all persons in the occupation group perform identical work functions, but it approximates that ideal. On economic grounds occupation is an imperfectly best way to describe the work that people do. On social grounds, occupational titles give insights into another aspect of poverty—social status.

The model also attempts to capture two hypothetically powerful determinants of earning rates: productivity and discrimination. Our economic theory attributes all important differences in earning rates to differences in the value of marginal product. But the marginal product would be difficult to measure for an individual worker and probably impossible to measure for all workers. Lacking true measures of productivity, we resort to a proxy by assuming that some important differences are correlated with age. It is not unreasonable to consider that in some occupations productivity increases with age as the person accumulates experience and higher skills. We can think of workers becoming more productive over time and raising their earning rates. This process might continue up to some point in the older working years when there may be physical limitation or failures to learn new techniques.

This would tend to lower productivity relatively and result in declining earning rates.

Discrimination results when two persons with the same level of productivity do not have the same earning rate. Thus, discrimination is interpreted as an irrational deviation from the association of earning rates and productivity. Such irrational deviations might occur with respect to many different characteristics other than productivity, such as physical attractiveness, or youth, or old age (thus confounding the proxy measure of productivity), but we choose to focus on the two variables: color and sex. As will be noted below, there are other measures of discrimination with respect to these variables.

A comprehensive analysis of the role of wage adequacy in determining poverty would, as noted above, take into account the interaction of family units with the economic system. For analytical purposes, however, it is preferable to begin with individual workers with undefined family status. The theory underlying the operation of the labor market does not differentiate between single women and married women, for example, and wage adequacy must be assessed in terms of the capacity of any worker to be the sole source of support for a family. Obviously, the concept of adequacy is meaningful only if we know how many persons are to be supported. A criterion for wage adequacy must, therefore, be arbitrarily designated. We take, as a point of departure, the criterion that any person who works a full year should earn enough to support a family of four persons.

The data base for the model is the 1/1000 sample of the 1960 Census. The particular elements selected for analysis were all persons, 14 years of age or more, who reported that they had worked 50–52 weeks in 1959. These persons are grouped in categories defined by the 3-digit U.S. Bureau of the Census codes for occupation. In some occupational categories there were fewer than 50 persons in the group and occupation groups were combined to obtain larger cells. In a few groups it was necessary to include persons who worked less than 50 weeks but their earnings were weighted appropriately to measure a full year earning rate.

Within each occupational group the amount of full year earnings is the dependent variable in the equation:

$$Y = b_0 + b_1 A + b_2 A^2 + b_3 C + b_4 S + b_5 D_1 + b_6 D_2 \qquad (1)$$

where A = age in coded form:
    0. Age 14 - 24
    1. Age 25 - 34
    2. Age 35 - 44
    3. Age 45 - 54
    4. Age 55 - 64
    5. Age 65 or over

C = 1 for white
    0 for nonwhite

S = 1 for male
    0 for female

D_1 = 1 for one through 4 years of high school
    0 for grade school or college
D_2 = 1 for one or more years of college
    0 for grade school or high school

The age term is put in quadratic form to allow for earnings to be hypothesized as rising to a maximum in middle age and then dropping off in the later working years. The dummy variables for color and sex serve to shift the earnings-age parabola up or down according to the magnitude of the effect of discrimination by color or sex within an occupation. The education variables are included to modify the occupation title as a descriptor of the work done. Many occupational groups contain a mixture of people with a variety of levels of educational attainment.

An example of an occupation group in which earnings for 50–52 weeks worked was significantly related to many of the hypothesized independent variables is "stock clerks and storekeepers". The regression estimates are:

$$Y = 618 + 1265A - 212A^2 + 816C + 1415S + 419D_1 + 853D_2$$
$$(493)\,(213)^* \quad (46)^* \quad (321)^* \,(309)^* \quad (238) \quad (338)^*$$

$$n = 241 \qquad R^2 = .22 \qquad * = \text{significant at 5\% level}$$

The estimating procedure required one recalculation of the regression coefficients, dropping all terms for which the original estimated value was not significant at the 5 percent level. In the case of this example D_1 was dropped and the revised estimates are:

$$Y = 1015 + 1241A - 219A^2 + 873C + 1353S + 540D_2$$
$$(440)^* \ (213)^* \quad (46)^* \quad (321)^* \ (309)^* \quad (289)$$

Figure 1 shows the estimated full year earnings profiles for four subgroups of workers in the "stock clerk and storekeepers" occupational category. The expected value of earnings for white males at all age levels in this occupation exceeds $3,000, the poverty level of income for a 4-person family in 1959. In the sense that the earnings of a white male who is the only worker in a family could support four persons above the poverty line, we say that this group is not underwaged. Nonwhite males less than 25 years old are underwaged, however — their expected full year earnings are

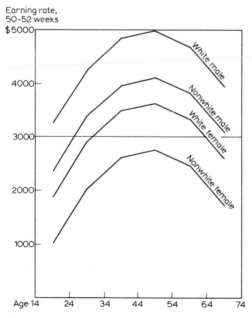

Fig. 1. Estimated full year earning rates for stock clerks and storekeepers by age, color, and sex, 1959.

less than $3,000. In the same way, younger and older white fe-
males and all nonwhite females are underwaged.

Estimates derived from the model, such as those shown in Figure 1, can identify subgroups within the population subject to
being underwaged even though they may be employed over a full
year.[2] The underwaged subgroups can be identified by occupation, age, color, and sex. Clearly, there is a conflict between our
social goals as they are expressed through attempts to alleviate
poverty and the structure of our social and economic system.
When conditions exist such that a full work effort by a person
cannot support a family of four persons above a minimal subsistence standard of living, the gains from pursuing "workfare" as
a solution to the poverty problem are not obvious. The following
sections describe four different types of occupations and the extent to which the workers in these occupations are subject to
being underwaged.

OCCUPATIONS IN WHICH EARNINGS VARY ONLY WITH PRODUCTIVITY

Considering age as a proxy for productivity there are some occupations in which earnings vary as productivity rises and falls, but
there are no statistically significant discrimination effects on
earning rates. This does not necessarily mean that discrimination
does not occur, however. Among sales engineers, for example,
there are no nonwhite workers and there are no female workers,
and the regression model used is not a satisfactory test of discrimination effects. Table 1 lists occupations in which there are no
apparent discrimination effects other than selectivity in employment.

The two occupations that have the lowest mean earnings, news-
boys and baby sitters, are perhaps trivial because very few mature
adults earn their living by working in these occupations and most

[2] Some deficiencies in the data require caution in interpreting the estimates
from the earnings model. Occupation is determined by the job held on the
date of the Census in 1960. Earnings are observed for the year 1959, not
necessarily in the same occupation. Although most persons worked full time
in 1959, others worked part time, and it is not possible to differentiate
between full and part time workers.

478

Table 1

OCCUPATIONS IN WHICH EARNINGS ARE RELATED TO AGE AND NO OTHER VARIABLES

Code	Occupation Title	Mean Earnings	Poverty Groups (50—52 weeks earnings < $ 3000)	Percent White	Percent Male
390	Newsboys	788	Ages 14—24, 25—34, 65 and over	96	96
801	Baby sitters, private household	867	All age groups	81	0
324	Messengers and office boys[1], [2]	3,374	Ages 14—24, 65 and over	72	94
474	Mechanics and repairmen, radio and television[1]	4,286	Ages 14—24, 65 and over	95	96
535	Upholsterers[1]	4,406	Ages 14—24, 65 and over	96	90
470	Mechanics and repairmen, air conditioning, heating and refrigeration	5,057	Ages 14—24	100	100
180	Sports instructors and officials[1]	6,130	None	95	76
074	Draftsmen	6,156	None	99	98
421	Electricians[2]	6,175	None	98	99
523	Structural metal workers[1]	6,354	None	96	98
285	Purchasing agents and buyers (n.e.c.)[2]	6,483	None	100	93
530	Toolmakers and diemakers and setters	6,878	None	99	100
082	Engineers, civil	7,383	None	99	99
084	Engineers, industrial	7,478	None	100	99
092	Engineers, sales[1]	9,541	None	100	100
162	Physicians and surgeons	13,421	None	94	90

1   Regressions based upon weighted values of earnings for 50—52 weeks worked and shorter periods
2   Occupation groups combined; see Table 1 Appendix

479

APPENDIX TO TABLE 1

Electricians combined with apprentice electricians

Purchasing agents and buyers, nec combined with buyers and shippers, farm products

Messengers and office boys combined with express messengers and railway mail clerks, telegraph messengers

Sports instructors and officials combined with athletes

of the young persons typically work only part time. Young persons working full time are more prevalent, however, in four occupation groups subject to wage inadequacy. Young persons, age 14–24, who earn their living as messengers and office boys, upholsters, or mechanics and repairmen in radio and television, or air conditioning, heating, or refrigeration, can expect to have poverty level earnings.

It may be argued that young persons who are in the underwaged earning segments of these occupations do not need to be in poverty because they should not be trying to support four persons. This argument presumes that young persons should not proceed very rapidly in family development, or if they do, their peril of being in poverty is their own problem, not a social problem. The fact is that many young persons do marry early and have children and become part of our poverty population as a result of being underwaged.

OCCUPATIONS IN WHICH EARNINGS DO NOT VARY
WITH PRODUCTIVITY BUT ARE SUBJECT TO DISCRIMINATION

Table 2 lists the occupations for which the regression estimates indicated that there were no significant differences among workers of different ages, suggesting no changes in productivity, or at least, no changing returns to productivity. Among these occupation groups, the regressions are straight horizontal lines differing in their height according to sex and color.

Inspection of differences in earning rates among subgroups in

Table 2

OCCUPATIONS IN WHICH EARNINGS ARE RELATED TO OTHER VARIABLES BUT NOT TO AGE

Code	Occupation Title	Mean Earnings	Poverty Groups (50–52 weeks earnings < $3000)	% White	% Male	Marginal Earning Rates White-Nonwhite	Marginal Earning Rates Male-Female
823	Chambermaids and maids, except private household	1,651	All in the occupation	34	1	406	—
705	Sewers and stitchers, manufacturing	2,694	All females	96	8	—	1,701
843	Hairdressers and cosmetologists	2,991	All females	91	15	1,802	2,342
963	Garage laborers and car washers and greasers[1]	3,118	All nonwhites	47	96	725	—
710	Spinners, textile[2]	3,214	Females without high school education	100	37	—	1,427
831	Elevator operators[1]	3,264	All females	72	75	—	1,454
832	Housekeepers and stewards, except private household	3,333	All females	90	30	—	2,453
964	Gardeners except farm and groundskeepers	3,495	All nonwhites	79	97	1,014	—
815	Bartenders	4,108	All nonwhites	97	93	3,219	—
120	Musicians and music teachers	4,136	All females	94	50	—	2,480

Continued Table 2

Code	Occupation Title	Mean Earnings	Poverty Groups (50–52 weeks earnings < $3000)	% White	% Male	Marginal Earning Rates White-Nonwhite	Male-Female
444	Inspectors, scalers, and graders, log and lumber[1,2]	4,234	None; earnings vary with education	97	100	—	—
694	Painters, except construction and maintenance	4,412	None	89	90	1,708	1,640
401	Bankers	4,735	All females	90	83	—	3,264
973	Warehousemen	4,783	None	81	99	926	—
965	Longshoremen and stevedores[1]	4,947	None	57	96	1,489	—
495	Painters, construction and maintenance[2]	5,007	None	91	98	1,816	—
653	Filers, grinders, and polishers, metal	5,097	Nonwhite female	94	93	1,661	1,927
314	Dispatchers and starters, vehicle[1]	5,102	None	98	92	—	2,276
685	Mine operatives and laborers (n.e.c.)[2]	5,227	None; earnings vary with education	92	98	—	—
323	Mail carriers	5,256	Females with elementary education	93	98	—	1,852
415	Cranemen, derrickmen, and hoistmen	5,314	None	88	100	1,942	—
850	Firemen, fire protection	5,507	None, earnings vary with education	96	100	—	—

Continued Table 2

Code	Occupation Title	Mean Earnings	Poverty Groups (50–52 weeks earnings < $ 3000)	% White	% Male	Marginal Earning Rates White-Nonwhite	Marginal Earning Rates Male-Female
321	Insurance adjusters, examiners and investigators	5,745	None	98	82	—	1,411
301	Agents (n.e.c.)	5,870	None	98	86	—	2,693
405	Brickmasons, stonemasons and tile setters[2]	6,096	None	89	99	2,865	—
075	Editors and reporters	6,542	None	98	70	—	2,693
640	Brakemen, railroad	6,603	Nonwhite without college education	94	100	3,855	—
154	Personnel and labor relations workers	7,168	None	97	71	—	2,571
145	Miscellaneous natural scientists[2]	7,598	None	98	94	7,080	3,452

1 Regressions based upon weighted values of earnings for 50–52 weeks worked and shorter periods
2 Occupation groups combined; see Table 2 Appendix

APPENDIX TO TABLE 2

Spinners, textile combined with knitters, loopers and toppers, textile

Painters, construction and maintenance combined with paperhangers

Mine operatives and laborers (n.e.c.) combined with blasters and powdermen

Brickmasons, stonemasons, and tile setters combined with cement and concrete finishers; apprentice bricklayers and masons

Miscellaneous natural scientists combined with agricultural scientists, biological scientists, geologists and geophysicists, mathematicians, and physicists

Inspectors, scalers, and graders, log and lumber combined with sawyers

these occupations indicates that sex discrimination is even more pervasive than color discrimination. Three occupation groups have mean earnings below $3,000 and each of these occupation groups consists primarily of female workers who are underwaged. In several other occupational groups, a substantial proportion of the workers are females but only females have earning rates below the $3,000 level. Note especially the data for elevator operators, housekeepers and stewards, musicians and music teachers, and bankers, indicating differences in earning rates between males and females ranging up to $3,264.

Discrimination by color also has a powerful effect on earning rates and wage adequacy. One group stands out as an example of a culturally determined poverty occupation. Owners of automobiles use the services of garage laborers and car washers and greasers at prices that create poverty in an occupation that is highly discriminatory. The expected earning rate for this occupation is $3,118, just over the poverty level for four persons, and 53 percent of those in this group are nonwhite. Because of discrimination in earning rates, all nonwhite workers have an expected earning rate below the poverty line and thus they are underwaged. The same phenomenon occurs among gardeners and bartenders; nonwhite workers in these occupations have estimated earning rates below $3,000.

According to this analysis, discrimination by color and sex plays a very important role in the socio-economic structure of wage

Table 3

OCCUPATIONS IN WHICH EARNINGS ARE RELATED TO AGE AND OTHER VARIABLES

	Occupation		Mean Earnings	Poverty Groups (50–52 weeks earnings < 3000)	% White	% Male	Marginal Earning Rates	
Code	Title						White-Nonwhite	Male-Female
803	Laundresses, private household[2]		1104	All persons in the occupation	29	5	191	1088
875	Waiters and waitresses		1926	All females, males 14-34, 55 and over	89	17	—	1027
890	Service workers, except private household (n.e.c.)[2]		2072	All persons in the occupation	67	56	—	1197
835	Kitchen workers (n.e.c.) except private household		2236	All females, all males 14-24, or 65 and over, all males 25-34, 55-64 without high school	68	41	—	1107
902	Farm laborers, wage workers[2]		2262	All females, males with elementary education, males 14-34, 65 and over with high school	82	95	861	990
824	Charwomen and cleaners		2450	All females, all males 14-24	76	32	—	2491
842	Practical nurses[2]		2489	All females, except 25-54 with college	81	2	—	1985
810	Attendants, hospitals and other institutions		2517	All persons 14-24, all 25-34 and 65+, except college males, all females 35 and over except college	73	32	—	727

Continued Table 3

Code	Occupation Title	Mean Earnings	Poverty Groups (50–52 weeks earnings <3000)	% White	% Male	Marginal Earning Rates White-Nonwhite	Male-Female
674	Laundry and dry cleaning operatives	2617	All nonwhite females, all white females without college education, non-white males, 14-24, 65 and over with elementary education	62	35	690	1954
830	Counter and fountain workers	2696	All females, all males 14-24, 65 and over	85	37	—	1053
812	Attendants, professional and personal service (n.e.c.)[2]	2737	All persons 14-24, 65 and over; all 25-54 without high school	77	54	—	—
825	Cooks, except private household	2846	All females, all males 14-24, nonwhite males 25-34, and 65 and over without high school	72	49	518	1719
970	Lumbermen, raftsmen, and woodchoppers[1]	2926	All nonwhites 14-34, 55 and over; nonwhites 35-64 with elementary education; all whites 65 and over	68	98	1819	—
200	Farmers (owners and tenants)	2961	All persons with elementary education, whites 14-24, 65 and over, and all nonwhites with high school education	95	97	1653	—

Occupation							
Janitors and sextons	834	3076	All females, all males 14-24, 65 and over, nonwhite males 25-34, 55-64	69	89	866	1556
Cashiers	312	3129	Females 14-34, 65 and over	94	25	—	1516
Attendants, auto service and parking	632	3224	Males 14-24, 65 and over without college. Nonwhite males 25-64 with elementary education	88	99	854	2178
File clerks	320	3280	Females 14-24	92	18	—	731
Dressmakers and seamstresses, except factory[2]	651	3286	Females 14-24, 65 and over, nonwhite females, 25-54, males 14-24, 65 and over without college	86	38	996	1862
Members of the armed forces, and former members of the armed forces	555	3541	All persons 14-24 without college. All nonwhite 25-34 without college	93	99	753	—
Bank tellers	305	3567	All females with elementary education. Males 14-54 with elementary education	99	30	—	889
Weavers, textile[1]	720	3573	Males 65 and over, females 14-34, 55 and over	100	62	—	1149
Packers and wrappers	593	3587	Males 14-24 with elementary education. All females 14-24; females 25-34, 65 and over without college	90	46	—	1262
Bookkeepers	310	3604	Females 14-24, 65 and over	97	18	—	1311
Telephone operators	353	3681	Females 14-24	100	4	—	2037

Continued Table 3

Code	Occupation Title	Mean Earnings	Poverty Groups (50–52 weeks earnings < 3000)	% White	% Male	Marginal Earning Rates White-Nonwhite	Male-Female
150	Nurses, professional[2]	3708	Females with elementary education; or age 14-24 with high school	94	4	–	1414
714	Taxicab drivers and chauffeurs	3756	All persons 14-24, 65 and over. All nonwhites 25-34, 55-64	74	98	1050	–
985	Laborers (n.e.c.)[2]	3806	All nonwhite females, non-white males, and white females 14-24, 65 and over	73	97	1032	1145
342	Secretaries	3900	None	98	3	–	2329
185	Technicians, medical and dental[2]	4042	Nonwhite females without college, nonwhite males and white females 14-24 without college	88	39	1005	1094
023	Clergymen	4081	All nonwhite; whites age 14-24	96	98	2474	–
111	Librarians[2]	4134	Females 14-24	95	19	–	1692
814	Barbers	4151	All nonwhites	93	98	–	1821
631	Assemblers[2]	4191	Females 14-24, 25-34 with elementary education	91	60	–	1309
325	Office machine operators	4264	Females 14-24	93	35	–	1931

Code	Occupation	Code	Description			
350	Stock clerks and storekeepers	4283	Nonwhite males 14-24; females 14-34, 65 and over; nonwhite females without college	90	90	873	1353
370	Clerical and kindred workers (n.e.c.)²	4425	Females 14-24; females 25-34, 65 and over without college	96	48	517	1833
333	Payroll and timekeeping clerks	4428	Females with elementary education, males 65 and over with elementary education	99	38	—	1516
775	Operative and kindred workers²	4470	Females 14-24, all other nonwhite females with elementary education, white females 25-44, 55 and over with elementary education	91	77	757	1851
851	Guards, watchmen, and doorkeepers²	4470	None	95	99	—	—
343	Shipping and receiving clerks	4486	Nonwhite females; white females 14-34, 55 and over	92	89	1198	2141
995	Occupation not reported	4590	Nonwhite females without college, other	85	71	1234	1983
171	Social and welfare workers, except group 2	4628	Females 14-24	91	40	—	1119
383	Hucksters and peddlers²	4662	All persons 14-24, all females 25 and over with elementary education	100	57	—	8944
643	Checkers, examiners, and inspectors, manufacturing	4664	Females 14-24, females 25-34, 65 and over without college	97	64	—	1929

Continued Table 3

Code	Title	Mean Earnings	Poverty Groups (50–52 weeks earnings <3000)	% White	% Male	Marginal Earning Rates	
	Occupation					White-Nonwhite	Male-Female
182	Teachers, elementary school	4684	Nonwhite females age 14-24	89	29	977	1024
472	Mechanics and repairmen, automobile[2]	4750	Nonwhites 14-24, 55 and over	93	100	1203	–
715	Truck and tractor drivers	4774	Nonwhites 14-24, and 55 and over with elementary education	87	100	1622	–
650	Deliverymen and routemen	4810	All nonwhite females, white females 14-34, 55 and over, nonwhite males 14-24, 65 and over	93	99	1686	2496
675	Meatcutters, except slaughter and packing house	4931	All females	95	97	–	3405
394	Salesmen and sales clerks (n.e.c.)	5015	Nonwhite females, non-white males 14-24, without college, white males 14-24 with elementary education	98	73	1183	3560
480	Mechanics and repairmen (n.e.c.)[2]	5076	Nonwhite females 14-24, 65 and over; nonwhite males 14-24, 65 and over without college	93	99	1156	1116
712	Stationary firemen	5176	Nonwhites 14-24, 65 and over	90	100	1584	–

490

184	5192	Teachers (n.e.c.)	Females 14-24, 65 and over	100	68	—	1453
411	5214	Carpenters[2]	Females 14-24, all other females without college	96	99	—	3644
721	5277	Welders and flame cutters	All nonwhite females with elementary education; or 14-44 with high school; nonwhite males, white females 14-24 without college	91	98	1033	1797
340	5309	Postal clerks	Nonwhite females 14-44	81	88	813	1821
425	5335	Excavating, grading and machinery operators	None	95	100	—	—
545	5389	Craftsmen and kindred workers (n.e.c.)[2]	Females 14-24, 65 and over	96	89	—	2445
853	5395	Policemen and detectives[2]	14-24 with elementary education	95	98	—	—
525	5566	Tinsmith, coppersmiths, and sheet metal workers[2]	None	92	99	—	—
191	5590	Technicians, other engineering and physical sciences	All females 14-24; males 14-24 and females 25-34 with elementary education	99	92	—	1426
465	5619	Machinists[2]	Nonwhite females, white females 14-24	97	99	1297	2344
192	5736	Technicians (n.e.c.)[2]	Females 14-34	95	88	—	3037
453	5849	Linemen and servicemen, telegraph, telephone, and power	Nonwhite females, nonwhite males and white females 14-34	100	98	3326	2125

Continued Table 3

Occupation		Mean Earnings	Poverty Groups (50–52 weeks earnings < 3000)	% White	% Male	Marginal Earning Rates	
Code	Title					White-Nonwhite	Male-Female
014	Artists and art teachers	5943	All nonwhite females	96	82	4056	–
190	Technicians, electrical and electronic[2]	5956	All persons 65 and over; females 14-24, 55-64	99	95	–	1982
414	Compositors and typesetters[2]	5980	All nonwhite females; white females and non-white males 14-24, 65 and over	97	92	2680	3384
270	Officials and administrators (n.e.c.) public and administration[2]	5996	Females with elementary education; males 14-24 with elementary education	100	78	–	1995
713	Switchmen, railroad[1]	6032	None	98	98	–	–
253	Credit men[1]	6155	Females 14-34	100	76	–	3971
260	Inspectors, public administration	6194	All persons 14-24; females 25-44, 65 and over	97	97	–	3298
510	Plumbers and pipe fitters[2]	6200	Nonwhites 14-24 without college	97	100	2452	–
512	Pressmen and plate printers, printing[2]	6225	Females 14-34	98	97	–	3295
183	Teachers, secondary schools	6296	All persons 14-24 without college; females 25-54 without college	93	72	–	2426

430	Foremen (n.e.c.)	Nonwhite females without college	99	94	1443	2719
195	Professional, technical and kindred workers (n.e.c.)[2]	All persons 14-24; nonwhite females 25-34, 65 and over	97	86	1947	1900
250	Buyers and department heads, store	Females 14-24; females 25-34, 65 and over without college	99	79	–	3112
393	Real estate agents and brokers	Females 14-24, 65 and over	98	84	–	3136
385	Insurance agents, brokers and underwriters[2]	Females 14-34; females without college 35-44, 65 and over; males without college 14-24	97	91	–	4350
520	Stationary engineers	None	99	100	–	–
001	Accountants and auditors	Females 14-24	97	85	–	1853
021	Chemists	All persons 14-24, without college; females 25-34, 65 and over without college	96	92	–	1959
060	Professors and instructors, subject not specified[2]	Age 14-24	97	89	–	–
454	Locomotive engineers[2]	None	99	100	–	–
290	Managers, officials, and proprietors (n.e.c.)[2]	Nonwhite females 14-34 and all others without college; white female without college	98	89	2363	3844

Continued Table 3

Occupation		Mean Earnings	Poverty Groups (50–52 weeks earnings < 3000)	% White	% Male	Marginal Earning Rates	
Code	Title					White-Nonwhite	Male-Female
083	Engineers, electrical	8253	None	99	100	—	—
085	Engineers, mechanical	8300	None	99	99	—	—
093	Engineers (n.e.c.)[2]	8627	None	98	99	—	—
105	Lawyers and judges	9112	All persons 14-24; females 25-34, 55 and over	99	94	—	5785

1   Regressions based on weighted values of earnings for 50–52 weeks worked and shorter periods
2   Occupation groups combined; see Table 3 Appendix

494

Laundresses, private household combined with private household workers (n.e.c.)

Service workers except private household combined with boarding and lodging housekeepers

Farm laborers, wage workers combined with farm foremen; farm service workers, self employed

Practical nurses combined with midwives

Attendants, professionals and personal service (n.e.c.) combined with attendants, recreation and amusement; bootblacks; ushers, recreation and amusement

Dressmakers and seamstresses, except factory combined with tailors and tailoresses, milliners

Nurses, professional combined with nurses, student professional

Laborers (n.e.c.) combined with carpenters' helpers, except logging and mining; fishermen and oystermen; teamsters; truck drivers' helpers

Technicians, medical and dental combined with dietitians and nutritionists

Librarians combined with attendants and assistants, library

Assemblers combined with graders and sorters, manufacturing

Clerical and kindred workers (n.e.c.) combined with baggagemen, transportation; collectors, bill and account; telegraph operators

Operatives and kindred workers (n.e.c.) combined with apprentices, building trades (n.e.c.); apprentices, metal working trades (n.e.c.); apprentices, other specified trades; apprentices, trade not specified, asbestos and insulation workers, boatmen, canalmen, and lock-keepers; power station operators; sailors and deck hands

Guards, watchmen, and doorkeepers combined with watchmen (crossing) and bridge tenders

Social and welfare workers, except group combined with recreation and group workers; religious workers

Hucksters and peddlers combined with auctioneers; demonstrators

Mechanics and repairmen, automobile combined with apprentice auto mechanics

Mechanics and repairmen (n.e.c.) combined with loom fixers; mechanics and repairmen, office machine; mechanics and repairmen, railroad and car shop; apprentice mechanics, except auto

Carpenters combined with apprentice carpenters

Craftsmen and kindred workers (n.e.c.) combined with bookbinders, decorators and window dressers; furriers; glaziers; jewelers, watchmakers, goldsmiths, and silversmiths; millers, grain, flour, feed, etc.; motion picture projectionists; roofers and slaters; shoemakers and repairers, except factory; stone cutters and stone carvers

Policemen and detectives combined with marshals and constables; sheriffs and bailiffs

Tinsmiths, coppersmiths, and sheet metal workers combined with boilermakers

Machinists combined with apprentice machinists and toolmakers

Technicians (n.e.c.) combined with photographers

Technicians, electrical and electronic combined with radio operators

Compositors and typesetters combined with electrotypers and stereotypers; engravers, except photoengravers; photoengravers and lithographers

Officials and adminstrators (n.e.c.) public adminstration combined with postmasters

Plumbers and pipefitters combined with apprentice plumbers and pipefitters

Pressmen and plate printers, printing combined with apprentices, printing trades

Professional, technical, and kindred workers (n.e.c.) combined with actors and actresses; airplane pilots and navigators; authors; chiropractors, dancers and dancing teachers; entertainers (n.e.c.); farm and home management advisers; foresters and conservationists; funeral directors and embalmers; optometrists; osteopaths; surveyors; therapists and healers (n.e.c.); veterinarians

496

Insurance agents, brokers, and underwriters combined with stock and bond salesmen

Professors and instructors, subject not specified combined with college presidents and deans; professors and instructors of agricultural sciences; biological sciences; chemistry; economics; engineering; geology and geophysics; mathematics; medical sciences; physics; psychology; statistics; natural sciences (n.e.c.); social sciences (n.e.c.); nonscientific subjects.

Locomotive engineers combined with locomotive firemen

Managers, officials, and proprietors (n.e.c.) combined with farm managers; conductors, railroad; floor men and floor managers, store; managers and superintendents, building; officers pilots, pursers, and engineers, ship; officials, lodge, society, union, etc.

Engineers (n.e.c.) combined with architects; engineers, aeronautical; engineers, chemical; engineers, metallurgical and metallurgists; engineers, mining.

rates that produce poverty level earnings among the fully employed. The measures of the effect of discrimination by color presented here are a small increment on a mountain of other evidence that nonwhites do not receive pay equal to that of whites for similar kinds of work performed.

Perhaps less well understood in terms of seeking ways to alleviate poverty is the importance of the inferior role to which women are relegated in the labor market. The "female-headed family" remains one of the more important subgroups of the poverty population. At the same time, since it is now widely accepted that women are an important segment of our total labor force, we expect that by working, women should be able to support themselves and, in most cases of necessity, their children as well, independently of a male breadwinner. The facts that many women are ill-prepared for any other than the most menial tasks in the hierarchy of jobs and that, even among the higher occupational levels, women are paid less than men, have been overlooked in our social strategy.

OCCUPATIONS IN WHICH EARNINGS ARE RELATED TO PRODUCTIVITY AND DISCRIMINATION

In this group of occupations, the regression estimates were significantly different from zero for both age variables and also for either or both of the dummy shift variables indicating discrimination by sex or color. In 14 of the 90 occupation groups shown in Table 3 the expected value of the earning rate is below $3,000 but in only two of these groups, laundresses and service workers, all persons have estimated earnings below the poverty level. In all other groups estimated full year earning rates fall below $3,000 only in specific subgroups defined by age, color, and sex. In several of the service occupations which have very low average earning rates, the estimated earning rates for all females fall below the poverty line.

Youth is a major factor associated with earning rates below the poverty level in almost all of the occupation groups. It is not at all unusual for persons 14–24 to be underwaged especially if they happen to be female or nonwhite.

OCCUPATIONS IN WHICH EARNING RATES ARE NOT RELATED TO PRODUCTIVITY OR DISCRIMINATION

In 19 occupation groups the regression model proved to be of no value in explaining variations in earning rates (*see* Table 4). Some of the occupations with very low earning rates seem to be dead-end, poverty-level jobs dominated by selective employment, dead-end in the sense that being older and presumably more experienced does not bring higher earning rates. The jobs that are most likely to produce poverty are housekeepers, receptionists, and attendants in physicians' and dentists' offices – all with very high rates of female employment. Porters, with a very high rate of nonwhite employment, fall in the same subpoverty category.

Table 4

OCCUPATIONS IN WHICH EARNINGS ARE NOT RELATED TO AGE OR OTHER VARIABLES

Code	Occupation Title	Mean Earnings	Percent White	Percent Male
903	Farm laborers, unpaid family workers[1]	$ 935	92	81
802	Housekeepers, private household	$ 1,079	71	1
341	Receptionists	$ 2,801	99	0
303	Attendants, physician's and dentists' offices[1]	$ 2,882	100	6
841	Porters	$ 2,924	20	100
360	Typists	$ 3,388	94	7
345	Stenographers	$ 3,702	97	4
410	Cabinetmakers[1]	$ 4,606	93	100
641	Bus drivers[2]	$ 4,735	93	95
492	Molders, metal[2]	$ 5,273	80	98
354	Ticket, station, and express agents	$ 5,489	100	82
450	Inspectors (n.e.c.)	$ 5,588	100	98
471	Mechanics and repairmen, airplane	$ 6,137	94	100
491	Millwrights[2]	$ 6,332	98	100
160	Pharmacists	$ 7,383	99	96
380	Advertising agents and salesmen[2]	$ 7,846	100	83
072	Designers	$ 8,030	95	88
175	Miscellaneous social scientists[2]	$ 8,705	100	80
071	Dentists	$ 12,536	100	100

1   Regressions based upon weighted values of earnings for 50–52 weeks worked and shorter periods

2   Occupation groups combined; see Table 4 Appendix

APPENDIX TO TABLE 4

Bus drivers are combined with conductors, bus and street railway; motormen, street, subway, and elevated railway

Molders, metal are combined with blacksmiths; forgemen and hammermen; heat treaters, annealers, and temperers; furnacemen, smeltermen and pourers; heaters, metal

Millwrights are combined with job setters, metal

Advertising agents and salesmen are combined with public relations men and publicity writers

Miscellaneous social scientists are combined with economists; psychologists; statisticians and actuaries

SUMMARY

The decade of the sixties has passed since the time period for which the earnings model generated estimates of wage adequacy. Our society experimented bravely with innovations in social policy over the decade but, we suggest, little has changed.

Our "war on poverty" brought a new public awareness of social and economic deprivation. We have tried to change the characteristics of those who are deprived through programs of community action, manpower training, and education. The basic objective of all of these social experiments has been to apply a treatment to people that would prepare them to interact with the market system. Our good intentions in these efforts could conceivably result in an improvement in welfare for the disadvantaged if, at the same time, we were willing to take other policy actions that would maintain a high level of demand for labor. The price of maintaining tight labor markets would be continuing inflation, judged to be excessive, or continuing price-wage control mechanisms.

So we continue to maintain a schizophrenic posture with respect to social welfare policy. We declare, sometimes loudly and sometimes softly, that we want to improve the lot of the disadvantaged and deprived. But we admonish the poor to help themselves by working hard, and we work-test them to make sure that they deserve our assistance. At the same time we endure a market system that has built into it a segment in which the full time earning rates for some workers are so low that poverty is a natural result of the functioning of the system. Which alternative social policy might be best is perhaps not clear, but there must be one that is better.

REFERENCE

Wilensky, H.L., and C. Lebeaux, *Industrial Society and Social Welfare*, New York: The Free Press, 1965.

500

Birth Control and
Economic Well-Being

JAMES D. SMITH

The will of the American people has been torn between saving face in Southeast Asia and fighting poverty at home. Our adversaries were more persistent than anticipated, and we have been unsuccessful in both ventures. We are gradually withdrawing from Southeast Asia, and we have been in full retreat on the home front for several years. Indeed, the number of poor increased by 1.2 million during the past year.

We refer to the annual transfer payment which would be required to bring all poor families up to the poverty line as the aggregate dollar deficit. The deficit has been variously estimated at from ten to fifty billion dollars. The wide range results from different definitions of poverty and assumptions about changes in labor force participation which might be induced by such a transfer. Measures of the numbers of poor persons and families are, of course, valid indices of the extent of poverty, and we employ them, but they do not take account of how far below its poverty line a given family is. A program which narrowed, but did not close, the gap between poor families' incomes and poverty lines would contribute to the reduction of poverty but would not be reflected in changes in the count of persons or families because they would still be poor. The aggregate dollar deficit would, however, be reduced by the program and for that reason may be a better index of program effectiveness than are head counts. Anti-poverty strategies can mostly be placed in two categories: those which attempt to fill the deficit with transfer dollars and those which are aimed at narrowing the width of the gap by increasing the earning power of the poor. The most promising of the transfer strategies is the yet unimplemented negative income tax. Although the negative income tax is basically a transfer scheme, its con-templated form would provide incentive to employment. Programs designed to increase the earning power of the poor range from retraining programs for adults to Head Start for the very young.

Of late, OEO has shown an increasing interest in strategies which decrease the gap by decreasing needs. The most important of these strategies is a birth control program. Since poverty is defined as an income below that needed to maintain a family standard of living dependent upon the age, sex and number of family members, a birth control program which reduced family size of poor and potentially poor families would reduce the deficit which must be filled with earnings and/or transfers.

In this essay a test of the limits of a birth control program in reducing the aggregate deficit income of the poor and their num-bers is undertaken. A simulation of birth control programs in ef-fect from one to ten years is performed using a 1970 sample population. The simulation is retrospective in that it takes a current population back in time and brings it forward again. It does this by operating on the known ages of children in families. A three-year-old-child in year n implies a birth in year $n-3$. If we postulate a birth control program in effect in year $n-3$ which includes a potential conception of a child with the family charac-teristics of this three-year-old, the simulation can prevent the birth and thus results in a population in year n which does not include the three-year-old-child.

THE SIMULATION MODEL

Two assumptions, one behavioral and one technological are made in the model. The behavioral assumption is that given a choice between conceiving a child who would be born into pover-

502

ty and not having that child, parents will opt for the latter. The technological assumption is that an acceptable, 100 percent effective contraceptive technology is available. Obviously, neither assumption is a perfect representation of reality, but reflects conditions within the affect of society; and both, it is believed, can be rather closely attained.

The simulation was run on a file constructed from the 1970 wave of the *Panel Study of Income Dynamics* [1]. The file has certain defects as a national sample, but they are considered minor for the level of precision required in the task at hand.[1] The main requirement was that micro-data about family characteristics, most importantly, age and sex of each member, and family income, be available.

The file contained a poverty score which was the ratio of family money income to family needs based in 1966 prices. The poverty score and the components of need were first adjusted to reflect 1969 prices. The poverty score used in this paper is higher than that used by OEO and other government agencies. Like the well-known Orshansky scores [2] it starts with a normative food need standard, which takes into account family size and the age and sex of its members. Unlike the OEO food need standard which uses the USDA economy budget, a budget intended for short-term use, the standard used here is based on the USDA "Low-Cost Plan" given in the *Family Economics Review*, March, 1967. The annual food costs from the low income budget are presented below after adjustments for inflation.

---

[1] The file is the residual after three years of a panel which started in 1967 as a representative sample of the U.S. noninstitutional population. Over the three years, substantial panel mortality took place. The sample population in 1970 was about 60 percent of its original size. However, studies conducted by the Survey Research Center, University of Michigan, indicate that families lost from the panel do not differ significantly from those retained. The sample weights in the file are those for the initial population adjusted only for first wave sample lossed, so estimates of aggregates tend to understate true values.

INDIVIDUAL LOW COST FOOD STANDARD

Annual amounts

Age	Male	Female
Under 4	229.16	229.16
4– 6	270.30	270.30
7– 9	323.18	323.18
10–12	376.06	370.19
13–15	434.82	405.44
16–20	551.21	423.07
21–35	440.70	381.94
36–55	405.44	370.19
56 and older	370.19	317.30

The above food cost for family members were summed to arrive at an annual food cost for the entire family, and then the USDA two-step adjustment, to take account of economies of scale in the purchase of family sustenance, was applied as follows to arrive at a need standard.

Single person	Food	Cost x 1.20 x 4.89 = Need Standard
Two persons	Food	Cost x 1.10 x 3.70 = Need Standard
Three persons	Food	Cost x 1.05 x 3.00 = Need Standard
Four persons	Food	Cost x 1.00 x 3.00 = Need Standard
Five persons	Food	Cost x .95 x 3.00 = Need Standard
Six persons or more	Food	Cost x .90 x 3.00 = Need Standard

For families headed by a person whose first or second job was on a farm, the need standard was divided through by 1.25 to compensate for lower costs in rural areas.

Table 1 displays the population by number of children living at home in the spring of 1970. The table classifies families, and persons in those families, by whether or not they were poor according to our definition. Poor families are those for which the ratio of family income to total family needs is less than 1. The term family is used to include one-person families – unrelated individuals living alone or in groups. Two columns in the Table are of special interest. In the column labeled *Dollar Surplus* we have taken the dollar income of nonpoor families and subtracted from it the need standard. It is thus the amount of income they have over and above what they need to be just above the poverty level. The other column *Deficit Dollars* shows amounts by which families are be-

504

Table 1

DISTRIBUTION OF FAMILIES AND UNRELATED INDIVIDUALS BY NUMBER OF CHILDREN IN FAMILY* AND POVERTY STATUS, 1970

Number of Children	All Families		Nonpoor Families		Surplus Dollars (billions)	Poor Families		Deficit Dollars (billions)
	Families (millions)	Persons (millions)	Families (millions)	Persons (millions)		Families (millions)	Persons (millions)	
0	29.7	52.1	22.7	40.4	$136.3	7.0	11.8	$ 9.2
1	9.6	30.1	7.1	22.3	41.8	2.5	7.8	5.8
2	9.1	37.4	6.0	24.6	36.4	3.1	12.8	8.9
3	5.0	25.8	2.8	14.6	21.2	2.2	11.3	8.3
4	2.9	17.6	1.1	7.1	8.1	1.8	10.6	7.7
5	1.4	10.3	1.0	7.1	4.8	0.5	3.2	1.6
6	0.9	7.2	0.5	3.9	2.8	0.4	3.4	1.0
7	0.4	3.5	0.2	1.8	1.5	0.2	1.7	0.7
8 or more	0.1	0.9	**	0.4	0.2	0.1	0.5	0.3
Not Known	0.2	2.0	**	0.5	0.3	0.1	1.4	0.5
Total	59.2	187.0	41.3	122.6	$253.6	17.9	64.4	$44.0

* Unrelated individuals living alone or with others are considered one-person families.
** Less than 50,000 million.

low the poverty level. The sum of that column is the amount which, if distributed to poor families in a frictionless system, would just get them out of poverty. As pointed out in an earlier footnote, the weights included in this file do not take account of sample depletion after the first year. Therefore, the actual values shown underestimate the true amounts. This does not trouble us in assessing the relationships between birth control and poverty in our simulation model, but the underestimation should be kept in mind when using the absolute estimates. An estimate of the correct aggregates can be had by multiplying the figures shown by 1.16, the reciprocal of the combined retention rates in the sample population for the two years following the weighting year. Doing this produces an estimate of a total population of families (including unrelated individuals) of 65.1 million. This compares very favorably with the 1970 Census estimate of 65.7 million [3, No. 76, p. 47]. The total dollar surplus resulting from this adjustment is $294.2 billion and the total dollar deficit, $51.0 billion. This deficit is substantially higher than the deficit which results from the application to the OEO poverty lines which use the economy food standard to CPS data. The deficit reported by the Census is only $10.1 billion [3, No. 76, p. 12].

The simulation was carried out by passing the file and searching each family record for a child aged one and a poverty score of less than one. If those conditions existed, the child was deleted from the record, thus meeting the assumptions of the model that a family would opt to contracept rather than bring a child into poverty. After the child was deleted, the family's need standard and poverty score were recomputed. The full pass constituted one conception year of the birth control program. That is, it changed the population in 1970 to conform to what would have been the case had the birth control program been operative in a period roughly nine to twenty-one months prior to the spring of 1970. The statistics of Table 1 were then recomputed. They appear here as Table 2. The next pass of the modified population repeated the same operation as the first. Thus, large families who were poor in simulation year n and had a child of age n would have that child deleted. Each successive simulation pass then, as it were, pushed the starting date of the birth control program one year further into the past.

506

Table 2

DISTRIBUTION OF FAMILIES AND UNRELATED INDIVIDUALS BY NUMBER OF CHILDREN IN FAMILY* AND POVERTY STATUS, 1970, AFTER SIMULATION OF ONE-YEAR BIRTH CONTROL PROGRAM

Number of Children	All Families Families (millions)	All Families Persons (millions)	Nonpoor Families Families (millions)	Nonpoor Families Persons (millions)	Surplus Dollars (billions)	Poor Families Families (millions)	Poor Families Persons (millions)	Deficit Dollars (billions)
0	29.7	52.1	22.7	40.4	$136.4	7.0	11.7	$ 9.2
1	9.6	27.9	7.4	21.5	43.9	2.2	6.4	4.9
2	9.1	35.7	6.2	24.1	38.1	2.9	11.6	8.3
3	5.0	25.0	2.8	14.4	21.8	2.2	10.6	7.7
4	2.9	17.0	1.1	6.8	8.1	1.8	10.2	7.7
5	1.4	10.1	0.9	6.5	4.5	0.5	3.6	1.8
6	0.9	7.1	0.5	3.8	2.8	0.4	3.2	1.0
7	0.4	3.4	0.5	1.7	1.5	0.2	1.7	0.6
8 or more	0.1	0.9	**	0.4	0.2	0.1	0.5	0.3
Not Known	0.2	1.9	**	0.5	0.3	0.1	0.4	0.5
Total	59.2	181.1	41.9	120.3	$257.6	17.3	60.8	$42.1

*   Unrelated individuals living alone or with others are considered one-person families.
** Less than 50,000 million.

A comparison of Tables 1 and 2 shows that the numbers of poor persons declined from 60.8 million to 56.5 million. The decline took place in families with varying numbers of children, but the largest declines took place in families with from one to three children. This suggests that a larger proportion of small families who are poor are bunched up just below their poverty lines than are poor larger families. The cause of this is that large families have larger income deficits so that the deletion of one child is more likely to reduce the number of poor persons by only one person. Smaller families, with smaller income deficits, are more likely to have the entire family lifted out of poverty by the deletion of a child, thus, the reduction in the number of poor by the contraception of one birth is more likely to be greater than one.[2] Of course, no reduction in the number of poor people in families with zero children took place. It is, of course, reasonable to believe that there are older couples now poor, who raised large families by consuming a lifetime of income and are now poor without any accumulated goods or financial savings. It would require a more elaborate simulation, over a longer span of years than we have used, to include them in the effect.

In Table 3 we summarize each of the simulated 1970 populations which emerge from birth control simulation periods which cover from one to ten conception years. Over the ten-year period there is a steady decline in poor families, poor persons, and deficit income. Comparing the present, simulation period 0, with the present, simulation period 10, it is apparent that a substantial

---

[2] The mean income deficit computed by the OEO method on families estimated in the CPS in 1970 by number of children under 18 is as follows. *See* [3, No. 67, p. 80f.]:

Number of Family Members Under 18	Mean Income Deficit
0	$ 850
1	1216
2	1305
3	1589
4	1733
5	1844
6+	2170

Table 3

SUMMARY OF TEN-YEAR BIRTH CONTROL SIMULATION

Simulation Period Years	Poor Families (millions)	Poor Persons (millions)	Dollar Deficit (billions)
0	17.9	64.4	$ 43.0
1	17.3	60.8	42.1
2	16.5	56.5	39.0
3	15.8	52.8	36.1
4	14.9	48.6	33.7
5	14.3	44.9	31.4
6	13.7	41.6	28.6
7	12.8	37.0	26.6
8	12.2	33.8	24.7
9	11.6	30.3	22.2
10	10.7	26.0	19.4

diminution of the dimensions of poverty has taken place. The number of poor families has declined 40 percent, from 17.9 to 10.7. Even more striking reductions in the numbers of poor persons, 70 percent, and in the deficit, 55 percent, are found. Detailed tables of the ongoing simulation are found in the Appendix. In Table 4 characteristics of the poverty populations before and after a ten-conception-year simulation are presented. As would be expected the impact of the birth control program is to make poverty much less of a young family problem. The proportion of the poor that are young and nonwhite decreases, but the change in the nonwhite component is less than had been expected.

Comparing the figures in Table 1 with the ten-year simulation, it is clear that large families had substantial declines in their average deficit, but because they are relatively less prevalent than families with fewer numbers of children, the absolute decline in the deficit is greater for the latter. A summary of the changes by number of children in the family is presented in Table 5.

Table 4

DISTRIBUTION OF POVERTY AND DEFICIT BY SEX, AGE, AND RACE, 1970, BEFORE AND AFTER 10-CONCEPTION-YEAR SIMULATION (FAMILIES AND PERSONS IN MILLIONS)

Sex and Age Of Head	White Families	Persons	Deficit (billions)	Nonwhite Families	Persons	Deficit (billions)
Before Simulation						
Males						
<20	0.4	0.9	$ 0.9	0.1	0.3	$ 0.4
20<30	2.3	8.0	4.7	0.5	1.9	1.3
30<40	1.9	9.7	5.4	0.6	3.8	1.8
40<50	1.5	8.3	4.4	0.5	3.3	1.6
50<60	3.8	9.8	7.3	0.9	3.4	3.0
Females						
<20	0.2	0.3	0.3	**	0.2	0.2
20<30	0.3	0.8	0.5	0.3	1.2	0.9
30<40	0.4	1.7	1.6	0.4	1.9	1.5
40<50	0.5	2.1	2.0	0.4	1.7	1.8
50<60	2.1	3.4	2.8	0.6	1.5	1.5
After Simulation						
Males						
<20	0.3	0.7	$ 0.1	0.1	0.2	$ 0.2
20<30	0.9	1.6	1.2	0.1	0.3	0.2
30<40	0.3	1.1	0.6	0.2	0.8	0.3
40<50	0.6	2.8	1.6	0.3	1.4	0.7
50<60	3.5	8.3	5.9	0.6	1.7	1.7
Females						
<20	0.2	0.2	0.1	**	0.1	0.1
20<30	0.2	0.1	0.1	0.1	0.1	0.1
30<40	0.1	0.2	0.2	0.1	0.6	0.4
40<50	0.3	0.9	1.0	0.3	0.9	1.0
50<60	2.0	2.8	2.1	0.6	1.2	1.1

** Less than 50,000

510

Table 5

CHANGES IN NUMBERS OF POOR AND INCOME DEFICITS AFTER 10-YEAR SIMULATION BY NUMBER OF CHILDREN IN FAMILY

Children	Before Birth Control			After Birth Control			Decline		
	Families	Persons	Deficit	Families	Persons	Deficit	Families	Persons	Deficit
0	7.0	11.8	$ 9.2	7.0	11.8	$ 9.2	0	0	$0
1	2.5	7.8	5.8	1.7	4.9	3.8	0.8	2.9	2.0
2	3.1	12.8	8.9	1.2	4.8	3.5	1.9	8.0	5.4
3	2.2	11.3	8.2	0.5	2.1	1.8	1.7	9.2	6.4
4	1.8	10.6	7.7	0.1	0.6	0.5	1.7	10.0	7.2
5	0.5	3.2	1.6	**	0.3	0.1	**	2.9	1.5
6	0.4	3.4	1.0	0.1	0.8	0.2	0.3	2.6	0.8
7	0.2	1.7	0.7	**	0.3	0.1	**	1.4	0.6
8 or more	0.1	0.5	0.3	**	0.1	0.1	**	0.4	0.2
Not Known	0.1	1.4	0.5	**	0.2	0.1	**	1.2	0.4
Total	17.9	64.4	$44.0	10.7	26.0	$19.4	7.2	38.4	24.6

There is little that appears to be needed on the technological side. At least the course and pace of biological science is toward a rapid development of all the contraceptive power society may wish to use. Nor does there appear to be an economic problem in making the technology available to those who wish it. The problem which policy must address is the behavioral one. What can be done to induce people to want to use the technnology, to forgo conceptions which produce poverty families or bring children into extant poverty families.

Economists have long recognized the incentive provided by money. Some observers of the problem posed by family size on attempts to reduce poverty have suggested that the federal income tax exemption for dependents be tapered so that after three or four children the exemption dropped to zero for additional children. As an incentive scheme, this approach has two defects. First, for the bulk of the poor, it would make little difference since their incomes are already nearly fully exempt. For the near poor, it imposes a serious penalty for past errors which are not correctable.

An alternative approach would be to pay people not to conceive. Let us say that the society decides that it is worth $200 to have a poor family not conceive a child in a year. Let us further say that we agree to pay the $200 to every couple with a wife under fifty and to female heads under fifty who have one child, if they had an income no greater than 150 percent, of the government established poverty line. Each year the taxpaying unit completes its federal income tax form, it would certify that no birth had taken place during the preceding year. When the return was processed, the $200 would either be remitted to the taxpayer or applied to the reduction of tax due. No change would be made in the present exemption system. If a family had a child, they would lose the payment for nonconception, but they would be entitled to normal exemption. Ideally, an aborted birth by natural or unnatural means would be treated in the same manner as a nonconception.

DISTRIBUTION OF FAMILIES AND UNRELATED INDIVIDUALS BY NUMBER OF CHILDREN IN FAMILY* AND POVERTY STATUS, 1970, AFTER SIMULATION OF TWO-YEAR BIRTH CONTROL PROGRAM

Number of Children	All Families		Nonpoor Families			Poor Families		Deficit
	Families (millions)	Persons (millions)	Families (millions)	Persons (millions)	Surplus Dollars (billions)	Families (millions)	Persons (millions)	Dollars (billions)
0	29.7	52.1	22.7	40.4	$136.4	7.0	11.7	$ 9.2
1	9.6	26.9	7.5	20.8	46.4	2.1	6.1	4.7
2	9.1	34.8	6.4	24.1	40.4	2.7	10.7	7.7
3	5.0	24.1	3.2	15.3	23.6	1.8	8.8	6.6
4	2.9	16.6	1.2	7.3	8.9	1.6	9.3	6.6
5	1.4	10.0	0.9	6.5	4.4	0.5	3.4	1.8
6	0.9	6.9	0.5	3.9	2.9	0.4	3.0	1.0
7	0.4	3.4	0.2	1.7	1.5	0.2	1.7	0.6
8 or more	0.1	0.9	**	0.4	0.2	0.1	0.5	0.3
Not Known	0.1	1.8	**	0.5	0.3	0.1	1.3	0.5
Total	59.2	177.4	42.7	120.9	$265.1	16.5	56.5	$39.0

* Unrelated individuals living alone or with others are considered one-person families.
** Less than 50,000 million.

APPENDIX

DISTRIBUTION OF FAMILIES AND UNRELATED INDIVIDUALS BY NUMBER OF CHILDREN IN FAMILY* AND POVERTY STATUS, 1970, AFTER SIMULATION OF THREE-YEAR BIRTH CONTROL PROGRAM

Number of Children	All Families		Nonpoor Families			Poor Families		
	Families (millions)	Persons (millions)	Families (millions)	Persons (millions)	Surplus Dollars (billions)	Families (millions)	Persons (millions)	Deficit Dollars (billions)
0	29.7	52.1	22.7	40.4	$136.5	7.0	11.7	$ 9.2
1	9.6	26.3	7.6	20.4	48.3	2.1	5.9	4.6
2	9.1	33.6	6.6	23.8	44.3	2.5	9.7	7.0
3	5.0	23.3	3.4	15.6	25.9	1.6	7.7	5.7
4	2.9	16.1	1.4	8.0	9.8	1.4	8.1	5.6
5	1.4	9.7	0.9	6.4	4.4	0.5	3.3	1.7
6	0.9	6.8	0.5	3.8	2.9	0.4	2.9	1.0
7	0.4	3.3	0.2	1.7	1.6	0.2	1.6	0.6
8 or more	0.1	0.8	**	0.4	0.2	0.1	0.5	0.2
Not Known	0.2	1.8	**	0.5	0.4	0.1	1.3	0.4
Total	59.2	173.8	43.5	121.0	$274.4	15.8	52.8	$36.1

* Unrelated individuals living alone or with others are considred one-person families.

** Less than 50,000 million.

DISTRIBUTION OF FAMILIES AND UNRELATED INDIVIDUALS BY NUMBER OF CHILDREN IN FAMILY* AND POVERTY STATUS, 1970, AFTER SIMULATION OF TWO-YEAR BIRTH CONTROL PROGRAM

Number of Children	All Families		Nonpoor Families			Poor Families		
	Families (millions)	Persons (millions)	Families (millions)	Persons (millions)	Surplus Dollars (billions)	Families (millions)	Persons (millions)	Deficit Dollars (billions)
0	29.7	52.0	22.7	40.4	$136.5	7.0	11.7	$ 9.2
1	9.6	25.9	7.6	20.2	49.6	2.0	5.8	4.5
2	9.1	32.3	6.9	23.6	48.4	2.2	8.7	6.5
3	5.0	22.4	3.6	15.7	28.8	1.4	6.7	5.1
4	2.9	15.5	1.7	8.6	11.7	1.2	6.9	4.6
5	1.4	9.4	1.0	6.5	4.8	0.4	2.9	1.6
6	0.9	6.6	0.5	3.8	2.9	0.4	2.8	0.9
7	0.4	3.2	0.2	1.7	1.6	0.2	1.6	0.6
8 or more	0.1	0.8	**	0.4	0.2	**	0.4	0.2
Not Known	0.2	1.7	**	0.5	0.4	0.1	1.2	0.4
Total	59.2	169.9	44.3	121.4	$284.9	14.9	48.5	$33.6

* Unrelated individuals living alone or with others are considered one-person families.

** Less than 50,000 million.

APPENDIX

DISTRIBUTION OF FAMILIES AND UNRELATED INDIVIDUALS BY NUMBER OF CHILDREN IN FAMILY* AND POVERTY STATUS, 1970, AFTER SIMULATION OF FIVE-YEAR BIRTH CONTROL PROGRAM

Number of Children	All Families		Nonpoor Families			Poor Families		
	Families (millions)	Persons (millions)	Families (millions)	Persons (millions)	Surplus Dollars (billions)	Families (millions)	Persons (millions)	Deficit Dollars (billions)
0	29.7	52.0	22.7	40.3	$136.4	7.0	11.7	$ 9.0
1	9.6	25.6	7.7	20.0	51.0	1.9	5.6	4.4
2	9.1	31.3	7.0	23.1	52.1	2.0	8.2	6.3
3	5.0	21.5	3.8	15.8	31.7	1.2	5.7	4.6
4	2.9	14.8	1.8	9.0	13.3	1.1	5.9	3.7
5	1.4	9.0	1.1	6.5	5.2	0.4	2.5	1.3
6	0.9	6.4	0.5	4.0	3.0	0.3	2.4	0.9
7	0.4	3.1	0.2	1.6	1.7	0.2	1.5	0.5
8 or more	0.1	0.8	**	0.4	0.3	**	0.4	0.2
Not Known	0.2	1.7	**	0.5	0.4	0.1	1.1	0.4
Total	59.2	166.0	45.0	121.1	$295.0	14.3	44.9	$31.4

* Unrelated individuals living alone or with others are considered one-person families.
** Less than 50,000 million.

continued APPENDIX

DISTRIBUTION OF FAMILIES AND UNRELATED INDIVIDUALS BY NUMBER OF CHILDREN IN FAMILY* AND POVERTY STATUS, 1970, AFTER SIMULATION OF SIX-YEAR BIRTH CONTROL PROGRAM

Number of Children	All Families		Nonpoor Families			Poor Families		
	Families (millions)	Persons (millions)	Families (millions)	Persons (millions)	Surplus Dollars (billions)	Families (millions)	Persons (millions)	Surplus Dollars (billions)
0	29.7	52.0	22.7	40.3	$136.4	7.0	11.6	$ 9.0
1	9.6	25.3	7.7	19.8	52.0	1.9	5.4	4.4
2	9.1	30.1	7.2	22.6	55.5	1.8	7.5	5.5
3	5.0	20.4	3.9	15.2	33.7	1.1	5.2	4.0
4	2.9	14.2	2.1	9.6	14.7	0.8	4.5	2.8
5	1.4	8.5	1.1	6.2	5.5	0.4	2.4	1.2
6	0.9	6.1	0.5	3.9	3.2	0.3	2.3	0.8
7	0.4	2.9	0.2	1.5	1.8	0.2	1.4	0.5
8 or more	0.1	0.7	**	0.4	0.3	**	0.4	0.2
Not Known	0.2	1.5	0.1	0.6	0.4	0.1	0.9	0.4
Total	59.2	161.7	45.5	120.0	$303.4	13.7	41.6	$28.6

* Unrelated individuals living alone or with others are considered one-person families.
** Less than 50,000 million.

continued APPENDIX

DISTRIBUTION OF FAMILIES AND UNRELATED INDIVIDUALS BY NUMBER OF CHILDREN IN FAMILY* AND POVERTY STATUS, 1970, AFTER SIMULATION OF SEVEN-YEAR BIRTH CONTROL PROGRAM

Number of Children	All Families Families (millions)	All Families Persons (millions)	Nonpoor Families Families (millions)	Nonpoor Families Persons (millions)	Surplus Dollars (billions)	Poor Families Families (millions)	Poor Families Persons (millions)	Deficit Dollars (billions)
0	29.7	52.0	22.7	40.3	$136.5	7.0	11.6	$ 9.1
1	9.6	24.9	7.7	19.5	54.4	1.9	5.4	4.3
2	9.1	29.1	7.4	22.0	61.2	1.7	7.0	5.2
3	5.0	19.4	4.1	15.2	40.0	0.9	4.2	3.4
4	2.9	13.5	2.2	9.9	18.6	0.7	3.6	2.2
5	1.4	8.1	1.1	6.2	7.9	0.3	1.9	1.0
6	0.9	5.8	0.7	4.3	4.6	0.2	1.5	0.5
7	0.4	2.7	0.3	1.9	2.2	0.1	0.8	0.4
8 or more	0.1	0.7	0.1	0.4	0.3	**	0.3	0.2
Not Known	0.2	1.5	0.1	0.7	0.5	0.1	0.7	0.3
Total	59.2	157.6	46.4	120.5	$326.3	12.8	37.0	$26.6

* Unrelated individuals living alone or with others are considered one-person families.
** Less than 50,000 million.

continued APPENDIX

DISTRIBUTION OF FAMILIES AND UNRELATED INDIVIDUALS BY NUMBER OF CHILDREN IN FAMILY*
AND POVERTY STATUS, 1970, AFTER SIMULATION OF EIGHT-YEAR BIRTH CONTROL PROGRAM

Number of Children	All Families Families (millions)	Persons (millions)	Nonpoor Families Families (millions)	Persons (millions)	Surplus Dollars (billions)	Poor Families Families (millions)	Persons (millions)	Deficit Dollars (billions)
0	29.7	52.0	22.7	40.3	$136.6	6.9	11.7	$ 9.2
1	9.6	24.8	7.8	19.5	55.1	1.8	5.3	4.2
2	9.1	28.2	7.5	21.7	66.0	1.6	6.5	4.8
3	5.0	18.6	4.2	14.8	44.2	0.8	3.8	3.2
4	2.9	12.6	2.4	9.9	23.2	0.5	2.8	1.7
5	1.4	7.6	1.3	6.5	10.1	0.2	1.1	0.6
6	0.9	5.4	0.7	4.2	5.7	0.2	1.2	0.4
7	0.4	2.5	0.3	1.8	2.6	0.1	0.8	0.3
8 or more	0.1	0.6	0.1	4.5	0.4	**	0.2	0.1
Not Known	0.2	1.3	0.1	0.7	0.5	0.1	0.6	0.2
Total	59.2	153.6	47.0	119.8	$344.5	12.2	33.8	$24.7

* Unrelated individuals living alone or with others are considered one-person families.
** Less than 50,000 million.

DISTRIBUTION OF FAMILIES AND UNRELATED INDIVIDUALS BY NUMBER OF CHILDREN IN FAMILY* AND POVERTY STATUS, 1970, AFTER SIMULATION OF NINE-YEAR BIRTH CONTROL PROGRAM

Number of Children	All Families		Nonpoor Families			Poor Families		
	Families (millions)	Persons (millions)	Families (millions)	Persons (millions)	Surplus Dollars (billions)	Families (millions)	Persons (millions)	Deficit Dollars (billions)
0	29.7	51.9	22.7	40.3	$136.6	6.9	11.7	$ 9.2
1	9.6	24.5	7.8	19.4	56.5	1.8	5.1	4.1
2	9.1	27.4	7.6	21.3	69.5	1.5	6.0	4.3
3	5.0	17.6	4.4	14.7	49.6	0.6	2.9	2.5
4	2.9	11.8	2.6	10.1	26.7	0.3	1.7	1.1
5	1.4	7.1	1.3	6.5	11.7	0.1	0.6	0.3
6	0.9	5.1	0.7	4.1	6.2	0.1	1.0	0.3
7	0.4	2.4	0.3	1.8	3.0	0.1	0.6	0.3
8 or more	0.1	0.6	0.1	0.4	0.6	**	0.1	0.1
Not Known	0.2	1.2	0.1	0.7	0.7	0.1	0.5	0.2
Total	59.2	149.5	47.7	119.2	$360.9	11.6	30.3	$22.2

* Unrelated individuals living alone or with others are considered one-person families.
** Less than 50,000 million.

APPENDIX

DISTRIBUTION OF FAMILIES AND UNRELATED INDIVIDUALS BY NUMBER OF CHILDREN IN FAMILY* AND POVERTY STATUS, 1970, AFTER SIMULATION OF TEN-YEAR BIRTH CONTROL PROGRAM

Number of Children	All Families		Nonpoor Families			Poor Families		
	Families (millions)	Persons (millions)	Families (millions)	Persons (millions)	Surplus Dollars (billions)	Families (millions)	Persons (millions)	Dollars (billions)
0	29.7	51.9	22.7	40.2	$136.6	6.9	11.7	$ 9.2
1	9.6	24.3	7.9	19.3	57.9	1.7	4.9	3.8
2	9.1	26.4	7.9	21.6	75.1	1.2	4.8	3.5
3	5.0	16.7	4.6	14.6	53.7	0.5	2.1	1.8
4	2.9	11.0	2.8	10.3	29.9	0.1	0.6	0.5
5	1.4	6.6	1.4	6.2	12.6	**	0.3	0.1
6	0.9	4.7	0.8	3.9	7.1	0.1	0.8	0.2
7	0.4	2.2	0.3	1.8	3.5	**	0.3	0.1
8 or more	0.1	0.5	0.1	0.4	0.7	**	0.1	0.1
Not Known	0.2	1.1	0.1	0.9	0.9	**	0.2	0.1
Total	59.2	145.4	48.6	119.4	$377.9	10.7	26.0	$19.4

* Unrelated individuals living alone or with others are considered one-person families.
** Less than 50,000 million.

REFERENCES

1 Institute for Social Research, *A Panel Study of Income Dynamics*, University of Michigan, 1970.
2 Orshansky, Mollie, "Counting the Poor: Another Look at the Poverty Profile", *Social Security Bulletin*, January, 1965.
3 U.S. Department of Commerce, Bureau of the Census, *Current Population Reports, Series P – 60*.

A Program to Abolish Poverty

WILBUR J. COHEN

WILBUR J. COHEN

THE BACKGROUND

The war on poverty in the United States has been going on since the earliest colonial times. Many of the men and women who came to the colonies and later to the United States did so in order to obtain religious freedom, or because they opposed militarism, dictatorship, or ethnic annihilation. Others came because they believed the United States was a land of opportunity where they could escape economic bondage.

The moving frontier, the opening up of the Northwest Territory and Oklahoma, the purchase of Louisiana and Alaska, the *Homestead Act*, and similar activities of the National Government for over 150 years have all been part of the war on poverty.

Similarly, the movement for publicly financed education so strongly supported by labor unions for the past 150 years was viewed by the unskilled and skilled not as a movement for the elite, or for classical education, or leisure, but as a way of improving the economic status of the workingman's children.

The *Federal Vocational Education Act* of 1917 (the *Smith-Hughes Act*) was a partial recognition of the point that vocational training of young boys and girls would enable them to become economically independent. Over the years the expansion of vocational education has been a strong counterbalance to the other fundamental reasons for educational programs.

European programs to deal with some of the causes of poverty had an important effect in the United States. The social insurance programs initiated by Chancellor Bismarck in Germany in the 1880's stimulated interest in workmen's compensation legislation, health insurance, and old age pensions. With the spread of such programs to England (1908–11), the interest increased in the United States.

The Royal Commission to study the British poor laws reported in 1909. The minority report, largely written by Beatrice and Sidney Webb, advocated many reforms including the "breakup of the poor law" into categorical programs with special objectives and special appeal. These views attracted sympathetic support in the United States, and the Webbs' philosophical and pragmatic approach became the American way.

Categorical programs to compensate for work connected disabilities and deaths (workmen's compensation) became the major social reform measure of the first two decades of the century. It took until 1946, however, for the last State (Mississippi) to join the procession.

The movement for mothers' pensions was also a major social reform movement in the early part of the century (1905–15) due to the high mortality rate of fathers. Widowhood and orphanhood were undoubtedly the major causes of poverty at that time. It is a sign of some substantial progress that orphanhood is no longer a major cause of poverty in the United States. Improvement in factory safety, nutrition and public health, coupled with improved wages and working conditions, better housing, family planning, as well as life insurance and survivors insurance benefits under social security, have almost eliminated poverty due to the death of the breadwinner.

Movements to enact health insurance (1912–17 and 1932–50) were initially unsuccessful as was the movement for unemployment insurance (1920–30). But viewed over a longer span these movements brought results after initial defeats. The passage of the Wisconsin unemployment reserves legislation in 1931 and the passage of the disability insurance benefits under social security in

1956 were the beginnings of other categorial programs to deal with the poor and with poverty.

The depression of 1929 changed the entire situation in the United States. Fiercely independent and selfreliant men and women became unemployed and dependent. Existing private and public welfare programs were inadequate. Able-bodied people were seeking help and were frustrated, humiliated, and open to any panacea. Dr. Townsend preached the gospel of the transactions tax to enable people to tax and spend themselves into prosperity. Senator Huey Long preached his gospel of "share the wealth" and "everyman a King", Out of these pressures and tribulations came the *Social Security Act* of 1935.

The *Social Security Act* in itself is the most important anti-poverty program (outside of the economy itself) which exists in the United States. It is estimated that if the social security program was abolished some eleven million persons would be added to the number in poverty — an increase of over 40 percent in the number. Although the social security program is not solely devoted to reducing poverty, it has increasingly over the years played an important role in the anti-poverty war. Other measures are needed, however, to complete the war on poverty. Most significant among these are additional financial support for education and a health insurance program.

Both these objectives were realized to some extent in 1965 when the Congress enacted the *Elementary and Secondary Education Act* and *Medicare*. The ESEA of 1965 culminated 95 years of controversy over Federal aid to education. The Medicare law culminated 55 years of vigorous and intense ideological struggle over "socialized medicine" and "regimentation" of doctors and hospitals (which did not occur). Both laws opened up the possibilities of further extension and expansion. Although this had not occurred by 1971, the probability is such that by the middle of the decade of the seventies, some new factor or personality will produce the inevitable expansion.

A great step forward occurred, when despite all doubts and difficulties, Mollie Orshansky quantified the extent and levels of poverty in the United States. The figures which she produced, backed by the independent research prestige of the Social Security Administration, gave a new dimension to the war on poverty. It was no longer a general war of undescribed dimensions. Now it became a specific war all mapped out with numbers, percentages, details, and clarity. Quantification enhanced clarification. Miss Orshansky's first figures, published in the mid-sixties, have now been taken over by the Census Bureau. They are a part of the regular statistical series of the government. The permanent war on poverty is feasible for the first time, instead of the recurrent war which had ebbed and flowed in previous years.

The legislative and programmatic effort to reduce poverty took a new turn in 1964 with the enactment of the *Economic Opportunity Act*, popularity known as the "war on poverty". The commitment which Walter Heller obtained from President Kennedy in 1963 for such a program was carried out by President Johnson. He selected Sargent Shriver, President Kennedy's brother-in-law to be the commander of the forces in the field. Although there are numerous books on the origin of the program, the full story of the origins and emphases of the 1964 program have not yet been fully told. Whatever may have been the expectations of those who participated in its conception (I was one of them), it should be said, to the surprise of many young people of the 1970 generation, that *the* war on poverty in the United States did not begin in 1964 and it will not be won either solely or primarily by the *Economic Opportunity Act* of 1964 or various adaptations or amendments to its present provisions. As important as the 1964 law was in creating some new instruments to deal with enhancing the political and legal power of the poor, its importance fades into insignificance when compared with the social security program, economic growth, and general education and health legislation.

The most important program, in my opinion, to emerge from the E.O.A. of 1964 was not the general community action program but legal services for the poor which was broken off from it. By opening up new constitutional and procedural questions, it is changing the entire structure and process of programs for dealing with the poor and with poverty. This process is still underway. The recent increase in applications for law school admission is, in part, indicative of the interest of many young people to use the law as a social change agent rather than as a method of underwriting the status quo.

While the Headstart program in the E.O.A. legislation was an important program development which received wide community support, it was not really anything particularly new, with the notable exception that "parent involvement" became a significant element in the program. Day care and early childhood development programs had been around in one form or another for some time. A major factor in encouraging more widespread development of early childhood education programs was the interest in having mothers on welfare go to work. This could not be achieved without providing facilities and services for their pre-school children.

The continually increasing interest of women with children in going to work has certainly made early childhood education acceptable and more economically feasible. It has coincided with a renewal of interest by child psychologists into the tremendous potential for enhancing learning, motivation, and creativity at the youngest ages.

The legislation of the thirties and the sixties has shown that still more needs to be done to abolish poverty; the institutional mechanisms at last are at hand; the administrative experience has been obtained; the options have become clear; the costs are within our ability to pay. Where do we go from here?

A COORDINATED PLAN

The United States is rich in material and human resources. In 1971, the annual gross national product exceeded $1,000 billion; the average annual income of families will be approaching $9,000. Moreover, abundance is growing.

During the period 1935–69, the gross national product increased at an average annual compound rate of 4.4 percent. From 1910 to 1969 (including the depression and two major wars and post-war adjustments), the average annual rate was 3.1 percent. There is every reason to believe that our economy can continue to increase at an average as much as 4.75 percent for the next two decades.

Per capita incomes have grown in the United States over the years. From 1913 to 1929, per capita income increased an average of 1.7 percent compounded; from 1929 to 1967, an average of 2.0 percent; from 1960 to 1967, an average of 3.3 percent. It appears that for the next two decades we could expect an average annual increase between 3 and 4 percent.

Historically, poverty has been the result of inadequate production of goods and services. This situation still exists in most of Asia, Africa, and South America. By contrast, the abolition of poverty in the United States is no longer a problem of productive capacity.

The nation has the material resources to eliminate poverty. In recent years, remarkable progress has been made toward the twin goals of the abolition of poverty and the provision of economic security for all. In addition, there are sufficient resources to assure the overwhelming majority of Americans (whether at work or retired, whether widowed, orphaned, disabled, or temporarily unemployed) continuing incomes paid as a matter of right — incomes sufficient to assure a modest level of living, not just enough to meet the low standard that is used today to define poverty.

Although there are different standards of poverty, the Social Security Administration index is the most widely used. For an urban family of four persons, the poverty level was $3,944 for the

Table 1

POVERTY LEVELS FOR VARIOUS FAMILY SIZES, 1970

Size of Family	Total	Urban Non-Farm Male Head	Urban Non-Farm Female Head	Farm Male Head
1 under 65	$ 2,005	$ 2,092	$ 1,935	$ 1,778
1 65 and over	1,852	1,879	1,855	1,597
2 under 65	2,589	2,619	2,522	2,225
2 65 and over	2,328	2,349	2,336	1,996
3 persons	3,080	3,113	3,003	2,635
4 persons	3,944	3,970	3,948	3,387
5 persons	4,654	4,684	4,639	4,002
6 persons	5,212	5,263	5,220	4,491
7 or more persons	6,407	6,486	6,317	5,521

Source: U.S. Department of Commerce, Bureau of the Census, Current Population Reports, *Consumer Income*, Series P-60, No. 77, May 7, 1971.

year 1970, compared with $2,974 for 1959. These figures are adjusted for family size and price changes on this basis. Table 1 presents the poverty levels for various family sizes for 1970. In 1959, there were about 39.4 million people living in poverty; in 1970 the number was down to 25.5 million — a decline of 14 million persons. In 1959, 22.4 percent of the U.S. population was below the poverty level; in 1970 this figure had declined to 12.6 percent. Table 2 presents the number and percent of persons below the poverty level, 1959 to 1970. Tables 3, 4, and 5 present more detailed information on the poor.[1]

We have, however, not only the resources, but also much of the institutional framework to build upon to make poverty a thing of the past and to better the economic security of all Americans. With a comprehensive and coordinated plan, the job of eliminating poverty can be accomplished.

During the 1960's improvements in the social security program have brought higher benefit payments to a great majority of retired older people, widows and orphans, and the long-term disabled. Twenty-six million people — one out of every eight Americans — receive a social security check every month. Because

Table 2

PERSONS BELOW THE POVERTY LEVEL BY RACE, 1959–70

Year	Number Below Poverty Level (in millions)			Percent Below Poverty Level		
	Total	White	Other	Total	White	Other
1959	39.5	28.5	11.0	22.4	18.1	56.2
1965	33.2	22.5	10.7	17.3	13.3	47.1
1969	24.3	16.7	7.6	12.2	9.5	31.1
1970	25.5	17.5	8.0	12.6	9.9	32.1

Source: U.S. Department of Commerce, Bureau of the Census, Current Population Reports, *Consumer Income*, Series P-60, No. 77, May 7, 1971.

[1] Figures for 1971 became available while this article was in press. The difference between the totals for 1970 and 1971 was not statistically significant. What was significant was that the number of persons in poverty rose in 1970–71 for the first time in a decade.

529

Table 3

NUMBER OF PERSONS IN UNITED STATES BELOW THE POV-
ERTY LEVEL, 1970, IN FAMILIES AND UNRELATED INDI-
VIDUALS (IN MILLIONS)

Characteristic	Total	White	Nonwhite
All persons	25.5	17.5	8.0
In families	20.5	13.4	7.1
Unrelated individuals	5.0	4.1	0.9

Source: U.S. Department of Commerce, Bureau of the Census, Current Population Reports, *Consumer Income*, Series P-60, No. 77, May 7,
1971.

Table 4

FAMILY STATUS OF PERSONS IN UNITED STATES BELOW
THE POVERTY LEVEL, 1970 (IN MILLIONS)

Characteristic	Total	White	Nonwhite
All persons	25.5	17.5	8.0
Head of family	5.2	3.7	1.5
Children under 18	10.5	6.2	4.3
Other family members	4.8	3.5	1.3
Unrelated persons	5.0	4.1	0.9

Source: U.S. Department of Commerce, Bureau of the Census, Current Population Reports, *Consumer Income*, Series P-60, No. 77, May 7,
1971.

of their social security benefits, about two-thirds of these beneficiaries are able to maintain a level of living somewhat above the
poverty level. Nevertheless, about eight million social security
beneficiaries still live in poverty, even with their benefits.

Yet, substantial progress has been made in reducing the number
of the poor, in improving the level of living for people whose
incomes are just above the poverty level, and even in improving
the position of those who are still below the poverty line.

The striking reduction of poverty during this decade is attributable to economic growth, to the various measures taken to make it possible for more people to participate in the economy through job training, rehabilitation, and improved educational programs, and to the major improvements that have been made in the social security program.

Nearly 30 percent of the poor lives in households with an aged or disabled person at the head. Most of these people could be moved out of poverty through further improvements in the social insurance and assistance programs. One of the greatest challenges comes in finding solutions for the rest of the poor – those who lived in households where the head worked all year but was still poor or could find work only part of the time or had no job at all. We can find solutions to this problem by a coordinated program.

First: A successful national attack on poverty is dependent on continued economic growth and economic development.

We could reduce the poverty group from 25 million to about 15 to 20 million in the next 10 years with continued economic growth, and the expansion of employment in areas where under-employment now exists. This involves changes in tax policies, housing, and other programs.

We should close the tax loopholes and shelters which provide favored tax treatment of certain industries and activities. The increased tax yield should then be allocated in part to increased public expenditures (for example, in health, education, and welfare), in part to some reduction in the highest marginal tax rates, and in the further reduction of taxes among the very lowest income groups. The combined effect of these changes would be both to help increase consumption and investment and to sustain a continuing overall increase in the gross national product.

In addition, economic policies which prevent periodic recessions must be encouraged. Interruption of economic growth by recessions increases the number of persons in poverty. Between 1969 and 1970, the number of poor persons increased by about 1.2 million, or 5.1 percent. With proper planning and effective programs, such an increase in poverty could have been prevented.

While economic growth by itself cannot eliminate poverty, it creates the climate within which other constructive policies to improve living standards effectively can take place. Consumer

Table 5

SIZE OF INCOME DEFICIT FOR FAMILIES AND PERSONS BELOW THE POVERTY LEVEL, 1970

Size of income deficit		All Races			White			Negro		
		Total	Male head[1]	Female head[1]	Total	Male head[1]	Female head[1]	Total	Male head[1]	Female head[1]
Families										
Number	thousands	5,214	3,280	1,934	3,701	2,604	1,097	1,445	625	820
Percent		100.0	100.0	100.0	100.0	100.0	100.0	100.0	100.0	100.0
$ 1 to $ 249		12.6	14.7	8.9	13.5	15.2	9.6	10.1	13.1	7.8
$ 250 to $ 499		12.3	13.8	9.7	13.2	13.9	11.2	9.9	12.8	7.7
$ 500 to $ 999		21.3	21.8	20.3	22.5	22.6	22.2	18.8	20.0	17.8
$ 1,000 to $ 1,499		16.7	17.2	15.8	16.4	17.0	14.9	17.4	17.9	17.0
$ 1,500 to $ 1,999		10.9	9.4	13.6	9.9	8.6	13.0	13.3	11.7	14.5
$ 2,000 to $ 2,999		15.2	13.2	18.6	15.0	13.6	18.5	15.5	11.8	18.4
$ 3,000 and over		11.1	9.8	13.2	9.5	9.1	10.5	15.1	12.8	16.8
Median income deficit		$ 1,110	$ 989	$ 1,350	$ 1,024	$ 955	$ 1,219	$ 1,316	$ 1,109	$ 1,492
Mean income deficit		1,419	1,309	1,604	1,337	1,279	1,475	1,621	1,427	1,769
Deficit per family member		361	333	407	370	348	428	344	291	387

TABLE 5 (continued)

Unrelated Individuals

Number thousands	5,023	1,431	3,592	4,121	1,088	3,033	840	301	539
Percent	100.0	100.0	100.0	100.0	100.0	100.0	100.0	100.0	100.0
$1 to $249	16.5	16.5	16.6	17.3	17.4	17.3	13.1	13.0	13.0
$250 to $499	20.4	16.5	22.0	21.5	16.9	23.1	16.1	15.7	16.2
$500 to $749	17.1	15.1	17.9	17.2	15.7	17.7	16.3	12.0	18.8
$750 to $999	14.6	13.0	15.3	14.0	13.3	14.3	18.0	13.7	20.4
$1,000 to $1,499	16.2	16.7	16.0	15.7	14.8	16.0	16.0	22.3	16.2
$1,500 and over	15.0	22.1	12.2	14.2	21.8	11.5	18.2	23.3	15.4
Median income deficit	$ 690	$ 787	$ 660	$ 663	$ 750	$ 635	$ 813	$ 916	$ 774
Mean income deficit	806	917	762	785	896	745	894	983	844

1   For unrelated individuals, sex of the individual.

Source: U.S. Department of Commerce, Bureau of the Census, Current Population Reports, *Consumer Income*, Series P-60, No. 77, May 7, 1971.

aspirations for better housing and medical care, more education, or more adequate retirement protection provide incentives for economic growth and the reduction and eradication of discrimination and inequities.

The reduction and eventual elimination of poverty requires continued emphasis on the belief that improvement in economic and social conditions are interrelated, important, and achievable.

Second: Opportunities for work — meaningful, productive, self-supporting work — must be expanded.

Economic security is perhaps best defined as a job when you can work and income when you can't. Most fundamental is the opportunity to work. Job opportunities must be made available for all who can work, and programs that improve the ability of the individual to earn must be expanded.

Well-planned and useful work, not made work, can be provided. There are over 5 million useful, public service jobs that could be developed — jobs in hospitals, and nursing homes, jobs that would contribute to improved roads, parks and recreation centers, jobs that would help relieve the pains and anxieties of children, the aged, and the disabled.

For those whose capacity to earn is low, and for those who have a potential capacity but are unable now to get a job, much can be done to improve programs that prepare them for full participation and full opportunity. Educational activities, job training, health and rehabilitation programs, manpower retraining and relocation, and special programs could enable the disadvantaged young to compete in the labor market.

Third: Racial discrimination — in jobs, in education, and in living — must be ended.

Table 6 presents the evidence on discrimination in our society.

Justice and opportunity must become a reality for every American, regardless of race, creed, sex, or national origin. Every effort must be made to diligently carry out the constitutional obligations and statutory requirements of the *Civil Rights Act* so there is equality for every boy and girl and every family in the nation. In addition to its other insidious effects, discrimination by race, sex, religion, or national origin is economically wasteful, costing the nation a loss of about $30 billion a year in terms of the gross national product.

534

Table 6

PERCENT OF POPULATION IN UNITED STATES BELOW THE
POVERTY LEVEL, 1970, SELECTED CHARACTERISTICS

Characteristics	Total	White	Nonwhite
All persons	12.6	9.9	32.1
Male head family	7.1	6.2	18.3
Female head family	32.5	25.0	54.5
Nonfarm family	9.6	7.5	28.6
Farm family	18.6	16.2	58.1
Inside central cities family	10.9	7.8	23.6
Outside central cities family	5.7	5.0	21.4
Northeast families	7.0	6.1	17.4
South families	14.8	10.5	37.5
Families	10.0	8.0	29.3
Unrelated persons	32.7	30.7	48.1
Age 45−64 families	7.3	5.5	25.3
Age 65 and over families	16.3	14.1	40.8
Four person family	7.4	5.5	27.6
Seven or more family	22.8	16.6	44.3
Less than 8 years education	25.3	21.0	40.3
College	2.0	1.9	2.7
No earners	39.2	33.2	79.8
Two earners	4.0	3.0	12.2
Craftsmen & foremen	3.3	3.0	8.4
Farmers & farm laborers	27.3	23.6	67.1
No children in family	8.0	7.3	16.9
Five children or more in family	29.8	21.5	54.7

Source: U.S. Department of Commerce, Bureau of the Census, Current Population Reports, *Consumer Income*, Series P-60, No. 77, May 7,
1971.

People must be equipped for full participation in our economy
and in all aspects of American life because this is the only worthy

goal of a free and democratic society. We must not buy our way out of facing the tough problems of providing opportunity by the acceptance of a permanent class of the disinherited, condemned to live on a dole when they want to be a part of society and equipped to move ahead. Jobs are basic to economic security and the first task is to see to it that everyone is given the chance to learn and to earn.

Fourth: Family planning services must be available, on a voluntary basis, to those with lower incomes and less than a college education, as they are to the higher-income, college-educated person in the suburb.

In the period from 1960 to 1965, low-income women of child-bearing age had an annual fertility rate of 153 births per 1,000 women. The rate for the rest of the female population was 98 births per 1,000. This rate of 98 per 1,000 is consistent with an ultimate family size of about three children – considered to be the size that most Americans, regardless of race, economic status, or religion, desire.

Thus, it is considered likely that the poor would bear children at the same rate if they had access to the same family planning services available to the nonpoor. And, on that basis, it is estimated that in 1966, among 8.2 million low-income women of child-bearing age, there were 450,000 births of what might be called unplanned-for children. Among these 8.2 million women, there were about 1 million receiving family planning services, and 4 million who were not but indicated they would if they were available. To provide family planning services to these 4 million women would cost about $120 million a year. This is an investment we could afford.

Fifth: Opportunities for education at all levels must be expanded.

The vitality and economic growth of our society depends, to a major extent, upon the effectiveness of American education. We must assure equal access to high-quality education from preschool through graduate studies. The cost of educating every American must be recognized as an investment in a stronger, more vital nation. To raise the necessary funds, the property tax must be eliminated as a source of revenue for education, and the Federal government must contribute at least one-third of the total cost.

Quality preschool opportunities, for instance, are essential for disadvantaged children if they are ever to have the hope of succeeding in regular classroom studies. Less than one-third of the nation's 12.5 million children age 3–5 are enrolled in nursery schools or kindergartens. The proportion of children from low-income families enrolled is even less than the average.

The need for modern and effective technical and vocational eduaction is also self-evident. We need a vastly expanded and a strengthened vocational education system, as well as imaginative new ties between school and the world of work in agriculture, commerce, and industry.

Unless children born into poor families have the opportunity to learn and develop skills, they will not only be poor children but will face the high probability that they will be poor adults and they themselves will raise poor children.

The revolution of rising expectations, which has been developing in recent years, has reached a stage where it is now possible to predict radical changes in our allocation of national resources in the near future.

Increasing affluence made possible by increasing productivity, amid poverty and pollution, has had a deep and pervasive influence on many individuals in our country. As a result, widespread support has developed for the belief that major social needs can be met if there is a different allocation of the national product. Programs that were once advocated by a small minority of people are now supported by many.

Once education was considered a privilege; not a right. Good health was considered a responsibility of the individual, not a right secured by the community. And a minimum income was limited to those who worked and for those who couldn't work, welfare was considered a gratuity.

Today, education, good health, and the assurance of a minimum income for all individuals and families are considered by many to be rights to be guaranteed by law. Once this was discussed only in books dealing with Utopia. Today, the revolution in our ideas about rights and guarantees is fast crowding in on the long-held concepts of the differentiation between individual and community responsibility.

In the area of health, the idea of national health insurance has gained widespread acceptance. The passage of *Medicare* brought to an end one of the most bitterly fought ideological battles in the political history of this country. Today, the emotional content is no longer present, and the major issue is how to deliver access to health services for everyone. Even the American Medical Association, the most active adversary of publicly-sponsored national health insurance legislation, has presented a legislative proposal which is designed to broaden and improve health insurance coverage.

Sixth: The social security program should be improved.

A job today not only provides current income but carries its own insurance against the loss of that income. This social insurance device is an institutional invention of first-rate importance. It is based on the idea that since a job underlies economic security, loss of income from the job is a basic cause of economic insecurity.

Under social insurance, while a worker earns he contributes a small part of his earnings to a fund, usually matched by the employer. And then, out of these funds, benefits are paid to partly make up for the income lost when the worker's earnings have stopped. Under this "income insurance", the payments made are usually related to the amount of the earnings lost and are thus designed to maintain, in part, the level of living obtained by the worker while he worked. Cash payments are made under social insurance programs to make up, in part, for earnings lost because of retirement in old age, disability, and the death of the family breadwinner.

In the United States, the largest and most important of the social insurance programs is the federal system popularly called social security. This program insures against the loss of earnings due to retirement, disability, or death and pays benefits to meet the great bulk of hospital and medical costs in old age.

This year nearly 95 million persons are contributing to the social security program. In addition, about 5,500,000 employers pay contributions. Over 26 million persons receive benefits each month.

In 1969, total benefits paid out under the social security program were $33.4 billion. For 1971, the figure will exceed $37 billion. Ninety percent of our population aged 65 and over are eligible for monthly social security benefits. More than 95 out of 100 young children and their mothers are eligible for monthly benefits, if the family breadwinner should die. And 4 out of 5 people of working age have income protection against loss of earnings because of the long-term, severe disability of the bread-winner. When the federal civil-service system, the railroad retirement program, and state and local government staff retirement systems are taken into account, nearly everyone now has protection under a government program against the risk of loss of earned income. In addition, many are earning further protection under systems that build on social security.

Social security provides a highly effective institution for income maintenance — one that is acceptable to the public, has a very low administrative cost, and is practically universal in application. But is needs improvement, particularly in the level of benefits.

To bring benefits and contributions up to adequate standards, the following proposals should be adopted:

1. *An increase in benefit levels.* Benefits should be increased by an average of at least 5% per year. The minimum benefit should be increased.

2. *A method of keeping the system in line with rising earnings.* Benefits should be paid based on average earnings over a worker's five or ten consecutive years of highest earnings, rather than on his lifetime average, so that the benefits will be more closely related to the earnings actually lost at the time the worker becomes disabled, retires, or dies.

3. *A way to make the program more effective as the basic system of income security for those who earn somewhat above the average, as well as for average and below-average earners.* The present ceiling on the annual amount of earnings counted under the social security program should be increased from the present $7,800, in stages, to $15,000. Then, automatic adjustment of the ceiling should be provided, to keep it in line with future increases in earnings levels.

4. *Provide protection against the loss of earnings that arises because of relatively short-term total disability.* Disability benefits should be paid beginning with the fourth month of disability without regard to how long the disability is expected to last. Under present law, the benefits begin with those for the seventh month of

disability and are payable only where the disability is expected to last for at least a year.

5. *Improve protection for older workers by liberalizing the definition of disability for workers aged 55 or over.* The revised definition should permit benefits to be paid to a worker aged 55 or over if, because of illness or injury, he can no longer perform work similar to what he has done in the past. Under present law, the definition of disability requires that the worker be unable to engage in any substantial gainful activity.

6. *Improve work incentives by liberalizing the retirement test provision under which a beneficiary's earnings reduce the benefits he receives.* In 1972, an individual could receive his full benefits if his annual earnings are less than $1,680. This amount should be increased to $3,000. The reduction also should be limited to one-half the amount earned above the exempt amount, regardless of the total amount of earnings.

The increase in the earnings-base ceiling proposed would result in higher income for both the cash benefits and the Medicare parts of social security and would go a long way toward financing the proposed reforms.

If the cash benefit program were to remain entirely self-financed, the ultimate contribution rate paid by employees and the rate paid by employers for the total social security program would have to be increased somewhat to meet the cost of all the proposals outlined. General revenue financing could be used to meet part of the increased costs.

Ways to relieve low-wage earners from the burden of the higher rates should be explored. One way would be to amend the income tax laws so that, for low-income people, a part of the social security contribution would be treated as a credit against their income tax or, if no tax were due, could be refunded.

These benefit increases and the other program improvements would help all workers and their families. Their most important effect would be to reduce the number of poor in the future and to provide a level of living somewhat above poverty for most beneficiaries. But the effect of these changes on today's poor would be very significant.

Seventh: Our health services must be improved.

High-quality health care must be available to all — in the inner city as well as the suburb. We must reduce the high toll of infant mortality: a more effective method must be found for financing prenatal and postnatal care for mothers and children. We should also:

1. *Provide under Medicare for protection against the heavy cost of prescription drugs.*

2. *Cover disabled social security beneficiaries under Medicare.*

3. *Put the entire Medicare program on a social insurance prepayment basis, so that medical and hospital insurance both would be financed from social security contributions and a matching contribution from the Federal Government.*

Eight: We must improve other social insurance programs.

Other social insurance programs — unemployment insurance and workmen's compensation — although not administered by the federal government, require federal standards. Coverage of both of these programs should be expanded, and benefit levels in many states should be substantially improved.

The introduction of federal benefit standards into unemployment insurance, where there is already a federal-state relationship, would not be structurally difficult. In workmen's compensation, which has been entirely a state matter, it would be necessary to establish some new device, such as a federal program providing a given level of protection, which employers would not have to join if they presented evidence of membership in a private or State insurance arrangement with an equivalent level of protection.

Ninth: Our welfare system must be radically overhauled.

Drastic changes must be made in the existing welfare system — in the scope of coverage, the adequacy of payments, and in the way in which payments are administered.

Although work opportunities and improvements in social insurance can bring economic security to the overwhelming majority of people, they cannot do the whole job.

The federal-state welfare programs have been confined to certain categories of recipients — the aged, the blind, the permanently and totally disabled, and families with dependent children when a parent is either missing from the home, dead, disabled or unemployed. In addition, the states have been allowed to define the level of assistance provided in these programs, and may have set the level below any reasonable minimum, and payments vary widely among the states. General assistance for those not eligible under the federal-state categories is entirely supported by state and local money and with few exceptions is very restrictive.

There were in 1971 about 12 million persons receiving assistance payments — about 11 million under the federally aided programs, and about one million persons receiving general assistance not financed with federal aid. This figure would be approximately double if the states took full advantage of the federal eligibility standards and removed from state plans and administrative procedures the restrictions that now bar needy people from getting assistance. Moreover, because of the low level of assistance standards in many states, a high proportion of those receiving assistance are still below the poverty level.

But criticism of existing public assistance programs is not confined to inadequate coverage or inadequate amounts. The list of criticisms is long, going to the nature of the program itself and its administration. The determination of eligibility for one is an unnecessarily destructive process, involving the most detailed examination of one's needs and expenditures and frequently prying into the intimate details of one's life. Moving from detailed budgeting to broad categories of allowances and to simplified determinations of income and resources would help to protect the dignity and self-respect of the assistance recipient.

One problem that has haunted assistance and relief programs for years is how to provide adequate assistance without destroying economic incentive for those who can work. Reasonably adequate welfare payments, particularly to a large family, will sometimes turn out to be more than can be earned by a full-time worker with low skills.

Under aid to families with dependent children, the federal government assists states to make payments to families with the father unemployed. In the 29 states that do not take advantage of this federal offer and continue to provide aid only if the father is dead, disabled or absent from the home, the assistance program is correctly criticized on the grounds that it sets up an incentive for the unemployed worker to leave home.

Support for an assistance program that applies to all in need and that pays an adequate amount has been faced with hard going because of the incredible longevity of myths about those whom the programs are supposed to aid: that the poor live high on welfare handouts and that the poor are lazy and don't want to work.

The myths persist despite the fact that over 3 million of those on welfare are aged or disabled and over 7 million are children, and despite the fact that 80 percent of working-age men who are poor but not on welfare have jobs, and about 75 percent of them are in full-time jobs.

President Nixon, in August, 1969, proposed a dramatic reform in the welfare system which included:

1. A federally financed and administered assistance plan to replace the aid to dependent children program, which would pay each working and nonworking family in the United States a minimum income. For a family of four without any income, the amount paid would be $1,600 a year with $300 additional for each child.

2. States would be required to supplement existing federal payments to families with dependent children.

3. A work-incentive provision which allows the family on assistance to keep the first $60 a month earned, and also 50 percent above $60 up to a maximum level, set according to the size of the family.

4. A work component which requires all family heads to register with the state employment office and accept suitable jobs.

5. An expanded day-care program for the children of working mothers and a job-training program to enable the parents to prepare for full-time employment.

6. Federal minimum payment standards for the three million aged, blind, and disabled receiving welfare.

As in the case of Social Security changes, the proposal includes several needed revisions, but does not go far enough. For example, by maintaining some form of federal state cooperation in financing payments, the plan retains the state-by-state inequities prevalent under the present system. It does not include over one million poor people who do not have families and who are not covered under existing welfare programs.

Tenth: the services that will help people out of poverty must be brought to the people — where and when they need them.

Family planning services, visiting-nurse services, day-care services for the children of working mothers, community action programs, and consumer and legal aid must be available where needed. City hall — and Washington — must be closer to the people they govern. There must be an adequate program of consumer and legal protection for the poor. There must be an end to practices that short-change the poor in the grocery store, in the welfare office, at the landlord, in the neighborhood department store, and in the courts — in all the waystations that add up to life in the ghetto.

It is important, too, that credit union facilities be available to the poor and that credit unions take even greater responsibility for the consumer education of their members.

Eleventh: Extreme variations among the states must be eliminated.

A major problem in overcoming poverty in the United States is the wide variation in incomes. The increased militancy of the poor and disadvantaged in recent years is clearly the product of awareness of the economic and financial ability of the nation to eliminate poverty and the extent of affluence and concentration of income and wealth.

But even if poverty were abolished in the United States overnight, glaring inequalities in services among states would continue to exist due to past practices and institutions. Medical and educational services would still vary by states and localities unless other measures were taken to minimize these inequalities.

Table 7 presents ten major elements which indicate the inequalities among the states which must be reduced and eliminated.

A DEMANDING TASK

The problems of poverty and economic insecurity in the United States do not lend themselves to easy, magic solutions. They require a combination of deliberate, carefully designed, wide-ranging approaches, for the problems themselves are not simple. Being poor means more than not having enough money. If often means poor in spirit, hope, health, and intellectual resources.

The abolition of poverty will cost additional money. The aggregate monetary deficit of the 25 million poor persons was $11.4 billion in 1970. But the total cost of eliminating poverty, with

544

Table 7

INEQUALITIES AMONG STATES IN INCOME, HEALTH, EDUCATION, AND WELFARE

Characteristic	Highest State	U.S. Average	Lowest State
1. Per Capita Income as % of National Average	124.6	100.0	60.2
2. Physicians, per 100,000 pop.	234.0	163.0	78.0
3. Infant deaths, per 1,000 live births, 1969	30.6	20.7	13.2
4. Birth rates per 1,000 pop., 1969	24.2	17.7	15.4
5. Per capita expenditures for education, 1969	$ 390.0	$ 234.0	$ 157.0
6. Percent pop. urban, 1969	87.2%	70.9%	35.8%
7. Welfare aid per child, 1970, month	$ 72.0	$ 50.0	$ 12.0
8. Percent pop. 65 and over, 1969	13.3%	9.6%	2.5%
9. State and local tax collections as % Personal Income	13.0%	10.3%	8.2%
10. Property tax revenue as % of Total Tax Revenues, 1968–69	61.9%	40.0%	16.1%

Source: *Ranking of the States, 1971*, National Education Association, 1971; Public Assistance Statistics, December, 1970, U.S. Department of Health, Education, and Welfare, Social and Rehabilitation Service.

appropriate work incentives, would cost more than $11.4 billion initially. But the cost should be reduced as the number in poverty declines. The 1959 deficit was $18.2 billion, which declined to $11.4 billion by 1970 — a drop of $7 billion (*see* Table 8).

As improvements in health and education continue, we may expect some declines in the costs of poverty. Our expenditures as a nation for health, education, and social security have been rising and are likely to continue to do so (*see* Table 9).

The additional costs of abolishing poverty are in the range of one to two percent of the gross national product. We can afford the money. But money must be accompanied by far-reaching public and private programs that provide opportunities for the poor. For those who are able to work, greater emphasis must be placed on jobs, education, and training. For those who cannot or should

Table 8

AGGREGATE INCOME DEFICIT OF PERSONS BELOW THE POVERTY LEVEL, 1959, 1969, 1970 (IN MILLIONS AT 1970 DOLLARS)

Family Characteristic	All Persons			White			Nonwhite		
	1970	1969	1959	1970	1969	1959	1970	1969	1959
Total Deficit	$11.4	$10.7	$18.2	$8.2	$7.7	$13.1	$3.3	$3.0	$5.1
1. Families	7.4	6.8	13.1	4.9	4.5	8.9	2.6	2.2	4.2
A. Male head	4.3	3.9	9.5	3.3	3.0	6.7	1.0	1.0	2.8
(1) No children	1.3	1.2	2.5	1.2	1.1	2.1	.2	.2	.4
(2) With children	3.0	2.7	7.0	2.1	1.9	4.6	.8	.7	2.4
B. Female head	3.1	2.8	3.5	1.6	1.5	2.2	1.5	1.3	1.4
(1) No children	.2	.3	.4	.2	.2	.3	NA	.1	NA
(2) With children	2.9	2.5	3.1	1.4	1.3	1.9	1.5	1.2	1.3
2. Unrelated individuals	4.0	4.0	5.1	3.2	3.2	4.2	.8	.8	1.0
A. Male	1.3	1.2	1.6	1.0	.9	1.2	.3	.3	.4
B. Female	2.7	2.8	3.5	2.2	2.3	3.0	.5	.5	.6

Source: U.S. Department of Commerce, Bureau of the Census, Current Population Reports, *Consumer Income*, Series P-60, No. 77, May 7, 1971.

546

Table 9

PUBLIC AND PRIVATE EXPENDITURES FOR HEALTH, EDUCATION, AND WELFARE, PERCENT OF GROSS NATIONAL PRODUCT, 1950–70

Fiscal Year	Total	Health	Education	Welfare
1950	13.5	4.6	4.1	4.9
1955	13.3	4.7	3.7	5.1
1960	16.0	5.3	4.4	6.5
1965	18.0	5.9	5.2	7.1
1967	19.0	6.2	5.7	7.4
1968	19.6	6.5	5.8	7.6
1969	20.3	6.7	5.9	7.9
1970	21.6	7.0	6.3	8.5

Source: U.S. Department of Health, Education, and Welfare, *Social Security Bulletin*, December, 1970, p. 16. Total adjusted to eliminate duplication resulting from use of cash payments received to purchase medical care and educational services.

not be expected to work, improvements must be made in the social security program, which, combined with private benefit plans, constitute the most effective institutions for income maintenance. They cannot, of course, do the whole job. The present welfare system must be drastically overhauled to adequately serve those whose needs are not met by other programs. Programs for the more effective housing of low-income persons, eradication of slums, and the elimination of hunger and malnutrition must be accelerated. Concomitant with improvements in existing programs, the search must continue for new and imaginative programs that will meet the demands of the decade ahead.

Setting the elimination of poverty as a national goal is a huge and complex undertaking. The nation has the economic capacity, the technological capability, and the intellectual resources to accomplish this goal before the end of the next decade. But the most difficult task will be sustaining the determined commitment of the nation to the American promise: Full and equal opportunity for all to share in the good life that can be offered by a dynamic, prosperous, democratic society.

Theory of Expectations

GEORGE KATONA

Recognition of the role of the human factor in economic affairs constitutes the central feature of behavioral or psychological economics. This new discipline concerns itself with the behavior of the human actors — consumers, businessmen, government policy-makers — rather than with the interrelationship among such results of their behavior as supply, demand, prices, interest rates, etc. One, though only one, of the important human factors that manifest themselves in economic action is to be found in the expectations of the actors. In this paper the theory of expectations is summarized, as it has developed from psychological assumptions tested by empirical research over the past 25 years. The theory relates to the origins and results of expectations as well as to the various ways in which they change. With respect to the impact of expectations on overt behavior, the discussion is restricted to short-run cyclical developments.

The simplest features of the basic model of human behavior may first be restated as they apply to the analysis of economic behavior. Personal intervening variables mediate between changes in the environment (stimuli) and people's responses to these changes (overt behavior or action). Intervening variables influence both the perception of the stimuli and the responses. They are of particular importance when a person has substantial discretion of action and when a problem arises about how to respond, rather than when the response is habitual or is inhibited by powerful constraints. Attitudes constitute important intervening variables; they are generalized viewpoints with affective connotation, indicating what is good and favorable or bad and unfavorable. Attitudes are learned, that is, acquired and modified by past experience. Certain attitudes are acquired in early childhood and are fairly stable over very long periods of time, while others may change frequently and even suddenly under the impact of new experiences. People's time perspective extends both backward and forward; expectations constitute the forward-looking subclass of attitudes of particular importance for economic behavior. Just as other attitudes, expectations have an affective component in addition to their cognitive and predictive content.

A more complete model would have to include the consideration of enabling conditions and constraints as well as of sociocultural norms and variations in value systems and in personality traits. The inclusion of these variables makes it a complex task to analyze the determinants of individual behavior or of behavioral changes over long periods of time. A change in attitudes and expectations that occurs among very many people at the same time and influences their behavior over a short period of time will be shown, however, to be dependent on fewer variables, and thus more amenable to study.

Intervening variables may be deduced from differences in the response of different individuals to the same stimuli, or from differences in the response of the same individuals at different times. Alternatively, indications of intervening variables may be obtained by questioning individuals about their motives, attitudes, and expectations. If the individuals questioned represent a sample of a chosen universe, data can be obtained on collective attitudes and behavior.

The role of expectations in behavior was emphasized by economists much earlier than by psychologists.[1] Because much of economic behavior, and especially investment decisions, relates to the

---

[1] The earlier neglect by psychologists of the concept of expectations is documented by Theodore Newcomb in this volume [27].

future and it takes a long time before most major outlays bear fruit, economic theorists in Sweden and elsewhere have long postulated the importance of expectations. Yet the gains to be derived from the inclusion of the role of expectations in the study of economic processes were delayed by the following circumstances: (*a*) the absence of any attempt to measure prevailing expectations and their changes; (*b*) the application of the concept of expectations to entrepreneurs only and not to consumers; (*c*) widely prevailing notions that individuals' expectations were uncertain, fleeting and volatile, or that they cancelled out when very many people were considered; and (*d*) the prevalence of an inappropriate theory on the formation of expectations. Over the last 25 years it has been demonstrated, however, that it is possible to obtain quantitative measures on changes in the distribution of both business and consumer expectations and that these changes are of importance for economic trends because they frequently reinforce each other rather than averaging out.

Regarding points *b* and *c* it may suffice to recall that J.M. Keynes specifically excluded the consideration of consumers' income expectations because they were "likely to average out for the country as a whole" and because they were so "uncertain" that they could not "exert much influence." Even business expectations were said by Keynes to have "a very precarious basis" and to be "subject to sudden and violent changes" as "determined by the uncontrollable and disobedient psychology of the business world."[2]

On the basis of these assumptions many economists were inclined to search for "certainty equivalents" to be substituted for the uncertain expectations. This was done by assuming that expectations of future sales, profits, prices, etc., were formed exclusively on the basis of recent past changes in those variables. Acceptance of this inadequate theory (*see* point *d* above) led to the conclusion that past profit and price movements, for instance, about which objective data were available, might be substituted for expectational variables. The psychological and therefore allegedly subjective and nonmeasurable factors were then excluded from economics.

[2] [24, p. 95, 315, and 317].

The "proxy theory" is discussed here not only because it serves to explain the neglect of empirical studies of expectations and because dissatisfaction with this theory represented the starting point of this author's studies involving the psychological analysis of economic behavior.[3] In addition, while not acceptable as proxy variables for expectations, past experience with income or prices must be considered as a factor contributing to these expectations. Finally, the proxy theory is still widely held, and has even been called the "rational theory of expectations". In this theory expectations are made an endogenous variable by postulating that they can be modified *only* by past changes of the same variable coupled with a consideration of past forecasting errors.[4] As recently as 1970–71 monetary economists at the Federal Reserve Bank of St. Louis substituted in their econometric model past price trends for price expectations by assuming that inflationary expectations, which in their opinion had been giving momentum to inflation, derived exclusively from past price increases (*see* [2] and [8]).[5]

ON THE PSYCHOLOGY OF LEARNING

The psychology of learning offers major clues about the formation of expectations. Some expectations are based on repetition. A person may expect those things to happen that have happened

[3] Those early studies were reported in two papers published in 1946 and 1951 [12, 14] as well as in a book published in 1951 [13]. The following paragraphs rely heavily on those publications, in which several studies of expectations by economists are cited. The author's studies stemmed from his investigation of the psychology of learning [11].

[4] This view probably originated in Philip Cagan's study in which "the expected rate of change in prices . . .is assumed to be a function of the actual rate of change" [4, p. 35] and "the expected rate of change in prices is revised . . .in proportion to the difference between the actual rate of change in prices and the rate of change that was expected" (p. 37).

[5] In its November, 1971, *Monthly Letter* the First National City Bank attributes the recent high interest rates overwhelmingly to price expectations which "denote the rate of price inflation that market participants expect will occur." How is this important variable determined so as to provide evidence for the role of price expectations? By substituting past price movements for price expectations! To repeat the words of the *Monthly Letter*, "Price expectations are proxied . . ."

before and the frequency of his past experience — the number of reinforcements — as well as their recency may determine the strength of his expectations. Having experienced the sequence $a-b-c-d$ several times, the occurrence of $a-b$ may arouse the expectation that $c-d$ will follow. This is particularly true of individual expectations, but collective expectations may also arise in this form. To the survey question "Why do you expect prices to go up" under certain circumstances some people reply, "Because thy have been going up for quite a while." The more frequent and the more recent the past experience, the stronger the resulting expectation.

But repetition (memorizing, stamping in, conditioning) is not the only form of human learning. There is learning which differs from the simple establishment of bundles of reflexes or stimulus–response bonds. Problem solving may enter into the process and result in an understanding of certain relationships, which may then produce the acquisition of insights not previously present. If and when a person perceives himself to be in a crossroad situation, he may try to solve the problem and to understand what is going on and what will happen. As a result of these processes he may arrive at expectations which do not represent extrapolations of past occurrences.

An important instance of problem solving consists of the reorganization of one's perception of a situation as the result of major new developments which make habitual behavior questionable or inappropriate. In such circumstances one may expect a reversal of ongoing trends, or developments that have never before been experienced. Expectations people derive from established principles and theories may be viewed as indirect results of problem solving undertaken by others.

The outbreak of a war or the end of a war may be mentioned as extreme examples in which a reorganization of the psychological field is called for, and people's expectations will commonly result from attempts to understand the consequences of the new developments. Many lesser events, concerning the people themselves or the general situation, may also provide the impetus for reorganization and problem solving. Insightful learning may occur suddenly, without any reinforcement, or slowly and gradually. Its results will be important in determining collective economic behavior if the impetus affects very many people at the same time, that is, if the precipitating circumstances are widely known and perceived as significant.

A new understanding and the arousal of changed or new expectations do not happen without reasons of which people are aware and which they consider valid. True, people's understanding of what causes what may be erroneous, and the expectations may be without justification when considered by experts in the light of their knowledge of manifold circumstances of which people in general are not aware. The extent of human intelligence involved in problem solving should not be overestimated. The formation of new expectations is not always based on a careful consideration of all facets of a situation. Problem solving makes use of shortcuts and stereotypes; the search for reasons may be superficial and inadequate.

It also follows from an understanding of the learning process that expectations are not fleeting and volatile in the sense that they change constantly without good reason. When they change, and especially when they change radically, the change appears well justified. Unless good reasons are seen for a change, the same expectations may be maintained for long periods of time. Neither consumer not business behavior should be assumed to consist of a continuous revision of decisions due to ever-changing expectations.

During the last 20 years many economists have also found ample reason to contradict the assumption that it was permissible to substitute past for expected magnitudes. Econometricians have recognized that expectations may be regressive as well as extrapolative. For instance, an increase in the sales of a business firm may make for the expectation of a further increase or for the expectation of a decrease. (To be sure, some writers have called regressive expectations indications of a departure from rationality!) In a formal sense expectations may be in the nature of expecting (a) a continuation of a prevailing trend, (b) its reversal, (c) the absence of any change following previous change, or (d) change following stability. (In the last classification we recognize the possibility of, say, inflationary expectations arising at a time of price stability.) Furthermore, extrapolative expectations may be subdivided into cumulative, accelerative, or elastic as well as noncu-

554

mulative, decelerative, or inelastic expectations.[6] Past increases or decreases may evoke the expectation of smaller — or alternatively greater — increases or decreases.

What contributes to the formation of expectations about any variable is not restricted to what has happened to the same variable in the recent past.[7] There is hardly any limit to the factors that may serve to change expectations; income or price expectations may be influenced by taxes, interest rates, political and international developments, the urban crisis, etc.

Reasons for changes in expectations have been studied during the last two decades. In quarterly surveys conducted by the Survey Research Center questions were asked about the news heard and recalled, as well as about why people expected whatever they did. In reply to the question, "Why do you think so", following a report on an expected improvement or deterioration in the economic situation, greatly different answers were obtained in surveys conducted at different times. There have been certain developments, which have remained major news most of the time during the last 25 years. But even in these areas the saliency of the news has varied from time to time. In addition, unique events were found to be salient at different times. At certain times news of changes in taxes, interest rates, or stock market prices, as well as of nonmarket developments such as news about Vietnam, the urban crisis, or pollution was found to have influenced expectations. The reasons for changes in expectations can be determined after the fact, but a change in expectations cannot be predicted from earlier objective developments. No shortcut exists which would replace the need to interrogate samples of consumers and businessmen about their expectations and their reasons for holding them [22].

The analysis of expectations and their use for forecasting is greatly facilitated by the principle discussed before, which may

[6] J.R. Hicks introduced the concept of elastic expectations as early as 1939.
[7] Doubt of the validity of this assumption has been expressed by James Tobin in this volume [32]. He recognizes the possibility of "revisions of income expectations resulting from information other than that conveyed by current income." Similarly, R.J. Gordon says that "Expectations may not be a simple function of a variable's past values," but nevertheless proceeds to make this assumption [9, p.125].

here be restated: Only when very many people see a reason for change do major changes in expectations occur that can be relied upon to persist. Only in that case can temporary changes in mood be excluded from consideration. Only in that case will an observed change in expectations have predictive value.

EMPIRICAL DATA

We interrupt the discussion of theoretical issues in order to present research findings on the frequency of different forms of change in expectations and their origin. We shall discuss consumers' expectations about prospective trends in business, their income, as well as in prices. In all three instances data are available which permit a comparison of perceived past changes with expected changes on the part of representative samples of consumers.

Expectations about the direction of change in business conditions fall in the category of those which occasionally change very substantially. We present in Table 1 survey data on both past and expected changes at two points of time which were radically different from each other.

Both regarding business conditions during the preceding 12 months and the following 12 months, survey respondents were asked to choose between the answers "Better", "Same", or "Worse". The answers received and presented in the two upper parts of Table 1 are summarized in the third part which indicates the proportion of respondents who gave the same answer to both questions (48 percent in 1969, 37 percent in 1971). If this proportion were close to 100 percent a proxy theory would be adequate. But different answers to the two questions were very frequent.

Early in 1969 most consumers thought that business conditions were good or even that they had improved during the previous 12 months. At the same time, very commonly expectations were less favorable than perceptions of past trends. Extensive questioning indicated that in 1968 the cessation of the bombing of North Vietnam as well as the election of Nixon to the presidency contributed to optimistic views, and that the introduction of the tax surcharge was not viewed pessimistically. (The surcharge will be

Table 1

PAST AND EXPECTED CHANGES IN BUSINESS CONDITIONS

	Early 1969	Early 1971
Past change[a]		
Better	36%	18%
Same	49	25
Worse	10	54
	95%	97%
Expected change[b]		
Better	19%	31%
Same	65	48
Worse	10	17
	94%	96%
Relation of expected to past change		
Same	48%	37%
Expected more favorable	14	44
Expected less favorable	30	12
	92%	93%

a   The question was: "Would you say that at the present time business conditions are better or worse than they were a year ago? ,,

b   "And how about a year from now, do you expect that in the country as a whole business conditions will be better or worse than they are at present, or just about the same? "

Note: Don't Know answers are omitted; therefore columns do not add up to 100%.

Source: Survey Research Center, quarterly surveys.

discussed later.) In 1969, however, disappointment about the new Administration's economic program and the absence of any prospect of an end to the war in Vietnam, as well as news of accelerated inflation and increased interest rates, led to a deterioration of consumer sentiment. (Later in 1969 fears about unemployment arose, and it was possible to predict the recession of 1970 far in advance.)

Early in 1971, on the other hand, consumers were well aware

that business conditions had worsened during the preceding 12 months. The data presented in Table 1 may, at first glance, indicate a major turning point. But most respondents expecting an improvement in business conditions explained their opinion by saying that "Things can't remain as bad as they are" or "Something will be done to improve the situation", rather than by citing good news. At the same time bad news about inflation and unemployment continued to be mentioned very frequently. On the basis of these findings, not shown in Table 1, the conclusion was reached that while many consumers felt that the worst was over, they saw no reason to expect a real or substantial improvement. The reliability of data about expectations must be judged in conjunction with data on the reasons for the expectations.[8]

An obvious matter must be given some emphasis: When people say that they expect business conditions to be unchanged, they may mean different things, for instance, in 1969 the continuation of good and in 1971 the continuation of bad conditions. Similarly, the answers "Better" or "Worse", in response to questions about expectations, must be evaluated relative to perceived conditions.

Income expectations have been found to fluctuate much less than expectations about general business conditions. It could be demonstrated consistently over many years that past gains exerted a great influence on many people's income expectations. Nonextrapolative expectations were, however, not uncommon even with respect to income trends.

As a typical illustration of the relation of past to expected income, we shall cite data obtained in 1967 on longer-run developments and expectations (Table 2).[9] At that time 63 percent of a representative sample said that they were making more money than four years earlier, and 51 percent of the same sample that they expected to be making more four years later. This differential may be explained by the refusal of many people to commit themselves as to what they thought would happen that far in the future. (Those without definite expectations are excluded from Table 2.) As the table shows, 39 percent of the sample expected

[8] For detailed survey data, *see* the annual monographs [23].
[9] For these and a great variety of additional data on personal financial expectations, *see* [23] and [20].

Table 2

PAST AND EXPECTED CHANGES IN INCOME AND PERSONAL WELL-BEING

Current income compared to 4 years earlier	Income 4 years hence compared to current income	Frequency
Higher	Higher	39%
Higher	Unchanged or lower	17
Unchanged or lower	Higher	10
Unchanged or lower	Unchanged or lower	15
All those with definite expectations, 1967		81%

Current personal financial situation compared to 4 years earlier	Personal financial situation in 4 years compared to the present	Frequency
Better	Better	31%
Better	Unchanged or worse	14
Unchanged or worse	Better	10
Unchanged or worse	Unchanged or worse	21
All those with definite expectations, 1968		76%

Source: Survey Research Center, quarterly surveys.

that past favorable income trends would continue and 17 percent that they would not. Similar findings were obtained with respect to past and expected improvement in people's overall financial situation rather than just their income. Because of inflation, a sizable proportion of people whose incomes have gone up did not consider themselves as being better off; yet the great majority with perceived improvement expected still further improvement.

The sizable proportion of people with extrapolative expectations were found to constitute a subgroup with important characteristics. The "higher" — "higher" group and especially the "better" — "better" group could be shown to behave differently from all other trend groups. These were the people who stepped up their discretionary expenditures to the largest extent, who incurred installment debt for purchases of durable goods most frequently, and who were most ready to accept innovations.

Explanation for the presence of nonextrapolative expectations was readily found. Some people with favorable past trends expected to retire during the next four years and others spoke of problems of health or of secondary earners in the family probably giving up their jobs. Furthermore, past favorable trends were sometimes characterized as temporary and were not expected to recur. More significant results were obtained when an explanation of extrapolative expectations was sought. It could be shown that even when the influence of income and age was partialed out in multivariate studies, past progress was associated with the expectation of further progress. Most people in this category explained their past income gains with reference to their own efforts.[10] When asked why they were making more than four years earlier, they said that they had worked hard and deserved their progress rather than that their income gains were due to inflation, or to steps taken by the government or their trade union, or that "everybody" had made income gains in the preceding years. (Answers of the latter types were given much more frequently in prosperous Western Europe than in the United States.)

It appears, then, that extrapolative expectations do not arise automatically. People who believe that their own effort has contributed to their progress are those who expect their progress to continue. Trust in one's own ability and a feeling of self-reliance are found to be the major explanations of extrapolative income expectations.

The arousal of expectations of rising prices is likewise not an automatic consequence of experience with rising prices. Runaway inflation, as it has occurred in a number of foreign countries, is characterized by the perception of an entirely new situation and a break with past habits and stereotypes. In the United States, where hyperinflation has not been experienced in this century, price control and rationing strongly influenced people's price expectations during World War II when patriotic attitudes favored the acceptance of controls. In the years following the war the

[10] See [20, p. 53 ff.].

notion that what goes up will come down was widespread, but disappeared after the outbreak of the Korean war. In 1950 people saw what they considered good reasons to expect rising prices. Later in the 1950's and in the first half of the 1960's both the proportion of consumers reporting that they had experienced general price increases in the preceding 12 months and the proportion expecting price increases during the next 12 months fluctuated greatly. Yet an increase in the former proportion frequently did not result in an increase in the latter proportion. In the years 1969–71 the notion that this is an era of inflation has become widespread: Many people have felt that there were good reasons why prices would be higher a year later, still higher five years later, and higher yet in ten years. But slow and gradual, rather than rapid and substantial, price increases were expected, and the extent of the anticipated price increases continued to fluctuate according to the news heard.

The extent of expected price increases was determined by the Survey Research Center at frequent intervals and was found not to be dependent on the extent of perceived past price increases. When both the extent of price increases during the preceding 12 months and expected increases during the next 12 months were tabulated in brackets (1–2%, 3–4%, 5%, 6–9%, 10% or more), in 1969 and 1970 less than one-half of members of representative samples were found to fall in the same bracket. The proportion expecting price increases, larger or smaller in extent than in the past, fluctuated mainly according to economic trends and news heard about government policies. It was found not to be true that the longer the inflation, the more frequent and the more substantial are the expectations of still higher prices. Nor did expectations of inflation induce consumers in general to try to beat it by buying in advance [21]. (Advance buying has occurred occasionally in automobiles and in a few other specific goods the prices of which were confidently expected to go up in the near future.) During the recession of 1970–71 consumer sentiment was adversely affected by the awareness of continuing substantial price increases, and yet price expectations remained fairly conservative. At the same time, consumers' discretionary expenditures were depressed and the rate of personal saving, especially in savings accounts, was unusually high.

561

Thus with respect to prices, just as with respect to economic trends and personal income, it appears necessary to measure people's expectations directly. And in every instance, as indicated earlier, data must be collected on the reasons for changes in expectations, because they contribute to an understanding of ongoing developments and to the prediction of forthcoming trends.

MICRO AND MACRO DATA

A brief discussion of the relation of individual to collective behavior is in order. It is the individual who thinks, learns and feels. Data on attitudes and expectations can only be collected from individuals and must be aggregated in order to provide information that serves the purposes of economic research. Micro-data relating to individuals do not suffice because economics as a discipline has macro-aims. To illustrate in a simple manner: Economics is concerned with an increase or decrease in the total number of cars bought, or to be bought, in a given period, but not with whether or not John Smith or Jim Miller bought or will buy a car. Change in the proportion of families with rising incomes or perceived financial progress — but not the progress of any one individual — is relevant for economic trends.

Collective behavior stems from individual behavior. And yet the whole may differ from the sum of its parts. The macro-model of behavior is much simpler than the micro-model. Many extensive differences in individual personality traits, as well as great variations in the information acquired by individuals, may be neglected in the study of social learning and of changes in the attitudes of all consumers. Social learning is more selective than individual learning. What very many people learn at a given time represents only a small part of what individuals learn. This is not due simply to idiosyncratic elements in the acquisition of information by individuals. More importantly, similarities in the information transmitted and in the information to which people have access relate only to certain parts of the information received by individuals. Mutual reinforcement among many people will extend only to certain rather than to all features of environmental change. A unifying characteristic of social learning consists of the affective connotation of what is learned. It may happen that practically everybody in a country learns at a given time that the economic news is good or bad, that business trends are favorable or unfavorable, pointing to an upswing or a downswing. At the same time manifold details about exactly what has or will become better or worse vary from individual to individual, depending on the individual's prior knowledge, his personal experience, and the group to which he belongs.

Furthermore, data on collective behavior, group attitudes, and social learning are more reliable than data on individuals. This is particularly true of data obtained by means of sample surveys in which a respondent may be questioned for a short time only (say, for an hour). To get the answer to such a fairly simple question as when an individual family will next buy a car, it may be necessary to collect a great variety of information. In addition to the number and ages of family members and of earners, the location of the residence and the job, the age and condition of the cars owned, family income and assets, it may be relevant to obtain data on such matters as health, family cohesion, personal satisfactions, aspirations, and hobbies. Furthermore, individual data may be volatile because they are subject to changes in the mood of the person answering certain questions. Several of these considerations may, however, represent random factors when the question relates to the car buying plans of all families or the trend in multiple car ownership. Unless there has already been an extensive family discussion about buying a car — which at any given time is true of a small minority only — some individuals will be ignorant of certain considerations which they themselves will take into account when the problem of buying a car becomes salient to them. Even depth psychology and unlimited time of questioning may then fail to provide reliable answers. Scientific research is selective, and what is selected for study depends on hypotheses developed by scholars. The process of testing hypotheses is much simpler with respect to group behavior or the behavior of all the people than of any individual. The influence of presumed crucial factors — e.g., a move to suburbia, or a wife resuming work — on multiple car ownership may be reliably tested for very many people, but not for any one person. If the many individuals questioned constitute a sample representing a universe such as all consumers, or the young or the high-income consumers, one may arrive at data of significance for economic trends (despite the sampling errors inherent in aggregate data obtained from surveys).

Similarly, individual data on whether or not business conditions have improved or deteriorated reveal widespread lack of knowledge. But the marginal change in the distribution of such data — an increase or decrease in the proportion saying "better" or "worse" — indicates trends in the perception of all people that commonly coincide with what has actually happened according to available statistical data.

To mention the extreme case: This author has occasionally been ridiculed for inserting questions in interviews about what business trends will be during the next five years. The question is asked of all people in a representative sample, including uneducated laborers and isolated sharecroppers. A substantial proportion of respondents are ignorant and the "forecast" they make is of little interest. Nevertheless, changes in the distribution obtained from all people have revealed affective notions which reflect changes in optimism or pessimism. Without necessarily going as far as Kenneth Boulding suggests when (in his essay in this volume [3]) he attributes to this author the principle that "the summation of ignorance produces knowledge", it must be pointed out that there is a great difference in the reliability of survey data on changes in collective attitudes as compared to data on individual attitudes.

For the purpose of understanding and predicting short-run changes in economic trends, then, a fairly simple model of human behavior appears to suffice. It does not follow that micro-data of a much more complex nature are of no interest to economic research. In a variety of additional studies it was found necessary to take into consideration data on situational determinants, sociocultural norms, and even personality traits. Such information was needed, for example, for (a) studies of longer-range economic trends, such as the difference between post-World War II affluence and prewar conditions; (b) international comparisons, such as differences in American and Western European affluence; and (c) an analysis of factors influencing the acquisition rather the allocation of income. Studies of the impact of social problems (race, poverty, violence, etc.) or of changes in life styles on economic behavior likewise call for a more extensive consideration of micro-data and of the attitudes and behavior of certain subgroups of the population. For the purpose of understanding changes in value systems and goals, micro-data must be collected which go far beyond those required for the analysis of short-run economic trends.[11] Finally, the collection of data on personality traits is called for in studying the poverty sector and especially the crucial problem of identifying the forces that lead certain individuals to get out of poverty.[12]

FULFILLMENT OF EXPECTATIONS

To return to the theory of expectations: It may be thought that there are two kinds of expectations, (1) expectations about what a person himself will do, and (2) expectations about what will happen to him. Examples come readily to mind. Price expectations as well as expectations about economic trends (e.g., "There will be an improvement in business conditions") belong in the second category, while buying intentions (e.g., "I expect to buy a car during the next 12 months") in the first category. Clearly, however, there are expectations which fit into neither category. Income expectations (e.g., "I expect my income to increase during the next year") may be due either to what a person expects others will do (e.g., employers, trade unions) or what he himself expects to do (e.g. change of job, other family members starting to work, etc.). Consumer sentiment, that is, feelings of optimism and confidence or their absence, is assumed to change as the result of both external and personal developments, the latter including matters that can be influenced by the person himself.

More important than the formal classification of different types of expectations are the deductions drawn from the system of classification. It has been assumed that personal expectations are more

[11] Regarding studies of acquisition of income and the relation of social to economic indicators, see the paper by B. Strumpel in this volume [31].
[12] *See* J.N. Morgan's studies of the behavior of the poor. His and Wilbur Cohen's papers in this volume [25, 5] point to the relation of psychological to economic studies in the area of poverty. It follows from Cohen's analysis that the fight against poverty must be conducted without impairing incentives and aspirations.

definite than nonpersonal expectations and that the probability of fulfillment is greater for the former than for the latter. The average person, so it was thought, should know more about his personal prospects than about business prospects and could have some control over what he does, but not over what others do.

Empirical findings do not confirm the assumed difference in the rate of fulfillment of the two kinds of expectations – except, to be sure, regarding expectations about a person's actions in the very near future. If survey respondents were to be asked, for instance, whether they would go to a movie the night of the interview or whether they would buy a car withing a few weeks, a very substantial fulfillment rate would doubtless be obtained. But expectations about probable actions in the near future are of little interest to economic research. A person's planning horizon may of course extend quite far into the future, and some personal expectations may thus be fairly definite over long periods of time. I may have definite plans to go to Europe in six months, and the fulfillment of this expectation may be impaired only by such unexpected developments as an accident or illness. In most respects, however, planning periods have been found to be rather short. Yet even when no definite plans exist, expectations may nonetheless prevail. Personal expectations as determined in surveys represent a mixture consisting of contractual obligations, fairly definite plans, as well as the assessment of probabilities, and even vague notions and hopes. All these represent predispositions to action which, although they do not determine future behavior, do influence it.

Turning to expectations about what will happen regarding matters over which a person has no control, we find that some of them are very definite. This will be so, as said before, if the expectation is based on reasons which the person understands and considers valid. People often expect with much greater confidence that prices will go up, than that their income will go up or that they will purchase a car in a few months.

The major test of the fulfillment of expectations consists of a comparison of changes in collective expectations with changes in subsequent overt actions of very many people. If at time point three the proportion of optimists is found to be larger (smaller) than at an earlier time point two, and at time point two larger (smaller) than at an earlier time point one, an increase (decrease)

566

in discretionary expenditures, which depend on willingness to buy in addition to ability to buy, may be predicted. The predictive value of changes in attitudes and expectations, when subjected to such an "aggregate test", is the result of more than just an increased rate of purchases by optimists. The purchases of people who were not optimistic at time point three but became optimists later may also play a role in the outcome of the test.[13]

Expressed buying intentions for automobiles were observed to be carried out in a rather large proportion of cases, even if they related to periods as long as 12 months. Further, among people who answered "No" to a question about intentions to buy cars during the next 12 months, the great majority were found not to have purchased a car in that period. Nevertheless, cross-section tests did not prove very satisfactory even in this case. Since the great majority of those in a representative sample say "No" to the question — or attach zero probability to their buying a car — even a small proportion of this large group purchasing a car in the absence of having expressed the intention to do so, results in a very great proportion of actual car puchases not explained by earlier buying intentions.

With respect to the aggregate test, it should be mentioned that the proportion expressing the intention to buy a house, a car, or a major household appliance will not correspond with the proportion actually buying in a subsequent period. But a significant and enduring increase or decrease in the proportion of the intenders has been postulated to indicate an improvement or deterioration in predispositions to buy. This was the assumption which led this author to initiate survey questions on intentions to buy toward the end of World War II. But even in this respect, the experience was far from satisfactory. Expressed buying intentions represent a fairly late intercept in the decision-making process. For a sizeable

---

[13] Tests of the predictive value of expectations expressed by individuals, or such groups of individuals as all optimists or pessimists (the "cross-section test"), are impaired by a variety of factors. For instance, the classification of some individuals as optimists or pessimists at one given time may be subject to error because some individuals are "at the margin". Similarly, what is a discretionary expenditure varies from individual to individual. Several reasons impairing the outcome of the cross-section test have been enumerated in [15, pp. 254 ff.].

number of people, the time period between intending and buying is too short to provide the basis for useful predictions. More importantly, at certain crucial times change in the rate of fulfillment of intentions, rather than change in their frequency, appears to be relevant. Thus in 1969, when expectations about what would happen and, therefore, consumer sentiment had deteriorated sharply, buying intentions as determined in the Bureau of the Census surveys did not decline at all. Yet, because of a continued worsening of attitudes, many expressed intentions were not carried out. It follows that data on intentions to buy need to be corrected by data on other expectations. Perhaps the reverse is also true: In periods of sustained upswing the techniques currently used to measure changes in expectations proved to be somewhat insensitive and may need to be corrected by intentions data. In general, however, expectations regarding matters over which the person himself has no control have proved to have the greatest predictive value.

The distinction between expectations about what a person will do and about what will happen to him is relevant for aspirations, which usually relate to the former. Aspirations and expectations are not the same and do not function in the same way. Aspirations may be less realistic than expectations: During a recession, for instance, short-run income expectations may be pessimistic, while aspirations toward a higher income and an improvement in the standard of living may persist. Aspirations are also more closely related to perceived values norms and less subject to the influence of situational determinants than expectations.[14]

FORECASTING

Clearly, the probability of the fulfillment of expectations and

[14] The dynamics of change in aspirations will not be discussed in this paper, although it is relevant to the theory of economic behavior. It may suffice to mention here that this author has found applicable to economic behavior the theorem, derived by Kurt Lewin from psychological experiments, that the level of aspirations is raised by success and lowered by disappointment and failure. For the theoretical implications of felt success or failure and their relation to saturation, see especially [18].

the predictive value of expectations increase if (*a*) the observed change in expectations is substantial and lasting, and (*b*) the observed change continues in the same direction during the subsequent period for which predictions are made.

Both circumstances were observed frequently. But periods also occurred in which the changes in sentiment were minor or fluctuated from one period to the next. It was found that insignificant or one-time changes could not always be disregarded because under certain circumstances information about the reasons for the changes provided valuable clues. But, in general, the predictive value of expectations is based on the following proposition: When a trend of change in expectations is established, it will be reversed only slowly and gradually − unless major unexpected developments take place. The first part of this proposition is derived from the theorem about the slowness and gradualness of social learning. It takes time, usually at least several months, until news or information different from that prevalent in the preceding period spreads to many people and is reinforced by word of mouth. Therefore, a long-lasting improvement (deterioration) of collective expectations will commonly be followed by a plateau or by insignificant ups and downs before a sustained deterioration (improvement) occurs.

In order for collective expectations to change abruptly, powerful stimuli must affect very many people at the same time. That major new developments may impair the fulfillment of expectations hardly requires any elaboration. If the period to which the expectations relate should witness the unexpected outbreak of a war, for example, it is clear that all bets would be off. Incidents in the cold war may also change the outlook suddenly, as was the case at the time of the U-2 incident (while, on the other hand, collective attitudes toward Vietnam have changed slowly). Abrupt changes in expectations also result from such things as riots, or an unexpected proposal to change income taxes, or a substantial sudden change in interest rates. Finally, and obviously, a prediction made for a certain quarter may prove false if a large strike should occur in that quarter.

There are good reasons to propose the hypothesis that a sudden and substantial change in collective expectations will occur when major new developments are unfavorable and not when they are favorable. Slow and gradual social learning may be the rule unless shocking news creates fear. The slow adjustment of consumer attitudes that occurred in response to the sudden and unexpected introduction of a price-wage freeze in August, 1971, which was considered good news by most Americans, is in line with this hypothesis.

For the purpose of analyzing the consequences of new events attitudinal studies provide important clues. By ascertaining the reasons for expectations, it is often possible to make conditional predictions. For instance, it could be stated during the last few years how attitudes and subsequent behavior would change if the war in Vietnam were either to accelerate or come to an end, or if the rate of price rises were to increase or decrease. Information on what kinds of development people regard to be either favorable or unfavorable constitutes an important part of attitudinal studies.

When expectations are fulfilled and predictions derived from expectations prove correct, is it then justified to speak of self-fulfilling expectations? One may argue that if people think that the next year will be a poor one, their own subsequent actions may actually produce the outcome they foresee. Although in a certain formal sense this statement may be viewed as correct, it has implications that need to be contradicted. It may be implied that the expectations alone produced the downturn in the economy, regardless of underlying factors. This would be analogous to the classic economic example of self-fulfilling expectations: In 1933 adverse rumors about the condition of a bank, even if the rumors were not justified and the bank was sound, are said to have caused runs on the bank which brought about its collapse. By contrast, we have argued that collective expectations endure only if people see good reason for their expectations, which means that the expectations must have some basis in real conditions. The same is true of inflationary expectations and their alleged consequences, stocking up and hoarding, which may make them come true. Such price expectations will not prevail among very many people over long periods unless they have some foundation in prevailing conditions and developments. Therefore, it may be said that expectations do not represent the sole causal factor but constitute a "filter" that modifies the impact of objective developments.

The notion about self-fulfilling expectations may also relate to the publication of findings on prevailing expectations. When survey data are published, for instance, on people expecting a downturn in business conditions, many people who previously had not given any thought to the matter may become concerned and may change their behavior accordingly. In this statement it is assumed, first, that survey findings are generally accepted and relied upon (which was not the case either in 1957 or in 1969!). Second, the statement attributes far too large a degree of power to printed matter, or to information received over the radio and TV, in changing and crystalizing attitudes. Without denying that the publication of survey data may reinforce certain attitudes, a more important consideration is a different possible consequence: If government and business, thanks to the publication of survey data, should know in advance of a threat to the economy, they would then be in a position to counteract it.

No doubt it would be the greatest triumph of research on expectations if unfavorable predictions derived from them were not to be fulfilled because policy-makers had instituted effective countermeasures. We have not yet reached this phase because reliance on indications derived from consumer expectations is still fragmentary. Moreover, there appear to be severe limits to fine tuning of economic policy.

EXPECTATIONS ABOUT GOVERNMENT POLICY

We must consider one specific important kind of expectation, namely, the expectation of either the success or the failure of policy measures instituted by the government. We shall look first at measures of fiscal policy. Again, the notion that reactions by business or consumers are mechanical or automatic must be contradicted. While an increase or decrease in income taxes reduces or augments aggregate purchasing power and ability to buy to an extent corresponding with the change in disposable income, the extent to which effective demand changes depends on people's reactions and therefore on their attitudes. It is possible that as a result of a tax increase or decrease (a) consumer spending will not be affected at all, (b) that it will rise or fall to an extent far exceeding the tax-induced change in income, (c) that it will change in the same direction as purchasing power but to a much smaller extent and, finally, (*d*) that it will move in the opposite direction from the change in incomes.

Some empirical findings relevant for an assessment of reactions to tax changes should have been known a priori: First, the incomes of very many people change all the time, and the direction of change in wages, salaries, and profits may or may not coincide with that of the tax-induced change. (Both in 1964 and in 1968 earned incomes rose, in the first case reinforcing and in the second case counteracting the tax-induced change.) People do not segregate the money available to them according to its source. Assumptions that people will use tax-induced gains differently from other gains are not realistic.[15]

Second, tax changes do not occur suddenly. Tax proposals are usually widely discussed even before legislation is introduced in Congress, and congressional deliberations take a long time. Therefore, a tax increase or decrease should have an effect on consumers long before their purchasing power has changed, and anticipatory effects may either dissipate or augment the later impact of change in ability to buy.

Third, policy measures may have a substantial impact on consumer sentiment, affecting not just personal income expectations, but also people's general economic outlook. This form of influence is difficult to foresee in advance, but it is possible to collect empirical data on how people view a proposed tax change long before the tax measure is enacted.

Extensive empirical data are available and have been published on reactions to the tax cut of 1964 and the introduction of the tax surcharge in 1968.[16] The findings will be recalled here very briefly, in capsule form.

Attitudes toward the tax cut and therefore people's behavior varied greatly from 1962 to 1965. When President Kennedy first proposed a tax cut, neither people's attitudes nor their behavior changed at all: most people thought that what was proposed,

[15] There may be perceived differences between the two kinds of income gains in the sense that tax changes may be viewed as temporary or one-time measures, while increases in earned income are often seen as gains leading to further gains. Those differences may influence the impact of tax changes on attitudes (see the third point above).

namely to reduce government revenues at a time of deficits and the need for a variety of increased expenditures, would be impossible and, therefore, would not be done. The opinions of the masses changed very slowly; only fairly late in 1963 and early in 1964 did the majority of people expect a tax cut and become convinced that it would have a favorable effect on the economy. Consumer spending and especially the incurrence of installment debt rose in the months *prior* to the reduction in tax withholdings. When the tax withholdings were actually reduced, many people were disappointed at the size of their personal gain, which they considered insignificant compared to their expectations. (Many experts then spoke of a lag of spending behind income changes.) Later in 1964 and in 1965, large increases in earned income and generally favorable attitudes toward the tax cut prompted a substantial increase in consumer spending.

Discussions of a tax increase began in 1966. In that year and in 1967, the threat of paying higher taxes and the notion that the tax increase would adversely affect economic conditions contributed to pessimism and, therefore, to restraint in discretionary expenditures. Again, there occurred slow and gradual social learning: By the first half of 1968 the majority of people thought that the surcharge would have a beneficial effect on the economy. In May, 1968, these findings together with data on other perceived reasons for optimism (the cessation of bombing in North Vietnam, for instance) made it possible to conclude that the major retarding effect of the surcharge had already taken place in anticipation of the tax increase, rather than that it would occur during the following few months when disposable income was actually reduced

[16] See *1967, 1968* and *1969 Survey of Consumer Finances* [23], and [19]. An interesting sidelight on the widely-prevailing disregard of anticipatory reactions is shed by the history of the financing of studies on the subject. Diligent attempts by this author to obtain funds from the government or from foundations were of no avail in 1963; he was told that the tax cut legislation might not pass and money should not be wasted studying something that might not happen. In February, 1964, immediately after the tax cut became law, however, the Council of Economic Advisers under the chairmanship of Walter Heller took the initiative in securing funds for extensive attitudinal and behavioral studies to be carried out by the Survey Research Center [17]. Because of lack of funds, only small studies were carried out in 1962–63, financed by the Survey Research Center itself.

[23].[17] Shortly after the surcharge was enacted, it was viewed by the majority of taxpayers as having only an insignificant effect on their personal finances, which were seen as improving under the impact of rising earned incomes.[18]

It appears, then, that a consideration of psychological factors is essential for an evaluation of the efficacy of measures of fiscal policy. The impact of higher or lower interest rates on the economy is also dependent on the attitudes and expectations of businessmen and consumers. Sometimes rising interest rates have generated the expectation of a further increase and, therefore, had the "perverse" effect of stimulating borrowing by business firms. Regarding the major form of monetary policy, an increase or decrease in the money supply, the situation is far from simple. One possible way change in the supply of money may affect consumer spending is via the stock market. A somewhat different influence is expressed by B.W. Sprinkel in his recent summary of the monetary view as follows: "If the stock of money [demand deposits and currency] is rapidly increased, they [individuals and businessmen] find they have too much money. Therefore they increase spending" [30, p. 104]. Neither of these propositions, either that consumer spending is directly and regularly influenced by stock market movements, or that consumer spending is a function of liquid asset holdings, has been proved. Studies by this author show that stock movements may influence some people under certain circumstances but not other people under other

[17] *See 1968 Survey of Consumer Finances,* p. 79.
[18] Two recent analyses of the tax surcharge of 1968 failed to consider expectations adequately. Robert Eisner [6] explains the failure of the surcharge to reduce consumer spending by referring to the permanent income hypothesis: A temporary change in taxes would not change people's expectations about their future income. His discussion takes no account of anticipatory reactions or expectations other than income expectations. Arthur Okun [28] concedes that the expectation of the tax increase may have played a role in determining consumer behavior and even that "the anticipation might have been worse than the realization." But he incorrectly states that such "conjectures defy systematic verification" (p. 175).

In this connection we may recall earlier widely publicized findings of the Survey Research Center according to which in 1950 the anticipation of large expenditures in Korea created inflationary expectations, while the actual increase in those expenditures in 1951 did not.

circumstances, depending upon attitudes toward the stock market. Liquid asset holdings do, of course, constitute an enabling condition for spending, but success in adding to one's savings may sometimes raise one's aspirations to add to them still more [16, p. 213 ff.]. Therefore any conclusion about a necessary unidirectional relation between growth in money supply and consumer spending is precarious.[19]

EXPECTATIONS AND RATIONAL BEHAVIOR

Analysis of expectations, of their changes, their impact on economic behavior and their origin, must be incorporated into the mainstream of economic thought. Expectations are a central concept of behavioral economics, which disregards some traditional distinctions between endogenous and exogenous factors. Yet in the past economic analysis made great progress even while restricting its scope to rational behavior or, at the least, taking rational behavior as its starting point. The question must be raised as to whether the analysis of behavioral changes and their determinants runs contrary to the major tenets of rational analysis.

This question is to be answered in the affirmative only if restrictive assumptions are made as to what is and what is not rational. The first of these is the assumption that economic behavior is "calculating". If economic behavior is seen as consisting exclusively of continuous and careful cost-benefit analysis, significant aspects of expectational dynamics are disregarded. Notions that consumers and businessmen have definite expecta-

---

[19] Empirical relations that have been presented between changes in money supply, or in wealth, and consumer spending are far from conclusive. At several crucial times (e.g., 1957, 1969) consumer attitudes were found to deteriorate and growth rates in discretionary consumer demand to decline before monetary restraint began or the stock market turned down.

This is not the place to discuss consumer reactions to the new economic policy (price-wage freeze, etc.) initiated by President Nixon on August 15, 1971, at a time when this paper was almost completed. It may suffice to say that what has been said about the major role of people's attitudes and expectations in contributing to the success or failure of government policy fully applies to what happened in 1971.

tions about all relevant factors at all times and are capable of discounting all future costs and benefits are unrealistic.[20]

Yet the concept of rationality need not be expressed in the extreme terms just indicated. Suppose we ask whether the consideration of expectational dynamics makes economic analysis irrational, rather than whether it conforms with rationality. If the term irrational is assumed to mean unexplainable, or subject to unforeseeable, random, or idiosyncratic considerations, the answer to the new question is an unequivocal "No". Analysis of expectations and of the reasons for their changes reveals economic behavior to be sensible, understandable, and subject to scientific study. Consideration of changes in expectations does open new vistas to economic analysis but does not obviate the goal of science, which is to develop broad generalizations that are verified by empirical studies. Economic analysis, to be sure, will no longer rest on alleged immutable principles of human nature, but rather on principles of human behavior.

The main advantage of the theory of rational economic behavior consists in its simplicity. No doubt, a behavioral theory that incorporates the major tenets of the theory of expectations is more complex. Yet the task of developing such a theory does not appear to be beyond reach. Such important tools of model building as abstraction and generalization should make it possible to provide a reasonably simple theoretical framework which is based (1) on the malleability of human behavior and the principles of social learning and (2) on principles of motivation, incentives, and constraints. (Only the first point, but not the second, has been discussed in this paper.) Postponing this major task for another occasion, two short references to important essays in this volume may be made here so as to illustrate the relation of expectational theory to the theory of rationality.

James Tobin [32] is right in emphasizing that scholars must assume the prevalence of purposeful behavior. Economic behavior is not a succession of unplanned, random, or idiosyncratic occurrences. Tobin is justified in pointing to differences in the saving

---

[20] In extensive studies no evidence was found about people having expectations of their life-time income or about consumers attempting to achieve a preferred distribution of consumption over their entire life.

576

behavior at different stages of the life cycle as revealing the presence of some foresight and thus indicating the need for embedding the study of expectations "in a theoretical framework of rational accumulation". But what rational accumulation is must, in itself, become an object of study rather than being postulated a priori and assumed to be the same in all societies at all times.

Tobin closes his recent discussion of the theory of consumption and saving with the following remarks:

> Pretending, even if somewhat counter-factually and unrealistically, that decisions are made on a rational basis — or with some purpose to them . . . — is a worthwhile way of proceeding. If it isn't a worthwhile way of proceeding, then I would like to know what other way we should proceed. [33, p. 160]

The answer to Tobin's query is simple: The underlying theory must be broadened so that it includes generalizations derived from psychological considerations and from findings about the function of attitudes and expectations.

"Everybody does what he thinks is best at the time" is Kenneth Boulding's formulation of the broadest principle of behavior [3]. He continues with a most valuable analysis of the psychological ramifications of the concept of what is best. Perhaps it may be useful to enumerate in the same volume the considerations that have emerged from studies by this author as modifying and clarifying the preference funtion or betterment function. First, striving for improvement is not a constant mode of behavior. Very frequently behavior is simply habitual with no genuine decision-making whatsoever. Second, the aim of improvement may relate not only to one's economic position but to self-fulfillment and nonmaterial satisfactions as well. Third, people are often satisfied with small steps toward what they consider desirable goals, without an extensive search process and without trying to achieve the optimum. Finally, progress or improvement may relate not only to personal needs and wants but also to those of groups to which one belongs. It is possible for a broad "We" to take the place of the "I" and for the aim of betterment to be directed, for example, toward better schools and hospitals, or toward such goals as progress in the fight against poverty, racial discrimination, and pollution.

ON TESTING THE PREDICTIVE VALUE OF EXPECTATIONS

Supplementing the paper, a few words may be said about the methods of testing the predictive value of expectations, which topic is discussed in several papers included in this volume.

What are the purposes of the Survey Research Center's quarterly surveys on changes in consumer attitudes and expectations? The most general answer to this question is that the surveys serve the purpose of testing propositions of behavioral or psychological economics. Therefore, first, evidence is sought about the contribution of attitudinal and expectational variables to an understanding of what has happened. This is done regarding various forms of discretionary expenditures by consumers, which are assumed to be dependent not only on ability to buy but also on willingness to buy, as well as regarding the incurrence of installment debt and change in the rate of financial saving.

Second, the quarterly survey data are used to make predictions about things to come, mainly in the short run but also, partly on the basis of long-range expectations, over several years. Fulfillment of predictions represents the best test of new propositions, and an analysis of the reasons for either fulfillment or nonfulfillment promotes scientific inquiry. (In addition, the predictions based on anticipatory data serve practical purposes and contribute greatly to financing the expensive survey program!) Each quarter a report is issued, and published, containing not only data on changes in consumer sentiment and their reasons, but also predictions about what is expected to happen during the next six, nine, or twelve months to such important and highly volatile forms of economic activity as the number of cars bought and an increase or decrease in installment debt incurred.

Some of these predictions appear of much greater importance than others. One may distinguish two kinds of periods, one in which ongoing trends continue and, two, crucial periods in which turning points occur. In the first type of period, projections of past trends or even a naive model would yield correct predictions, and it is hardly possible to demonstrate an advantage of anticipa-

578

tory data. This author postulated as early as in 1951 that there are basic differences between forecasting on the basis of anticipatory data and forecasting by means of extrapolation and projection, in that the former serves primarily to provide an early indication of turning points (*see* [15, pp. 171–75] and [16, pp. 85–90]).

Naturally, the question arises about how to summarize the predictions made at specific dates. Although this has been repeatedly done in the annual volumes entitled *Survey of Consumer Finances*, for instance with respect to early warnings issued about the recession of 1958 or the recession of 1970, econometricians had some justification to criticize the methods employed as judgemental. Each quarterly survey contains some forty questions, of which only five are used to obtain the summary measure called the *Index of Consumer Sentiment*. The predictions, as published every quarter, stem both from data included and from data not included in the *Index*; some judgement may enter into the selection of the data used. (But the selection was always made in advance and was explained by principles of behavioral economics such as habituation, generalization of affects, etc.) We at the Survey Research Center failed to construct a comprehensive index or to specify a complete mathematical model to be used for purposes of prediction. Construction of an explicit, detailed model for testing is difficult because the basic theory of anticipatory data specifies the kind of variables that should influence certain forms of spending and saving, not the extent of their influence, which may vary from time to time.

The method of predicting employed by the Survey Research Center differs from the common econometric methods of prediction. The requirements of econometricians are clearly expressed by Adams and Klein [1] who demand that anticipatory data be properly integrated into the framework of structural equations so that their contributions to improving the prediction of components of GNP may be demonstrated. To be sure, if this is done over a time span of 40 or 60 quarters, the demonstration relates both to crucial periods and the more frequent periods in which ongoing trends continue. Furthermore, there exists a second difficulty, not yet solved up to now. The *Index*, the only part of the Center's anticipatory data used by econometricians, was constructed as a trendless variable indicating short-run changes in willingness to buy. It neglects short-run changes in ability to buy as well as the long-run trend toward higher incomes and population growth, which are postulated to interact with changes in willingness to buy in influencing discretionary expenditures. The *Index* alone indicates the direction of forthcoming changes. It can hardly be expected to contribute much to the prediction of the size of a dependent variable expressed in billions of dollars (e.g., automobile expenditures) unless it is appropriately transformed.

Therefore the net contribution of the *Index* to forecasting, that is, its contribution beyond that of other variables included in an equation, depends greatly on the specifications set up for the regression equations used. After studying these specifications it appears gratifying that Adams and Klein [1] found a modest net contribution of attitudes to improving their forecasts and hardly surprising that Shapiro [29] found only a negligible contribution to the quality of the forecast derived from some of his models. Fair [7] finds that the *Index* makes a significant contribution to his forecasting model which is based on equations resembling closely the equations first proposed in studies carried out at the Survey Research Center by Eva Mueller [26], who used only two explanatory variables, lagged *Index* and lagged income.

A crucial difference between psychological economics and the traditional theory of consumption, consisting of the appraisal of the impact of inflationary expectations on consumer demand, must be reflected in the tests of predictions. It has been frequently postulated in the past that the expectation of price increases would enlarge demand because consumers would hoard and stock up or buy in advance of needs when they expect prices to rise, so as to beat inflation. Empirical findings made in the United States over the last 20 years indicate, however, that the expectation of price increases has induced most consumers most of the time to postpone some of their discretionary expenditures and thus to reduce demand. This was the case because consumers regarded inflation as an adverse development which would restrict their ability to buy. (This was found to be true even of people who expected their income to increase more than prices.) Moreover, the expectation that because of higher prices they would have to spend more on goods and services must have led many people to cut down on expenditures that were desired but not nesessary. In the last 20 years the *Index of Consumer Sentiment* declined the more widespread and the more substantial the expectations of rising prices were.

It is not assumed that inflationary expectations must always reduce demand. The relation between inflationary expectations and changes in the direction of consumer demand has been established at times when slow and gradual rather than substantial price increases were expected. (This was the case even in 1969–71 when fairly rapid inflation coincided with record personal savings.) The predictions derived from the *Index* are based on findings about consumer behavior rather than on alleged principles of rational behavior.

(The author wishes to express his gratitude to the Ford Foundation for a grant that has greatly contributed to the preparation of this paper.)

REFERENCES

1   Adams, F. Gerard, and Lawrence R. Klein, this volume.
2   Andersen, Leonall C., and Keith M. Carlson, "A Monetarist Model for Economic Stabilization", *Federal Reserve Bank of St. Louis Review* (April, 1970), 7–25.
3   Boulding, Kenneth E., this volume.
4   Cagan, Phillip D., "The Monetary Dynamics of Hyperinflations", in Milton Friedman, ed., *Studies in the Quantity Theory of Money*, Chicago: University of Chigago, 1956.
5   Cohen, Wilbur J., this volume.
6   Eisner, Robert, "Fiscal and Monetary Policy Reconsidered", *American Economic Review*, 59 (December, 1969), 897–905.
7   Fair, R.C., *A Short-Run Forecasting Model of the United States Economy*, Lexington, Mass.: Heath Lexington Books, 1971.
8   Francis, Darryl R., "Some Lessons to be Learned from the Present Inflation", *Federal Reserve Bank of St. Louis Review* (October, 1970), 6–11.
9   Gordon, Robert J., "Inflation in Recession and Recovery", *Brookings Papers on Economic Activity*, 1 (1971), 105–166.
10 Juster, F. Thomas, and Paul Wachtel, this volume.
11 Katona, George, *Organizing and Memorizing*, New York: Columbia University Press, 1940.
12 Katona, George, "Psychological Analysis of Business Decisions and Expectations", *American Economic Review*, 36 (March, 1946), 44–62.
13 Katona, George, *Psychological Analysis of Economic Behavior*, New York: McGraw-Hill, 1951.

581

14 Katona, George, "Expectations and Decisions in Economic Behavior", in D. Lerner and H.D. Lasswell, eds., *The Policy Sciences*, Stanford: Stanford University Press, 1951.

15 Katona, George, *The Powerful Consumer*, New York: McGraw-Hill, 1960.

16 Katona, George, *The Mass Consumption Society*, New York: McGraw-Hill, 1964.

17 Katona, George, and Eva Mueller, *Consumer Response to Income Increases*, Washington: Brookings Institution, 1968.

18 Katona, George, "Consumer Behavior: Theory and Findings on Expectations and Aspirations", *American Economic Review*, 58 (May, 1968), 19–30.

19 Katona, George, "Attitudes Toward Fiscal and Monetary Policy", *Public Policy*, 18 (Winter, 1970), 281–288.

20 Katona, George, Burkhard Strumpel and Ernest Zahn, *Aspirations and Affluence*, New York: McGraw-Hill, 1971.

21 Katona, George, "The Impact of Inflation on Consumer Attitudes and Behavior", *Conference Board Record*, 8 (March, 1971), 48–51.

22 Katona, George, "Consumer Durable Spending", *Brookings Papers on Economic Activity*, 1 (1971), 234–239.

23 Katona, George, Jay Schmiedeskamp, and others, *1967, 1968, 1969 and 1970 Survey of Consumer Finances*, Ann Arbor, Mich.: Institute for Social Research, annual publication.

24 Keynes, J.M., *The General Theory of Employment, Interest, and Money*, New York: Harcourt, Brace, 1936.

25 Morgan, James N., this volume.

26 Mueller, Eva, "Ten Years of Consumer Attitude Surveys: Their Forecasting Record", *Journal of the American Statistical Association*, 58 (December, 1963), 899–917.

27 Newcomb, Theodore M., this volume.

28 Okun, Arthur M., "The Personal Tax Surcharge and Consumer Demand", *Brookings Papers on Economic Activity*, 1 (1971), 167–204.

29 Shapiro, Harold T., this volume.

30 Sprinkel, B.W., *Money and Markets*, Homewood, Ill.: Irwin Press, 1971.

31 Strumpel, Burkhard, this volume.

32 Tobin, James, this volume.

33 Tobin, James, Rebuttal to "Wealth, Liquidity and Consumption" in *Consumer Spending and Monetary Policy*, Boston: Federal Reserve Bank, 1971.

582

Contributors

F. GERARD ADAMS

Professor of Economics, and
Director, Economics Research Unit
Wharton School of Finance and Commerce
University of Pennsylvania
Philadelphia, Pennsylvania.

BERND BIERVERT

Assistant Professor of Economics
Cologne University, and
Director of Consumer Surveys
Forschungsstelle für empirische Sozial-
ökonomik
Cologne, Germany.

KENNETH E. BOULDING

Professor of Economics
University of Colorado
Boulder, Colorado
President, American Economic Association,
1968–69.

WILBUR J. COHEN

Dean, School of Education, and
Professor of Education
The University of Michigan
Ann Arbor, Michigan
Secretary of Health, Education and Welfare
1968–69.

583

WILLIAM C. DUNKELBERG   Assistant Professor of Economics
Graduate School of Business
Stanford University
Stanford, California.

ROBERT FERBER   Research Professor of Economics and
Marketing, and
Director, Survey Research Laboratory
University of Illinois
Urbana-Champaign, Illinois.

DEBORAH S. FREEDMAN   Assistant Professor of Economics
Department of Economics
The University of Michigan
Ann Arbor, Michigan.

HAROLD W. GUTHRIE   Professor of Economics
University of Illinois
Urbana-Champaign, Illinois, and
The Urban Institute
Washington, D.C.

F. THOMAS JUSTER   Vice-President for Research,
National Bureau of Economic Research
New York, New York.

GEORGE KATONA   Program Director,
Institute for Social Research
Professor of Economics and Psychology
The University of Michigan
Ann Arbor, Michigan

DANIEL KATZ   Professor of Psychology
The University of Michigan
Ann Arbor, Michigan.

LAWRENCE R. KLEIN   Benjamin Franklin Professor of Economics,
Wharton School of Finance and Commerce
University of Pennsylvania
Philadelphia, Pennsylvania.

ALBERT LAUTERBACH   Regional Economic Adviser,
International Labor Office,
United Nations.

RENSIS L. LIKERT   Director Emeritus,
Institute for Social Research

584

Professor Emeritus, Sociology
Professor Emeritus, Psychology
The University of Michigan
Ann Arbor, Michigan, and
Chairman of the Board
Rensis Likert Associates, Inc.

E. SCOTT MAYNES
Professor of Economics
University of Minnesota
Minneapolis, Minnesota.

JAMES N. MORGAN
Professor of Economics, and
Program Director
Institute for Social Research
The University of Michigan
Ann Arbor, Michigan.

THEODORE M. NEWCOMB
Walgreen Professor of Human Understanding
Professor of Sociology
Professor of Psychology
The University of Michigan
Ann Arbor, Michigan.

FRANCESCO M. NICOSIA
Director, Consumer Research Program
Survey Research Center
University of California
Berkeley, California.

FOLKE OLANDER
Senior Researcher
The Economic Research Institute
at the Stockholm School of Economics
Stockholm, Sweden.

GUY ORCUTT
Professor of Economics
Yale University
New Haven, Connecticut, and
The Urban Institute
Washington, D.C.

ROBERT W. PRATT, JR.
Manager, Business Research and Forecasting
Operation
Major Appliance Business Group
General Electric Company
Louisville, Kentucky.

GUNTER SCHMOLDERS
Professor of Economics
Cologne University, Germany.

GERHARD SCHERHORN

Professor of Economics
Hochschule für Wirtschaft und Politik
Hamburg, Germany.

HAROLD T. SHAPIRO

Professor of Economics, and
Co-Director of Research
Seminar in Quantitative Economics
The University of Michigan
Ann Arbor, Michigan.

JAMES D. SMITH

Professor of Economics
Department of Economics
The Pennsylvania State University
University Park, Pennsylvania.

BURKHARD STRUMPEL

Associate Professor of Economics, and
Program Director
Institute for Social Research
The University of Michigan
Ann Arbor, Michigan.

GORDON F. SUTTON

Professor of Sociology
University of Massachusetts
Amherst, Massachusetts.

JAMES TOBIN

Sterling Professor of Economics
Yale University
New Haven, Connecticut
President, American Economic Association,
1971.

PAUL WACHTEL

Research Associate
National Bureau of Economic Research
New York, New York.

KARL-ERIK WARNERYD

Professor of Economic Psychology
The Stockholm School of Economics
Stockholm, Sweden.

KLAUS WIEKEN

Director, Institut für Venbraucherforschung
Cologne, Germany.

ERNEST ZAHN

Professor of Economic Sociology
University of Amsterdam
The Netherlands.

Publications of George Katona

Organizing and Memorizing, Studies in the Psychology of Learning and Teaching. New York: Columbia University Press, 1940. (Republished in 1967 by Hafner Publishing Company, New York)

War Without Inflationn, The Psychological Approach to Problems of War Economy. New York: Columbia University Press, 1942.

Price Control and Business, Field Studies Among Producers and Distributors of Consumer Goods. Bloomington, Indiana: Cowles Commission and Principia Press, 1945.

Psychological Analysis of Business Decisions and Expectations. *American Economic Review,* 36 (1946), 44–62.

Contribution of Psychological Data to Economic Analysis. *Journal of the American Statistical Association,* 42 (1947), 449–459.

Effect of Income Changes on the Rate of Saving. *The Review of Economics and Statistics,* 31 (1949). 95–103

Analysis of Dissaving. *American Economic Review,* 39 (1949), 673–688.

Psychological Analysis of Economic Behavior. New York: McGraw-Hill, 1951.

Expectations and Decisions in Economic Behavior, in *The Policy Sciences: Recent Developments in Scope and Method*, edited by Daniel Lerner and Harold D. Lasswell. Stanford University Press, 1951, 219–32.

Psychological Data in Business Cycle Research. *American Journal of Economics and Sociology*, 12 (1952) 11–22, (With L. R. Klein).

The Quantitative Study of Factors Determining Business Decisions. *The Quarterly Journal of Economics*, 66 (1952), 67–90, (With James N. Morgan).

Consumer Attitudes and Demand: 1950–1952. Ann Arbor: Survey Research Center, Institute for Social Research, The University of Michigan, 1953, (With Eva L. Mueller).

Rational Behavior and Economic Behavior. *Psychological Review*, 60 (1953), 307–18.

The Sample Survey: A Technique for Social-Science Research, in *Research Methods in the Behavioral Sciences*, edited by Leon Festinger and Daniel Katz. New York: Dryden Press, 1953, 15–55, (With Angus Campbell).

Economic Psychology. *Scientific American*, (October 1954), 31–36.

A Study of Purchase Decisions, in *Consumer Behavior*, I, edited by Lincoln H. Clark. New York: New York University Press, 1954, 30–36.

Variability of Consumer Behavior, in *Contributions of Survey Methods to Economics*, edited by Lawrence R. Klein. New York: Columbia University Press, 1954, 49–89.

The Predictive Value of Data on Consumer Attitudes, in *Consumer Behavior*, II, edited by Lincoln H. Clark. New York: New York University Press, 1955, 66–75.

Consumer Expectations, 1953–56. Ann Arbor: Survey Research Center, Institute for Social Research, The University of Michigan, 1956, (With Eva L. Mueller).

Attitudes Toward Saving and Borrowing. *Consumer Installment Credit*, Part II, Vol. 1, National Bureau of Economic Research and Federal Reserve Board, 1957.

Business Looks at Banks: A study of Business Behavior. Ann Arbor: The University of Michigan Press, 1957, (With Stanley Steinkamp and Albert Lauterbach).

Business Expectations in the Framework of Psychological Economics (Toward a Theory of Expectations), in *Expectations, Uncertainty, and Business Behavior*, edited by Mary Jean Bowman. New York: Social Science Research Council, 1958, 59–74. (From a conference held at Carnegie Institute of Technology, October 27–29, 1955, under the auspices of the Committee on Business Enterprise Research.)

Attitude Change: Instability of Response and Acquisition of Experience. *Psychological Monographs*, 1958, Vol. 72, No. 10, 1–38.

The Psychology of the Recession. *American Psychologist*, January, 1959, Vol. 14, 135–143.

The Powerful Consumer: Psychological Studies of the American Economy. New York: McGraw-Hill, 1960.

Changes in Consumer Expectations and Their Origin. *The Quality and Economic Significance of Anticipations Data*, National Bureau of Economic Research. Princeton: Princeton University Press, 1960, 53–89.

Survey of Consumer Finances — Monographs prepared and published annually, from 1960 to 1970 by the Survey Research Center, Institute for Social Research, The University of Michigan, Ann Arbor, Michigan, (With Staff).

The Relationship Between Psychology and Economics, in *Psychology: A Study of a Science*, Vol. 6, edited by Sigmund Koch. New York: McGraw-Hill, 1963, 639–676.

The Wealth of the Wealthy. *Review of Economics and Statistics*, Vol. 46, 1, (February 1964), 1–13, (With John B. Lansing).

The Mass Consumption Society. New York: McGraw-Hill, 1964.

Private Pensions and Individual Saving. Ann Arbor: Survey Research Center, Institute for Social Research, The University, 1965.

What is Consumer Psychology? in *American Psychologist*, Vol. 22, No. 3, (March 1967), 219–226.

On the Function of Behavioral Theory and Behavioral Research in Economics. Communication, *American Economic Review*, Vol. 58, No. 1, (March 1968), 146–150.

Consumer Behavior: Theory and Findings on Expectations and Aspirations. *American Economic Review*, Vol. 58, No. 2, (May 1968), 19–30.

Consumer Response to Income Increases. Washington, D.C.: The Brookings Institution, 1968, (With Eva L. Mueller).

Consumer Behavior and Monetary Policy. In *Geldtheorie und Geldpolitik*, (Festschrift for Günter Schmölders), pp. 117-132. Berlin, Germany: Duncker & Humblot, 1968.

Attitudes Toward Fiscal and Monetary Policy. *Public Policy*, Vol. 18, No. 2, (Winter 1970), 281–288.

Aspirations and Affluence: Comparative Studies in the United States and Western Europe. New York: McGraw-Hill, January, 1971, (With Burkhard Strümpel and Ernest Zahn).

The Impact of Inflation on Consumer Attitudes and Behavior. *The Conference Board Record*, March, 1971, 48-51.

Consumer Durable Spending: Explanation and Prediction. Washington, D.C.: *Brookings Papers on Economic Activity*, 1, 1971.

The Human Factor in Economic Affairs, Chapter 7 of *The Human Meaning of Social Change*, edited by Angus Campbell. New York: Russell Sage Foundation, 1972, 229–262.